STRINDBERG'S LETTERS

VOLUME II

STRINDBERG'S LETTERS

VOLUME II

1892–1912

selected, edited and translated by

Michael Robinson

THE UNIVERSITY OF CHICAGO PRESS

THE UNIVERSITY OF CHICAGO PRESS,
Chicago 60637
THE ATHLONE PRESS LTD, LONDON

Published 1992

The Publishers wish to express their thanks to the following individuals and bodies for their support in the publication of this book: H.M. The King of Sweden and The King Gustavus Adolphus VI's Foundation for Swedish Culture; The Swedish Academy; and The Anglo-Swedish Literary Foundation through the good offices of the Embassy of Sweden in London.

01 00 99 98 97 96 95 94 93 92 92   1 2 3 4 5 6

ISBN: 0 226 77727-8 (*Volume I*)
ISBN: 0 226 77728-6 (*Volume II*)
ISBN: 0 226 77725 1 (*the set*)

Library of Congress Cataloging-in-Publication Data
Current in Publication Data are available
from the Library of Congress upon request

This book is printed on acid-free paper

Typeset, printed and bound in Great Britain

CONTENTS

VOLUME I

VOLUME II

VI

Letters 285–326 November 1892–11 August 1894

The German years of Strindberg's second sojourn on the continent were filled with incident yet superficially chaotic; not until the end of the decade, in *Inferno, To Damascus,* and the posthumously published autobiographical novel, *The Cloister,* did they yield their worth in literature. It was a period of ferment and occasional conviviality. Although his friendship with Ola Hansson, who had encouraged his move, soon collapsed, Strindberg immediately gained a fresh circle of associates, including the Finland-Swedish writer Adolf Paul, the Pole Stanislaw Przybyszewski, the Norwegian painters Christian Krogh and Edvard Munch (whose one-man exhibition of 1892 scandalized Berlin even more than Strindberg's plays), the German poet Richard Dehmel, and Dr Carl Ludwig Schleich, a pioneer of local anaesthesia. Through them Strindberg became aware of the *fin-de-siècle* currents in literature and art out of which the modern movement emerged, and he began to negotiate the difficult transition from Naturalism to Modernism, which is the ultimate achievement of these otherwise apparently unproductive years. They met at a tavern which Strindberg christened *'Zum schwarzen Ferkel'* (The Black Pig), where they were joined by Bengt Lidforss and an emancipated young Norwegian woman, Dagny Juel, who became the erotic focus of the group. She eventually married Przybyszewski, but not before she had been the mistress of both Munch, who often represented her in his paintings, and Strindberg.

In counterpoint to this Bohemian existence was his attachment to a young Austrian journalist, Frida Uhl, who wrote criticism and reviews for the Imperial court paper, the *Amtliche Kaiserliche und Königliche Wiener Zeitung,* which was edited by her father, Friedrich Uhl. Although only twenty, the convent-educated Frida, who came from a family of wealthy landowners, married Strindberg in May 1893. The ceremony took place on Heligoland, and the honeymoon was spent in Gravesend and London, where the pair had misplaced hopes that *The Father* would be put on by J. T. Grein at his Independent Theatre. Strindberg detested England and soon returned to Germany, leaving Frida behind to administer his affairs. He went first to Rügen via Hamburg, then visited his parents-in-law in Austria, and finally met up with Frida again in Berlin, in August. The remainder of their brief marriage was a series of often farcical vicissitudes, in the course of which, in May 1894, Frida bore him a daughter, Kerstin, while they were staying on her grandparents' estate at Dornach, on the banks of the Danube, between Mauthausen and Grein.

Although *Creditors* had been successfully produced at the Residenztheater in Berlin, in January 1893, Strindberg had little time during these years for literature or the theatre. He was mainly occupied with painting, photography, or chemistry where, in accordance with his Monist theory of matter, he sought to prove that sulphur was not, as generally supposed, an element but divisible into a combination of hydrogen and carbon. He also tried to transmute copper and iron sulphate into gold, and conducted experiments into the nervous system of plants and the composition of air. His main work during this period was the Baconian scientific tract *Antibarbarus*, but in 1894 he began a second collection of Vivisections, this time in French. These were designed to make him better known in Paris where *Miss Julie* had been performed at the Théâtre Libre in January 1893, and *Creditors* in a production by Aurélien Lugné-Poë at the Théâtre de l'Œuvre, in June 1894. One of them, 'Des arts nouveaux! où le hasard dans la production artistique' (The New Arts, or The Role of Chance in Artistic Production), outlined the basis of his technique for tapping unconscious processes in art. As in the many long and intriguing letters which he addressed to his old friend Leopold Littmansson during the early summer of 1894, its speculations on the relationship between chance and design were an instance of his search for the new poetics on which he would eventually base many of the major dramas that he composed between 1898 and 1907.

In the meantime, however, his relationship with Frida was again deteriorating, and he also suffered from acute feelings of guilt over regularly defaulting on the monthly payments he was obliged to send Siri and the children in his first marriage. On 14 August he lamented to Littmansson the 'terrible discord between what I am and what I am thought to be by those about me; the disproportion between my abilities and what I do; my shame over unfulfilled obligations; the unjust hatred, persecution, nagging, the eternal harrassment, the encroachment of material things. I'm sick, nervously sick; hovering between epileptic attacks of furious work and *paralysie générale*.' The next day he left for Paris, alone, having sent a collection of his paintings on in advance.

285. To BIRGER MÖRNER

Friedrichshagen bei Berlin, 5 November 1892

My dear Mörner,

Do you know if Rod[1] has done anything about *The People of Hemsö*? I sent him my portrait the other day with an inscription. Will you write and tell him the prospects for bringing out a novel now are favourable since I am going to be played in Paris. At the same time, could you find out if he's read

Am offenen See (By the Open Sea) in the *Freie Bühne*,[2] otherwise I'll send him a copy.

It would also be a good idea to mention McCarthy's essay on Aug Sg in a recent issue of the *Fortnightly Review*[3] in case he wants to write something, or to give a lecture about me.

The manuscripts for the 'Mörner Book' are all here at Ola Hansson's, exactly as they left their Creator's (B.M's) hand.[4] And that's where they'll probably remain.

Lidforss has *also* stopped communicating with Ola H!

It's true I shouldn't need to certify my change of address like some maid, but it had been trumpeted abroad in any case![5]

Are you satisfied with your lot; are things going as you'd like them to? For the moment Fate seems to have wearied of persecuting me.

Trusting that you won't publish my letters.

Yours,
August Strindberg

P.S. If you know the med. student G. Brand,[6] give him my regards!

286. To STANISLAW PRZYBYSZEWSKI

Stanislaw Przybyszewski (1868–1927), Polish novelist and playwright. He came to Berlin, where he studied architecture and medicine, as a political exile in 1889. He wrote a highly praised paper on the structure of the *cortex cerebri* and established himself in a *ménage* with a young Jewish girl, Martha Foerder, with whom he had three children. However, he soon turned to literature with a series of essays on *Chopin and Nietzsche* (1891) and *Ola Hansson* (1892). These were followed in 1893 by a novel in German, *Totenmesse* (Requiem), in which he asserted the primacy of the subjective self and proclaimed, through its hyperneurotic hero, that 'in the beginning was Sex'. Its modish Satanism helped introduce Strindberg to such *fin-de-siècle* currents in both Germany and France. In 1893, Przybyszewski married Dagny Juel, the young Norwegian with whom Strindberg had been erotically linked earlier that year. This relationship aroused deep guilt feelings in Strindberg, and the powerful emotional charge of these Berlin years, reinforced in 1896 by the news of Martha Foerder's suicide, contributed much to one of the central motifs of his autobiographical fiction *Inferno*, in which Przybyszewski appears as the Russian Popoffsky (see Letter 376). After several visits to Scandinavia, Przybyszewski returned to Poland in 1898 to preach the aesthetics of a pure art and become the leader of the New Poland movement, though not before writing *Homo Sapiens* (1894–96), a trilogy of novels about his Berlin period in which Strindberg figures as the painter, Iltis. According to Przybyszewski, Strindberg still wrote to him as late as March 1897. However, this is his only extant letter to one of the key figures of the Inferno period; according to a note on the manuscript in Frida Uhl's hand, it was never sent.

[Original in French]

Berlin, 1 December 1892

Cher Stanislas,

I may well be leaving without any great fuss, but not without saying goodbye. Therefore come and see me more often these last days in Berlin.

The tragi-comic husband has become the ridiculous lover[1] and since the role is quite insupportable for me, I escaped to the Black Pig to paralyze my excited spermatozoa with bad alcohol.

May so-called Heaven grant that nothing worse lies in store for me, and that my journey extends to no more distant a country than golden Prague! I am dreadfully tired of all these torments, and would prefer never to have been born.[2]

Yet, in spite of everything, my brain always remains free of my sexual instinct, so that I am discovering all the divine misery of love and submitting to it.

And though I foresee that the break between us must one day or the other be complete, I delight in the present, and endure it.

So, until soon or never!

Auguste Strindberg
'The ridiculous lover'[3]

287. To ADOLF PAUL

Adolf Paul (1863–1943), Finland-Swedish writer. Paul studied the piano in Helsinki under the Italian virtuoso Ferruccio Busoni, whom he followed to Berlin in 1889. Once there, however, he turned to literature with the Strindbergian novel *En bok om en människa* (A Book About a Man, 1891). This was followed by a succession of stories, novels and plays, including the historical drama *Karin Månsdotter* (1899). In the early 1900s Paul went over to writing in German, in which he was equally prolific. He published his *Strindberg Erinnerungen und Briefe* in 1914 (an enlarged edition appeared in Swedish as *My Strindberg Book*, in 1930). Their personal acquaintance was in fact brief and confined, apart from a few letters during the 1900s, to 1892–94, while Strindberg was based in Berlin and Austria. During this period Paul was often cast in the role of Strindberg's literary amanuensis and errand-boy, and his resentment is apparent in his memoir, which also contains material transposed from his story 'Med det falska och det ärliga ögat' (With False and Honest Eye, 1895). Sixty-four of Strindberg's letters to Paul have survived.

Weimar, 5 December 1892. 5.30 p.m.

My dear Paul,

After visiting the park,[1] which I found quite decent, if somewhat small, I returned to the hotel and froze. Went to bed. Missed lunch, as I'd foreseen, since I can't bring myself to consort with a head waiter, three waiters in tails, etc.

Lay here till now, 5.30, famished, frozen. Increasingly petrified that I might starve and freeze to death in this room from an inability to press the bell and say what I want!

I knew this from previous experience. Panic at the thought of the accumulating bill paralyses me.

To carry on begging in Berlin after leaving without saying goodbye is pointless, and revolts me.

Weimar was a drunken fantasy!

Could have done business in Dresden, made contacts. In Prague ditto. And in Vienna I can get Fru Prager[2] to translate *The Bond* and *Playing with Fire*, and have them put on at a matinée. I've got *Neue Freie* there, etc., and numerous acquaintances. At least I wouldn't starve to death there. And would have Italy to the south.

There's nothing to be done in Weimar, for I can't work while travelling. So, get hold of (??) 100 Marks!

Meet me in Dresden; and ask Fru v. Borch either to meet me there or let Piersons know I'm coming.[3]

We'll find some furnished rooms straight away. And then move on.

I can hold out here for 2 more days, no longer.

In haste. Yrs,
August Strindberg

288. To KARIN, GRETA AND HANS STRINDBERG

Berlin, 3 January 1893

Beloved Children,

A Happy New Year!

from
Your friend,
August Strindberg

289. To BIRGER MÖRNER

[26 January 1893]
Ganz Privat![1]

Dear Mörner,

New Year 93, after *l'année terrible* 92,[2] seems likely to be a turning point in my tragicomic life.

In Berlin I am decidedly up through *Creditors*,[3] and so sure of my two new plays, *The Bond* and *Playing with Fire*, which will soon go on at the Lessing, that I consider myself 'saved', financially too.

Last Sunday, in the basement of the Rathskeller, where we dined after the performance in a larged mixed gathering and I was toasted, there was a moment when, relapsing into childish and Christian humility, I wondered whether I'd deserved this good fortune, so much so that I almost forgot to doubt the genuineness of the acclaim and sympathy which everyone was pouring over me.

I became almost sentimental, perhaps not least because I hadn't dined for three days, and had been walking around in summer socks in this dreadful cold.

Strange, lovable nation this, that bows down before foreign talent, sincerely, without resistance or a trace of envy.

We – Drachmann, Heiberg,[4] Munch,[5] Paul and I – attended a banquet recently at Lehmann's, Sudermann's publisher, the day after Sudermann's première. Drachmann proposed a toast to Sudermann – the great Sudermann – and Sudermann, in thanking him, acknowledged the great debt he owed the Scandinavians, his teachers, who this time had brought *das Licht* (Berlinerwitz: '*Nordlicht*') to Germany.[6]

It was a literary-historical moment.

I've heard from several sources in Paris that as a result of performing *Mlle Julie*:[7]

For a whole week – a long time in Paris – my play has been *the* subject of debate in conversation and the press; much enthusiasm and a deal of hatred; but in the end the ones who maintained they understood nothing were unmasked as liars or asses.

My name is known and the results are already visible: a publisher (you were sent a copy),[8] invitations to write for the best journals, and *The Red Room* to appear in a week's time![9] Etc.

In London I have an offer to stage *The Father*,[10] and an agent is taking my plays for England and the Colonies.

In Rome my best plays are being translated into Italian, so I'm hard on Ibsen's heels.

I haven't read a Swedish paper since before Christmas. I assume people are flattering themselves that I've suffered a defeat and gone to ground. How have people been reacting? Is the place itself?

Has Viktor Rydberg had another attack like the one following *The Weapon Smith*?[11] How are Staaff and Geijerstam? And Norén and Småland's Petter? And Linck? And Gullberg, Bonnier *et fils*?

Was Spada[12] as unjust as usual in what he wrote?

I probably won't see Sweden again for a long time. This is a good place to be. I'm going to Finland this summer. And in the autumn to Paris. *Voilà*!

Please make sure that just for once the Sg Book is decently illustrated, using one of your photographs, but not the one with the goatee. I'm 44 and hence becoming vain!

I have had a grim winter, suffering hunger and cold, but I know my children were better off than I was, and that consoles me. They ought to have things even better now – and, I hope, a future which befits my children!

Adieu! Tell Lidforss he's welcome, and remember me.

Your friend,
August Strindberg

290. To FRIDA UHL

Maria Friedrike (Frida) Cornelia Uhl (1872–1943), Strindberg's second wife. Her father was editor-in-chief of the *Amtliche Kaiserliche und Königliche Wiener Zeitung*, the official Hapsburg court newspaper, and had quarters in the Royal Palace in Vienna, while her mother had returned to live with her wealthy parents, the Reischls, on their estates by the Danube. Frida first met Strindberg in January 1893 at the supper party held to celebrate the première of Hermann Sudermann's *Heimat* in Berlin, where she had recently embarked upon a career as a journalist. They met again the following month at the home of Otto Neumann-Hofer, where the young convent-educated woman invited Strindberg to visit her in her lodgings the following day. They became engaged in March, although from the outset their relationship was unpredictable and volatile. Indeed, following their marriage on Heligoland and a brief, working honeymoon in England, where Strindberg grew increasingly impatient with her attempts to organize his life and to act on his behalf with publishers and theatres, much of their short marriage was spent apart, and hence conducted by letter which (as he once pointed out to her) was a recipe for confusion. Their one child, Kerstin, whose birth in 1894 seems to have delighted Strindberg more than it did Frida, held them briefly together, but their parting in Paris at the end of that year, although not planned, turned out to be permanent. Frida went on to have an affair (and a son) with the German playwright Frank Wedekind, and another with the painter August[illegible] when she returned to London in 1910. She opened a cabaret clu[illegible] called The Cave of the Golden Calf, with decor by Wyndham Lewis and Jacob Epstein, and then went briefly to the United States. But following the First World War, she lived mostly at the family home in Austria. Although it is wrong to follow his own hints and regard Strindberg's second marriage as entirely frivolous, it is nevertheless true that its ultimate value was the material it offered his writing, beginning with *Inferno* and continuing in *To Damascus*, *Advent*, and *The Cloister*. Frida wrote her own version in a two-volume account, abridged and translated into English as *Marriage With Genius* (1937). The letters published there are often cut and adapted by Frida to suit herself. Strindberg's share of the surviving correspondence amounts to one hundred and fifty-seven items.

[Original in French]

Berlin, Kleine Kirchgasse 2–3, 8 February 1893

Mademoiselle,

If you are still here, please let me know! I must apologize for so many stupidities, which arose from my temporary indisposition; I must thank you for an unforgetable evening; I must tell you that I didn't forget the rose, but left it behind on purpose, so as to have an excuse for coming to get it the following day, although my courage failed me at the decisive moment.

In short, I have many things to tell you, even at the risk of losing your respect, which I value less highly than your sympathy.

Awaiting a kind word, I beg you, Mademoiselle, to regard me as your very devoted,

August Strindberg

291. To FRIDA UHL

[Original in French]

Berlin, 20 February 1893

Dear Mademoiselle and Friend,

I don't know how to tell you how much our walk in the Park has tamed the evil spirits which persecute me; I can only thank you and congratulate myself.

You call yourself my old friend![1] Granted! But you will never be as old as I am, or such a child.

But I must see you every day even at the risk of compromising you, and supposing I have compromised you – be assured of this! – I would be ready to give you the honourable satisfaction one expects of a man of honour! Is that enough?

Your old young friend,
August Strindberg

292. To FRIDA UHL

[Original in French]

Berlin, 16 March 1893

Beloved Child,

The moment has come when I must tell you everything, even at the risk of incurring your displeasure.

A respectable love, which ends in marriage, has its economic side, that I don't dispute, but marriage mustn't be a business arrangement![1] You have played the role of my kind old aunt, and the game amused me, because everything you do becomes you. But you're now set in the role, you have abused the power I gave you, and I've become your ridiculous slave.

I fancy my heart is younger than yours, my spirit more liberated, but when I read your prescription for married life, marriage as you conceived it filled me with horror.

From pity to contempt is but a step: you already despise me, and your permission to be unfaithful to you wounded me, for it proves you do not love me.[2]

From this day forth, I forbid you to concern yourself with my affairs in any way, and we'll see if our love cannot feed upon its own fire, without this horrible fuel.

This doesn't mean to say I intend to neglect my affairs, on the contrary; I've been busy with them since yesterday, and will get everything sorted out by May, in accordance with the conditions you have given me.

My love is admirable because it is for you; but you love the disorder of my affairs, because you thereby gain the upper hand in this battle of the sexes for the preservation of individual identity.

You have cast your silken net over my head, I am already wriggling in it, and if things continue as they have up to now, my Omphale, I can foresee the moment when your Hercules will take hold of your spindle![3]

You are convinced it is your motherly love for me which moves you! But what does a little creature like you know about what goes on in a human soul under the mask of noble sentiment! The powers of darkness play their hateful game, and only the seer sees clearly!

I am a seer, and I won't permit my own creative power to become the plaything of a young woman, enchanting enough to seduce a god!

However great your power may be, you won't enslave me, Viviane,[4] for it was I who taught you my magic arts!

Away from here! With the air in his wings, your eagle, plucked and pecked at by the small fry, will nevertheless rise into the blue heavens, where the good little angels cannot follow him!

A.

293. To BIRGER MÖRNER

Heligoland, 9 May 1893

Dear Mörner,

Thanks for your good wishes!

I am newly married, on Heligoland, and things are fine![1]

But our poor Bengt is stuck in a hotel in Berlin, ruined by that damned woman Dagny Juel (who was also my mistress for three weeks!).[2] I learnt today in a letter from Paul that the proprietor of the hotel is threatening him with the police, and as you know, in Germany they bring in the police if one can't pay one's bill promptly.

Bengt went on the spree in Copenhagen (with Hamsun), came here (to Berlin) drunk, and has been drunk a whole month. Found his beloved Dagny as Aspasia at 'The Black Pig', where she slept with just about everyone.

It would be a good thing if you could recall Dagny, for her parents' sake.

She has taken a room on a street in the brothel district,[3] and is so afflicted by moral insanity that she too will soon be arrested.

Oh, it's a novel! She lays waste families and men, compels men of talent to embezzle money, to leave house and home, their duty and careers!

It shouldn't matter to me, for I've donated her as a mistress to someone else, and don't care about morality. But for Bengt's sake, for her own and other people's, including her family . . . get someone to fetch her!

And if possible let someone – if necessary his father – telegraph 300 Marks to Bengt. He's so sodden with drink that he's incapable of writing for any money himself!

This needn't come between us – don't get angry – and don't tell anyone else. Lure him home for the conferment of his doctorate, if possible! – That will give him a lift.

You mustn't think he'll suffer any mental damage, for he's never lived so rich a life among such gifted company before. And such experiences!

Thanks for the books, by the way!

Your friend,
August Strindberg

294. To ADOLF PAUL

[21 May 1893]

Dear P.,

Incarcerated on *die Fraueninsel*[1] my address is:
Gravesend by London.
12 Pelham Road.
England.
All right![2]

Yrs,
August Strindberg

295. To BIRGER MÖRNER

London: 84 Warwick Street,
Eccleston Square S.W.
8 June 1893.[1]

Dear Mörner,

Since I assume you've seen Lidforss in Lund, will you please let me know the result of the Berlin expedition and L.'s present situation.

In his last letter to me, he simply asks me to deny the facts I gave you in a private letter.[2] To which I now reply: those facts I supplied were based on Lidforss' own verbal reports to me, especially concerning Aspasia's establishment on Karlstrasse, which Lidforss found alternately liberated and *scheusslich*.[3]

Besides, I was on Heligoland and wrote my letter under the influence of Paul's, which mentioned L. and the police, a disease a Polish friend had got after sleeping with Aspasia, and a disease which L. had got after contact with another woman, etc., etc. Since my letter was well intended, that justifies my action. And if I deny the information I gave you, I'll make a liar of L., and he wouldn't want that. I don't understand why L. got angry, since he had little respect for Aspasia himself, and had his own ideas about summoning her home for, like me, he felt sorry for her and her family, and for anyone else who got caught on her lime-twig without the strength in their wings to break loose, as I did! He smiled broadly over all the extravagant, liberated expressions she allowed herself, and rationalized away his quite serious passion as a mere matter of instinctive secretions, which he repressed only from an honourable desire not to transmit his disease to her. But he must have suffered from the fact that we others enjoyed what he in all honesty could not bring himself to enjoy.

However, how did things go for him in Lund, and what's he doing? R.S.V.P

And you?

Now living and working in London!
Farewell for now!

Yrs,
August Strindberg

296. To FRIDA UHL

[Original in French]

Sellin, 26 June 1893

Dear Frida,

Rügen at last![1] where I flung myself head first into the sea to drown my *diables noires*,[2] but only half successfully.

And this evening, Sunday, 25 June, I received your letters full of love and tears for me! It breaks my heart to think of you worrying about me – an old good-for-nothing, who eats, sleeps and loafs around without the energy to earn a serious living. What oppresses me is the fear that I overestimated myself in marrying (wedding) you, and that – sooner or later – I may leave you in distress. I've no hope, and a stifling lethargy hangs over my soul, which has gone to sleep. Maybe I'm exhausted by excessive work, sorrow and distress. My spring love (*secunda primavera*,[3] alas!) roused me for a while, but the past haunts me and sows discord in my life. A dread of the future pursues me, and I no longer have the strength to stretch out my hand for the fruits which must be waiting for me after so many years of toil.

For the moment I am obsessed by the natural sciences, and cannot concentrate upon *belles lettres* or my theatrical affairs.

Here everything is tranquil, the sea, the woods, men (even the women), except me. What are you doing? What are your thoughts? How are you? Frau Kainz[4] is dying! What a misfortune! Paul tells me Schleich has gone mad! Crazy! Happy man! *Au revoir*! Till when?

Your August

297. To FRITZ KJERRMAN

Fritz Josef Kjerrman (1858–96), journalist, after 1891 a subeditor at *Dagens Nyheter*. Only three letters to Kjerrman from Strindberg survive.

297. To Fritz Kjerrman

Sellin, Rügen, 1 July 1893

Fritz Kjerrman,

Dear Friend,

I am somewhat afraid of writing letters to Sweden, because people generally publish them, but this time I must, though I beg you, if it proves necessary to utilize the contents, to do so without reproducing them verbatim or in quotation.

Only today have I seen from an advertisement in D.N. that *Budkaflen* is translating and publishing *Beichte eines Thoren*.[1] Without having asked my permission. I'm less concerned about the actual theft than the harm a Swedish edition can do to other people.

Briefly, the book's history is as follows.

When in Denmark, in 1888, I thought my life was over, I wanted, for my family's sake, to leave behind a document containing an account of my marriage, which showed that I wasn't a seducer or adulterer suffering a well-deserved punishment nor a madman who (after *The Father*) ought to be shut away. – Plans to that end were then in hand, and the 'Defenceless Woman' could count on 4,000,000 friends in Sweden, and I on none.

So that my heirs shouldn't happen to sell the manuscript out of greed, I wrote it directly in French. Unread by anyone, I deposited it under seal with a friend, and later with a relative.[2]

Following my return to Sweden in 1889, Gustaf af Geijerstam let fall during a drinking session that he had it in mind to portray my marriage. When he saw nothing to stop him, I considered I had a somewhat greater right, since I knew a little more about the matter than he did. I let Ola Hansson and his wife read the manuscript. They recommended immediate publication, and I sent the French text to Savine.[3] The Hanssons considered the case highly instructive and thought that many people would find the story useful. But then I regretted what I'd done and countermanded my instructions to Savine in Paris, who had taken it.

But during my last year in Sweden 1891–92, at the time of my divorce suit, when my children were being brought up in a sodomite household and all my attempts to save them were frustrated by the untold enemies my writing had conjured up, I decided, as the innocent party who was fined and threatened with prison, to see that justice was done myself. But I never attempted to bring out the book in a Scandinavian language, for I didn't want it vulgarized.

Well, it's a cruel book, as cruel as life, as love and woman, but the genre has been sanctioned ever since George Sand's *Indiana* and Fru Benedictsson's *Money*, in which her husband's embraces are portrayed right down to the hairs on his chest. (When Fru B. died, her publisher advertised *Money* with an assurance that it portrayed her marriage.)

As far as *Budkaflen*'s crude behaviour is concerned, I should like to see publication halted even if one has to allude to the book's impropriety, for it is improper to publish the book in Swedish, but not so in German or French, since the characters are unknown abroad. I feel sorry for the decent W.[4] and his family.

Can't he do anything, without being seen to?

I'm not bothered about the question of literary theft, and that swine can keep his ill-gotten money! I remain a Swedish citizen and literature is, after all, still regarded as property, even if it's not counted among those things which can be stolen.

Though you may regard this letter as a private communication, please at least let those few friends, whose sympathy I value, know something of its contents!

August Strindberg

298. To MARIE WEYR

Marie Weyr (1864–1902), Frida Uhl's eldest sister, married to the Austrian sculptor, Professor Rudolf Weyr. Strindberg sometimes addressed her as his 'mother-in-law' for the solicitude she showed him and her sister. (At her own entreaty, Strindberg called his real mother-in-law, Marie Uhl, 'Mutter' or 'Mamma'. See *Inferno*, p.225.) Of the letters which Strindberg addressed to her, nine have survived, together with seven telegrams.

[Original in French]

Sellin, Rügen, 22 July 1893.

Dear Mizi,

At the risk of incurring the displeasure of my beloved Frida and of being held in contempt by my relatives in Austria, I have decided to write this letter.

This is how things stand:

After a month of happiness and work on Heligoland, we conceived the idea of going to England to see how the land lay regarding my plays, etc. Frida, our treasurer, with her head fairly up in the clouds of married bliss, assured me we had the necessary means for the journey; thus we set off.

In England we fell into the clutches of genteel robbers, and after a month were cleaned out.

Unable to speak the language, and overwhelmed by the great city and the enormous heat, etc., I was struck down by some malady, and on the verge of being really ill.

We therefore decided I should go on ahead to Rügen to rent a flat for the summer. Frida was to follow me in a week or two. So off I went! But then I received some letters from Frida about a theatrical venture in London too grandiose to make any sense. And she wanted six weeks to organize it all. I've been waiting here for one frightful month, suffering from loneliness.

Now she declares it her firm intention to remain a whole year in London to launch a theatre, and urges me to come to London.

Frankly, it's all the same to me whether I live in England or some other country, but I'm afraid Frida might have fallen into the clutches of some cunning adventurers.

At any rate, and to crown our misfortunes, I myself have had no luck, rather the opposite. Unable to work, in despair over this involuntary separation, I have neglected my finances and suspect that Frida has had no success in her speculations with my manuscripts. I am expecting some money from Sweden and Norway, but the publishers have either gone on holiday or to sleep in the present universal heatwave and – I can wait no longer!

Forgive us our youth (?) and folly, but come to our rescue, if you can! Frida is suffering, and I am half mad with anxiety. I am ashamed to die, but the situation is intolerable. Deliver me from this prison, and let me go and find my lost lamb. If there are 500 marks in the world, find them for me, dear sister, and I swear never again to build my hopes on empty air.

I admit we are both a little mad, but we are sincere, we love one another, and the future will be ours.

I kiss your hands and beg you to embrace your parents for me – and don't say anything to Frida, it would cost me my happiness.

Your brother in spite of all,
August

P.S. Frida tells me she's placed most of my manuscripts for fabulous sums!

299. To FRIDA UHL

[Original in French]

Mondsee, 7 August 1893

Dear Frida,

I've just received your letter with Burckhardt's contract and the rest.[1] I can't say it gave me any pleasure, for nothing has done that since we parted. You are ambitious like me, but I believe you're consumed by your ambition, which will envelop anyone who comes near you. I try in vain to imagine a future dedicated solely and exclusively to science.

From time to time, I reproach myself with having taken your person and your career too lightly, with having repressed you. But never having read a word of yours, I didn't know the value of your talent. Now that I've read your articles, with their colourful, vibrant style, I'm aware you are somebody, and that I was wrong to tease you.

Well, for your part, you have been treating me like an idiot, at first playfully, then from habit, and finally in earnest.

It seems to me we are now more or less quits, even though I've given you the right to tell me all kinds of 'truths', founded or unfounded, without allowing myself the right of reply.

Now that I'm about to return to Berlin, I feel as if I were returning to darkness, for I fear you won't join me there. I can see it all again, this Berlin, its *Künstlerklause*[2] where we played the gypsy, the Neustädtische Kirchstrasse, where our love blossomed in the spring sun and storms. Love wild and springlike, sometimes grandiose, sometimes sad. The sublime struggle of two souls who fought to avoid the unavoidable, two cells that had to merge with each other and lose their individuality.

And now it's all over. Finished! Is that possible?

I regret only one thing, that I didn't kill myself a short while ago in London, in your arms, with my head on your breast. I did think of it, but found the place so squalid. Here, by the Mondsee, I dream of death.[3] In the water – it's so pure – or on the bed in the bathing pavilion – you know the one! But at the last moment your image haunts me and hope smiles at me.

You are throwing away love for fame, but let me tell you that, when the hour has come and fame is yours, you will want to spit it out, for everything about you will be empty, deserted, and you would gladly give all your laurels for a wreath of roses. When life is generous enough to offer your both, why discard one of them, and that the sweeter? I could tell you the laurel has sharper thorns than the rose.

Is it all over?

And why? A riddle with no answer! You love me as long as I am weak and unhappy, and you hate and detest me when you scent the man, the male in me. You hate and despise men. Your flesh desires the man and your soul rejects him. Amazon that you are!

You sensed that I adapted myself to your desires. As if I made myself, without knowing it, the woman, leaving you the man's role. Why?

Because otherwise you wouldn't love me! And I had to have your love.

Having lost all hope of winning you back, I'm tempted to tell you my secret thoughts every time my behaviour was incomprehensible to you; it would amuse me to divulge what goes on in a man's soul when in the grip of love. But what good would it do? You would only misuse it!

I am the man of the future, so masculine that I do my utmost to conceal it; that's why I play the misogynist. My instincts are so sound that they always lead me in the right direction where an excess of love awaits me, peppered with a woman's cruelty.

What is it you want? At times maternal love, gentle, golden love, a sheep-like love? Is that right?

It seems so to me – and again, not! And the moment you won it, you would despise it, and desire another kind.

Chaste Love? Nonsense!

You despise me – and rightly so, up to a point! I wonder whether you would love me more and differently if I were to behave roughly and show you the beast, the cannibal! You have no need of intellectual love, since you yourself possess intellect – –

Can two people go on living together, once they've said all there is to say? Forget it!

And then: why don't I come to England? I don't quite know, really. There's nothing for me to do there; I'm afraid of jeopardizing my new career; I dread my love, which will make me your slave once more.

So, I shall go to Berlin! And then? And then?

Have you considered the consequences of a separation? Vengeance, revenge!

And everything will collapse! Irreparably!

Make up only to break up. One prostitutes oneself, offering a spectacle to a public impatient for a second *Plaidoyer d'un Fou*.[4]

And the revelations and recriminations. One dies of shame and comes back to life in order to avenge oneself.

It is life itself that is at fault, life beautiful and cruel!

August

300. To ALBERT BONNIER

[21 November 1893]

Dear Herr Bonnier,

By today's post, I am sending the first sheet of a work called *Antibarbarus*, for which I laid the foundations in 1883, but which has been composed over the last three years. Four sheets, comprising the first part, are ready, and the three other sheets are being translated. The whole work should amount to 10 parts of 4 large octavo sheets each, and ought to be ready in a year or so.

However, it could well be no easy task for you to decide whether or not you want the work for it is a natural scientific philosophical work, and our philosophers in Sweden are uneducated people, who know nothing of science, while our scientists are not philosophers.

For a moment I thought of getting Nordenskiöld to read the first sheet. He's a chemist and was quite sceptical ten years back, but I don't know where he stands now. Professor Blomstrand in Lund might not be bad; many years ago, in *Research Today*,[1] he hinted at the direction my work takes, but he's a specialist, and doubtless careful of his position.

Maybe it wouldn't be a bad idea to try Nordenskiöld. He's suffered a certain, though less severe, martyrdom for his theory about cosmic dust, which was heretical.[2]

Seventeen years ago Carl von Bergen would have been the best person, but although he remains sceptical of science, he has returned to an abandoned point of view.[3] Viktor Rydberg is a complete ignoramus, and as a positivist Anton Nyström has espoused science as a religion.

However, there is a small circle of chemists, philosophers and doctors, both practising and theorizing, here in Berlin, who have been listening to my lectures from the 'Green Sack',[4] as the material is called, for the last year; they believe in the correctness of my theories and are prepared to support my views in lectures and journals. It might therefore be sensible for you to await publication of the first part in German. As long as the printers don't release the proofs, there's really no need to fear a rival Swedish edition.

Or might you reach a decision after hearing the opinion of two by no means young doctors,[5] one of whom is a surgeon with a private clinic and a well-known writer on medical matters, particularly renowned for his opposition to Koch and his vaccine?[6]

These men are familiar with the entire work and know pretty well where it is heading. I have no illusions about an edition of more than 1,000, and the royalties will doubtless be eaten up by my debts.
[28 lines omitted]

Yours sincerely,
August Strindberg

301. To BENGT LIDFORSS

[10 January 1894]

Dear L.,

Do you know what *Sansclou* are? Buffon says that fructified eggs have been found in men's seminal tubes.[1] *Sansclou* is a *Dröppel.* A *Dröppel* is an accumulation of male seed in a vagina. Now if a man mounts a woman over-filled with semen, he can get another man's semen in his penis or testicles, and then the seeds germinate, and the *sanscloued* man finds himself in a perverse state of pregnancy which, however, is halted by bringing down the temperature (ice bags!). The female probably has no eggs! Everything is in everything, and everything is in flux, even semen. Wombs are only birds' nests in which the male ♂ lays his eggs. *Ergo*: if the male has his eggs ready and waiting, he can lay them in a vessel warmed to a temperature of 37° Celsius. Tell this to Schleich, and we'll see if my egg grows in his brain pan, as in the past!

Yrs,
August Strindberg

[Postscript omitted]

302. To CARL LARSSON

Ardagger via Amstetten, Nieder-Oesterreich,
16 January 1894

Dear Carl Larsson,

I resolved at first not to reply to your letter, since all contact with Sweden makes me vomit, and I have recently witnessed the infamous manner in which private letters have found their way into print![1] But I recognized certain tones from the good old days in your lines; although they can of course never return, they can never be undone either.

But! Why should I return home? Who believes what I preach? And in this age of the masses, when the majority is in the right, Sweden is right to worship mediocrity and in so doing admire itself. Four years ago I let myself be lured back: 'come to us, down to us, and be close to us, like one of us'. At the time my situation abroad left me well on the way to being liberated from the slavery whereby publishers and editorial hacks could decide what I wrote. But I gave it all up and went back.

At home people were so blind that the better I wrote, the more profound my research, the worse my writing was seen to be. Witness Herr Sohlman's enlightened criticism of my masterpiece *By the Open Sea,* and ditto the learned Doctor Sjögren's, in which he discusses me together with a Herr Chicot![2]

Jealousy also played a part. Old Rydberg was to have rewritten my *Master Olof* as a novel,[3] and my *Somnambulist Nights* was ignored while his 'Grottesånger'[4] was taken to be 'the modern poem'. My socialism from 83 and 84 was no good, but Rydberg's met with approval, even though it was cut from my cloth.

I wasn't even a dramatist once Geijerstam created Molander[5] and the Women supplied the Royal Theatre. No one mentioned my *People of Hemsö* because what I wrote came from books, but Geijerstam's tales of the skerries, stolen straight out of my mouth, became classics. 'It wasn't *The Red Room*' which stirred up literature, G. wrote, in his derivative *Erik Grane,* it was *Erik Grane.* And Strindberg was dethroned while Fru Leffler, Fru Benedictsson and Fru wxyz were elevated to the lady chair.

The mediocrities had sought each other out, and when they perceived that they *were* mediocrities, they transformed themselves into geniuses – and Sweden was incarnated in that monstrosity Småland Petter, who received an honorary degree from Lund!

When I returned, I found I was the only sane person in a house of fools – a madhouse would be too fine.

[42 lines omitted]

Since I left Sweden, I've had many 'destinies and adventures'. In Berlin, where I was much bigger than I knew, I was supported by admirers of my writing, so that I was able to send my children what I earned from theatres and publishers. It was a rich and stormy life, during which I grew unbelievably, learning much.

But what good does that do me in Sweden where people stick out their tongues and say Bah to everything they don't want to understand. I have the wind in my sails – and at last the time has come when I don't need Sweden! I've publishers in Berlin, Paris and Milan, and am played and read all over the world – to the ends of the earth!

I've never had it better than I do now, and I can't see why I should exchange better for worse!

I live by the Danube, in the country, with my mother-in-law's parents, where people are intelligent enough to treat me as I deserve, and where Austrian good nature is united with French charm and tolerance.

In a word: things are fine as they are, even though I can't pay my debts! And I look forward without any qualms to the birth of the first child in my second litter, which probably won't be a Swedish subject.

On the other hand, what I fear in Sweden, were I to return, is that, as before, people would tear my marriage to pieces. That was my Achilles heel in the past, and they found it, but I didn't prove a shit like Achilles! Of course I long for pine trees and grey rocks when spring comes, but my loathing for that country, its climate and people outweighs it.

Besides, I refuse to take my young wife there, to be greeted by distraints and trials. She's quite aware of the situation and smiles at it, but I should find the reality painful. And I won't return home before I'm entirely rehabilitated! Or until I can obtain redress myself.

Is there really anyone apart from you who misses me? I doubt it! And I take your letter for what it is, a surge of desire to bathe in the atmosphere of the past. I often have such moments, especially when I haven't spoken my own language for three months. My wife can't speak a word of Swedish, and isn't going to be my translator but my wife.

If you've something pleasant to tell me, I'll gladly hear about it, but not about the baseness of those hacks; anyway, I always receive a lot of letters about them, long ones too, which only serves to heighten the pleasure of my present situation.

Things are going well for you, and you were allotted the free 'places' in the National Museum to paint.[5] (Is it to be anecdotes *à la* Heidenstam (Charles XII's boot) or our, your and my Swedish People, with a bird's eye view of the infinitely small?) Living as you do in Stockholm, you no doubt see Hasselberg! Give him my regards. He was my last and best friend in Sweden, and the only one who kept my spirits up, when the others trampled on me, or spat at me.

My other friends have emigrated, I hear; I advise you and every talented man in a country 'where it is fatal to have talent' to do the same.

Your friend,
August Strindberg

303. To BENGT LIDFORSS

[25 January 1894]

Just a word before I let the matter drop. Though I shall leave it unanswered, I gather from a letter posted in Lund that Aspasia, in a fit of rage which doubtless turned quickly back into love again, has portrayed your situation as very gloomy, indeed as hopeless. It seems, too, as if certain informers, whose existence you don't even suspect, have painted Poland's[1] marriage as a *ménage à trois*, in which you are the third party –

With that all communication with Lund ceased, as did my correspondence with Sweden as a whole. Following the article in the *Revue des Deux Mondes*,[2] Sweden has caught hysteria and is menstruating. Hedlund is to be invested with a gold medal; Ranft[3] is putting on Geijerstam's crappy play, *Other People's Business*, in Gothenburg, and D.N. has been told the piece is genuine Swedish (i.e. shit). Fru Wahlenberg is writing a novel about me! Tor Hedberg a play! Staaff and Geijerstam a dramatic lampoon. Ola Hansson-Marholm a novel.[4] Albert Bonnier is publishing my letters, *Aftonbladet* and the whole country are yap-yapping away!

But I don't give a shit about the place! No more should you! Haven't you got in touch with the *Freie Bühne* in Berlin yet? – While in Friedrichshagen[5] you probably couldn't help abusing me, which perhaps disgusts you now. Remember, too, that everything you tell the Marholm is immediately sold to German magazines in the form of novels and stories!

Write, create, and you'll be free and have *Machtgefühl*.[6]

[no signature]

304. To CARL LARSSON

Ardagger via Amstetten, 26 January 1894

Dear Carl Larsson,

It's all very well our discussing how vapid Sweden is, but it seems as if we've grown apart, and don't understand each other any more.

To say I'm being 'modest'[1] when I reproach those journeymen for following in my footsteps is nonsense for I'm actually reproaching them for snapping at my heels, for stealing from and abusing me. On the other hand, my 'modesty' – or pride – forbids me from resolving such a vapid question as who is the greatest – only Swedes could be preoccupied with questions like that.

But you see, the reason why I don't bow down before Viktor Rydberg, any more than I raise my stick to him, stems from the fact that my development owes nothing to him. I read his *Last Athenian*[2] when I was young, but found it quite unbearable, *Lesefrüchte*[3] of a man never born to be an artist, but who wanted to be one whatever the price.

I came across his *The Bible's Doctrine Concerning Christ* when I was 34, but had gone to school at 16 with Strauss, Renan,[4] and other original masters, to whom Rydberg was, and remains, an apprentice.

Since then I've read nothing of his. The generation which learned from Rydberg was: Wirsén, Anders Flodman, Frans Hedberg, Hugo Nisbeth, Frans Hodell,[5] and Richard Gustafsson, plus Carl von Bergen. For me, Viktor Rydberg is therefore the illustrious progenitor of all that's vapid, and that's why he hates me, persecutes me, and reviles me, while I simply don't give a shit about him! *Voilà*!

But my spirit haunts him, day and night; he can feel himself rotting away, fears he'll fall apart, and pulls himself together by trying to kill me with *The Weapon Smith*, only to become so frightened that I wouldn't really die that he fled to Gothenburg in a fit of persecution mania. (We both spent that winter[6] at Djursholm.) No, Rydberg embodies the barren woman's terrible envy and hatred for someone who is fertile.

And what haven't I shaken out of my trousers! Even though Sweden was stony ground! Novels and poetry, plays good and bad, Histories of Sweden and China, and four children, a fifth on the way, and *two* wives.

To Rydberg and the other great Swedes, I'm the Black Balder at whom they've been shooting for fifteen years. Who will find the mistletoe? Loki![7]

Farewell, and enjoy what's vapid! I'm now hanging up on Sweden!

Your Friend,
August Strindberg

305. To ADOLF PAUL

Ardagger, Whit Monday [14 May] 1894

Dear Paul,

I do believe you're afraid! But I assure you, Poland is *ganz* harmless because when he starts lying, he loses his edge. This is his situation. That whore Juel hooked Birnbaum [*sic*], the editor of the *Freie Bühne*.[1] Poland praised his friend Munch's paintings there in such an idiotic way = spinal marrow and neuroglia, *gebährmutter*[2] and my old *Sonnengeflechte*,[3] that Birnbaum was sacked and the whole circle split up.

What's the good of them praising each other when no one reads them? Ola H. may have praised that Cuckoo Rydberg[4] (honorary member of the Swedish Publishers' Association!), but no one reads him in Germany!

I'm sure Fru T.[5] damaged my prospects with Lautenburg, but with my nine kingdoms, I can afford to lose Norway.

That Poland hates me because I mounted his Juel before she knew him, I can understand; but on the other hand, I really can't take all his future marriages into account every time I have intercourse!

Even Lidforss isn't dangerous; he's pathological and probably looking for a nail or a branch after his latest exploit, for such deeds will give him no peace.

He described his life with Poland when they lived three to a room. Poland drunk and asleep, B.L. and Juel sitting undressed on the edge of the bed – without coupling (?).

Then along came Bäckström[6] with his millions. Accused Poland who defended himself by saying Aspasia had slept with four different nations in a month. B. sought out Lidforss, who confirmed it! That might have seemed it where I was concerned! But their hatred for me has deeper grounds.

I now erase Lidforss from the ranks of the living! He no longer exists for me!

I found his most recent exploit quite appalling, and refrain from relating it.[7] I once called him a 'disgusting person', which I repeat!

But Asch and Schleich?

Impatiently

Yrs,
August Strindberg

306. To ADOLF PAUL

[27 May 1894]

Dear A.P.,

That may be what A. and S. said,[1] but what did they do? *Nichts*, probably!

L.[2] took me by surprise at first, but now he interests me. And psychologically, how can he explain his behaviour towards me? If I were to publish his latest letter in Lund, written when he was translating *Antibarbarus*, where he agrees with me 'in the main', I wonder what he'd do? – What did he say to you about his article in D.N.? Do L. and Poland think I *can* be exterminated? They're destroying themselves, for they know that whoever touches me dies, as when one carelessly fingers an electric accumulator. Without my needing to raise my hand! Look how L. blew himself up! They attack me in Stockholm, I'm dead for a day, then up I pop in Karlstad;[3] then they kill me in Christiania,[4] and up I pop in Paris, where Bigeon[5] has just published *Les Revoltés Scandinaves*, in which I am the only Swede. I fell in Rome,[6] was whistled in Naples, and rose like a sun in Copenhagen;[7] was booed in Berlin by Aspasia and the cuckolds, and popped up straight away in Moscow.[8] Last Autumn, *A Madman* was put on trial in Berlin and pirated by *Budkaflen*; once again I was a *todte Mann*.[9] Then Pow! Cherbuliez, the secretary of the French Academy, writes a whole essay about Aug Sg in the *Revue des Deux Mondes*. No, they can't eradicate me! I've Paris dangling on a hook now, the next season is mine. I'm going there this autumn, when everything is ready. *Dramatique*, vol. 2, will appear any day now with *The Bond*, *Playing with Fire*, *Creditors*, and my portrait on the cover. *Le Figaro* has interviewed me about Zola's candidacy.[10] No, they won't exterminate me, but I can exterminate my enemies, you just watch how meekly they'll bite the dust – but fast this time. I've learned how to improve on chance!

If you're in touch with the Bureau,[11] announce a new novel: *Everybody's Aspasia* by Aug Sg. Set in Berlin. But dear, and cash only. If they'd rather have *Vergangenheit* IV[12] first, they can, and for a decent price (500 Marks, cash down, unabridged!) considering it's *unpublished in Sweden*! Will you undertake negotiations?

Today my wife presented me with a daughter!

Yrs,

August Strindberg

307. To GEORG BRANDES

Ardagger via Amstetten, Nieder Oestreich,
31 May 1894

Most respected Herr Doctor,

The solitary soul is accustomed to fly to you when overwhelmed by stupidity, malice and envy, but I don't come like faithless youth, asking your help only to stab you in the back with renewed vigour.

You may know that a recent work of mine, *Antibarbarus*, has caused the Swedes to depict me as first a rogue and then a madman – for them the notion is a mere fifteen years old! – All I'm asking is that you get this letter,[1] discreetly, into a Danish paper, preferably *Politiken*. If you know a Danish chemist who is educated enough to see that I have simply taken Monism, the doctrine which we all profess, to its logical conclusion, and who is willing to write a short introduction, that would help!

There is in fact not a single paper in Sweden honourable enough to print a word in my defence, even if it's reviled me beyond measure! Haeckel's letter doesn't say much, but it nevertheless acknowledges that I am not mad, and that a *geistreicher*[2] Chemist entertained similar ideas, also that I can rest assured in my success. I have witnessed many interesting things, but none more so than this last one: to see a whole country's chemists so blinded by jealousy that they cannot acknowledge their own views when they see them put forward by someone they find offensive!

I am no dilettante where chemistry is concerned; as a boy I did laboratory work, as a medical student I studied on a regular basis, etc. (See *The Son of a Servant* I, II.)

With followers in Berlin among practising doctors, I might have smiled at the sneers of idiotic Sweden, but this time my personal freedom is threatened, and my relatives are beginning to concern themselves about me. I'm depending on your help, and hope to be able to return the favour, perhaps this autumn when I go to Paris, where I now have my finger firmly on the pulse!

Yours ever,
August Strindberg

308. To GEORGES LOISEAU

Georges Loiseau (1864–1949), French writer and dramatist whose play, *Péché d'amour* (Sin of Love), written in collaboration with Michel Carré, had been performed at the Théâtre Libre. Loiseau later managed the Casino at Deauville, but between 1892 and 1895 he devoted much of his time to translating, editing, and revising Strindberg's works, including *Creditors, The Bond, Playing with Fire,* and *A Madman's Defence,* working either from Strindberg's French or from German editions. Many of the letters with which Strindberg bombarded him contain plans for productions of *Sir Bengt's Wife* with Sarah Bernhardt, and *Lucky Peter's Journey* at the Théâtre du Châtelet, but neither scheme came to anything. By 1895 the two were wary of each other, and their collaboration ceased, although Strindberg contacted him in 1898 concerning *To Damascus,* and again in 1900 and 1901 over *Easter* and *The Dance of Death.* But by then Loiseau was no longer interested, and passed the typescripts on to Lugné-Poë, who mislaid them. Over one hundred of Strindberg's letters to Loiseau survive.

[Original in French]

Ardagger via Amstetten, Basse-Autriche
3 June 1894

Cher Monsieur, et Ami,

In haste, the most necessary answers instead of by telegram.[1] *Ohne Versöhnung* = means, simply: Without reconciliation! That is to say: As friends; in a non hostile frame of mind.

Tekla is afraid of parting from this redoubtable man as an enemy. That is all! No trace of a lewd implication!

He who has seen his shadow, will die.[2]

In our mythology, it was a portent of death if one saw oneself (*Sosie*?)[3] Here I am symbolising (!): Tekla, who leads an unconscious existence as women do, who commits crimes without hesitating, and who cries afterwards, with a sincere heart, is brought by Gustav to reflect on herself, becomes unmasked before herself, is made conscious. She is thus torn apart by the disharmony that enters her life when she discovers what she is and what she believed herself to be. Hence she sees herself; and she is going to die.

Moreover! Tekla is not a monster, since there are no such things as monsters; she is an egoist, naive, spoilt, hungry for power, etc., like other people.

And furthermore, regarding the cuts, I am writing at once to Monsieur Bang,[4] and in Swedish, and I give you two, the director, and the others concerned, a free hand. The actors who have to deliver the offending words are the best critics in this case.

Finally, and in order to counter the anticipated attacks:

Tekla is the double of Laura in *The Father*. *The Father* and *Creditors* were both published two years before *Hedda Gabler*, who resembles Tekla. Hence I am not the epigone. This is worth remembering, since every year I am accused of having copied this female figure, who is truly my own, from Ibsen. But it's a pity that Volume II will not appear. What's to be done? Edit *Creditors* as a booklet! And sell it at the performance! I lay no claim to any author's rights!

Creditors has been played once in Copenhagen, and M. Bang turned down the role, that's true.[5]

And the piece was played in Berlin 50 times last year; a great success.

Besides, if you are after an analysis, read the essay by M. Adolf Paul on the performance of *Creditors* in Berlin in the book on S-g.[6] It's not bad.

And finally – my regards to M. Poë, and to the other participants. Rameau[7] will have a success as the psychological assassin, the lover of vivisection!

And my thanks to you, from

Yours sincerely,
August Strindberg

309. To LEOPOLD LITTMANSSON

Ardagger via Amstetten, Basse-Autriche
19 June 1894

Dear Lyktnanntson,

We're now getting on for fyfty, have danced away our mylk teeth and should be thynking of our tail end, yet I can't help laughing when I thynk of this joke called lyfe, which is nevertheless pretty serious between tymes.

That's why I'm wryting to you again to fynd out if you're alyve and would lyke to put me up over the summer – pension la Kymmendö as it were. So I can learn to speak French as well as a Swede can.

I really am damned big now; my byst is in the Finnish (!) National Museum,[1] and in 2 waxworks[2] with a whorelike mane of hair and dirty clothes (like Hjalmar Hyrsch[3] once had); have been hyssed in Naples and played once (1!) 'In Rome' (and *The Outlaw*), as well as crytycyzed by Sarcey[4] yn Parys, etc.

But Hjalmar ys also big; there's a sketch of him in *Hvad nytt från Stockholm*.[5]

I've been married twyce but remain a monogamist; have also unmasked the whole Unyverse along with God, Jesus and the Angels.

Ekström[6] is very big; has 6,000 *kronor* in the Bank and dines in the Gothic Rooms at Berns with Prince Eugen, where the Red Room was before; but he hasn't any front teeth left, only a skunk collar.

Anyway: if you live outside Paris and I'm welcome, please let me know straight away.

Yours,
August Strindberg

310. To ADOLF PAUL

[21 June 1894]

Dear A.P.,

A new plan means cancelling *Antibarbarus*.[1] Am pushing on to Paris, where the whole book will appear at once, in French. Now you're writing an opera libretto, haven't you thought of going further than Mascagni[2] and Convaljen[3] and using modern blokes in stylish outfits, and no folk dress. He, She, and the Other in redingotes, with a table and chair. What do you say to *The Bond*? (Imagine the twelve jurymen as a chorus for baritones and bases!) What choruses, ensembles and Solos with Leitmotifs! Beat Mascagni's world record!

A. Sg

311. To GEORG BRANDES

Ardagger, 26 June 1894

Dear Herr Dr Brandes,

I didn't believe life had any more surprises in store for me, but when this curious Lidforss business arose, I discovered I was only flattering myself. At first, I tried to find it interesting, but then I fell back into my old groove, and found it tragic. Why tragic? – About four years ago in Lund, I was sought out by a young man who worshipped me. This was Lidforss, at the time an amanuensis at the laboratory of plant physiology there. Two years previously he had read my *Flower Paintings and Animal Pieces* and discovered in its popular format the key to a new science; he swore he would quote Strindberg in defence of his Doctoral thesis. We botanised in Lund, talking for 24 hours at a stretch about biology, botany, everything.

I returned to the Stockholm area and we carried on a long correspondence about science, in which L. assumed the role of disciple, sending me plants and books and offering me his most powerful microscope, etc. as well as visiting you with Mörner about the Strindberg book in which, of course, L. was to write on 'Sg as Scientist'.

Then sex reared its head!

I was living in Berlin, a widower waiting for the wind which would cast me up on dry land. As I had no home, I sat like other castaways in the tavern so as to have someone to talk to. Then along came a Norwegian painter[1] with a woman: the painter preened himself before me (he didn't know I already had two women, since I didn't think that anything to boast about). The woman was curious about Sg, the woman hater, and her lover arrogant. In short, I did my duty to my self – and then retired. This hurt the woman.

Now L. arrived in Berlin and presented himself as the woman's suitor. I rated L. higher than that, and told him everything – even that his bride had had four different nationalities over her in a month.

He proposed all the same, and was turned down! Then I married elsewhere and moved away!

We'd previously coupled the woman with a Pole, and L. became their *Hausfreund*. (Later the Norwegian and a Prussian[2] also became Friends of the newly weds.)

A long pause!

Then L. popped up again after being evicted from the Polish camp, and sought me out.

He translates *Antibarbarus*. Goes around with me every day while we're reading the proofs, makes some comments on matters of detail of course, but agrees with me on all the major issues. When the book is ready for publication, we parted as friends. Six days later I read his article in *Dagens Nyheter*, which must therefore have been written the day after my departure to have made it up to Stockholm, been printed, and come back down to the Danube.

Initially, I was struck by the false signature, B.D., instead of the usual B.L.[3] But then I thought: well, he still feels some shame.

But there was something in the article which gave me reason to believe that B.L. is the one who's mad. In his epigraph, 'Themistocles wandered at night because he could not sleep', he has described himself. For this has nothing to with me and my habits; I lead a regular life and go to bed at 8, 9 or 10, while Lidforss is a notorious nightbird.

And if one reads the quotation in full, it runs: 'Themistocles wandered at night because *Miltiades' victory* would not let him sleep in peace.'

This is what came out against his will.

But the Swedish papers embroidered upon it, and sought the cause of *my* mental disorder in *my* sleeplessness.

Well, you've experienced something similar, and *die perfide Jugend*[4] doesn't change.

It's true one can outgrow and overtake one's teacher, but in 2 days – that's impossible!

So he carried a knife in his pocket during our last days in Berlin, and is a *Strassenräuber*![5]

Nor can he defend himself by saying he had compassion for the ravings of a madman and spared him on that account, for his letters show that he took my science seriously, something his next work was to have demonstrated.[6] But by then I was ready to publish the results of my experiments in the physiology of plants, particularly concerning their transmutation (in the primordial leaf) and *nervous system* (not soul!), which B.L. acknowledged in his letters was my discovery, and something entirely new!

You needn't answer this long letter; but please preserve it.

In the past I didn't usually defend myself, but then I saw a whole collection of myths grow up about my person (cf. Fru Marholm's imbecile article in the Strindberg book!), ineradicable legends which had quite disastrous consequences for me; therefore I began to parry and counter attack. Then people went on about revenge and said I was vindictive; they even had the audacity to demand I go and place myself against a wall while they shot at me undisturbed.

If there's any sign of *Politiken* suppressing your article, take it back and seek another outlet – perhaps Swedish! – or Norwegian!

I shall probably be in Sweden next week, and it would be good not to have to return a miscrowned madman.

Thank you, however, and may things be better for you than they are for me!

Yours ever,
August Strindberg

312. To RICHARD BERGH

Sven Richard Bergh (1858–1919), painter. The son of a distinguished landscape painter, he studied at the Swedish Royal Academy of Fine Arts and then spent several years in France, including a number of visits to the artist colony at Grèz-sur-Loing. He established himself as a portrait painter whose interest in psychology was evident in *Hypnotic Seance* (1887), with its evocation of the widespread contemporary interest in suggestion and hysteria, and though he proved receptive to the influence of Gauguin, and played a decisive role in the development of Swedish National Romanticism in the landscapes he produced at Varberg on the Swedish west coast between 1893 and 1896, it is his studies of his contemporaries and friends (e.g. *Ellen Key* (1891), *August Strindberg* (1905), *Gustaf Fröding* (1910) and *Hjalmar Branting* (1912)) that have endured, his most frequently reproduced painting, *Nordic Summer Evening* (1899–1900), notwithstanding. Bergh was a leading force among the artists who seceded from the Academy in 1885, and he became secretary of the Artist's Union on its foundation in 1886. During the 1890s he devoted a great deal of time to teaching at the school of art which he established in his own atelier in Stockholm, and he was also an active polemicist, engaged in the discussion of numerous cultural, social and political issues. He made a last important contribution to the cultural life of Sweden through his appointment in 1915 as director of the National Museum.

He and Strindberg first met in 1889, and they maintained a friendly correspondence from 1891 until the latter's death. Bergh was a welcome visitor at Strindberg's Beethoven evenings during the 1900s, and he regarded the writer, whom he described as 'an old, wounded but proud lion', as 'the most interesting model I have ever had. I read in his face, with its many lines of fate, as in a marvellous book'. Although sitting for Bergh tried Strindberg's patience, their friendship survived the experience, and he clearly valued Bergh's opinion of his later works. There are eighty-one extant letters from Strindberg to Bergh plus twenty-six from Bergh to Strindberg.

Ardagger via Amstetten, 9 July 1894

Richard Bergh,

Having drunk a glass of milk, I've regained the strength to think, and confess the following:

I have, as they say, Paris on a hook; I'm even negotiating with the Châtelet about *Lucky Peter* and 'Saint Peter',[1] and can hence espy money on the horizon. But my temperament, my habits, and an anxiety about my person, the self's instinct for its own preservation, drives me away from Paris.

On the other hand, my economy is such that for ten months I haven't been able to send anything to the children in my first marriage (my oldest daughter already writes abusive demanding letters – at fourteen! – right!) – and since the birth of a child here as well – I've got to emigrate – for I can see no source of income, and it's no longer possible to go on living here free of charge, not after I ejected my rich old in-laws, who at least got the impression that I wasn't a fortune hunter.[2]

In brief: on the one hand Paris, with three theatres open to me, *The Father* coming up this autumn, and all the rest: publishers including Ollendorff and Charpentier (!).[3] First-class company: Cherbuliez (who wrote about me in *Revue des Deux Mondes* and caused this last storm of hatred in Sweden), Coppée,[4] who writes me unsolicited compliments now that I've taken the sting out of his Anti-Scandinavianism with 'France et Suède', Zola! about whose candidature I was interviewed by post for *Le Figaro* – and replied! Mme Adam. The Marquise Saint-Denys, etc. And then Sarah Bernhardt, who lives in the same village as my friend, Österlind,[5] who lives with his friend, Charpentier, in Brittany. In short, all that!

On the other hand, I'd rather beg in Sweden, beg freedom for myself and my family by way of a sinecure that wouldn't bind me in any way.

If you pass through Gothenburg and know Algot Carlander, just mention that now is the time for his brother-in-law Krusenstjerna[6] to speak to the King in Marstrand (as he promised).

The customs officer at Sandhamn is about to retire, and might do so straight away. I could have the job (I don't give a damn about the title) and then in a year's time be pensioned off with a house and salary for the rest of my life!

If that isn't on, then give me a 1st Class lighthouse, which is about to be closed down! Or re-open Korsö lighthouse outside Sandhamn, and close it again in a year.

I could have Korsö anyway, since it's disused and might be converted into five rooms and a kitchen. This is my dearest wish. Listen, the lighthouse could be equipped as a meteorological station with a post specially created for me there as superintendent, but with my own telegraph! Hey! I've been a telegraphist! So there![7]

Ask around! – But no begging lists or anything like that!

A foreign country is enemy territory, and not speaking your own language softens the brain etc., etc.

Hope this letter reaches you before you leave.

Yrs,
August Strindberg

313. To RICHARD BERGH

[9 July 1894]

Richard Bergh,
(Cont.)

But this time without v. Steijern and Geijerstam, for reasons you're partly aware of.[1] The price was too high, and when the bill arrives, gratitude ceases and business starts.

Again: you wonder why I'm asking you to deal with Carlander and don't come myself? I've been awaiting money for the journey for 6 weeks, damn it! Another week and it will be too late![2]

Should anything else 'be done' for me, nothing seems more suitable or honourable to our country than this: Give me a theatre!

Sweden lacked a drama; I created one, and one which will soon take the world record.

I seem to remember reading in D.N. this winter that compared to P.S., G. af G.,[3] Knut Michaelson and Fru Wahlenberg, I am no dramatist; but they can take that back. The fact is, I wasn't played between 70 & 80; 90–1910 ditto. In order to write plays there must be some prospect of having them performed. The theatre should be small and simple, a converted courtyard or large room. Not built, only hired. Lindberg, the Engelbrechts and some others could be assembled, with Lindberg as director of the 'Strindberg Theatre'; that's what it's to be called, and only Strindberg will be performed there. In Berlin an old actor founded a theatre and simply called it the Wallner-Thomas Theatre after himself. Only Strindberg because Sg isn't performed anywhere else; and because the 'others' are performed elsewhere, especially if they write shit – they have it Royally!

However, an enterprise like this mustn't be founded from below, so that it smells of partisanship, but from above.

I don't know if I can still count on my friends in Gothenburg. Last winter Bååth[4] left a letter of mine unanswered and Warburg took the opportunity (after I'd sent him 2 letters) of addressing some stupid remarks to me, which certainly had mass support before he dared come out with them. – They concerned Rydberg; I may not have written Goethe's *Faust* like V.R.,[5] but I am incontrovertibly Sweden's foremost dramatist. Can't one unite on that basis?

I'd like the appeal for a theatre to be signed by:

Prof. Ljunggren,[6] Nyblom, Snoilsky, Rydberg (N.B. I've never attacked him, and he shouldn't be angry with me just because he attacked me!), Wennerberg[7] – Wirsén – etc. (K. Warburg starting it off.)

Is that possible?

I'd be there with you now if I could afford the journey, but I've hardly enough for a stamp.

Yrs,
Aug Strindberg

314. To LEOPOLD LITTMANSSON

[14? July 1894]

My dear Friend,

If you really want a serious discussion, I'll doff my fool's cap which conceals a Buddha, or a Dominican – and then we can talk seriously.

First about you!

You once had a seed of Buddha in you, and felt something wanted to grow in your belly, a desire to propagate your soul in other people's brains . . . to evolve into a superman and tame the beast. You're an Arian as the Persians are, and a Parsee;[1] you should see your portrait which I found in a travelogue of Persia. You had blue eyes but the teeth of a tiger, vainly concealed by a long tiger moustache. As you well remember, you loved meat; you always wanted a rare Chateaubriand, while I preferred pigswill like herring salad. But you reacted against your predatory nature and became a vegetarian. You wanted women, too, perhaps more from vanity, like an oriental, than from desire, and you also frequently mistook the creative urge of your spirit for your body's. I concede that a woman's embrace resembles the joy of giving birth to a new thought or beautiful image, but this ungratified sexual desire and hunger is transformed into intellectual power.

(I wrote my strongest pieces, *Miss Julie* and *Creditors*, in 30 days, when condemned to celibacy.)

Were you weak? No, I don't believe so! But your violin is pathological! Did any of your ancestors have aborted musical impulses, which then possessed you? You're obsessed by that shit box, and always were. When you squeezed sounds from it, you buried the text beneath the noise, and its strings consumed every scrap of nervous energy intended for other purposes.

Your eyes were opened early, like mine, but your scepticism devoured your sinews; my scepticism rendered me sterile for seven years until, like Kant, I had to invent a categorical imperative and postulate. Everything is shit, I said, but suppose some of it is less shitty than the rest! I invented poets and socialists, reformers and blasphemers; begot with myself, like

Zeus, a whole Olympus of madmen and imposters, saints and children! Therefore I lived.

Do you know Nietzsche? No? Ah! –

The secret of life: The Will to Power; over minds!

Happiness: to be able to grow and to rule.

Unhappiness: not to be able to grow and to be ruled.

This is happiness, this feeling of power, to sit in a cottage by the Danube, surrounded by six women who think I'm a semi-idiot, and knowing that right now, in Paris, in the intellectual headquarters of the world, 500 people are sitting like mice in an auditorium, and foolishly exposing their brains to my suggestions.[2] Some revolt, but many leave there with my spores in their grey matter; they go home pregnant with the seed of my mind, and then spawn my brood.

In six months, I'll read a French book, a French paper, and recognize my offspring! Aha! Those are my grains sprouting!

That is happiness!

When I read last winter that a young Frenchman had had a play performed at the Théâtre Français,[3] and the paper said it had been inspired by *Miss Julie*, I felt my power, like Merlin, the magician!

I understand your velocipede! An extension of muscles and wings, an ever-present danger overcome; an ideal body, better than the one God gave us, but – there's your violin again in another guise. Fontanelles! Everything which ought to come out of the brain's anus, you extract by way of artificial fistulas! This illusory sense of power on the velocipede, I once experienced on horseback, round the bar table, where I shone, dreamt it in the pulpit, on stage! Now I have it at my desk with my pen; and only there. I never play the master in my daily life; it's too small! And it encourages one to waste one's strength: cracking a nut with a sledgehammer. My former wife could do what she wanted – but I also *wrote* what I wanted, and therefore my mind was never dominated, only my sexual drive.

Are you going through a crisis again? – I always move off, as soon as I notice someone stroking my wings! And I'm always ready to pull up my tent-pegs when the atmosphere starts to get oppressive! As it is now!

The flesh was your 'tragic flaw', and the family mine. But one has to go through everything – and put it all behind one! *Vorwärts*![4]

I've reached the point where I must make a choice![5] Either turn into a philistine, plant vines and cabbages, become an heir, and eat myself sick, or – Excelsior!

Listen!

Don't come here! I'll come to Paris! If you're really in earnest and want to be someone, to do something, then take up your cross and follow me. Once I have a disciple, I'm going to the Ardennes to rent a house and found a monastery. Rules and habit (a variation on the Dominicans!) already worked out. I'll fill the house in 30 days, and with rich young men who'll buy a really old monastery – in France – and equip it with a library, ateliers, a laboratory, organ room and garden!

Rules: complete freedom, but no women. Purpose: that the individual, by reducing his living costs to a minimum, can liberate himself from his digestive organs in order to be able to grow in freedom to the highest stage of human development. Etc. Etc.

And then, yesterday, the following books were advertised in the *Journal des Débats*:

Fr. Jollivet-Castelot. *La Vie et l'âme de la matière. Études de dynamochemie.*

and

Claude Hemel. *Les Métamorphoses de la matière!*[6]

Both from Sociéte d'Éditions, 4 rue Antoine-Dubois!

Oh buy them – they cost 3 F.50 each – I haven't a sou! Have a read and then send me them! They bear me out, you see!

I am ill! –

You ask what I want of you! – I need someone who believes in me, and you need an earthmother to extract your progeny for you! Isn't that 'fair play'? No illusions!

Shall we be serious from now on? Our best 30 years are before us, when we ought to be wise and delight in the happiness power brings!

Am enclosing a book! See what a new world it opens up! *Es ist eine Lust zu leben!*[7]

August Sg

315. To LEOPOLD LITTMANSSON

[15 July 1894]

My dear Leopold,

(Cont.)

Léon Daudet[1] may not be on the wrong track in *Hæres* when he maintains that man goes through his ontogeny (like sulphur) not only in the oviduct but also later on in life – like this: the young man under thirty duplicates his mother with a woman's hysteria, lust, vanity and everything vile; from 30–40 he recapitulates the father with his ambition, strength and insensitivity; only after fifty does the self appear, as it has been engendered by these father and mother doubles.

So *à nous la vie*![2] (As Zola said when he turned 50 and began to ride a velocipede!)

A monastery, without walls, would have the aim (I repeat myself!) of producing a fine specimen of humanity by combatting the beast in man: the suppression of the vegetative and animal functions in order to further the emotional and intellectual.

The cultivation of the spirit by isolation and shutting off contact with impurity; emancipation from expensive and unprofitable habits. Simplicity in food and drink.

I've allowed 1 franc a day for living expenses.

Every brother can obtain this by half an hour's work.

The monastery will have no servants; no cooking. Everyone will clean their own room, so they know when it's available and hence free from servants and filth (= maids = the filthiest). Whether or not food should be cooked is a problem. Uncooked food decomposes and ferments more easily in the stomach, as it should, and cooked food gives indigestion and ruins the teeth. Mainly vegetarian food.

10 cent.	Morning: 1 quarter of milk and 1 roll.
30 cent.	12 a.m.: lunch: Cold ham, sausage, 2 eggs, a piece of cheese, an apple, a roll; 1 glass watered wine.
10 cent.	Evening: 1 quarter of milk, 1 roll; an apple, cheese.

= 50 centimes: rent 25 cent. Fuel, light, washing, etc. 25 cent. = say 1 franc.

The same habit for all, but with a distinction between grades. Black monk's cowl, with hood; many pockets containing: Comb, toothbrush, soap; 2 small towels; 1 pair of socks; needle and thread; buttons; tinder-box; writing materials and paper; twine; postcards, stamps;

For travelling: always ready packed: a case containing: a lightweight hammock, a blanket; gutta-percha; nails; needles; drinking vessels; plates; knife and fork, etc. And to eat = Pemmican bread (baked from dry meat extract, flour with bran, currants, egg white, milk and powdered peas. Strongly spiced).

No one should expect personal freedom in the monastery since its aim is the training of superior beings, and training means the suppression of the baser instincts. But subordination to the rules is voluntary, and there will be no disciplining of individuals or verbal reprimands.

Anyone who violates the rules will exclude themselves. (Not for minor infringements, however.)

The regulations embody advice and directions for the formation of a harmonious, wise and worthy being who seeks in his spirit to emulate his fine outward behaviour.

All loud talk, shouting, sneering and laughter is prohibited. Outbursts of anger or violent emotion which interfere with reason are forbidden.

No one has the right to greet or address a brother who indicates he wishes to remain alone in contemplation.

The Prior's power is limited to following the rules, upholding them, and seeing they are applied. No assemblies, no speeches, no feasts in order not to disturb the individual in his self-development and exert mass suggestion upon him. Anyone who wishes to consult the Prior shall notify him in advance, when the Prior shall appoint a time.

The monastery shall be subsidized by voluntary gifts, by the work and legacies of the brothers. All the sciences, arts, and literature may be cultivated, but in every case with the specific purpose of their development, seeking new paths.

Particular stress shall be laid on fostering a collaboration between philosophers, scientists and historians in order to seek the solution to the riddle of life, which must be solved.

Those inventions in most urgent need of discovery so as to liberate the spirit from its bonds and raise it over time and space are: the one-man aeroplane (my invention), not the airship; the telescope (without lense and reflector), etc. (see my *Antibarbarus*); the art of making gold and diamonds (it's already possible to make silver, although people think it's only 'reproduced', and silver has thus lost its value). Hence money will be overthrown!

People are to be enticed away from the cities and from luxury; hence the overthrow of industry and luxury goods. We shall thus return *in part* to the simple, modest life of the savage, and become philosophers like the Redskins and the Hindoos. Less food, less work, a greater and higher intellectual life.

(Rousseau was right, and will soon come again.)
[25 lines omitted]

I've chosen the Ardennes because it's on the main Cologne-Paris line by which people come from the North and East, and from the West, from Paris!

This is my dream! When we've trained ourselves to produce the highest form of human being, then and only then shall we reveal ourselves! Like the salvation army! We'll build a white Viking ship in gold and other colours; dress ourselves in white ceremonial attire and row down the river Aisne; sail when the wind is with us with blue silken sails down the Oise and into the Seine; pass through Paris without disembarking, playing new instruments, which I'll invent, and new melodies, which I'll let nature (chance) invent; singing songs in scales with quarter tones and in eighths, which no one's ever heard before; and so we'll sail into the Marne and up again to Aisne, our home!

But before then, training! Seeking, ruthlessly, without fear!

Scepticism! Yes! Of the old! But belief in the new: your scepticism seems like fear of ridicule, as mine sometimes is! Also a lack of tension in the clockwork, so that the wires slip the tackle and the machinery goes backwards, the weight tumbles down, goes 'bom', and comes to a standstill. And when you wind it up, it comes tumbling down again!

What if I can't get away? Then you come here! 24 hours by train from Paris. Via Pontarlier – Zürich – Munich – Salzburg – Vienna.

Amstetten is between Salzburg and Vienna! From there one travels the stretch to Ardagger by carriage. – Wonderful landscape with the Danube and Alps.

Fine hotel, rural, etc.

But I live in Dornach, directly opposite Ardagger on the other side of the Danube.

Or the Orient express: Paris – Nancy – Strassburg – Stuttgart – Munich – Salzburg – Vienna! If it stops in Amstetten!

Heavens, give me a glimpse of those two books, otherwise I'll die! I'm so dreadfully poor!

begs

Your

August Strindberg

[postscript omitted]

316. To GEORG BRANDES

[16 July 1894]

Dear Dr.,

I've just seen two new books in the *Journal des Débats*, whose titles suggest something Antibarbarian. Perhaps your chemist would be interested in them:

François Jollivet-Castelot: *La Vie et l'âme de la matière. Études de dynamochimie.*

Société d'Éditions Scientifiques, 4 rue Antoine Dubois (Paris)

3 francs 50

Claude Hemel: *Les Métamorphoses de la matière.*
3 F.50 *Ibidem.*

In haste, Yrs respectfully,
August Strindberg

317. To LEOPOLD LITTMANSSON

Ardagger, 22 July 1894

Dear Friend,

You are still living in the past, and your thoughts are preoccupied with shadows that no longer exist: humanity, virtue, vice – whether secret or not – happiness and unhappiness, etc. The only thing that exists is the self (*le culte du moi*), and I know nothing about the world and 'other people' except through my self. Every individual is the centre of his 'od-circle',[1] everyone sees their own rainbow, and two people cannot stand on the same longitude and latitude at once.

'Have you noticed that when one sits down on a bench while out walking and begins to draw in the sand with one's stick, what finally emerges is a mass of concentric circles in which I (you) are the central point? Why *unbewusst*[2] draw these circles? That point is the self's first movement out into space: the desire to mark out one's territory . . . and above all make oneself the central point' (thus I recently began an essay on the self).[3]

Why do I find one landscape dead and unattractive and another beautiful and harmonious? Because the one reflects my self and the other doesn't.

Why is gazing into the face of a loving woman, a woman who loves me, so wonderful? Because it reflects my soul as it is in moments of ecstasy, generosity, and creation, and as I cannot see myself at such times, I see myself in her. Or in your child's face, when it listens to your words of wisdom, or receives a present and beams with gratitude!

I! and the others, only in so far as they form coordinates which determine where my self is.

I think you're going to have to let yourself be taught by Schopenhauer, Hartmann, Feuerbach[4] and Nietzsche, and I've the feeling that with you, I'm still talking to a ghost from my hideous youth: with Strauss[5] and V. Rydberg, Spinoza and Mendelssohn,[6] Büchner[7] and Parker![8]

Rhapsodies: (1) Your tragic flaw is your insincerity towards yourself! With your scepticism towards others, you showed your desire for power early on = strength and instinct to rule = Buddha = the strong self. You loved my weak, gelatinous brother Axel because he submitted to you, but you gladly avoided me, or wanted to reduce me to a position of inferiority by your criticism.

(2) You had the seeds of growth in you, but you didn't cultivate your self with brutal egoism. You couldn't invent several persons out of yourself; you couldn't pull yourself up by your own hair, as Münchhausen and I could, and lift yourself out of your scepticism; you couldn't seek out your ur-self and use it to discipline the other conventional selves which others had poked down into your soul; you couldn't stand above your self.

(3) You must still be weak because you set your sights on something outside yourself, on the possibility of an eighty-year-old woman's money.[9] And you're in a terrible cul-de-sac of contradictions when you can't see that my idea for a monastery offers salvation from being dependent upon money! I was confronted by the same dilemma ten years ago: either increase my income and be done for as a genius and a person, or reduce my expenses. With superhuman efforts, I managed the latter.

(4) I had the idea of, first, writing the Rules of the Order and then appealing to the President of France and the King of Belgium for permission to have it legalised as a mendicant order.

For Raskolnikov (Eugene Aram!)[10] is not my style, and nor is making money out of ideas.

(5) If necessary beg, borrow, as scholars (and Luther) once did. On behalf of poor students!

(6) Besides, one can earn 30 francs a month without damaging one's soul. One can get permission from the police to play in the streets; and if I create a new instrument for you, on which you can use your violinist's technique, you and I could make enough for a month in one day.

(7) Buddha and the others succeeded! For they achieved their aim of becoming the straw and muck in the great spiritual dung heap from which our Jonah gourds have grown and now give shadow to the world.

(8) Children! What is a child? A human being by 9! My children are over nine, and hence no longer exist for me as children! I grieved for them as for the dead, when they no longer smiled at me with their kind, friendly milk teeth.

(9) My fourteen-year-old daughter already writes impertinent, heartless, brutal dunning letters to me, and is delighted when someone writes something nasty about me in the papers! And I've loved this child more than myself, and she has idolized me.

Hosanna!

(10) Father and Mother? – What have I to do with you? And children?

(11) I hover between extremes of pleasure and pain!

Yesterday, when I read the two books you were so kind as to send me, I thought for a moment there must be a God, who had sent me these ravens with food for my soul! There were my own ideas! One author pronounces his belief in the possibility of making gold! But compared to me both of them were infants!

(12) It's not poverty that depresses me, even though my letters have to

wait in line for a week to get a stamp. I find wisdom in an encyclopedia from 1840 and torn-up newspapers in the toilet. But I've such an enormous mass of material, both lived and researched, in notes and in my head, that it grows if I take a walk or lie in a dark room.

(13) What now keeps me going is the thought of my *Antibarbarus*, whose exoteric part is complete in manuscript, its esoteric in notes = thousands of pages and jottings.

It contains everything: a new physics, astronomy, coelestography, the physiology of plants, and finally alongside them: a science of man.

(14) But I'm fearful of coming too late!

(15) Has Wronski[11] published anything? From certain expressions he seems to have something in common with theosophy and other well-known fads, Volapük[12] – or universal-arcana-revelatory-arabian-philosophies.

You seem to want to arrange, to systematize and trilogize, the great confusion which simply is, and is marvellous in its disorder = freedom. I daren't write that dangerous word which begins with α and ends – in Greek – with α,[13] and which is the secret of creation. Have you read *By the Open Sea*? Am sending it in German just in case.

Ivan[14] became a myth for you because he was blond! But there was jiggery-pokery there too! Gesticulator! And now he has had ten fine years in the bosom of Abraham without needing to work – and yet! The sacrifice for Adolf! Oh shit! The old man was a fiendish beggar and filled his lair with masses of money, like an old fox!

I don't know what fate now holds in store for me, but I feel 'The Hand of the Lord' poised above me. A change is in the offing, upwards, or straight down to the centre of the earth, who knows about such things!

Sometimes these letters, so unusually long for me, contain a presentiment of the decrepit horse trotting wearily to its resting place! I've also relapsed into superstition; hear ravens in my garden; children weeping on the other side of the Danube; dream of bygone days, and feel a yearning to fly, in some tepid substance between air and water, dressed in white, hearing no human voices, free from the humiliation of hunger, having no enemies, neither hating nor being hated . . . see what weakness, fatigue, surfeit.

Prison attracts me, but the prelude: brutal lawyers who would poke around in my soul, asking me questions I don't want to answer – no!

I'm now waiting here for something to set me in motion from without! Divert me in the meantime! Please –

Yours,
August Strindberg

318. To TORSTEN HEDLUND

Torsten Hedlund (1855–1935). See headnote to Letter 272. In *Inferno* Strindberg described Hedlund as his 'occult friend who played such a decisive part in my life as my mentor. He gave me advice, comfort, and chastisement; and, in the periods of acute poverty that recurred from time to time, he it was who stood by me and provided me with the means of subsistence' (p.167). He also suggested that it was Hedlund who re-opened their correspondence in 1894 whereas it was in fact Strindberg who wrote to Hedlund here, eliciting a reply that he henceforth referred to as the '*Donaubrevet*' (The Danube Letter), and to which he attributed an almost occult significance in its reception at a turning point in his life. In 1895, after he had settled in Paris, Hedlund replaced Littmansson as his main correspondent, and the result was perhaps the most significant and extraordinary of all the sequences of letters in which Strindberg successively engaged. Through Hedlund, who arranged with the Gothenburg businessman August Röhss for Strindberg to be sent a regular sum over a limited period (see Letter 363), he secured the financial support he required to pursue the extended experiment in self-analysis and artistic renewal to which, on one level, the Inferno crisis amounts. More pertinently, he acquired in Hedlund, whom he was never to meet, and whose age even, he seriously mistook, a correspondent with whom he could be at once intimate and yet distant; he was cast as a kind of blank screen onto which Strindberg projected the substance of his inner life as, by way of associations, dreams, fantasies, chance and those 'strange coincidences' which he discovered all about him, he sought to read the unconscious text of his life. These letters are the crucible in which Strindberg's post-Inferno outlook was forged, filled with literary, mythological and religious allusions, and in many respects a first draft of the material out of which *Inferno* and *To Damascus* emerged. The specifically business side of the correspondence is generally kept separate from the letters in which he conducts his psychological and literary experiments, and nowhere does Strindberg so obviously open and close an epistolary sequence to suit the purpose of a particular phase of his life as in the eighty-three letters he addressed to Hedlund between October 1895 and November 1896. Unfortunately, only two of Hedlund's letters (one of these the '*Donaubrevet*') have survived.

Ardagger via Amstetten, Nied. Oestreich,
23 July 1894

Herr Torsten Hedlund,

Two years ago you wrote to me after the publication of *By the Open Sea* and asked, or at least wondered, if I was a theosophist. My work seemed to exhibit a certain similarity of outlook.

You will recall my reply![1]

But a further coincidence has now occurred which cannot be mere chance: I wish some light shed on it, and am therefore asking you to illuminate the following for me. You perhaps know that in April I published the first part of a work called *Antibarbarus*, in which I simply drew all the logical conclusions inherent in Transformism and Monism. I thought I had expressed the secret thoughts of my contemporaries and didn't expect to be received as a charlatan or lunatic; thus I was feeling somewhat depressed when Haeckel, in Jena, wrote to say that these ideas about the transformation of matter were not unfamiliar to him, for he had heard them from a recently deceased chemist whose work he respected, etc.

Two months then passed. A week ago I read in the *Journal des Débats* that the following books had recently appeared (My Swedish is a little muddled, but I've been unwell and *aufgeregt*!):[2]

François Jollivet-Castelot (Mac-Iwnard): *La Vie et l'âme de la matière. Essai de physiologie chimique.*

Claude Hemel: *Les Métamorphoses de la matière.*

I got hold of them and was astounded!

On the title page, Castelot calls himself: Chimiste, membre de la Société Astronomique de France, et Du *Groupe Indépendant d'Études Esotériques.*

From what I can see, this man repeats all the ideas of my *Antibarbarus* without knowing it; he even dates his chapter on transmutation November 1893, exactly as I did! Except that he was in Douai and I in Brünn.

He declares openly that Tiffereau[3] made gold in 1853, that he believes the problem can be solved, and publishes some rather puerile laboratory reports.

(In parenthesis: I have now come a lot further in my esoteric studies: the published part of *Antibarbarus* only contains the exoteric. I can transmute iron into Nickel and Manganese, and produce Iodine, etc., but am avoiding alchemy so as not to arouse comment.)

However: Castelot touches on Spiritism; believes in Crookes,[4] but hits out at theosophy.

He seems to belong to a tendency with a party behind it, has high hopes, etc. The publisher is Société d'Éditions scientifiques, 4 rue Antoine Dubois, Paris; the book costs 3 francs 50.

If you're interested, get hold of the book, read it, and let me know if the man is a theosophist or belongs to your grouping. I intend to get in touch with the man, because he owns a laboratory, but I don't want anything to do with Spiritism or theosophy. Or will you tell me in a few, clear words what theosophy is. My *Antibarbarus* is beginning to attract disciples, but I must have immaculate credentials, and don't wish to sail under false colours.

So many strange things are happening in the world at the moment, and it is difficult to untangle the threads. I am willing to try everything, but not retain it all.

Yours sincerely,
August Strindberg

319. To LEOPOLD LITTMANSSON

[23? July 1894]

Dear Friend,

This is how things stand: my marriage B is dissolved; and my predicament as a divorcé is desperate, since I cannot depart because I haven't the money for the journey. The cause: much the same as the first time round. All women hate Buddhas, persecute, disturb, torment, humiliate and insult them with all the hatred of inferiors, because they themselves cannot become Buddhas; on the other hand, they are instinctively drawn to maids, servants, beggars, dogs, especially mangy ones, and worship buffoons, dentists, rank-and-file writers, agents in timber – anything mediocre.

And their love: see *Creditors*.

English doctors have recently observed that if two children sleep in the same bed, the weaker imbibes strength from the stronger.

There's marriage for you: the brother-and-sister bed!

I'm not an anti-Semite,[1] for I love Arabs and am married to an Arabian – there are no longer any Jews, no more than the Greeks are Hellenes. What are called Jews are made up of every kind of nationality – mostly the descendents of niggers, like the Josephsons: (Ludvig = Uncle Tom; and Ernst is crossed with an Alexandrian! Karl Otto's wife has a boy who turns black every summer); Armenians like Seligmann: Kazan Tartars like Albert Bonnier (Isidor isn't a relation, they adopted him in Denmark); Papuans like Karl Warburg; Albanians like the Rubensons; Persians like the singer, Jacobsson; Turks like Otto Samson; Mexicans like little Josef †[2] with the chair leg on Kymmendö, etc.

After the crusades, no Easterners dared enter Europe except under cover of the Synagogue, therefore they called themselves Jews or adopted the Jewish faith, the mosque being prohibited!

As for staying with you! I'm not sure I can be a guest, for I tend to be ungrateful and can't tolerate the least pressure from those near to me, which is why, like everyone else, I rapidly feel a natural hatred for my benefactors. But I may come nevertheless.

Perhaps my ingratitude is also based on the fact that I always think I've given more than I've received; and when I die one day, I'll regard it as the cancellation of a debt which people owe me. I've taught them all kinds of devilry, occupied their thoughts during moments of leisure, and entertained them; I've avenged many of their injustices, liberated spirits languishing under other people's wickedness, revealed the ruses of oppression, and demolished false reputations which concealed where real talent lay!

Is it, then, surprising that those who are so greatly indebted to me should hate their benefactor and, like true Christians, project their guilt onto him, turning him into the ungrateful one *par préférence*?

It is this fear of being considered an egoist, sensual, etc., which prevents you from daring to choose. Have you seen anyone work for you, give you something, think on your behalf? No, not without payment or calculation! And yet you believe you are duty-bound to work for others (I'm not counting your family, which is only an extension of the dominant self).

The others!' Why are the others always better than you? When the others go whoring, it's a legitimate instinct; when you do, it's a vice; when the others amass money, it's a virtue, thrift; when you do, it's avarice; when the others get drunk, it's all right; when you do,it's not! Etc. Etc.

Read Nietzsche's *Beyond Good and Evil*!

And Jesus! That wretch! Who couldn't survive on his own, as John the Baptist could. He had to have company, but whose? Not a single talented man among all those louts; only Paul, and he didn't want to go about with Jesus, and Jesus avoided him.

Jesus = Underclass; the friend of those with no talent; the friend of the intellectually inferior, the idiots.

No! Nietzsche! *Ich*! *Die Welt für mich*![3]

That his brain exploded is no more astonishing than that a wooden tub cracks when the roots of the bush it contains grow too long. In my childhood, we had to bind a bowl containing a persian lilac with iron, and yet the bowl still cracked!

Comte's brain also burst – afterwards, yes, when he thought more incisively than the other philistines, whose beefsteak brains could easily be crammed into a bone case!

No, Leopold, you're still under the sway of the law, the Gospel, and it sometimes seems to me as if your ancestors' seed must have contained Christian blood! I'm devilishly prejudiced against Christianity. I am the Antichrist!

But Jehovah – wow! – he's the God for me! An eye for an eye, and an ear for an ear! Strike them all down, The Lord knows his own. I know nothing more sublime than David's Psalm to Jehovah, in which he prays for his enemies; *hoc est*, he implores Jehovah to punish (can also be called'avenge'!) his enemies! He specifies the punishments he would like; he gives God a hint that he would most like to see his enemy struck down with this sickness or that, his dwelling burned, his wife violated, his children flayed alive. That is strength, displayed quite openly.

You want to be a monk and have a family. Like that brewer's hand, Luther! No! The family isn't for us! This constant, daily accommodation to lower forms of existence: women and children, consideration for and compromises over the agglomeration wife-maids = natural allies, gradually pulls us down.

Watch two men talking seriously together. A woman joins them. Note how the men's faces begin to grimace like an ape's; the silly smile, the fiddling with their clothes, necktie, cuffs, so as to adorn themselves for the female, to please! And what is said amounts to Jig![4] with gin on the table so their spirits don't sink! Then they look round for a bed! Always Jig!
[52 lines omitted]

August Strindberg

320. To LEOPOLD LITTMANSSON

[25 July 1894]

Dear Friend,

Since 5 p.m. on Saturday I've experienced such things (like before, exactly like before), which still can't fail to make a certain impression. A long letter to you remains unsent. Briefly: since I have 2 families α and β, and can't provide for either of them, I must establish myself as a mendicant friar. The trick is: how to pull up the new roots! But it's surely possible! – Thank you, however![1] Now I don't need to flee in one coat, without a valise! And I am coming! Only waiting for a letter from the Alchemist,[2] who is young, rich, and has a laboratory!

Strange that I scented this imminent major *fin-de-siècle* current in science. Now I'll become these young Frenchmen's prophet (Ibsen), for they are babes-in-arms compared to me! I've broken the world record, and am Champion of the World[3] in that field! – I may even be inclining to Jig again now that my depression has passed! In any case gin! Oh God (?), what is truth and purity? Jig! *Machtgefühl*! *Alles*!

Aug Sg!

321. To LEOPOLD LITTMANSSON

31 July 1894

Brother Thomas,

You're wearing out my grey matter with your sterile arguments and your female logic. You take no delight in intercourse because you feel and speak like a woman on behalf of woman against man!

You immediately stood on the opposite side to me, instinctively (please note), and felt sympathy for the dregs and for serving wenches.

Chateaubriand and Lamartine were no Buddhas but sots, *dont les défauts flattent la femme*, and their outward brilliance duped *les sottes*.[1]

Wronski has every reason to feel humble when he's come up with such Bosch! Bosch – it's nothing, and his suffering was well-deserved. His conceit and stupidity are so enormous, they quite take my breath away!

He was lyttle, and therefore humble. *Nur die Lumpen sind bescheiden*![2]

My crash here is complicated. Parents-in-law and Great-ditto are ultra Catholics. They insisted on baptizing the child a Catholic, but we young ones didn't want that. At first they tempted us with earthly gold; then they evicted us. After which they baptized the child in secret! Then the 30 Years' War broke out, and I, as *Alter Schwede*,[3] defeated the Catholics in a great battle. But then they got the priest to declare our marriage was only a concubinage (the very word!) because my wife's a Catholic and I'm divorced, with a wife still living. Wanted to make a bigamist of me! Etc. Etc. Also hints that no more children should be born, etc.

Sakyamuni[4] wanted to go to Benares to purge himself of all this impurity, but first he needed 100 Rupees to pay the earth mother and the doctor, and only had 70. So he couldn't go respectably. His wife scented the registered letter; the earth mother was sharp, and Buddha had to 'lend' the woman the rest. So there he sat without a rupee, while in Parys he was considered a scoundrel, even though he wasn't one. However, now write and ask Österlind to send 100 pistoles (Austrian). I'll repay them – or leave right away, if there's a new crash!

Sakya has nothing from his wife, who has nothing herself, and no guarantees. I don't know who on earth is keeping back the money, but it never reaches me. I wrote my liver and lungs out for Albert, or Albortus Magnus, but the New Year accounts I received only sold me to the devil. I wrote *Lucky Peter*, which was performed 100 times, and received a bill for 500 *Riksdaler* for the music followed by a statement revealing a deficit, though it helped Uncle Tom[5] amass a fortune. (A wytticysm against Massa's wyll.)

In Berlin an agent took my plays; they were performed all over the place, to be followed by a bill for the printing costs. And yet you wonder that I want to set up as a mendicant friar!

How the hell does one sell oneself to the good? Jalmar[6] once wanted to teach me how to sell Otto[7] to the devil, but I almost went mad with remorse, and no longer settle accounts. Ekström fynally sold out! I have only liquidated (i.e. not liquidated) lyke the European and Eagle, on whose account Otto received the Order of Vasa.

Well, God (?) help us all! not least your dyvoted

Brother,
Stryndberg

322. To LEOPOLD LITTMANSSON

31 July 1894

Dear Friend,

Wo die Geldfrage fängt an, hört der Buddaismus auf.[1]

(Goethe).

So, a few practical matters again.

With my impending arrival in mind, I am now sending, *petite vitesse*,[2] a crate of large and small oil paintings which I intend to unload on some Swedes in the autumn. Am enclosing the accompanying text, which refers to the red numbers on the back of the canvases. It is in fact a new (that's to say, old) kind of art which I've invented and call *L'art fortuite*.[3] I've written an essay on my method.[4] It is the most subjective of all art forms, so that in the first place only the painter himself can enjoy (= suffer) the work because he knows what he meant by it, as do the chosen few who know the painter's inner (= outer) a little (= a lot). Each picture is, so to speak, double-bottomed, with an exoteric aspect that everyone can make out, with a little effort, and an esoteric one for the painter and the chosen few. It should be pointed out that the pictures were painted in a half-dark room, and cannot on any account stand a full light; they appear best in strong fire-light or a half-dark room.

All the pictures are painted using only a knife and unmixed colours, whose combination has been half left to chance, like the motif as a whole.

See the accompanying text!

In addition: 'The Weeping Boy'![5] – My son – far away, the thought of whom can drive me mad, living in the home of a Sodomite – because the whole of Sweden hated me and would not help, but acted as the knight in shining armour for the 'defenceless woman' (the Sodomite). Oh yes, there are discords in my past which could lead to suicide without it being a crime!

Like Abraham I have to sacrifice my Isaac in order to be able to hop from sprig to sprig until I reach the green one.

You appreciate that I modelled it myself.

Listen! I wrote to Castelot (the alchemist) some time ago, asking him to send his book to Nordenskiöld. He must have done so because the book mentioned the light of the Zodiac and the possibility that Saturn isn't the only planet with rings. Pow! N. goes and writes about his Earth Ring in *Politiken*![6] – You see the power of suggestion! *Machtgefühl*! Send the book on comets, then we'll see more! Castelot and Hemel are now at large in the Swedish press.

Should you have anywhere, hang the paintings if they arrive before I do. Take the two unnumbered ones (the numbers are in red on the reverse) as a present – variations on 'The Wonderland' and 'The Verdant Isle'.[7]

But what about my book, the new one,[8] which is meant to save 2 families?

Who translates Swedish? I don't know anyone!

Peace and salvation, but not through Wronski, for that's just shit, pure and simple. If you feel like a spirit in the presence of the inexplicable, go on a terrific bender for 48 hours like me, in good (= male) company, and you'll feel a radiance encircling your brow like the Northern Lights!

Your friend,
August Strindberg

[enclosure]

No. 1.
Exoteros!

A man in a billowing raincoat is standing on a cliff which is being washed by the ocean waves; far out on the horizon, the three white-painted, unrigged masts of a stranded bark.

Esot:

On closer inspection one sees that the man on the cliff has a slouch hat like Vodan (Buddha); that the crests of the waves resemble monsters, the clouds demons, and in the middle of the sky is an excellent likeness of Rembrandt. The three masts with their cross-bars[9] look like Golgotha, or three crosses on graves, and could be a Trimurti, but this is a matter of taste.

No. 2.
Exot.

A dense forest interior; in the middle, a Exot. hole opens out into an idealized landscape where sunshine of every colour streams in. In the foreground, rocks with stagnant water in which mallowworts are reflected.

Esot.

The Wonderland; the battle of light against darkness. Or the opening of the realm of Ormuzd and the exodus of the liberated souls to the land of the sun; under it the flowers (they aren't mallows) decay in *gnothi seauton*[10] before the muddy water in which the sky is reflected (Petter's Keys of Heavyn).[11]

No. 3. It has rained in the Alps which lie half-veiled in clouds
Exot. and mist. In the foreground, desert with slates and broom.
Esot. The desert wanderer's longing for wet rain, cool snow, clear ice. My eyes turn towards the heights, but the weary remain in the desert.

No. 4. The Verdant Isle. The sea tranquil and smooth before sunrise. The sky yellow and rose-coloured. Morning mists lie on the
Exot. horizon, but above them the tree tops of the verdant isle are visible, and are reflected in the sea.
Esot. Life's high summer (for me, Kymmendö 1880), therefore the isle itself veiled in white, yellow and rose.

No. 5. Flood on the Danube.
Exot.
Esot. The water is rising. Where is the Ark? Etc.

No. 6. Landscape.
Ad libitum.[12]

No. 7. A shit-green landscape, with shit-red rocks, a shit-yellow sky
Exot. and shit-black fir trees.
Esot: Sweden!

323. To GEORG BRANDES

[1 August 1894]

Herr Doctor,

I have now read the two French books[1] and find I've happened upon a Main Current[2] which seems to be making enormous headway. The scientific treatment of science was only to be expected now that Haeckel's work is thirty years old, and Chemistry is in decay, un-fertilized by Transformism. However, I now see there's a whole French literature in my genre. – Did you get both the French books I asked them to send you? Nordenskiöld must have received them, for Castelot wrote in his book about the light of the Zodiac and the possibility of there being rings around other planets besides Saturn! – I wonder if your Danish chemist[3] won't soon be left behind.

Now see from a book catalogue that *L'Or et la transmutation des métaux* by Tiffereau and Franck appeared in Paris in 1889. 5 francs. Castelot quotes an Ed. Robin and a Dr Gibier, who are both unknown to me, but in my genre!

Yours sincerely,
Aug Sg

324. To LEOPOLD LITTMANSSON

Ardagger, 1 August 1894

Dear Friend,

Yes, the child is saved, with the help of two wet nurses and a maid, and therefore I'm lost and must go into exile . . . but in that case the book! The Book! Will you really translate it? If so, I'm saved, for I have French and German publishers to hand!

Right, my friend! But in this order, so that if you suffer a miscarriage in the middle, the best bits will be ready:

1. Woman's Inferiority to Man.
2. The Small.
3. The Battle of the Brains.
4. Nemesis Divina.
5. My Anniversary Celebration.
6. Voltaire.
7. Soul Murder.
8. Hallucinations.

But please! write them all in your best hand on quarto paper, on one side only, and as legibly as possible!

Where are we heading? Towards the annihilation of the individual. Hence the hellish anxiety we now feel, as things go downhill, about reproducing our souls and thereby attaining immortality. Ambition, you see, is the soul's desire for self-preservation. (Children as a means of survival are so problematical since in order to differentiate themselves, and live as individuals, they vomit out everything they get from the father (there's nothing to be had from the mother!) and can, moreover, disgrace one's name rather than preserve it.)

I lived in and for my children over a long period, was ready to sacrifice everything, including my talent, but when I reached 40 and the moment when my children emancipated themselves – then I cast off again!

What you say about woman is quite archaic (Jos. Seligmann 1860).[1] I've seen all my contemporaries' wives and those of the following generation; I have the largest collection of material, the most acute powers of observation and deduction, and am an authority!!! And I was always able to preserve my great brain from the influence of my sexual instinct, so that I loved, coupled passionately, but thought lucidly all the time – and then wrote!

And I overthrew the Gynolatry of Ibsen-Bjørnson in Scandinavia and North Germany. Those emancipated women went under one after the other from indignation and impotent fury. Fru Benedictsson slit her throat; Fru Edgren was probably murdered; Fru Kovalevsky is said to have taken poison; Fru Adlersparre exploded; Fru Svedbom[2] capsized like an umbrella in a storm; Fru Andersson-Meijerhjelm[3] fled from buggery (and gave a lecture in Versailles the other day!). *Deus (?) afflavit et dissipati sunt!*[4] (And that cunt C. O. Berg[5] is in Långholm, where he wanted to put me in 1889 [*sic*].)

So; *Allons travailler!*[6] Not discuss things by post! Isn't that right?

Yrs,

Aug Sg

325. To LEOPOLD LITTMANSSON

[4? August 1894]

Dear Friend,

Just because the French are *Aristokratie des Geistes* and nix *des Geldes*[1] (= false bills, Panama and Kropp shares, Capital Bonds in Nord*,[2] pirating and forced contracts), I long to be there. Where Verlaine, a convicted criminal, who was never able to manage his money, is celebrated because he has talent. Morality begins with mediocrity.

As for my relationship to Nietzsche, he has never buggered my soul. For proof see *A Book About Strindberg*, where it's clear that 'The Small' and 'The Battle of the Brains', etc., were written before I or anyone else in Scandinavia had heard of him. See also G. Brandes on Nietzsche, in which N. writes of having read Sg's *Mariés*, and has only one thing against the book, namely that he discovered his own thoughts there.[3] (*Mariés*, written 1884.)

Here's another choice! With your fiddle you can walk or cycle round the world with a violin case on your back. Listen!

Prince Esterhazy lives in Hungary, at Totis near Pressburg. He's so damned rich that he has his own orchestra, theatre, library and stables with 1,000 horses, and a subterranean church full of wyne. This Prince saw *Creditors* in Berlin and was carried away (I never met the man – didn't even touch him! Far less . . . !); he thought *Cavalleria rusticana* and *Creditors* the summits of modern art. So . . . let us emulate the Troubadours, make our way there anonymously, as *fin-de-siècle* Buddhas, and have them discover us.

You can play and I'll recite some Scandinavian (pseudo) *fin-de-siècle* pieces, which I'll write beforehand in German.

Then we'll unmask: you'll become court conductor and composer with the Iron Crown of Hungary on your tail-coat, and I the royal librarian and Alchemist!

No philistine life, that! But you're aware of how the Hungarians play the violin: without bar lines, not in D minor, and *immer tempo rubato*,[4] like people whining.

I had dinner one day at the Hotel Bristol in Berlin (didn't pay myself, of course). The champagne was flowing and I felt radiant. – All of a sudden I heard a sound from the adjoining room which made me think I had the Northern Lights in my ears. It sounded like people weeping and wailing, and now and then sobbing and laughing, etc. It was a band of Hungarian violinists playing for Krupp, who was dining out with his friends for 50,000 *Riksdaler*.

This is a fine choice! Not ascetic! Aristocratic as in the good old days when players and fiddlers bowed down to princes, and not as now to the mob.

You could walk right in and ask for a place in the orchestra, audition, and become God!

But you must have a fetching hair cut, preferably a Scandinavian one to counteract the effect of your blond moustache, for the Hungarians hate the Germans. Or a French one, with a Spanish goatee.

Hungary is flat and the Danube excellent bicycling country.

Spend a week writing a one-acter in French and tell your mother-in-law you're going to become a writer but need to make a study trip in order to meet me. And that you're starting off by translating me so as to practise your French, learn style, and get to know some publishers and theatre directors. That'll make the old woman proud and happy! Then adopt a French pseudonym and become French.

Charpentier, who's waiting for *By the Open Sea*, and Sarah Bernhardt both live in Österlind's village. That's the place for us, if only I could borrow the money to get there!

But we'll see if my pictures can't be sold in the Scandinavian Club.

Charpentier and Ö. are keen cyclists.

Strange: you chose twice: from the bank, alone; but to the Shakers – with Jallmar!

World of contradictions. Jigg-Jallmar and the Shakers. I could understand your not waiting a year and taking your exam – just; but I found your retreat to America incomprehensible. After all, you had money even though Selig.[5] hung on to it! – However, that time you chose with Jallmar's help. Well, one was young then, and the choice not really necessary, but now, with age approaching, and death! The muddy pit![6]

The paintings go off tomorrow. Accompanied by some yellow Bikupa for stock (take good care of it), and a winter coat.

The paintings can be sold cheaply, 100 francs apiece maximum. I sold for something like 1000 francs last year in Sweden, and had an exhibition (slated, but not by the painters, the *Vortschrittler*).[7] And the funny thing is, I was the first to paint symbolic landscapes; now see how all the realists have turned with the wind!

Aug Sg

326. To TORSTEN HEDLUND

Ardagger, 11 August 1894

Herr Torsten Hedlund,

First, my thanks for your letter, which was hardly expected, for my compatriots' insane hatred has led me to anticipate almost anything but a reply, and a friendly one at that.[1]

So, my response, but rhapsodically, for I'm still tired.

In so far as you are a Monist and believe that everything is in everything, heat and cold, hate and love, why do you then draw such a sharp, dualistic distinction between black and white magic?[2]

Do you know why? Have you been honest enough with yourself to see that it could derive from the fact that you and your group have abrogated the white for yourselves, and therefore the black must be black in a derogatory sense.

And if hate and love are one, why must my so vocal hate, an expression, too, of great strength, express itself in a negative form, and be so clearly different from your love?

When I was a young man, I was extremely religious, with a predisposition for the ideal, as it's called. At times I found all contact with material things repulsive – at times. When I was called to table, I became angry because I was reminded of the fact that I was an animal; I went to bed without food on purpose, in order to have pure dreams; self-tormented and self-observed, self-punished; this world appeared so strange to me that I often wondered from where, from what better world, I had come, since I found everything about me so vile, yet had nothing with which to compare it.

I joined the Pietists, who sought the health of the soul and preached love. But adherence to a group, which proved to be the most wicked of all, the most despotic, began to oppress me, and when I took things really seriously, and went beyond the others in annihilating the self, they saw I was becoming more saintly than themselves, and hated me.

– Down to us, but not so deep that you become higher than we are!

These people had no love. They were a group of unbelievably selfish egos with an overwhelming majority, who thought they'd found the only Truth.

They had to follow the herd, because they were weak; they probably thought they loved their fellow men, and grew used to the idea, but didn't really.

Then I discovered my ego was also justified, and threatened in its self-justification, and I forced my way out, and grew away from them – who knows what powers we have within us?

But my young flesh had suffered unjustly, and been held in check; now sensuality claimed its due, though always controlled by my desire for intellectual enjoyment, which was greater!

Now, when we see everything slipping and sliding over into everything else, virtue into vice, etc., I wonder if my unconscious régime – to the spirit and flesh their own! – didn't guide my fate in the right direction!

I have always been afraid of flying, and wanted to feel the ground beneath my feet. How often, after great spiritual exertion, when I had long breathed only pure air, have I not had a need, a desire, to roll in the mire, briefly but thoroughly. And it has been like a beneficial mud-bath. With fresh loathing for matter, I would return to my work with greater delight and new strength. Thus I have lived two lives: an exoteric and an esoteric, and when I now reflect on my behaviour in public, where I have always sacrificed my person to ridicule, to contempt, to pity, it seems as if I've been driven by a fear of losing my best self.

But I also needed the ground beneath my feet in my thinking. First a mass of raw material, observations, preferably my own, because I cannot depend on other people's. Not going round and round in circles but ground between stones. First physics, then metaphysics, like Aristotle. But not metaphysics without physics.

And curiously, that's where we part company, even though, as a Monist, you ought not to see any grounds for difference.

And you still use the word materialist, even though the concept doesn't exist. If spirit and matter are in fact one, then the so-called materialist is just as much an idealist as the latter is a materialist.

But driven by the instinct of the self for its own preservation, I was also afraid of joining any group and being absorbed into the collective self which the others constituted.

When I started out as a writer, I never sent my books to famous men. I wanted no contact with other souls. In 1879 I knew nothing of Brandes and his followers. They extended the hand of friendship to me and declared me a member of their party, but as I knew nothing of their programme, I trespassed against it in my next book, and was expelled without knowing what I had been a member of.

I fled 'Young Sweden', who sought me out, adopted me, elected me their Chief and wanted me to obey their orders. Expelled as a renegade – from what?

I never sought out Bjørnson; he sought me out, baptized me in the name of something I knew nothing about; and when his strong but coarse soul began to devour mine, I fought free – a far more painful operation than might be thought, but one which saved me.

When family ties oppressed me, I broke them, at the risk of perishing; but I didn't die.

Don't you think this instinct to preserve the freedom of the self and to grow freely was both justified and invaluable for my development? If I'd become a theosophist in 1884, I would once again have been fettered. If I'd maintained bonds of friendship, ties of blood, I would have stifled my development simply out of consideration for others.

No, I shall remain apart from, and outside, every grouping, take to the woods as an outlaw, set things ablaze, and risk, as always, being put down like a wild animal, a vandal in everyone's eyes.

Therefore, when you offer me your help now, I have to reply:

– Thank you, but no! I should then be tied; later on I might be ungrateful, suffer on that account, and so be unfree again!

As for *Antibarbarus* and what it represents!

Chemists demand proof! – Have you ever seen anyone accept it? – I've extracted carbon from sulphur, sent it to a chemist, to two! No reply!

But I've analysed it myself and discovered carbon. Using their own methods!

When they find carbon, they call it an 'impurity'!

I can extract silver from lead! But then they say: lead is silvery.

No, one gets nowhere there!

Finally: does the development of the organisms and that of mankind support your doctrine of the five stages of development? I can't see it! – So the question is: how do you know that's so?

To me the whole system seems to be a freehand sketch, and any attempt to classify what is continually in flux, to organize what is indecipherable, to systematize, arrange and above all divide as finely as into black and white, is illogical and insensitive.

If I place the black race below the white, this is grounded on my experience, which has shown the blacks to be inferior to the whites. But you! . . .

And this craving for power! The theosophists, who haven't gone the long, laborious Propylaeum of science, are within the temple and know it all, without knowing anything! That is simply religion again, faith without knowledge, the annihilation of reason, but not of the self, for the group self is placed above everyone who doesn't belong to the group. It's just like the Pietists of my youth!

There is also something dishonest in this desire to expropriate everything, everyone's ideas, including what is foul! And a short cut: They don't enter the perilous race across the river, but go round by the road; and arrive first.

They declare all mankind's questions solved, without having tried to solve any of them.

You believe I am facing a new epoch in my life. I think so too, for I am as restless as a crab when it changes its shell – but I've no idea what is on the way!

Therefore I put myself as usual into an unconscious state, let the forces do their work, and wait in a state of the most enthralling quietism.

Yours sincerely,
August Strindberg

[Postscript omitted]

VII

Letters 327–394 29 August 1894–November 1896

The next two years of Strindberg's life were spent mainly in Paris, and seemed initially to lack any real sense of direction. Having left Frida in Austria with their daughter, he went first to Versailles, where he stayed with Littmansson. Within days, however, he was consorting with a set of new acquaintances, including a Danish painter and confidence trickster, Willy Grétor, the publisher Albert Langen, who brought out a French edition of *A Madman's Defence* in 1895, and the German playwright Frank Wedekind, whose mistress Frida was later to become. Grétor admired Strindberg's paintings and set him up as an artist in Passy, in a luxurious apartment belonging to his absent mistress, Rosa Pfaeffinger. Briefly solvent, Strindberg sent Frida 250 francs, and she joined him in Paris in mid-September. Their reunion was brief, however. The following month she returned to Austria to care for Kerstin, and never met Strindberg again. Their parting seems not to have been planned, but on 8 November Strindberg sent Frida a savage letter, in which he accused her of behaving like a prostitute; when challenged, he refused to withdraw his accusation and, though they continued to correspond until September 1896, she now determined on a divorce.

While in Paris Frida had, as usual, attempted to further Strindberg's literary career, but although he tried to place a number of newly translated or recently written articles in the French press, he showed little direct concern about literature or the theatre. He became friendly with the dramatist Henry Becque, visited Rodolphe Salis' cabaret, Le Chat Noir, and let Lugné-Poë put on *The Father* at the Théâtre de l'Œuvre in December 1894, but, apart from his painting, his abiding interest remained his scientific studies.

To his own satisfaction at least, he confirmed that sulphur was a ternary compound, composed of carbon, oxygen and hydrogen, and he also claimed to have discovered the structure of iodine. Articles on his research appeared in *La Science Française* and *Le Temps*, he enrolled as a student in the Faculty of Science at the Sorbonne, where he was permitted to conduct some experiments, and he corresponded with the eminent French chemist, Marcelin Berthelot. He also met the astronomer Camille Flammarion, with whom he discussed his celestiographs, taken without the assistance of either a camera or lens, and published a series of speculative works, including an *Introduction à une chimie unitaire*, *Sylva Sylvarum*, and *Jardin des Plantes*, on different aspects of the natural world. Above all, however, he sought to make gold, and found in *fin-de-siècle* Paris a haven for his interest in alchemy and the occult. An enthusiasm for telepathy, *doppelgänger*, the Cabbala, and both white and black magic was widespread in France among writers like Huysmans, Mallarmé and Villiers de l'Isle Adam, for whom it appeared an extension of the preoccupation with hypnotism and suggestion that had characterized the preceding decade. Strindberg associated with a number of adepts among the different schools, including the celebrated magus Dr Papus (Gérard Encausse) and François Jollivet-Castelot. He contributed an essay on 'The Irradiation and Extensibility of the Soul' to Papus' journal *L'Initiation* and was a regular contributor to Jollivet-Castelot's *L'Hyperchimie*, where he published his findings on 'The Synthesis of Gold', in 1896.

Whether in science or the occult Strindberg was preoccupied with the possibility of a fundamental unity of organic and inorganic matter. From the outset, his hylozoic concept of nature abutted both mysticism and the Natural Philosophy of German Romanticism, but underlying his present concern with the transmutation of matter was a desire for personal rebirth or metamorphosis, and what Gunnar Brandell, in his important study of Strindberg's Inferno crisis, has identified as the wish to create a new cosmos. Moreover, once Strindberg had accepted that the world he was investigating was a work of art, shaped by the hand of an artist-creator who fashioned it according to obscure but interpretable rules, he found it possible to resume the creation of imaginative literature himself.

This process of renewal was something that Strindberg likewise discerned in the paintings of Paul Gauguin, with whom he associated regularly during 1894–95, in a circle of artists that also included Frederick Delius and Alphonse Mucha. Strindberg wrote an introduction to a catalogue for an exhibition of Gauguin's paintings, which reinforced the notoriety gained from his occasional forays into the Parisian press, such as the polemical article 'On the Inferiority of Woman to Man' in the *Revue Blanche* for January 1895.

During most of this time Strindberg was impoverished and in poor health. In January 1895 he became an in-patient at the Hôpital Saint-Louis, where he was treated for the psoriasis of the hands which often afflicted him during periods of acute mental and emotional stress, but which had been exacerbated by the repeated handling of dangerous chemicals. Meanwhile, two separate collections were made on his behalf during 1894–95, one among the Swedish colony in Paris and the other in Sweden itself. The shame and hurt they caused him contributed greatly to the feelings of guilt which brought on the most severe of the five mental crises that can be discerned in Strindberg's life between July

1894 and November 1896. Old anxieties and residues of guilt from his Berlin period – not least his continued failure to provide for Siri and his first family – arose to torment him in May 1896 when he heard a rumour that Stanislaw Przybyszewski had been arrested for murdering his common-law wife, Martha Foerder, whom he had abandoned to marry Dagny Juel. Strindberg also believed that Przybyszewski had followed him to Paris and was now seeking to murder him. The acute attack of persecution mania which these fears heralded induced a series of bizarre and terrifying events that were monitored by Strindberg in a sequence of long letters to Torsten Hedlund in Gothenburg during July 1896 as well as in the *Occult Diary* which he started to keep while staying at the Hôtel Orfila, a student pension that was to become the *locus classicus* of this period in Strindberg's life through the account he gives of it in *Inferno*. It was there that he first began to take the works of Swedenborg seriously, and became aware of the mysterious powers that he henceforth took to be determining the course of his life.

The diary, which complements the letters he wrote over the next twelve years, is a kind of collage of strange occurrences, remarkable coincidences, and provoking dreams through which Strindberg tries to trace an order and logic in events, but it gives a very partial view of his life at this time. For although it is certainly true that he suffered periods of acute mental distress and material poverty during these months, Strindberg was never in fact quite as isolated as he makes out, either then or retrospectively in *Inferno*. He had many contacts both in Paris and by post, and carried on a voluminous correspondence not only with the obliging Torsten Hedlund, who acted as his confidant and helped provide him with much needed funds, but also with Anders Eliasson, a doctor who practised in the town of Ystad on the Southern Swedish coast. Strindberg stayed briefly with Eliasson in June–July 1895 and again in August 1896, after fleeing first the Orfila and then Paris in panic.

Following this second visit, which is recorded in *Inferno* and exploited in *To Damascus*, Strindberg left Ystad for Austria on 28 August 1896. He had been invited to visit his daughter, Kerstin, who was now living with her grandmother. He remained there three months, seeing Kerstin regularly, reading Swedenborg, whose descriptions of hell he recognized in the landscape where he was staying, and experiencing a general improvement in his health. Frida, however, refused to join him, and when his father-in-law indicated that he had outstayed his welcome, Strindberg left for Sweden, there (as he wrote in *Inferno*) 'to face the fire of the enemy at yet another station on the road to atonement'.

327. To FRIDA UHL

[Original in French]

Versailles, 29 August 1894

Dearest,

Yesterday dinner at Laurent's, Champs Elysées, to meet Langen,[1] Henry Becque, and an intimate friend of Langen's, a Dane,[2] who knew me from Denmark. Langen lives like a rich man, with a *valet de chambre*[3] and all the rest of it. He's definitely going to take *Le Plaidoyer*, which is awaited with curiosity by the literary world and well-known here through Cherbuliez' article. He's looking for someone to write a preface. Becque will revise the text. (L. paid G. Brandes 6,000 Marks for his Shakespeare!)[4]

B. proved a jolly fellow, witty and amusing, and said some charming things about *Creditors*. Like everyone else, he'd gone to hiss the Scandinavians but confessed himself won over. He knew exactly what I'd written about him and laughed over it.[5] He's invited me to *La Plume*.[6]

When I got home, I found a letter from Zola, who is waiting to shake my hand.[7] I am now launching my paintings, one by one; some people are going to set me up as a painter and sculptor (of busts).

Your letter arrived this very moment! about the little one! What bad luck, and what vicissitudes this child has. I'm awaiting further news, and fear these worries will depress you. But what's to be done? You won't heed my advice.

I shall probably stop over in Paris for a fortnight in order to attend to my affairs and oversee our interests, thus hastening your arrival.

August

328. To FRIDA UHL

[Original in German]

[31 August 1894]

From Monday I shall be spending a week at 112 Boulevard Malesherbes as the guest of a rich Danish painter[1] who today bought 'Wonderland' and 'Alpine Landscape' for 400 francs, and has told me I am a painter. So, should I send you 200 francs and you come? Remember that on 15 September I'll get paid for *Plaidoyer*! And paint more. My friend here said I should certainly exhibit at the Champs de Mars, that 'Alpine Landscape' is a masterpiece, but the 'Meadows' picture was worthless. Oh God, what is what? What?

Your
August

329. To FRIDA UHL

[Original in French]

Versailles, 2 September 1894

Frida,

I've just looked over your letters to Versailles and my general impression is that you love your child above everything, and that you were born for family life. This, then, is the dilemma! If you establish yourself as a journalist, you'll have to abandon home, child, household, and me; and if you get involved with a circle of interesting people, you'll lose your good taste for family life, whose troubles and cares will fill you with disgust for your home and child.

Besides, theatres, exhibitions, in short Paris, will mean that life will become more expensive, particularly as we shall be forced to find somewhere to live near Paris, where the tradesmen are all swindlers, corrupted by the exploitation of foreigners.

Above all, these damned theatres – *mein Verhängniss*![1] [*sic*] – never come down before midnight, and there are no trains then! Moreover, a married woman who goes about alone, here, in this cynical atmosphere . . . well, you know!

An alternative suggestion! Forget the idea of a regular column; write occasional pieces, when you feel so inclined. Accompany me to dinners; write book reviews at home; or better still, write books. What you lose, the household gains, me, the child, and above all – my economy. I shall do bad work if I have to keep an eye on the maids, the child, the household, and alone, especially during the evenings, I shall miss our fine moments of tranquillity and intimate conversation, and have recourse to the tavern, which is expensive and immoral.

So: let us settle down in a village close to Paris, but somewhere quiet and simple . . . and make it a rule never to go into society alone. Emancipation is unknown here, and an emanicipated woman means a prostitute.

My finances are on the mend, but without the mother of the house to watch over them, everything will vanish. This doesn't mean you'll become my serving-maid, and stay at home while I go out, still less that I'll remain at home alone while you go out.

Besides, what good is the theatre? By the time you've written your piece, the main German papers will already have reprinted the reviews in the French papers. And what interest is there in the acting? – To study it! What did I study in order to write my plays? – In any case, there are Sunday matinees, when the great performers appear in their principal roles.

It wasn't a Notebook but a folder of yellow Bikupa.[2]

Now there's some money, save yourself, and quickly, before it gets frittered away! Save yourself, and you'll also be saving your child – from Dornach!

Tomorrow I'll be on my own in Versailles! My friend[3] is going away. And I've said no to Paris. The great city is the death of me.

It seems as if my economy functions best when I live expensively, with a heavy outlay; to draw in my belt depresses me, and takes away my energy. – It's all there. Just take it!

August

330. To FRIDA UHL

[Original in French]

Versailles, 4 September 1894

Dear Frida,

Alone in my house in Versailles, I have plenty of time to reflect upon our future. M.L.[1] and his family left yesterday morning; I spent the day in Paris. And with the same result as before. The air must be poisoned, for I was overcome by an indescribable sense of unease, my nerves flared up, and I fled to Versailles. Shall I be able to bear Paris? And then I wonder again: What am I doing here? In the long run, I shall go out of my mind, and there are moments when I would like to flee. Where? To Sweden!

There are also moments when I want to return to Dornach, to live together with you as an invalid and painter on the money I have earned here. Will you? Until the child is better? So far as the trial is concerned,[2] I could get a doctor's certificate! – The money is certain, and with money it's possible to arrange things in Dornach so as to spend the winter there. Paris is so depressing, depressing like London, and I've done what I needed to do. A business trip, that's all, and a successful one.

We can live like a prince and princess on this money at Dornach, but like beggars in Paris. Just think, in Paris we'd never be able to see our friends after this unsuccessful lottery of a debut.

Once again! Do you want me to come back? With money one can have books, journals, papers, all the little things that make life tolerable. Imagine! Tiled stoves, beautiful lamps, curtains, carpets, above all, nurses! – a glass of wine in the evening, fine evenings together. Here, you'd be tied to the house, with dreadful servants, endlessly exploited. A dear and soon vanished illusion. The gabble of famous men for an hour, instead of their books at home. Do you expect to find inspiration here? There's nothing! And with the child, you'd never be able to go out. In the evening, exhausted, you wouldn't want to leave your child and your comfy bed. In the land of the enemy, where no one understands what you say, where they mock at everything.

Will you?

And to make the journey with the child? How can you think of it, when she is ill?

Admit that it was money which lay behind most of our domestic quarrels.

And besides: here we shall have a muddy, damp autumn. Tramways, lorries, stations, barrel-organs, bad tobacco, adulterated milk!

I miss the Danube, in spite of everything! It was 'a Home' after all! Here: the street!

Think it over!

Your August

331. To FRIDA UHL

[Original in French]

[6 September 1894]

Send me a telegram if you want me to return to D.[1] or somewhere near D., where we could find each other again.

I've everything I want, and I want to leave everything! to rejoin you and resume an existence *à quatre diables*.[2] Remember my words of yesteryear: better an ill-matched marriage than nothing. It's too quiet here. No one pesters or torments me; I long to endure a good matrimonial quarrel in which you are without doubt the master! *Chère maître*,[3] call me back and I'll return like an ass laden with gold. – Schleich has written some charming things to me, and Asch has unleashed a furious offensive in *Die Zukunft*.[4]

[no signature]

332. To FRIDA UHL

[Original in German]

Passy, 9 September 1894

Dearest,

Two days and two nights alone; without speaking a word; without hearing my own voice! In the middle of Paris.

Listen! There's something rotten here – about Langen too! And . . . I'm coming back to you.

A demi-mondaine atmosphere, which doesn't suit us. I live in a cocotte's flat that still stinks of perfume. The woman[1] is in the country; the Dane has lodged me here in her name and as her friend. It would be a fine thing if the police were to come demanding papers and an explanation.

The Dane wants me to introduce myself as the friend of a woman I've never seen.

I: 'Thanks a lot. Then I'd be *l'homme entretenu,*[2] M. Alphonse, to the police and the concierge!'

Becque, who was present, thought the role a perfectly honourable one. *'Mais vous voilà installé en parisien tout à fait.'*[3]

To Alphonse is honourable!

Tomorrow I'll have ten paintings ready to go off to – Sweden! Will tell you another time why they can't remain here![4]

Langen arrives the day after tomorrow!

As soon as you get this letter, wire me where to find you. And I'll come! Preferably Schliersee!

Dornach may be 'finished' for you, us!

Frida! Believe me! It's dangerous for us here!

I'm a sheep in so far as I generally believe other people to be at least as honest as myself . . . but my animal instinct seldom deceives me. And I hear, remember, piece together, see and think!

Loneliness and my respectable life make me attentive! and alert!

Just one thing! The pictures were bought a week ago. I've seen the letter myself. The money was to arrive the following day! Then a day later . . . then . . .

It is not yet in my hands! I can guess where it is!

But the one doesn't rule out the other. And Sweden, Denmark and Finland are open to me for my paintings. Paris too!

And I've made progress!

It's three weeks since we parted in Grein! And what weeks!

In Versailles, ugh! In Paris, phew! No, child, the world has gone downhill since my youth!

Let us live in our little poeticized world, work and believe – that we are better!

Where shall we meet?

Your
August

333. To BIRGER MÖRNER

[7 October 1894]

As usual Bang[1] was being stupid when he wanted to be smart. Naturalism isn't dead; it's thriving here in Zola, Goncourt, Hervieu, Prévost,[2] Huysman [*sic*], Becque, etc. Naturalism, or the poetic portrayal of nature, can never die before nature dies. But Maeterlinck, a caprice, a bibelot that amuses me in a tired moment, is still-born. To go back to fairy tales and folk tales is sometimes diverting, but cannot be the inevitable consequence of the development we have experienced up to now. And it won't become a school; for it doesn't contain a single discovery about human nature: writing folk songs nowadays is imitation and a fad. So you've nothing to fear as a writer, although you are a natural 'bang'. Anyone who follows Maeterlinck's unknown *Nachklang*[3] form is lost as an independent writer. He's already repeating himself with his golden hair and the constantly murdered brother and sister; he's lost his naïveté and is an old Coquette. – There's room here for everyone, old Sardou and young (?) Strindberg, Zola and Loti,[4] Tolstoy and Hervieu. Simply be true to oneself, even as one develops. Besides, every fad passes so quickly and becomes old-fashioned faster than the new (ten years ago!), which becomes classic. What have we to do with Novalis and Tieck *noch einmal*![5] And Grimms' fairy tales? Damn it all, it will be back to Geijer and Afzelius[6] and Atterbom – one more step and we'll go from Tor to Frans Hedberg again! Ugh! – – – – – – –

Have you sent the bundle of Chinese material to Dahlgren,[7] as I asked?

Did you get last Sunday's number of *Le Figaro*[8] which I sent you, and see that I've become a French journalist? I shall soon be flooding the papers here with Vivisections in French, written 6 months ago. You may think I'm part of the great world now, but I'll take to the woods again all the sooner. To write in French in *Le Figaro* was the realization of a youthful dream. *Was mann in Jugend sich gewünscht!*,[9] etc. How's your play going?[10] Have you looked up Poë while he's in Stockholm? Otherwise he'll soon be back here again! I have three plays accepted here for the winter! *Le Lien* by Antoine, *Père* by L'Œuvre and *Jouer avec le feu* by les Escholiers. Have you read a letter from Paris about my painting in *Politiken*?[11] What sort of thing was it? I'm living in a way I've never done before, and find it so strange that I feel like Jeppe on the Hill;[12] no doubt I'll finish up under the branch of a tree again, my faithful old branch. Remember how in spring 1885, Norén and Småland Petter[13] made such dreadful fun of me when people found out I'd become a French writer (in *Le Monde Poétique*)! What do they feel now? – Unfortunately I can only reach my objectives, not enjoy the consequences. Please answer my letters, otherwise I'll think you've broken off our correspondence and want to end it.

(What does Broomé say?[14] R.S.V.P)

[no signature]

334. To FRIDA UHL

[Original in French]

All Souls' (*et morticules*) Day, 1894[1]

Dearest,

I don't know, but it seems to me as if the past alone is bearable and the present moment always painful. I hated the rue de l'Abbé de l'Epée before and now . . . I love the Jardin de Luxembourg and its carps, I love Passy, of which I have such mixed memories. It's very possible my affection (love, maybe?) for you gilds all these things with its shimmer. Yes – Passy was good. The Quartier Latin good – then, and now I endure it while regretting the past, both good and bad!

But I'm desperate! Nothing doing! Not a word from Sweden, from my good friend of bygone days. And he was my last hope![2]

Therefore I sold myself body and soul this morning by promising to write on Henry Becque for *Zukunft*, so as to gain a place for my article in *Le Journal* and the review of the *Plaidoyer*. I'm ashamed, and feel I've stooped, descended; this feeling of degradation may yet drive me to flight.

I've no more illusions regarding money. Everything has fallen apart, in Germany, in Scandinavia, Italy, England, and it's impossible to recover what's lost, time is passing, and we with time. In making oneself modern one always gets left behind; it's only the imitators who win at this game.

Besides, what does it matter. I've done my work, and have nothing more to add.

A *ménage* in France is impossible. Thaulow[3] pays more than a thousand francs a month. Yet lives like a bourgeois, without a vestige of luxury. And with only one servant girl, which means his mother takes their boy to school. In fact they have two children, but only one servant; and that's in Dieppe, where I've found a quite splendid house with seven beds, furnished, for 65 francs a month. Just imagine Paris or its outskirts!

When will we meet again? And where? – Haven't I worked, what more can I do? Your youthful illusions will plunge us into despair rather than renew our hopes, considering the tremendous crisis in literature, where even the Academicians are currently fighting with one another to get their articles into the papers.

The *Plaidoyer* won't appear before the beginning of November. A whole month, and its success highly debatable!

What's to be done?

What's the situation on the Danube?

I don't believe Burckhardt's fable,[4] the Court Theatre went along with *Creditors*. But never mind, that's what always happens!

This time our parting threatens to be unexpectedly long![5]
What do you think?

August
(*Morticole.*)

Paris, 14 l'Abbé de l'Epée.

335. To FRIDA UHL

[Original in French]

Paris, 4 November 1894

Dear *Sonnenkäfer*,[1]

What a miserable existence! I detest mankind, but I can't stand being alone – hence: bad company, alcohol, late nights, Chat Noir,[2] despair and all the rest of it, above all paralysis. What's the point of my being in Paris? There isn't any! They'll perform me whether I'm here or not, and my novels are translated all the same. The papers are chock-full. There's nothing doing there.

Why should I lure you here? Would your presence give me courage and the strength to act? Perhaps! While you were here, there was money. With you gone, I lost interest in everything.

This is the situation: Lecture.
Paintings
Plaidoyer. (New edition)
Vivisections.

But we must act! Nothing will happen without strenuous efforts.

Couldn't I sell my *Vivisections* in Germany?

It seems as if I've come to Paris a year too soon, this Paris where I am *détraqué*![3] Wouldn't it be wiser to take a break for three months and return when *Plaidoyer* and *By the Open Sea* have paved the way? It doesn't matter where you do your translating, and you can write literary *feuilletons* anywhere. In three months it will be easier to move around with the child; it will have teethed by then, and no longer require a wet-nurse.

A three month break, and it will be time to exploit the *Plaidoyer*, *By the Open Sea*, my paintings, and *Vivisections*; the way to Paris will be open. Spring will be here, and without wood and coal it will be 100 francs a month cheaper. Won't you be sensible for once, and look on your trip to Paris as a reconnaissance? You don't want to! And you think I'm lying! I assure you, however, I long for Paris, but only when the time is right!

In fact I'm unwell, nervous, and times are hard. Have a little patience, a little more, and we shall reap the fruits! You won't? Then something must be done, for I can't let myself live on your work.

Littmansson has been to see me and we have a plan to found a Chat Noir or a Procope[4] Strindberg; I shall paint the walls and put on *The Keys of Heaven* as a shadow-play; my guitar will be there; Littmansson will direct the music according to the latest mode; the audience will be made up of Scandinavians, etc. We'll summon Drachmann, etc. Then we'll be back at the Ferkel, with chronic alcoholism and all the rest of it. To sink so as to rise, to die in order to live! The Tavern in place of the family. *La joie de vivre*! After four days, alone, I'm already a wastrel. A six-hour lunch with Becque; a whole day from morning to night with Littmansson; an evening and half the night with 'Geissbart'.[5] It's disgusting, of course, and yet, alone in a city, the tavern saves me from suicide, or draws me towards it, so much the better!

Not a sound from Sweden!

So, can you reach a decision based on what I've written, incoherent though it is?

We've been parted for a fortnight now; you have the child, and I – the tavern!

Sunday afternoon, full of hypochondria and the bells of St Jacques!

Without saying goodbye, and till when?

August

P.S. All the books have arrived. Thank you!

336. To FRIDA UHL

[Original in French]

Paris, 6 November 1894

Dearest (Dear Ladybird),[1]

I've just been reading my *Antibarbarus*, published and in manuscript, and I now understand the great disharmony in my existence. This is me, and the other is not.

And I fear death, because my Work will vanish bit by bit, science will overtake me, and I shall be of no account.

So it must be published. Where? And how? A lecture? That isn't me. Everywhere impossibilities!

Write? But I have written so much. Paint, yet I have painted so much. The tavern, Chat Noir, etc., clowning? No, I abhore the tavern, and yet am condemnded to it!

Two days later! – Yes – You want to keep me as a good comrade at the expense of the child? No, my dear, I've heard that before, it's why, after having undergone the vilest humiliations at the hands of my wealthy relatives on the Danube, I emigrated.

Latterly, here, I went through the same story when you wanted to use your beautiful eyes to get something from M. Langen.[2] Which was? That he paid me what he owed me. And when he stopped visiting us, you were jealous of his mistress. My thanks for your charity. For you've given me to understand that I've you to thank for M.L.'s favours. Always obliged to someone, whether I owe them anything or not! Comradeship with a woman, we know very well what that amounts to! And I see no chance of future happiness while you carry on with your bachelor habits. A married woman who has rendezvous with unmarried men is no longer a respectable woman, that's a fact. After my marriage to you, I gave up all my women friends, platonic or otherwise, but the moment you take the liberty of living as you did in the past, I shall return to mine.

You don't appreciate this because you live instinctively, and can't distinguish right from wrong. You can't make me jealous because I don't know the man in whom I have anything to envy, but if you continue to make me ridiculous, I shall take my revenge straight away!

I had to tell you this! Because with me, revenge is an innate feeling, something irresistible, which plays the role of justice, an instinct to restore the equilibrium, and you know very well that I need make no great effort to find consolation –

That's that! Enough! Think it over and don't forget it!

[12 lines omitted]

August

337. To FRIDA UHL

[Original in French]

[6 November 1894]

Report: General paralysis. Following a dinner yesterday with Österlind. Before that the Café Napolitain with Charpentier, Catulle Mendès,[1] Babin, the assistant ed. of *Des Débats*, who wants an interview; Zola's intimate friend, Desmoulins, who's undertaken the article for *Le Journal*, invited me, and is organizing a Strindberg banquet, which I shall call off. There's the tavern for you! Without it, nothing! and with it: everything! Österlind, poor but kind, is doing what he can! So, be thrifty!

Grétor has returned, and Langen is going away for three months!

I'm now counting on *Le Journal*, and a permanent position as editor. An absinthe at the Café Napolitain sets everything in motion – even *la morticole*. Tell me something about *Das Häusel*'s[2] garden, my cucumbers, etc. There's a flower pot with no flowers in the east window of the dining room, where I cultivated gold. Take good care of it!

Today's bad letter[3] not rescinded. *Das ist gut.*[4]

[no signature]

338. To FRIDA UHL

[Original in French]

[8? November 1894][1]

I don't know what is happening to me, but I fear for our future. I have allowed myself to be duped out of politeness, but there are limits which one doesn't exceed without suffering the consequences. And if I don't heed the call of self-preservation, sooner or later I shall be lost. You are forever fighting against me, and I merely defend myself; but I no longer find any pleasure in these domestic battles. Your arriving in Paris and telling me you no longer wanted to see the man who had avowed his love to your sister, etc.

You want to live with a ponce's[2] furniture; I get rid of it, and you continue to demand it back.

After endless discussion, you finally admit that M. Langen has insulted me by his late night visits; you say you asked him to discontinue these visits, yet I know you invited him to spend an evening reading manuscripts together until midnight, for four hours, starting at eight, and this on the very day when you assured me it wouldn't happen again. You offer to be his secretary, and declare yourself ready to go to him every morning.[3]

This whole web of lies, of deceit, is bound to end in a tremendous crash, the sooner the better.

At this moment I am possessed by a single emotion, just one, the last: to defend my honour, take my revenge, and rid myself of what is degrading me.

Do you act consciously and by design or is it your immoral nature that compels you? In London you established your reputation by dining in public with an unmarried man,[4] and you a young wife; in Berlin you are notorious, in Vienna as well, and you've made a fine beginning in Paris.

Wherever I take you, you damage my affairs by exploiting my connections for your own interests, at the expense of mine.

What good is there in playing the comedy of love, when we hate each other? You hate me as your superior, someone who has never wronged you, and I hate you because you behave like an enemy.

If I were to continue the struggle against you, I should have to espouse your corrupted morals, which I don't want to do. So I shall go, never mind where.

As soon as you're alone and have no wish to debase me, you'll see that you're no longer driven by the same energy as before. Your strength lies in doing evil, but you need a permanent victim, one who likes to play the simpleton. I no longer want the role. Find someone else! *Adieu*!

August S.

Yes, you've always exploited my connections with others, and yet you call me the most ungrateful of men.

Divine insouciance led me into a marriage where I was treated like a beggar, lower than the servants, so much so that my children curse me. A fine philosophy!

There it is: '*La confiance, voilà le seul système qui réusisse avec nous*'![5]

Remember a certain letter, written in London and addressed to me on Rügen! And put yourself in my situation.

339. To RICHARD BERGH

14 rue de l'Abbé de l'Epée, Paris.
26 November 1894

My dear Richard Bergh,

Well, I took your advice and set off for Paris, where I found myself better known and appreciated than I'd supposed; I've now, finally, been invited to gala performances and banquets, but shall probably slip away – to Varberg, to fulfil various commissions and await publication of all those of my major works for which I have publishers, also for my plays to be performed. Moreover, I'm tired and unwell, and need to undergo a cure of *smörgåsbord* and punch.

I don't really know very much about my marriage. It was never taken that seriously, as you no doubt noticed in Berlin, and is probably heading towards its dissolution – though I'm not yet sure. It was sometimes great fun, and pleasant enough, but language, race, our notions of right and wrong, and different habits sometimes created enormous tensions.

Some time ago I sent you an article from *Le Figaro*: 'Sensations détraquées', in which I tried, in a favourable mood I'd worked up, to anticipate the capacities of a future, more highly developed mental life, which we still lack, and which I can only conjure up momentarily – before falling back, exhausted by the effort, into my old frame of mind.

What impression did it make on you, with your delicate nerves?

In Paris – at the Café Napolitain, where I have my ear of Dionysus[1] every evening between 6 & 7 – it silenced everyone! It was new, *extraordinaire* but mad. Since my talent wasn't in question, nor its originality, my madness only served as seasoning, and I'm now addressed as 'Cher Maître' –

This is all very fine, but one should only put in to Paris now and then; to stay here is dangerous. The devil himself can't hold his own against the place, and the desire to be an immediate success, to be appreciated, inevitably reduces one to the level of 'the others' in the end.

Conscious of this danger, and tired of the loneliness that comes from being in a crowd, I shall flee as soon as I can.

There's always the hotel in Varberg, of course, and bearing your past words in mind,[2] I'll make my way there – to work. If you'd like to listen to me during the long winter evenings, I have a great deal to tell (about the latest in painting, too, which can be of direct interest to you). Where art is heading, I don't know. People are constantly seeking the new but what they find is mostly the same old thing, new though this may become every quarter of a century.

If you've a moment, write me a card. And my regards to our friends!

fr.
August Strindberg

Why don't you exhibit your latest things here? At the moment there are shows at *La Plume* and the rue Le Peletier.

340. To FRIDA UHL

[Original in French]

14 rue l'Abbé de l'Epée, Paris.
3 December 1894

No, I won't take back a word, and there's more I could add, but that can wait for another time.

I thought you had been punished for your arrogance, but you threaten me with the law. Heed these words: before a tribunal you will be crushed, and for life, for I have preserved the evidence, and this time I've lost the gift of mercy. So be humble; repent and mend your ways.

Your speculations seem to have miscarried. Too bad, though I can now understand your talk about begging. Fortune has favoured me, and if you want to continue living with me, and for your family, I shall put the two ground floor rooms here, where Thaulow used to live, at your disposal. I'll stay in the other two previously occupied by M. Bang.[1] I'll take care of the hotel bills and we shall eat alone.

But all this on condition:

that you cease to have rendezvous behind my back

that you never see either M. Grétor or M. Langen, whom I've sent packing.

that you never make propaganda here for your German friends or lovers, considering the unpopularity of Germans in Paris.

that you don't wander about the town on your own or with people who would compromise you

that you stop speculating in men and your shady business deals

that you stop your flirting, which backfires like all the promises one breaks

that we speak French together as best we can

that instead of contributing to dubious journals, you help me translate myself from French into German, and that between times you devote a little care to domestic matters.

Etc.

I appreciate that you suffer when parted from your child, and shall only be happy when we can all be together again under our own roof. But this means waiting a month or two.

If you read the enclosed newspaper, you'll see the situation a little more clearly. And I hope that in the New Year, we'll get help from Sweden.

One thing is certain, the production of *The Father*; H. Bauër,[2] Lugné-Poë, and the actors are so sure it will be a success that they expect it to run a whole week in Paris.

That means: money! Then a tour to London, Brussels, all over France, etc. Also: *La Nouvelle Revue* has taken 'The Silver Marsh' for 15 January, which you will translate into German.

Futhermore, 'The Romantic Organist' is being translated for the *Revue des Deux Mondes*, etc. Then *Getting Married*, two volumes, from Charpentier, etc.[3]

I am no longer 'the same person', and never will be. That '*Confiance*'[4] is over, and I regard you with disgust after your latest, unspeakable behaviour. If you wish to come and wipe out the bad impression by behaving properly, you are welcome, on the terms stated. Otherwise, *adieu*!

August

[Postscript omitted]

341. To AURÉLIEN LUGNÉ-POË

Aurélien-Marie Lugné-Poë (1869–1940), French actor and theatre director. In 1886, while still at school, he helped found the amateur *Cercle des Escholiers*; he appeared at the Théâtre Libre under Antoine between 1888 and 1891, and then at the Théâtre d'Art with Paul Fort, whom he succeeded in 1892. He developed it into the celebrated Théâtre de l'Œuvre, where he worked from 1893 to 1929 as director and principal actor. Often in collaboration with such artists as Toulouse-Lautrec, Maurice Denis, Edouard Vuillard, Pierre Bonnard and Paul Sérusier, he staged the work of Maeterlinck, Hauptmann, and Jarry, and was also the prime mover in bringing contemporary Scandinavian drama to the Parisian stage. He produced Ibsen's *Lady from the Sea* with the Escholiers in 1892, and followed it with Bjørnson's *Beyond Our Power* and Ibsen's *Rosmersholm, An Enemy of the People, The Master Builder, Little Eyolf, Brand, Peer Gynt* and *John Gabriel Borkman* (with designs by Edvard Munch). In 1894, he took *Pelléas et Mélisande* to Stockholm, but not *Creditors* or *The Father*, the two Strindberg plays he produced. Following the Inferno crisis, Strindberg continued to send his plays to Lugné-Poë, but the latter no longer seemed interested even in the symbolist-inclined works that accorded best with his theatrical style. However, after Strindberg's death, in 1921–22, he mounted successful productions of *The Dance of Death* and (again) *The Father*.

[Original in French]

Paris, 14 December 1894

My dear Director,

If I sinned against established convention, I say: Forgive the foreigner! I am neither ungrateful nor unmannerly, only what do you want with my poor person when you have my work?[1]

I beg you to think of me as a sick man and accept that I have substantial reasons for seeking solitude. I shall give my sincere thanks to the performers this evening, after which I should like as a rule to call on them during the day, for I am obliged to sleep at night.

I've not been devoured by M. Loiseau, nor by anyone else, not even the grossest of mammiferous females. In fact he has given me a great deal of support, for which I'm grateful.[2]

Therefore do not count too much on a *détraqué* like

your greatly obliged,
August Strindberg

342. To AURÉLIEN LUGNÉ-POË

[Original in French]

16 December 1894

My dear Director,

First of all, thank you for the success that you have brought me!

But why must I serve as Ibsen's gun-dog?[1] I've been his victim for ten years, yet *The Father* was composed and performed four years before *Hedda Gabler*, though nowadays people like to see her as the original of my Laura, whereas the opposite is in fact the case.

M. Antoine accepted *The Father* as early as 1888: he buried it, and now that I've been resurrected, I'm once again to be entombed beneath my enemy.

Allow me to say that you have been exploited now and then to serve some pretty base and vile interests, of whose motives you are unaware.

After the generous hospitality accorded me by France, I acknowledge my debt to your country and to French literature, and would very much like my name to be of service to the younger French dramatists were one of my plays to act as a vedette for a young Frenchman. On the other hand, being exploited by the detractors among my fellow countrymen, who are simply oxen or insects, I find extremely humiliating.

In the hope that we shall always understand one another and enjoy a collaboration which these trivial Scandinavian altercations ought not to disturb do, please, believe in my gratitude and my affection.

August Strindberg

343. To FRIDA UHL

[Original in German]

Paris, 7 January 1895

You asked me in your last letter to write; I wrote, and am writing yet again, because today I've been admitted to the Hôpital St Louis to find a cure for my nerves and hands, and I don't know when I'll be able to use a pen again.[1] Yes, I'm like a child, and can no longer dress myself, nor eat, nor hold a book.

Thus it was to end: by begging from the Scandinavian Society, for *The Father* only brought me 300 francs, in spite of ten performances – why, I don't know. Yes, Frida, a Christmas Eve like mine and most of the other evenings – I couldn't send my children anything . . . Alone, so alone, it is solemn but weird; perhaps it would have been better never to have shared my life with anyone, since the memory of the good times is so cruel. And I remember our last Christmas in Dornach, with the mistletoe that once killed Balder; you gave me everything and I gave you nothing.

I saw you last night in a dream. At first you were a tall lady in black, in mourning; and then you became your own little self, and the black veil fell, and you smiled, but not with your ladybird smile, which so filled my heart with joy – but, but . . .

I often ask myself if you were consciously my enemy. And then I reply: 'What if you were?' You were a merry, pleasant enemy, of whom I was so fond, even if I gradually succeeded in learning how to conceal it fairly well.

I now feel that I'll not see you again, the same feeling as when we parted on that stone island, surrounded by darkness and the noise of traffic.

However that may be, write me a few lines about yourself and the child. Why part as enemies? Let us be modern! Treat me as your discarded lover (they are always more innocuous than husbands) and suppose that I'm gallant enough to bestow the role of victor upon my lady.

In a word, let me talk with you by post, for I really am desperately unhappy. My address is:

Hôpital Saint-Louis
Pavillon Gabrielle
Paris.

Don't be angry about the valise![2]

It's such a long story. The hope that you would come, *Paralysie*, the search for a locksmith who could make a key etc., etc. It'll be despatched tomorrow! Forgive me, and don't think I did it out of malice, for I have no such common instincts!

Where are you living, where is the little one, what are you doing, and what do you hope for from this wretched life!

Oh God! 'A Happy New Year!' – That is what we wished each other in Dornach that time. But it is too hideous! It's enough to make one weep. Weep, if you can. I still can, alas!

[no signature]

344. To LEOPOLD LITTMANSSON

[9 January 1895]

The doctor who looked at my bleeding hands, which can no longer button a shirt, believed for a moment it was 'leprosy',[1] i.e., incurable. But even if that isn't the case, it's still difficult to cure after six years of treatment by so many doctors. It's painful and distressing, and my nervous system is rotten, paralytic, hysterical, with fits of crying that have nothing to do with drink. The devil knows, but I feel humanity has sometimes treated me so swinishly that I weep over myself, from sheer self pity, just as if I were watching someone else go through hell without deserving to, and I can see myself objectively, something the he-and-she asses and colts call my subjectivity, as if that were something bad.

But my great brain and grey matter aren't rotten; they work so subtly and delicately, and with a little help I could turn the earth on its axis, which according to a pamphlet recently published in Paris, '*Est-il bien vrai que la Terre tourne? Non!*',[2] really does seem to be standing still. I haven't read it. Can you get hold of a copy? Yesterday evening, *Le Temps* carried an article 'On a Third Gas in Air'! Ekazote! – *Siehst Du*![3]

[no signature]

345. To FRIDA UHL

[Original in French]

17 January 1895

The struggle going on within me and between us is the eternal struggle for the preservation of the personality, the self. And from my experience, there is no use compromising – it is a question of submitting or parting.

I take it that a part of me requires a wife, child and family, and since I hate any attempt upon my independence, I am a misogynist. And you – the same. I love you, otherwise I wouldn't be married; and I detest this love, for my soul is threatened. I dream of a hermit's life, but I cannot bear it. I should like to shut myself up in a monastery – but to see only men? – I don't know! The mere presence of this '*mère*' (of the order of St Augustine) comforts and soothes me.[1] The '*chaleur du sein maternel*',[2] as Baudelaire (I think) calls it, does me good, but it isn't enough. Between you and me stands your upbringing, your ambition. But your ambition can never be satisfied at my expense. You will never be happy until the moment when someone tells you that your work is better than mine. That will certainly happen, without its necessarily being true. And the suspicion that it isn't will make you unhappy.

In spite of everything, your path will be easy since all my enemies and detractors are on your side. But when you are really honest with yourself, you will always appreciate that I am your creditor, even if I don't present the account, and you'll hate me with that savage hatred, which you know so well.

What is to be done? Get divorced? – But suppose you aren't successful, and you discover you've sacrificed so much for the sake of an illusion?

And if you are successful and we are married, then, then! . . .

I see no way out. You have eaten of the apple and will never know happiness again.

What is still worse, the struggle between us will never end. Parted, you will always strive to compete with me or to take your revenge! That's the eternal torture!

Love vanishes, but hate never dies! Sad!

Why do you seek revenge? Don't you know revenge incites revenge?

Don't make me cruel, for that saddens and demeans me; and I suffer from doing evil, particularly to those I love!

[no signature]

346. To ALLAN ÖSTERLIND

Allan Österlind (1855–1938), Swedish painter, resident in France since 1877, where he received the Legion of Honour in 1895. He and Strindberg first met in Grèz in 1885 and, though no more than an acquaintance, Österlind recommended *By the Open Sea* to his good friend, the publisher Georges Charpentier. He also encouraged Strindberg to come to Paris in 1894, assuring him that he 'would certainly soon conquer the metropolis'. Österlind may have helped Strindberg financially with the journey, and his portrait of the writer, drawn from a photograph which Strindberg sent him, adorned the French edition of *Creditors* that Ollendorff published in 1894. Besides Charpentier, who was also Zola's publisher, Österlind knew both Sarah Bernhardt and Antoine, and the Café Napolitain where he and Strindberg used to meet was a fashionable venue for the literary establishment and others. Only the one letter from Strindberg to Österlind has survived.

[24 January 1895]

Dear Ö.,

When you go to the Napolitain tomorrow (Friday), won't you carry on to the Auberge des Adrets on the Boulevard Saint Martin, on the left hand side from the Madeleine, just below the Théâtre Porte St Martin, so that I may while away a little time in talk. It's so horribly gloomy here! I'll be there at 6.15 and wait until 7.

Yours,
August Strindberg

I must be back in St Louis by 8!

347. To FRIDA UHL

[Original in French]

[20? February 1895]

You took pity on me and wanted to comfort me in my great misery. In return I slapped you full in the face, and you must have suffered, I know, because I'm suffering terribly, though without feeling any remorse.

You took pity! Can one pity an enemy?

We believe it's all over! But as long as the child exists, there will always be points of contact, always this invisible bond that brings us together through our memories. This is hell itself, the eternal punishment in which we shall torture each other to death, because we tried to deceive nature. Think about your life for once, your unconscious behaviour, which will drag you down to ruin. How can you explain these simple facts: I introduced you to my circle of friends in Berlin; I've lost them all, and you still have them; in London, the same; and again in Paris! – Don't I have reason to shun you?

And yet I'm afraid of having made you suffer; I'm afraid . . . in spite of my doubts about your feelings in my last letter. You see: the world belongs to the wicked and the cruel! The art of cruelty is a divine gift, one that hasn't been vouchsafed me, and as the son of the servant cast out into the desert, I am born for the desert, where I shall perish alone. Or else I shall have to create a god who will protect me against evil spirits!

It is four months, a third of a year, since I last saw you – people say you've been in Paris during that time – and half a year since I saw our child. I have acquired a horror of life and people, I have been on the verge of becoming a worthless wretch, I have been exposed to every kind of temptation, and I have resisted them – thanks be to God, perhaps? I no longer know anything, for this last few months my tormented and trivial existence has revived in me my old yearning for a life lived on the heights.

Don't be my enemy! Simply leave me in peace! Leave me alone with my sorrows!

And tell me you no longer suffer, that I haven't hurt you!

[no signature]

348. To PAUL GAUGUIN

Paul Gauguin (1848–1903), French painter, sculptor, print maker and ceramicist. Although Strindberg met Gauguin's Danish wife, Mette, in Copenhagen in 1887, he only encountered Gauguin himself in late 1894. However, he had undoubtedly seen some of his paintings before that date, for Mette Gauguin was Edvard Brandes' sister-in-law and also previously related by marriage to another of Strindberg's friends, the Norwegian painter Frits Thaulow. Both Georg and Edvard Brandes owned paintings by Gauguin, who spent part of 1884–85 in Copenhagen; they were thus displayed in houses where Strindberg was at least an occasional visitor.

Gauguin had returned to Paris from his first visit to Tahiti in August 1893. He brought with him a number of paintings, which he exhibited at the Durand-Ruel Gallery. The exhibition was a failure, and most of the paintings were then hung in his atelier at 6 rue Vercingtorix, which is where the two men finally met. Strindberg had been drawn there by his friend, the composer and civil servant, William Molard, and his Swedish wife, the sculptor Ida Molard-Ericson, who lived in the atelier below Gauguin's. During his stay in Paris, the Molards provided Strindberg with a relaxed and friendly retreat (it was there he spent the Christmas Eve described in Chapter One of *Inferno*, for example), and Ida Molard also helped organize the collection which made it possible for him to receive proper treatment for the psoriasis of the hands to which he alludes in this letter.

Between the end of 1894 and Gauguin's final departure for Tahiti in June 1895, the two men saw each other regularly. They were the centre of a group of artists, including the composer Frederick Delius, the Czech poster designer Alphonse Mucha, the Polish painter Wladyslaw Slewinski, and the French poet Julien Leclercq, which met almost daily at Madame Charlotte Futterer's *crémerie*, 13 rue de la Grande Chaumière in Montmartre, opposite the small hotel at No. 12, where Strindberg stayed during the first half of 1895. Both intellectually and in their situation as artists separated from their wives and children, the two men had much in common. They shared an interest in Anarchism as well as in the current reaction against Naturalism and Impressionism, in which they both played a significant role, and Gauguin was already the enthusiastic reader of Swedenborg, and of Balzac's Swedenborgian novel *Séraphita*, that Strindberg would shortly become. Moreover, the *Nabis* group of Pierre Bonnard, Maurice Denis, Paul Sérusier and Edouard Vuillard, with whom Gauguin associated, frequently worked with Lugné-Poë at the Théâtre de L'Œuvre (not least on Alfred Jarry's *Ubu Roi*, in 1896), and his well-documented attendance at the première of *The Father* there on 13 December 1894 is thus hardly surprising.

The status of this letter, however, is problematic. Clearly Gauguin had asked Strindberg to write a preface for the catalogue of his paintings to be sold by auction at the Hôtel Drouet, on 18 February 1895. The request was opportune since Strindberg had recently caught the public eye with the publication of *Le Plaidoyer d'un fou*, in January. This had been the subject of an enthusiastic article by Leclercq in the *Revue Encyclopédique* for 15 February while Strindberg's essay on 'On the Inferiority of Woman' in *La Revue Blanche*, again in January, had stimulated the editors of *Gil Blas* to solicit the opinion of fifteen celebrities on the subject. Although addressed to Gauguin personally, the letter bears the imprint of a public statement, moving as it does from an initial refusal to oblige Gauguin, via a personal history of recent French painting, to a final declaration of solidarity with Strindberg poised to embark upon the kind of artistic journey that Gauguin is portrayed as having undertaken. In any event, Gauguin was delighted with what Strindberg wrote; he took up the correspondence in a letter of 5 February, and the exchange was published as the desired preface, after having first appeared, in a slightly different form, in the daily *L'Éclair*, on February 15 and 16. Although Strindberg's letter was originally thought to have been written in Swedish and translated by Molard, it is more likely that the latter merely corrected inadvertencies of style and grammar in the French of both writers before publication in the catalogue. Thus the version published in Volume 54 of Strindberg's Collected Works is Molard's translation from his own re-working of the French text in *L'Eclair*. There are no other known letters from Strindberg to Gauguin.

[? February 1895]

My dear Gauguin,

You insist on my writing the preface for your catalogue in memory of the winter of 1894–95, when we lived here behind L'Institut, not far from the Panthéon, above all close to the Cimetière Montparnasse.

I really would have liked to give you this souvenir to take with you to that Island in Oceania where you intend to seek a setting more in harmony with your majestic figure. But from the outset, I feel in an ambiguous position, and my immediate response to your request must be:

'I cannot', or put more brutally: 'I don't want to'.

At the same time, I owe you an explanation for my refusal, which doesn't stem from a lack of good will or an idle pen, for it would have been easy enough for me to blame my notoriously afflicted hands, on which the hair has still not yet had time to grow.

Here it is:

I cannot understand your art, and I cannot like it. Your art (which this time is exclusively Tahitian) eludes me, but I know this confession will neither surprise nor hurt you, for you seem to me to derive strength from being hated by other people. Anxious to be left in peace, your personality delights in the antipathy it arouses. Admired, you would have followers, and people would classify you, pigeonhole you, give your art a label which would, within five years, be used by the young as the term for an out-of-date form of art, which they will do everything to make still more out-of-date.

I have tried to do this myself; I made a serious effort to classify you, to fit you in as a link in the chain, to establish the course of your evolution – but all in vain!

I remember my first sojourn in Paris, in 1876.[1] The city was sombre, because the country was in mourning after recent events and felt apprehensive about the future. Something was fermenting. Among Swedish artists, Zola's name was still unknown, for *L'Assommoir* had not yet been published.[2]

I was present at a performance of *Rome vaincue*[3] at the Théâtre Français, when a new star, Madame Bernhardt, was crowned as a second Rachel, and my young artist friends had dragged me off to Durand-Ruel's,[4] to see something completely new in the art of painting. A young painter, then unknown, was my guide, and we saw many wonderful canvases, most of them signed Manet and Monet. But as I had other things to do in Paris besides looking at pictures (in my capacity as secretary to the Library in Stockholm, I had to track down an old Swedish missal in the library of Sainte-Geneviève), I regarded these new paintings with calm indifference. But the following day, without quite knowing why, I returned, and discovered 'something' in these bizarre manifestations. I saw a swarming crown on a jetty, but I didn't see the crowd itself; I saw an express train speeding through the Normandy countryside; the movement of wheels in the street; frightful portraits, all of ugly old men who had not been able to sit for them in peace. Struck by these strange paintings, I sent one of my country's papers an article in which I attempted to reproduce the impressions that I thought the Impressionists had been trying to render, and my article had a certain success as a piece of nonsense.[5]

When I returned to Paris for the second time in 1883, Manet was dead, but his spirit survived in a whole school that was struggling for supremacy with Bastien-Lepage.[6] During my third visit to Paris in 1885, I saw the Manet exhibition. This movement had now broken through. It had made an impact and was now classified. At the triennial exhibition the same year, there was utter anarchy. Every conceivable style, colour, and subject – historical, mythological and naturalistic. No one was interested in schools or tendencies any longer. Freedom was the order of the day. Taine[7] had declared that beauty was not what was attractive, and Zola that art was a segment of nature seen through a temperament.[8] Nevertheless, in the midst of the last spasms of Naturalism, one name was on everyone's lips, that of Puvis de Chavannes.[9] He stood quite alone like a contradiction, painting with the soul of a believer while at the same time easily accommodating himself to the contemporary taste for allusion (the term Symbolism was not yet in use), an inappropriate label for something as venerable as allegory.

It was to Puvis de Chavannes that my thoughts turned yesterday evening when, to the southern strains of the mandolin and the guitar, I contemplated the walls of your atelier with their medly of sun-drenched paintings which haunted me last night as I slept. I saw trees which no botanist would recognize, animals of which Cuvier[10] never dreamed, and figures which you alone could have created.

A sea that might have flowed from some volcano, a sky in which no God can dwell. 'Monsieur' (I said in my dream), 'you have created a new earth and a new heaven, but I don't feel at home in this world of yours. It's too sunny for someone like me, who loves *le clair-obscur*. And your paradise contains an Eve who isn't my ideal, for I really do, even I, have an ideal or two of woman!'

This morning I went to the Luxembourg Museum to have a look at Chavannes, who kept coming back into my mind. It was with profound emotion that I contemplated *Le Pauvre pêcheur*, as he attentively seeks the catch which will gain him the faithful love of his wife, who is gathering flowers, and their idle child.

This is beautiful! But then I noticed the fisherman's offensive crown of thorns. I hate Christ and the crown of thorns. I tell you, Monsieur, I hate him! I will have none of this pitiful God who turns the other cheek. I'd rather have Vitsliputsli,[11] who devours the hearts of men beneath the sun, for my God.

No, Gauguin is not a rib from the side of Chavannes, nor from Manet's or Bastien-Lepage's. Who is he then? He is Gauguin, the savage who hates a burdensome civilization, something of a Titan who, jealous of the Creator, makes his own little creation in his spare time, the child who takes his toys to pieces in order to make new ones. Someone who abjures and defies, preferring to see the heavens red rather than blue, as the crowd does.

Indeed, now that I've warmed myself up by writing, it seems to me I'm beginning to get some idea of Gauguin's art.

A modern writer has been reproached for not depicting real human beings, but for *simply* constructing his figures himself. *Simply*! Bon voyage, Maître! Only do come back to us and look me up again. By then, perhaps, I shall have reached a better understanding of your art which will enable me to write a real preface to a new catalogue for another show at the Hôtel Drouet. For I, too, am beginning to feel an immense need to turn savage and create a new world.

349. To ANDERS ELIASSON

Anders Eliasson (1844–1900), a doctor from the spa town of Ystad in Southern Sweden, where he had a wide practice, especially among the poor. Eliasson first met Strindberg during his visit to Lund and Skurup in 1891, and after hearing of the various schemes to aid him financially, he wrote, offering his assistance, in 1895. As a result, Strindberg visited Eliasson, at the latter's cost, in June 1895. Frank but volatile, unsociable yet a good drinking companion, Eliasson immediately became one of Strindberg's anchors during the Inferno crisis, a free-thinking counterpart to the theosophist Torsten Hedlund. Over the next two years he received one hundred letters from Strindberg, many of them what he called his 'chemical sonnets' comprising his experimental formulae for gold. He stayed with Eliasson again in August 1896, a visit which is treated imaginatively in chapter seven of *Inferno*, where Eliasson appears as a providential scourge, an implement of the powers and theatrical *Deus ex machina* in a battle of the brains in which the modern scientist is pitted against the *fin-de-siècle* occultist. Eliasson treated Strindberg for his nervous disorder, prescribing cold showers and sulphonal; according to *Inferno*, he also took away his missal and Bible and told him to read things that would not excite him, such as world history or mythology. Eliasson was deeply wounded by the portrait Strindberg drew of him, not least the suggestion that he had designs on the writer's life, and that he once came home covered in blood, carrying a two-month-old foetus. He responded in a long letter, dated 16 November 1897, but never sent, in which he refuted Strindberg's comments point by point, and asked: 'Who is it, what is it, that has sown this blind hatred in you, that has distorted our entire relationship?' What, if anything, he made of Scenes Two and Sixteen of *To Damascus I*, set in a house which recalled his own, is not known; all contact between them ceased in 1897, although Strindberg continued to interest himself in Eliasson's fate. Writing to Gustaf af Geijerstam in September 1897, he remarked: 'Towards me he was a good but hard friend, whom I was given "for my sins".'

Paris. 12 rue de la Grande Chaumière,
(Montparnasse).
[1? April 1895]

Dear Eliasson,

One shouldn't believe everything one reads in the papers. The fact is, I spent approximately a month in the Hôpital Saint-Louis, thanks to begging off the Swedish colony in Paris, but to no avail since the affliction in my hands is incurable. You were the first to mention the word Syphilis,[1] and the famous Hop. St Louis, which specializes in all known skin diseases, began with that, but they found nothing, thus confirming Anton Nyström's diagnosis.

However, I was discharged, or expelled, because I couldn't pay.

My financial *misère* doesn't stem directly from my sickness, since it followed inevitably upon my being unable to transform my personality in accordance with public taste, etc.

Thank you for remembering me, and ask some favour in return if there's anything I can do here.

Yrs,
August Strindberg

350. To KNUT HAMSUN

Knut Hamsun (1859–1952), Norwegian novelist. In their exploration of the unconscious life of the mind, Hamsun's early novels *Hunger* (1890), *Mysteries* (1892) and *Pan* (1894) reveal the impact of Strindberg, whom he acknowledged as 'about the only Scandinavian writer who has made a serious attempt at presenting modern psychology'. Hamsun contributed to the 1894 *A Book on Strindberg*, but the two were never close (according to Hamsun, Strindberg regarded him as 'too powerful a personality'). However, Hamsun responded to Strindberg's plight in Paris by assisting Jonas Lie in mounting an appeal on his behalf; Strindberg's response, his only surviving epistle to Hamsun, was brief.

[6 April 1895]

Keep the thirty pieces of silver and let us be done with one another for life.

August Strindberg

351. To JONAS LIE

[17 April 1895]

Jonas Lie,

Only two words.

I am not ungrateful though I am very poor. I haven't refused help, but I have dismissed Hamsun, who abused my destitution in order to subject me to moral abuse. That's the whole of it.

Your
August Strindberg

352. To BIRGER MÖRNER

Paris, 12 May 1895

Dear Mörner,

Thanks for your letter!

An appalling winter of sickness, want, loneliness and much work; often fruitful, often not.

Yesterday I completed some work in the laboratory of the Sorbonne[1] by discovering the formula for iodine, also a method for manufacturing it from coal-tar derivatives. I'm going to preserve the starched shirt cuff on which I noted the reaction, so crucial.

Were I a businessman, I'd take out a patent, but I'm not going to; instead, I'll write an article for *La Science Française* to which I contribute and where I have disciples.[2] This is what iodine looks like from the inside, even though it's been thought an element up to now: $C_6H_4O_2+H_2O$ or $C_6H_6O_3 = C_6H_6$ or $C_6H_4(OH)$. (So: hide this letter!)

I began to get wind of this discovery 5 years ago, then did my calculations and have now achieved its synthesis and an analysis which tallies with the formula for Iodine I gave in *Antibarbarus*.[3]

I think this will make my future more quickly than I'd supposed. But, you fellows, if you've arranged a stipend for me, let me have it now, tomorrow, for I'm tied by debts, can't move from Paris, and have only one pair of trousers with a hole in the knee, which I had to cover with my hat when I was up at the legation.

I'll finish the iodine article[4] this week, and then I'd like to get away from town, for it's so hot here that I can neither work nor eat, much less drink, and my bed's scorching.

I'm not ungrateful, but I think I deserve to live. I'd like to go home to Sweden, but don't know whether I'm married or divorced (my marriage is invalid in Austria, and there I'm a bigamist!).

Am awaiting clarification!

We'll see where fate casts me next. I'm tired of these casts, with my belongings scattered over half of Europe, housed in hotels here and there.

Give my regards to Öhrvall and tell him that stuff about helium and argon is all really bosch.[5] Or rather, don't. Ö isn't enough of a sceptic, he believes blindly in the old leaven.

Farewell for now!

Yours,
August Strindberg

353. To FRIDA UHL

[Original in French]

22 May 1895

You have a strange way of writing letters; it takes me three to answer one of yours.

Finally, and to make an end of it, I am this very moment handing over your things, these last reminders, to the Concierge at Passy. The lock's been repaired, there's a key, and everything is in order.

Do you think the little one will cry when she sees me? That's what I'm afraid of. Only children love me instinctively, by nature.

It's a year now since she came into the world. A terrible but all the same productive year for me.

When I've completed my work on iodine, I shall return to botany for the summer. I've made progress, thanks to my friends, who have given me a splendid microscope and some books. And I've established the existence of nerves in plants. Then I shall start on astronomy. I've been elected a member of two astronomical societies,[1] and many are only waiting for a bold man to stop the old earth in its mad course through the void without it losing its atmosphere. So don't lock me up if I continue with my coelestographs and so forth!

You got angry because I suggested you translate me! Why? Am I inferior to the whippersnappers you deign to translate? Besides, weren't we agreed on this at the time of our marriage? Now I no longer have need of it, and our social contract is annulled.

It's possible I shall write a book alongside my botanical studies this summer. This will be my farewell to worldly life, for I'm preparing to enter a monastery in the autumn. You laugh? Laugh!

Aug Sg

For the last time: hold on to my luggage! I swear I'll be by the Danube in a fortnight at the latest!

354. To ANDERS ELIASSON

Paris, 7 June 1895

Dear Eliasson,

Many thanks![1] I'm setting off right away, via Berlin, and shall be in Ystad on Tuesday, Wednesday or Thursday.

There was one thing in your first letter which rather disturbed me: you spoke of my broken spirit. My spirit isn't broken, it has never been so lucid and clear; on the contrary, I have broken spirits of a lower kind, who threatened my own, more legitimate, freedom. And I have also broken down old prejudices in science, penetrated the Sorbonne itself, planted the flame of doubt there, won followers, admirers, slanderers. Disciples are now working in four different laboratories to establish the formula of Iodine: in Paris, Rouen, Havre, Douai and a fifth in Lyon. I have adepts in Prussia, Austria, England and Italy, and once had a disciple in Sweden who called me Master; of course he finished up a Judas, because he had a wicked nature and led a wicked life. His name is B.L.,[2] by the way, the translator of *Antibarbarus*.

Be on your guard against the myths, go on trusting in me, and don't try to interfere with my inner freedom, for then I take flight.

You can restore my lungs, for they suffer from an induration which can have consequences that I shouldn't entirely regret. I'm tired and need rest. That's all!

I don't like luxury and hate immoderation. I shan't burden your home very much or for long, as they claim to have established a stipendium for me in Sweden, which should guarantee my existence!

So, thank you and au revoir!

Your friend,
August Strindberg

P.S. I'd be happiest if I could have your cottage!

355. To TORSTEN HEDLUND

12 rue de la Grande Chaumière.
[18? October 1895]

Herr Torsten Hedlund,

Since you yourself brought the matter to my attention, I sent you a number of *L'Initiation*[1] in which, without wishing it, I am accounted one of the occultists. You know my thoughts on that subject, but since you found our endeavours converged, I wonder if you would like to publish the book I have been preparing since 1883, and which has cost me my earthly well-being. What is the book about? A new cosmos, such as I began with *Antibarbarus*, but several tones higher, since through suffering and battles I now have the strength to be myself, the courage not to hide behind mockery against the mockers.

My manuscript, which amounts to a couple of thousand sides in the form of notes and diverse essays, ought to provide the material for a book in large octavo of 300–400 pages.

Plan:

I begin by searching out the primal elements of the world and their transmutation into one another in the volcanoes. I descend into the depths of the ocean with the Deep Sea divers and observe the origin of life out of water. Ascend into the air with the Balloonists and use their observations to reach my conclusions about the atmosphere and the way in which the earth took shape, as well as its relationship to the firmament and the other worlds beyond our own.

Return to earth: begin with the stones and the first forms of life. Dwell on the zoophytes, and particularly on the parting of the ways between plants and animals.

Move on to the plants, which for me are living beings with nerves, perhaps sense perceptions, and conceivably: consciousness.

To the Animals.

Ascend to the firmament which for me, and supported by observations and proofs actually based on the accepted laws of nature, is not what others believe it to be.

From there to man, who is not only an animal; who like the earth itself, has perhaps had previous incarnations.

If I finally encounter God, perhaps you as a Pantheist won't want anything further to do with me, but we'll see about that when the time comes!

I merely want to say: I am not contracted to Albert Bonnier except for novels. And I want no contact with him or his worldly soul during the writing of this work, for I am very susceptible to impressions, especially unpleasant and inhibiting ones.

I intend the style to be like Michelet's in 'The Sea'.[2] My own observations, own experiments, excursions into nature, other people's observations, etc. A book which everyone can read, even children, and written so that it doesn't require illustrations.

With regard to my unpopularity, I'm not counting on an edition of more than 1,000, from which at 60 *kronor* a sheet, I ought to receive approximately 1,500 *kronor*.

You know something of my chemistry. If you'd like to look through some essays on cosmogony and botany, I'll send them. But as I'm completely destitute, and see no prospect of being able to write this book, I have to suggest that during the four months I need for the actual writing, you pay me 350 *kronor* a month while I'm supplying you with manuscript.

Since I have to leave my hotel on the 27th and don't yet know if I shall be returning to Sweden or going elsewhere, I should be grateful for a very prompt reply.

Yours respectfully,
August Strindberg

P.S. I hope you won't consult any 'scientists' or let any such person read my manuscripts.

Also that you don't despise my science, for I have been a scientist since I was 14, and am now 47.

356. To TORSTEN HEDLUND

[26? October 1895]

Beg those who can to save me from distress, humiliation and degradation!

Everyone has abandoned me, the evildoers are persecuting me and trying to reduce me to despair in order to make me return to what was even worse.

Seek help for me, otherwise I shall perish.

Yours ever,
August Strindberg

357. To TORSTEN HEDLUND

12 rue de la Grande Chaumière, Paris.
30 October 1895

Herr Torsten Hedlund,

Your letter has made me very happy, and strong.

You give me a livelihood for two months and don't demand my soul in return. Thank you!

Since you wrote to me in the summer of 1894, I've gone through so much, and been close to annihilation, but at last I've received a definite impression that someone is guiding my destiny, and that this someone is nearer than we think, perhaps as near to us as the sun, which is very near, as is proved by the fact that the speed of light has been considerably reduced.

I also seem to have become childishly superstitious, which delights me. When I announced my coming book to you, that is, following my letter, I received a gold pen with silver accessories (weighing a thousand grammes!). From where? Wholly unknown friends in Spain![1]

Just chance, nevertheless it makes an impression, and now I shall write golden words and white, like silver and albumin.

I don't regret my past life, for I didn't control my fate. And I believe my teacher Sakya[2] was wiser than Christ precisely because he was rooted in the earth. I've been bound with blond ropes and black braids,[3] with the rosy arms of children, but have severed all my bonds so the blood ran. Only let my temptations cease! This isolation is terrible and my suffering unspeakable, but I'd rather burn up than return to sin, sanctified or not!

No promises! But for Christmas you will have the manuscript, to read, or publish?

Prompted by a last seed of doubt, I'm sending you a magazine in which you can see what such sober people as engineers think of my Chemistry![4]

Farewell for now, and believe my soul has benefited from meeting you.

August Strindberg

358. To TORSTEN HEDLUND

Paris, 10 November 1895

Dear Herr Hedlund,

Yes, you are to write to me, for I must have contact with someone who is striving whither I strived in my youth, I must be reminded that there are people who approve of my work. The way in which I am received at home was beginning to demoralize me. Continual disapprobation, opposition on principle, so that when I said white they said black, and vice versa, petty criticism, which increased in proportion to my knowledge and talent, all this fostered in me a hatred commensurate with my boundless contempt. In spite of that, I often long to return to the landscape I love, where I've sometimes had great thoughts, but I can't return home, for the past drags me down. I tried last summer but failed!

On the other hand, in the disturbing bustle of this Babylon, where frippery and pettiness, baseness even, occupy the foreground, it is extremely hard not to lose oneself, to be enticed into the conflicts of this vanity fair, and I often ask myself: why don't you found the Monastery which all those weary of the world are seeking, a sanctuary offering solitude amidst companionship, where one might by strict rules, asceticism, and symbols, preserve the spirit from everyday influences. I have long thought of such an institution, based on a moderate amount of work and – why not – on begging sanctioned by governments, but only for those who are entitled to, who wear the habit of the order. This would hardly be abused since the humiliation involved is greater than any pleasure. I have also thought of becoming a hermit, but with that come temptations from which the desert could not shield an Anthony.

I want to get away from the milieu where isolation, persecution and poverty have driven me, but I don't know where to. I've thought of a Catholic monastery, but that means confession, and an obedience that I loathe.

I'm disciplining myself for my future work, for which I have hitherto felt myself more or less unworthy, especially following our last exchange of ideas, and your great expectations, hence these reflections.

This work is so vast that it overwhelms me; I can't hold it together; I undertake research among my own notes, or rather, discoveries, and after having rummaged around amongst my papers for several hours, I admit defeat and can only fling myself on my bed. Even so, some wicked people have deprived me of half of them, along with my books and instruments. I told you recently that I had some chapters ready. I've read them through again. They retain the sparse, slipshod, arrogant style that one acquires when making discoveries. I wanted you to read them, but as exoteric material. Maybe it's my mission to go the superficial, outer way, to continue as a 'Gladiator'[1] – after all, there must be shock troops, *Enfants Perdus*,[2] who go before the flag, and are there to be shot down.

It's evening and I'm tired after my day's work; that's why my letter rambles so. My soul is also discordant. Here are a few suggestions, though I don't know whether they represent my innermost desires:

If you have a 'friend' in Paris, let him come and read it.

Were I to send you my manuscript, I would never know another peaceful night.

Should I have a copy made, and send that? But that's not what you ought to read!

Should I come to Fredrikshavn? And we meet there – or incognito in Gothenburg, or nearby. I've so many good friends in Gothenburg whom I couldn't see without lapsing into a previous frame of mind.

I'm afraid of travelling, for my soul gets mauled about in contact with other people's. And the filth, the physical filth, I find degrading. My ears have to hear and my eyes to see what I don't want to.

Here, I've arranged a more isolated life for myself than one might imagine.

Before 6 p.m. I see no one. I take my early morning promenade alone through Montparnasse Cemetery or the Luxembourg Gardens. Eat breakfast in my room. – In the evening I go and have dinner with a quiet family,[3] and by 9 o'clock I'm back home. Never read a newspaper of any kind; don't look at posters, never go to the theatre, and don't give permission for further performances of my plays. I've been played here three times but haven't been to see a play, not even to the theatre.

I do everything to avoid contact with people, and see Paris only every other month.

These really are appalling times we're going through. The old positivists, who grew weary, told the young: 'The Universe contains no more secrets. We've solved every riddle.' And the Young believed this, and became dejected, despaired.

I remain sceptical about Theosophy. It's supposed to derive from Buddha, and I was educated by three Buddhists: Schopenhauer, v. Hartmann and, finally, Nietzsche. Perhaps therefore we do have points of contact. The way Madame Blavatsky appropriated and degraded the subject made me wary of it. As a Buddhist I am, like Buddha and his three great disciples, a woman hater, since I hate the earth because it binds my spirit, and because I love it. Woman is for me the earth with all its glories, the bond that binds; and the most heinous of all the evils I have seen is the female sex. The obstacles she creates, the hatred, the low calculation, the crudity, above all the inhuman hatred for a spirit which wants to grow, to rise. 'Their instinctive villainy', as Schopenhauer, the master, says.[4] – To love a man = to degrade a man in his own eyes and raise him in the eyes of the world just enough to meet the needs of her own vanity. The instinctive dishonesty: if, in spite of everything, he amounts to something, it is she, so stupid and immoral, who has made him what he is! What could she give, who has nothing! He took where there was nothing, for he created out of nothing.

They are sweet illusions, Lord, all too sweet. But shall I never learn how to mortify my flesh? It is still too young and fiery, but in that case let it burn itself out! And no doubt it will! But the spirit then! Maybe it dies too!

If everything is one, the flesh is also justified! No, I answer myself, and so the whole edifice collapses!

I see no escape! – Bachelor life strikes me as in part filthy. Family life is the most beautiful – but!! but! even filthier when one pokes about in it! Outside it – absolute degradation, where one meets the beast.

I'm returning to my book! Although it isn't a book; it's a life! – I'd like to train my soul, collect and purify myself before commencing work.

Strange! The inkwell and the pen haven't arrived. The deed of gift, from a company in Barcelona, sought me throughout Europe, and eventually found me in Paris. It announced the imminent arrival of the gift, which the goldsmith was to hand over on 12 October. I replied, giving my address, maybe a little excited by the unusual event. No reply! For a fortnight! – The letter seemed genuine: it referred to an artistic, symbolist work with an epigraph that it didn't cite. An elderly man had got someone to copy the letter out, but had signed it himself in a trembling hand. He was the company chairman, and called himself Daniel Grant![5]

This silence hasn't failed to make an impression on me!

You can see from all this that I'm in ferment and cannot reach a decision.

Advise me!

Yours sincerely,
August Strindberg

359. To MATHILDE PRAGER

Mathilde Prager (1844–1921), Austrian writer and translator of, among others, Ibsen, Strindberg, and Georg Brandes. Strindberg first approached her with the idea of promoting his work for a German-speaking audience after hearing of an article on *The Red Room* which she contributed to the May 23 issue of *Das Magazin für die Litteratur des In- und Auslandes* in 1885, under the pseudonym Erich Holm. Over the next ten years she figured as Strindberg's main German translator, until superseded by Emil Schering at the end of the 1890s. Among other works, she produced versions of *Creditors*, 'Short Cuts', *Somnambulist Nights, The People of Hemsö, Life in the Skerries* and *The Keys of Heaven*. The one hundred and sixteen extant letters from Strindberg to Prager are respectful and mainly businesslike, with little of the character or insight displayed in the best of his correspondence with Schering.

359. To Mathilde Prager

12 rue de la Grande Chaumière, Paris,
29 December 1895.

Dear Madam,

This is how matters stand. I am just publishing here, in French, the two first sheets of the work I mentioned,[1] and now that I've read them through, I find it too scientific for the *Neue Freie*. However, I am only publishing 300 copies, as a manuscript, comprising the first four chapters, with the intention of giving them away free to friends, supporters, and disciples, as well as to patrons from whom I expect help with the printing costs, though these are modest = 120 francs for 64 small pages with cover.

There is something else that deters me from the *Neue Freie Presse* – What is now appearing is only a series of extracts from a number of often re-written, lost, and even stolen manuscripts. It assumes in the reader a knowledge of my earlier essays which have been published here, there and everywhere, above all of *Antibarbarus*. But I also refer to notes which are being withheld or have gone missing; my theories are supported by proof taken from notes, laboratory reports, and books to which I no longer have access, and whose absence has driven me to despair during proof reading.

I shall therefore only send the printed sheets which will be ready next week, bearing the inscription:

Réimpression et traduction libre[2]

I have in fact ceased to deal in literature, and am not seeking a publisher, because I don't want a master, ask for no remuneration, and am leaving the rights of reproduction entirely open, while reserving for myself the right to write as I please! Poverty and freedom.

I expect nothing good of a review of the *Introduction*[3] in *Neue Freie*, because the requisite knowledge, and perhaps the good will, is lacking. I am therefore sending you this resumé.

In 1888 I published *Flower Paintings and Animal Pieces* in which, beneath the book's undemanding exterior, I cast doubt on the dreadful descriptive science then in fashion.

1894 *Antibarbarus* I. Part II never appeared, and I had to leave my books, instruments and papers, and come to Paris to seek sympathetic and understanding people, whilst making a living by writing in the papers and journals.

In January 1895 I entered the Hôpital Saint-Louis because I couldn't even dress myself, and needed to heal my suffering hands. Certain people, who feared my presence in Paris, spread a rumour that I'd burned my hands by the careless handling of explosives (Anarchist) so as to get me deported. Then I was questioned by reporters from *Le Matin* and *Le Temps*.[4] I used my misfortune to talk about my Chemistry as well as to write in *Le Temps* on the composition of Sulphur. On his own initiative, the editor (Perrau) sent a cutting of my article to Berthelot. I felt compelled to write to Berthelot,[5] who answered politely and not unfavourably.

This was the signal, and all those timorous souls who had been silently of my mind, now came forward. Obalski in *Science Française*, Gautier in *Le Figaro*, Dubosc in *Le Travailleur Normand* wrote it up, and hundreds of papers reprinted it.

I expanded on the subject in an essay to Berthelot, in an article in *Le Figaro* (27 February), and another in *Science Française*.[6] After that I went to the laboratory of the Sorbonne and by carrying out experiments with Carbon Bisulphide, I obtained absolute proof of the composition of Sulphur, having already established the presence of Carbon at an analytic laboratory.

In May, I wrote about Iodine in *Le Temps*. This made a great impact and even caused a tremor on the Bourse because a cartel which had bought up all the Iodine in the world (for 14 million marks) feared a Crash. An agent came running to me and asked me to sell my 'secret' for an incredible sum. But since there was no secret, I told him to make his own Iodine. He called in a chemist and put Naquet[7] in charge, at which point I departed for Sweden.

There I drew up a Summary, an abstract of all my findings and speculations. This was the *Introduction*. It is, so to speak, only a catalogue, and incomprehensible to anyone who hasn't read my book = *Antibarbarus* and all my essays.

Thus, while it would be of great value to be accorded the same recognition there as here, I fear NFP's reviewer – you can probably guess or know why.

It has been a long year of suffering, struggle and work for me, and although I see no sign of an improvement, I approach the New Year fully equipped for the fight, prepared for the worst.

With my thanks for this year, and wishing you a Happy New Year!

Yours very respectfully,
August Strindberg

360. To ANDRÉ DUBOSC

André Dubosc, an engineer at a chemical factory in Rouen. Dubosc was on the editorial board of *La Science Française* and had written to Strindberg following an article there on his experiments with sulphur. 'If the hypothesis you have presented can be proved,' Dubosc observed, 'it probably explains many hitherto unexplained phenomena in the manufacture of sulphuric acid and sulphides.' Strindberg visited Dubosc in Rouen in April 1895, and carried on what, in *Inferno,* he terms a lively correspondence with him until July 1896. Although Dubosc seems at first to have regarded Strindberg's gold making with scepticism, in July 1897 he asked permission to reprint his *Synthèse d'or* (Synthesis of Gold) in a Rouen paper. Nineteen of Strindberg's letters to Dubosc survive.

[Original in French]

12 rue de la Grande Chaumière.
[29 December 1895]

Gold.

Tiffereau[1] and Castelot have always obtained a small amount of gold by boiling silver and copper with Nitric Acid

This is it:

C^2H^5 $(OH)^2$ = Cuivre = 65.
$C^2H^5AzOH^2$ $(OH)^2$ = Argent = 107.
C^2H^52 $AzO^2(OH)^2$ = Or = 197.

It is beautiful and so simple!

A happy new year!

To you!
August Strindberg

361. To TORSTEN HEDLUND

Paris, 24 January 1896

I meant the copy as an expression of my thanks, for I have you to thank for its publication. But I didn't know how to resume contact![1]

I drew back, involuntarily, like a spider when its web is touched by human hands. A spider's web is in fact an organ, an exteriorized web of nerves (which is also to be found in a plant: *Sempervivum Arachnoideum*).

And it was not your hands, but someone else's, when you contemptuously let fall the word: fantasy.

It was to do with the moon – a detail! You didn't understand that a transparent body can conceal a source of light, and therefore you corrected me.

Place a small object, a farthing, on the table and hold a prism of cut glass between your eye and the object, at the right distance, and the object will disappear, through total reflection. Observe the moon, a star, or a light through a magnifying glass; alter the distance the right amount and the moon etc. will disappear, be veiled! Etc.

I have 2,000 pages of manuscript. Can't reply to every objection to my book, which will only be abstracts.

I was grieved by the loss of contact with your soul. I'd broken with people here. Was close to perishing, but in my isolation, I found a previous acquaintance, who sometimes still conceals himself, that is, the personal God who has watched over me, struck me like Job, even worse, but who no doubt has had his reasons. Whether or not he also has enemies, I cannot say, but that's how it appears.

I once wanted to live near you during the work's publication – so as to be able to respond to the thousands of things I cannot write or publish. And I called you my Friend because you allowed my soul to grow without trying to 'see how'. But then you got impatient like a child; you wanted to uproot the sprout to see if it had grown, and were then no longer my friend.

That's quite logical.

Do you believe I fear to avow my God openly now that I've finally found him? No! But this courage you called a Gladiator's! It was hard!

I consider the immortality of the soul to be entirely self-evident. I feel I am immortal: consequently I am.

That the body decomposes, which isn't certain, proves nothing to the contrary!

The butterfly larva creeps around and eats like we animals. One fine day it falls ill, its powers decline, its body is consumed, but in a final effort it weaves its own shroud and builds its grave. Then it decomposes – necrobiosis! Death-Life! Life-Death! Because there is no difference between life and death! I've opened chrysalides and put them under a microscope! There is nothing there but a white, unformed, inchoate substance which resembles the saponification of a corpse, and smells like one. Out of this slime, from 'adventitious points', the butterfly grows and leaves its grave. This is more than a symbol, and yet as such it reveals the creator to be an artist who amuses himself by speaking in beautiful signs to people who only partly comprehend!

Yes, a storm is raging! The evil hate and persecute me, but that's no doubt the intention!

Rejoice even in the discoveries that 'science' makes! They serve us! – Two years ago I was to be locked up in a madhouse – by madmen – for taking photographs of the celestial bodies without a camera or lens – and now people are taking photographs through planks! – without a camera or lens![2]

We'll see where I've got to the next time we meet – by post! It looks as though I'm being called away from here, from Paris, somewhere! and the

Evil ones are making my life bitter, like the Maenads, who killed Orpheus because he didn't admire them.[3]

What is now taking place is terrible, but that is doubtless how it should be!

Farewell, and thank you for your help, comfort, and support.

Yours sincerely,
August Strindberg

362. To TORSTEN HEDLUND

[22? February 1896]

Good Herr Hedlund,

You rescued me just in time, when I'd abandoned all hope, and I've still not had a chance to get over it, or to be able to rejoice in a danger overcome.

Got away from my hotel and all the bother, but could only make it as far as another hotel, which oddly enough is called the Orfila after the great Chemist 1820–30, who confirmed the nature of Sulphur for me.[1]

Yes, I am ill and prefer the country to a small town where one is always tortured if one doesn't want to lead a hectic life with just anybody. I experienced that in Ystad last summer where people were so kind as to demolish the wall of the house next to the one in which I was living, with the result that I fled and – no exaggeration – my house collapsed a couple of days after my departure.

I think we ought to meet, for an acquaintance by post is no good in the long run. A misunderstood word, a vague rumour, a neglected communication, and that's it. I assure you I was already afraid you would be offended at my turning to *Handelstidningen* without asking you to act as a go-between. But I had to approach the Editor-in-Chief directly, because that's what they prefer; I meant to tell you what I'd done, but was paralysed, thought: Herr Torsten H. will find out in any case, etc.[2]

My nerves are in disorder, mainly perhaps because of how my work has been dismembered. One fragment in German (*Antibarbarus*), another in French (*Sylva S.*), two more in Swedish. There is no continuity, and I have continually to reply to objections that have been answered many times in advance. If I only saw a way of carrying on with Pt 2 of *Sylva* and abandoning physics, so as to be able, like Aristotle, to proceed to metaphysics, mankind, and God along with the secrets of creation.

You say Karma![3] Why not say plainly: God. That demands courage for it isn't fashionable. It depresses me, however, that none of the existing religions can satisfy me, least of all Christianity. – I am closer to the God of the Old Testament, for He too can hate and strike, but also forgive, and

He comforts us in our sorrows by letting us understand the purpose of the evil that befalls us.

I have been systematically visited these last months; at first I raged and shook my fist at heaven. But then I read Job and submitted to God, not men, and bore my fate more calmly, expecting no other reward but the sublimation of the senses which sorrow affords. Tears are like spring rain, which leads on to growth.

From your letter you seem at a loss as to what direction my fate should take. Decide, I shall follow blindly, like Tobias his guide. One thing seems clear: I must get away from here! I think I ought to live in sight of you, for the hatred I've aroused is inhuman, and my enemies are invisible and too numerous!

I should also like to know how your theosophy compares with the scientific occultism of *L'Initiation* (Rochas,[4] Papus, etc.), which is seeking contact with tradition and a key to the mysteries. I believe theosophy's concern with human improvement and the solving of social problems encroaches upon the rule of God, since what exists, especially evil, exists by His will, either as punishment or regeneration. He alone governs, and no one has the right to question his government.

I should very much like to go to your place in the country, even though I find your west-coast landscape dismal; however, it's good to be dismal.

Only one request, on which my mental health depends: I must live where I cannot hear people's voices, nor see nor speak to anyone before five or six in the evening.

Finally: don't have too high an opinion of my task in life! I am more modest than you think, although I well know that great powers are at work in my weak soul; therefore, when I compare myself to others, my confidence can seem like pride!

A final word, which ought to be the first: Thanks!

Yours sincerely,
August Strindberg

Expédié par August Strindberg, 60 rue d'Assas, Hôtel Orfila. Paris.

363. To TORSTEN HEDLUND

Paris, [5?] March? 1896

Dear Herr Torsten Hedlund,

I abandoned literature in order to escape being superficial; but no one, least of all I, escapes his destiny. I shall, however, try, and suggest this consortium[1] as follows: that I write a series of letters directly from memory and my notes, without a thought for the paper and its readers, but so that every letter will form a chapter in a future book, which, if you like it, I then offer you, and for no honorarium unless it promises to bring in something.

But in that case I shall only send it on condition that you retain the manuscript, for I can only write something well once.

If needs be, those passages which the editor thinks ought to be excluded could be bracketed in pencil.

I leave it to you to decide whether we should use the same type-face as the paper.[2]

If so, the format would be as for *Sylva Sylvarum.*

Popularly, yes, but can absolutely new, heretical thoughts be popular, or become so?

So I'll begin!

If a whole article is rejected, please preserve it as well.

Yours sincerely,
August Strindberg

364. To TORSTEN HEDLUND

60 rue d'Assas, Paris, 28 March 1896

Dear Herr Torsten Hedlund,

My isolation since December has been a great discipline for my inner life, but it won't do any longer. I am becoming sterile from overproducing thoughts that must find an outlet, and am forced – driven – to get to grips with this material and with other people, so as not to be left hanging in the air.

I think Alingsås[1] would be just the place for a veritable 'mud bath' with factory owners and engineers. I won't drown, for it seems I can't!

Yes, the time has come to perform the miracle – for the people, and it can only take place with *eine Thatsache*[2] by way of industry, not now via exoteric science; that will no doubt discover me later.

Only a violent reaction can cure me, for I am suffering from an excess – of asceticism, self-mortification, isolation. Therefore: Alingsås!

Today I finished reading a book about India and no longer know where I am. It seems to me as if the author of *Sylva Sylvarum* (and all the rest!) is someone other than I, and that this 'I' is a Hindu. (I suspect my mother of having been a Tschandala, for my uncle was a complete gypsy type whose living likeness I have seen in Denmark, in East Prussia, and by the Danube.) Consider this description of Benares (*Dans l'Inde*, par André

Chevrillon, Paris, Hachette, 1891 = 3 francs 50): 'Within the walls, above the gates, there are niches protecting deformed gods, monsters with the heads of elephants and androgynous bodies entwined by arms. Here and there wells from which rises a stinking odour of rotten flowers . . .'

'One slips on a mulch of flowers, one proceeds through filth, holy jasmines which rot in the water of the Ganges, which is sprinkled upon the altars . . . In the midst of the seething mass of humanity screeching apes caper about, tied to the roof trusses, and cows wander around quite freely, eating flowers.'

'The Brahmin worship these living forces of nature . . . Indra, Varuna, Agni, Surya are elemental spirits, not petrified or fixed in definite attributes, not comprehended as particular and immutable beings but flowing, billowing, transforming themselves into one another – This dawn sky is also the sun; the sun is also fire, fire is lightning, which is storm and rain.'

(Description of a Coppar Vase.)

'What do these chasings represent? At first one has no idea: one sees only a maze of tangled lines, coiled together by chance. Gradually the skein unravels, and obscure figures emerge (the great disorder and the infinite coherence): gods, genies, fish, dogs, gazelles, flowers, plants, not grouped according to any design but flung together all pell-mell like a lump of mud dragged up from the seabed, a shapeless mass in which one glimpses a claw, a scale, a fin . . .'

'Unintentionally, by a particular endowment of their spirits, the objects of the external world seem to them infinitely entwined. To the Greek, on the other hand . . . '[3]

Who is Siva?

'A lord of death, but also of life. He is love and terror, good and evil, he is the great ascetic, the scholar and the philosopher, a gay and wild man of the mountains, a drunken Bacchus who dances at the head of drunken fools.

He has five faces (not only two!), six arms, three eyes, one thousand and eight names!'

Who is Krishna?

'An Orpheus, Adonis, Hercules, Jesus, ascetic and libertine.'

What is this? It is mankind. I, you, he, she. – I have seen a hundred portraits of myself and always asked: is this me? – I have only seen one bust of myself of which I said: that's how I'd like to look![4]

Whenever I examine myself, I find all the bad things people have said about me untrue, and all the good also untrue.

But I can't root out my selves – I discipline the one with the other, but never absolve myself of responsibility, have a highly sensitive conscience, could die of shame hence I believe the self exists. You know how jealous I am of my self, how I'd rather suffer the agonies of loneliness than rub up against other people and have it consumed by theirs. But now I'm sick and must undergo a cure among men and women!

So, to earth again, for a while – then back out into the desert, to return once more to earth.

Yours sincerely,
August Strindberg

365. To BIRGER MÖRNER

60 rue d'Assas, 21 April 1896

Dear Mörner,

Those fifty francs came from above to save me from an abyss of unpaid bills, which is, however, bottomless, so it would be good if Richard Bergh were to put in an appearance soon.

I am making gold, and like all makers of gold, I'm poor.

Am sending some more, however, finer than the last lot.[1]

If you consult a chemist, he'll say it's iron. No need to tell me, I'm aware of that, but it is partly gilded iron. And if it doesn't resist the reagents, that's because it's gold in an unfinished state, and we will be able to finish it off later. It ought to be observed by sunlight, and freshened up over a cigar or some ammonia.

If you know a chemist, ask him to perform the following basic experiment:

Green vitriol in distilled or ordinary water.

Immerse the strip of paper, hold it over the cigar or bottle of Ammonia (at a moderate temperature), or better still both in turn. When gilding occurs, it dries out completely at a moderate temperature. It is iron, but there's gold there too. My theory: green vitriol always precipitates gold from gold salt solution. Precipitate (for me) = reconstruct. Therefore green vitriol itself gives *some* gold!

When you've done this, I'll send the more highly developed experiments!

So, an answer: is there any trace of *gold*? *gold*?

Not iron, for that's always there!

Why is there gold in Ädelfors and Falun? Because of the green vitriol!

Farewell again, and thank you!

Yours,
August Strindberg

[Postscript omitted]

366. To ANDERS ELIASSON

Paris, 23 April 1896

Elias,

You who have sometimes at least lent me an ear, listen to this; and look – but in sunlight and with a magnifying glass. Green vitriol precipitates gold in the form of a brown powder that resembles rust. For me, to precipitate in a solution means to reconstitute a decomposed body. Iron is thus integral to the new formation of gold.

In nature iron always exists near gold.

Before the gold mines of California and Australia were discovered, all the gold was extracted from iron pyrite and all auriferous sand from ferric oxide substances; if one finds gold in gneiss, iron pyrite is never far away.

Basic Experiment

Immerse a strip of paper in green vitriol (blue, fresh) in a solution of distilled water (blue, not reddish-yellow solution). Let it drip a little. Hold the paper over a bottle of Ammonia. Dry carefully over a cigar (not a strong flame). Don't crack the film which is formed by the Ammonia.

Why a cigar? Because it affords Ammonia, heat and nicotine, which reduce gold salts.

Now do the following test.

Immerse in oxalic acid which dissolves rust but precipitates gold. Observe how the gold flakes don't disappear.

Variant: When a blue film is formed by the Ammonia, immerse in oxalic acid and using a piece of dry paper, fish up the flakes, which now glitter like gold – natural-coloured Iron Oxalate. It is no good dissolving this glittering gold substance in aqua regia for that introduces ferrous chloride, and I cannot separate that from the small amount of gold. Why? I don't know, but $FeCl^2 4H^2O = 197$.

$Au = 197$.

Advanced Experiment:

The paper is first immersed in a choice of

Chromic Acid potash (weak solution)

or

$CuO^2H^2 + CrO^3$
Etc.

Then in Green vitriol, and then Ammonia.
But work in Sunlight!
A more advanced stage would be: Albumenized paper, or Cholesterin.

If this isn't a sign of gold, what is it?
$Fe(NH^4)^2(SO^4)^26H^2O = 392$
According to the chemists!
But 392 = 196 x 2.
And 196 = Aurum.

That's it, for now!

Your friend,
August Strindberg

If the specimens I sent have faded, freshen them up over a cigar!

367. To TORSTEN HEDLUND

Paris, 15 May 1896

Dear Herr Torsten Hedlund,

Am enclosing a short chapter that was overlooked in the great clear out, but which must be included in the first part, because if the elementals[1] on the East Coast are allowed to let off steam, I don't think I'll ever get to see another one.

For the sake of our undertaking, order from Per Lamm here a photograph of the main entrance to the Jardin des Plantes from the rue Linné, where the crown of the Cedar of Lebanon is visible alongside those terrible bronze lions, which are pure visions.

Use this plate for the title page and print it right away as summer reading, but distribute it yourself, and don't let Bonnier have anything to do with my affairs; and don't have any secret dealings with him, for this slave market, in which one can be sold like cattle, has always outraged me, and forced me to behave ungratefully, and so to suffer.

Remember the barely 5 months income I have left, and put my impatience down to that.

On Easter Sunday, when I went to eat dinner with my suffering friend[2] (who became my enemy) in a dark, cheerless room, I found him there, alone. Overcome by a mood which I cannot explain except as a reaction against this frightful melancholy, I greeted him by saying: 'You here? Aren't you on the cross?' (Easter!)

He didn't reply, although he understood.

Some days later he and I were sitting in a pavement café, reading the papers.

A rough man, dressed like a worker, came up to the table and abused my friend coarsely in front of everyone, of which I only caught:

– You promised to pay for the cross (sic!) a fortnight ago . . .

When my contrite companion was finally left in peace, I asked him:

– What cross was that, and who was that dreadful man? He replied:

– It was the carpenter who made the cross for Joan of Arc.

Translation: Last January my friend (= enemy), who is a painter, was working on a painting for the Salon representing a crucified woman (= feminism). The model's name was Joan of Arc, and she was – a 'model'. When the picture was half-finished the crash came; unpaid rent, etc. The man took enough morphine to kill 2, but didn't die. The cross was confiscated, and the picture never finished, etc.

Why should one expect an immediate explanation for hitherto inexplicable things, and then drop the matter? Anyway, the man didn't die, but on his return to life he had a new soul. From having been a merry fellow, whose thoughts only dwelt on worthless things, and whose art lacked all interest, he became a serious man who never smiled, and who produced a profound work of art.

One day, when he noticed how deeply I had influenced him, he was at first extreemly grateful and acknowledged our relationship, but then he developed a grudge. Left me, satiated, and is now educating a disciple. It's all quite logical, and I don't blame him.

There is a Swedenborg Society here with a chapel, library, reading room and publishing house. I visited it the other day, and saw two portraits of the theosopher.[3] But they are only casings, and say nothing except that our souls are stuffed into holsters that don't fit, and therefore we feel as ill at ease here on earth as one does in ill-fitting clothes.

Swedenborg is very much in the ascendant here, and is regarded as the first theosopher of modern times, before Allan Kardec;[4] and I frequently read that I hail from the land of Swedenborg, etc. Therefore I've read Balzac's *Séraphita.* How great and wonderful it is! Set in Norway, it deals with a Swede, a descendant of Swedenborg. And this Swede is like Swedenborg's angels – androgynous. She has revelations – – – but whatever you do, read it! – This is Balzac, the novelist who had at least 2,000 incarnations, though an insignificant little man, a coffee drinker with a pot-belly and a misogynist who was always in love, who lived like a munk and dreamt of a hotel, which he got just as he was dying – not before!

My gold is gold, for it contains no other metal and amalgamates with mercury, which isn't the case with iron. This has been acknowledged by my chemists who are now at work on it, competing for the honour of coming first. 'My mission is finished',[5] and I won't pursue it any further.

Whatever you do, publish my *Jardin des Plantes* so that I can write my book about all that I have 'seen' and experienced since last December. Including the lumps of coal I found on three occasions in my stove and am preserving. I showed them to the painter Munch recently. He said (without knowing anything): Who 'made' those?[6]

He thought they resembled the Norwegian fairy-tale figures of a Klitteman (?).[7] And the third was a Buddha, he said. When he heard it was *only* coal, he smiled.

I shall ask him to sketch them!

I observe, make notes, and wait! 'There's something in it.' That is all I know!

Yours sincerely,
August Strindberg

368. To TORSTEN HEDLUND

60 rue d'Assas, 17 May 1896

Dear Herr Torsten Hedlund,

Yes, you must write as you wish, for there is always something good in your letters, because you are striving, and because you give your best incarnation in your letters. But you must allow me, without ill-will, to reply, so you can see the other side, and thus profit from the exchange.

In your last letter there were, not for the first time in my life, two big, horrible words, dangerous words because they open the madhouse doors: Megalomania and Persecution Mania.

As you know, I've been married to two insignificant women, both of whom wanted to shut me up because I wasn't prepared to admire their petty souls, and yet couldn't stand them treating me as an idiot.

Now, if a man finds great powers at work in him, and humbly acknowledges that these powers aren't his own but come to him from above, such a man is not a Megalomaniac, especially if he has demonstrated that these powers have found a fertile soil in him.

But the little woman who gains the mistaken impression that she is above this man, because he has placed his least important, exoteric incarnation in thrall to her motherliness, is deluded and has *Grössenwahn*.[1]

If a man really is persecuted, so that everything he does is torn to shreds, mocked, smeared with filth; if he is persecuted with lawsuits, threats of imprisonment, and false accusations of Anarchism, is hunted from land to land, threatened with the madhouse, hounded by debts, harassed in public places; and his enemies turn up in the hotels where he is living and warn the landlord, etc.; if this man, who is persecuted, gets the impression that he is being persecuted, then this is no delusion or mania.

But if someone has committed a minor crime, and is afraid of the consequences, such a miserable wretch easily gets the idea that the person he wronged is persecuting him, and if this isn't the case, then the wretch is suffering from persecution mania, and can end up in the madhouse, where he instinctively seeks refuge; or else he wants to annul the testimony of the person he's wronged by having him declared insane.

I have experienced all of this; and one day I shall write about it.

Please, treat any information about me from here with great care.

Last autumn I told you that I spent the evenings with a 'quiet family'.[2] I went there – for a year – because when I was wretchedly ill the woman of the house had begged together the money to send me to hospital. Bound by gratitude, I saw only what I wanted to – good! Spoke well of the house, so that people sought it out – and it gained a certain authority. When their impudence had finally exceeded all limits, and my soul was revolted, I left, without malice. But I wasn't forgiven for it. 'Ingratitude' – of course, and the whole pack was let loose on me. Just recently I heard that Ellen Key sent a woman there to ascertain my state of mind. (What has that to do with her?) You can imagine what she was told.

Is it right to speak well of bad people – simply because they've given you money and compassion? Aren't you bought by your gratitude? – You create an authority, out of gratitude, and then, when they abuse this authority, you're punished.

In the end one doesn't know how to behave in this life.

Why do you always urge me to extirpate my self?

It is my most sacred duty to care for, cultivate, and observe this self, otherwise it will be dragged down to the level of those disgusting little selves that give nothing, only suck one dry, cling to one, and daub one with filth.

Finished reading about the great pyramid. Who built it? – A pastoral people who knew nothing of mathematics, astronomy or mechanics? No! Probably the same race that built Fingal's Cave, the stone burial chambers, the Cyclopean walls: in short, the giants. According to Genesis, God's sons came down to earth and multiplied with the daughters of mankind. From them came the giants. Ovid, that sceptical, highly-educated Roman, who wrote a great Cosmogony and the *Metamorphoses* (= Transmutations) believed in giants and the Golden Age. He was no fool and didn't scoff at the idea!

Yours sincerely,
August Strindberg

369. To MATHILDE PRAGER

60 rue d'Assas, Paris. 12 June 1896

Madam,

I had a particular purpose in sending you the *Revue philosophique des Hautes-Études*,[1] for the old tales about my insanity are abroad again, and my relatives[2] are being urged to have me confined because I really have made gold.

L'Initiation is edited by a doctor, Dr Encausse (Papus), who has been Chef de laboratoire at the Charité, a perfectly sound and very learned man.

The editorial board also includes Colonel A. de Rochas, who is Administrateur at the École Polytechnique, a famous physicist who has published a classic of psycho-physics, *L'Extérioration de la sensibilité*.

Also: Barlet,[3] an excellent chemist; Jollivet-Castelot, a chemist; René Caillé,[4] etc. –

In the literary section you will find Maurice Beaubourg, L. Hennique, Catulle Mendès, Rodolphe Darzens, *et al.*[5]

So you can see that this is no ordinary collection of spiritualists; we are now engaged in studying the unknown, once it became apparent that the known was no longer worth studying.

I am not a spiritualist, but it has been observed that in my research I have gone beyond routine science and established the transition to scientific occultism, which continues from where Crookes, Charcot, Bernard, etc. left off.

This is the situation –

And so far as my gold is concerned, this has been analysed and authenticated as gold, though not yet quite finished. Many chemists are engaged on it, and we await their conclusions.

In spite of that, and since human stupidity always comes up with *Grössenwahn*,[6] I could easily be committed to a madhouse. If that happens, you know the pretext, but you won't be able to discover the real egotistical motives so quickly.

I fear nothing, for I've gone through everything life has to offer, and come out unscathed.

Yours respectfully,
August Strindberg

[Postscript omitted]

370. To TORSTEN HEDLUND

Paris, 26 June 1896

Dear Herr Torsten Hedlund,

Someone is tampering with my destiny, and I believe we shall soon have proof that I'm not suffering from persecution mania but really am being pursued; please keep this letter, and private!

It has been a characteristic of my life to assume the form of novels, without my rightly being able to say why. I don't meddle in other people's destinies, for even when young I realized this was criminal and brought its own punishment. But I have always been like a lime-twig; I attract small birds, they finger my destiny, stick fast, and then complain. My everyday manner, my exoteric person, must appear naive, inexperienced, and people easily get the idea that I am stupid. From laziness or for convenience, and from a strange disposition to accommodate myself to whoever I'm with, I often let myself be duped rather than defend myself, and people easily seem to get control over me. Also because I suffer from defending myself and readily identify with the person who is wronging me and – feel so ashamed at his behaviour that I cannot bear to see him humiliated. Hence my novels, which are concocted by other people.

I'll be brief.

When your remarkable letter reached me by the Danube,[1] I was literally in hell – a hell of spiritual and physical filth constituted by my surroundings: wickedness the like of which I'd never seen, etc. In the end I fled to Versailles and had to paint pictures to survive. Fell into the hands of an international gang of thieves who both forged paintings and effected their sale!

Before I discovered the nature of these bandits, I'd already sold to them.[2] After the discovery, I drew back. By then they feared me, however, and denounced me as an anarchist, etc. The hospital saved me.

Six months later the Museum in Berlin happened to buy a Rembrandt – and its director was dismissed – while the Museum in Budapest bought a forged Raphael, and as a result the affair was raised in the Riksdag, and the museum's director went mad with fright. At the same time, the papers announced the discovery of a Rubens outside Berlin and a Murillo in Brittany. More recently, a Rubens in Poland, and at this very moment a 'Descent from the Cross' by Rembrandt is up for sale in Paris for ½ a million francs.

The sellers have grown so brazen that when one points out its resemblance to a Rembrandt in Munich, they declare the Munich picture to be the sketch and this one here the painting.

In short, it's bound to leak out, and if someone starts delving into the matter, I won't be able to deny having produced paintings for these people, nor that I lived in the very flat in Paris which housed their workshop.

What's even worse, I didn't want to turn informer, nor could I, because my own position was delicate, and people close to me were suspected of being accessories to the deception. If there's an investigation, I'll certainly be arrested, and knowing what I do of the law, it's uncertain if I can exonerate myself.

The worst of it is, these criminals live in perpetual fear that I'll inform on them, and in order to neutralize my words in advance, they seem prepared to use that old method of getting rid of a troublesome witness – the madhouse.

Living among respectable people, you doubtless think this is a novel – yet it's a very realistic and ordinary tale of this *fin-de-siècle* generation, for whom everything is permitted. And if the scandal breaks, you'll see names you'd never have dreamt of seeing in an affair like this – – – for the gang is extremely clever, and has realized the wisdom of implicating all kinds of people, both great and small.

Hide this letter, I beg you – and carefully!

You ask if Mörner understands me. He was among the first who glimpsed what I was about, but – – – I am now prevented from saying precisely what I think because he's done me some great favours. I don't really know why he's now broken off our correspondence, but please make him give you the valuable long letter (several sheets!) which I confided to him, but which belongs to you. Among other things, it concerned deposits of ore that I'd divined during my many and long journeys throughout Sweden and elsewhere in Europe; also new methods of extraction; coal, etc. One item was as follows (I remember it almost word for word!):

'You who have an arc-lamp . . .' examine the powder deposited inside the cylinder. For this has been identified as silicon and cannot be derived from the glass. Thus, carbon in the filaments is transmuted into silicon, producing a diamond powder which is at least good enough for polishing (carborundum?)

In fact I specified the island of Runmarö and the surrounding area as a source of silver because I'd observed traces of lead and the rocks are like those around Sala![3] Also a dark, gabbroic island between Gothenburg and Marstrand where there *must* be deposits of ore (by analogy with the Erzgebirge,[4] etc). And much, much more.

Don't be sceptical! not even of my coal figures! And when you've found their likeness in the story books, let me borrow them; I'll photograph mine so you can see. The originals wouldn't survive transportation and handling in customs. (Kittelsen, Werenskiold,[5] Asbjørnsen, etc.)

Do you remember *Go mikki*,[6] as practised by Buddha's priests? Which represents the principal incarnations of Vishnu?

The priest puts his hand in a wide sack and with rapid finger movements forms a fish, a tortoise, a wild boar, a cart, a snare, a garland, etc.
108 figures.
From where does his hand get this monstrous artistic creative power?
Well, observe your pillow in the morning in a semi-dark room after you have been asleep, but *without thinking* about what you might see! and without doing anything to the pillow. I've shown mine to several artists and will take some photographs later on![7]

This is my method: no seances, no mediums! Simply to observe nature and not be afraid of understanding, nor of believing all manner of things!

Was the young sculptor[8] I sent you my friend or my enemy? I felt he was the latter.
Until soon!

Yours sincerely,
August Strindberg

371. To TORSTEN HEDLUND

Paris, 30 June 1896

Dear Herr Torsten Hedlund,
Impossible for me to exist with a collective god in whom I was part owner, for then I'd be able to make slight changes in my destiny, and that I cannot do. And I consider it pride, arrogance, to want to enter into partnership with our Creator and preserver.
No, I experience God as a quite personal acquaintance who has 'sought' me so openly these last years, so obviously, that I've awakened, though I still don't always understand what he wants of me. I don't believe it is to go forth and preach in person, for every time I have stepped forward, my tongue has been paralysed and my reason gone dark. Nor are human honour or happiness vouchsafed me, and I now avoid growing attached to anything, so as to be ready to leave all this behind. At Christmas I owned some small things, the kind one accumulates while living in a place for a year, but I have freed myself from everything – a few books still weigh me down, but they will go; my stock of paper is mostly used and deposited – so I am free. There's pen and ink everywhere.
I have gnawed away all emotional ties, and am almost ready to depart.

In order to establish once and for all whether omens exist, please put this letter carefully by and look out for 13 or 14 August this year. My dream diary[1] runs as follows: '20 May (this year) I dreamt that Jonas Lie was carrying a gilt clock in circumstances I've forgotten.

On 22 May I was walking along the Boulevard St. Michel lost in thought. Stopped in front of a watch-maker's and said (aloud): Look, there's Jonas Lie's clock.

On 26 May, I was driven by an inexplicable curiosity to go and see Jonas Lie's clock once more. It had stopped, and the date on it read 13 August.'

Therefore: remember 13 August! If nothing happens, all the better; if something remarkable happens, then – go on taking note.

I've never seen you in person, nor your picture. Saw you in a dream a while back; you were like Tor Hedberg, but smaller, and with a full beard! (perhaps closer to Frans Hedberg). I feel my end is approaching! We'll see if I'm right.

Jardin des Plantes? I asked in my last letter if you wanted to print the botany from *Sylva Sylvarum*. Haven't got anything else, and I don't want to let the occult material be defiled in Sweden.

On the enclosed piece of paper is the embryo of a walnut tree: seen through a loupe or microscope.[2]

Seems to be a symbiosis of two individuals, as lichen is of an alga and a mushroom, which is a mammal.

The letter, yours, which I sent Mörner and de Laval[3] ought to be recovered, if necessary with the help of a Lawyer, for it could be abused –

Mörner hasn't replied to it, nor to any of my later letters, but I noticed from my brother-in-law that M.'s goodwill has played its part. M. has qualities which can bring their possessor great misfortune. I've told him as much long ago, but what good is that against *fatum*?[4]

Yours sincerely,
August Strindberg

372. To ANDERS ELIASSON

60 rue d'Assas. [1 July 1896]

Thanks for the card.

Don't forget to go to Türke's Weinstube (*Zum schwarzen Ferkel*), No. 76 Unter den Linden, but entry from Neue Wilhelmstrasse. It's the classic Ferkel, where Heine, Schumann, E. T. A. Hoffmann and later Drachmann, Krogh, Munch, Heiberg and *Ego* once had their haunt. Remember me to the landlord and you'll hear the tale of the Pole[1] and much more besides, for it started there in that wine cellar, and is of fatal complexity.

Schleich is also to be located there, and can be reached by telephone (the landlord will ring!).

If you want some atmosphere ask for the Künstlerklause on Dorothéenstrasse.

Write me a beer mat[2] or two. (Avoid a Finn called Paul. He'll compromise you.)

Yrs!
Aug Sg

373. To EDVARD MUNCH

Edvard Munch (1863–1944), the Norwegian painter. He first met Strindberg in Berlin in late 1892. He was likewise seeking recognition in a climate that seemed responsive to the Scandinavian avant garde. However, the exhibition which opened on 5 November 1892 at the *Verein Berliner Künstler* was closed a week later 'in the name of decency and proper art', an act which led indirectly to the formation of the Berlin Secession. Munch sought to express the disturbing interior of the mind rather than the comfortable, mainly bourgeois interiors of realism, and apart from Strindberg's plays and autobiographical fictions, it is his paintings and lithographs, including those of Dagny Juel and Stanislaw Przybyszewski, which constitute the most significant artistic record of the Ferkel period. During 1893–94 Munch produced several of his most celebrated works, among them *Woman in Three Stages, Madonna, Jealousy, The Day After, The Cry,* and his portrait of Strindberg. They met again in Paris in 1896 when Munch made the well-known lithograph, labelled 'Stindberg', and Strindberg contributed a rhapsodic commentary on Munch's paintings to the *Revue Blanche* as an introduction to his 1896 exhibition there. He also put Munch into both *Inferno* (as the Danish painter 'handsome Henrik') and *The Cloister*. Following their break that year in the wake of the Przybyszewski affair, they ceased to meet, though Munch did illustrate some of Strindberg's works in the January 1899 issue of the journal *Quickborn*.

[1 July 1896]

I've heard from Berlin that Pb has been arrested 'for gassing his wife and two children.'[1]

There's your beautiful Dagny, whose knight you still long to be!

If you want to do something with me to help her victim, Pby, I'm ready, but it will have to be right away if it's going to influence the verdict; otherwise it's – Plötzensee![2] Reply!

August Strindberg

374. To ANDRÉ DUBOSC

[Original in French]

[4 July 1896]

Orfila[1] says:
Gold salt with yellow Ferrocyanide gives Prussian Blue. *Ergo*![2]

Proust[3] says:
Gold hammered into leaf dissolves in Hydrochloric Acid.
(*Probatum est.*)[4]

Ego dixi:[5]
Gold hammered into leaf dissolves in Nitric Acid.
What then are all these so-called characteristic reactions worth?
Nix![6]
Factum est:[7] I have made Gold!

Ammoniacal Iron Sulphate is a white powder! So it is not that!

[no signature]

375. To EDVARD MUNCH

[4 July 1896]

Yesterday news from Berlin that he's been arrested for abortion, with fatal consequences for the mother and child.

But read in my paper that Our King had dined with old man Bäckström,[1] so he's sure to be out soon!

Therefore no *blague*,[2] at least!

Aug Sg

376. To TORSTEN HEDLUND

Paris, 6 July 1896

Herr Torsten Hedlund,

Your letter has aroused me, but not unpleasantly, rather put me in a solemn mood. Life is short, had intended to write a book, but feel I haven't the time, and shall therefore send you my memories and experiences from these last amazing years, helter-skelter, as letters.[1]

But I beg you – first strike out these three fatal words and concepts –

fantasies, *Grössenwahn*[2] and persecution mania, and new horizons will open up for you, as they did for me when I struck out superstition, chance and strange coincidences.

Nothing comes of nothing, and fantasies, like dreams, possess full, higher reality. A person who has great powers eventually becomes aware of them, and will always appear conceited. Someone with so-called persecution mania is persecuted, either in actual fact or because he feels the hatred of his fellow men, which is real.

Now! Your letter suggests that you know my life has been threatened. How do you know that? – I received several warnings from Berlin, and knew what was going to happen; talked openly about it, and no one contradicted me, though many smiled and others said: persecution mania. The reason! My path crossed that of a young man, who lived in darkness. He became my disciple, my friend and my 'Paladin', as he called himself. Well, a woman entered my life when I was unattached, and became my mistress for a short period. Thereupon she grew arrogant; I turned my back on her, and she hated me.

Eventually, she met my disciple: through him she got me back, and he got me through her. They now marry, and develop a boundless hatred for me: the ablactation of the individual, or his declaration of independence. They persecute me; in the end I lash out, and then the chase is on!

The man has long arms, the woman even longer. In a roundabout way they reach me here in Paris, and I'm boycotted. Then I hear something which arouses my sympathy: destitute and parted from his wife, my disciple was forced by his dire straits to return to Berlin alone, and move in with his first wife, who was now married to the Paladin's brother. The situation was horrible: the same woman, and now with his brother, who was the child's stepfather. Through the Paladin's fellow countrymen, I tried to rescue him from his misery, and bring him here to Paris. There isn't time, however, for a letter from one of the Paladin's friends describes how he (the Paladin) has been arrested on suspicion of having murdered his first wife and his two children. The rumour was confirmed, though with some variations, and at the present moment no one knows the man's fate. Now I confess that at first the information allayed my fears, in short – I'm not ashamed, that's how I am – it delighted me! Not because I was afraid of dying, for I'm immortal, but because I found the idea of dying by another's hand demeaning. My next feeling was compassion. Said to Munch that we ought to contribute a portrait and biography, a literary *Ehrenrettung*,[3] to a French Journal whose pages are open to us – but we weren't able to.

Now for a 'strange coincidence' which can only be 'explained' (?) in an occult fashion.

When Munch and I philosophized over P's feelings in prison, I took it into my head to say:

– Do you know what will torment him most? The thought: how pleased Strindberg will be!

And in my mind I followed his mood, imagining how he cursed my children! from revenge!

A few days later I read in a French paper that an elegantly dressed man (not yet apprehended) in *Berlin* had amused himself by stabbing three children about the loins with a knife. Of these three children two were girls, two years apart, and the youngest a boy!

Did you know I have two girls in my previous marriage, two years apart, followed by a boy, who is the youngest!

Do you know that in *envoûtements*[4] (our old laws call them 'bewitchings', from casting spells), the power which has been set in motion can strike to one side, even backwards!

Or are there demons? – No, better unexplained! But keep the word in your heart, and the event in your memory.

(Insert.) (While I remember it)

Even if it means going to a great deal of trouble, please try and get hold of Westermark-Rosén's picture.[5] I've read so much about him, and find the affair most curious! I think I know him, but may be mistaken! Do! We haven't much time, and must use it to clarify things for other people's sake.

Munch and I were deeply shaken for several days, and Munch confessed:

– Life is strange; you, Strindberg, were saved. (So there *was* a plot to murder me!)

This was in his atelier. M. had two portraits of P. One of them was of a head severed by mist, with yellowish, criminal features and underneath some bare bones; painted long ago.[6] (M. had also been the woman's lover!)

Was it strange if I thought I'd been saved by a guiding hand? And that I remembered the following episode from 1887–89, which I'm afraid to mention, because I'm usually punished when I tell anyone about it.

A man,[7] who'd been a friend and helper in my younger days, had got the idea that he was still my superior, notwithstanding I'd developed and he hadn't. Out of arrogance and curiosity, he had to go and poke around in my fate and (in league with my relatives) write a letter to Bavaria in which he tried to trick me into visiting him (to be taken into care as a madman, as my family subsequently admitted).

I escaped the danger that time, but two years later I boldly went to see him, for I love danger and piquant situations. What happened? – Well, I soon observed that I was a prisoner on the island; was refused a boat, etc. And now my executioner began to torture me. (If this isn't a novel, nothing is!) I gathered up all my strength of soul and self-command and . . . it wasn't I who conquered, although I did so, deferential, friendly, meek as a dog, tolerating insults with a smile, as when the man pronounced all my writings worthless and forced me, in his wife's presence, to listen to him reading his own poor verse, his father's poems, and finally parodies of mine.

As a result, the man's hatred was transformed into true brotherly love, and he was naive enough to say that I was the only person whose company he could stand! But his wife, who had by then been suffering for seventeen years at the hands of this executioner (deserved or undeserved?) was seized with compassion for me, and gave way. Alone together for a moment, she explained tearfully that the man was insane, had had fits, and that she was only awaiting the catastrophe. Told me that one of the man's sisters had recently been detained in a madhouse (then I began to prick up my ears!).

I gradually broke free, brought my family up from Denmark, and settled down on a neighbouring island. Two months later his brother stuck his head in a stove and was committed to Vadstena hospital for the insane. (But note, this was also after having forged his brother's signature (the one on the island); and this Brother, my executioner, had used his brother to write anonymous letters under an assumed name.)

A year later another (third) brother took his own life, convicted of having had criminal relations with his pupils, male ones too! (Note this: at the precise moment when my executioner was trying to influence a judgement which would save my children from a perverse mother, whom he defended.)

I was sent for to comfort my tormentor, who was broken by sorrow and shame, and even though the spears sometimes whistled about my ears, I comforted him as David did Saul. (I even played the guitar for him.)

But at the time I was, like him, blinded by the prevailing belief in 'natural explanations' and thought the problem could be solved merely by turning it on its head!

You mustn't say *grössenwahn* if I now see an invisible hand in this episode.

But I ask myself: Is my life to end just now, when I am almost ready to undertake a great task, not salvation's but (yet perhaps!) . . . what? prove with facts, as banal as gold, that it is possible to derive an infinite interest from life once we see it truly and appreciate its design!

(Insert, while I remember! Death lies in wait!)

Saw in the paper – without malice, since I'm far too aware! (conceited!) – that a Danish painter, Locher, had 'impersonated' me at an artist's ball in Gbg! For research purposes, please follow this man's career and work. The point is: it's supposed to be possible for someone to be 'possessed' by the spirit of the person they impersonate, particularly when it occurs in an atmosphere like this. I've seen many examples, and if you open your eyes – without malice! – you'll find numerous incarnations of me in Sweden!

Now: so you can follow the destinies sketched here, I must give you their names. Paladin is a Pole called Pzybyscewski [*sic*], a writer married to the Norwegian Dagny Juel (he and someone else 'fell in love with her name'; she actually looked like a vulture). The executioner's name is Ossian Ekbohrn, a customs inspector on Sandhamn. I find it painful to give their names, but between us, and given its importance, I must.

Follow their fates, so that when their names appear in the papers, you'll recall what I've written here!

Something else! If you want to see the creative power of nature, then melt lead (lead is an element, a carbon; lead suboxide looks like tinder and burns like tinder; gold is a yellow lead which has lost 10×, from 207 = Lead to 197 = Gold, but at the same time has been condensed from dead weight 11 up to 19; lead acetate is a form of sugar and poisonous like sugar, for if you swallow a sugar lump you get colic, and can get stomach ulcers; lead oxide, litharge, is on the way to being gold, looks like poor gold, red with too much copper, etc.) and pour in water with a drop of sulphur. But small amounts at a time like hail. I won't say use it to 'see' things, but note how every human and animal form is reproduced there. Occultists explain creation like this: God is an artist who worked over a long period, sketching and throwing away half-finished, unsuccessful rough drafts; hence the gaps between species, sometimes without intervening stages, sometimes with them. And why not? According to Genesis, God created man in his own image. We therefore bear some resemblance to God, and are right to conceive God according to our outer and inner selves.

Therefore he forbade all reproductions, because they were caricatures. And I have often believed deep down that artists are apes, conceited, rebels, lecherous, impudent, dishonest. Generally look like bandits, and love dressing and shaving like bandits!

Or the Creator plays with them; he smiles at their imaginary creative ability, and when he grows angry, he lets them feel the hollowness of their ambition. (Savonarola!)

Do you know what an artist's darkest hour is? When he doubts his 'calling'; doubts his greatness, divines his hollowness, and suspects he is the victim of a delusion!

Lead! the shapes it assumes are more than that, they are traces of the Creator's experiments since he, like everything else, must have evolved! (When you've got some worthwhile results, let me have them to compare with mine! If we find two the same, then we *know* the hand is there, and can believe in it! Suppose we find some like my charcoal figures? What then?

Read what I write without criticism, without resistance, and don't prevent me running on, for I am growing as I write this, and maybe you will too.

Why to you? – I don't know! Perhaps because you sent me the Danube letter!

The Danube boasted demons with the enormous capacity for evil that all savages possess. It was purgatory for me, for while there I learned to loathe filth and acquired a yearning for the white, though I was on the point of becoming evil, and committed a couple of wicked deeds that were immediately punished. (Letters from there about this are to be had from Leop. Littmansson in Versailles, c/o Per Lamm, 212 rue de Rivoli, Paris. Remember that one day!)
[44 lines on gold-making omitted]

'Strange Coincidences'

Green vitriol precipitates gold from its Salts!

Oxalic acid precipitates gold from its Salts!

Acetic acid precipitates gold from its Salts!

How have photographers stumbled on the idea of combining them?

Look: they transmute silver into gold. And when lunar caustic turns violet in the light, it becomes gold.

Violet is related to gold, not silver.

Exp: Take a solution of tartaric silver oxide and precipitate it with tartaric iron. According to the book, it precipitates as a yellowish silver. Carry out the experiment, take the yellow silver to a goldsmith and simply ask:

– How many carat is this gold? But don't let him know the procedure! Do this!!!

If you send me the Geological map (costs 2 *kronor*) of your family estate, I will tell you what metals are to be found there! Not by occult means, yet, but I know the entire geology of Sweden at first hand, and that of Europe, along with the rest of the world, from books.

Objects made of ivory get a beautiful gilding if one fishes up my gold flakes with them; also mat or unglazed porcelain.

(While I remember!)

If I die suddenly: herewith the right to publish all the letters I've written you, with all the consideration they show for others, and which others have never shown me!

Also the important letter to Mörner – de-Laval![8]

To be opened and read when something strange happens to B.M.!* Not before!

*Guess who! Not difficult![9]

Some advice! Doctor Eliasson is asking me to return to Sweden!
Should I or shouldn't I?
Answer: No!

I boil oxalic acid and introduce green vitriol to the solution. The deposit is Gold.

(To be cont.)
Botany to follow!

377. To TORSTEN HEDLUND

Paris, 7 July 1896[1]

Orfila:

In the Hôpital Saint-Louis, abandoned by everyone, hated by my own wife (the authoress) because my play, *The Father*, had been a success at L'Œuvre, I made the acquaintance of the Pharmacist and by means of incomplete combustion, I established the presence of carbon in sulphur. Encouraged by his conversation and borrowing his books, I took the carbon and went to an analytical bureau near the Hospital, and requested an analysis without saying what it concerned. The following day I received a certificate, confirming it was carbon. This satisified me, and a number of other chemists as well, but not everyone. The papers stirred things up. But I still had doubts, and was uneasy.

One morning I awoke having dreamt, I've forgotten about what; went at random, but directly, to a second-hand bookshop on the Boulevard St Michel, took a volume from the stall outside, opened it at page 124 and read: 'Sulphur has been classified among the elements, but the ingenious experiments of Davy and the younger Berthollet[2] seek to establish that it contains hydrogen, oxygen and . . .'

I bought the book, in two volumes. It was Orfila's *Chemistry*. I knew something of Orfila the toxicologist already, but now I blessed him.

A few days later, I discovered his beautiful monument in the Cemetery at Montparnasse.

Shortly afterwards the Hôtel Orfila, whose resemblance to a monastery appealed to me. Over the entrance were two tablets set in the wall, designed for commemorative inscriptions; they were blank, however. When I was hounded out of the rue de la Grande Chaumière, I immediately put up at the Hôtel Orfila, and it was there (you may believe this or not) that I solved the question of gold.

And his chemistry always helps me in my hour of need.

Among other things, I have a chemist friend in Rouen,[3] who blows hot and cold, and isn't firm in his belief, but nevertheless sometimes comes dashing out to weigh in on my behalf, and weighs in stoutly. When I sent him my first specimen of gold, he refused to accept it, saying it was Ammoniacal Iron Sulphate.

But Orfila says not, for this body is a white powder, and no shining gold scale.

And again (this was the trump card): Ammoniacal Iron Sulphate is obtained by precipitating a solution of Gold (!) in a compound of nitric acid and ammonium chloride with iron sulphate.

Imagine: Gold in order to obtain an iron preparation! This surely indicates the relationship between iron and gold.

My chemist in Rouen remained silent. Then he thought to pull the rug from under me: It isn't gold, because it can be dissolved in Hydrochloric acid!

I was nonplussed for two months, and had forgotten Orfila, because I suppose I must have at least 12 other chemistries.

Then one day I open Orfila who states: Genuine gold leaf is dissolved in Hydrochloric acid. (And in Nitric acid too!) Pow!

I promise you, when all other chemistries are silent, Orfila speaks. It's an unpretentious book in 2 volumes, fifth edition, Paris 1831.

The man was born in Minorca, and one of his names was Bonaventura.[4]

It's probably his house I'm living in, and his spirit still seems to visit it!

'Strange Coincidences and
Inexplicable Events:'

During my travels in Sweden, I visited Kinnekulle.[5] Left the coachman at 8 o'clock in Råbeck and went on foot straight over the mountain. Came down to the station at Gåssäter; but no coachman. I lay down on a bench, hungry and tired, until 5 p.m. But on the mountain, I found this scrap of paper.[6]

When the coachman came, he'd had something to eat and drink, and left me to my fate.

Why have I kept this scrap of paper for so many years?

I must have thought it curious even then!

Stockenström, who wavered between a sincere search for enlightenment and banal pleasure seeking, was walking along the rue de Rennes with me. Suddenly he stopped in front of a print dealer's and cried out: There it is again! He meant some plates depicting pansies (see the enclosed).[7] Returning home the previous evening, he'd noticed how the pansies in his back yard gazed at him with large eyes.

I went back later and bought one; asked discreetly who the artist was, where they came from, etc. They knew nothing at all about them.

And yet it is a Seer who saw this the first time. The strange thing is, of course, that S 'saw' it at once yet swore he'd never passed along that street before, so a hazy impresssion might have stayed with him.

(It's strange! Since your letter yesterday, your person has been totally transformed in my mind. I don't know how old you are, but you may have noticed that I've been treating you as a younger man. Now, after yesterday, you turn out to be my age, or even older, stronger, in some respects superior to me, so that I'm almost ashamed at having taken you for a young man who knows little of life. When you mentioned last winter that you were married, I couldn't grasp it. – Such a young man! – Where did I get that from? With the new picture, you now resemble my brother-in-law in Vienna, the sculptor Weier [*sic*],[8] who did the 'Train of Bacchus' round the Hofburg Theatre, even though (?) he's a man of deep religious feeling and enormous passions.)

I once told you that I felt so impersonal and irresponsible that all the evil people said about me seemed to me untrue. I must add: and true! Terribly true! And yet not so!

Concerning *Grössenwahn*![9] The other day a Norwegian composer related the following story:

When Bjørnson had written his *Gauntlet* and thundered against the immorality of the young, a man asked him if he hadn't sinned himself in his younger days.

Bjørnson replied: 'Me? That was something else. I came like a young God.'

I was meant to smile at that, but couldn't and thought aloud:

– What tremendous powers that man must have had to feel the distinction so clearly! To be able to say that, one must feel it, and then it's a fact!

Anecdotally, you know I once broke with Bjørnson – but do you know why? He was an errand boy, and for people of no consequence, who were using him to castigate me. That was the reason! For prior to that, I'd put up with much more from the man because I found him justified, like an Old Testament prophet; but he was sometimes demeaned by the pettiness of the age.

His *Gauntlet*! Yes and no! But I always believed in monogamy of course!

Occultists say that love between men and women should be taken extremely seriously, for the relationship is established for eternity when the two become one (the angels). That's why widows are burned in India, and adultery is punished with death.

On the basis of our own costly experiences, Fru Anton Nyström and I once agreed that marriage should be indissoluble. If one has learnt from experience and wants to pass it on to the young, they mock you. Why should the young always be foolish? Perhaps one *must* go through the swine age first, and eat pig swill until it makes one puke.

I'm almost certain that's the case, and intend to preach neither morality nor immorality to the young; both because it's futile, and perhaps wrong.

An episode which had unpleasant consequences for me. I was invited to Doctor Encausse's (Papus) in Marolles-en-Brie (N.B.) on Tuesday, 24 June. The visit was put off until the Thursday. That morning I met the Doctor and his wife at the Gare de Vincennes, and we made our way to Brie. The atmosphere was somewhat gloomy. On arriving at the villa, the Encausses were greeted by three items of bad news. The maid was in bed with scarlet fever; some unknown creature had killed the best duck, etc.

When I got back to Paris that evening I read in a paper that a house in Brie (!) in Valence, the same direction as Marolles but further away, had been possessed by ghosts for two days; furniture had been thrown about, voices heard, and a sick woman subjected to immoral language.

The police, doctors and priests conducted thorough investigations. Journalists went down! The papers reported the affair in grave terms; Papus and the Abbé Schnebelin (an occultist) went there, and found it had all ended – the same evening I left Brie. And the unpleasant thing is that it began on the Tuesday, when I'd been expected. Particularly unpleasant in my hotel, where people knew I was going to go to Brie that Tuesday – and because they think I'm some kind of sorcerer.

However, this house provided a good opportunity to give the academies a drubbing. (See the enclosed articles!)

Whatever's behind the story, don't rush to any conclusions, but wait until something similar occurs in your life.[10]

Wednesday, 29 April, I found the nine of spades on the rue Ségnier. This card means death! – Around midday I received a black-edged letter (from the chemist Vial).[11] In the evening Madame Charlotte Futterer[12] told me a man had died in her house, and that he had literally fought with death, dressed, got up, and wanted to go out onto the boulevards. Later the Shah of Persia was murdered; Vegesack died in Paris.[13] On the night of 14 May, I dreamt that a severed head was fixed back onto its trunk and started speaking. The man like a drunken actor pursued me and was behind a screen which I knocked over on top of him, but first pushed a Pole (!) I know in front of me. In the morning there was blood on my hand, and I thought I'd killed a mosquito. On my morning walk, when I went to see Munch, I saw a lot of blood spilled on the Boulevard Port Royal.

Note the Pole! A month later the catastrophe with the Pole, his wife and children.

On the night between 17 and 18 April I dreamt that the late Rudolf Wall gave me a silver coin as big as a 5 franc piece, but whiter. I asked what it was. He replied that it was American, but genuine! The following day I received a letter from America in which an old, but quite forgotten acquaintance, whom I haven't seen since 1884, told me among other things that he'd once tried to reach me by letter to commission a biography of Leif Eriksson for 3,000 dollars.[14]

I dread August, partly because the heat will have come, and that gives me suicidal mania; partly because the summer will be over and I've a dreadful winter in front of me, partly because I'm finished. This presentiment means I daren't begin a book, and am therefore writing these letters instead. I don't believe in any outward change in my destiny, and I've no desire to possess anything I would regret leaving. No, I've been preparing for death of late, and shall depart from here with genuine joy, as after a good fight, a task successfully accomplished, or a sentence served.

However, I do have occasional moments of doubt. Is it possible, I ask, that such a training isn't going to lead to some great task? I don't know.

(Note: I donate my many manuscripts to the library of the Jardin des Plantes. Should they be refused, I want them to go to Gothenburg City Library! Remember that, if the need arises! And that they are kept together; not pigeonholed according to subject so they disappear, as happens at the Royal Library in Stockholm.)

(Cont.)

378. To TORSTEN HEDLUND

[18 July 1896][1]

I am going to continue, whether you wish me to or not. I am writing this to clear my mind and unburden myself, most of all perhaps to maintain my interest in life.

Hallucinations, fantasies, dreams seem to me to possess a high degree of reality. If I see my pillow assume human shapes those shapes are there, and if anyone says they are only (!) fashioned by my imagination, I reply:

You say 'only'? – What my inner eye sees means more to me! And what I see in my pillow, which is made of birds' feathers, that once were bearers of life, and of flax, which in its fibres has borne the power of life, is soul, the power to create forms, and it *is* real, since I can draw these figures and show them to others.

And I hear a sound in my pillow, sometimes like a cricket. The noise a grasshopper makes in the grass has always seemed magical to me. A kind of ventriloquism, for I have always fancied that the sound came from an empty hall beneath the earth. Supposing that grasshoppers have sung in a field of flax, don't you think that Nature or the creator can fashion a phonograph from its fibres so that their song re-echoes in my inner ear, attuned as it is to hear more acutely than it normally does by suffering, privation and prayer? But this is where 'natural explanations' fall short, and I am abandoning them forthwith!

The coal figure resembling a 'mountain troll' shattered when I placed it in the sun. According to folk tales, trolls shatter when they see the sun.

In order to ascertain if I was the only one to remark these figures, I showed them to my acquaintances (Cf. Munch).

But I wanted to know if animals were also able to see these figures. There were some house sparrows which I fed with bread on the roof outside my room. I now placed the kobold beside the bread, and lo and behold: the birds didn't come.[2]

In folk tales they are called trolls; we say elementals, and think we don't believe in trolls.

If you observe the empty shell of a crab, the first thing you'll notice is an amazing resemblance to a set of false teeth, with two or three different kinds of teeth. Look at the outside of the shell and you'll see some figures. I first noticed this in Berlin in 1894 and pointed it out to an educated Swedish scientist.[3] At first his eyes flashed as if he'd 'seen' something, then he gave a stupid, bestial smirk.

The reality of these figures may be confirmed from the enclosed copies, and you can place a piece of paper on a crab's shell yourself, and rub it with a piece of soft charcoal. Or take a photograph. If you come up with the same pattern, then this is no hallucination but something constant![4]

These figures were recorded in Paris this winter. The one I saw in Berlin was an illustration in a book on Heligoland, and resembled a calf's head.[5] These from Paris resemble the head of an ox or goat with human features.

I don't know what it means!

When Linnaeus expected or had received something pleasant, he was afraid to mention it: *Ne audiat Nemesis!*,[6] he wrote afterwards. What is Nemesis? Other people's hatred, a jealous hate, which has the power to destroy my prosperity. I have always been afraid when things have gone well for me and always been unhappy at a stroke of good fortune, for those closest to me have hated me, and I have always been abandoned just at that moment. People do not flee unhappiness as they do happiness, and the happy man is the most unhappy.

I've won a victory, but daren't say so, yet my friends must sense it, for I've rarely felt such violent hatred. In order to neutralize it, I'm keeping quiet, and would rather be taken for an idiot than arouse still greater hatred.

Once again threatened with a police interrogation, a trial, the madhouse. And you think these realities are hallucinations?

I'm a little agitated before the explosion comes, but as soon as I look reality in the eye, I grow calm. How many times haven't I been threatened already, how many lawsuits, but someone always came to my rescue. I'm now prepared for everything, so let's see if I'm not helped this time too! If not, then it was decreed thus! Have just read in the Old Testament that when the Israelites built their idols, they had an image of envy! Does that mean they used the image to arouse this raging passion in their enemy, and thereby destroyed him?

If the earth is a penal colony to which we have been banished, then we are all villains. In that case, it is right to think badly of one's neighbour, and to hate him as the representative of evil. And when I find myself at ease in company and love my neighbour, I'm a long way from hating evil.

Should I love my neighbour as myself? I hate myself and hate my neighbour as myself, for if I love my neighbour, I love myself, but I don't, and what's more, I may not.

'Do not I hate them, O Lord, that hate thee? and am not I grieved with those that rise up against thee?

I hate them with perfect hatred: I count them my enemies.' Psalm 139.

Today I received a message from a dead man. Literally, because it read 'From the Author', who's dead.[7]

This message delighted me in several respects.

In Genesis it says that God created a space (*étendue*?) and separated the higher waters from the lower, and called the space heaven (*cieux* = clouds?). There were now two waters, one above heaven and one below. And God commanded that the lower waters be gathered together in a basin that the dry land appear. And the dry land in the lower waters was called Earth.

This means that unbeknownst to us the higher waters remained above heaven! Did dry land appear there too, and another earth? Is it from thence we come and thither we go? Our memories of a golden age; the solemn delight of children when they leave the town for the country, which has always seemed to me a better world, awakening recollections of a half-forgotten existence.

However, when I see sea and sky merge in the blue air, making the horizon invisible, it seems to me to be a single substance, all water, or all air; they are reflected in each other. And is it from the higher waters that clouds, rain, dew, *frost flowers* come?

Is it possible that communication can take place between these realms? These ideas are prompted by a phenomenon hitherto inexplicable to me.

Birds conveyed in a balloon do not suffer from a lack of oxygen.

How is it that the millions of swallows which breed in Sweden arrive and vanish without anyone witnessing their periodic return? I am forty-seven, and have never seen the swallows arrive.

Suddenly, there they are, but they never come sweeping in in flocks.

Just once, in Denmark, I saw some two thousand swallows ready to migrate. A couple of hours later they had vanished. They'd 'taken off'.

When I think of how every spring kites hang in the air at a great height and wind their way down in a spiral, it now seems to me as if they were descending from above, growing accustomed to our atmosphere as it were, before sinking right down. When the Eldkvarn in Stockholm burned down in the 1870s,[8] a lively discussion arose in the press among Zoologists concerning what species of bird had appeared in swarms above the conflagration. Those who favoured 'natural explanations' said they were the miller's pigeons, but other people said they'd definitely identified them as oyster catchers (*Haematopus ostralegus*), a mysterious, shrieking bird that I know well from the Archipelago.

It would be interesting to read about the phenomenon, and establish precisely what birds were seen, and whether or not it was so late on in the autumn that there couldn't have been any oyster catchers, because they migrate!

This is an idea which has haunted me.

Another thing. Where do swifts spend the winter? The other swallows are supposed to be in Egypt, but who knows if they are the same ones that we see! Swallows die in cages!

Where do ice-cold winds come from when the sun is blazing? Here in Paris during June it was cold, while the sun blazed down. A north-easterly wind, from Scandinavia in other words, but people were collapsing from the heat there, so that's not where the cold wind came from. And cyclones, when the wind blows from every direction, but mostly from above. And waterspouts? And ebb and flood? From above!

It appears to me that heaven is much nearer to us than we think, perhaps because I'm closer to it!

Yes, I'm not mistaken about my approaching end. It seems to me more likely than ever, although I don't know why!

My soul rejoices at the thought that there's a place up there, resembling this in fact quite beautiful earth, for to pass directly to an infinite realm has never appealed to me. I imagine it to be like Switzerland, and shall never forget my first impression of Switzerland as the train descended from the

Jura; I thought I was seeing cloud formations of a wondrous beauty, but – then it dawned on me: they were the Alps! It's heaven itself, said my children. And my wife burst into tears.

My stay in Switzerland was like a year of Sundays. A serene and moving peace, solemn as Whitsuntide; and the great bell of Lausanne sounded as if it came from another world, and doubtless still does. And the Föhn, which is thought to come from Africa, now seems to me to have come from above, for even though it had crossed the alpine snows, it was still warm.

Look here at the way children come into the world from above, and how beautiful they are, only to become so abominable later on; observe, too, the skull which receives them at the portal to this world of sorrow and filth.

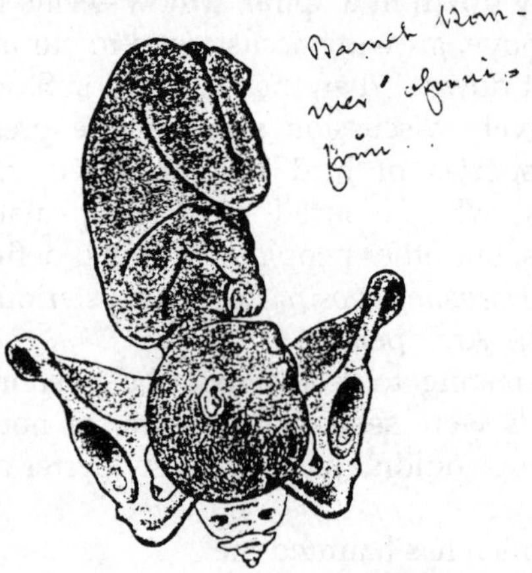

And can you see the basket or urn (a cinerary urn?) in which the child is borne? Its purity of style? I can't remember what it reminds me of! A Roman burial urn?

Strabo[9] held that the Great Pyramid was so miraculous that it must have been lowered from heaven. It looks like a crystal of alum or ammonium alum. Ammonia derives its name from Ammon because salt was first discovered in the desert near the temple of Ammon (?). If one takes the figure on page 19 of Svenonius' *The Mineral Kingdom*,[10] where there is a schematic reproduction of a crystal according to Haüy's[11] 'building brick theory', and compares it with the reproduction in Piazzi Smyth's *The Great Pyramid*,[12] the inner resemblance between Pyramid and crystal is also striking.

Job XXXVIII and XXVI are thought to refer to the Pyramid, likewise Leviticus XIX 35–37, where God says he has himself given meteyard, measure and weight, which were of course established by the Pyramid. Imagine if everything has been 'made' by the hand of an Artist-Creator who, with practice, came ever closer to perfection while himself undergoing his own evolution. And making sketches in the process (for example the figures on crabs, the human foetus in the sting ray, which is a mammal and suckles its young, the incomplete faces on a number of the larger snails, like certain forms of Strombus. See the rays with human features in Brehm's *Animal Life*, where the creatures seem to have wings. Axel Jäderin said he'd seen human malformations, living, at the Eugenia Home, among them one with a face like a paper kite (the ray!)).

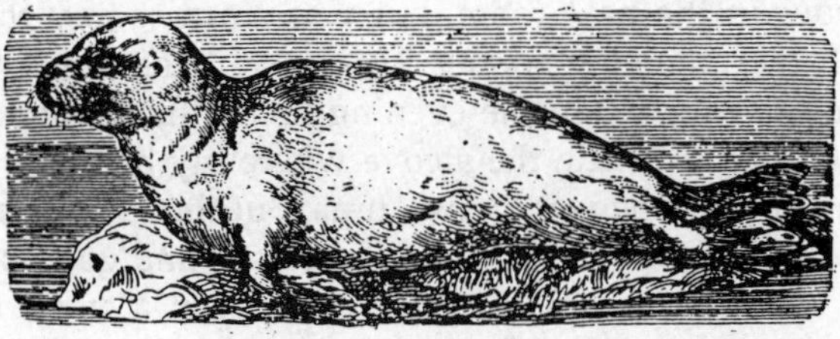

I know someone who looks exactly like this seal. Have you heard a seal when it calls (not shrieks) from a rock, and have you seen one weep?

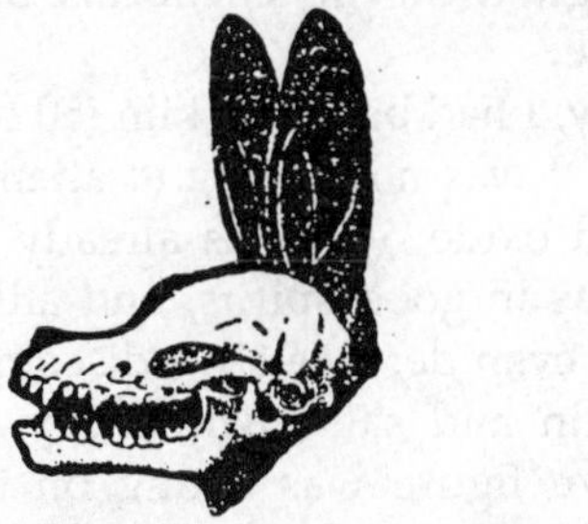

This looks like a ghost, but is a bat; reality really is more weird than imagination.

And what about this gorilla? Is it the Sphynx?

So beautiful, monumental in all its horror!

(Cont.)

379. To TORSTEN HEDLUND

4 rue de la Clé, Paris. 19 July [1896],
3 p.m.[1]

Escaped with my life, unless that is, my wounds prove fatal. So much the better!!!

It had been silent on the floor where I'm living. Suddenly I noticed I had a neighbour in the next room, but was surprised by the fact that he occupied both the adjoining rooms. Throughout the day I heard him on the right of my desk; at 10 in the evening he left that room and went and lay down in the room beside the alcove where my bed is, a foot from me with only the width of the wall between us. But then I was amazed to hear someone else in the deserted room get undressed and go to bed. There had consequently been two people in there all day, in a small room without speaking to one another. Why! Because they wanted to remain concealed – from me! The night between the 14th and 15th I was exceedingly nervous, heard a rustling against the wall, woke up many times, was sick, felt I was suffocating, and thought it was my chemicals, but it couldn't have been, for they were on the stove.

Yesterday, Saturday, I had bought a kiln (50 *centimes*) and some crucibles (for 30 *centimes* each). I was now going to attempt the synthesis of gold in fire by means of lead oxide, which is already on the way to being gold. Despite the heat I was in good spirits, and although I was working with soda and potassium cyanide, I felt no discomfort. But every time I left the stove and the kiln and sat down at my desk, I felt uneasy, partly because this unknown figure was sitting on the other side of the wall, an ell from me, moving his chair, and partly because I was suffocating. I was gripped by a deep feeling of unease, a fear of something silent, hostile. At 12 o'clock I ate from a tray, standing at the chest of drawers. Read the papers. Lay down on the bed to rest, but found none: heard the voices of a man and a woman in the adjoining room but deliberately speaking in the unmistakable low tone that conspirators use.

Got up: received a pleasant letter.

A calm came over me. Read Isaiah, Chapter 54, opened at random, which seemed as though it had been written specifically for me:

'For a small moment have I forsaken thee, but with great mercies will I gather thee. In a little wrath I hid my face from thee for a moment; but with everlasting kindness will I have mercy on thee, saith the Lord thy Redeemer . . . Behold, they shall surely gather together, *but* not by me; whosoever shall gather together against thee shall fall for thy sake.'

Wonderfully comforted I sat in my chair and meditated. But it became oppressive and my eyes grew heavy.

Then I recalled that two days previously one member of the artistic community here had been robbed on the upper deck of an omnibus, after having been rendered unconscious by some drug.

Since I had nothing to steal, it suddenly flashed upon me:

– The Pole was originally said to have murdered his wife and child with 'gas'. But as I pointed out to Munch at the time, there was no gas main in their flat![2]

So it was that kind of gas, was it! I recognized the taste of prussic acid in my mouth.

At 6.30 I ate my dinner on a tray on the edge of the chest of drawers. Went out for a stroll in the Luxembourg; but my legs were paralysed from the thighs down and my back so bent that I had to drag myself to a seat.

Back home I wanted to write but was unable to with the stranger sitting beside me.

At 10 I went to bed, and immediately afterwards the other one crossed over and lay down beside me. But now the other individual awoke and made a noise.

I lay awake and heard them signalling to one another with coughs and special tapping sounds. Lit the lamp again after feeling as though I was being drawn between the poles of a powerful electric machine, or as if I was being suffocated between pillows.

There was no sign of the *garçon* whose window faces mine, and I realized that I hadn't noticed the noise he normally makes when going to bed; noticed, too, that I had heard nothing of a third neighbour. Shut in between what I surmised were two murderers, I came to a decision: got dressed, went down to the proprietor, said that the chemicals in my room were making me ill, and requested another.

He was friendly, gave me something to drink and a different room, directly under the stranger, without my ever having breathed a word about him.

I now heard the stranger leap out of bed: – He's going to flee, I thought, because he thinks the police have been called.

He didn't flee, however, but struck the floor once with a chair, and dropped something heavy into what sounded like a valise. I fell asleep, woke up, and could only remember having dreamt about Ola Hansson.

It was a grey, miserable morning: yellow-grey! like murder and the fear of discovery!

At 11 o'clock I packed and a quarter of an hour later I fled, giving as my address: Dieppe![3]

And now I'm lying on a bed on the ground floor of a garden house with the doors open and hollyhocks and acacias outside. It's the first breath of summer I've had. And now I'm waiting for something new, or the end, or else another pursuit.

Who are you to believe? you ask! Not the godless but me, for I'm so terrified I daren't commit a wicked deed, since it would be punished immediately.

The absent one gets the blame. Well, blame me, then; but when you accuse me, either directly or indirectly, give me an opportunity to reply and defend myself. But better not!

Business matters: The hotel here with *full* board = 135 francs, therefore much cheaper than the Orfila and Chaumière, though it turned out dear because to begin with evil people said I was mad, and to be thought mad costs money.

My lungs and heart seem to be ruined; not by recent events, but by two years of handling poisons, Sulphur, Iodine, Bromine, Chlorine and Cyanide. I've grown thin, detest food and strong drink, and will probably end up paralysed.

Don't divulge my address, because they'll come round and turn the owners against me; then they'll also give me rotten food, steal my laundry, and salt my bills!

If I die here I have *no one* to take care of me. I beg you, send a telegram and reclaim my body, for I consider it a punishment to be cut up in the dissecting room and have the caretaker sell the pieces to the shops. Cremation is cheapest (50 francs). Failing that, ever since my youth I have had an inexplicable and childish desire to be buried in Montparnasse![4] This costs 500 francs which could surely be obtained from Bonnier as an advance on my Collected Works. I don't want to lie in Swedish soil, for it is cursed, and I don't want my grave defiled my enemies.

Haven't you noticed that Sweden is where the banished dwell, the damned, who must sit in darkness and see how the world is run without anyone paying heed to them? The land of nonage, of the disenfranchised, the mute. Hence this demonic hatred, jealousy, savagery: devils with a mission to torment one another.

For a long time I had been asking the Lord if I should leave Paris, but received no clear reply.

Nevertheless, 14 days ago I was walking along the rue de Luxembourg and looked up one of the avenues: in the distance above the tree tops high up on the roof of a house, I saw a hind, pale-chested and with fine markings; she turned her head and twitched her ears. I saw her on several occasions (in reality it was only the chimney stacks, of course). Finally I traced the house and found it was the one with Jonas Lie's clock.[5]

From my window in Orfila I could see a blank wall with a stench pipe and two toilet windows; but if I approached the window, I could see 150 toilet windows, a garden, another, a long rising valley, a chapel, and at the top a church tower with a cross, and on the cross a weather cock. When spring came, the trees spread their leaves and hid the filth. Then out of the foliage I heard school children playing and shouting with joy; sometimes from the greenery concealing the chapel came church music as if from angels.

I always regarded this cross which crowned everything allegorically. But I didn't understand the cock. Now, these last weeks, I've seen it move: it turned its head towards me, and flapped its wings as if urging me to flight. But I objected: while my enemies are upon me, it would betray a lack of trust in God to flee. And so I stayed.

Tonight, when I came down into the new room, I opened the window, looked out, and located the Plough with the Pole Star. Wondered: are you meant to go North?

I still don't know what God intends with me! Must I go to Ystad, where the asylum in Lund awaits me? Perhaps I must also pass this Golgotha? In order to learn still more.

[no signature]

380. To EDVARD MUNCH

[19 July 1896]

The gas apparatus seems to be based on Pettenkofer's[1] experiment: blowing out a light through a wall.

But it works badly.

Last time I saw you, I thought you looked like a murderer – or at least an accomplice.

[no signature]

381. To TORSTEN HEDLUND

Paris, 20 July 1896

You say I am seeking gold and honour. I am bound to reply that you are being deluded into believing this by the fiend. For if so, I've a strange way of going about it. I'm not seeking gold, I've already found it, and given it away; and once there's a way of manufacturing gold cheaply, it will become valueless. My formulae are already published here, and my specimens in circulation.

And another thing: perhaps you don't know this, but I'm still a rich heir by my second marriage, very rich; and people make up to me because they think I'll embellish their gold with my renown. But as you see, I've set myself up as a beggar, and not fallen for the temptation.

As for my search for gold, I pursued it because I believed my mission was to overthrow the golden calf in its very symbol, gold. Other standards of value may come, but if so they must be based upon these notes and formulae, not this transmutation of iron. This is usually called a noble ambition, and I shall smile without pity when all those who have hoarded gold metal in their cellars discover it's only an iron oxide hydrate, and no good even as a cooking pot.

As for worldly fame: Have I sought decorations or the Academy; high-born company or preferment?

I have even foregone happiness, or the only pure and rejuvinating pleasure in life, for I have relinquished my children, knowing that in law I could have kept them!

No, sir, I have never lived for this life, which has always seemed to me something provisional; I never hoarded things in a cellar but was considered a spendthrift – on others!

As for astrology, I have never attached any importance to it because I didn't know whether the planets were bodies or projections of light.

But from my reading of *La Lumière d'Egypte*,[1] I can't help finding some strange coincidences.

I was born in Aries.[2]

This sign represents Sacrifice. After a life's work such as mine, my reward is to be butchered. Every success the result of suffering; every trace of happiness smeared with filth; every encouragement a mockery, every good deed punished with the cross. But it also means: Spring, something new. Who knows? Cabbalistic = the head (senses = the gates) and brain (= thought). Biblical = Benjamin: 'Benjamin shall ravin as a wolf: in the morning he shall devour the prey, and at night he shall divide the spoil' (Jacob's blessing).

Manilius[3] says: 'The Ram, glorious in its golden fleece . . . ' The golden fleece is thought to have been a sheep's skin on whose woolly side flakes of gold were fished up by the gold panners of Colchis, a technique still used today by French gold panners in their country's rivers.

N.B. My first performed play, *In Rome*, deals with Jason, whose statue with the golden fleece was Thorvaldsen's first. My Cabbalistic stone is the Amethyst. Such stones have always enchanted me, and I finally got one a year ago (but pawned it in Paris for 3 francs). Amethyst (pale violet) and Chrome Yellow were my favourite colours when I painted. Were also my first wife's colours, and suited her best.

Aries is the planet Mars with martian destruction. 'Out of his mouth went a two-edged sword . . . '

The epigraph of my first work (*The Freethinker*): 'I am not come to bring peace but the sword.'

External appearance: tall and thin; long neck. Character: fiery and passionate.

Quarrelsome, irritable and ready to do battle.

Illnesses: Headache, measles and fevers. (Fits.)

Among plants Broom (my great favourite), holly, thistle, garlic, mustard, onion, poppy, radishes, pepper. (Fits exactly.)

Stones: Pyrite (note!), Sulphur (!), ochre and all ordinary red stones. (Pyrite, Ferrous Sulphate = Fe^3S = Gold.)

There's something in this!

Where do vultures come from in the desert when an animal in a caravan dies? Every traveller's tale agrees that the birds are not to be found in the vicinity; aren't to be seen during the whole desert journey before an animal drops down dead. Then they come from above. 'From above!'

If I now possessed a copy of Olaus Magnus,[4] I would see it differently. There's wisdom yet in the traditions of the Old Wise Men, which is why he was driven into exile when the 'dark rays' of Protestantism fell across our land.

Since I now have access to the Jardin des Plantes at all times of the day, and can see the animals arise from their night's sleep and go to rest, see them in every possible situation, even when they think they are unobserved, I now perceive their existence in a completely new light. My most recent view – namely, that they have been created by the hand of a great Artist, who made sketches, rejected them, began again, and developed both himself and his skills in the process – is fully confirmed here. But He reveals himself as so completely free that he disregards all laws, all conformity to law, and shows himself to be the Great Artist who expresses the highest independence and freedom in his 'caprice'. But the small detest this, and as soon as they see someone wanting to remain independent or break the simple rules of etiquette and eat standing at the corner of a chest of drawers, they become so uneasy that they want to lock him up.

In the books on insanity, which are written by idiots who haven't the intelligence to go mad, it says, among other things, that an abhorrence of meat, particularly when roasted, is a symptom of insanity.

I've sometimes felt an aversion to meat. As early as 1877 the shock of seeing blood on my plate when I was served with roast beef in a restaurant caused me to get up and leave. I've had several instinctive impulses to turn vegetarian.

Another symptom is irresolution.

Since I go over matters at length, in the past with myself and now with God, before realizing a decision, I appear to be irresolute, and since people with a craving for power have always wanted to govern my destiny, I've developed an instinctive method of self-defence by making detours and leading people astray. This offends those who want to curb me, and when I've fooled them, they get angry and refer to the madhouse manual.

Have you ever seen anyone so set upon as I am? The ram, the scapegoat! It seems as if all the collective fury over the banishment and sterilty of the Swedish nation has fallen upon the scapegoat. When I've been so hunted, and hunted with spears, and finally turned round and bitten back, they have screamed again: He bites!

But I don't entirely understand this last hue-and-cry. It's so long since I wrote anything that might annoy specific individuals, and I gave up literature mainly in order not to provoke people, since it was ultimately my children who suffered from their vengeance. But this unnatural hatred now? Can my chemical theories, otherwise regarded as harmless idiocy, so inflame people's minds?

I now believe these idiots have awoken to the terrible suspicion that I might turn out to be right! That the ignominy in which my name has been shrouded could be expunged, and that I might end up by becoming 'renowned'. Yes, that's probably it! And hence I always fear success, for it enrages the hosts of hell.

But if, in the event of my coming out unscathed, I am modest and give the glory to God, these fiends are enraged still further, and shriek:

– He has *Grössenwahn* and thinks some God's protecting him. If I'd said: Look, you wretches, how strong I am!, the fiends would also say: He has *Grössenwahn* . . . [5]

Therefore it doesn't seem to matter what I say, and this wickedness must be there to serve me, and make me good, so that I can finally endure success without pluming myself, and glorify God only in silence.

Like you, these last few days I have also had a suspicion that something is germinating, something happening to my advantage. Certain faint signs have pointed in that direction, and the events of the last fortnight have been a training, not for misfortune, for I can bear that, as you have seen, but for – a new life. The break with the disgusting world of the *Crémerie* (Procuresses, Sodomites, Thieves); my departure from the Orfila, where I'd been tormented by devils for six months; giving up bad habits like Absinthe (Wormwood!); isolation, weaning myself of a need for other people's company and unnecessary conversation; gaining the patience to bear minor inconveniences more easily (I fled from the Orfila leaving behind all my linen apart from one shirt, nearly all my books, all my chemicals, and the new kiln and crucibles), and to go without.

Isn't all this providential, a training for something new, here – or there!

It sometimes seems to me as if people are convinced I've solved the problem of gold, and are therefore seeking to kill me. This feeling may be without foundation, but I don't think so. Doctor Encausse (Papus) told me recently that he'd been offered money to divulge the secret, but as he has other, higher interests he directed them to *L'Initiation*, where it has already been published.[6]

You exhort me to live for this world! That is materialism, and not for me, who have staked my whole existence on death, or a life after this one. I don't understand how you can say such a thing. But it seems as if you still can't distinguish between the black and the white, which you sometimes used to confuse.

Black magic is practised by godless or arrogant beings who make themselves one with God. God in us, yes, in so far as we are emanations of His being, that is one thing; but God the fixed point outside us, by which alone we can accomplish anything, the Creator above us, and we his creations with traces of his being, under him, that is how I understand the matter.

[no signature]

382. To TORSTEN HEDLUND

[24 July 1896]

Dear Herr Torsten Hedlund,

After having slept calmly all week, I was awakened last night at 2 a.m. by a door being closed above my head and feet tiptoeing as at the Orfila, but half a minute later I started up almost stifled, and with my heart threatening to burst.

I stood on the floor and now felt as though I were standing under an electricity machine; and that I would fall down dead if I didn't hasten away. But every time I went back into the room, I was stifled. So I remained outside for three hours.[1]

Now, this morning, after having been out and come back home, I have the same stifling feeling and the same pressure on my shoulders, especially the left one, and strains in my upper arms, pains in the pit of my stomach.

I don't know what it is! But it's obvious that I am being attacked in some way, for the same system of coughs and knocks as at the Orfila is being repeated here.

Is it the Pole with his gas apparatus or electrical engineers with accumulators and reflectors?

I don't know for sure, but I noticed at once when a stranger entered this hotel.

I don't want to flee, but will doubtless have to in the end.

What does it matter if I die; my spirit will be the more vital as a result, and become a still greater torment to my enemies.

But, but . . .

Do you see now that I'm no maniac, that I *am* being persecuted, and that the first person to use that word intended to persecute me and wished to conceal a crime, his own and other people's!

Who would believe that? And will I be tempting God if I remain? Yes! Then I want to tempt him, force him to reveal Himself to me so clearly that I shall never lose faith in Him again.

Jacob wrestles with God; and God asks: What is thy name?

And he answers: Jacob.

And God says: Thy name shall no longer be called Jacob but Israel: for as a prince hast thou power with God and with men, and hast prevailed.[2]

This is incomprehensible to me, but that is my fault!

Yours sincerely,
Aug Sg

P.S. Since this was written, I've fled to Dieppe, where the attacks have continued and I became ill. c/o M. Thaulow, Dieppe.

383. To TORSTEN HEDLUND

Ystad, 1 August 1896

Dear Herr Torsten Hedlund,

For mine, for yours, for the sake of all seekers, read the two articles I am sending you, and see that miracles do happen in our time.[1]

The cyclone in Japan is a 'miracle' like the cyclone in the Jardin des Plantes the same day Andrée took off and balloons were hurled to the ground in and around Paris, and I fled to Dieppe.[2]

The idea of the double can possibly give you the key to Francis Schlatter and my story about the German, Herrmann, which you probably thought was crazy.[3] Maybe also explain (?) the mysteries of our existence, our double life, obsessions, our nocturnal life, our bad conscience, our moments of groundless (?) fear, our persecution mania, which perhaps isn't a mania and we really are persecuted – by what you and the occultists call elementals or lower beings, which envy us our existence, and drive us to suicide in order to take possession of what you call our Astral Bodies.

The Black Death has returned; those demonic countries Japan and China are ravaged by it.

My health is ruined, and I'm awaiting death! Ought we to meet before then?

If you've let yourself be led astray by wicked people, and have in all good faith released a storm of hatred against me, then recall it, for I don't want you to feel discomforted.

If I die, don't presume I've fallen by human hand, for it was written. And don't be impatient to judge me. Wait, and you will see that I was wrongly accused, that I wasn't mad, that I didn't serve the Black but the White.

My mission is over and my sentence served.

Attacks of angina pectoris recur every night at 2 o'clock. Last night I succeeded in controlling them without getting up. But it returns during the day.

What happened to me in Paris will doubtless remain a riddle; and ought not to be investigated. That I wrestled with death is certain.

Doctor Eliasson has given my body a thorough examination and found it sound and strong. Whether he says this out of consideration for me, I don't know. I can't judge.

And my spirit has never been so clear-sighted as now, so solemnly calm when I am not disturbed – by others.

Write me a letter, but write yourself, for you have white in you.

Your last letter was full of untruths which you had from others who had selected you as a medium!

Farewell, just in case . . .
Yours sincerely,
August Strindberg

384. To TORSTEN HEDLUND

Ystad, 18 August 1896

Dear Herr Torsten Hedlund,

Between the 13th and 14th there seems to have been a turning point in my life without my being able to account for what and from where. Yesterday I received a letter written at that time which recalled me to life.[1] But this means I must take leave of science – for a time.

I was cast up like a shipwrecked man on this coast beneath the Plough without knowing how I got here, and now here I sit, asking: how did I get here? What am I doing here?[2]

Your letter's just arrived!

Yes, I trusted in the power which was guiding my Fate, right up until the end, but I thought he was angry with me and had unleashed his instruments of punishment, and that belief taught me resignation, but also fear and dread.

I haven't described my last crisis to you, but shall do in a book – a novel, if you want to call it that. I think we're closer to one another than before – but – but . . .

I thought I was being punished either because I had delved into the forbidden (though science has always done that, even if it hasn't always gone unpunished), or because I sought to avoid life's 'toil without reward', and because I tried to sever the bonds that *should* bind me to the earth and to mankind; should! – The rebel!

Often in my researches I encountered a hand which blew my papers about and beclouded my solution, and in the blowpipe bubble on the charcoal, I saw a leering face which stuck out its tongue and mocked me. But I began the experiments again, telling myself: These are enemies who must be overcome.

I am therefore giving up my scientific studies on a trial basis, but as a momento, I beg you to print these three pages I'm sending you,[3] in 100 copies, so that I may escape writing 100 letters on the same subject in response to inquiries, and because I would like proof that I haven't been mad in believing I had made gold.

Write when you have time, for I have every reason to be rightly suspicious.

Yours sincerely,
August Strindberg

385. To TORSTEN HEDLUND

Ystad, 20 August 1896

Dear Herr Torsten Hedlund,

Your letter of yesterday seems to have crossed with mine of the day before, and has therefore already been answered in the main, quite apart from the fact that my whole correspondence with you constitutes a reply.

A sick man who is waiting for death, who has been torn to pieces by these unknown and half-known soul hunters called 'people', who cast veils over defenceless sleepers, what is he good for?

Did I not tell you that I considered my researches into hidden things were forbidden, and that I have been punished for them; did I not give you plainly to understand that my occultism has cost me my health and almost my personal freedom, and that I regarded it as criminal to continue? That, lost in the selfish pleasure of my developing ego, I had neglected and withdrawn from unrewarding work, severed bonds that may not be broken, and that my first step towards reconciliation with life and the powers would be to resume the yoke, to work for my daily bread, and seek to procure the same for those I had brought into the world, and who are in need.

To abandon myself now to an organized fight, when I've recently been carried wounded from a battle, the like of which I've never seen, is something for which I lack the strength – as yet.

In wanting me to be a prophet, you continue to overestimate me.[1] I lack the call, but have sometimes felt it my mission to be a preacher in the wilderness, most of whose words fall upon the dry sand, and who will end by having his head served up on a platter. Besides, do you really think my past life lends itself to the evolution of a sermonizer or a moralist? Not me!

Let the crusade go forth, I shall help, but on a small scale, where I am at home; I want to see the banners unfurled in full sunshine before I adjure anyone.

You aren't aware of my last development; you don't know that I couldn't find consolation in the Book of Job a day longer, for I suddenly realized I was no Job; no righteous man who must be tested, but a robber who had ended on the cross because his deeds deserved it, and who had to be punished.

You think I've clung to my egoism – but I tell you, that isn't so. However, I must begin to give, perhaps sacrifice, my person for those who are closest to me by nature. And like you, I must find a way of splitting myself in two, become a sober, well-behaved working man and alongside him, if I'm able, let a silent, esoteric *Übermensch*[2] grow up at the edge of the field. I implore you, implore because I've been nourished by your hand and encouraged by you in times of trouble, felt your salutary displeasure in moments of pride, to let me gather together the rags of my soul and my body; let me first undertake a crusade against my old self, then I shall be ready to follow the banner – provided it is white.

Even if it's borne by a Joan of Arc, sent to put men to shame for their decadence or awaken their ambition, that won't prevent me – though you don't believe it.

Moreover, purely practically, my period of respite is over;[3] the highway is no longer open to beggars, and with the last of the gold, I am getting down to work – for bread!

Since this is the last time, my thanks to you for helping me a long stretch of the way in my evolution.

My instinct tells me that we ought not to meet now – we have given the best of ourselves, and the worse or meaner part, we can keep for ourselves, or those who are meaner.

Yours sincerely,
August Strindberg

P.S. When can I expect copies of *Jardin des Plantes* 2?

If you don't publish the Falu process,[4] please let me have the manuscript back!

Don't take this to mean the end of our correspondence!

386. To TORSTEN HEDLUND

Ystad, 23 August 1896

Dear Torsten Hedlund,

Forgive this letter, but I have to write it.

You asked recently if I had any money. I replied that I was bankrupt in that respect too. You added that there was still some money in your keeping.

If you'll let me have it, I shall try to regain my health, get down to work, and seek to make my way.

My luggage in Paris seems to be lost, my manuscripts included, hence I have nothing to give you – now when I am about to put everything right, so long that is, that it's not too late.

I am still being suffocated, and must make for the mountains and the sun in order to be able to breathe. The sea is alien to me now!

Another thing! You said recently that people are looking for:

The Zola of the Occult.

I feel the call. But in a grand, elevated tone. A poem in prose: called

Inferno

The same theme as *By the Open Sea*. The destruction of the individual when he isolates himself. Salvation through: work without honour or gold, duty, the family, consequently – woman – the mother and child!

Resignation through the discovery of the task assigned to each and every one of us by Providence.

Think this over! But keep it a secret!

'We' all have the madhouse ahead of us!

Yours sincerely,
August Strindberg

387. To F. U. WRANGEL

Count Fredrik Ulrik Wrangel (1853–1929), writer and chamberlain to Queen Sofia of Sweden. Wrangel first met Strindberg as a student, but it was not until the 1890s that the two became better acquainted. In 1895, at Jonas Lie's instigation, he helped organize the collection made for Strindberg in Sweden. The following year he visited Strindberg in the Hôtel Orfila, and later acted as intermediary when the latter sought to sell a number of letters he had received from illustrious correspondents, including Heidenstam, Bjørnson, Nietzsche and Haeckel. In 1906, Wrangel was forced to go into exile after losing the Queen's travelling funds at the tables in Monte Carlo. Strindberg remained grateful to Wrangel for the help he had given him during the Inferno crisis, and in 1911 he invited his now relatively impecunious friend to translate *Christina* into French for Lugné-Poë to put on with Suzanne Desprès in the title role. Nothing came of the idea, however. Wrangel published his recollections of Strindberg in *Minnen från konstnärskretsarna och författarvärlden* (Memories from Artist Circles and the Writers' World, 1925).

22 September 1896

Good Wrangel,

In this wilderness without steamer, railway or coach, your longed-for bill of exchange for 200 Fl. is about as useless as the pot of gold which the Arab found in the desert.[1]

Civilization has ceased to exist here; if one wants to send a parcel, the wrapping paper has to be ordered 24 hours in advance, and so on. Therefore please write and tell me (1) how to get any money against this bill in Austria, and (2) if it's good for anything anywhere else than Austria, and if so how!

In future, may I, to save a lot of time and trouble, always have banknotes in the currency of the country in which I'm living. One loses less on the rate of exchange than on trips and correspondence. S.V.P.

The letters could well be sealed until 1 January 1900 without any harm, and only the Nietzsche published. Otherwise there'll be a terrible racket!

There are a couple of chests stored at my brother Oscar's on Riddarholmen with letters and newspapers to do, as I now remember, with the whole *Getting Married* affair, mostly abusive. Much of it won't be to my advantage, I imagine, but as a providentialist, I submit and consider what has happened, whether good or evil, to be unavoidable. My brother would be glad to get rid of these chests, and if the Society of Authors would like to reclaim them by way of this letter, they have my consent and may take them as a present, the chests to be sealed until 1 January 1900.

I've one chest here covering my sojourn in Germany – Berlin, Brünn, Rügen, Dornach (Ober-Oestreich) 1892–94, which you can have too if you pay the carriage.

There's a chest of letters and newspapers at Madame Charlotte Futterer's, 13 rue de la Grand Chaumière, Paris, our *Crémerie = La Purée Artistique* concerning my stay in Paris 1894–96.

Likewise a packet at the Hôtel Orfila, 60 rue d'Assas, concerning the same.[2]

(In the chests at my brother's there is, among other things, a collection of French provincial newspapers from all the French provinces covered by my Peasant journey, and these – some 100 of them – could be of interest at some future date. Likewise a sketch book with buildings (peasant) from the same journey, etc.)

I repeat again – if you find anything of special interest in the way of autographs for yourself in the previous consignment, you can nab it for your own collection as a souvenir. If anything too intimate has been carelessly overlooked act *à discrétion*.[3] I've no secrets, and can bear the judgement of the world. But for other people's sake!

My impressions of Austria? Well, I'm more at home here than in Sweden, and feel as though I was born here, for I've planted trees and brought forth a child here.

Besides, all the rabble of the world has passed this way along the Danube so I feel really at home in my role as tramp (though with a passport, issued, what's more, by your *aimable* brother in Paris).

Here 'everything is in flux'[4] and is always new, every tenth minute. Today I was summoned to the court in Grein – I've no idea why, but I am always being accused of things, often without knowing why. Of course I shan't go, and the gendarmes will be after me. Then I'll shake the mud of the Danube off my feet, and tramp on!

Your politics! Good God! What's that all about? A seat in the Riksdag? That's probably all it amounts to, isn't it?

So! let the little letter of credit be for the moment, but ready to be called upon the next time I am hounded out of my lair!

Kindest regards,
August Strindberg

Saxen bei Grein (address probably Klam again tomorrow!)

Give Jean J.[5] my thanks.

Tell Fallström[6] too that I've forgiven him 77 times and do so a 78th, but that my sympathy isn't for sale.

388. To ANDERS ELIASSON

23 September 1896

I think I've finally found the solution to the problem with this formula.
$Fe(NH^4)^2(SO^4)^2, 6H^2O = 392$

This is the formula for ammoniacal iron sulphate, which ought to appear when green vitriol is precipitated with Ammonia.

Now watch: (one more time).

$Fe(NH^4)^2(SO^4)^2, 6H^2O = 392$

The *Molecule* of Gold (according to the tables) = 392.

What then is molecule and what is atom?

Cf.

Sulphur's Atom = 32.

Oxygen's Molecule = 32. (Atom = 16.)

What then is sulphuric acid? $SO^4 = O^5$ or O^6.

[no signature]

389. To TORSTEN HEDLUND

25 September 1896

Dear Herr Torsten Hedlund,

Before I receive your answer to my letter on the Ystad stones and V. Rydberg,[1] I must write the following.

This morning, Friday 25 September, I received a parcel of books: Hesiod, the Eddas, Dante's *Inferno* (and had also ordered the Rigveda and Grimms' *Fairy Tales*). Found my old edition of Linnaeus' *Gotland Journey* in the attic and on page 51 I came across an engraving entitled 'Stone Giants'. 'When one was some distance from them, they looked like statues, half-length portraits, horses and all manner of weird things.'[2]

At 11 o'clock I read in *Dagens Nyheter* about the V. Rydberg foundation for research into mythology.

Need I assure you that I was entirely ignorant of this project, and that I was in no way speculating on Rydberg when I wrote my last letter?

However, Linnaeus' journey in Gotland has strengthened my belief, and if I only had his *Scanian Journey*, I would surely make a breakthrough.

Linnaeus is for me and for the world in general one of the greatest Seers that ever lived. He featured in a French biographical dictionary last winter as a mythical being, an heroic spirit alongside Aristotle. For the specialization, or engineer's science, which has brought about our present Babylonian confusion where things are so far gone that a mineralogist can't understand a zoologist, hadn't yet been invented. And he possessed imagination, which is now lacking, wherefore the senses of a whole generation or two have been dulled.

Yours sincerely,
August Strindberg

New Address: Klam bei Grein
Ober-Oestreich.

390. To TORSTEN HEDLUND

Klam, 12 October 1896

Dear Herr Torsten Hedlund,

'If you want to learn to know the invisible, observe with open eyes the visible.'[1]

With this advice from The Secret Doctrine (*Talmud*), I am continuing along the even way my destiny more modestly directs me, leaving metaphysics, which is 'beyond my Power',[2] and returning first to the Ystad stones, then to meteorites.

Strengthened in my belief concerning the petrified nature of these stones, I wonder if you might not have a theosophist friend in Southern Sweden who would be willing to collaborate with a faithless Tschandala like myself, and photograph whole groups of them, which I would then examine for constants, perhaps comparing them with stones from Easter Island, the Gobi, and India. (In the British Museum, but probably reproduced somewhere.)

As you remember, my guess was original beings, the Creator's Sketches for what became people, but so as not to alarm you, I focused on a detail, their hats.

You will recall that last spring I asked you to look at a crab which has a whole set of teeth and an elementary figure on its back.[3] When you have an opportunity, would you please look in Gbg Museum at a large species of snail, the Strombus, and note the human-like figure at the blunt end, when one places the snail on its 'belly', and in semi-darkness.

These last six weeks I have grown a whole ell as a result of studying Swedenborg, where I found the word 'Correspondences' which gave me the key to my method: see resemblances everywhere. They exist, and with reason. This is Bernardin de St Pierre's 'Harmonies', which I found in his marvellous book *Œuvres Posthumes*.[4]

If you have a Sunflower in your garden, please (bearing in mind St. Pierre's beautiful '*harmonie*' between the Sun and the Sunflower) cut the medulla of the stalk and look at the figure in the medulla, white on white. Then make a cut in the root and observe the figure there.

B. de St Pierre contains the following idea, based on observation.

Saw into a tree and you'll see a ring for every cycle of the sun.

Cut a root (of beet) and behold: there is a ring for every lunar cycle during the growth of the root!

The sun = the celestial; the moon = the subterranean. Apollo and Diana.

Isn't that beautiful!

Why is there an eagle in the root of a fern? Perhaps it isn't an eagle!

Tell this to those people who find my Death's-Head Moth so amusing.[5]

A moth, the *Zens(era) Æsculi,* which lives on horse chestnut trees, has these markings on its thorax  This is the sacred number 7. And the *Æsculus* is palmate (its leaf has 7 fingers), with 7 stamens in its flower.

If you observe the base of one of the leaves now falling from a Chestnut tree, it has 7 brown spots which are thought to be ducts. The Chestnut (Horse) is the only tree I know belonging to the *Heptandria.* (Apart from the beautiful Chickweed Wintergreen.)

Gbg museum probably has a *Zensera.* (The larvae live inside the tree.)

But there are several butterflies with these markings. Linnaeus calls one of them *Vanessa Gamma* because it is marked with a Greek gamma Γ or γ, without any butterfly books, I don't know which. What does this mean – occult?

And so to the walnut again. Look at the profiles of Ask and Embla inside the *Juglans Regia.*[6] *Juglans* = *Jovis Glans* = Jupiter's Acorn. I have a head of Zeus here which resembles the *Zeus Otricoli* as Darwin reproduced it in his book on faces.[7] See for yourself!

But isn't there a *Juglans Fraxinifolia* (Ash leaved) which shows the affinity between the Walnut and the Ash?

When I saw the meteorite in the Jardin des Plantes from the Alpes Maritimes I said to myself right away: these figures were handmade. (I mean the Widmanstettersche figures.) Then I saw some bowl-shaped indentations as if made by a hammer, and was amazed. But read afterwards on the notice that the village smiths had extracted iron from the boulder. And stood corrected.

But now I have reproductions of other meteorites which haven't been exposed to smiths, and they also bear these bowl-shaped indentations. Is it writing? Yes! How should one investigate it?

See Svenonius' *Mineral Kingdom,* page 187, on 'The Imprint of Raindrops and Birds' on Sandstone.

See the sketches of elf-stones in *Wärend och Wirdarne,* with their bowl-shaped indentations.[8]

I've a Death's-Head Moth on my table behind a shoemaker's glass. Anyone who wants to see a ghost can see one there!

A query: Stuxberg has translated that book about the Sea Monster. Does Stuxberg now believe in it? And is Stuxberg 'hopeless'? If not, he could well help me to 'see', since he's sitting in the middle of Paradise.[9]

Otherwise a great deal is happening to me even though things are quite calm, and I am keeping my diary – while waiting for the as yet remote time when I can write my book.

It sometimes seems to me as if I had been vouchsafed a longer life, or rather been condemned to one!

What a crisis Fröding has gone through![10]

It is one symptom among others, and a reaction against Heidenstam's *fin-de-siècle* childishness, which supposedly represents Satanism.

The words 'spiritual agony' haven't been heard for a long time, but I know many who are starting to sleep uneasily at night, and begin to perceive the body has a soul.

Yours sincerely,
August Strindberg

391. To TORSTEN HEDLUND

Klam, Friday 30(?) October 1896

Dear Herr Torsten Hedlund,

The butterflies are taking me so far that I don't know where it will all end; but I'm following without fear. The male *Zensera Æsculi* has 7 spots and the female 6. (*Æsculus* has 6 *or* 7 stamens.) But I've now discovered another species, the *Amphidasis prodsomaria*, whose larvae are geometrical and live on Alders. (Cf. the Erl king.[1] The alder is eldritch and furnishes divining rods like the Hazel.) The butterfly has 4 dots on its thorax, and when I consult my flora, I see the Alder has 4 stamen. The larvae have four pairs of legs under the abdomen, and can 'lie out' for hours on a twig of alder.

Apropos the number 7, the sacred Ladybird (Indra's creature) has 7 spots, *Septempunctata* (See The Sw. People).[2] A Brown Fritillary has Sanskrit or Tibetan lettering on its wings.

The beetle *Cicindela Campestris*, the green and beautiful 'Sandrunner', has 5 spots, a band and a half-moon. The larva has lettering (oldest Chinese style) on its back and lower down a sign like this:  .  . The Puppa, which hangs in a hole in the ground, sticks out two arms with hands to retain its hold on the grave. The hands have real fingers. Coppar on its shards. I am very interested in the creature, but have no books.

Read in a French paper that I've been driven out of Paris, by women. And that the other misogynists are appalled. The newspaper (*L'Événement*) referred to Orpheus, who was torn to pieces by the Maenads. If this was a plot to get me out of Paris, then it was tantamount to attempted murder. (At 2 a.m.!) In other words, I'm not insane! But for all that there was a cyclone the following day.[3]

The immediate cause of this woman-hate, that is, women's hatred of me, was my article in the *Revue Blanche* just before the murder attempt.[4] The article dealt with Munch's paintings of women, and mentioned Orpheus and the Maenads. However, I forgot Eurydice, and she can gladly stay where she is – in the underworld.

A friend, Jules Lermina,[5] went on my behalf to the widow Kahn[6] in the rue de la Clef with a letter from me, and asked for my things. The monster refused until I had signed a *décharge*.[7] I signed this a fortnight ago, and sent it off. But my things still haven't arrived, including all my washing! The charmer has probably stolen my luggage, definitely hung on to the 100 francs, and was prepared for people to kill me. (When I went to see her the day after that night, she refused to receive me and pleaded – illness!) My opinion of the fair sex has not been altered one iota, I assure you!

Another thing. I read in D.N. about Gustav Adolf's picture. All right, that may be the exoteric explanation, but it doesn't preclude the esoteric question: whose hand directed this chance event.[8]

But the details don't add up to me. Aren't there cassettes which contain two plates? What if it's the same plate, exposed twice!

And then a request. As a publisher, you must have a copy of all the alphabets of the world, which I could borrow or have!

A question of conscience: If one has enemies who are seeking to take one's life, should one let oneself be struck down without resistance? Is self-defence allowed?

Assuming that *envoûtement* is possible, would it be a sin to '*envoûte*' one's enemies? They're allowed to murder unchecked, but I'm not allowed to do as they do. Why?[9]

I don't know if *envoûtement* is possible; if so, then witch trials and burnings will begin again. And above all: false accusations of witchcraft. Whoever is unlucky then is lost. But that's probably where things are heading!

I believe someone is tormenting me from a distance, and others believe the same of me; but they're mistaken.

This very moment I came upon the following about *Vanessa Gamma* in a book.

'Gamma, or Robert le Diable, with wings showing a C (also the third letter) in matt silver on the wings. The larva lives on nettles, *Caprifolium*, gooseberries, hazel, elm. Has a white band on the back and is called *la bedeaude* (the vergeress) by Réaumur – – – 'These brilliant Vanessas have inspired superstitious (?) fear.'

After hatching, these butterflies emit a red excretia which resembles blood, and have given rise to tales of a rain of blood. A great commotion in Aix in 1608 (What occurred that year or shortly afterwards? The Thirty-Years' War?). A rain of blood under Childebert in Paris, another under Robert le Diable.[10]

What is one to think of these winged creatures? Goblins or living representations of Immortality? It now remains to see what the Swedish Butterfly Book and Stuxberg have to say about the Gamma –

The curious thing is, in my illustration there's a Hebrew character on the thorax 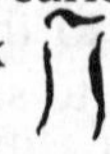 together with something obscure to the right. (Look in Gbg Museum.) What is it?

Henry IV of France was assassinated in 1610. (1608 Vanessa's rain of blood.) 1608 saw the formation of the League and Union, the beginning of the 30 Years' War. (Henry IV's murder signals the beginning of the 30 Years' War, for he was murdered by the Jesuits, and Ravaillac[11] hated Protestants.)

Robert the Devil, as the butterfly is also called, was likewise murdered, and after Vanessa's rain of blood.

I take it Childebert was murdered, or did Vanessa's rain of blood point to the beautiful Brunhilda's future rain of blood – (It rained blood in Sentis during the time of Childebert; what took place?).

It's quite natural for a butterfly to emit a bloodlike fluid, but why just then, and so that everyone noticed it; then?

N.B. When I sat down to write this letter, I knew nothing of Vanessa's bloody deed. But five minutes earlier, I'd cut my hand so that the table top of white, unpainted wood was covered in blood. And on a knife with a past!

In the sandy woods of Ystad last summer, another Vanessa (*Moris*) attracted my attention by its striking behaviour.

What's to be read on these two Neuroptera?

Hasn't one of them got some Chinese 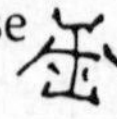 ?[12]

Forgive me for not sending *The Secret Doctrine*.[13] Just carelessness!

Yours sincerely,
August Strindberg

392. To F. U. WRANGEL

Klam, 12 November 1896

Dear Wrangel,

Since it's gone to press, all right![1] I don't know what '*Écran*' is because I haven't the text here. The verses are from Svedbom's Reader, 'The Saga of Little Rosa and Long Leda'.[2]

Is my linden playing?
Is my nightingale singing?
Is my little son weeping?
Is my husband ever happy?

Your linden is not playing;
Your nightingale is not singing;
Your son weeps both night and day.
Your husband will never, never more be happy.

And so to the eternal, insoluble question of money. Until August of this year I existed on a subvention from an unknown source. Since then I've been existing on the autograph swindle, as it's been so finely called, but that spring has run dry, and times look dark. It would therefore be good if there was a quick sale!

After the end of the year I see absolutely no way out, and all attempts to resolve the problem have stranded. Though I console myself with the thought that *die Armuth kommt von den Ewigen Göttern*,[3] I must nevertheless think of the morrow.

To involve literature with the racket of publishing is a type of speculation from which others besides myself have suffered, therefore we wither so quickly after a precocious flowering. And if a great and distinguished literature is ever to come into being, we must either publish it ourselves or rest content with the manuscript and a few fair copies, and leave all sordid profit-making to the business man. And live on what? On other work, begging or private favour – preferably work. Pegasus under the yoke! Well, it will probably be the acid test, and anyone who cannot speed before the plough had better give up.

It's a little late for me to change direction now, when I've started on the downward slope, and I'll opt for the begging bowl and manuscript.

I am preparing a book in manuscript – which I'm writing for myself and *de Enkelte*;[4] without a thought of publishers, papers, old maids or Courts. I don't know if I'll have time to complete it, but hope the interest it arouses will give me strength.

Yours,
August Strindberg

393. To TORSTEN HEDLUND

[23 November 1896]

Your appearance in my life always seemed to me like a mission, and your person, which I do not know and have never seen, always remained an abstraction to me. Therefore I permitted you to write to me as a superior to a subordinate, and this permanent humiliation was for me like a training in self-control; not in humility, for in Inferno we are all just as much devils in each other's sight, and the one brother can take the other in hand.

But you sometimes forgot your role as an abstraction, and from being a helper, you set yourself up as master, abused your temporary power, failed my unbounded confidence, and swelled with pride. Then it was my duty to warn you, and I said: do not tamper with my destiny so high-handedly or you will end in discord. I said this in a friendly way, and quite modestly, but you replied arrogantly: 'Higher powers are at my disposal.'

With that your Fall seems to have begun, and your role in my life to be played out. So I believe.

When I once said: You have probably not done as much wrong as I, I should have said: Your less complicated fate has not forced you in justified defence of your personality to strike as many enemies as I have had to. You took this to mean I had confessed my sins to you, and thought yourself saintly.

My apparent humility before you, by whose hand Providence gave me bread, had the unfortunate consequence for you that you mistook yourself, the tool, for the Lord of life and death, and interfered in my destiny with a heavy hand, with what consequences for your inner life, you must yourself wait and see.

An improvement on the text: I wrote: 'Is this letter from a younger and more inexperienced man to someone older and more experienced?'[1] I will cross that out and put: 'Is this letter from a sinful man to a fellow sinner?' Judge? With what right? Saviour of souls? On what grounds?

You forget that you have played the Tempter to me, when you showed me heaven and said: fly thither!

Do you never think I may have had a mission like yours in other people's lives, perhaps in your own? No, you won't grant me that.

Your craving for power, your egoism, your prophet's megalomania are the grossest I have ever come across!

You say: Believe in me and my party or you are black, damned, and will die. Above all: Black! This is supposed to be brotherly love, the sacrifice of the self (have you ever sacrificed your self?), compassion.

Have I, on the other hand, ever interfered in your spiritual life? Have I desired a conversion of you? I proclaim or tell what I can see, but have never preached to you, never pursued your soul, never punished, merely given you a warning, once, and then you became angry!

In the past I saw you in my mind as Azariel.[2] Now you have changed, and I last saw you as Ariel! And you have been given another mission: to torture, tempt, and be withstood.

Aug Sg

394. To GEORG BRANDES

[30 November 1896]

Passing through only to depart again early tomorrow, [I] wonder if Dr Brandes would like to meet me this evening in some unpretentious place since am not dressed for visits.[1].

AUGUST STRINDBERG ANCIEN ATTACHÉ À LA BIBLIOTHÈQUE ROYALE DE SUÈDE MÉDAILLE DE LA SOCIÉTÉ IMPÉRIALE RUSSE DE GEOGRAPHIE MEMBRE DE LA SOCIÉTÉ ASTRONOMIQUE DE FRANCE, DE LA SOCIÉTÉ DES AUTEURS ET COMPOSITEURS DRAMATIQUES A PARIS ET DE L'ALLIANCE FRANÇAISE 12, Rue de la Grande-Chaumière (Montparnasse). PARIS

VIII
Letters 395–450 December 1896–May 1899

On his return to Sweden Strindberg soon settled down in the small university town of Lund, where he rapidly became the centre of a group of young journalists and students, among them Bengt Lidforss, with whom he was now reconciled. He continued his reading of Swedenborg, in whose *Arcana Coelestia* he discovered an account of earthly punishments by spiritual tormentors that tallied with his own recent experiences. He also began to correspond with his three-year-old daughter Kerstin, in Austria, and was approached by Gustaf af Geijerstam, now literary editor for the publishers Gernandts, about publishing any new work he might have. Shortly afterwards, he embarked upon the autobiographical fiction *Inferno,* which he wrote in French and used to sift and organize the events of the last three years. His health had now improved although he continued to record numerous perplexing and disturbing experiences in his *Occult Diary,* and to speculate on their meaning with his new friends in Lund. Meanwhile, in Stockholm, Harald Molander had revived *Lucky Peter's Journey,* the first production of one of Strindberg's plays in Sweden since 1890, and an improvement in his financial situation enabled him to return to Paris in August 1897, in greater comfort than on his previous visit.

His purpose this time was to find a publisher for the French edition of *Inferno,* but he encountered a surprising reluctance on the part of the Paris occultists to support him in his search, even though he was trying to make gold again after a period in which he deemed any such attempt immoral. However, in the young poet Marcel Rjéa he found a new collaborator, someone who not only revised his French but also managed to place his book with *Mercure de France*. Strindberg, meanwhile, began work on a sequel, *Legends,* covering his recent life in Lund, and Gernandts brought out the Swedish edition of *Inferno*. To Strindberg's old admirers, who remembered him as the author of *The New Kingdom* and *Master Olof,* it came as a huge disappointment, and seemed to represent a complete rejection of his earlier views, but it sold well. Moreover, having completed *Legends* and part of *Jacob Wrestles,* he took the decisive step of writing for the theatre again. The play was *To Damascus,* the first of his later masterpieces and one of twenty plays that he wrote between 1898 and 1901. 'I seem to have regained the grace of being able to write for the theatre,' he told his new friend, Axel Herrlin, and thus encouraged, he left Paris for the last time and returned to Lund, where he remained for a further fourteen months while he wrote the second part of *To Damascus, Advent* and *Crimes and Crimes*, once again utilizing the experiences he had accumulated during the previous six years. He also celebrated his fiftieth birthday, which brought him many tributes from old friends like Hjalmar Branting and Carl Larsson; he now resumed contact with them, as he did with his children in his first marriage.

In January 1899, Strindberg revisited Stockholm for the first time since 1892, but stayed only four days. Back in Lund he wrote the first of his later history plays, *The Saga of the Folkungs* and *Gustav Vasa*, which were aimed at the contemporary Swedish theatre, where the genre was again in vogue. Only then, after hearing from Geijerstam that Gernandts wished to publish a collected edition of his novels and stories, did he finally take the plunge and return to the city he had left so ignominiously almost seven years earlier. Within three days of leaving Lund, he was back in the Stockholm Archipelago, in what he described as 'the most beautiful landscape in the world'.

395. To ANDERS ELIASSON

Kramers, Malmö, 1 December 1896

Elias (as doctor and friend),

I am in Malmö and intend to go to Skurup so as not to be far from you, and under Lars Nilsson's care, because he has been through what I have, and believes in its reality.[1] My condition is grave, and I expect a rapid dénouement.

Yes, the witch trials have already begun![2] Yesterday evening, in Copenhagen, during a lengthy colloquy with Georg Brandes, the latter told me that, two years ago, Huysmans, Zola's great successor (*La bas* and *A rebours*) accused Stanislas de Guaita[3] publicly in a newspaper of having used *envoûtement*[4] on him (i.e. Huysmans) by 'torturing him in the chest' at a distance. What do you say to that?

Huysmans is the greatest and most learned of sceptics who's finally learnt to doubt his sterile denial of unknown powers.

Among my papers is a number of *L'Initiation* in which Colonel Rochas, the *administrateur* at the École Polytechnique, proves the possibility of *envoûtement*. And there is also a pamphlet by an Englishman called Digby (17th Century),[5] a doctor, who demonstrates its possibility in a long and subtle essay.

The last four nights I have taken sulphonal, with varying success. Met a Danish doctor on the train who said (1) that the Sulphonal dose is 1 gramme (you wrote 3 grammes); (2) advised against sulphonal as bad for the heart.

He had given a man sulphonal who then leapt up from his sleep, raving mad, and out through the window.

Was thun?[6]

I hope to meet you soon, in Skurup or Ystad. Have arranged things so as not to be a burden on anyone.

T. H-d[7] wrote and suggested we return each other's letters! This worried me, for what has he to fear? Or has he something to fear?

So! Until we meet!

Yrs,
August Strindberg

396. To KERSTIN STRINDBERG

Kerstin Strindberg (1894–1956), Strindberg's daughter in his second marriage to Frida Uhl and the 'Beatrice' of his *Inferno*. About one hundred of the one hundred and six extant letters and cards from Strindberg to Kerstin were written over a four year period, beginning in December 1896 when she was two years old. She thus afforded him what he sometimes sought, an addressee to whom he could write as fancifully as he wished, and who could not reply, at least in person, although, of course, much in these letters was addressed to her grandmother, Marie Uhl, and – ultimately – to Frida. However, Kerstin had little to do with her mother: after a childhood spent near Linz, she came to Stockholm shortly before the First World War in order to learn Swedish so as to read her father's books in the original. In 1917, she married a German lawyer and publisher, Ernst Sulzbach, with whom she had a son, Christoph, in 1919. The marriage was dissolved in 1925, and she returned to Sweden, where she spent the remainder of her life. She became more and more of a recluse, and was eventually removed to a mental home in which she lived for several years. Twenty-one letters from Kerstin to Strindberg have also survived, together with seventeen written on her behalf by Marie Uhl.

[Original in German]

Skurup, St Nicholas' Day 1896

Dearly Beloved Child,

I hear you call, but do you hear me? Driven without peace, harried like a wild animal, I ask my fate: what do you want of me? And do I get a reply?

In my desolate, cold, alien country, where I appear to myself like a ghost, where people flee from me, I long for you, but without hope. Why? Fate will not have it so!

This is what my country looks like – air and corn and windmills:[1]

How different in beauty to Klam and Saxen. Hills and forests and the beautiful castle! and the gorge![2]

What are Therese and Feldmann and Misto doing?[3]

Today is St Nicholas' Day![4] And I am so far away from you, my child; I cannot give you anything but my best wishes and prayers that you will be nice to Grandmama and everyone else.

Farewell! And write to me often, often!

Your friend, August Pappa.

397. To MARIE UHL

Marie Uhl (1844–1925), Frida Uhl's mother whom, at her own request, Strindberg normally addressed as 'mother' rather than as 'mother-in-law'. She lived apart from her husband at Dornach and Saxen on the Danube, where Strindberg visited her in 1893 and 1896. They generally got on well and shared a common interest in Swedenborg and the occult. She is portrayed in *Inferno* and figures as 'The Mother' in *To Damascus*. Fifty-three letters from Strindberg to her have survived, all written between 1893 and 1909.

[Original in German]

Lund, 16 February 1897

Good Grandmother,

You are a true materialist, and I can't quarrel with materialists.

I merely said that I find Bachelor-Hermit-Bohemian life repulsive in its filth, and that I can only breathe fresh air in one family, my own. Now that I spy a scrap of bread on the far horizon, my thoughts immediately turn to founding and providing for a family, and not to Aspasias or Messalinas. That is surely proper and my little daughter must rejoice, since it may preserve her father from a life of idle debauchery.

What has all this to do with cycling and cold water, you materialist?[1]

As far as Paris is concerned, I have no ties.[2] I shall rent a laboratory where I have the *right* to work and can train disciples, if there are any. In this laboratory, surrounded by friends and followers, I shall work for the Nobel Prize.[3] My Paris friends, the chemists, expect this of me!

So you can see that for the time being there's no money in it, only overheads. Nothing but hopes! However, this spring, in Paris, *By the Open Sea*, *The People of Hemsö*, and 'The Romantic Organist' will be published by three different publishers, and I shall get 1,000 francs for them.

It seems to me that here in Sweden my mission will soon be over. I have pupils; I have sown; it only requires time to germinate.

My heart remains in Dornach, but my head must probably go to Paris.

Here I give of my spirit, in Paris I receive. – And if I ever again seek a wife, she must be French – for reasons . . .

And without a wife and home, I shall go under. Condemned to drinking! Imagine that three days ago my nights of terror began again, and after I had spent three quiet, solitary evenings at home. So back to the tavern again, and when I come home half-drunk at 12, 1, 2, 3 o'clock, I sleep like an angel and am fresh and out of bed at 8 a.m.

Nevertheless, just to say that in the evenings and the mornings I drink milk like a cat. But how will this end? In the hospital? Don't know!

Anyway, don't worry! – Let us await what fate and the spring will bring.

August

398. To MARIE UHL

[Original in German]
Lund, 23 (?) February 1897

Dear Grandmother,

Do you also believe I would let you be torn to pieces by my arrival in Klam? I will risk being chased off as a beggar for the little lass's sake!

So please don't give my letters to Frida! She sends them straight on to her lawyer; and it already seems to me as if someone has maliciously betrayed and exploited our Bonaparte Fairy Tale,[1] which we played with Kerstin. I sense it, I know it!

You don't know Frida's love-hate for me. If, in her boundless love and compassion, she could have me confined, she would. And now, when everything is going well for me, I'm afraid. Don't you understand that? As long as I live and develop, she can have no peace; as long as I wander about here as the living refutation of her calumny, she can never rest easy!

So: in two![2]

Am now reading Bulwer's *Zanoni*![3] With terror! It is all there: I, Frida, the little one. Moreover, the demon persecutes the unfortunate Zanoni (a reincarnation) whenever he seeks to rise above material things and immerse himself in solitude and pious thoughts. But if he mixes with cheerful people, the demon flees! Exactly as in my case!

And Zanoni has an occult child, who always looks at him with its large, calm eyes. And her mother flees Zanoni from fear of 'the Unknown' in him. He is a Rosicrucian, makes gold, is two thousand years 'young', cannot die because he has drunk the elixir of life. He seeks his Viola unceasingly, and she flees although she loves him! Read this book!

Fillida (Aspasia) is there too!

August

399. To VILHELM CARLHEIM-GYLLENSKÖLD

Vilhelm Carlheim-Gyllensköld (1859–1934), astronomer and physicist, renowned for his research into the aurora borealis. His most important work was *Sur la forme analytique de l'attraction magnétique de la terre exprimée en fonction du temps* (On the Analytical Form of the Attraction of the Earth Expressed as a Function of Time, 1896), considered by many to be in its time the most significant contribution to the field since Gauss. Gyllensköld became Professor of Physics in Stockholm in 1911, and also wrote a number of popular studies in astronomy. He came to Strindberg's attention in 1888 when he submitted a play, *En sommarnatt* (A Summer Night), to the Scandinavian Experimental Theatre. Strindberg praised the play but was soon corresponding with him on scientific topics. Following Strindberg's return to Stockholm in 1899, a close friendship developed. Gyllensköld was one of the regulars at Strindberg's Beethoven evenings, and Greta Strindberg was told by her father that she would find Nils Andersson (see headnote to Letter 453) and Gyllensköld the only two of his friends on whom she could rely after his death. As Strindberg's literary executor, Gyllensköld catalogued *Gröna säcken* (The Green Sack), as Strindberg called his voluminous collection of drafts and notes on literary, linguistic and scientific topics. He also made an inventory of the *c.* 7,000 items in Strindberg's library as well as of the precise location of the objects in, on and around his desk, which proved invaluable when the Strindberg Museum was established in 1960. He made copies of letters both to and from Strindberg, and edited two volumes of hitherto unpublished writings. Three other projected volumes were stillborn, however, and Gyllensköld's final years were overshadowed by controversy concerning what was sometimes regarded as his idiosyncratic custody of Strindberg's literary remains. Their surviving correspondence amounts to some one hundred and seventy-three items, one hundred and thiry-seven of them by Strindberg. There are also a number of notes in which Gyllensköld left a record of Strindberg's conversation.

8 Grönegatan, Lund, 12 April 1897

Carlheim-Gyllensköld,

I was asked the identical question a year ago, and by someone who, without being an astrologer, had nevertheless observed as you did that there was something in the mysterious influence of the planets.[1] I responded: born 22 January 1849, hour unknown (perhaps my brother Axel Sg in the Life Insurance Company Nordstjernan knows), in a house on Riddarholmen which has been pulled down, but lived my first years at 74 Drottninggatan (I remember I always associated it with 74 Hornsgatan = Debtor's prison). The strange thing was, the man who drew up my horoscope told me my ruling planet (I've forgotten which one; you tell me!), and in a book entitled

Les Mystères d'Egypte (newly published by Chamuel, 4 rue de Savoie, Paris), I found under this planet my character and my predelictions right down to my precious stone, the amethyst, and my favourite plants, mint and rue.

I remember now that my brother Oscar on Riddarholmen has a book in which our father noted the births of all his children, perhaps he also entered the hour.

When you've drawn up my horoscope, write to Torsten Hedlund in Gbg and ask him for the horoscope he drew up for me. Then you can compare them.

As for people's apparent hostility, I have personally become resigned, but only because I experimented with Pythagoras' theory of pre-existence and reincarnation, and I now believe this assumption has been confirmed by experience and observation. That my fate worked out so painfully for me doubtless arises from crimes committed before I was born, and I am absolutely convinced we are in Inferno, especially after I discovered life here on earth depicted in detail in Swedenborg's descriptions of hell.[2]

The school of thought which you have stumbled upon represents the immediate future, and its serious scientific representatives are assembled and active in the journal *L'Initiation* (Chamuel, Paris, 10 francs per annum). I published several articles there last year that would certainly interest you. One, entitled 'A Glance into Space',[3] has been translated in the forthcoming new collection of *Published and Unpublished* (Volume 4).

This is a vast subject, and I must refer you to my *Inferno*, which will appear this autumn, where I have assembled my experiences and observations from these last 2 remarkable years.

It's very unlikely I'll come north; you come south!

Peace!
August Strindberg

400. To KERSTIN STRINDBERG

[Original in German]

Lund, 4 May 1897

Dear Little Glow-worm,

You glimmer in the distance and even look for gold in the drawer of the wash-stand – and find it. And so you are living in Dornach on the Danube again; good, then I no longer need to wander Klam-wards in my thoughts, but can go directly to the little cottage where you were born, where I kissed you farewell three years ago.

But dear child – wasn't it your birthday one of these last days? Surely! So take my good wishes, my little one, I can't send you anything else.

Am tired and weary from so much scribbling, but glad, too, that I am writing. Inferno (Hell) doesn't prosper without Beatrice,[1] but then it begins in real earnest.

Green and cold! Still confined to Lund.

Great student festivities on 1 May. I was invited along by the youngsters; wore a white student's cap with a black band and a yellow and blue cockade – felt back in my youth again, and drank punch for 14 hours.

When is your picture coming? I am so longing for it.

Tell Grandmama that so many strange things are happening here that nearly everyone is convinced the higher powers have returned to visit the earth. I know only one unbeliever here, and he has already been brought to his senses. Something new is on the way, people are quaking with fear. Swedenborg has proved correct, and he alone explains everything that is going on. The Sâr Péladan[2] is the reforming Catholic occultist, and his book, *Comment on devient Mage*, is the greatest and most beautiful reading there is for a Catholic.

He is a white prophet (not black!). With him Protestantism will probably disappear from the world.

When I have published my *Inferno*, I shall certainly enter a monastery: Frres Saint Jean de Dieu – male nurses and monks.

It has come to that!

Farewell! Greetings to Ur-grandmama, grandmama and great aunt. Little mother doesn't want any greetings!

August P.[3]

401. To GUSTAF AF GEIJERSTAM

Lund, 25 June 1897

Dear Geijerstam,

Here is the book![1] It is what it claims to be, a genuine diary with digressions.

I am giving the Swedish Version to Gernandts on condition:

That the book's appearance resembles the manuscript, but without borders.

That the small quarto format is thus retained, but with the text placed further in on the page so that it amounts to approximately 150 pages, and the book doesn't look like a pamphlet or a seed catalogue, but a proper volume. A skilled master printer can gauge this!

The Swedish Version should not include

a) The Prelude
b) The printed extract.[2]

While Fahlstedt[3] is doing the translation, could someone please make me a copy of the French original – straight away.

N.B. The French original remains the property of the Author (the manuscript, that is).

The price should be set according to the manuscript, but only calculated to 20 printed sheets. And I request 50 *kronor* per sheet per 1,000 copies. The publisher should set the selling price accordingly, as is right, and not the other way round! The translation to be paid for by the Author.

The royalties to be paid: half on acceptance of the manuscript, half when printing is completed, which ought to be by 15 September. If that is not the case, the sum falls due 15 September all the same. Moreover, I also request discretion! on Falhstedt's part as well, so nothing leaks out!

If you are unsure as to the book's authenticity, I can let you have reports by two trustworthy authorities (docents) that it is taken from my diary, and not a fabrication.

You will appreciate that I am waiting impatiently for a reply before you go abroad, also my anxiety about what is the only manuscript.

Yours,
August Strindberg

The manuscript is being dispatched tomorrow, Saturday, and will be with Gernandts on Sunday. Have it sent on to you, and read it before you leave Stockholm!

402. To JOHAN OSCAR STRINDBERG

Lund, 19 July 1897

Dear Oscar,

After a long and apparently unforgivable silence,[1] which could surely be explained, and certainly will be in the major new book I am publishing this autumn, only these words in your anxiety over your best-loved son.[2] I have a premonition that all will be well, and these last few years I have so often been proved right! Especially since the Powers who control our destinies have given me the clearest proofs of their existence and good intentions, even in the evils that befall us.

If I remember rightly, Nils is my godson! Should they be of any use, my good wishes at this time must serve as my christening gift!

Your old Friend,
August (once 'The Eagle')[3]

403. To GUSTAF AF GEIJERSTAM

[19? August 1897]

Dear G. af G.,

It seems as if the Powers have been propitiated since I, *Coram Populo,*[1] made my *confessio mea culpa;* for the very moment your letter arrived, I received notification from Copenhagen that Georg Brandes had read *Inferno* for Hegel and *absolutely* recommended publication. Thus the curse on my affairs seems to be broken. My fear about the book's reception has also passed because, although I don't know Brandes' precise opinion, I nevertheless find his recommendation to publish very reassuring. What have we to learn from this? Tell me, or rather don't!

Has Fru Marholm read the manuscript?[2] Well, so be it! I don't think she can do me any harm, not even by the grossest indiscretion.

A strange coincidence! Bengt Lidforss, who recently returned from Christiania, encountered Edvard Munch there, who told him that he had abandoned painting for the time being in order to write a book which would be called 'Hell'; for he believes that we are 'down there' already.

I'm already curious about your story.[3] If it's anything like your *Medusa,*[4] I congratulate you!

I shall now probably go to Paris; to publish; and then write my *Legends,*[5] for which the material is ready, 'from life'. So many curious things occur here every day.

Farewell, thanks for this! and my regards!

Your friend,
August Sg

404. To GUSTAF AF GEIJERSTAM

3 rue Bonaparte, Paris, 10 September 1897

Dear G. af G.,

While waiting for the proofs, I have been studying occultism here and, best of all, became acquainted with Allan Kardec, whose work I did not know.[1] In certain respects, he seems to me to carry on from Swedenborg, and I find his 'natural explanations' satisfactory. His *Livre des esprits* (3 F. 50, Éditeur Leymarie, Paris) gives me most of what I need.

Strangely enough, that book contained something of direct relevance to me. You may remember that in *Inferno* I relate the curious story of Francis Schlatter, the American miracle-worker and his double in Paris, my friend the German painter, who came from America when Schlatter disappeared (Schlatter's skeleton was found this year in Mexico); the story about the cross and Joan of Arc, his signature, etc.[2]

Well, this man's real name was Herrmann; he was very mysterious and so full of lies (?) that I thought he wasn't quite right in the head.

Imagine my surprise when, in the *Livre des esprits*, page 84, I read the following about *Doppelgängers*:

'Tel est par exemple celui qui est rapporté dans la Revue spirite du mois de février 1859 page 41, sous le titre de: Mon Ami Hermann(!). Il s'agissait d'un jeune Allemand, du grand monde, doux, bienveillant et du caractère le plus honorable, qui tous les soirs, au coucher du soleil, tombait dans un état de mort apparente; pendant ce temps son esprit se reveillait aux Antipodes en Australie, dans le corps d'un mauvais chenapan qui finissait par être pendu.' (Cf. my Herrmann, who slept till 6 p.m. on Good Friday. – '*Sind Sie nicht gekreuzigt*?' See *Inferno*).[3]

What is one to make of this?

Is the *Revue Spirite* for 1859 in the R. Lib. in Stockholm? What else does it say about the man?

Do you think I ought to insert this in *Inferno* as a footnote?

Is Herrmann a reincarnation?

When Jules Lermina saw my Herrmann, he said (in the Hôtel Orfila): 'That one comes from the galleys.'

Since the question of Mysticism will now be much discussed this autumn on account of Ola Hansson's *Studies in Mysticism*[4] and my *Inferno*, I recommend as *Vorschule*:[5]

Lotus Bleu – } *L'Initiation* – }	only this year.	10 F. per annum
Allan Kardec: *Livre des Esprits*		3 F. 50.
Russel Wallace: *Les Miracles et le moderne Spiritualisme*		5 F.
W. Crookes: *Recherches*		3 F. 50.
Aksakov: *Animisme et Spritisme*		10 F.

All from Leymarie, 42 rue Saint-Jacques.

And so: farewell for now!

Yrs,
August Sg

405. To KARIN, GRETA AND HANS STRINDBERG

29 September 1897

Dear Children,

Have you received the 200 *kronor* which I had Gernandts send you through Geijerstam a week ago? Hope to be able to send you more soon, but that's not for sure. – How are you, and how are things otherwise? – I'm staying on in Paris another month, but haven't decided where to go then. I ought really to have replied about Hans' chemistry, but I didn't want to disturb his studies with new things, which will follow in due course. And one must know the elements first! – Best wishes!

Your friend,
August Sg

406. To KERSTIN STRINDBERG

[Original in German]

Paris, 11 October 1897

Dearest Child,

How come you are having thoughts of death, you too? I am already there, and a few days ago had a vision in a dream which made me long to transmigrate to the other side; but I need do nothing about it. It looks as if I am gradually vanishing. In six weeks I have become as thin as a skeleton, and that pleases me. I have neuralgia, am poisoned with carbon monoxide. And long to see the Alps. Will perhaps go to Vevey, on Lake Geneva.

I live here like a monk in a cell with a window under the roof as in Marie Antoinette's prison, and there are bars, too. It's all right, and costs only 27 francs a month. But eating alone twice a day in a restaurant is a penitence! which is also how I take it.

In a week my *Inferno* comes out in Swedish. Then it would be better for me to be lying in my grave than living on the gallows! I shall be called a charlatan or fool!

Cold and filthy! And will be like this until March! No, I must see the pure, high, snow-capped Alps! and then die. I desire no more of life, for it can give me nothing but filth! even if it is gilded.

What kind of a changeling are you, since you are such a miraculous child?

Be always only kind and good, and you will get by in this world!

Greetings!
August

407. To KERSTIN STRINDBERG

[Original in German]

Paris, 4 November 1897

Dearest Child,

I saw you in a dream last night and must write straight away and thank you for the visit. But I'm no butterfly, I'm only an old gadfly, and can't get away once I've taken root; unfortunately!

In a few days you will be immortal in Germany as Beatrice;[1] you are already so in Sweden, where 'Hell' is now loose. That you didn't enter heaven is my fault.

I'm going north, back to my lair. It's bitterly cold here, and my hands are burnt black by the flames. (I am smelting gold every now and then!)

Your
August

408. To GUSTAF AF GEIJERSTAM

[7 November 1897]

Dear Gustaf af G.,

My book came out a week ago, and when I didn't hear anything, I grew anxious; have otherwise spent these days in a solemn mood awaiting confirmation of my good opinion of the Powers and my fellow men. And then, today, Sunday, your letter arrived – and my belief in an invisible protector was confirmed. No incarceration, therefore, no prosecution![1]

But as for coming to Stockholm, I must heed my inner voice, which says no! If it were a penitential journey, with prison a possibility, it would be something for me. But to go out among people and expose, exhibit, my person, which is not yet sufficiently trained to resist influences from without, is something I may not do, especially as you hint at some kind of celebration, which I cannot accept.

On the other hand, I shall probably go to Berlin, partly to supervise the proofs of *Inferno* which (according to a letter from Bondi[2] today) is only half set and won't be appearing for another fortnight so that 'misprints' may arise.

Partly in order to make a *Pilgerfahrt*[3] and put things to right where I have sinned.

Am sending *Legends* today by registered post, which is, however, not to be published under that title, but as: '*Inferno*: Part Two'. Since it is shorter, I am only asking 1,500 *kronor* (it says francs on the packet!) divided thus: 500 Finnish *Marks* to my children, 7 Gräsviksgatan, Helsinki; 100 *kronor* to my sister Elisabeth Sg. by way of Axel Strindberg at Nordstjernan;

(not Oscar Sg., Riddarholmen, who as a businessman usually 'charges'. Oscar oughtn't even to know about it!). Further, 50 *kronor* to Doctor Edvard Laurent, Djursholm, a debt from 1892, accompanied by a friendly word merely giving the sender's name.

The remainder I would like in a bill of exchange *à vue*.[4] I can assure you that I wasn't speculating by hanging on to the manuscript; it was diffidence, doubt, and the fear of its being rejected.

I understand this Bondi business! Sjstedt (Osborne)[5] has seen B. and written to say that B. and S., who's read the manuscript, expect a success!

Now about *Legends*! My Lund friends know what I've been writing and were in favour of it – at least in August. But then came this extraordinary reaction of Verdandi's, which I found insane.[6] They must sort that out for themselves! And I ought to show no consideration. The same goes for Ekbohrn and Eliasson as well as for Torsten H-d; it was their mission to torment me, but it is highly probable that it was also my mission to be a scourge to them! And the odd thing is: this time I haven't a trace of a guilty conscience, of 'ingratitude'. *Ich dien', och wir dienen högre Magter*.[7]

But now, I beg you: let *no one* read the manuscript; not Emanuel, not Gerda L-s,[8] so that no inopportune distortions go the rounds. You can see there's no unkindness in my account – and my friends in Lund ought to value my discretion when they see what I *haven't* divulged!

(A small point: the reader is asked to put his sandwich down whilst reading. Compare: *Inferno* Part I, which was all sticky!)

I fear that woman's printing house Idun, for it seemed to me the book had been read before it was published – by Maenads (what brutality!)

In parenthesis: Will you please send me Tavaststjerna's *On the Border*[9] (is that its name?), in which he portrays his sojourn on the 'Astral Plane', i.e. 'madness'. You can imagine what enormous interest it should hold for me, who haven't read it.

Do you know that Fröding[10] has been there?

Do you know that Ernst Josephson[11] (who hasn't a trace of paralysis) went over the edge because he and Österlind abused those powers that we possess, though without knowing it? and like me took pride in it?

In the *Livre des esprits* Allan Kardec has explained madness as a punishment and not an affliction; in certain cases, it can be a blessing, e.g. for the suffering one forgets!

I have again encountered 'Mon Ami Herrmann'[12] here. He is now a famous artist and does etchings for *Pan*.[13] Still full of hate: *'Ich hasse! hasse Alles und Alle ohne mich.'* – I replied: 'That's strange, because I hate myself!' – *'Nein, Ich liebe mich!,'* he replied; *'aber ich hasse Alle die Andere* [*sic*]!'[14]

He had experienced many curious things, and wondered himself whether he had a 'double'. Slept terribly at night, and now went to bed when the sun rose, probably from an instinctive fear of his nocturnal excursions.

However, it was salutary for me to see myself at an earlier stage in his present situation. He's now reading my *Inferno* together with a doctor (French)[15] who has done three months in La Salpêtrière; who shared my views; was informed about occultism. To my question what he (the doctor) thought about Swedenborg's 'visions', which he knew, he replied smartly: 'They weren't "visions", Swedenborg found himself on *le plan astral*.'[16] This modest word means: in contact with the world of the invisible.

People are thus clear about the occult here.

Once again: my thanks, dear Gustaf, and may my good fortune lead to yours!

Your friend, August Strindberg

409. To WALDEMAR BÜLOW

Waldemar Bülow (1864–1934), journalist and, from 1891, editor of the radical *Folkets Tidning* (The People's Paper) in Lund, where he succeeded his father, Jöns Christian Bülow, who founded the paper in 1856. A humorist and lover of nature who was also actively engaged in both local and national politics, particularly over the question of suffrage, Bülow met Strindberg when he visited Lund in the early 1890s, but the two became good friends only on Strindberg's return to Sweden in late 1896. During 1897 he lodged briefly at Bülow's house in Lund, and celebrated his 50th birthday there in 1899. However, following his return to Stockholm later that year, their correspondence dwindled to the polite exchange of annual good wishes. Bülow, who was not uncritical of the direction taken by Strindberg's writings after the Inferno crisis, was the subject of the chapter 'My Sceptical Friend's Travails' in *Legends*, and not above adding to Strindberg's collection of occult tales and strange coincidences with the odd, specious story. Over fifty letters and notes from Strindberg to Bülow have survived.

Paris, 20 November 1897

M.D.W.B.[1]

Just to please you, I am going to answer that stupid question (from S.A.B.).[2]

In *Inferno* I have portrayed my own experiences. Howcan you plagiarize what you have experienced from someone else's book? What you have experienced yourself is yourown, and anyone who wants to divest you of it is a thief.

The basic idea or point of view, the problem of Evil, is taken from – myself, from the Postlude to *Master Olof* (the verse edition of 1877), which dealt with Satanism before it became fashionable in France. (That's why this Mystery Play now precedes *Inferno* in the German edition.) The title,

'Inferno', I have indeed plagiarized – from Dante, but only because the Swedish word, Hell, didn't correspond to my conception.

I first read Huysman's *En route* on 18 September this year (see a letter about it to G. af G.).[3] The first part deals with the Author's religious musings in different Catholic churches, where he is captivated by the music. In the second part, he describes his retreat in a Trappist monastery.

What resemblance is there between that and my book?

His move from Satanism to Catholicism is common to all occultists, and the Sâr Péladan, Papus, and the whole school have gone the same way. Moreover, since I hadn't read his book, it couldn't have influenced me.

The same thing happened to me when *The Red Room* appeared; people said I'd plagiarized Zola, yet I didn't know who Zola was, and mixed him up with Zacher Masoch [*sic*], whom I didn't know either.[4]

Huysmans I do know and admire, and am not surprised to find that two contemporary authors of the same age and with the same education should evolve in a similar direction.

Huysmans began as a Zolaist, a direct pupil. Then he became an individualist (*A Rebours*), then a Satanist, and finally a convert. Consequently, our development appears identical. With the difference that I was a Satanist in the 70s, believing that evil was the power which governed the world (see *The Son of a Servant*), and have never been a straight naturalist.[5]

This is for you and my friends in Lund. I've sent something on these lines to the paper in Malmö.[6]

Yours,
August Sg

P.S. This critic can't have read Huysman's *Là bas*, otherwise he'd never have mentioned it in connection with *Inferno*.

410. To MARCEL RÉJA

Marcel Rjéa (1873–?), French poet and doctor, author of *L'Art chez les fous* (Art and the Insane, 1907). Strindberg met him in 1897 through Paul Herrmann, when Rjéa agreed to revise the French manuscript of *Inferno* for publication in France. Several of Strindberg's encounters with Rjéa and Herrmann are recorded in *Jacob Wrestles*, and Rjéa in turn left a brief essay, 'Souvenirs sur Strindberg'. Eighteen of Strindberg's letters to Rjéa survive.

[Original in French]

[20? November 1897]

Cher Monsieur Rjéa,

The manuscript of this volume was delivered to the editor on 24 June

1896.[1] On 18 September I read Huysmans' *En route* and was struck by the coincidence of two human fates developing in a parallel direction and finally converging upon the same point. What I have recounted in *Inferno* is lived, hence my property, and the idea which animates these observed facts dates from 1877 when the mystery play that forms the introduction was published in Sweden as the epilogue to my drama *Master Olof*.[2] The accusation of plagiarism on my part is thus of no moment, but what does deserve the attention of the thinking man is this constant in the movement of occultism towards religion. Whether one approaches occult questions with scientific curiosity or not, one will be crushed like Maupassant or impelled onto the way of the Cross like the Sâr Péladan, Huysmans and possibly even Papus, who has ended a Martinist, that is, religious.

A. Strindberg

411. To AXEL HERRLIN

Per Axel Herrlin (1870–1937), philosopher and psychologist. Herrlin became Docent in Philosophy at Lund in 1892, and moved to Gothenburg in 1906. From 1912–35 he was Professor of Psychology, again in Lund. His early studies in the thought of the Renaissance were followed by the series of works for which he is best remembered, *Själslifvets underjordiska verld* (The Underground World of the Mind, 1901), *Snille och själssjukdom* (Genius and Mental Illness, 1903), and *Tillräknelighet och själssjukdom* (Responsibility and Mental Illness, 1904). Herrlin shared Strindberg's interest in spiritism and the occult, and became a close companion during his Lund years. 'Now I am no longer alone,' Strindberg wrote in *Legends*, 'this young scholar seems to me to have come as a messenger from the powers, I can share everything with him, and in comparing our experiences, we give each other mutual support.' In later years Herrlin wrote several articles about Strindberg, including a valuable study of his intellectual relationship with Bengt Lidforss, whom Herrlin also knew well. Sixteen of the letters which Strindberg addressed to Herrlin have survived, the majority of them from 1898.

3 rue Bonaparte, Paris, 31 January 1898

Dear Herrlin,

Your letter came at last, as I knew it must. But for a long time I thought Ebbe had enticed you to Florence, believed on one occasion, too, that the world had tempted your youth, which would hardly be strange.[1]

So there you are, on the road to Christ.

Were I to try and define my own standpoint, however, I don't think I'd succeed. Since our last letters, I have been working with *The Imitation of Christ* and Swedenborg's *Vera Religio Christiania* [*sic*], which I found was just the same as Protestant pietism. Instead of bringing me peace, both these books filled me with the anguish of my youth; and when finally Swedenborg permitted (*sic!*)[2] the heavenly beings to partake in theological disputations and put Calvin in a brothel, etc., what I would call my godly self rebelled, and a war of extermination began. I found *The Imitation* easier for it is intended for monks and those who have taken the spiritual life as their calling. I, who am bound to the earth and its duties, to my children, may not 'despise the world' but am doomed to root about in the earth, with a small but steady side-long glance upwards. Religion as I practised it before Christmas degenerated into a vice. So I closed Swedenborg and *The Imitation* and gained a relative peace, accompanied by a certain sober pleasure in life.

I don't yet know if these stern demands represent temptations laid in our path; I don't know if there are several powers which fight against each other, but so it sometimes seems to me, and as if the Protestant God has got hold of you and the Catholic God of me. For since the Solesmes scandal last August,[3] everything I have seen of Catholicism and its adherents has only drawn me closer to it. It is a religion for children, and if we be not as little children, etc. Protestantism seems to me the religion of the rebel, the freethinker's endless reasoning about faith, dogma, and theology, but not religion.

That the Powers and Principalities are in conflict here is certain, and what is taking place up above is reflected down here.[4] Zola's significance I don't know. I often believe that this is an epoch which must condemn itself in his person, but don't know. The man is certainly not imitating Christ, and may stand condemned. We'll see! He no doubt represents one Power, but whether it is the one that will conquer – who knows? Here in Paris the air is so full of hate that one becomes ill. Remarks are made about a Bartholomew Night and Calas, but Dreyfus is no Calas, and Voltaire has been repudiated by everyone, even the anarchists.

Protestants and Jews are uniting, and it looks as if the Thirty Years' War has broken out – – –

Probably no one knows anything about the Dreyfus-Zola Affair, which seems only intended to hypnotize us while the Powers operate elsewhere.

The day before yesterday someone had written 'Saint Louis et Jeanne d'Arc ayez piti de la France!'[5] in enormous letters on the church of St-Germain l'Auxerrois, whose bell rang on Bartholomew Night (at 2 in the morning)!

I've portrayed my long, spiritual torture and contrition, which has lasted 5 months, in Part II of *Inferno,* to appear in February, and in Part III,[6] which I'll send you in manuscript, though I beg you not to mention its existence.

Once, last autumn, I saw you in a dream; you looked strange and there was a stream between us.

I believe your dead Father is guiding you: led you to Italy to become an anti-Catholic, or be tempted.

That idea of Eliasson's often comes back to me: that religion is occultism and forbidden, for as soon as one begins to probe the secrets of belief (and after all one has the right to know what to believe) one is smitten with angst and impiety, and comes close to madness.[7]

Peace returns with moderation and gravity, and care as to what I think and say. But the intimacy of *The Imitation* was followed by impiety, and a relapse into hate.

Chateaubriand's *Génie du Christianisme* calmed me.

I came across *La Clef des Grands Mystères* (Germer Baillere, Paris, 1861. Hector, the chemist in Malmö, has a copy) by Eliphas Levi (the abbé Constant) three days ago.[8] I urge you to read it, but then to throw it away, for one must know what one should avoid. I can't say whether it was written by an angel or a devil. However, it contains all Blavatsky's secrets and much more; it is also the bible of the Papusists, and rightly so: Blavatsky is an epigone.

Guaita died![9]

Life here is horrible!

Fägersköld! Isn't that the repudiation of free love? Isn't it? Taube's death has become of secondary importance! The death of Fägersköld's child is the important thing![10]

Materialism may well be a propaedeutic, but only as a terrible warning. Therefore I don't launch into Zola, especially as that is a stage I've put behind me. Perhaps he is to play *Esprit correcteur*, but not *instructeur*![11]

So, farewell, and good luck! as much as one can expect. If we could only attain clarity and wisdom, it would be easier to distinguish the voice of truth.

Yours affectionately,
August Strindberg

412. To GUSTAF AF GEIJERSTAM

Paris, 2 March 1898

Dear Gustaf af G.,

On reading the proofs of Part II, I see that we have miscalculated the amount of manuscript, and that the book will look like a paltry little pamphlet. Since a Part III I'd begun misfired, and I've been forced to cut short my religious musings, I'm sending you this fragment, to be incorporated in Part II. With that my religious struggles are over and the whole Inferno saga at an end. It also has a natural ending in Part III, where I thank Swedenborg and *The Imitation* for their help!

But Part III must be distinguished as 'Section II' in the text because it is linked to *Part* II, which it retracts. I can always clarify this in a postscript.

I leave whatever increase in my royalties to you, but please let me have it quickly – for I am *destitute*! – And my play[1] is creeping forward beautifully, giving me high hopes that I have now passed the summit.

Tell Fahlstedt in no uncertain terms that his translation is shameless. I can be coarse, but not banal, oafish or operetta-like. Which is what he is. 'Bon vivants' and such like phrases have never passed my lips or left my pen. And that flabby tone isn't there in my text!

In the hope you will soon be well again, and with best wishes,

Yrs,
August Sg

P.S. Let Adler[2] have the manuscript, so I can have some money!

413. To GUSTAF AF GEIJERSTAM

Paris, 8 March 1898

Dear Gustaf af G.,

Herewith a play,[1] I've no idea of its worth.

If you find it any good, then chuck it in to the theatre.

If you find it impossible, then hide it away in Gernandts' safe.

But the manuscript remains my property. It's my one and only money-box.

In haste. Yrs.
August Strindberg

414. To AXEL HERRLIN

Paris, 10 March 1898

Dear Herrlin,

It was fortunate that you got hold of the proofs, for on no account would I have wanted to harm you unintentionally. Changes will now be made, though I'm awaiting a letter from Geijerstam.[1]

Yes, what is this? Who stages these performances for us, and to what end? Are they real? Is there a hell besides this one? Or is it just to frighten children? My nearly seven months long crisis hasn't brought me much nearer certainty, except on a few points. Thus, I know what is expected of me as regards ethics, but the demands seem to be gradually intensifying. Alchemy and occultism, divination and research into what is hidden, are absolutely forbidden, but not speculative chemistry. On the other hand, I seem to have regained the grace of being able to write for the theatre, and have just finished a large-scale play, which I'm grateful for having been allowed to do. I thus recognize this is a gift which can be taken away from one if one misuses it.

As regards religion, I have had to stop at a moderately warm relationship with *Jenseits*,[2] which cannot, it seems, be approached too intimately, for otherwise the punishment is religious fanaticism, and one is led astray. But I'm not certain when it is a temptation to be withstood or a call to be obeyed. My earlier fatalism has thus been transformed into a belief in providence, and I see quite clearly that I am nothing, and can achieve nothing, on my own. But I shall never attain complete humility, for I don't have the conscience to kill my own person.

Now business: I shall probably have to come up to Lund again quite soon to consult some Swedish books for a play, set in the Swedish Middle Ages, which I am going to write for the autumn. Will you ask that friend of humanity, Brand,[3] if I could borrow a room in his house when I arrive, to spare me a hotel, until I've found rooms for the summer!

I imagine much has changed in Lund since I left, and that there has been time for the weeds I sowed myself (with *Inferno*) to grow over my memory. But I must take that as it comes!

Give my regards to all my friends!

from
Your devoted
August Strindberg

415. To GUSTAF AF GEIJERSTAM

[15? March 1898]

Dear Gustaf af G.,

New plan!

On my journey to Lund (or Copenhagen) at the beginning of April, depending on money, I shall stop off for a few days at a Benedictine Monastery in Belgium,[1] where I've been invited. I want to record my impressions in *Inferno II*.

You can see what a '*clou*'[2] this will be.

So: a delay!

Why have a fiasco of a book when we might have a success!

To weary the public by reappearing with another Part III in the autumn won't do! Two stout blows, and then full stop! I can have the account of the monastery ready in April. So the book could be out 1 May. Or – for the autumn!

The painful impression which Part II makes in its present form must be alleviated by the Luxembourg[3] – and the Monastery.

I am now awaiting the play!

Hillberg could well read it, and Ranft![4] There are a lot of settings, but they're all used twice!

And so, first and last and eternally: Money! Money! Money!

Your friend,
August Strindberg

416. To GUSTAF AF GEIJERSTAM

Paris, 17 March 1898

Dear Gustaf af G.,

Just received your letter about the play![1] – You were the first to read it, and your verdict delights me!

Yes, it is certainly a fiction but with a terrifying half-reality behind it. The art lies in the composition, which symbolizes 'The Repetition' that Kierkegaard speaks of:[2] the action unrolls forwards to the Asylum; there it kicks against the pricks and rebounds back through the pilgrimage, the relearning, the eating of one's words, until it begins again at the same point as the action stops, and where it began. You may not have noticed how the settings unroll backwards from the Asylum, which is the spine of a book that shuts upon itself and encloses the action. Or like a snake that bites its own tail.[3]

I suggest the following alterations: The Lady hasn't cursed him; but by reading his book, she has eaten of the tree of knowledge; she begins to reflect, loses her *unbewusste*,[4] discovers the difference between right and wrong, is filled with discord, and thus loses her charm for him. I am thinking of having them agree to separate in the final scene, which will be extended. Shall I part them? Yes! For the relationship is foul, but as instruments of torture for each other, they could go on being attracted to one another. I also want to arrange some details. Her knitting must be finished. The line 'Shall we talk about you now?' is taken up again when she wakes to say herself: 'Now we ought to talk a little about me, perhaps.' His conversion to a religious frame of mind after the terrible blow at the Doctor's, when he discovers he has been in a lunatic asylum, must be apparent in the last scene, in greater contrition. Etc. Etc.

1000 *Kr.* is an awful lot of money! I thought it would be 100! But in that case, the drama must look magnificent! Like poetry!

A performance! After all, it's meant for the stage. And has the same dcor twice! Let Hillberg read it. He'll understand it best! Lindberg[5] never will!

And so back to money!

I must have 300 francs by the 25th. G. can find that.

But on 7 April, Maundy Thursday, I'll be celebrating Easter at the monastery of Maredsous. I want to see who Christ is, and find out if I belong to his flock. Ought therefore to leave here on the 5th. Can I depend on it?

Gyldendahl has suggested that Adler and I bring out a Danish-Swedish Dictionary.[6] I've agreed! It is no more than I deserve. Will consequently be heading north via Maredsous (near Namur, in Belgium). To Copenhagen, then, to atone for my sins there too!

Many thanks, however! The play must be performed: *c'est du théâtre*![7]

Your friend,
August Strindberg

P.S. Delete the Docent![8]

417. To WALDEMAR BÜLOW

Paris, 1 April 1898

My Good Friend,

To your question: 'What have I done since I am being persecuted?' no one can reply but yourself, and no one else has the right to reply, least of all I, who have done more than you to deserve the wild hunt to which I was recently subjected.

It isn't people who are persecuting you; people are too lazy and egotistical to waste time on persecuting others – no, it is someone else, the Unseen One, who you have defied. Moreover, as a source of popular enlightenment, your paper gives you greater power than others have; therefore you are being treated more severely. And you are fighting against a new age, which is being born. You are following your father's old-fashioned ideals, which is why, somewhat arrogantly, I called you 'antique'.

Brand recently sent me a book on the Jesuits in which I found some lines that afforded me relief.

The author, Jean Wallon, writes in his preface: 'In 1867 . . . I foretold in an article called *'De l'athéisme providentiel'* that God now intended to conceal himself, in order to force people to seek him out more diligently.'

This neglect of the Powers because they were in hiding began in 1867 with Renan and Taine and Zola (Darwin was no atheist). But now the return of the Powers is at hand, and God is being sought both high and low, whether by God we mean a moral world order or an avenger or the reconciler. And those whose arrogant curiosity led them to delve too deeply into forbidden mysteries, like the occultists (and myself), saw more than they wanted to, and the Sphinx savaged them, one after the other. But occultism led back to a conception of God and the certainty that there are others who guide our destinies. That is my current position; I haven't been able to get any further, but it seems to me that with the return of the Powers, the old demands for order and discipline, etc. will revive. I even believe that the old morality will come back, but making considerably stronger demands. And as someone who is under the continual supervision by the invisible ones, I believe I must deny myself some of life's little pleasures, which have been my misfortune, most of all – wine!

When I now make my way home, it's likely I shall be an ascetic in that respect; and as I've been shut up all winter, I want to go straight to the country; also because after *Inferno*, Lund has become unbearable, and because there must be an end to tavern life.

I've elected to set up camp at Anarp, or some other station between Lund and Malmö.

Therefore, please would you immediately inquire after something for me, but away from noisy neighbours and free from a sugar-refinery or tavern, especially Sunday dancers.

One room, I don't need more, and with meals nearby. Or set up house with one or more teetotallers and an old woman to do the housekeeping (e.g. Elna).[1] But this must be done quickly, because I'll probably be leaving very soon!! And don't want to be in Lund, for if I'm giving up drinking, I shan't be going to the tavern either to listen to a lot of stupid nonsense about nothing, or expose myself, in all of which I was once a master.

I hope you received the 100 *Kr.* I sent! That's the end of the matter – I've deeply regretted that I gave in to the temptation, when I was in duty bound not to open my mouth.

Please keep this letter private!

I sent the passage on *L'athéisme providentiel* to Brand for him to send on, but he'd gone; therefore I'm copying out the best bit again. It gives us the semblance of an excuse!

Keep the peace with the Powers now, and don't pursue those unfortunate people who are under a bann. Being a Pietist isn't funny! Then you'll be left in peace, and sleep well at night. But you ought to move house to get away from that old, unhealthy atmosphere!

You can give the clothes away. But not the toilet things!

So: Greetings and Peace!

Your friend,
August Strindberg

418. To ELISABETH STRINDBERG

22 Tomegapsgatan, Lund,[1] 12 April 1898

Dear Sister,

Have you any idea how your situation might be changed?[2]

I live like a student in one room in Lund, and have no home to offer you. Nor would my company profit you, for I am in the same situation as yourself!

It is surely our condition to be oppressed, and after carrying on what I now realize was a vain struggle for almost fifty years against a dependence on other people, I have had no alternative but to accept it. That is how it has to be; and for some hidden purpose, which is probably not evil. Submit to your fate! That is my only advice! You must have seen that moving somewhere else doesn't help; and that one cannot escape one's destiny! What's the use of trying?

Your friend,
August

419. To ALGOT RUHE

Algot Ruhe (1867–1944), dentist, novelist and playwright, member of the so-called *flâneur* school of writers who, during the 1900s, produced a personal literature, centred on the experience of urban life, and exploring social and erotic themes. Ruhe was also a contributor to *Stormklockan*, the radical organ of the Young Social Democrats, and the Swedish translator of the works of Henri Bergson, about whom he wrote a monograph in 1914. In his *Socialism och livsglädje* (Socialism and the Joy of Life, 1910), Ruhe sought to combat the pessimism which had overtaken the Swedish workers' movement following the general strike of 1909. Ruhe came to Strindberg's attention after his article 'August Strindberg et son œuvre dramatique' appeared in the February 1898 issue of the *Revue d'Art Dramatique*. Twelve letters from Strindberg to Ruhe have survived.

Lund, 20 April 1898

Dear Herr Ruhe,

Just before I left Paris, I learned that Julien Leclercq,[1] who is handling *By the Open Sea*, has called it 'La Femme du Nord' in French. In what indicates either a complete ignorance of the book or a speculation on French curiosity, I discerned something ominous and sought to prevent it through Davray at *Mercure*.[2] The original title of the French translation was *L'Extrême Rocher*, which I thought a good one. That was three years ago. But Geijerstam's new book, *The Last Rock*,[3] which will probably appear in French, has ruled this out. I think 'Surhomme' would be good, particularly as the end of the book gives the lie to this very transitory contemporary figure, who lacked all basis in reality. I thus second your opinion, and would like *Mercure* to be informed of this as soon as possible, above all so as to prevent the impossible and misleading 'Femme du Nord', which I would be inclined to see as a piece of feminine malice or stupidity on the part of J.L.

With thanks for your assistance in this matter

Yours truly,
August Strindberg

420. To ELISABETH STRINDBERG

Lund, 23 April 1898

Dear Sister,

My last letter was written in haste, and I had no time to ask you various things, such as: what are you doing in Motala? Is there anything you want? How do you envisage a change in your situation? Where would you feel at home? Will you let me know?

As regards your impressions of being persecuted, they are just like the ones I had when I was ill, and lack all foundation; though perhaps not all, for it seems we persecute ourselves. If you've read my book *Inferno*, you will have seen what lay behind my feeling of persecution, which consisted chiefly of self-reproach. And you can also see the way in which I sought to find resignation.

I don't know whether your case resembles mine, and have no right to inquire or admonish; but I can give you one piece of advice: try to discover what Providence has in mind with the sufferings that afflict you.

Don't move away from where you are in a hurry, for that won't help. You cannot run away from yourself – or from Him who visits you.

However, write and tell me what you want to do!

Your friend,
August

P.S. Here's a little money! When I get more, you shall have more.

421. To KARIN, GRETA AND HANS STRINDBERG

Lund, 24 May 1898

Dear Children,

I am very glad to hear that you are happy, and that things are not going badly for you.

As for my prospects, they are quite good. I have recently completed a big play in five acts,[1] the best I have written, and it has given me and my friends who have read it great hopes. Since it is a new genre, fantastic and brilliant as *Lucky Peter* but with a contemporary setting and a completely real background, it may turn out to be our salvation, though it can also happen that the public will find itself a little lost at first.

I am now waiting for a reply from a major theatre which has 'bitten', and was hoping to have been able to send you some money for the summer holidays by now. In the meantime, I am enclosing 115 marks, of which you may keep 15 for yourselves, that is 5 marks each for fishing rods and other such summery things.

I shall probably remain in Lund over the summer.

If I am unable to send you any great sums, I shall nevertheless send several smaller ones, for better something than nothing, and I'm hopeless at accumulating small sums. Better to send them as they come.

If you see from the papers that I've moved away from Lund, write there in any case, for your letters will be sent on. And if you should get into any unexpected financial difficulties, then telegraph or write and let me know, and I will help you if I can, there is more chance of that now than a year ago.

Have a fine summer, and let me hear from you; also give me your address in full when you know it!

Your friend,
August Sg

P.S. As it's difficult to get Finnish money here, I'm sending 100 *kronor*. So you should take 100 marks for the household and share the rest! This way you'll get a little more!

422. To GUSTAF FRÖDING

Gustaf Fröding (1860–1911), Swedish poet. When this letter was written, Fröding had already produced the five collections on which his reputation as a lyric poet rests; he had also succeeded Birger Mörner as the editor of *A Book About Strindberg,* to which he contributed a sensitive assessment of Strindberg's poetry. However, the two men never met: Fröding's mental health had long been unstable, and when it finally gave way later that year, he was committed (by his doctor, and Strindberg's friend, Hjalmar hrvall) to hospital in Uppsala, where he remained until March 1905. Basing his account on reports received from Bengt Lidforss, Strindberg had portrayed one of Fröding's earlier mental crises in *Legends,* and was led by their common interest in Swedenborg and the occult to regard him and his hallucinations as a parallel to his own Inferno experience. In the light of his subsequent afflictions, the court action brought against Fröding for immorality in the collection *Stänk och flikar* (Daubs and Patches, 1896) seemed to Strindberg not only reminiscent of his own experience over *Getting Married* but also further evidence of the emblematic nature of Fröding's fate, and in *Gothic Rooms* he again treated his case as a symptom of the times.

Lund, 5 June 1898

Dear Herr Fröding,

I had been expecting your letter for some time, and now it has come to set me free, partly from a scruple of conscience concerning the thoughtless way in which I released your story,[1] which is why I am taking this opportunity to ask your forgiveness, partly for other reasons.

I agree with you entirely that we must communicate with each other, but how can we do that by letter? Couldn't we meet and live near to one another for a while, and then go our separate ways again? Does that attract you? If so: Uppsala for me or Lund for you? Lund is an ideal place in which to spend the summer: peaceful, clean, fresh, verdant, southerly, and lighter for our melancholy spirits than Uppsala; the Sound also opens out quite invitingly. The memories it holds makes Uppsala absolutely hideous to me, but Lund would be good for your health.

Think it over!

By way of preparation, a few words about the important questions that you touch on in your letter, and in your poems on the Grail,[2] which I had just put down when your letter arrived.

Something is going on in the world of the Spirits: 'The Return of the Powers'. Is it God himself? I don't know, I don't think so. I believe the dead conduct affairs, and therefore the Governing Body may possibly have shortcomings, for which others are responsible. Consequently, I don't cease to complain every now and then, because I cannot understand why I should be punished for crimes I haven't committed, or suffer from an undeservedly bad reputation, for perversity, for example, when I am not a pervert. Perhaps it's because I have carelessly repeated loose, unsubstantiated rumours about other people who may suffer from this vice, which is beyond my understanding; or maybe because, in *Getting Married II*,[3] I fell in with the mania of the times for liberation, and sought to lighten the burden of guilt of those unfortunate people?

A word of advice, and don't take the lessons of long experience amiss. Do not use the word hallucination (not even the word delirium) as if it stood for something unreal. Our hallucinations and delirium possess a certain kind of reality, or rather, they are phantasmagoria, induced by the Invisible One, and consciously designed to frighten us. They all have a symbolic meaning. For example, you know the projections of alcoholic delirium are always the same: flies and rats. The direct progeny of filth. (The Lord of the Flies! etc.) Consequently, if one wants to dismiss the meaning of these visions simply by saying it is *nothing but* delirium, one is mistaken. The matter cannot be brushed aside like that.

I'm certain that your visions are also to be found in Swedenborg, and if you could write them down from memory, you would be doing yourself, me, and many others a great service. I should interpret them for you; you would see that they contained a common element, that they are meaningful and well-intended. When I came across descriptions of my own experiences in Swedenborg, I was liberated. Now, when I am attacked at night, I lie there and tick off these torments against my bad deeds; I immediately think: 'That's what you get for that! Take care, and don't do it again!' And so I regain my peace of mind; until I sin again. But you mustn't think I am only being punished for wine and women; no, every bad word about others, even if it's true and common knowledge, arrogant thoughts, and many more such things are closely scrutinized. I don't believe in another Gehenna apart from this one, yet I don't know. And Swedenborg's hell is an exact description of life on earth; I don't believe we leave here until we have suffered our allotted portion. But we two, we seem to have a mission, and it is no use trying to escape our calling by leaping into the sea like Jonah. We must go forth and prophesy, and risk being disavowed like Jonah. My development isn't as absurd as it appears.

'Pull down!', said the Spirit. And I pulled down!

'Now build', says the Spirit, 'since you have basked in the sun in the fresh air of the Esplanade!' (The burned site!)[4]

And now I shall try to build.

As for my religion: I suppose I'm nominally a Christian, an amateur Catholic, a creedless Theist, I don't know! Yet! But through occultism,

Swedenborg, Saint-Martin,[5] Eliphas Levi[6] and the Cabbala, I have a wholly satisfying explanation, a scientific explanation, of the miracle, and believe in every kind of wonder, for such things occur every day, and I am keeping a record of them. And I believe that Christ is a God, who overthrew Zeus, and who may have been Zeus' son. That is how he is foretold in Aeschylus' *Prometheus Bound*, which I urge you to read.[7] But note carefully that Prometheus specifically prophesies his special redemer (*Erlöser*), who was of course Hercules, and specifically mentions Zeus' son, who will overthrow Zeus. Who in fact overthrew Zeus, leaving him not a single altar? Who has succeeded him in Hellas, Rome, Europe? Christ! Who else?

This in haste!

Thank you for approaching me; and think out how we ought to meet!

In haste. Yours,
August Strindberg

423. To EMIL SCHERING

Emil Schering (1873–1951), German writer and translator. According to Schering's own account, he was so taken by a performance of *Creditors* at the Residenztheater in Berlin in 1893 that he decided there and then, though still a student, to become Strindberg's German translator, and promptly set about learning Swedish. They first corresponded in 1894 in German, but from May 1898, when Schering began to figure prominently in his literary plans, Strindberg switched to Swedish. Over four hundred of his letters to Schering survive, the majority written between 1902 and 1907, but Strindberg never abandoned the formal mode of address. They were published in German by Schering in 1924 as part of the 48–volume edition of Strindberg's works which he brought out between 1910 and 1924. During the first decade of this century, Schering functioned as Strindberg's factotum and impresario in Germany, tirelessly supplying him with books and negotiating with publishers, journals and theatres. However, in placing Strindberg's works he was not averse to providing the extracts he made with his own titles, and editing them accordingly. Nevertheless, although his translations have often been criticized, his significance for Strindberg's reception in Germany was enormous, and helped make possible the great wave of Strindberg productions there between 1915 and 1926.

Lund, 1[9] June 1898

Dear Herr Schering,

In order not to leave anything unanswered in your latest, detailed letter I shall take it point by point.

Dr Jonas' letter has gone astray.[1]

It's impossible for me to promise you an original story for your journal,[2] since I cannot determine my disposition. Take something out of *Sylva Sylvarum*: why not 'The Death's-Head Moth' and 'Cyclamen'. Or 'Towards the Sun' from *Published and Unpublished*. In my opinion that short item contains the whole equation whereby my life can be solved: my estrangement here on earth, where my whole life has been a provisional arrangement, a guest appearance; where I have never felt at home, but believed in a life to come, even during my short atheist period (a psychic experiment that immediately failed).

Couldn't 'Loki's Blasphemies' in Dehmel's[3] translation be included? The Gods of the Age (= The Dominions, Powers, Principalities), whom I couldn't love, because I believed they jealously came between mankind and the God of Eternity. The Russian peasant oppressed by officials and never able to reach the Tsar, his Father, with his complaint, affords an image of my conception.

On your word I am willing to appear in the same number as Munch.

There isn't a copy of the Berzelius article.[4] The original is at the publishers, and will appear in July.

Then I have what is perhaps a somewhat impertinent request. Will you let me have two copies of your translation of *Damascus*, to be used in translating it into Italian and French? In that way, I'd gain a year, and not risk missing the theatrical season. Zacconi,[5] who is performing my plays in Italy, has asked for *Damascus*, and Lugné-Poë is also waiting for it. We should of course gain by a performance in Paris, since that would influence the German theatre directors!

And so, with my respects to Frau (Fräulein?) Schering,[6]

Yours sincerely,
August Strindberg

424. To KARIN STRINDBERG

Lund, 20 June 1898

Dearest Karin,

It isn't easy for me to say how happy I am that you have yourself thought of adopting some religion. You know of course that I have always allowed you complete freedom where spiritual matters are concerned, partly because I myself was unsure, partly because I didn't believe I had the right to influence you. I am all the happier that you have discovered Catholicism, for after having found in Protestantism not a religion but theology, argumentation and free thinking, which ends in godlessness and doubt, I consider it the only faith for us Westerners.

'The faith of our fathers', that is Catholicism, and the Protestants now seem to be returning to it in droves after having lost their way and dissolving into as many sects as the philosophers, both past and present.

But a piece of advice: never reason about religion, Karin. If anyone brings the subject up, then, politely but firmly, interrupt them, and don't be afraid of confessing: 'I am a believer and do not discuss these sacred things. The truths of religion are axiomatic for me and can thus not be proved, and do not need to be proved, and if one attempts to prove an axiom, one gets tangled up in the absurd. Religion is thus as exact a branch of learning as mathematics, which is predicated upon unproved and unprovable axioms, which must nevertheless be taken 'in good faith' if the whole of mathematics isn't to come tumbling down.'

But, Karin, let your religion be a living, guiding principle for your thoughts and actions. Look at my unruly and vacillating life, grounded upon a lack of religion.

And have recourse to prayer: that is the miracle, as I finally discovered. It is so wonderful, that we receive all we pray for, so long as we only pray sensibly. It is true, Karin, that I have finally received all I should have.

And moreover: don't believe that He who guides our destinies is evil. Those seemingly 'evil powers' that torment us when we have done wrong, cannot be evil since they persecute and punish evil with remorse and the like. Were these powers evil, they would encourage our vices and persecute what is good, but there has been no evidence of that! So they, too, are ruled by good!

Whether I shall ever bind myself to some form of religion, I don't know, but if so, it will be Roman Catholicism.

I would so much like to have been able to send you some money, but I still see no sign of any. Perhaps, however, a little later this summer. My best wishes to your brother and sister from

Your friend, August.

425. To EMIL KLÉEN

Johan Emil Kléen (1868–98), Swedish poet and journalist. Already a good friend of Bengt Lidforss, Kléen first met Strindberg at the end of 1896. Their friendship developed rapidly into what some contemporaries saw as almost a father-son relationship, and Strindberg certainly treated Kléen with unusual tenderness and care. Kléen visited Strindberg in Paris in January 1897, where he reported on the Dreyfus Affair for *Malmö-Tidningen*, while during the last weeks of Kléen's life, as he lay dying from tuberculosis of the throat, Strindberg went to the hospital almost every day to read to him and keep him company. Kléen, whose Bohemian figure may be glimpsed in numerous literary works of the time, appears briefly in *Legends*, where Strindberg records a New Year visit to his parents' house outside Lund, and again in *Gothic Rooms*, where he describes his death. However, his principal literary memorial was the foreword he contributed to a selection of Kléen's mildly decadent, symbolist-inspired poems, published in 1906. Twenty-six of Strindberg's letters to Kléen have survived.

Lund, 9 July 1898

Dear Kléen,

I am sorry I wasn't at the station, but my agoraphobia kept me at home. Thank you, however, for the papers, which Wistén[1] gave me straight away.

I hope you've now recovered your voice so that after completing our penitence, we can resume our colloquies.

Nothing new in the literary world. The Red Man and Schlatter[2] have written; S. had also done some drawings; evidently Kleksography applied to sketching.[3]

My play[4] has repeatedly ground to a halt; I meant to burn it as totally worthless, although I'm nearly at the end of Act 4. But I'm carrying on. It was conceived in hate and deals with hateful people. Although it has a sturdy framework and diverse compositional tricks, it disturbs me and makes me ill. *Tristis sum*![5]

Can I count on you to read it when it's finished? We'll have to see if it will do as a sketch.

While you're in the country, will you please collect what information you can about the Corncrake; particularly about its migration.[6]

Can you hear any singing in the rye fields?

Do you know an amateur photographer who would photograph the Ystad stones in Arpis Park? If so, he'll become immortal!

Herrlin is now the only person I see; and I eat both lunch and dinner in my cell since I've given up Åke Hans'![7] *Tristis sum*!

I long for Switzerland to regenerate my body after punch and *brännvin*, which make me gloomy and bad-tempered, and my soul spiteful and dull.

If the play misfires, I'll be stuck in Lund. – Alack!

Write and tell me how you are, and your impressions of your enforced penitence. If you're very bored, I could slip over and talk to you at the station for a few hours. Haven't the time or peace of mind for more!

Yours,
August Strindberg

426. To EMIL KLÉEN

Lund, 22 July 1898

Dear Kléen,

When I left the station in Lund after our meeting, the scales quite literally fell from my eyes and the stone from my heart, so that I noticed how I was overcome by a delightful, positive feeling, and floated home to my four sandwiches, and was happy.

Isn't it therefore logical to conclude that my unseen Mentor doesn't think it in my best interests to leave Lund before the right moment comes to do so?

However: since then I've been studying Péladan's *Vice Suprême*, 1884 (N.B.), and find it highly remarkable. The same Satanism = belief in evil, the same despair and way of blaspheming as the characters in *The Red Room*. But in Péladan + the factors of the *Übermensch*[1] and western Occultism from the Cabbala and Eliphas Levi, which anticipates Theosophy – Péladan's views on the nature of woman also coincide with mine in *Getting Married*. Therefore I have reason to suppose that I represented a mainstream in my time, whether or not the source has been a subterranean one.

And Péladan is the prophet of the Third Republic, its Jeremiah, while Zola is an historical novelist who prophesies (in retrospect!) the Second Empire, after the event![2]

And there are real prophecies in *Vice Suprême*, even about the rue Bruxelles,[3] where something very nasty has been going on.

If you come tomorrow, Saturday, I promise not to introduce any alien elements.

Yours,
August Strindberg

A few French papers would cheer my loneliness!

427. To KERSTIN STRINDBERG

[Original in German]

Lund, 29 August 1898

Dear Child,

Back in Lund, I only now received your two dear letters, which have made me very happy.

My journey passed off like this: after five days of torture in Heyst,[1] where I was forced to live together with 200 people and eat six different courses for dinner, sitting at table for over an hour, I was ready for monastic life. Went to Maredsous, a foundation of extraordinary beauty, as big as Melk.[2] Was received as a guest in a very friendly way. Slept there, ate in the refectory together with the 100 monks. All was peace and tranquillity, apart from me. For there, too, one got 5 courses with beer and wine on the table for us guests, and that was too much for me, so I left and came back here.

It made a beautiful and unforgettable impression, but we guests disturbed one another. Perhaps it's harder to live as a monk in everyday life, and for the time being I shall stay where I am. During the journey, it was my curious fate only to be with Austrians, Bohemians and Hungarians, and Heyst was packed full of ladies from Vienna and Buda. The children had a carnival, which interested me a lot, and I thought I could see you in a triumphal waggon. In any case, I swam in the Baltic and bathed away the heat.

That business in Honolulu has something to do with ghosts, and the braggart who asked after me is called Hugo; the abducter of princesses, however, is Albert.[3]

The night I slept in the monastery was – Bartholomew's Night! (24 August!) Imagine! But I wasn't afraid, since I went to the night mass and was forced to receive consecrated water and even to make the sign of the cross, otherwise they would have killed me as a Huguenot. The fathers were very friendly, but they drank wine and took snuff, which I didn't like. They were a bit too worldly for me.

And so it is autumn again! and chilly.

Still tired after this tearing around, I can't write any more today! Farewell, and read your Bible; it contains everything, and I consult it every day for advice!

Your August P.

428. To EMIL KLÉEN

Lund, 2 September 1898

Dear Kléen,

So much has happened this week, but in spite of various things I remain attached to my faith – as an experiment!

I believe in the Tsar's good intentions;[1] I also believe the Henry debacle[2] came just to discredit the army with the war party, to frustrate the idea of revenge and compel France to attend the peace congress. I believe, too, that Dreyfus is guilty, and that Zola should not be turned into a martyr and crowned as a truth teller. You know why I think that, and it would strain my belief in God when and if Dreyfus should be rehabilitated – but then? Then? what am I to believe then? *Credo quia absurdum*![3]

Georg Br. seems to have met with a little Damascus down there. And Fröding?[4]

I am still being tortured at the Central Hotel as a tourist in expiation for my dissatisfaction with my situation at 22 Tomegapsgatan, to which I'll nevertheless return!

Am reading Péladan with growing admiration but mixed feelings. A lewd moralist! A paradox! who castigates his carnality yet enjoys his flagellation.

Here's the bill of exchange; that's how it always ends! Even this letter!

Yrs,

August Strindberg

Are you coming to town tomorrow?

429. To GUSTAF BRAND

Carl Gustaf Adolf Brand (1857–1953), doctor. He and Strindberg first met in 1892 through Per Hasselberg, when Brand offered to buy the majority of the paintings in Strindberg's 1892 exhibition at Birger Jarl's Bazar. Although he gave Brand two of them, Strindberg received only 200 *kronor* for eight other canvases that he eventually carried off. In spite of this the two became good friends after Strindberg's move to Lund, where Brand was completing his medical studies. Brand then settled in Belgium, where he married and was converted to Catholicism at the Benedictine monastery of Maredsous, which Strindberg visited in 1898. Brand also acquired Agnes de Frumerie's 1895 bust of Strindberg, which the latter regarded as the best ever made of him. In 1900 he sent Brand *To Damascus I* in the hope that he would get it translated and published in Brussels, perhaps with Maeterlinck's assistance, but nothing came of the idea. Numerous postcards to Brand have survived (Strindberg once described the genre as Brand's 'forte'), but no extended correspondence.

[28 September 1898]

Dear Br.,

No, I'll not get away from Lund in a hurry! Therefore I'd be grateful if my laundry was sent here (carriage unpaid).

Kléen is now in Mörsil with consumption. No sign of Strömstedt. Mortensen has gone to Gbg. so I'm quite alone.[1]

Greetings, peace!

Yrs,
Aug Sg

430. To GUSTAF BRAND

[16 October 1898]

Dear Br.,

Much obliged for my washing! And you paid the carriage too! So, a big thank you! All pretty monotonous here! *Nichts passirt*![1] [*sic*] Greetings and my respects.

Yrs,
August Strindberg

431. To GUSTAF AF GEIJERSTAM

Lund, 17 October 1898

Dear Gustaf af G.,

After reading through *Damascus* again, it seems to me that the 2 parts with cuts could both be premièred on the same evening between 7 and 11. If it proved a success, it could then be split up.

Will you now, however, let Ranft, Hillberg, Lindberg and Molander each have a copy as soon as it's printed.

And tell Molander that of the scenery only the Kitchen, the Doctor's courtyard and the Rose Room really matter. The rest can be run up anyhow. The change from summer to winter can be done with set pieces, with the tree in the foreground, and otherwise by lighting if the scenery is kept in an abstract, shadow-like, colourless tone, which is in keeping with the play.

This time, too, I should like the cover to be plain, without any advertising. If the publisher wants to advertise, he can put a fly sheet in each copy.

How are things with you, good friends? A little snow on one's sorrows, and then the sun comes and fades even the most blood-red pain![1]

Your friend,
August Strindberg

432. To GUSTAF AF GEIJERSTAM

Lund, 23 October 1898

Dear Gustaf,

When I returned home yesterday evening, I remembered a child's prayer at the end of an enjoyable day: 'Thank you Dear Lord for the lovely time I've had today.' And that came closest to conveying what I wanted to say.

It was pleasant and good to re-establish contact with my past, and I thank you warmly for coming and delivering me from my melancholy and lonely dejection. And my thanks to Nennie,[1] who denied herself, and allowed you to make the journey.

One thing: would you please send Ibsen a copy of *Damascus*, and simply say: Strindberg is ashamed that as a prominent Swedish writer, he did not join in the tribute to the Master, from whom he learned much.[2] But he was feeling depressed and did not believe his tribute could honour or delight anyone, anywhere.

Will you do that?

If you take on the task of dealing with my various publishers over new editions and a volume of Selected Writings or a Strindberg Album,[3] I hereby authorize you to act as you see fit!

Hoping you are now safely home again with your family!

In haste. Yrs,
August Strindberg

433. To GUSTAF AF GEIJERSTAM

Lund, 29 October 1898

Dear Gustaf af G.,

I understand your silence! But my bellies[1] are now screaming for money! And in another week I shall probably have completed the first part of my novel, 350 pages and in a form that could be served up as a book on its own, if need be.[2]

The question is: should I move to Stockholm? then? And write the second part? so both come out in one volume, a real thunder-clap of a book?

And: can't I offer it to *Sv. Dagbladet* now at a high price, as a *feuilleton*?

And work in Sthlm for a production of my play and the appearance of the birthday album?

Here in Lund I lose all *Geist*,[3] find no stimulation. If you meet Tor Hedberg, give him a friendly word of thanks from me.[4] For he wasn't obliged to write so promptly, and we are competitors, though he, at least, is a loyal one!

Have you kindly sent copies to the theatres I mentioned?

I haven't received a copy yet! Yes, one!

How have Ranft, Hillberg, Lindberg and Molander responded?

In haste. Yrs,
August Sg

P.S. Had already written this when your letter arrived!

Now I'm awaiting your reply!

And thank your firm for the welcome gift!

Let me get away from here!

Away!

The air is stifling! My faculties embittered!

434. To GUSTAF AF GEIJERSTAM

Lund, 2 November 1898

Dear Gustaf,

Here is the first part of *The Cloister*, which is only the introduction.

I beg you not to let any unauthorized person read it!

You appreciate that I'm sending it because I'm in need of money!

It's worth a thousand *kronor*, even if I were to die, because it can be served up on its own.

Let me have something as soon as possible! My young ones are howling! And so am I!

What do you think about my Stockholm trip?

The Cloister mustn't come out before April, and I may even fit in a drama between times!

The proofs of *Damascus* are a disgrace. Not even my corrections corrected.

Anyone who now wants to know the saga of my life can read, in the following order:

The Son of a Servant
Time of Ferment
In the Red Room
Le Plaidoyer d'un Fou
The Cloister 1
Inferno
Legends
The Cloister 2

That's quite something!

Once again: Have those theatres received the copies that I wrote about?

And Ibsen? That really is sincerely and disinterestedly meant! And you're not to ask anything for me of the old boy 'in return'![1]

What you said about him concerning me aroused my sense of justice. That's all!

Yours,
August Strindberg

435. To EMIL KLÉEN

Lund, 10 November 1898

My dear Friend,

I only just found out where you are;[1] and immediately went and sent you some autumn roses.

I've been worried about you, and had a feeling that you've suffered greatly. Strömstedt could have sent us a word, to all of us who are concerned, and particularly to me, to whom you brought such happiness, and whom you sustained with your friendship during the long, cheerless departed summer.

Sent you *Damascus* to Mörsil! Don't know if you've received it!

Here a redeeming mist has settled upon the summer's fallen splendour; the wind is silent and still, as if the air were holding its breath, and nature is as solemn as at Christmas time.

My life is just the same. It creeps on, day after day, in work, and now and then I have some beautiful thoughts. Am writing a fairy-tale tragedy[2] without fairies or sprites; only the great, unfathomable Unseen One working his magic.

Providence has been good to me of late, but I can hardly take pleasure in that, for my wickedness has grown old along with me. Have serious intentions which nevertheless unfortunately miscarry, so often running aground on submerged rocks, so often.

Lund is noisy, and the squabbles and quarrels of people who are never satisfied disturb the peaceful muses.

With my respects to your good parents, I wish you peace in the struggle, and hope in your suffering.

Your Friend,
August Strindberg

436. To ANON

Anon. According to Torsten Eklund, the probable addressee was Leonard Ljunglund (1867–1946), who edited *Hvad nytt från Stockholm* and was interested in philosophy.

Lund, 15 November 1898

Sir,

I will not and cannot comment on my writings in direct statements to the papers.

If the question of Nemesis as such interests you, may I refer you to the Autobiography of the Danish writer Goldschmidt,[1] and his book on Nemesis, even though he frequently confuses Nemesis with Providence.

Yours faithfully,
August Strindberg

437. To GUSTAF AF GEIJERSTAM

[19? December 1898]

Dear Gustaf,

Herewith the Mystery[1] in the spirit of Swedenborg!

I've never been so uncertain whether I have succeeded or failed as now. Have no idea whether it's good or bad!

Tell me straight!

And then: to Ranft with it before having it copied!

As you can see, however, this means Over-Production! What's to be done about that? We'll shelve it, and not a word in the papers!

My journey?[2] I don't think I may! Fear 'the repetition' of so much past unpleasantness that I prefer solitude! We'll see, however!

In any case! Read *Advent* straight away and, please, send me a word by telegram, such as: 'Approbatur, Cum Laude, Non sine', or the like. Just a word! But not coloured by friendship. Criticism, Sir!

In any case: Happy Christmas to you and your family!

Yrs,
August Strindberg

438. To ELISABETH STRINDBERG

Lund, 22 December 1898

Dear Sister,

I am sending you the enclosed 25 *kronor* in time for Christmas, all I can manage for the moment.

And then just one word: you are not being persecuted by people, but by Someone Else, the one who persecuted me with the good intent that I should forget myself and think a little of others; reduce my demands on people and consider my duties towards life.

When I discovered this, I *began* to recover my peace of mind, and when I realized my misdeeds and repented, life started to go well for me, so that I was able to fulfil my duties to my children. I regard this as a miracle, and yet it was so simple!

Happy Christmas now, and seek peace in the only place where it is to be found!

Your friend,
August Sg

439. To KARIN, GRETA AND HANS STRINDBERG

Lund, 26 December 1898

Dearest Children,

It was kind of you to send me such a long letter for Christmas, which is lonely here and not particularly cheerful. So now I'm up to date with your affairs, both big and small.

You two, Karin and Greta, are no longer children, however, but young ladies, ready to go out into life.

As I've never followed advice myself, I won't give you any; for you doubtless know yourselves what brings happiness and what unhappiness.

Instead, I offer you my services, and you know of course that I have contacts, particularly as regards the theatre and literature, so when the time comes, you only need to get in touch with me. It's strange, I always imagined it would be Karin who would want to go on the stage, and Greta who would be the domestic one.[1] But I was wrong, as you see!

I have now put aside everything else and am devoting myself exclusively to writing for the theatre, so as to fulfil the promise I showed as a dramatist in my youth. I've recently finished a serious fairy-tale play in the style of Andersen's Stories,[2] and tomorrow I am going to begin one on Swedish history.[3] So you see, I don't mind Greta going into the theatre, for the Stage is after all my own art.

That I once abandoned you may have appeared reprehensible in the eyes of the world; however, I don't consider I have any right to repent of it, for I acted as if at the bidding of a higher power. And it now probably seems as if you have profited from being able to develop in greater freedom, freedom from my nagging, and freedom from the solicitude of parents who, with the best of intentions, want to direct their children's destinies. We should probably have fallen out by this stage, whereas now I count on your regarding me as a friend, who doesn't want to force his ideas on you or interfere with your spiritual life, and on whom you can rely if misfortune strikes.

Best wishes for a happy New Year, and don't forget

Your friend,
August Sg

P.S. Here is a little New Year's money for you to put in your pockets! Write if you're in need of the rent, and so on!

440. To GUSTAF AF GEIJERSTAM

Lund, 3 January 1899

Dear Friend G. af G.,

I have been left astounded by your letter and wonder: have I really written something good, or as good as you say? Now and then I certainly had my suspicions, but the depressing horrors of isolation deprived me of the courage to hope!

Now some answers, at random, to your questions. Why 'Advent'? Well, as you can see, I adopted a purely Christian, childlike point of view and conjured up the Christ-Child (you mistakenly call him 'the Angel') as the peace offering, the Only One who can undo all our evil, which we cannot do ourselves, however great our penitence and remorse (the idea was your brother Emanuel's, and does him honour!).

I've stressed this in the Christ-Child's line – 'Blame me!' Advent is also the arrival of the happy news that the Evil One was compelled, through Christ's descent into 'hell', to serve good, and that The Evil One (who is legion) is only an *Esprit correcteur* (Swedenborg's idea!), not an evil principle; in this way the Dualism of 'Good and Evil' is abolished. In the last Christmas Eve scene in Hell, Advent is explained as 'the hope or tidings that punishment is not eternal'.

The Judge and his wife are great criminals, who think they can buy the 'kingdom of heaven' and display the imagination's infinite capacity for fooling people into believing they are righteous. This fantasy is a form of punishment (according to Swedenborg) by means of which mankind is kept in a state of impenitence in order to suffer the torments of hell.

In short: the problem of Evil, both the Evil One and the Evil Ones, solved (?) from a monistic point of view.

Your suggestions for renaming the characters seem too abstract to me! If you remove the present Cover to the Manuscript, you'll see another, earlier title! Have a look![1]

By all means let Stenhammar[2] read it; but I don't write librettos! However, entractes and music accompanying my prose, together with a concluding chorus, would be fine! If he wants some songs, let him specify where!

You are also depressed! What is it? Something new or old?

I spent my Christmas Eve alone in my room with a jug of milk, and without bitterness, but meditating gratefully upon all the fine Christmas Eves Providence has given me! However, the best ones were with my own children around our own Christmas tree. Many have never experienced that! Our pretensions diminish with the years, my friend!

I both want and don't want to come to Stockholm! It is too painful! The peep-show of the past is terrible!

Once more, thank you for this last year, and good luck in your undertakings!

Your Friend,
August Strindberg

441. To HJALMAR BRANTING

Lund, 23 January 1899

My good Branting,

First: thank you for both past and present. Then, in answer to your direct question,[1] which I am certain was well meant, as follows:

I have never been anything but a writer, and the fact that in recent times we writers wanted to be prophets and politicians was, I think, to exceed our competence. 'No programme' was my old motto and still is. I reserved for myself the same freedom to develop that I granted to others. It is thus quite by chance that I am fighting alongside you as a friend of peace and universal suffrage, and you must not regard me as a political person.

Some people have a need for religion, others don't. I must have contact with *Jenseits*[2] in order to gain perspective and *lointain*[3] in my canvases, and I cannot breathe in your physical vacuum.

So: that is where we part company, and consequently we must see life and other things differently.

As regards the purely practical measure you propose, namely to persuade a majority in the Riksdag to award me a writer's stipendium: I don't want to be the poet of the majority, or the farmers, any more than I want to be a court poet. As for accepting anything from those farmers, whom we are seeking to bring down by means of the franchise for abusing their power like proper tyrants, I find it perfidious to run with them at the same time as one conspires against them.

So! Thank you once again, but I must decline!

I was once impolite to your wife – neglected to answer a letter – therefore, late in the day though it is, my apologies, which I ask you to convey together with my respects and kind regards.

Yours,
August Strindberg

442. To CARL LARSSON

Lund, 24 January 1899

Carl Larsson,

Now I must go to Canossa again! I left your last letter to me unanswered;[1] but I've been punished both by years of scruples – for it was the first time you asked a modest favour of me, you who have done me so many – and by your friendly memoir in Sv.D.[2]

Such tolerance as you show there for my faults may indicate that you consider me irresponsible or deserving of indulgence. It may also have some secret cause, such as my inability ever to forgive myself for an unworthy action or to accept praise. To me the latter always seems meant for someone else, and I don't believe in it. But my life is a cripple lacking half an ell of spine. The years between 20 and 30 are missing in me;[3] the best part. And I cannot make sense of my fate. At 19 I discover what is in Sweden the uncommon gift of writing for the theatre. I was then a half-pious soul who went down on his knees and thanked God for his grace, and began dutifully to cultivate this costly talent. But imagine yourself painting enormous canvases which never get accepted for exhibition but which you are forced to roll up and carry to the attic, where they lie around and grow old fashioned. That is what I've had to do over and over again. And it isn't true that I misused my gifts, for my most beautiful plays, *The Secret of the Guild*, *Sir Bengt's Wife*, *Damascus* and *Advent*, are never performed! while the less attractive ones are to be seen now and then, only to disappear! leaving a damp stain after them!

Where I have done wrong, I now confess my fault and feel ashamed, but where I am without guilt! – and used to feel anger, real anger! – I nowadays do not, or not so much, and simply wonder what it all means!

This jeremiad was to ask your forgiveness for my ingratitude towards you! Do you accept my apology? Answer: Yes!

Good! Then my thanks for your long and good friendship; all good wishes to you and your family, and hoping to see you in the near future!

Your friend,
August Strindberg

443. To KERSTIN STRINDBERG

[Original in German]

Lund, 1 February 1899

Dear Little One,

I have just returned from Stockholm, where I spent a few days after having celebrated my birthday. I'm now sending you some cuttings, for you to keep until you're big enough to be able to read your own language; then you'll find out who your father was in his country, and consequently in yours.

Your sister, Greta, has now made her debut – at 17. Young people begin early these days, and I'm waiting to hear something astonishing about you too one day – for instance, that your first symphony has been performed at the Royal Opera in Vienna.

So I'm back again in Lund, listening to the deadly silence and seeing the darkness. Stockholm was bright and gay, too gay, but it was pleasant to see again all my good old friends from the eighties gathered together. But otherwise tragic to wander the streets where I endured my childhood, youth and middle age. Pompei and Herculaneum beneath the ashes; not a house I could call my home.

All is over up there! *For ever*![1] And I'm now writing another play;[2] an all too human drama in which all the people are angels and do the most appalling things – just as in life! The wicked are too cunning to break the law!

What has happened to you people down there by the Danube, that you weep so much? Have you nailed your saviour so firmly to the cross, that he can't help you? Or what is it? And you have something which we do not, a figure full of compassion and grace! You know her, I do not!

And so: farewell!

Your Father

444. To RICHARD BERGH

Lund, 5 February 1899

Richard Bergh,

Didn't have time to thank you for your monograph on Nordström, but do so now. Am sending you Munch's latest, horrible masterpieces, which I detest.[1]

In seven years he hasn't had a new idea, not even found anything new to caricature.

After nature, the spirit in nature! That is what Nordström has discovered, and therefore he surely represents the logical continuation of Naturalism.

And then: thank you for the other day! I can still hear in the silence so many stifled remarks, which ought to have been completed; but the next time I come, I shall keep to the present, and not root around in the past.

Have just read Kipling for the first time.[2] The man's a perfect example of the present age. He's 'half-mad', and all his heroes are 'mad'; there's Whisky everywhere, too.

But Kipling is occult, i.e., he believes in the soul of man and touches lightly upon the Inferno problems which I framed!

So! Farewell until later on in May!

Yours,
August Strindberg

P.S. Read the Sâr Péladan!

445. To GRETA STRINDBERG

Greta Strindberg (1881–1912), actress, Strindberg's second daughter by Siri von Essen. Following his divorce from Siri in 1892, he did not see Greta until 1899, when she came to Stockholm to be converted to Catholicism ('I feared seeing her again,' he told Carl Larsson, 'but found only joy'). Although more extrovert than either Karin or Hans, she surprised him by choosing to become an actress. After appearing in several amateur productions, she made her professional debut in Helsinki, in 1900, as Sigrid in Frans Hedberg's *The Wedding at Ulfåsa*, the play in which Strindberg had failed as an aspiring actor in 1869. She moved to Stockholm to further her career in 1906, and shortly afterwards became engaged to her cousin, Henry Philp, whom she married the following year. The two saw much of Strindberg in his last years when Philp was his personal physician and Greta appeared in several of his plays. In 1907 she played Lisa in a revival of *Lucky Peter's Journey* and in 1909 the title role in *The Crown Bride*, written for her eight years earlier (Luise in *Midsummer* was another role written with Greta in mind, as was Judith in *The Dance of Death*). She was to have played the Queen opposite Anders de Wahl in the Swedish première of *Gustav Adolf*, but the project was abandoned. In 1912 she repeated her success as Kersti in *The Crown Bride* at Folkets Hus in Stockholm, in one of six productions given on 22 January to mark Strindberg's birthday and coincide with a torchlight procession of workers in his honour the same evening. Whereas he had previously communicated with her through Karin, Strindberg wrote Greta numerous letters during his final years, often to do with the theatre company with which she toured the provinces in 1909–10, performing, besides *The Crown Bride*, the première of *The Black Glove*. Her only child died at birth in 1911 while Greta herself was killed in a train accident a month after her father's death, and two months after Siri's. Eighty-three of Strindberg's letters to Greta have survived besides those addressed to all three children in his first marriage. There are also seventy-two letters from Greta to Strindberg between 1904 and 1911.

Lund, 6 February 1899

Dear little Greta,

It was good to receive a letter in your hand for once, and I was, moreover, delighted to hear that your debut went well![1]

My birthday has been celebrated here, and you have all been liberally toasted: a speech in the Gothic Rooms[2] in Stockholm; one here in Lund, and finally one in Carl Larsson's studio in Stockholm. At the latter, I replied by proposing a toast to his six children, who were present and sitting at a little childrens' table; whereupon Larsson got the six little fellows to stand up and give three cheers, which they did well. And so now I've conveyed their toasts to you!

I was up in Stockholm, which I hadn't seen since 1892, *after* my birthday. We talked business there, and a big collection of Selected Stories, which ought to bring in some money, is on the cards. But you must let me know if you've used the letter of attorney that I gave you for my Collected Works two years ago.[3] My Collected can't appear until after my death, and you oughtn't to squander that capital. Remember that Topelius' children got 125,000 *kronor* for their Father's work after his death. If you've mortgaged that document, we ought to redeem it at once. And it isn't essential, for you are my only legal heirs, even if there is no will. When my Selected Stories are published, I shall stipulate that you be paid direct from the firm at regular intervals; and perhaps a lump sum straight away for any debts!

While I remember it, I want to ask you something: if you ever hear anyone say anything disparaging about Albert Bonnier, you shouldn't join in the slander, nor try to discover whether or not it is well-founded, for this man once saved you, when you were small and in dire straights. He let us have 8,000 *kronor*. Which he didn't need to do.[4]

Even if I haven't been able to be grateful, you must try to be. You must be better than I am!

Farewell again for now, and best wishes to Putte and Karin

from
Your friend,
August Sg

446. To LEOPOLD LITTMANSSON

Lund, 21 March 1899

Good Leopold,

Since I let myself be disciplined by the spirits, I have gained another view of the world and of myself. I now believe that 'the others' are better than I, and my wicked deeds rendered my judgements of people hard and foolish. This is a confession. Believe me, the unwritten letter to your wife in Versailles still weighs upon my conscience as a black deed – against you! But at the time I was an egocentric scoundrel, led by injustice to believe that I was justified in accepting what was offered me, with no obligation to repay this with my person! I was niggardly with myself in general, and still lived according to the Old Testament principle of an eye for an eye. Unaware that everything in life is conditional, I clamoured for justice! In short, I was an AS![1] Enough said?

However: our youthful Kymmendö dream from 1873 (?) of appearing together on a Poster in Paris is now going to be realized![2]

But it occurs to me, why not have our names side by side with an & in between? And also, why didn't you become a writer? For you could construct a drama, conceive characters, and make them talk. I think it was because you didn't believe in anything; you could be enthusiastic about something for a moment, but then you squittered out! Or else – I just don't know, which is the most likely!

So! *En route*!

A detail! Please specify in the parenthesis about Beethoven's D minor Sonata, that it is particularly bars 96–107 of the Finale which should be ground out.[3] These notes always act like a centre bit drill upon my conscience. It should sound as if the player was practising these bars, that is, repeating and repeating them, with pauses in between. And so over and over again! (Did you notice that my play is based upon this sonata; fugal?). In the Prostitution scene, please choose moderately coarse words: *fille, drôlesse, ces dames*, etc.[4]

Hail and peace upon your birthday! I congratulate myself that you were born 52 years ago!

Do you need someone to revise the text? It would be a pity if you do, because in that case we'll be duped again!

Your friend,
August Strindberg

447. To GUSTAF AF GEIJERSTAM

Lund, 22 March 1899

Dear Gustaf,

Much obliged for the money!

Receipt enclosed!

Have just received the 2nd set of proofs of *Intoxication*;[1] but as they weren't accompanied by the 1st set, I can't read them, since reading the 2nd lot presupposes one can check that corrections have been made to the 1st lot. So as to gain time, I'd now like them checked at the publishers.

As for Ranft and *Intoxication*! The ending doesn't please him because it's decent (= moral), and because the woman isn't allowed to put the man down. Ten years ago my plays were rejected because they were immoral, even though they weren't. Is that my fault?

The last act is Swedenborgian, with hell *déjà*[2] on earth, and the hero of the play, the plot-maker, is the Invisible One. Does that blockhead R. understand that? No!

And then I suppose he wants to cut the prostitution scene, which I've been keeping up my sleeve for ten years! The dignity of woman, of course!

Gynolatrine – oh latrine! – latrine (A trimurti.)[3]

I'm furious, and considered getting angry with myself, but can find no justification this time! Will try again, however!

Hope Ernst[4] has got the stamps now!

Peace!

Your friend,
August Strindberg

448. To GUSTAF AF GEIJERSTAM

Lund, 9 April 1899

Dear Gustaf,

Your trials seem to be unusually prolonged and are of such a particular kind that my thoughts are oddly inveigled onto that newly-discovered track which leads to something we once called Fate, and which I now term Providentia. I may say no more! and cannot! But wish you strength and resignation to bear what you can hardly avert.[1]

I am writing my Folkung play about Magnus the Good (alias Smek), and have reached the middle of the third Act without knowing how I got there, or what it's like. For posterity, probably! – This is a secret for now!

I am collecting my Miracles;[2] for miracles occur here every day, in broad daylight, and to anyone and everyone!

So my new book will soon be ready!

Farewell!

Your friend,
August Sg

449. To KARL OTTO BONNIER

Lund, 3 May 1899

Good Karl Otto,

Firstly, I want to thank you for being so obliging over the gathering together of my diverse writings, for without your good will the project would certainly have come to nothing.[1]

Then, and since the day of reckoning has arrived, I wonder if I might trouble you with the following request. Many years ago I received a loan from Prof. Dietrichson.[2] This money was paid out by Herr Albert Bonnier. I repaid part of the debt by proof-reading and translating for Dietrichson; but the account was never settled. Can you now look in your books and see how much I owe, or will you ask Dietrichson how much he considers I owe him, including interest (if he takes that into account).[3]

As I know you won't deny me this favour, I thank you in advance, and sign myself as before,

Yours,
August Strindberg

450. To AUGUST LINDBERG

11 June 1899

August Lindberg!

The Vasa play[1] is now finished! I dread sending anything by steamer and have made three suggestions to Gustaf af G. That you, he and I meet in

Stockholm and you kindly read it, so that we can decide at once if the play ought to go to Ranft (Master Olof here is a brilliant role for you; otherwise you have Erik XIV and Göran Persson to choose between, fine lads both!) or to the Royal Theatre. This play is better 'made' than *The Saga of the Folkungs*! and doesn't lack punch!

Otherwise I suggested to G. af G. that he entice you out to him; or that you and he should meet in Stockholm. Best if I come! Don't you think?

G. af G. is staying on Skytteholm in Lake Mälaren, via the steamer *Säbyholm*!

I am in Lund!

Yrs,
August Strindberg

IX

Letters 451–608 June 1899–May 1908

Following his return to Stockholm, Strindberg was often to be found consciously reforging his links with the past. Indeed, with the exception of one brief, enforced journey to Denmark and Berlin in 1901, he lived a much more settled life, although he did move numerous times within the city, and spent several summers in the Archipelago, usually at Furusund.

He brought with him the personal, syncretic religious faith that had evolved in him during the years immediately following the Inferno crisis. While sometimes severely tested, it generally sustained him throughout the remainder of his life, as did a number of close friendships and the renewed contact he enjoyed with several members of his family, including his eldest brother, Axel, and, following her move to Stockholm in 1906 to further her stage career, his second daughter, Greta. Music also came to occupy a central role in his life, both as a listener and a dramatist. His admiration for Beethoven led to his forming what he called 'Beethovengubbarna' (The Beethoven Boys), who gathered wherever he happened to be living to play and listen to music mostly (but by no means exclusively) by Beethoven. The personnel varied but the core of the group comprised Axel Strindberg, Richard Bergh, and Vilhelm Carlheim-Gyllensköld. On occasion they were joined by the violinist Tor Aulin, the sculptor Carl Eldh, Karl Nordström, or the actors August Palme, August Lindberg, and Ivar Nilsson. Whenever he was in Stockholm, they were joined by Strindberg's loyal friend from his Lund days, Nils Andersson, with whom he also carried on a regular correspondence.

However, for Strindberg the central experience of these years was his encounter with the twenty-two year old Norwegian actress Harriet Bosse. He saw her as Puck in *A Midsummer Night's Dream* and promptly offered her the role of The Lady in the première of *To Damascus*. Shortly afterwards he offered her the role in his life. She accepted, and they embarked upon an often tempestuous marriage; but although they separated several times, their relationship continued even after they were divorced in 1904. Its complex course can be followed in the prolific correspondence which Strindberg addressed to her, as well as in his *Occult Diary*. A daughter, Anne-Marie, was born in 1902, and their time together also produced a series of major female roles, often written especially for Harriet.

These were in fact enormously productive years for Strindberg. They included four novels, among them one – *Black Banners* – which scandalized the literary establishment with its vituperative portrayal of a number of his contemporaries, including Gustaf af Geijerstam. He also wrote a further volume of autobiographical fiction, *Alone*, a collection of poems and another of fairy tales, two volumes of short stories on historical themes, a hybrid work of scholarship and speculation entitled *A Blue Book*, and twenty-five plays, including several of his very finest. But even though his work had some success on stage, especially where *Gustav Vasa* and *Crimes and Crimes* were concerned, the Swedish theatre was unable to accommodate so varied a body of work, and it was especially his most experimental plays that failed to reach an audience. Even *Miss Julie* was not performed professionally in Sweden until 1906, and while his growing recognition in Germany, achieved mainly through the efforts of Emil Schering as a translator and impresario, and Max Reinhardt as a director, went some way towards easing his financial situation, it ultimately served only to underline the lack of proper recognition at home. Thus, when he was approached by a young actor, August Falck, in 1906, with the idea of starting his own theatre, Strindberg entered into the project with enthusiasm. During the first five months of 1907 he wrote the four Chamber Plays, *Thunder in the Air*, *The Burned Site*, *The Ghost Sonata* and *The Pelican*, and on 26 November he and Falck opened the Intimate Theatre at Norra Bantorget in central Stockholm, shortly after *A Dream Play*, with Harriet Bosse in the role of Indra's Daughter, had received its world première at the Swedish Theatre. As his plans for the theatre were realized, his relationship with Harriet came to an end. In 1908 she remarried and Strindberg's correspondence with her ceased, though only after he had prepared the ground for the final stage of his life, to be lived in new quarters at 85 Drottninggatan, barely four hundred yards from the site of his most permanent childhood homes, at 12 and 14 Norrtullsgatan.

451. To ADOLF STRÖMSTEDT

Adolf Strömstedt (1860–1928), who appears in Chapter One of *Legends* as 'my friend the doctor, my psychiatrist'. Strömstedt, who was still a student at the time, was one of Strindberg's closest acquaintances in Lund, and may well have been responsible for inducing him to settle down in Skåne, alongside their mutual friend, the poet Emil Kléen. Strömstedt later moved to Gothenburg, and their contacts became occasional though affable. Seven of Strindberg's letters to him survive.

Furusund, 6 July 1899

Dear Friend,

Exceedingly kind of you to lift the veil that has concealed your fate since we parted in Lund. In Lund, where we have fought our last fight, you and I; for my term there really is at an end. I am now living in the most beautiful landscape in Sweden, *Insel der Seligen*,[1] Furusund, and shall settle in Stockholm this August to await *The Folkungs*[2] and my Collected Works. So I broke loose at last, and my prophetic spirit wasn't mistaken that time when I asked you to take your exam soon, so that I might return home to my own land, where my roots are. Yes, this is the milieu where I grew up, and I am rediscovering myself here and there every day.

Have finished *Gustav Vasa* 'at home' and am now writing *Erik XIV, con furore*; the last act of *The Folkungs* will be published in the next number of *Varia*, for July. So: a better prospect of my meeting you in Sthlm than you me in Borås! Farewell!

Kindest regards,
August Strindberg

452. To KERSTIN STRINDBERG

[Original in German]

Furusund, 8 July 1899

My dear Child!

I am astounded! You are in Den Haag?[1] At the Peace Congress? And with whom? Are you there with the 'fury of peace', Bertha von Suttner,[2] or what? Your photograph was certainly signed at Den Haag!

Your Rose Room[3] letter has just arrived, and I'm answering it in rose coloured ink.

Yes, your picture! Grandfather's flashing eyes and your own face! Really special! and that is what's best! But you mustn't tyrannize me, and demand to know everything!

Anyway, I'm writing and writing, every day, to get lots of money for your brothers and sisters; young ladies need beautiful clothes, and young Hans has got a bicycle.

Greta is coming to Stockholm next Monday to be confirmed into the Catholic Church, in no way my doing, for as ever I'm a Christian without a specific creed. I don't know if I shall meet Greta, for she is bringing her mother with her, whom I never want to see again; besides, I can't, it could cost me a spell in prison.

I am now living here amidst the most beautiful scenery in Europe. A lady writing last year in German described it as '*Insel der Seligen*'. It is certainly beautiful, and young people and children wander around in light clothes, beneath oaks and birches, in green meadows, lawns, groves, woods and by the shore. And the sun shines hot. The sea is quite warm. In the evenings

I sit on the verandah with my sister.[4] Steamers and sailing ships pass by on their way to Russia, Finland and Lapland, which enlivens the picture. My sister often plays Beethoven, for me the summit of music, while my brother-in-law and I smoke and drink punch. Your cousins are beautiful, pleasant, sweet girls of 16 and 17, with strong family feelings, that is, they feel a loyalty to all their relations and bid you welcome to their beautiful villa. My brother-in-law, a Doctor of Philosophy and well-to-do man (consequently no Strindberg but a Philp), is a director of the bathing society, where I never go. I am now writing a tragedy, *Erik XIV*, taken from Swedish history. Gustav Vasa's son, Erik wanted to marry Elisabeth of England; later he courted Mary Queen of Scots – and ended up marrying a Corporal's daughter from Stockholm (who sold nuts in the market). He ended his days in prison, poisoned by his brother Johan III. A fine story! – Now you know more of my secrets than anyone else. But you are never satisfied, and demand to know still more (like a jealous woman), you would like to know more than I know myself, you little tyrant!

But enough ticking off, and peace! Kiss of peace and all's well, as in Den Haag!

Your Pappa August

453. To NILS ANDERSSON

Nils Andersson (1864–1921). Of all the friends that Strindberg made in Lund during the late 1890s, Andersson proved the most loyal, and their correspondence was one of the most intimate and voluminous of his final years. Over one hundred and fifty of Strindberg's letters to Andersson survive, ninety-seven of them written between May 1907 and April 1912. A lawyer by vocation, Andersson held a series of administrative and legal posts (he was both Clerk to the Justices and Mayor of Lund), but he is now remembered as an enthusiastic amateur musicologist and collector of folk music. Many of the *c.* 12,000 melodies that he gathered on field trips throughout Sweden were published posthumously as *Svenska låtar* (1922–40), the most comprehensive and important of all collections of Swedish folk music. Sixty-eight of Andersson's letters to Strindberg have also survived.

Furusund, 7 August 1899

Dear Nils Andersson,

I dare write you this letter because our long talks last winter have given you the grounds for understanding it.

When I decided to come to your wedding, I was overwhelmed by an inexplicable feeling of dread, which lasted several days and nights. Finally, I woke up one morning resolving not to go: and that very moment, my oppression ceased; I became dead calm, and a work I had begun, which had dried up, began to flow again. It was as if I'd escaped an unknown danger, and I felt glad and thankful.

Yesterday, Sunday, I opened the Bible and my eyes immediately alighted upon Kings I, Chapter 13, verse 15ff.

'Then he said unto him, Come home with me, and eat bread.

And he said, I may not return with thee, nor go in with thee: neither will I eat bread nor drink water with thee in this place:

For it was said to me by the word of the Lord: *Thou shalt [. . . not] turn again to go by the way thou camest.*'

With that, *I* knew for certain that this journey ought not to take place! Whether or not you approve my motivation, I cannot come!

However, you saw how I longed to meet you, and hence can judge that my friendship was not all too fleeting!

And now: good fortune in your great undertaking. You are approaching the greatest happiness life affords, even if it is as dreamlike in nature as the whole of existence!

Your friend,
August Strindberg

454. To NILS ANDERSSON

5 Narvavägen^{III}, Sthlm. 9 September 1899

Dear Nils Andersson,

I lost you at the time of your marriage and found you again in Lund a married man, fond of your home, happy and liberated from the tavern. And I congratulate you! for you are now embarking upon the best part of your life!

Mine is just the same. Mostly alone although I have at least 1,000 acquaintances here. As in Lund, my day passes prison-like until evening, with food on a tray. Do I feel at home? No, I'm not at home anywhere, have never been happy here in life, and believe, like Stagnelius,[1] who I've recently re-read, that I am an aeon sent down from some better sphere to be tormented here below. And yet things are going well; and I can work. Am now full of Karl IX, a real 'tough nut' to deal with.[2]

Ranft thinks he will be able to mount *Gustav Vasa* in October; with de Wahl[3] as Erik XIV! But you mustn't mention this to anyone yet!

There are moments when I long to be back in Lund, but that is only an illusion; for it is no longer the same; it had already changed by the end; and it doesn't matter where I am, for I can't get away from myself! So I shall stay where I am! and dream of three rooms and a kitchen with my own housekeeper – if only I could find an Elna (65, honest and considerate)! – then I wouldn't need to go to the tavern of an evening!

I don't like the theatres, or find them diverting either!

Hope to see you again in Stockholm this autumn!

Regards to all my old friends in Lund, and with respects to your young wife!

Yours affectionately,
August Strindberg

455. To ALBERT RANFT

Albert Ranft (1858–1938), actor and theatre manager. After appearing with August Lindberg's company, Ranft spent two periods as a director with the Grand Theatre in Gothenburg before moving to the capital, where he became known as 'Stockholm's Theatre King'. At one time he controlled a series of venues including the Vasa Theatre, the Swedish Theatre, Djurgården Theatre, the Southside Theatre, and the Östermalm Theatre, as well as the Grand in Gothenburg and, between 1908 and 1911, the Royal Theatre itself. Thus Strindberg had often to deal with him over practical matters, and though Ranft's own taste in drama was naive and unsure, the Swedish Theatre in particular became associated with his work. Under Ranft's rule, some fifteen of Strindberg's plays were performed there, including the premières of *Gustav Vasa, Erik XIV, Midsummer, Engelbrekt* and, most notable of all, *A Dream Play* in 1907, even if Victor Castegren's direction sadly failed to solve the problems with which the text confronted him. Thirty-two of Strindberg's letters to Ranft have survived.

19 October, 1899

Dear Albert Ranft,

I have to thank you for helping me reach the public with my *Gustav Vasa,* and for its arriving so well fitted out in every way.[1]

So far as the fairy-tale play we spoke about is concerned, that has been put to one side for *Gustav Adolf,* which is now in progress. In conversation with Molander yesterday, M. said he would ask you whether *Erik XIV* might not follow on immediately from *Gustav Vasa* while the public still had the characters fresh in their minds, and so that the Trilogy (*M. Olof, G. Vasa, Erik XIV*) would be ready for the spring. I should naturally be pleased if things started moving, and would go on more happily with my present task if nothing remaining on the shelf. As you know, *Erik XIV* is not at all costly. Molander also threw out some possible suggestions as to casting, which I and P. Staaff[2] accepted. It came out like this:

Erik XIV = Lindberg.
Göran = Hillberg.
Karin = Fru Sandell.
Måns Knekt = Gustaf Ranft.
Svante Sture = Svennberg.
What do you think?[3]

Another suggestion is that *Crimes and Crimes*, which has been sold to Berlin, Vienna and Breslau, could, if you wanted some variety in the programme, easily be put on with Svennberg, Gösta Hillberg (whom I and my friends greatly admired in *Gustav Vasa*) and Fru Håkansson.[4] Do you incline more to that?

In any event, having waited so painfully long, please let me come up once more before the summer! You know I have thirty plays ready, among them *Damascus*, which Molander has already found ways of doing with simplified settings, kept in a half-unreal tone that corresponds to the play's dreamlike character. Etc. Etc.

And so finally, once again a warm handshake by way of thanks and for the future!

Yours sincerely,
August Strindberg

456. To HARALD MOLANDER

25 November 1899

My dear Molander,

While there's still time, I'd like to make a few observations concerning the production of *Erik XIV*, and the way in which the roles are perceived.

(1) Måns Knekt ought to be seen as a *bona fide* man; underclass certainly, but sensitive about the dishonour he suffers through his daughter. The hatred he feels for her destroys his respect for the king. In the scene where Erik and Karin enter Måns' kitchen, Måns oughtn't to know what to do. Therefore he remains silent; but here there ought also to be a trace of vengeful pleasure in someone from the underclass who has got a 'master' beneath his heel.

In the final scene, at the wedding, Måns, after his entrance, starts off merely clumsy in his goodwill, and his awkwardness is wounding. At table he is sober (completely!) and only asks to speak out of embarrassment! N.B. his prompt recognition of Johan III is due to his being a soldier, which has taught him discipline and blind worship for his master, whoever that may be (provided he hasn't seduced his daughter!).

(2) The final scene must be played like this: while Erik and Johan [*sic*][1] philosophize over their fate, the eating and drinking should cease; the

lackeys stand upright and still; the dinner guests sit absolutely silent and absolutely still, looking like ghosts. At this point, don't you think there ought to be some plucked string music off-stage – muted – to heighten the atmosphere and motivate the silence and immobility of the guests, who are listening to the table music. My suggestion is the moving gavotte, or whatever it's called, which opens Act I of Bjørnson's *Mary Stuart*,[2] and ought to be in the archives of the R. Opera. Otherwise the music director of the Sw. Theatre ought to borrow Berggreen's *Folksongs and Melodies*[3] from the R. Library (my brother Axel at Nordstjernan has a copy!), and choose some old English or Scottish melody from there, one we haven't heard before, and arrange it for strings (but *Pizzicato*). The melody ought to be mournful, solemn!

(3) I've spoken to de Wahl[4] about leaving out the line: 'Do you want to be queen?', because it's superfluous, a mistake (or pure stupidity), and lets the cat out of the bag!

(4) Remember: 'Emotional tripe' instead of 'shit', etc.

Etc.

I'll come to the Dress Rehearsal on Monday.

Recommending myself to your best memory, and committing myself and my play to your especial care, I remain

Yours,
August Strindberg

31 Banérgatan, Sthlm.
Telephone: Ö.M. 29.46.

457. To OSCAR STRINDBERG

Sthlm. 2 January 1900

Dear Brother,

If you're in touch with Olle,[1] let him know I have a pile of excellent clothes that would probably fit him, now that I've put on weight.

I don't want to write myself because I'm afraid of hurting his feelings.

In haste. Yrs,
August

If he wants to come to Sthlm, I'll pay for his ticket, return too!

458. To HJALMAR ÖHRVALL

Hjalmar August Öhrvall (1851–1929), physiologist and, in his early years, one of the leading radicals in the Verdandi Society in Uppsala. Appointed Professor there in 1899. Öhrvall first met Strindberg in Stockholm, in 1884.

They corresponded briefly on scientific topics during the early 1890s, and though Öhrvall rejected his theories, Strindberg remained on good terms with him, and sometimes invited him to the Beethoven evenings which he arranged for his friends during his last years.

19 February 1900

My dear Friend,

I've heard a rumour that the Society of Stockholm Students in Uppsala is planning to elect me an honorary member. Whether or not there's any truth in it, I beg you to avert this in good time, for I have made up my mind never to accept any outward honours, office or titles.

The reason is fully explained in my latest writings, and I don't want to repeat it. That it isn't from pride is surely quite evident.

Please, do me this favour; but discreetly, without any fuss, and in good time, so that I don't have to hurt anyone's feelings by declining.

In haste. Yrs,
August Strindberg

459. To EMIL SCHERING

[Original in German][1]

31 Banérgatan, Stockholm, 26 March 1900

Grateful; but I am not an educator, only a poet who on his pilgrimage lives through all the stations of human experience in order to be able to portray humanity! Experimenting with standpoints and ideas; scientist and experimental object at one and the same time. Nothing more!

August Strindberg

460. To GUSTAF AF GEIJERSTAM

4 May 1900

My dear Gustaf,

Only this morning did I hear about the end of Nennie's saga! I am at a loss for words, and we are poor comforters; but if you have need of a sympathetic ear, you know I am ready to come and sit with you![1]

My regards to the boys – – –

And forgive my recent unsociability; but I have been absorbed in myself since Easter, and afraid of contacts!

Your Friend,
August Strindberg

461. To NILS ANDERSSON

8 July 1900

Dear Nils Andersson,

Such are life's ups and downs, this general uncertainty designed to keep us awake by means of a salutary fear.

I had counted on a cheerful (?) summer; caught a fever and cough as soon as I left town; and a black veil settled down upon nature, life and my fellow men. So I longed to return to my lair, which is where I am now, alone! As alone as when you and Gillberg[1] discovered me in Tomegapsgatan! One might have thought life would be a little brighter for me now, but that's hardly so. Unfortunately, my work no longer affords me the same pleasure as before. And in the end, it's no doubt life's meaning that one shouldn't enjoy oneself, but do what one can and remain calm – in a word, do penance. I also have a presentiment that in two years time I'll be out of the game, for I'm already drying up, and no longer sit down to write with the same feeling of delight as before. So I'll probably finish up impoverished once again! That's what it feels like!

However, I've gained this much, that when I depart this life, nothing will hold me here, and I shall miss nothing! That is something!

I've no business in Lund; I've done my time there and would only wander around the statue of Tegnér and to Åke Hans' like an anachronism!

So: I'm staying where I am, and cannot do otherwise!

Give my regards to De Wahl and ask him to read *The Folkungs* before we meet – this autumn!

Gillberg, who only lives amongst human misery and squabbling, can't help growing old before his time; or getting a melancholy view of life. My regards to him! And my other friends!

Yours affectionately,
August Strindberg

462. To EMIL GRANDINSON

Emil Grandinson (1863–1915), theatre director and writer. Apart from August Falck, Grandinson was perhaps the most responsive of contemporary Swedish directors to the demands of Strindberg's late dramas. Certainly, he was willing to seek new ways of projecting the hallucinatory inner reality of the post-Inferno plays on stage. In his *Open Letters to the Intimate Theatre*, Strindberg acknowledged that Grandinson 'went beyond Harald Molander's externals, and admitted I was right when I was right, seeing that the effect or the impact of the play depended on something other than what was piquant in the situation and the scenic effects'. The play in question, *To Damascus I*, was staged at the Royal Theatre in 1900, with August Palme as The Unknown and Harriet Bosse as the Lady. According to Strindberg it was 'a masterpiece of direction', and Grandinson, who had already directed *Crimes and Crimes*, followed it with *Easter* in 1901, *Charles XII* (1902), *The Last Knight* (1909) and *The Black Glove* (1911). Sixty-nine of Strindberg's letters to Grandinson survive, twenty-eight of them written during a six-month period in 1908–09 about the première of his historical drama *The Last Knight*.

Sthlm. 25 October 1900

My dear Grandinson,

The moment is almost upon us, and we must be prepared for some resistance to innovation by the public. Therefore, on further consideration, I suggest there should be no interval before the *Asylum*. – – – The audience must be kept in their seats and in the mood that long if they are to be drawn into the action. If we let them out to discuss things, and arm themselves for conscious resistence, then we can lose the play. The scene changes up to that point must take place in blackout, but without a curtain. As soon as the curtain comes down, an audience gives itself a shake and rejects what it's seen! As you know, in Germany they have only one interval: in the middle of the play.

If you agree, cancel Halldén's[1] superfluous interval music at once. But I go along with Bethoven's [*sic*] *Largo e Mesto* as overture.[2]

The winds aren't blowing as favourably for me now as they did last season. Therefore I'm prepared for hostility!

If you would divide the acts differently, then let me know!

Yrs,
August Strindberg

463. To LEOPOLD LITTMANSSON

1 November 1900

My dear Leopold,

Yes, I've been mulling over coming to Paris for two months, possibly combined with a trip to Switzerland; there's nothing really preventing me, but I don't think I have 'permission'; at least not for Paris! Your guest room in Versailles sounds attractive, assuming your wife has forgiven me my last excursion! But I don't know!

Will you start by giving me Antoine's full address, and I'll try to get the manuscript out of him.[1] (Street and number of his theatre or house.) As a last resort: does M. Roger, the Secretary to the Société des Auteurs, to which we both belong, undertake such tasks? Doesn't Antoine reply?

Another way would be . . . but that is too bitter for you, who haven't emptied every last cup of bitterness as I have. You can probably guess! Canossa on the rue de la Pompe![2]

What's the matter with your nerves? Is it your head like me? – – – A 'call' in life? A 'choice'? Old Søren Kierkegaard cured nerves with horse medicine! The choice and a calling!

Zarathustra doesn't cure anything! couldn't even cure his own Master![3] who was finally transformed into a Loon (he screamed like one at the approach of bad weather)! –

It would have been simpler if you'd asked your girls about the puppets,[4] and written the characters' names on a card! Now: Peace again!

Yrs,
August Strindberg

464. To NILS PERSONNE

Nils Edvard Personne (1850–1928), actor and theatre director. Personne had been engaged at the Royal Theatre since 1876 and became its leader in 1898, at the head of an actor's consortium. Under his regime, Strindberg's relationship with the theatre improved. Productions of *Crimes and Crimes* and *To Damascus I* in 1900 were followed by *Easter* and *Casper's Shrove Tuesday* in 1901, and *Simoom* and *Charles XII* in 1902. However, Personne refused both *The Dance of Death* and *Gustav III*, and their relationship was never more than an occasionally working one. There are nine extant letters from Strindberg to Personne, and four cards.

17 November 1900

Dear Nils Personne,

Thank you for your friendly words about my plays,[1] which I also take to be a definite acceptance. And I depend upon their being played next Lent. For if you fail me, it will cost me a year . . . and that's a long time to wait now, when life is rushing past.

Next year Shrove Tuesday is 19 February. If it's performed then, without flogging it to death, it could be revived in Easter Week. Or else wait for Holy Week!

Just a word about the girl (Eleonora's) part![2] You know my weakness for Fröken Bosse.[3] I miss the fund of poetry and 'Seriousness' which she possesses in her colleagues; and her childlike figure is well suited for a girl with a pigtail down her back.

The role of her brother is no bravura part, but Palme[4] would no doubt take it and give it a breath of his irresistible lyricism.

If you, *mon Directeur*, would honour me by playing Lindqvist and give that terrible creature a touch of humour, I would be eternally grateful!

I believe it requires a girl (but with short hair) as Benjamin, for young rascals of that age are extremely unpoetical.

So . . . we have never signed a contract before, and won't write one this time either, but depend on our word and common interests!

Yours,
August Strindberg

31 Banérgatan, Sthlm.
Tel.: Ö: 29.46

465. To HARRIET BOSSE

Harriet Bosse (1878–1961), actress. Born in Norway of Danish and German ancestry, she studied music in Stockholm and acting in Christiania before making her stage debut at the Fahlstrøm Theatre there, in 1898. After a further period of study, this time at the Paris Conservatoire under Maurice de Féraudy, she moved to Sweden and in 1899 was engaged by the Royal Theatre, where she made her first appearance as Loyse in Théodore de Banville's *Gringoire*. Having charmed Strindberg as Puck in *A Midsummer Night's Dream*, she was chosen to play The Lady in the première of *To Damascus*. Her subdued, allusive, non-declamatory style of acting made her an admirable choice for the part, and following her success Strindberg soon invited her to assume the role in his life. They married on 6 May 1901, but from the outset their relationship was marked by conflict, occasioned not least by the difference in their ages. When Strindberg claimed he had been forbidden by higher powers to embark on their honeymoon, the impatient and independent-minded Harriet left for Denmark on her own. Although Strindberg soon followed, they were shortly to part again, but even after their divorce in 1904, they continued to meet, and remained lovers until 1907. Indeed, even after her engagement to the actor Gunnar Wingård, whom she married in 1908, Strindberg continued to consort with her in telepathic intercourse on what he called 'the astral plane', and both his *Occult Diary* and the letters to Bosse, of which some two hundred survive, provide a detailed account of a relationship that was also sustained by Strindberg's deep affection for their daughter, Anne-Marie, born in 1902. Moreover, the role that Harriet played in Strindberg's life between 1901 and 1908 was also central to his development as a dramatist: he wrote several parts with her in mind, notably Indra's Daughter in *A Dream Play*, which was partly inspired by her exotic, Eastern features, Queen Christina, Swanwhite, and Emerentia Pohlhem in *Charles XII*.

Early on in their relationship, Strindberg invited Harriet to become the actress of the new century and in substituting an intense and eloquent spiritual inwardness for the stilted, declamatory style that prevailed when she arrived in Stockholm, she made herself one of the foremost actresses of the day, and played a key role in the emergence of the new drama. In addition to her many successes in Strindberg's plays, including Eleonora in *Easter*, Kersti in *The Crown Bride*, and Henriette in *Crimes and Crimes*, she triumphed in Shakespeare (as Juliet, Viola and Cleopatra), Shaw (as Ann Whitefield, Liza Doolittle and St Joan), Ibsen (Hilde Wangel), Maeterlinck (Mélisande), and as Elektra in Hugo von Hoffmannsthal's reworking of Sophocles' play, in which her performance was celebrated for its vivid combination of cruelty, passion and beauty. Following the failure of her marriage to Wingård, who committed suicide in 1912, she married another actor, Edvin Adolphson, in 1927, but this marriage, too, was short-lived. In 1932 she published the majority of Strindberg's letters to her with some cuts and a brief commentary. Unfortunately, only twenty-two of her letters to Strindberg survive.

19 November 1900

Fröken Harriet Bosse,

Since I shall not be at the theatre tonight, I wish to thank you now for what I saw at the dress rehearsal.[1] It was great and beautiful (Damascus), although I had imagined the character somewhat lighter, with little touches of mischief and with more expansiveness.

A little of Puck! – those were my first words to you! and will be my last!

A smile in the midst of misery suggests the existence of hope, and the situation doesn't turn out to be hopeless after all!

And now: good luck on this journey between thorns and stones! Such is the way! I am merely placing a few flowers upon it!

August Strindberg

466. To HARRIET BOSSE

5 December 1900

Fröken Harriet Bosse,

Having in mind that our Journey to Damascus ended today, I ordered some roses – with thorns of course – there seem to be no others! And am sending them with a simple 'thank you': now become the actress of the new century here with us! You have let us hear new tones, no matter where you found them! And let me hope to hear you again – next spring – in *Easter*, as I understand you've promised me!

August Strindberg

467. To GUSTAF AF GEIJERSTAM

Sthlm. 27 December 1900

G. af G.,

In order to avoid a break, which must nevertheless end in a time-wasting reconciliation, I am writing this letter.

You have probably noticed, just as I have, that when our heterogeneous mental spheres enter into repulsion, we become estranged from each other for a shorter or longer period, but that we finally meet again, against our will, as if we were predetermined to exert an influence on each other's destiny, to our mutual advantage.

Last spring, April I think it was, you experienced a longing to distance yourself from me, and you took your farewell in more or less the following words: 'Now I want to draw back and compose my own self, live my own life for a while, etc.' I understood you completely and kept away, without a trace of bitterness.

I have now reached the same point! And into the bargain, I feel something sick in your personality, which oppresses me and threatens to make me sick. I also experienced something menacing in your way of behaving, a desire, maybe with good intent – to interfere in my destiny!

You have, for example, sought to rule my sympathies and antipathies, to determine the company I keep, to force opinions upon me, and so on.

I am retiring, and I beg you: do not seek me before I seek you. I risk your refusing to see me then. Well, if so, I shall have to bear it!

You have recently declared yourself in favour of the great justification of individual liberty. In that case, respect mine too.

We can conduct our business relations by post. But even in that respect I could wish for a little more self-determination. Thus your wilfulness over the illustrations to *Somnambulist Nights* displeased me, when outsiders were consulted but not me, the author. The illustrator of a poem should follow the Poet, not put himself above him, not criticize him or find in the poet an opportunity to vent his own feelings, etc.

So I wish you a good end to this old year, and all the best in the coming new one!

As before, yours

August Strindberg

468. To VILHELM CARLHEIM-GYLLENSKÖLD

2 January 1901

Carlheim-Gyllensköld,

If you'd like to spend the evening with me on Saturday, from 7? p.m., along with Richard Bergh and my brother Axel, who will play a little Beethoven for us, then let me know by 'phone.

Yours,
August Strindberg

Ö:29.46

469. To EMIL SCHERING

Sthlm. 4 January 1901

Dear Sir,

The day before yesterday I sent you an untitled manuscript.[1] It was to be called 'The Vampire', but can now be included as a component in *The Dance of Death.*

Or do you think the whole play should be called 'The Vampire'?

Yours,
August Strindberg

470. To RICHARD BERGH

Sthlm. 30 January 1901

Dear Richard Bergh,

First: thank you for the books! *Beyond*[1] which I read yesterday, Swedenborg's birthday, with a heavy heart and put down in the evening with a sigh of gratitude, *de profundis*, from the depths of my soul . . . complements what Fru Skram's *Hieronymus*[2] offered the author of *Inferno.* May I lend *Beyond* to Fröken Bosse so as to initiate her into the world of *Easter*, where she plays a girl who is distantly related to Swedenborg's niece, Séraphita, so wonderfully portrayed by Balzac? My figure is called Eleonora, and has entered into telepathic rapport with the whole of humanity, realized 'Christ in Man', and suffers all the suffering of mankind in herself, most of all her father's, who is in prison for his crimes.

I would rather St Francis had been portrayed by Maeterlinck than by Sabatier.[3]

And then Maeterlinck! His book[4] was published in 1896, my Inferno and Damascus year! I was probably not permitted to read the book that year; now I have received it, after my Virgil – Swedenborg – had guided me through all the nine circles of Inferno.

What did Maeterlinck say in 1896, in 'Le Réveil de l'âme'? 'A time is approaching . . . when our souls will see each other without the intermediary of our senses.' '*On dirait que nous approchons d'une période spirituelle. . .*

Et l'on trouve partout, à côté des traces de la vie ordinaire, les traces ondoyantes d'une autre vie qu'on ne s'explique pas.'

'It is a matter of discovering a super-sensual (transcendental) psychology which is devoted to the direct relationships that exist between soul and soul *et de la sensibilité ainsi que de la présence extraordinaire de notre âme.'*

'Les signes et les mots ne servent plus de rien, et presque tout se décide dans les cercles mystiques d'une simple présence.'

Listen to this! 'People judge one another *par-dessus les paroles et les actes et jusque par-dessus les pensées. Car ce qu'ils voient sans le comprendre est situé bien au delà du domaine des pensées!*'[5]

This tells me I was right to distance myself from G.,[6] without needing or being able to explain why.

And it indicates to me that the afflictions of the mind are not all punishments or insanity.

Can you try and get hold of Maeterlinck's plays here in Stockholm! Someone ought to have them! K. Warburg? P. Staaff? O. Levertin? Tor Hedberg?

I want to translate one and get it performed! Maeterlinck is not 'passé' as G. maintained when he wished to obstruct my new theatre.

Won't you soon be ripe for Joséphin Péladan? The greatest, a man of beauty, who heralded *l'époque spirituelle* before Maeterlinck? In his novels *L'Initiation sentimentale, L'Androgyne, Gynandre, Le Vice suprême, Istar, Typhonia* (*à* 2 F. 50).

Will you come on Saturday evening from 6 p.m., with music if Axel can bring some Brahms? R.S.V.P.

Yours,
August Strindberg

471. To HARRIET BOSSE

Sthlm. 8 February 1901

Kind Fröken Bosse,

Happy to have had a talk with you at last about *Easter*, I now feel I forgot so much of what I wanted to say to you, and I am also afraid of appearing to want to interfere in your development. But as you so charmingly and kindly thanked me today, when it was I who wanted to thank you, I will start with a few words about Eleonora, and then go on to something else!

Family troubles have brought Eleonora to a state of mind, some would call it an illness, which has enabled her to enter into rapport (telepathic) both with her relatives and with mankind as a whole, and finally with the lower forms of creation, so that she suffers with all living things, or realizes the idea of 'Christ in Man'. She is therefore related to Balzac's Séraphita,

Swedenborg's Niece, whose acquaintance I meant to recommend to you as an introduction to *Easter* – had I not feared – yes! – making a nuisance of myself. I also intended asking you to read Hannah Joël's *Beyond*, Fru Skram's *Hieronymus*, and – above all – Maeterlinck's *Le Trésor des humbles*. But as I've just said, I was afraid you wouldn't appreciate instruction!

However, as regards the keynote of the role: serious, of course, but Eleonora must be kind and tender, and should prattle and babble with Benjamin, prettily like a child playing at being mother. Never hard or even severe, for she pretends she is so would-be-wise, and one never knows what she believes, though she has a cheerful, childlike trust –

To show she has brought an angel of peace with her, as her mother says, you must keep her bright, gentle, and above all not be harsh or preach like our pietists. And, note well, when Benjamin asks if she's a pietist, and she answers yes, she does so merely to cut short an indiscreet question, it's not a profession of faith.

For our pietists can't smile – and Eleonora can, because she believes in a good God who can forgive, even though he delights in frightening children.

You know, it may sound strange, but as in *Damascus*, I think I'd like 'a little of Puck', roguishness! Sad, by all means, but not severe!

I was impertinent enough today to advise against a tour. I can't really say why, but I knew that the people who wish you well above all others, your sister and brother-in-law,[1] had advised you against it. This no doubt influenced me!

And then: I beg you to read the enclosed play[2] and see whether your role there might attract you.

The piece has been submitted to the Opera, remember, but hasn't yet been accepted.

It's an attempt on my part to enter Maeterlinck's wonderful world of beauty, giving up analyses, questions and opinions, and seeking only beauty in colour and mood. I know I've only stopped at the threshold; I must burn the rubbish in my soul before I am worthy of entering.

Please read the directions carefully and play the melodies – the ancient tones of Swedish folk music. Kersti is not so hopelessly wicked that you need fear the contact.

Finally, I beg you not to involve anyone apart from your most trusted friends outside the theatre in this matter, you know from above who I mean!

Another time, soon, I hope to hear your impression of *La Princesse Maleine*,[3] and after you have read *The Crown Bride*, I shall introduce you to the delightful girl Judith in *The Dance of Death*.

August Strindberg

472. To RICHARD BERGH

14 February 1901

Richard Bergh,

Assuming I am well on Saturday, I would like to see you at my Beethoven supper. Have been ill – in an almost occult fever – with telepathic spasms – – –

My house is now full of Maeterlinck and Péladan.

Péladan is a Giant! He has written the missing Parts I and III of Aeschylus' *Prometheus* and translated Part II, or the extant middle piece.[1] He has surpassed the master! A piece of effrontery which has come off! How rare!

I have three of his plays; it is food for lions, and ought to be read by Per Hallström[2] and others.

I also have a novel, and am waiting for more.

Péladan and Maeterlinck come from the same root: Parisian Occultism derived from Balzac's *Séraphita, Ursule Mirouet*, etc., and Barbey d'Aurevilly (*Les Diaboliques*)[3] – So: respect for Maeterlinck! make way for Sâr Péladan.

Yours,
August Strindberg

473. To RICHARD BERGH

31 Banérgatan, 16 February 1901

Richard Bergh,

Yesterday evening you mentioned an Italian monastery where it's possible to find board and lodging.

1. Does one have to pay?
2. Where is the monastery?
3. What is it called?
4. Can one write to them?
5. And is only Italian spoken? Can't one get by with Latin or French?

I know a monastery that takes boarders in the Salzkammergut, but it's too near to my old battlefields, and would reopen old wounds.

In Maredsous, in the Ardennes, where I'm expected, you don't have to pay.

Even if I didn't enter it for life, I long to go there, away from here. And I believe my personal presence here at home only has an irritating, disturbing effect on other people's tranquil labours.

Now that I have fulfilled the promise of my youth and done my duty to my country, I think it would be becoming to disappear; I almost feel I owe it to public modesty to hide my lumbering, blundering self. And let my works speak! for themselves!

So: please, simply write the address on a card!

Yours,
August Strindberg

474. To RICHARD BERGH

Sthlm. 18 February 1901

Richard Bergh,

Yes, by all means ask Fru Nyblom, for with every day that passes I find this milieu ever more alien, and the isolation I seek under an unknown compulsion is closing in like darkness upon me.

By isolating myself from contact with the banalities of life, my sensitivity has increased and I shall soon not even be able to bear other people looking at me – – – I await a change in my destiny – a great crisis – a total break with the past. Perhaps the end of a road which now seems to me so dreamlike.

Therefore I am arranging my earthly affairs and preparing for my departure.

When you've read *The Crown Bride*, please let's meet so I may hear your impression.

Your friend,
August Strindberg

475. To HARRIET BOSSE

25 February 1901

Fröken Harriet Bosse,

You must retain a little patience with me and my correspondence, which ultimately has in view our great common interest: Eleonora. That is also the purpose of the books I keep sending you. You say that the role is so sensitive that it can scarcely stand being touched. Right, therefore I won't analyse it or take it apart, nor philosophize about it. On the other hand, however, I didn't want you to fall into the traditional method of portraying someone who is mentally ill. You surely won't do that, for you seem to be born with all the ideas of the new century.

I noticed, too, after you'd read Hannah Joël and Maeterlinck, that you'd discovered a certain relationship, an affinity of soul, a way of seeing the world and things – and therefore I'm content to suggest those things which can't be put into words.

Yesterday I sent you some Kipling; exclusively for the last story, 'The Brushwood Boy'.

Apropos Eleonora's double life in her dreams, where she makes contact with distant relations.

As I said: don't study the books, just glance through them, and you'll find help in the hints they contain.

Why did I send you the bizarre *Le Prince de Byzance*?[1] That's a very long story, which would need to begin with Eleonora's relative, Balzac's Séraphita-Séraphitus, the Angel, for whom earthly love does not exist because he-she is *l'époux et l'épouse de l'humanité*.[2] A symbol of the highest, most perfect type of man, which often figures in the most modern literature, and which is taken by some to be on its way down here to us. Don't demand an explanation now, but store the word in your memory. One day, when this type of relationship falls within your sphere of experience, the word may cast some light on the matter. (Fru Boberg touches on the theme in *Tirfing*,[3] and has probably been misunderstood.)

One detail, while I remember it! On page 15 of *Easter* there is a retort so cruel that – I am ashamed, and feel I wrong Eleonora by using it. May I trouble you to change that terrible word of Benjamin's, 'eat off' to 'sit out'.

And have it inserted, together with the previous corrections, in the prompter's and the director's copies 'at the author's request'.

[no signature]

476. To HARRIET BOSSE

1 March 1901

Kind Fröken Bosse,

Come and give me your impression of *Damascus III* before it has been diluted by something else.

I attach so much value to your opinion – because you have acted the role of the Lady, you understand![1]

Yours sincerely,
August Strindberg

Ö:29.46.

477. To KERSTIN STRINDBERG

[Original in German]

11 March 1901

My dearest, dearest, Child! Forgive me, but I was ill with fever when your last dear picture arrived. Do you think I could ever forget you, you who led me through Inferno as my Beatrice, by way of gorge[1] and path of lamentation, through anguished nights and evil days? Oh no! I am not like that, nor ever will be!

All plays contain changes of scene, and changes of dramatis personae too, but in the last act, they all reappear, and the author mustn't forget a single one of them. Such is the eternal law of drama, and of life! And woe to him who forgets it! So now you know!

God bless you and all who hold you dear!

Your *Father*

478. To AXEL STRINDBERG

Sthlm. 21 March 1901

Dear Brother,

Will you play some Beethoven for your friends in my rooms on Saturday at 7?

Since we've taken a flat and intend to get married in April the bachelor suppers have been replaced by well-filled family sandwiches. Otherwise everything as before!

R.S.V.P.

Yours,
August Sg

479. To EMIL SCHERING

[25? March 1901]

Dear Herr Schering,

Your inexhaustible good will follows us here like a warming spring wind; you are, as it were, holding a back door open to freedom for us prisoners.[1]

However, my bride is just as afraid of hubris ('υβηις) as I am. She is delighted by the hospitality that Germany extends her, but also fears it.

Moreover, as we are getting married on 15 April, all our attention is currently focused on that. Nevertheless, let us keep the question open!

The news about *Gustav Adolf* is so tremendous, that I quail!

Imagine, the day before yesterday I resigned myself to the cancellation of *Gustav Adolf* at the Swedish Theatre here. The storm last autumn was too strong. Luther means more here than Christ, Lutherdom more than Christendom. Protestantism in Sweden has ceased to mean tolerance and has degenerated into a permanent negation which has finally become positive intolerance. And then along came Halm's project! In that case, I must alter what I said before and agree willingly to a première abroad for a play that has been refused in Sweden!

A detail! Fröken Bosse asks if she might create the role of the little

Trumpeter in German![2] It doesn't matter if she speaks with a foreign accent, for the boy is Swedish. It would simply be a charming novelty!

You've now had the Pucks![3]

Yours sincerely,
August Strindberg

P.S. *The Strindberg-Blätter*![4] Is it wise?

Could you explain in them the simple fact (Cf. the letter to Albert Dreyfus)[5] that I am a Dramatist, have no constant 'opinions' (like Shakespeare) but incarnate the characters I portray. A Dramatist cannot have opinions, apart from those his creatures hold at any given moment!

A tendentious writer has opinions, therefore his characters have no life.

480. To HARRIET BOSSE

Easter Monday, 1901

Beloved,

Since I am resuming negotiations with Personne concerning *The Crown Bride*, I must have your definite answer as to whether you will accept the role or not. For if I request the role be given to you – I have already done so! – and you turn it down – well, then you would have humiliated me, and you wouldn't want to do that because 'it'd be a pity'! If you won't take my roles in general, you'll not take Swanwhite either.[1] Do you then wish to see another actress take the place you occupied in my soul, and become Swanwhite? who is you! Is that what you want?

The consequences! Herr G af G has said he's writing a role for you; Herr Nycander[2] has already written one; Herr P.S. will soon follow suit and Herr Tor H–g likewise![3]

You shouldn't refuse their roles; yet these men, who instruct their actresses themselves, will consequently enter into a spiritual relationship with you – while I remain without!

What then will become of the life of spirituality and truth we've dreamt of sharing? It won't happen! And what will we be left with? A marriage in which I wait on you at table while others cater to your soul!

This morning I walked along Narvavägen and looked up at the little window of your room. I was overcome by tears – of longing and sorrow – as for something lost, lost forever!

What gave me that idea?

Why do you want to leave me? And why do you prefer any other soul, no matter whose, to mine? Have I defiled you or your art? Has the Lady in *Damascus* or Eleonora degraded you?

Would Kersti[4] and Swanwhite do so?

You, who are young, were meant to grow with the new century and turn your back on the past. But you don't, you love the old, which was young twenty years ago!

Will you now give me a definite, irrevocable answer about your part in *The Crown Bride*?

Your
August Sg

481. To KARIN, GRETA AND HANS STRINDBERG

25 April 1901

Children,

Your impudence has now overstepped all bounds, and this is due to the miserable upbringing you have had since I left you.[1]

Greta has an engagement at the theatre, Karin will become a teacher this spring, or a governess. There remains Hans. Please send me Hans' latest school report at once! I will support him only if I'm convinced his genius isn't the same humbug as Karin's. Send it at once, and I'll see to the rest! I too have a right to live! And more than people who deserve to die in the gutter! And perhaps should end there! and end there!

If you can beg, you can work, and get paid for it, which I haven't always been, and you know there is always the workhouse or the poor house, something not everyone seems to be aware of!

August Strindberg

482. To HARRIET BOSSE

1 May 1901

Beloved,

I've just this moment read: 'I can well imagine the little lady's exultation and joy, if the Stranger – in spite of all her misgivings – were quite calmly to take her hand in his and set off with her towards – their goal.

And forgot the monastery.'

That is what you wrote on 4 March!

Has the little lady had cause since then to feel less happy? Since she has seen what great and good and beautiful things she has done for the Stranger?[1] The Stranger, whom she has filled with loathing for 'the beautiful pangs of conscience' and intoxicating Mosel wine.[2] The Stranger, whose belief in the powers of good she has restored, so that he now sees good and not evil in the hard lessons he receives. The Stranger, to whom she has given back the true joy of life, whom she has taught to appreciate the Ninth Symphony, where everything proceeds grandly and peacefully – lofty in its gravity – down to the final chorus of 'Joy', where it becomes banal and the Titan breaks into a popular song in order to make fun of the unthinking mob, who were oppressed by his mighty solemnity.

All this the little woman has done; but she no longer rejoices! Has she wearied of the pilgrimage despite the victories and fame she has won?

Is it possible? that she has grown tired of her half-finished work of art, the sight of which should have given her joy and edification every day of her life, and inspired her to think well of herself and her power to create beauty and goodness?

[no signature]

483. To HARRIET BOSSE

[28 August 1901]

I reached out my hand to you yesterday – that usually means: let all the bad things be forgotten; it usually means: forgive and forget! But you wouldn't accept it. May you never come to regret it![1]

How often at night, and always, haven't I taken your outstretched little hand and kissed it, even though it had scratched me, only from a mischievous, childish desire to scratch! I remember one night, I kissed your hand to sleep with a silent prayer, and you kissed mine in return. Then you made a remark – which I haven't forgotten! – – – Do you remember what it was?

There are words one is forced to say, even though one disapproves of them, and suffers from having said them. What you recently took so badly was one of them. But it was a stick of dynamite, placed on the line at the last moment to give warning of danger.

Remember how it was set off. You wanted to deprive my child of my name.[2] I remarked that if my child was called B. this might damage the child later on in life, so that its comrades might one day get it into their heads that it was illegitimate!

But long before this you had played with the poison. When it was clear that you were with child, the surprise you expressed was humiliating. You 'couldn't understand how it had happened' . . . Later you began to make insinuations that the child wasn't mine, couldn't be mine, simply couldn't be like me; in short, you played the poisoner. Then go back to that other time when we feared you were pregnant, and your outburst that night at the inn in Hornbaek, when you thanked God that you weren't, and spoke emphatically about 'justice'. Incredible!

Remember, too, the first days of our marriage. The day after our wedding you declared that I was not a man. A week later you wanted to let the whole world know that you were not yet Fru Strindberg, and that your sisters regarded you as 'unmarried'.

Was this kind? And was it wise?

If the child isn't mine, then it must be someone else's. But that wasn't what you meant; you merely wanted to poison me, and this you did unconsciously; that's why I brought you back to your senses with a bang.

Are you awake now? And can you resolve not to play with crime and madness again?

You say you have been having a difficult time. What do you think I've gone through? When I saw what I regarded as sacred being treated as a joke, when I saw the love between husband and wife so rapidly exposed to the public gaze – then I regretted that I had ever taken anything seriously, then I looked upon the whole of life as a colossal humbug! I well-nigh lost my faith – in everything! Came near to falling back into wickedness and decided to write farces, but colossal ones, farces about love, about a mother's love, about world history, and about what is sacred! I thought of writing a parody of *Swanwhite* for Anna Hofman[3] – but when I came to the Easter girl, I stopped.

You once asked God to bless me for having written that![4] Were you being serious then? And if so, how could you, a week after our wedding, exalt Lindelin[5] as your ideal woman? – – – And say you couldn't be an artist without being a whore first.

And then you glorified adultery, threatened to take a lover, boasted you could get one anytime – – – That was how you tried to give me back my faith in woman! – and mankind!

And now you ask: how can I love you in spite of all?

But such is love! It suffers all, but will not tolerate degradation!

Now, when our marriage should have been cleansed and ennobled through the child – you leave!

Where do you want your belongings sent? Grev Magnigatan or Blasieholmen?[6]

[no signature]

484. To HARRIET BOSSE

[29? August 1901]

In this ghost story which is called our marriage, I have sometimes suspected a crime. Does it surprise you if I momentarily believed that you were playing with me and, like Emerentia Polhem,[1] had sworn to see me at your feet.

I already mentioned this suspicion to Palme after the inexplicable scene at the dress rehearsal of *Damascus*.[2]

When you first came to see me in February, I still believed that you were playing with me, but that your feelings gradually changed and that you became sincerely attached to me. It is no doubt true that you had wicked eyes, and that you never gave me a friendly glance. But I loved you and always hoped I would finally win your sympathy.

Following the wedding, when I saw your spiritual decay; how your wickedness erupted, how cynically you regarded what was sacred to me, how you hated me; how you were seized by melancholy and despair – then I thought you were being tortured by a bad conscience, for that is how it normally manifests itself.

That you had betrayed the secrets of the yellow room,[3] I could understand, and forgive, although I was horrified and wept inwardly.

When I saw your portrait hanging in the shop windows between two similar pictures of a certain actor,[4] I shuddered. But when this actor was struck by a bullet in the breast, I supposed that a tutelary Power was assisting me and protecting our holy union.

I once thought you loved me; when you came back from seeing Inez[5] in the skerries – then there was harmony – and then, I think, our child was conceived.

In the evening, at table, you radiated a supernatural beauty and remarked: Just think, now I feel I am a woman! Our child was conceived in love, then, not in hate; in pain but not in pleasure! Therefore it is legitimate, and that is the difference between illegitimate and legitimate children! For children aren't born of pleasure seeking! (Whores don't have children.)

I have sought the explanation for your absolute reluctance to see Richard Bergh again as follows: that the secrets of the yellow room were confided to him last spring, and that you are now ashamed. I may be wrong. In which case he must have behaved indiscreetly towards you, and if so, you ought to have indicated this to me, so that I could have broken off relations without explanation.

This – our marriage – is the most inexplicable thing I have ever experienced, the most beautiful and the ugliest. At times the beautiful emerges by itself – and then I weep, crying myself to sleep so as to forget the ugly.

And at such moments, I take all the blame upon myself, all the guilt! When I then see you, melancholy, desperate, in May and June, in your green room, mourning your lost youth, which I've 'laid waste', then I accuse myself, then I cry out in pain because I have wronged you and been unjust, I kiss the sleeve of your dress, in which you stretched out your little hand, and entreat you to forgive me for all the sorrow I have caused you!

When I have stopped crying and the Angel of the Lord has comforted me, I can think more calmly. That is how all young girls have mourned their youth – and through these portals of grief have entered into motherhood, where woman finds her greatest, her only true joy in life, which she senses in advance – You have already sensed it!

But I, who shared this pain, may not share the joy!

Is it my fate to bring children into the world, to have all the worries and ingratitude, only for the joy to be snatched from me? In that case, don't say I am the one who flees happiness!

You once remarked, when I found our home ghost-like: 'If you knew what went on in this house, you would die of horror.' What went on that you knew about, but I did not?

Supposing our relationship is soiled by hatred and mistrust, well with autumn everything gets soiled, but the new spring that the child will bring will eclipse and destroy our selfish love. Can't we reduce our personal illusions and only be united in our common interests as parents and friends, and meet in our art, which is one and the same?

And haven't you given a thought to our child, who longs to be born in a home, that requires a *father* and a mother, tenderness, consideration, support and later, an introduction to life?

A child with a celebrated father growing up without knowing its father. And if you were to die, do you think I would be prepared to take over someone who had been brought up to hate me?

What does all this matter to you?

What will happen now? I don't know, but I long for an end, even if it be the very worst!

[no signature]

485. To HARRIET BOSSE

[4?] September, 1901. (Cont.)

'Forever, farewell!' Is it possible? And why? Because I wasn't kind.[1]

Wasn't I? Didn't I suppress my antipathies so as to please you? You got a grand piano, although I detest grand pianos; your room was yellow and green, even though I hate yellow and green; I bought Grieg, although I find him old-fashioned, and I requested Emil Sjögren,[2] in spite of my disliking him.

I accompanied you to Denmark, the worst country I know; I sat through the table d'hôte, which is a torture; I bathed off a sandy beach, something that figures in my worst nightmares. You were free to hold court at the pension, attended by cavaliers whom you yourself called crude, but I couldn't bring myself to act as cavalier to women who had been 'engaged' eighteen times. Finally – and this was the limit – you tried to force me to admire that ungrateful, faithless pupil of mine, von Heidenstam. Then, quite pardonably, I left the room!

Wasn't I kind, when I respected the secrets of the yellow room – your part in them – when I revered your 'secret room', as you called it (though it wasn't secret), while you at least once a day, with demonic pleasure, expressed your admiration for, and sang the praises of, a name that you, as a respectable woman, ought to have avoided mentioning! Where did you find such baseness? It was more cynical than the vulgar word I used, which wasn't aimed at you, still less at our child – it was merely a supposition that the word might one day be used by mean minded people about our child!

Why didn't I strike back?

Why, because I was kind, because I loved you – that was why I held my tongue and suffered – for such is love – but in so doing, I became used to keeping quiet – and finally felt myself being false to you. Duplicity, that was what our marriage gave us in the end. A volcano of stored-up, repressed opinions was created, and it had to explode – as it did in Berlin.

I can understand your amazement, after having lived in self-deception for four months – Self-deception is the word!

You were under the impression that you ruled me, because I was silent; you thought you impressed me with your malice, particularly during press week, when you sat on my sofa and dispensed wisdom from the middle of the last century. I accepted this as a trial – Hercules with Omphale[3] – and wanted to see how long I could put up with unkindly rudeness (in elegant form), and you looked so beautiful when you were malicious! as beautiful as a spoiled child! who one allows to pull one's hair! I grieved inwardly to see your and my degradation!

For it was degrading to see a man who had accomplished what I had in life being treated irreverently by a girl.

You speak of my delusions! I have never had any others than those you've given me.

Why did you go? No doubt you were ashamed of some bad deed which you thought you had sufficient strength of conscience to bear; but on closer inspection, your robust conscience couldn't stand it!

That is what I now believe!

[no signature]

486. To ANNE-MARIE STRINDBERG

Anne-Marie Strindberg (b.1902), Strindberg's daughter with Harriet Bosse. His relationship with his youngest daughter, born on 25 March 1902, was one of the delights of his later years, and generally survived the several crises he passed through with her mother. When the latter was working away from Stockholm, Anne-Marie sometimes stayed with Strindberg, even after their divorce, and a number of the one hundred and forty-seven extant cards and letters he addressed to her were also intended for Harriet. In 1926 she married a Norwegian, Anders Wyller, and they had two sons. A leader of the resistance movement to the German occupation of Norway, he died in London of cancer in 1940. In 1974 she married an old childhood friend, Gösta Hagelin.

[4 September 1901]

To my child! (The unborn little one)

My child! Our child! Our Midsummer child! Your parents went about their home, waiting for something, and as all waiting becomes long and maybe disagreeable, they believed that *they* were disagreeable.

They were waiting for something to come, they didn't know it had come already, in a silent, fragrant room beneath white veils with yellow walls, yellow as the sun and gold!

Then your mother was seized by a longing to see her mother's country,[1] a marvellous longing that tore her with a bleeding heart from hearth and home.

And you, child of the South and the North, were carried in the light green beech-woods by the blue sea!

And your beautiful mother rocked you on blue billows in the sea that washes three kingdoms – and in the evenings, when the sun was going down – she sat in the garden and turned her face to the sun to give you light to drink.

Child of the sea and the sun, you slept your first slumber in a little red ivy-clad house,[2] in a white room, where no word of hatred was ever even whispered, and an impure thought was unknown!

Then you went on a dark journey, a pilgrimage to the City of Sin,[3] where your father was to weep and your mother learn from his tears whither that road was leading . . .

Then you came home to the golden room where the sun shines night and day, and where tenderness awaited you, and then you were carried away! . . .

(End.)[4]

487. To EMIL SCHERING

Sthlm. 9 September 1901

Dear Herr Schering,

Briefly and to the point: to support a movement like Rauch und Schall [*sic*],[1] which belongs to the Chat Noir from the last century, *fin-de-siècle*, now in the new century, whither I have made my way with so much strife, is something I do not wish to do, indeed I may not!

In haste. Yrs,
August Strindberg

488. To HARRIET BOSSE

[12? September 1901]

Beloved,

You say you would die if you returned. That's what you said last spring – and people said: Look how radiant she is! I, who saw Little Bosse die, divined the resurrection, and though I suffered, I lived in hope!

I have seen the Great Woman, my wife, being born in pain, and never have I seen your beauty as I do now!

You say that you will turn wicked! No, my friend, your child will make you good.

Haven't you noticed that people have grown tired of being wicked, that everyone longs for goodness and beauty! Why do you want to go back, twenty years into the past?

What is it you wish to go through? As a mother and artist, you don't need to go through my bachelor life, do you? Or how am I to understand you?

Another time you said: Now I only want to live for my child and my art!

Do so! Give your child a home and a father, and give your art a friend and servant!

Harriet, let me see you again! I promise not to speak of anything except our artistic interests, and to prove to you how glad I'll be to see you, I am writing 'The Growing Castle', grand, beautiful, like a dream (The Dreamplay).[1] – It is of course about you – Agnes – who will free the Prisoner from the castle . . .

May I talk it into being with you?

How is the little one? (Our unborn child) – I go about here like the Organist on Rånö,[2] converting ruins into poetry. Yesterday I put the yellow room in order, as it was from the start, with the green bed and the blue one under the golden circle in the ceiling. And then I 'pretended' that the little one will be born in the green bed! where the violets on your nightgown are now waiting!

When I caught sight of that, I was filled with despair, for I suddenly realized what I had lost! – Soon I won't be able to play any more, and then I'll die!

[no signature]

489. To HARRIET BOSSE

21 September 1901

My dear Friend!

In three days or so, *Christina* will be ready for inspection by your beautiful eyes!

But won't you, so as to be a little *au courant*,[1] read something about Christina beforehand!

Fryxell[2] is the most readable, almost like a novel, and can be had from Birger Jarlsgatan, where you got *Pickwick* (you remember!).

Or something shorter! Odhner?[3]

It now has 5 regular, well-defined acts. 'The greatest and most exhaustive female role ever written.' Accordingly 5 magnificent costumes, among them Pandora's, out of Walter Crane,[4] you remember, which we intended using for *Swanwhite*.

I'm now collecting her portraits for you!

You could well look in at the Library and ask to see all the portraits of Christina – We only need the attractive ones, the pictures from her youth!

Michaelson has recently depicted the ugly Christina.[5]

What luck for the unfortunate queen that I still had your beautiful image here and in my heart while I was portraying her! And that we have you as an actress. (The new century's!)

Have you received *Swanwhite*? She can wait a year!

Write a few lines and stimulate my interest in the final acts with a friendly word. Tell me that the little one is alive! (I dreamed last night about a child's tiny severed foot in the sand!)

Have you received Emerentia?

Are you well? How is *King René's Daughter*[6] going? – When will *Charles XII* open?

Your Friend

What a mercy I can work! Otherwise – well! It was dark and dreary before – but now . . . even Sorrow has grown dark!

490. To HARRIET BOSSE

23 September 1901

Harriet!

Now I know it! God has given you power over me – and I submit. But don't abuse this terrible power which brings responsibility with it – use it only for good, and all will be well for us and our child. It is true, Harriet, that you literally hold my life in your little hand.

If you leave me, I shall die, possibly by my own hand, or else my reason will be extinguished. When I now ask you to come back, you understand that I am prepared to accept both good and bad at your hands – without complaint –

And when you last warned me about what you once had in store for me, I didn't believe it! For the child, motherhood, suffering have, unbeknown to yourself, fashioned a new, great, and glorious woman, of whom I caught a glimpse last time, and who made me happy!

You once told me about your sister Alma[1] and the complete change of personality that being a mother made!

This is what you have before you, too! And consideration for your child's future will compel you to hate all evil.

What pair is so favourably placed for married life as we are? Tell me that!

You said last time that you saw your role in my life as a mission! Well, I believe that! Fulfil your mission then, spur me on to goodness and beauty as in the past – and now and then punish my pride with your little acts of cruelty! I'll kiss your hand even when it strikes, for He who guides your hand wishes me well!

Your spirit is with me every hour of the day, and you watch over my conscience! When I am tempted to think or write something ugly, I see your beautiful eyes; then I blush, feel ashamed, and correct myself.

I can't divert myself, and when I seek company elsewhere, it feels like an infidelity to you, for my soul belongs to you alone.

Don't reject my life which I have dedicated to you, for then my death will cast a shadow over your bright path. Forgive me; everything, all the bad I've done you!

Sacrifice a little of yourself to me, and I shall sacrifice everything for you. I have wronged you in so far as I punished your *thoughts* when they were not good! I had no right to do that! You have probably kept some small, innocent secrets from me! I had no right to delve into them. Therefore I was afflicted with suspicion as a punishment!

A warm, kind-hearted person also said to me: 'You may have been too inquisitive!'

I have been! Forgive me!

And then: for what we have now been through, neither you nor I are to blame. 'It's not man's doing, but God's will that has been done.'

So let there be an end to accusations and this seeking after a cause!

Come back my friend! I shall serve you, obey you, except in what is wrong! I shall serve your child, I shall carry you both in my arms!

And by your presence, you will save my writing from filth and hatred.

You shall – I am now convinced of this! – fulfil your task – to reconcile me with humanity and with woman! Now you've become a woman and a mother!

Try! God will help us![2]

[no signature]

491. To HARRIET BOSSE

3 October 1901

My beloved little Wife,

After our conversation this evening, I was convinced that you cannot return to our flat – seeing you prefer four hours in the streets – and yet that you and I could live together, but following tradition – as Gypsies. I was the first to hate 'The Flat' – I, the son of the hut and the hovel – The Son of a Servant – Hagar's – the desert's!

Accompany me on my wanderings in the wilderness! Beloved! You were my child, my daughter! Now, a mother, now I am your child! As you said, so beautifully: 'You, Gusten,[1] lie under my heart!' – And it was after all my Inferno dream to fall asleep on a woman's breast!

And when this evening you said that the Little One had my eyes – as it slept on your arm, as you once slept on mine! Everything made new! A line through the past!

Let me arrange – I wrote to Personne this evening! – for you to play Iolantha[2] as your farewell performance, before we depart!

Or – free yourself from the Royal Theatre and return as Christina with Ranft in April? Or – whatever you will!

Would you like to go to Paris – with me? You may live in a pension if you want!

You may keep house, with Lovisa,[3] in Paris, if you want!

You may have a suite and eat out. Whatever you like!

Think it over – everything except the flat! that goes!

And I'll take care of your return to the stage! The autumn and winter in Paris, learning French, the only language which is worth our learning!

Let me be such as I am until our child arrives! Then – is the time for you to decide about your future.[4]

Your Gusten

492. To CARL LARSSON

40 Karlavägen[IV], 2 November 1901

Dear Carl Larsson,

For several days I've had intimations of you, expected you; for my wife and I visited the Museum recently and saw your frescoes again[1] (which have gained in tranquillity; discovered too that they should have been isolated from each other, and from the pillars, by painted frames. You know how a page without margins looks cluttered!). Anyway! Your letter arrived – not unexpectedly, in other words!

Reply: I cannot pose or make faces before a fragment of life, and I have written and had my ears boxed for so many stupid, impudent forewords that I've promised to keep quiet! I content myself with portraying human destinies![2]

You ask how things are with us. Well, we've had sickness, and storms of course, ever since July, when a new little Bosse began to announce her entry into this earthly life. But for a month now, things have been wonderfully peaceful, and our hopes seem likely to be realized in March – a year? and what a year? since you surprised us round a table in Banérgatan!

Life becomes ever more dreamlike and inexplicable to me – perhaps death really is the awakening! Who knows? Neither Moses nor the Prophets say anything on the subject.

My *Charles XII* will now be put on at the Royal Theatre in November, and my *Engelbrekt* this Christmas! at the Swedish![3]

If you come to town, please ring so we may see you in our home, which is open for visits! with a few friends! Yesterday we had guests! The Warburgs, Rich. Berghs, Staaff, Geijerstam, Svennberg, my brother Axel, the old guard! The Strindbergs gave a proper supper-party (one dinner jacket put in an appearance by mistake!). *C'est la vie, quoi*!

And so: best wishes to Fru Karin and the children!

from
Your old friend,
August Strindberg

493. To EMIL SCHERING

18 January 1902

Dear Herr Schering,

What shall I write, what say, about *Engelbrekt* and *Easter* and all the rest? Adversity makes me dumb, for I can't blame anyone, and I cannot alter my fate.[1] Sometimes one has the wind in one's sails, now I have it against me, and can only wait. Worst of all, I begin to lose interest in my work when I find no encouragement anywhere. Moreover, it seems to me that I have said all I have to say for the time being; particularly in a newly completed Dream Play, which has not yet been copied.

I am probably facing a change in my destiny, in which direction I don't know. Perhaps it marks the end of what is for me and others my so mysterious existence. I don't know!

However, I ought to have relayed my thanks to Fr. Eysoldt;[2] as I had already done so in my mind, I thought I had already done that. We have read her lively letter with much pleasure, and she has aroused my wife's interest in particular.

Schiller's *Demetrius*,[3] which you sent me, confirms my old experience that one must not plan in detail, for then one loses the joy of conception, and with that the urge to write it down disappears. One has been premature. This happened to me once.

I signed the address to Tolstoy.[4] Consequently our wretched Academy says I was 'envious'. Seeing an injustice doesn't make one envious! An injustice makes one indignant. But the Academy understands nothing about logic or language. Besides, I cannot envy what I despise; and I despise the Swedish Academy, that illiterate clique, so much that I would *never* accept an honour from them. My friends have known that for ten years!

Yours sincerely,
August Strindberg

494. To EMIL SCHERING

15 March (The Ides of March) 1902

Dear Herr Schering,

Tired, I can only thank you, and ask you to convey my very best congratulations, especially to Emanuel Reicher and Rosa Bertens.[1] And tell them that this has revived memories of our mutual success ten years ago. Those hopes to which we drank after *Creditors*, in the Rathskeller, in the spring of 1893, have thus required ten years to germinate and flower! What a terrible decade!

Convey my appreciation to Fru Eysoldt,[2] and to her fellow actors as well!

Charles XII played to full houses, but was nonetheless dropped from the repertoire, and performed as a cut-price Sunday matinée! That's how they treat me! Why?

What do Reicher and Bertens say to *Intoxication*[3] or *Damascus*? For, let us be modern!

Yours sincerely,
August Strindberg

495. To TOR HEDBERG

Tor Hedberg (1862–1931), the son of Frans Hedberg, Strindberg's old mentor at the Royal Theatre. After studying at Uppsala, Hedberg emerged as one of the leading writers and critics of his generation. During the 1880s his novels *Johannes Karr* (1885) and *Judas* (1886) were noted for their careful psychology and objective style, and in the 1890s he also began writing for the theatre. His comedy *Nattrocken* (The Dressing Gown, 1892) poked fun at Ibsen and Strindberg, but his major achievement was *Johan Ulfstjerna* (1907), a play inspired by the assassination of Bobrikov, the Russian Governor General of Finland. From 1897 to 1907 he was theatre, art and literary critic for *Svenska Dagbladet*, and between 1910 and 1921 he succeeded Knut Michaelson as head of the Royal Theatre. He was elected to the Swedish Academy in 1922. Thirteen of Strindberg's letters to Hedberg survive.

40 Karlavägen[IV], Sthlm. 10 April 1902

Tor Hedberg,

You were kind enough to answer my last letter; therefore my thanks! And I hope you will also reply to this one!

Through your review of Gorky's first book,[1] I got to know a writer with whom I feel a kind of kinship.

Who is he? His real name is Pieskow, and his works are mentioned in the big Meyer.[2] But not a word about the man! A mysterious news report the other day from Petersburg (Baku?) maintained that Gorky couldn't become a member of the Academy of Science because he had committed a crime against the state! – The Academy of Science? What does that mean? Is he a scholar?

The report seemed to me so uncalled for that I wondered if it might be a Nobel one from our Academy – it wouldn't be the first time the activities of that reptilian outfit had been visible in the press.

In my opinion, Gorky would be an appropriate candidate for the Nobel Prize; the right combination of beginner and master – and needy too. It would also be interesting to see if prosperity made him see life differently (which I doubt, however!).

At a recent dinner, I tried Gorky out on a Swedish Academician but was met with Minchiewizc [*sic*] or Sinkiewicz [*sic*]!,[3] whom even Karl Otto regards as lending library material.

Who is Gorky? asks

Yours sincerely,
August Strindberg

496. To EMIL SCHERING

13 May 1902

Dear Herr Schering,

Understand *The Dream Play*? Indra's daughter has come down to earth in order to find out how mankind lives, and thus discovers how hard life is. And the hardest thing of all is hurting others, which one is forced to do if one wants to live.

The form is motivated by the foreword; the jumble and confusion of a dream, in which there is, however, a certain logic! Everything absurd becomes probable. People flit past and a few traits are sketched in, the sketches merge, a single character dissolves into several, who merge into one again. Time and space do not exist; a minute is like many years; no seasons; the snow covers the countryside in summer, the lime tree turns yellow, and then green again, etc.

There was nothing about Chemistry in Goethe's *Ephemerides*.[1] So it remains to be discovered!

After having read *Götz*[2] recently, I couldn't take *Florian Geijer*;[3] though I struggled through it. It is all worked out, but the spirit is lacking! It is so meticulously studied, that one wishes it were less so. A work of art should be a little careless, imperfect like everything in nature, where not a crystal is without a flaw, not a plant lacks a miscarried leaf. Like Shakespeare. Serious play, but no labour and no learning in art!

I've stuck fast and think I'm written out – like 1892.

Yours sincerely,
August Strindberg

497. To HARRIET BOSSE

[3 July 1902][1]

Faced with the inevitable, I'm struck dumb and petrified; I no longer believe it possible to make you change your mind – It's probably meant to happen! whether as a passing trial or a judgement on me, I don't know. But I feel as though I won't survive this. I may have been suffering all the tortures of our separation for three months, but I feel the worst is yet to come!

The child kept me alive and at your side.

I can't remember what our arguments were about! So they must have been mere bagatelles, perhaps an excessive concern for the little one, and a pardonable anxiety.

That you regretted your lost youth, I could understand, but I had hoped the child would give it back to you, as it did to me. But no!

At this moment, I have nothing to reproach you with. Married life brings with it a certain constraint, and like you, I have sometimes longed to be liberated from such restraint, wished to be the sole centre of interest in my circle again, but I soon realized this desire was a chimera. My friends have all become indifferent to me as a result of your presence in my life. And I can feel the approach of absolute isolation, frightful and solemn!

Yesterday evening, I had intended to ask you quite simply and directly why I couldn't go with you to Räfsnäs. – Why do you want to send me off to Sandhamn to parade my grief before strangers?

But my tongue was frozen.

I don't know what will happen to me now. I shall no doubt remain in the only hiding place I have, the home I dreamt of! Whatever happens, I shan't touch anything! And whatever you wish to have is yours to take!

When I met with the furious north wind today, which could well prevent your journey, I wondered for a moment: Is it possible this cup might be taken from me? Is the inevitable perhaps not inevitable?

When one morning some time ago you entreated me from the depths of your soul to 'Help me!', I took this to mean: 'Help me to get away from this home to freedom!' Since this could best be achieved by my leaving or dying, I took it that you wanted me to make off with myself. But it was hard for me to hear you demand my life, and I replied harshly. Since then I have doubted whether you really meant to be so cruel. And I wanted – perhaps in the extremity of my despair – to interpret your cry for help as: 'Ask me to forgive you! And I shall forgive! I want to stay with you, but I can't until you come to my aid!' – I'm probably mistaken. But if that is what you meant, then I say: forgive me for misjudging you!

My feelings for you and the little one are absolutely unchanged, even though the horror of our separation paralysed me! Judge then the tortures in store for me! which already began before the child arrived and you announced you were leaving. I originally intended not to become too attached to the child so as to suffer less later on; but it was irresistible. And now I'm trapped!

Alone! For I learned everything through you, I saw the world only through your eyes, kept in touch with the earth only through you. Do you understand now that I can be destroyed by loneliness: 'I obeyed you and it went well for me.' You were given power over me by Providence, but only the power for good! When I thought you wanted to abuse your power, I disobeyed you! And therefore I find it so difficult to reproach myself for resisting – I had to keep on going – not go under, and one day you will be grateful to me for this! for otherwise I would have dragged you down too! And that I could never do!

Is your mission in my life now ended? Can there be an end to what we thought had no beginning?

Can Chrysaëtos[2] be dead, when our souls are immortal?

[no signature]

498. To HARRIET BOSSE

4 July 1902

My beloved Wife,

At first it was calm of course, as it always is after an earthquake and a thunderclap – – – but then it became slightly too calm, and I missed the patter of your restless little spirit on the floors; I missed the open doors, and most of all perhaps (?), the little cries from the nursery.

But when I think how irreconcilably horrible my feeling of loss would have been if we had parted as enemies yesterday, then I am happy, and this calm is as refreshing as a rest.

I had thought of seeing some new faces, but am afraid of losing you, of falling back again into prehistoric times on Banérgatan;[1] it seems to me like infidelity, even if I know you've surrounded yourself where you are now with people I've never met.

And, in my solitude I have you with me, but in company you vanish, and our contact is broken.

What did we fight about? Yes, about each of us retaining our own individuality when we were in danger of melting into one. You had the advantage, for you had friends – I was absolutely alone, captivated by you and the little one. This sometimes seemed awful to me. To be delivered unconditionally into your hands. Then I wanted to flee, but I wasn't able to. All this is very natural, as natural as the fact that love has both a time of blossoming and a seed time. One wants the seed, but one lacks the flower when the seed has come. *C'est la vie; qu'est-ce que vous voulez*?[2]

So: If you have room for me (and Bertha)[3] just say the word! Carrying on a futile struggle against the laws of life is absurd! The practical thing would now be to rent a 6 room flat, give up the months remaining here, and move from the country into a new place, where you would have your own room! Here the very walls are noxious!

And also stop philosophizing about our relationship; simply throw ourselves into our work, and devote all our other thoughts to the little one.

Now kiss my daughter! Rest your tired nerves! And let us continue our pilgrimage!

That is what I now think!

Your little husband,
Gusten

P.S. The money from Norway has arrived! Do you want it?

499. To EMIL SCHERING

10 September 1902

Dear Herr Schering,

Right, *Intoxication*,[1] in Berlin! But this time I as the author would like to be obeyed for once, for I know its dangers.

The greatest of these, and where we went wrong, is to give way to preaching or moralizing, in spite of the play's evident liberating tendency.

(1) Fru Eysoldt must appear psychically seductive; a Vampire who drinks souls; and needs no body. (Aspasia has no body!) Unconscious of good and evil: 'everything is permitted'. But as she doesn't take into account that deeds have consequences, she is at first surprised and enraged, then she discovers that everything isn't permitted – but makes the discovery with an elegant resignation, without remorse, but with a certain sadness! Otherwise the role is drawn in great detail, and Fru E. ought to take careful note of what the other characters say about her when she is off stage.

(2) Maurice's role is clear.

(3) Fru Cathérine is good-natured and tolerant; smiles at their weaknesses and (note well) never punishes!

(4) the Abbé is the most difficult. He should be – exactly like Fru Cathérine – but without being trivial! With humour then, and spirit. In the final scene particularly, roguish, tolerant; childishly surprised at

the enormous lack of scruples which has come to light! – 'After all, it is terrible . . . ' (to break one's word!).

And then: drawn from everyday life, without any *Räuber*-like gestures! Swedish: that is, a light scepticism behind everything! Not Norwegian! For your Norwegian cannot smile! He is hard, unforgiving. And then: don't suggest depths where there aren't any! or profundities which were never intended! In other words, not Ibsen!

Enough for now!

Yours,
August Strindberg

500. To LEOPOLD LITTMANSSON

Sthlm. 25 September 1902

Dear Leopold,

When the great Beethoven (the Greatest) grew old, he lived with a relative for whom he was always an object of ridicule, so that even the maids made fun of him. And when his final illness set in, he sent his preoccupied nephew for a doctor. The rascal didn't go to the doctor but to play billiards, where he drank up the money; and when he came home, Beethoven lay there dead. This perhaps helps us to understand why B., whose whole life was more or less in the same vein, has alone been able to express what those whom life has treated badly have felt, and why such people still gather together to listen to him. Axel usually plays Sonata 31,[1] and for three years now we've been going through the Sonatas almost once a week.

Ivan[2] joined us this summer for the first time. He is in Babylonian captivity in Isaac's office, where he has time to meditate on his destiny, which hasn't been kind to that kind man. But he doesn't envy Isaac, for the latter has 'never a happy moment': fussy and discontented, filthy rich!

Our last meeting was given over to philosophizing about the fate of people we know. This is what interests us at our age. We were all agreed on one thing: 'If life isn't Infernal then it's Purgatorial, or inexplicable.' And we concluded that it was right to 'envy no one, for no one is enviable'.

However: You are writing! Never too late, but often too soon! Only now have you something to relate!

Can't we publish what you've written in Swedish? For the friends you have, and those you might acquire? Will you send me your manuscript?

I am sending you my *Dream Play*, which represents my final word in all my musings on the riddle of the Universe.

Peace! When shall we build Fridhem[3] and till the earth and (adhering

6. August Strindberg, Self-portrait, Berlin, 893, aged forty-four

17. Frida Uhl, 1892, aged twenty

8. Mme Charlotte Futterer in her *crémerie*, 3 rue de la Grande Chaumière, Paris.

19. Bust of Strindberg by Agnes de Frumerie, Paris 1895 (See Letter 364

20. Torsten Hedlund

21. Hôtel Orfila at 60 rue d'Assas, Paris, Strindberg's residence between 21 February and 19 July, 1896

22. Strindberg in Lund, 1897

23. Carl Larsson

4. Gustaf af Geijerstam. (In a letter dated
 February 1894 Strindberg described Geijerstam
s: 'Born bald with glasses, paunch, pension
nd the eyes of a rabbit in need of a piss.')

25. Harriet Bosse with Anne-Marie Strindberg, born 25 March 1902

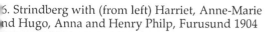

6. Strindberg with (from left) Harriet, Anne-Marie
nd Hugo, Anna and Henry Philp, Furusund 1904

29. Strindberg at his desk in Blå tornet

27. Harriet Bosse as Indra's Daughter in *A Dreamplay*, 1907

30. (right) Strindberg with (from left) Greta, Hans and Karin, Blå tornet, 1911

28. *The Father* at the Intimate Theatre, 1908

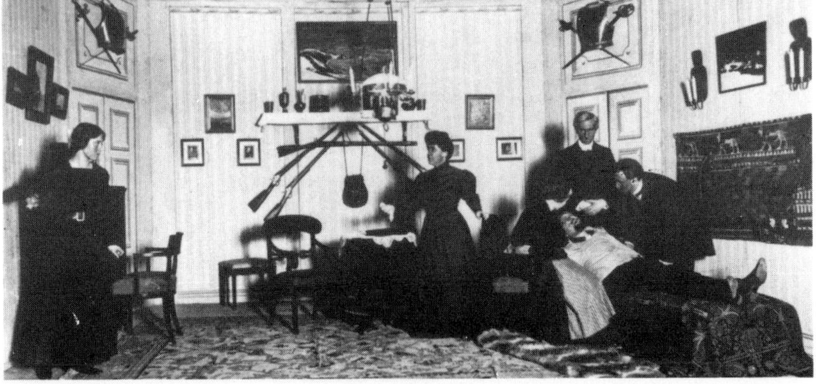

to no creed) philosophize of an evening? On the high rocks opposite the Customs House at Blockhusudden there are plots of land with a view over Stockholm and Vaxholm!

Yours,
August Strindberg

501. To LEOPOLD LITTMANSSON

4 October 1902

My dear Leopold,

I have been through what you are now experiencing twice,[1] and can understand your suffering. It is the greatest possible torment; the roof over your head comes crashing down and you have to leave its warmth and go out and wander – Then it's good to have Sakya[2] in mind.

When we spoke about your destiny last summer, we were agreed that you had a calling which you had failed to fulfil. Perhaps you are being tormented out onto the heights to prophesy. Jonah wanted to run away, but had to come forward. It is our sufferings people really want; to hear about our empty pleasures only offends them. Tell about what you know!

You will in any case be separated from your daughters when they marry. So prepare yourself for the inevitable and parry the blow in advance. Loneliness may not be pleasant, but it is sublime and also pure. Silence enables one to hear so many and such great things.

You saw my cell with the iron bars in the rue Bonaparte.[3] I suffered, but I was happy! And it was there the great matter of my life took shape.

You may well live another 25 years. That's a whole generation! And to forget, even what one holds most dear, only takes a year.

And besides, when reality fails then invent an existence for yourself, as I invented a character for myself when I grew tired of the one I had.

Write out your misery, then it will seem as if it never existed!

Yours,
August Strindberg

502. To EMIL SCHERING

8 October 1902

Dear Herr Schering,

What you write all sounds very hopeful, and it's high time (*höchste Zeit!*) because here the situation is reminiscent of 1892. Not one of my six, new, good plays has been accepted by any of the theatres: that is, neither *Gustav III, Christina, The Crown Bride, Swanwhite, The Dream Play,* nor *The Dance of Death.* Why? I don't know!

As for *Gustav Adolf*, there isn't a prompt book because the play has never been performed here. But my suggestion was the Shakespeare stage in Munich as a model;[1] costumes, make up, etc. can be borrowed from Devrient's[2] published *regiebuch*. Moreover, I could spend a week in Berlin and work one out – if *Intoxication* goes well, that is.

But it's not to be undermined by the production. The words are what matters, and we could play it with the backcloth and an arch throughout, as in *Damascus*. – We'll have to see!

So far Hertz[3] has been a reliable friend; I took care of him in Lund as a young journalist in an unpleasant situation. However, since he's 'young', perhaps it suits him to regard me as 'old-fashioned'.

More after *Intoxication*.

Yours sincerely,
August Strindberg

503. To EMIL SCHERING

25 October 1902

Dear Herr Schering,

I have no desire to publish a pamphlet on child care. And in any case, the century of the child was the 18th Century, when Rousseau wrote *Émile* and got mothers to suckle their children. (Everything Fr. Key asserts is a half-truth, if one investigates it.)[1]

However: if I do come to Berlin, it is partly in order to get away from Sweden and partly to study people and books, not to exhibit my person. My writings are myself! The man who writes them should be protected, and preserved from all kinds of prostitution. I know that my presence in person damages my interests because of visits not made, invitations refused, etc. For example: I cannot visit Herr Lautenburg,[2] even though I am indebted to him; I find him offensive, in spite of his friendly, clumsy kindness. And he would be revenged at once! The same goes for Neumann-Hofer[3] – – –

Going to Schwerin or Breslau is absolutely pointless, for I'd turn back on arrival![4]

That is how I am, and have been since early childhood, and I cannot change my nature now!

Personal freedom in poverty rather than the prospect of money by appearing in public!

I am afraid of what will happen if you announce my arrival for the 25th performance.[5] How can you be certain the play will run so long? Now I don't believe it will!

Why does the *Norddeutsche Allg. Z.* go on about autobiography?[6] Doesn't Goethe say in *Aus meinem Leben* that his entire work was a Confession? Isn't *Faust* a diary? 'One is none the worse for being like Goethe (in this respect anyway).'

Yours sincerely,
August Strindberg

504. To EMIL SCHERING

1 December 1902

Dear Herr Schering,

This is how things stand with my 'Next Work' (under an absolute promise of secrecy!).

After *Fagervik*,[1] I perceived that there had to be a pause in my writing, and as a way of killing time, I read right through world history. This strange *Geschichte*,[2] which has always seemed to me like a picaresque novel, now revealed itself as the creation of A Conscious Will, and I discovered Logic in its Antinomies, a Consequence of its conflicting Components.

Thus I found right at the beginning that the World Spirit revealed itself *concurrently* in several places on the earth without these places having any contact with each other. For example: at the very moment of the Mosaic Law on Sinai (1300 B.C.), India got the *Rigveda*, Greece Orpheus and Linus,[3] and China the Schi-King. This is not chance! – – – My investigations were continued Synchronically and 'The Conscious Will' in History was verified.

Then I sought the form. To begin with I wanted to write a Philosophy of History, but that was too dry for me! Then I was torn between Three Trilogies, each of them 3 x 5 acts (= 45 acts). Or short stories, or tales.

I proposed beginning in 1899 in the Hague during the Peace Congress with a meeting between Dr Faust and Ahasverus (*Der ewige Jude*); who then relate these short stories (perhaps).

For the moment I incline to Tales (in Andersen's poetical style).

Leaving aside all subsidiary questions of money or ambition, will you tell me what form your instinct tells you I should choose? Essay, plays, short stories, tales?[4]

The *Vasantasena*?[5] Yes, that dates from the same year as Christ and embodies the Christianity of India: Atonement through suffering. The Spirit of Christianity, without any knowledge of Christ!

I am entirely satisfied with the Faust Book you sent me! Thank you!

I already have Goethe's *Divan*! And will now borrow the other books from our Library.

But could you get me to keep:

Syncretism is beginning to gain ground!

1. The Proceedings of the Peace Congress in The Hague, 1899.
2. The Proceedings of the Congress on Religion in Paris, 1900.

This inaugurates the New Century and concludes the nineteenth century, the greatest century since the birth of Christ and the discovery of America.

What should we offer Schwerin? *Christina*?

Yours sincerely,
August Strindberg

505. To OTTO WEININGER

Otto Weininger (1880–1903), Austrian philosopher, author of *Geschlecht und Charakter* (Sex and Character, 1903), which he sent Strindberg through his publisher. For Weininger, a writer in the misogynist tradition of Schopenhauer and Nietzsche, woman lacked a higher spiritual life, and was only a sexual complement to man, the two poles of her character being represented by the mother and the whore. Elsewhere in his book, in which he refers several times to Strindberg, Weininger puts forward a theory of bisexuality which, he maintains, characterizes the vital activities of every organ and cell. This notion forms the basis of his theory of human character types, including the idea that 'male' and 'female' substances vary proportionately in different individuals. Sexual attraction is thus explained by the 'law of bisexual complementarity' whereby (for example) a ¾ masculine and ¼ feminine man would attract a ¾ feminine and ¼ masculine woman. Weininger committed suicide on 4 October 1903, after spending his last night in the house where Beethoven had died. Following his death, his book enjoyed great popularity, and went through twenty-six editions by 1925.

[Original in German]

Stockholm, 1 July 1903

Herr Doctor,

Finally – to see the woman problem solved is a deliverance for me, and so – accept my deepest admiration and my thanks![1]

August Strindberg

506. To LEOPOLD LITTMANSSON

Almvik, Blidö. 4 July 1903

My dear Leopold,

Carrying on a discussion by post isn't easy. Now I didn't say the theme of the Ninth is banal, because it isn't; I said the *Lied an die Freude* is banal,[1] because it is! It resembles 'Fröken Agnes was a Clever Girl', etc. Axel has just played the Ninth on the piano and confirmed this.

Mozart, *Simplicius Simplicissimus,* is not heavenly, but splendid in the G minor Symphony and in two movements of the Requiem. The rest is piano for one finger, or children's flute of Saxon porcelain. Of the whole of *Don Giovanni,* only Leporello's Aria and the Commendatore's chords mean anything to me.

Beethoven's scherzos are Mozartian tootles and Axel always has to skip them. His teacher, Haydn, is more profound and artistic. Yes! That's my view!

It was certainly lucky you encouraged Monnier![2] For otherwise it could easily have begun to look as though I was behaving badly.

Your French poetry! Thank you for my copy! But there isn't a paper here which publishes material in French, their readers are barely up to German.

You have *Mercure* and *La Plume* though!

In the Archipelago, bathing in the sea, writing Fairy Tales; with a wife and little one-year-old daughter – – – am on Blidö, off Furusund.

The gulls, rocks, flat-fish, everything is just the same!

C'est la vie! Quoi?

Axel's Charlotte[3] was buried this week. His daughter died two years ago, married, the Baroness Thott, leaving a daughter.

How strange it all is!

Your friend,
August Strindberg

507. To HJALMAR SELANDER

Hjalmar Selander (1859–1928), actor and theatre director. Since 1890, Selander had been touring the provinces with his own company, and his productions of *Master Olof* and *Lucky Peter's Journey* had both enjoyed considerable success. He wished to renew his performing rights on the latter, but Strindberg hoped to interest him in the newly-written and unperformed *A Dream Play*.

8 July 1903

Herr Director Hjalmar Selander,

On looking through *The Dream Play* again, I find that it only requires 12 projected back-cloths 3 ells in size plus a few ordinary back-drops which can be flown out while the stage is blacked-out with the curtain raised. (As was done in *Damascus* at the Royal Theatre.)[1]

The framing arch throughout the play is made up of a forest of Giant Poppies. A permanent inner stage of poppies with an opening of 3 ells in which there would either be transparent screens or a white screen onto which Sciopticon images could be projected. There are no costumes to speak of!

Isn't this cheaper and better than my tired old *Lucky Peter*? If you like, you could start by giving *The Dream Play* in Stockholm at the theatre in Folkets Hus, while I took care of subscriptions and the advertising.

I've already had a word with Branting![2] The only really important role is Indra's Daughter, and that can be played by any serious young girl who hasn't had her head turned by operetta, and the like. In Folkets Hus one can't have changes of scenery, but must operate with screens and the Sciopticon. I've also cut some characters and combined a number of walk-on parts.

If you're still not interested, you can have *Lucky Peter* for 400 *kronor* cash, and sole rights for the provinces, though for a limited period of course. And always assuming that Engelbrecht[3] doesn't turn up; in which case you could still go ahead, but with your rival that's hardly conceivable.

Yours faithfully,
August Strindberg

Address: 40 Karlavägen (not Blidö).

508. To EMIL SCHERING

[2 August 1903]

Dear Herr Schering,

Am reading Rich. Meyer's *Goethe*,[1] and see that G. wrote about the Metamorphosis of Insects. Now, to start with: What does the most complete edition of Goethe cost second-hand? And then, you Germans, who know everything, isn't there a single contemporary scientist who has described and reproduced the histolytic course of events within the pupa of a butterfly (and others)? I don't mean the change of skin the larva undergoes but its entire *histolysis within the pupa*. No Darwinist, no Haeckel, has dealt with this universal problem; individual life which continues after the chrysalis dissolves into a slime; this is the problem of immortality;

the indestructibility of individual energy; resurrection from the dead, the resurrection of the body too![2]

Yours sincerely,
Aug Sg

509. To KARL KRAUS

Karl Kraus (1874–1936), Austrian writer and the founder, in 1899, of the periodical *Die Fackel*, to which he became in time the sole contributor. Kraus had asked Strindberg to write an article in memory of Otto Weininger, following his suicide on 4 October 1903. Thus, 'Idolatri, Gynolatri' appeared in *Die Fackel* for 17 October, translated by Schering. Following its publication, Kraus' journal became a forum for Strindberg's work abroad, and Schering placed many pieces there over the next nine years. However, although Kraus regularly sent *Die Fackel* to Strindberg via Schering in Berlin, this remains the only exchange of letters between them. Following Strindberg's death, Kraus gave a reading of his works in Vienna on 4 June 1912 and, exceptionally (for he did not normally commemorate the death of a writer in this way), published an obituary in *Die Fackel* on 21 June.

[Original in German]

Stockholm, 12 October 1903

Herr Doctor,

I have already sent Herr Schering a short article for translation.

In return, may I ask you to be so kind as to lay a wreath on the dead thinker's grave; (herewith 10 *kronor* enclosed!).

Yours faithfully,
August Strindberg

510. To ARTUR GERBER

Artur Gerber (1882–?), Austrian writer and intimate friend of Otto Weininger, whose letters he published in 1919. Gerber had written to Strindberg on 19 October to inform him of Weininger's suicide. According to Gerber's letter, Weininger had observed: 'August Strindberg is the most important man alive. He also knows woman even better than you or I.' There are two extant letters from Strindberg to Gerber.

[Original in German]

40 Karlavägen, Stockholm, 22 October 1903

Herr Doctor,

I have understood our dead friend, and I thank you!

Several years ago, when I was in Weininger's situation and weighed up the intention of passing on, I wrote in my diary: 'Why am I going? Cato killed himself when he found he could no longer hold himself upright above the swamp of sin. Which is why Dante has acquitted him of suicide (*Inferno*). Now I (August Strindberg) am sinking, and I do not want to sink, therefore . . . Bang! – – –'[1]

I was on the way upwards, but a woman pulled me down. . .

However, I carried on living because I believed I would find that our union with the earth spirit,[2] woman, was a sacrifice, a duty, a test. We are not allowed to live as gods here below; we must wander in excrement and yet still remain pure etc.

Consider the case of Maeterlinck!

Just the same! He stood so high above matter (*Le Trésor des humbles*), and then along came the earth spirit – – – He has fallen so low that he trails his naked earth spirit around, exhibiting both it and himself! Isn't it tragic![3]

When Dr Luther got married, he wrote to a friend: 'I marry? Incredible! I'm ashamed! But it seems as if the Lord God wants me to remain a fool!'

Send me the biography and the other things! – When he died, Schering wrote to me: 'Weininger has sealed his faith with his death.' That's right!

I was near to doing the same thing around 1880; alone with my 'discovery'. It is no opinion, it is a discovery, and Weininger was a 'discoverer'.

The new era seems to be arriving with new truths; the zoological world view ended in veterinary psychology.

We strugglers, who strive once more after the immortal soul, are therefore called religious. Indeed I am; but I cannot adopt any single creed. Until I find something better, I am calling myself a 'Christian freethinker'!

Your unknown and far-away friend,

August Strindberg

511. To EMIL SCHERING

15 November 1903

Dear Herr Schering,

Your telegram's arrived!

Now look: *Gustav Adolf* is written for Swedes, it represents a Swedish episode from the Thirty Year's War, *two years* out of thirty; that's why it has a Swedish ending.

What happens after Lützen: why, the renewal of the alliance with Richelieu; the release of French troops into Germany – and the German countryside laid waste by the French and the Swedes. The Germans curse the Swedes for having enticed their arch enemy, the Roman (Gallo-Roman) into the country. Saxony is ravaged by that coarse lout Banér,[1] and every base instinct is released.

Can I, as a Swedish subject, write all this? And what has it got to do with the portrayal of Gustav Adolf?

I warned you about *Gustav Adolf*; it must appear incomprehensible and repugnant to a Prussian. What do the Germans know about Gustav Adolf's blood guilt stemming from Karl IX and the Lords at Linköping?[2] Yet that is my tragic theme! That's why I wrote: Take Luther instead! You know about him!

I re-read my Luther[3] yesterday! It gave me new vigour! It's the strongest and most youthful play I've written! No doubts like Master Olof, no scruples, no women round his neck, no parents in the way, no compromises with friends. And such is the historical, traditional Luther. I can see no point where I have broken with tradition! And I understand neither your fears nor Henriksson's![4]

Eingedeutscht werden, ja wohl, aber Gustaf Adolv zu verdeutschen, das mag ich nicht! Lieber nichts!

Mein letztes Wort! Amen! Hier stehe ich und kann nichts Anders![5]

Yours,
August Strindberg

512. To ALGOT RUHE

Sthlm. 23 November 1903

Herr Algot Ruhe,

I must thank you for your beautiful book.[1] I have been following you quite closely, with interest, almost with curiosity, wondering if you would solve the insoluble problem, which I thought last summer had been solved by Otto Weininger (*Geschlecht und Karakter*).

I, too, have tried to solve it with veterinary psychology, but failed; believing in the existence of the transcendental, I am nevertheless still preoccupied with the phenomenon, though I'm uncertain whether it might not be my beautiful projections that I worship in Her; whether She isn't simply a *tabula rasa* on which I write with my best blood-ink!

Your analysis far surpasses Balzac's, and you really ought to write for the French; in this country, one isn't allowed to address men; Swedish literature is designed for secondary schools and candidates for confirmation.

Now you understand how eagerly I look forward to your next book: *Après*?

Are the illusions of art also only illusions? We'll see!

Yours sincerely,
August Strindberg

513. To ARTUR GERBER

[Original in German]

Stockholm, 8 December 1903

Herr Doctor,

A strange, mysterious man, that Weininger!

Born guilty, like me! I in fact came into the world with a bad conscience; fearful of everything, afraid of people and life. I now believe I did wrong before I was born. What does that mean? Only the theosophists have the courage to reply.

Also like Weininger, I have become religious, from fear of becoming a monster. I also worship Beethoven, have even founded a Beethoven Club, where only Beethoven is played. But I have noticed that so-called good people cannot stand Beethoven. He is a tormented, restless spirit who cannot be called divine, yet he is most definitely other worldly.[1]

Weininger's fate? Yes, did he betray the secrets of the Gods? Stolen fire?

The air became too thick for him down here, is that why he suffocated?

Was this cynical life too cynical for him?

That he departed this life, means for me that he had the highest possible permission to do so. Otherwise such things do not happen.

It was so written.

Yours sincerely,
August Strindberg

P.S. Do not publish my letters before my death.

514. To HJALMAR BRANTING

1 January 1903[1]

Hjalmar Branting,

Thank you for your kindness; my best wishes for the New Year to you and your family too!

However, the moon is full once more; why not have a game of skittles next week, when the New Year has woken up a little?

Will you come by one evening and arrange it?

Yours,
August Strindberg

515. To HARRIET BOSSE

1 January 1904[1]

Harriet,

If you ask me why I didn't wish you a Happy New Year, my answer is: I did so in my heart all New Year's Day.

If you also ask why I didn't come to you, my answer is: I don't know!

I don't know why I flee from your home, when I come to see you; I don't know why I feel hostility when you are friendly in a particular way.

You betrayed me once to my enemies, you bore my head upon a platter and my heart in a bowl to these men of the world, and therefore things can never be the same again! To be my enemy's friend? How could I?

Don't touch my fate with wanton hands! Haven't I warned you often enough? But you in your arrogance had to do so – like all the rest!

I wept for forty days over your treachery, when you went around mocking the one who only wished to raise you up. You wish to descend, but I want to rise! You can't follow me, and I do not wish to follow you!

That is undoubtedly the secret!

My name
(given me by my mother and father,
which you could never pronounce.)[2]

516. To CARL LARSSON

25 January 1904

Carl Larsson,

It was Koppel's idea,[1] not mine! But I was willing!

To recover oneself! Yes, I needed ten years. One travels round the world and comes back to the same point, right. But one's not the same person, for so much has happened on the way, and that's the best part!

Yours,
August Strindberg

517. To HARRIET BOSSE

[9? April 1904]

My Friend,

So you really think an ordinary lawyer can achieve what we ourselves have tried to do but failed.[1] Though if you feel the bond is too tight, then so be it; although it seems to me you have availed yourself of your freedom with little enough care for bonds. The marriage ceremony could not bind us, but you think that divorce can separate us; very well then! I, who have felt myself bound by my vows, might well gain by it; then I can consort with whomsoever I want to, furnish my home as I want to, keep what servants I want, think and act as I want, without anyone having the right to pass adverse comment. It means recovering my personal freedom, and regaining my honour, which is now deposited in your hands, for if you behave badly, the dishonour is mine; every word you say about me is accepted as the truth itself, even if it isn't true; therefore you could murder me with a word – if I'd not placed my fate in God's hand. Once, when you misused the power which Providence had given you over me, I nearly said to you what Christ told Pilate: 'Thou couldest have no power at all against me, except it were given thee from above.'

You had been given power over me, but you abused it, and you believed it was your own, therefore you lost it.

As for our last encounter, you so poisoned me with your suspicion that I became suspicious myself,[2] and when I then looked back into the past, lo, it was nothing but deceit, and my entire emotional life was counterfeit; yet I now think you are suffering from remorse. Such was my Easter, when everything I had experienced with you turned to ashes.

You will appreciate how I long for freedom and honour regained! for restitution!

Well, so be it!

[no signature]

518. To AXEL STRINDBERG

[6 May 1904]

Dear Brother,

Richard Bergh has invited himself over this evening. Please arrange things so you can come. We long for some Beethoven, and Rich. is a rare visitor.

Your friend,
August

519. To HARRIET BOSSE

[27 May 1904]

Beloved!

Isn't it right to follow one's best feelings, especially when they enjoin one to do right?

Isn't it clear enough that we are being drawn to each other, in spite of all our differences?

And isn't Lillan[1] entitled to our consideration?

You fear this journey abroad, as you should, for you will come to feel how the child misses you; you may have to interrupt your journey and spend the summer in hospital in a strange country, far from us. That's what I believe may happen.

You ask for advice! Here's one idea. I'll let you have (?) my beautiful Isola Bella on Furusund.[2] You can take a cook and Sigrid. I'll remain in town with my servant; and come out and stay only as long as you want or we can manage.

We can, as long as we avoid the dangers, and we know what they are. Just as your acting career is your affair, so my writing must be mine; nothing in common but our home, our child and our friends. If we each have our own circle of friends, we shall drift apart and be unfaithful.

Alf and Inez,[3] whom I'm otherwise fond of, have a disruptive influence on our life. They can visit you when I'm in town.

But we must live as man and wife, for I love your body as I do your soul, and I know that our knowledge of each other has gained ground even though it took time, as I told you it would on our first night together.

And we must risk having a child, but a son this time, so you won't be disappointed afterwards. I now believe that after so much self denial, we will have one. And I also believe that when I long for your beauty as now, you will find what you have long been searching for.

Let us tempt fortune once more!

What will the world and our lawyer say? They will rejoice in their hearts.

For mankind weeps when it sees love shattered, even though it has no love for those who suffer!

[no signature]

520. To HARRIET BOSSE

[31? May 1904]

Beloved, and so be it! The sufferings in store for us will surpass everything we have endured so far.

You're about to make an Inferno journey to Paris, torn by your longing for the child, and will perhaps turn back or fall ill.

I am sitting with Lillan, who is calling for her mother, and when I can't console her, she gets angry. It's more than she can bear, and she doesn't want to eat at the same table with me because you aren't here.

There are moments when I think she will find life terrible, and leave us. She brought such joy and ennobled our union, gave us an interest in life. But she wants a home and parents, she wants to have relatives and see her parents together. It is only with the two of us that she feels at home. And only when *we three* are together do I see any light. We three, man, woman, child, were a world, justified, complete, sufficient unto ourselves, and therefore beautiful. When we drove out at midday on a Sunday, people bowed their heads, and we weren't obliged to drive behind the Prince that time, had we not chosen to, and found it proper.

And now we're parting! Do you really know why?

I don't! I've never been the one to leave! I've sat, waiting – as I am now!

You have been away seeking happiness in your freedom from me! Have you found it? Do you think there is such a thing as unalloyed happiness, or that it has its price? It can be bought with suffering and privation, but then it can be so intense that one can live on its memory for years to come. The memory of *one* Sunday morning still keeps me alive.[1]

[no signature]

521. To HARRIET BOSSE

[8 June 1904]

Now I am doing as I did in Karlavägen; I am adorning our home in homage to your spirit, which I know visits us, at least Lillan; and I believe your spirit can feel whether or not it is beautiful here. So it will feel at home, I had the walls of the large room papered in your favourite colour, the most delicate violet with three narcissi, and put up new curtains in a floral pattern with birds, as delicate in texture as a dream.

But if you were to come yourself for however long, I have a room on the first floor which is as friendly, as private, and as quiet as a bird's nest. And there I would make up a bed for a brother and sister on the floor out of our two mattresses, which have finally met out here after such a long separation. I would sew them together with silk yarn; and I would sew our bedcovers into one, and our sheets as well; then we would sleep on each other's arms, in each other's arms; if you came. But I know nothing! Have asked Millar[1] by letter, but he doesn't answer.

We live on a small island, green, bright, open, so one can hear the plash of the sea as one lies in bed. We live, literally, among primroses and orchids.

Lillan is well-behaved, never cries, is gentle and loving. When life is hard, she smiles and talks to me; and her warm, soft little hand guides me on over the stones. She seems on good terms with life and to have no fear of people, however justified. She makes their acquaintance by herself, preferably with grown-ups. The Chemist[2] is her good friend, and the other day she introduced herself to a German. Sigrid[3] couldn't tell what language they spoke.

I am now reading Emerson, who Maeterlinck so often refers to as his teacher. I am also reading Novalis,[4] who seems to come from the same regions as Maeterlinck; so I am not lonely. Consorting with spirits (in books), my kindred. Emerson has given me a satisfactory account of Swedenborg. And shown me his greatness.

Received *Das Theater*[5] from Schering yesterday, in which he has written on 'Strindberg's *Traumbühne*', and included two pictures from *Damascus*. He recommends it as a way of staging *Faust*.

Sigrid has written every day. She is a conscientious, kind human being and a fine person. Lillan obeys her without question. Moreover, there is peace in the kitchen!

Send a nice letter for once, when you do write. Hatred is vain, but goodness is all powerful! If people only knew that!

[no signature]

522. To HARRIET BOSSE

Sunday morning, 12 June 1904

Harriet,

Thank you for your friendly postcard with greetings from the Orfila and Mme Charlotte's! But have you seen my rainbow on the dyer's glass door in the rue de Fleurus, to the left of the Luxembourg Garden?[1]

The bow in the sky = No second Flood!

Great hubbub! Lillan has been stung by a mosquito, the naughty thing! Uncle Axel and Uncle Svennberg[2] are here. Beethoven evening! until I dozed off with the sun in my face.

Saw Antoine's programme for next season! *King Lear*, adapted by Pierre Loti (the little lieutenant!),[3] *Old Heidelberg*,[4] etc. No Maeterlinck.

How will this summer end? Everything is so uncertain, vague, threatening!

Have you thought something out yet?[5]

Gusten

523. To EMIL SCHERING

Furusund (Isola Bella), 13 June 1904

Dear Herr Schering,

Much obliged for the 400 Mk, Emerson and *Ofterdingen*![1]

Likewise the *Traumbühne*[2] and Harden.[3] I will add my name to the Harden, and am glad that in lieu of something greater, he has for now received this modest monument.

And then, since you Germans seem to have all knowledge in stock: are Newton's mystical writings on the Apocalypse available? Also Kepler's mystical text on the Earth as a living being, which breathes at Ebb and Flood (Systole and Diastole)? I think it's called *Cosmographia Mystica*[4] (see Brockhaus' Encyc).

Is there a Böhme?[5] *Ja wohl*![6] But his principal work? Whatever it's called.

Can I have these?

Is the English edition of Swedenborg's Scientific Works by Wilkinson[7] available (or in German), in particular *de Cultu et Amore Dei*, which is his Cosmogony, and *de Regno Animali* [*sic*], etc.

Emerson is a whole new education for me, to which Novalis is a corrective. But Emerson's mysticism has ceased to be mysticism, and is now limpid rationalism.

One thing, while I remember. If I die soon, will you collect the following works in *one volume* and publish them under the title 'The Son of a Servant':

1. *The Son of a Servant*.
2. *In Time of Ferment*.
3. *In the Red Room*.
4. (4th Part of this work in manuscript at Bonniers)
5. *Die Beichte eines Thoren*. (With appendix, *He and She*, correspondence, at Bonniers in manuscript.)
6. 'The Quarantine Officer's Second Story' (from *Fairhaven and Foulstrand*).
7. *Inferno*.
8. *Legends*.
9. *Alone*.
10. *The Occult Diary*, since 1896.
11. Correspondence, letters.

This is the only monument I desire: a black wooden cross and my story!

If you come here this summer, look in on Furusund! it's more beautiful than ever!

Yours sincerely,
August Strindberg

524. To RICHARD BERGH

7 July 1904

Richard Bergh,

Before I left town, I heard that Fröken Svensson[1] was planning to set up a modern Theatre this autumn under the patronage of Prince Eugen,[2] and that among other things, she intended to put on *The Outlaw*.

What *The Outlaw*, an old-fashioned piece and a weak one, has to do with modern Art, I don't know. The choice seems idiotic to me, or else malicious, since my youthful play will be ranged alongside Heiberg's *The Balcony*.[3] If she'd chosen *Creditors*, which is the prototype of all the later Balcony plays, I would have been more justly treated.

Now may I first of all be spared *The Outlaw*, and since you intervened with me about its performance last time (when it was mutilated), please convey my wishes to her. If she won't listen, I'll simply forbid the performance.

If she wants to put on one of my modern pieces, we can choose between *Miss Julie* (which is still playing at the Kleines in Berlin),[4] *Creditors, The Father, Comrades, The Dance of Death, The Dream Play, et al.*, but on condition that it is performed uncut. Will you tell her that?

Here I am now at Isola Bella with wife and child, sailing-boat, bathing-hut, fishing rod, opera terrace and sunshine, just as in the best and fairest summer days I've known. *C'est la vie, quoi*? While it lasts! I know nothing about the morrow, much less the autumn. I take one day at a time (*Carpe Diem*), like a date case. In a diary one can always peep between the pages in advance, but the sealed book of a date case makes that impossible. *Das macht ein Unterschied*.[5]

Is Värmland just as splendid and beautiful in the rain?

Don't take my harsh words badly now, but I've no wish to do anyone an injustice, not even myself! – With best wishes,

Yours,
August Strindberg

The Beethoven boys (Axel and Svennberg) had a soirée here recently which lasted until sunrise!

525. To RICHARD BERGH

[8? August 1904]

Richard B.,

Since Fröken Svensson is of the same opinion, we ought to be able to reach an understanding; and in the hope that we can, I suggest my *Dream Play*.

Two years ago, when I was on the point of founding a Freie Bühne with Hillberg, I arranged the staging of this piece in a cheap and practical way, so it could be put on in Folkets Hus.[1] For wherever we turned we were threatened by the disgraceful competition of the Royal monopoly if we operated with more than *one* décor. In order to avoid this, I painted (?) a permanent frame for the whole play: a *Forest* of Poppies. Then a permanent inner stage of flowers, in which I made an opening 3 ells big, behind which I placed some so-called screens (permitted by the royal authorities). These screens consist of painted canvases, four ells in size, on a frame. That accounted for the scenery. Surely one could find some wealthy man who would arrange for a youngster (Arthur Sjögren?)[2] to paint these bagatelles for 1,000 or so, if Fröken S. hasn't the money!

Moreover: if Fröken S. has a young girl with respectable manners and a serious cast of mind, the play is made. I recall a Fröken Palm, and was much taken with her excellent grounding!

Indra's Daughter needn't be beautiful! The other roles play themselves, and can be doubled in various ways. If you haven't got another theatre, I suggest Folkets Hus, and if they refuse: 'from below, when you will not from above!'[3]

Since the Philistines' theatres have been closed to me for the last two years, I'd be happy with whatever comes up. And with being my own contemporary, not with the 1870s!

If you have a proper theatre, however, then the *Damascus* stage is the one to use. (See 'Strindberg's *Traumbühne*' encl.)[4]

The summer is drawing to an end! Everything comes back and is repeated! Last Saturday my wife and I gave a supper party at Isola Bella – for the entire Philp family! Brilliant atmosphere! P. gave a speech and was young! Not a discordant note! What about that?[5]

Music, flowers, wine, ladies, speeches, youth, beauty . . . And then it was over! But first we had some evenings on the terrace with the music from *Carmen*, a dinner and a supper at the Philps, and an unforgettable game of skittles, which ended late at night with a race (I came first).

C'est la vie, quoi? Maybe this will also come back before the summer is over. *Que sais-je*?[6]

Yours,
August Strindberg

526. To JOSÉPHIN PÉLADAN

Joseph (called Joséphin) Péladan (1859–1918), French novelist and dramatist, self-styled Sâr Mérodack and member of the *Ordre Kabbalistique de la Rose-Croix*. With his religious eroticism, his aristocratic occultism, and his obsession with the androgyne, he enjoyed a modish reputation in *fin-de-siècle* Paris out of all proportion to his literary talent. Nevertheless, his influence may be discerned in several of Strindberg's works, including *Swanwhite, Christina* and *A Dream Play*. According to *Inferno*, Strindberg first encountered Péladan through his *Comment on devient mage* in 1897, and after reading several of his plays and many of the novels in the series *La Décadence latine*, he analysed Péladan's historical significance in *Gothic Rooms*, where he is described as the first of the symbolists. Strindberg seems never to have met him in person.

[Original in French]

Sthlm. 14 August 1904

Maître,

Happy to have received a line from your hand I greet you without fine phrases

A.S.

527. To NILS ANDERSSON

Sthlm. 15 August 1904

Dear Nils Andersson,

Mankind is in crisis as it develops towards a finer spiritual life, and the 'sickly' phenomena this entails are vulgarly called neurasthenia. As it grows, a child is sick, just as a crab is sick when it changes its shell.

I believe what your friend says possesses complete reality on a higher plane. Our sensors, or receivers, have become more acute, and we live in permanent rapport with the whole of mankind. We hear other people's thoughts.

When Professor B. at the Observatory in Stockholm sought his post, and every astronomer in Europe was engaged in reviewing his credentials, he felt he was in rapport with them. But he also felt the hatred of the other applicants, and this hatred was so powerful that it affected the flame in his night light. The doctors called it neurasthenia.

When last spring, 'by higher command' and following a long struggle, I published *Gothic Rooms*, I felt by and by which of those concerned were just then reading the book; felt their hatred and saw their situation from within. But I had previously asked Providence for a sign which would indicate either approval or disapproval of my work: And when the approval came, I was certain, and at the same time immune to this hatred.

Since then I have lived through what has been on the whole an unforgettable summer at Fagervik with my wife and child, and the whole Gothic Storm has passed without a trace.

But all the time there have been signs and warnings, trials and minor tribulations. The strange thing is that when one has been 'pardoned', the suffering is never more than one can endure, though one must remain modest, and watch one's thoughts. These visitations are an honour, but one may not take pride in them.

The idea that Christ appears in person is doubtless to be understood symbolically, as Christ in Man; it doesn't mean we have to embrace obscure doctrines or become 'pietists'. I am a Christian freethinker, and feel Christ as a Power, a source of energy, rather than a model, which I can never attain while I am bound to life among men on earth.

You ought to read the enclosed article on the power of prayer irrespective of how weak or strong one's faith is, particularly the introduction and conclusion. The journal isn't theosophist but Occult, and published by a practising doctor.[1]

Otherwise I recommend Carl du Prel's[2] books (Reclam's Universal Library). He is modern and scientific, and explains *all* your friend's phenomena according to the methods of contemporary science.

If your friend is weak and has wantonly acquired enemies, either from arrogance or pride, he ought to reconcile himself with them *in his mind*. They will sense this at a distance, their hatred will subside, and he will gradually find peace.

On the other hand, if he believes he has a calling and feels certain about it, he must endure the struggle, and will find peace in the midst of battle. 'The Lord is fighting for you; yours is the patience.'

Your Malaria can mean a renovation of – your soul, which according to the Old Testament resides in the blood!

Now don't take offence, my friend! Only do stop rooting around in old things, in ancient forms of music! Don't you see how this might bring with it something horrible, heathen, from pastoral or animal life, a satyr or faun?[3]

Peter, thou shalt be a fisher of men, and not of the fish in the sea!

Well, this is what a weary pen can come up with on the spur of the moment! Tell your friend to fight the fight, to have no fear yet not be proud; not to rage against suffering, but give vent to his thoughts like a freethinker, according to the promptings of his spirit, allowing new experiences to give them a new content, and perhaps to appease the powers with small sacrifices!

In the hope of seeing you again soon,

Your friend,
August Strindberg

528. To HARRIET BOSSE

2 September 1904

My dear Friend,

So as to put an end to this eternal dissension, let us loosen these bonds which now mean nothing, and which only oppress us. Then let us see what happens!

We need only obtain an affidavit that we have lived apart from autumn 1903 to spring 1904. Introduce nothing irrelevant into the case and bear in mind that a certain lack of concord in our natures is neither your 'fault' nor mine. And take care that you do nothing to cast a shadow over Lillan's legitimacy. If you do, my interest in her would be dead for all time; and the child would suffer martyrdom in school and all her days.

So, let Millar go ahead with the proceedings!

I hate this unnatural bond that makes my life dependent upon yours, my honour dependent upon your behaviour. But I don't hate you, and would like us to part as friends!

We shouldn't have any more children, for we must be free in order to grow in our art!

This is my profoundest and my final view![1]

Your Friend
August Strindberg

529. To HUGO GEBER

25 December 1904

My dear Geber,

Thank you for your kind Christmas greetings!

Here is the book, which I am offering you and your firm, under its proper title.[1]

I had no pleasure in writing this book, but it hung over me like a calling of which I am now certain – it had to be written!

I haven't read it through, so I beg you to keep a red pencil in your hand while reading, and correct any inadvertencies straight away.

Yours,
August Strindberg

530. To HARRIET BOSSE

New Year's Day 1905

Beloved,

I must thank you for Christmas Eve, which I shall treasure as one of my most beautiful memories – You let me see you in your rightful setting – alone, superb, but with your loveliest jewel – the child!

And you let me see the mother, undressing her child for the night!

That is how your bedroom should always look!

You, so proud, wanted to have a husband at your side! That was a mistake, which has now been put right! But it was for the sake of the child! I feel most honoured!

But I brought with me the prose and the past; not cured of distrust since the summer either! Our reunion seemed natural to me, but there was a strange and hostile world behind you, and it frightened me.

Strange that you, who live among my enemies, should harbour friendly feelings for me. But this is no doubt the incongruity which lies at the heart of any truly great love, this 'in spite of everything!'

Our visible bonds could be undone, but not the invisible one! I think things are beautiful as they are and, at a distance, I can see you come from a higher sphere. I don't believe we are really mortals but that we have been cast down from somewhere a little higher up; that's why we are so constrained by our bodily shroud, and feel so ill at ease.

Last night at 12 o'clock I felt your perfume like a sudden cry, to which I responded!

I wonder at times whether there isn't some little soul which longs to have us as parents again, and is driving us together . . .

[no signature]

531. To EMIL SCHERING

28 March 1905

Dear Herr Schering,

At last! Francé[1] has found it!

If I knew him, and if I could be sure he wasn't a conceited *Wissenschaftler*,[2] I'd send him my Collections of pictures in the comparative histology of Animals and Plants, but I daren't because I'd never see my valuables again. You see, I've cut out illustrations from some expensive books, which I don't want to lose, and mounted pictures of Animal tissues alongside those of Plant tissues, thus proving they are identical. Plants have precisely the same tissues as animals: smooth muscular fibres, arteries, veins, nerves, etc.

If W. Pastor[3] would take the trouble to buy two large illustrated works, a Physiology of Plants and a Histology, and compare the one with the other, he'd see all the connections. If he knew any Swedish, I'd let him borrow my Collections.

Just one example:

= a Cell of Spruce wood

= Smooth muscular fibre of a mammal.

Don't buy any more books! I see Francé has got there!

In haste,
Yours sincerely,
August Strindberg

532. To HARRIET BOSSE

Sunday evening, 17 September 1905

Dear Friend,

Anne-Marie is sleeping, the Stranger on the ground floor is playing the E minor,[1] Rosa[2] sits forgotten on my sofa with open eyes and in rose-red dress (Rosa was presented yesterday evening to Henning Berger,[3] who stopped by for a whisky), the house is silent, both Ebba and Sarah are quiet people . . . .[4]

But outside the window one can see the moon over *Gustav Adolf's* Church, Venus under the Pleiades over Lidingö, and Capella (that is your star, remember)! I have been in a kind of blessed rapture all day, as if an unknown messenger had succeeded in reaching me. I am now liberated from the coalmines of Sw. History;[5] feel I am back in the present, which is the best of all times, because the whole of the past is the mulch in which the present grows.

What will come now? A beautiful today is my reply.

If I had a pension, I would write idylls and pastoral verse. If you were here, I would write monodramas for you! Or arrange *Macbeth* and Schiller's *Maria Stuart*, etc. as monodramas.[6] But I'm afraid one might clip one's own wings. With three actors, I would create a theatre, and perform with screens and an arch. Think it over!

The difficulties you experienced to start with are over; it will all go smoothly now!

My book[7] won't appear before 1 October, but will be exceptionally beautiful to look at.

Eysoldt has been touring with *Miss Julie* in Switzerland. She is also going to play it in Berlin this autumn with Reinhardt at the Deutsches Theater!

Fru Nansen[8] failed here; a deadly silence, in spite of all the humbug, dinners and column inches.

Why is the New Royal Theatre costing 20 million when the Swedish Theatre and the New Vasa cost only 1?

Good night!

Your friend,
August Sg

533. To HARRIET BOSSE

24 September 1905

Dear Friend,

After a night with Young Sweden[1] – we broke up at 6 this morning – I am free of the yoke again, and beginning to think that I must employ the pound of talent I was granted as a man of the theatre and, since others don't wish to perform me, try to perform my plays myself.

So, and since you seem unable to escape from the theatre too, shall we create one ourselves, and tour? But I must have three players; if I have you and two others, I shall borrow some money, engage staff and have my miniature stage painted with screens.

There will also be monodramas, and adaptations of older works, great and beautiful things, the Classics, Shakespeare, Schiller.

Like you, I have to live in and on my work. Such is life's hard law. Have you recovered your calling? Or shall I wait a while longer?

The night was interesting, but a little tiring – everyone came except Melsted, who is awaiting a child from his wife. Ruhe is also awaiting one, but still came!

Anne-Marie is happy and well, was given a little present by Uncle Berger!

A free Norway![2] At last! Now we can talk about something else!

Bo Bergman is now the theatre critic for *Dagens Nyheter*!

Live well, dear child, and *courage Madame*!

Your friend,
August Sg

534. To HARRIET BOSSE

26 September 1905

Dear Friend,

Your Monodrama is already planned in 5 acts, only one character; I daren't write a play just now, for this time our plan wasn't to involve other people.[1]

I'm now writing the Sw. Stories during the morning and then I have the rest of the day for you! In that way I start by ensuring our welfare; then write as I wish.

If everything fails, we can drive the kingdom round with Thespis' waggon, you, me, and Anne-Marie.

I'm trying hard to do something good; perhaps there will only be one: it is difficult and new, therefore I find it amusing. We'll have to have a dresser and a director, who can say the odd line off stage from a book.

In places there will be piano music, based on a new system.

We could perhaps try it out in Finland!

But I need to know if Fru Wiehe[2] acted on her own all evening, and whether it was only mime. I've never been able to make that out.

That can never really be a genre; works for a while though, like *L'Enfant prodigue*![3]

However, with two characters I could create a little world, and with three move it!

Think about it!

Have you recovered? Let me know if Juliet[4] is going well.

Your friend,
August Sg

535. To HARRIET BOSSE

[4 October 1905]

Dearly beloved,

I feel my last letter hurt you, but I couldn't help it . . .

My disharmonies tear me apart; loneliness drives me to seek company, but after each encounter, even the best, I withdraw, wounded, and find myself feeling even worse: I am ashamed without cause, suffer remorse without having done anything, loathe myself without knowing why . . .

Today I feel an urge to depart this life; I believe I have fulfilled my obscure mission, fear being drawn down into unknown swamps if I remain here, believe a better home awaits me somewhere in the beyond . . .

I've been thinking about the dream you had the last time you were here: that I had died by my own hand . . .

That is no doubt how it will all end, but for no particular reason. I strive upwards, but sink down; want so much to do good, yet behave badly; my old self is at odds with my new one; I want to see life as beautiful, but it isn't, only nature is beautiful; I pity people but I cannot respect or love them, for I know them through myself. My only comfort now is Buddha, who tells me clearly that life is a phantasm, a *Trugbild*,[1] which we shall see the right way round in another life. My hope and my future lie on the other side, that is why I find life so hard to bear; everything here falls short and mocks one; it should only be seen from afar. This morning I saw my landscape from my desk, you know the one, bathed in sunlight and so divinely beautiful that I was overcome with ecstasy.[2] I wanted to go down and take a closer look; but then it disappeared behind the hills, and when I came nearer, it was no longer the same!! What one seeks, eludes one!

Wife, child and a home were the best; a hard school, but the only protection against bad influences; without this protection I drift, fall into anyone's hands; loneliness is not bad, but there I fall prey to my stern, chastising self, which wounds me . . .

Think kindly of me, it will help me!

It is four years ago since you returned home with our little unborn child! I think of it now with gratitude and loss.

Yours.

536. To HARRIET BOSSE

22 October 1905

Beloved,

Yes, I was alone and with you in our flat last Friday evening; this flat which tolerates no one but us! It darkens and wrinkles its brow at strange men; and it is only having men for company that drags me down. You remember my innocent remark last summer – how a woman's presence elevates a man, who then not only appears a better person but is one! In fact it is every man's dream to seek salvation through a woman, salvation from what is low and coarse.

Solitude – but solitude within the family and its natural circle of relatives, that is how I envisaged the comparative bliss life has to offer.

It is possible, however, that when they are alone women don't maintain so high a tone either, as they do when men are present! For the same reason!

When I'm with other men, I sometimes try to put a check on the conversation by a well-placed silence, but it always ends as the majority will, and I am dragged down into the depths, where I don't want to go.

Alone with just one other person, I usually win out!

So we have met again with the daffodil, the rod, and Swanwhite, which always belong together in my memories of that spring in Banér and Grev Magnigatan![1]

But what a long, roundabout way!

Lillan and I are now counting the days; she says 'three, five, ten days and then Mummy will be here!' She hasn't forgotten you at all!

You'll see when you come!

Until then, and then: A big hug!

from

Us both

Yesterday evening, Saturday, I was invited to Djurgårdsbrunn[2] to play skittles and have supper with Young Sweden and Carl Larsson.

Well – – – there were a couple of moments when we adopted a higher tone, and that was thanks to Ruhe. He really is the finest and most genuine of men; never discusses the kind of things he writes about! Strange! But then things deteriorated! Ugh!!!

537. To HARRIET BOSSE

4 November 1905

Dearest,

You've stayed away two days and I thought you had let go of me.[1]

And one waits so long, one becomes listless, and fears what one has been waiting for. Even Lillan has stopped counting on her fingers. Everything's at a standstill – nature and life; and people become like ghosts when the sun goes in.

Rich. B.,[2] to whom I gave my collected Plays a year ago, had not read *Christina* before. When he did so, he was amazed! 'That is a role for Bosse; why hasn't it been performed?'

Then he read *Gustav III*! Even greater amazement!

Now I've asked him to read *Damascus III*!

If I have to be discovered by those closest to me, how long will it take the rest?

Are you really coming next Monday? I can hardly believe it!

I presume you'll stay with Inez, and I'll have to wait until Tuesday!

But don't squeeze your child to death when you wake her up at 10 o'clock on Monday night, for she won't be able to stay awake; and great excitement is dangerous for both young and old.

Your
August Sg

538. To HARRIET BOSSE

2 December 1905

Harriet,

It seems as if our saga is finished and our mutual destiny sealed – the Angel of Death is stalking 40 Karlavägen; the piano is gone, the Inferno painting as well,[1] the other paintings will follow on Monday. But Lillan, too, is abandoning me, is hard and alien –

The most difficult thing of all is how my memories darken, and turn to ashes.

Swanwhite is dead – long ago – the Crown Bride has lost her crown – Indra's Daughter is beginning to feel at home down in the dirt and enjoys the sufferings of mankind – the Easter girl prefers the cabaret to tragedy. Such is life!

I no longer believe in our life together, for I don't believe in what has been. You were perhaps the only one who understood me, at certain moments . . . and yet!

I don't know where I am now being taken, but it is onwards, and not downwards! And I hope never to stand in your way again, I certainly don't want to!

Regard my last letter as unwritten, and resolve to seek happiness elsewhere![2]

I am tired of this world and now wish to grow accustomed to the idea of the end, and what comes after it.

This was only *Lug* and *Trug* and *Schein*,[3] and leaves no sense of loss, only revulsion.

If I live much longer, what we have shared will turn to smoke like all the rest, and the child will be as alien to me as the others.

That will be a kind of happiness, if only I can achieve it!

August Sg

539. To HARRIET BOSSE

Midday, 8 December 1905

Dear Harriet,

Do you think we can ever free ourselves from each other after the way in which we have mingled our lives? When you are anxious down there in a distant land,[1] my heart beats up here in my breast as if it were yours.

Sometimes I feel your warm breath pass over my cheek, and then I think you are speaking my name in a friendly way.

At times I have you inside my coat, and I am you –

Wouldn't severing one of our lives from the other be the most painful of operations?

What kind of Christmas now awaits us? In a fortnight?

August Sg

540. To CHARLOTTE FUTTERER

Madame Charlotte Caron, née Futterer (1849–1925) was the owner of a small *crémerie* at 13 rue de la Grande Chaumière in Paris. She had been abandoned by her husband and ran the restaurant with the occasional help of her son, Louis. It was the haunt of the Polish painter Wladyslaw Slewinski and Alphonse Mucha as well as of Gauguin, Delius and the French poet Julien Leclercq. Favoured artists could eat there on credit and pay with their paintings: its walls were adorned with works by Gauguin, Slewinski and in due course at least one canvas by Strindberg, who lived at 12 rue de la Grande Chaumière during 1895, and eventually used the restaurant as a setting in *Crimes and Crimes*, where the figure of Mme Cathérine owes something to Mme Charlotte. Strindberg always retained an affection for her, and they often exchanged New Year letters. In 1898, he sent her his photograph which, according to the eminent Swedish sculptor, Carl Milles, fanned her already tender feelings for him. On hearing of his engagement to Harriet Bosse, she abandoned the *crémerie* and withdrew to the provinces.

[Original in French]

Stockholm, 12 January 1906

Chère Madame Charlotte,

The years go by, life and us, our friends, everything. And everything changes. From what Monsieur Eldh,[1] who came to put the finishing touch to my bust, says, the Crémerie no longer exists. And you have retired to the seclusion of the countryside, along with your memories of bygone days in the Grande Chaumière; Goguin [*sic*], Leclercq are dead, the others disappeared, vanished to the four corners of the earth.

As for me, I remarried in 1901 and am the father of a little girl of four, well-established, well-fed, and living an agreeable enough life after so many years of tribulations, both great and small. See how life changes!

It has been a great pleasure, Madame, to hear your news and to be reminded of the days, both good and bad, of my terrible years 1894–96, and I wish you happiness and peace for the rest of your days, after the storms of life.

Accept, Madame Charlotte, my good wishes for the year now beginning, and do not forget your old regular of long ago

August Strindberg

541. To HARRIET BOSSE

11 March 1906

Dear Child,

You are so restless that I don't know where I have you. However, if letters aren't reaching you, it's the fault of the post office. Your Russian stamps are no good here; we have to redeem them.[1]

Nothing new, only that Craig[2] was here. We didn't understand one another; so I sent Berger to talk English and help him. I don't know the outcome. Berger said we didn't care for the ballet. Sv.D.[3] lashed out at Duncan; Craig seems to be in love with her and, like Schering, has vowed she must come here. I discouraged the idea. So they went away with a dreadful impression of Sweden and the Swedes. We made ourselves as horrible as we could.

Craig was like Oskar [*sic*] Wilde; *der war mir zu schön.*[4]

Lillan and Brita[5] come here every day, eat a sandwich, draw, and look at the bird book. The latest idea entails using a burning glass in the sun to set light to whatever remains of our keepsakes from Hornbaek. Then there's smoke and the scent of lavender; we've also burnt a hole in Brita's black dress; that was novel!

Today, Sunday, Lillan has gone out to dinner; *elle dine en ville*, at Uncle Oskar's (Holm).[6]

Sonst nichts![7]

Enjoy yourself! At least the sun is shining!

Your
August Sg

542. To HARRIET BOSSE

13 March 1906

Dear Child,

You are storming and pressing upon me today, the 13th, more than usual.[1] Lillan feels lost, longs for mummy, invited herself home to me today, but ate nothing. Suggested we go out for a walk or a drive.

Duncan is coming to the Olympia 1–7 May. Let her, I shan't go, and don't want to meet her. Berger and Engström got hold of Craig and wandered about for 24 hours, to Thiel's, and round Djurgården. I didn't see them again.

There's a great to-do here about the theatre, and how they might best be shot of me.

Ranft disappeared without trace. Michaelsen is now a candidate.[2]

The plays are now beginning to grow in me again; big, weighty, mature, and I shall write them all. *Idun* has put up a prize worth 4,000 *Kr.* for the Roy. Theatre, but I'll bypass that and go straight to the board!

Can you stand what's happening in Finland?

Buy some new books from the bookshop to read! That's company!

I've just finished two by D'Annunzio: *Child of Pleasure* and *Illegitimate.*[3]

Powerful and terrible! (Published by Bonniers.) Much 'coarser' than mine; painful, instructive.

Easter is approaching; birch in the air; suffering, the cross!

Your
August Sg

543. To HARRIET BOSSE

22 March 1906

Dear Harriet,

Your letter's just arrived! – But I still say, you have Ranft ready and waiting for you.[1]

Lillan is here every day! Now she resembles Greta[2] again, just like the last time you were in Finland! Isn't that strange!

On Sunday we shall celebrate her birthday with a calash round Djurgården – just like *the other time*! – and then dinner. Inez thinks you are all right, and I no longer complain on your behalf, for then she snaps at me. I don't understand how her mind works, and can't carry on a conversation with her. But don't say that, for then I won't be allowed to see Lillan, and will have a mass of explaining to do.

Berger has gone abroad – to get divorced – but also to stay!

Eldh has been very fortunate with his graven image of me; Rubenson[3] claimed the New Theatre wants a copy. (?)

Next week the Riksdag is voting on my stipendium, which it's thought will get through.

On Tuesday, the 27th, the Aulin Quartet has invited itself here to celebrate the anniversary of Beethoven's death; Stenhammar may come too.

Axel and Rich. B. were here yesterday; we devoted ourselves to the 7th Symphony and 'The Waves of Sound'.[4] Also the 9th, which will be given next week. It's good to see that Beethoven endures; otherwise everything passes.

Flee, if you can't stand it any longer! You have Ranft – and me, for the summer! Left on my own I'll probably take Alsvik (Inez' place).

Isadora has had Craig write to Berger that she is willing to build a box for me on stage, since I *must* see her.[5] I told B. that I didn't wish to see her. If you're not here to save me, I'll leave town.

Schering writes that Craig is Isadora's lover and is ruining her, which is why he's losing people's respect. Craig brought 'England's greatest composer', Shaw,[6] with him here.

Engström admired Craig's paintings.

Give my regards to Greta and say I hope they get a little money from my plays out of Wetzer[7] for the spring. No other authorization is required.

All good things to you now.

Your Friend,
August Sg

544. To HARRIET BOSSE

1 April 1906

My dear One,

Lillan has been ill, but is well now. There was talk of the isolation hospital, and I was prepared to accompany her, after I had offered the use of the Yellow Room.

Today she came to Sunday lunch alone, because Inez had the Fahlstrøm's[1] here. She drove home in a closed carriage, because when one asks for a coupé they always send a cab. She ate well, but was pale and got tired, and liked being carried. This morning she had an early Sunday visit from Pappa with flowers!

Today I finished the Prologue in verse for my new play![2] Strange: in the surging joy of conception, I picture the whole play as light, grand, beautiful! When I write it down, there's nothing of this, and it becomes something else. Writing is almost a sin. Putting things into words is to degrade them! turn poetry into prose! To reduce to the commonplace, in short! – That's why I suffer from writing, and happily turn my back on what I've written.

Am starting to think about the summer. To Furusund, or at least the Baltic.

Visit from Svennberg[3] yesterday! The women are weak at the Swedish Theatre next season. He's been engaged, and the men are strong. Ranft is worried, and will soon be going abroad.

Well, that's about all! It will soon be *Easter*!

Your Friend,
August Sg

545. To HARRIET BOSSE

14 April 1906

Dear Child,

Easter went well![1] What a miracle! Then I have nothing with which to reproach myself.

However, it's now Easter all year round, year in year out.

I want to move, but can't; feel as though I were walking in space, turn dizzy, lose my thoughts and memories, five years of them, stored in these rooms; come under the yoke of strangers, their tastes and fancies, have to pander to their weaknesses, mongrels, and maids. I feel I must either stay here or really seek unknown regions, away from all this, over on the other side!

The play escaped me! Went its way! Empty! But I must start on something else. The novel tempts me most. I loathe the theatre. Pose! Superficiality, calculation.

Read Shakespeare's *Shrew*. It was awful. Circus – false, clumsy, untrue. To think the public lets someone throw dust in their eyes like that. And how can Borgström[2] make anything of this hollow, empty role? Most people must go around like dozy cattle, and can be made to believe anything. Those hapless ones whose eyes have been opened – they ought to depart this life!

Balzac's type of novel tempts me most now. As in *Alone*. There one can explain oneself, develop an argument, interpret people, study them in depth, thoroughly.

Your Easter egg came this evening while Lillan was here. When the table was covered with eggs, we both laughed aloud, and papa couldn't even tell if the last one, which was no bigger than a pea, really was the last, even with his glasses on.

Tomorrow we're having a dinner here, with asparagus and *meringue glacée*, for Inez and Alf too.

19 degrees in the shade! Probably something to do with Vesuvius![3]

That's all!

Come soon now, and give me the courage to move to Stocksund, for I must get away!

Your friend,
August Sg

The two-roomer on 12 Grevmagnigatan, 3rd fl., is vacant.[4]

546. To HARRIET BOSSE

28 April 1906

My dear One,

It was you who made *The Crown Bride* possible,[1] and I thank you! Now there only remains *Swanwhite* and the whole program will have been realized; we achieved it, with patience!

Why are you sad? According to Indian books of wisdom, an inexplicable sadness foreshadows an imminent happiness.

But I know another heavy sorrow: when one can see into other people's lives and glimpse all the horrors that are hidden beneath a charming, respectable surface. Then one wants to die!

I am struggling to educate myself, but not getting very far. However, in the end, religion means this to me: the hope of a better world, the certainty of liberation, belief in God! There is little to expect here: 'for the good that I would do, I do not; but the evil which I would not do, that I do. But it is no more I that do it, but sin that dwelleth within me.

For I see another law in my members, warring against the law of my mind, and bringing me into captivity to the law of sin which is in my members . . .

O wretched man that I am, who shall deliver me from the body of this death?'[2] That is the collective lament of the human race!

I went to see your child this morning, with some presents. 'Pappa must stay!' she said. Then it's hard to leave! Homeless, and so young! Perhaps that's how it's meant to be!

I can now plan for the summer, because some money has turned up! It will probably be Furusund, because of the aquamarine water!

You'll be here again on Thursday! I'm happiest for Lillan's sake, for I'm mostly out of it myself!

August Sg

547. To HENNING BERGER

Henning Berger (1872–1924), a largely self-educated Swedish writer who spent the 1890s working in an office in Chicago. He returned to Stockholm in 1899 but lived from 1909 in Copenhagen. Berger's best works are characterized by their detailed observation of urban life both in Sweden and the United States, about which he wrote the first modern account in Swedish, *Där ute* (Out There, 1901). Berger's main achievement was the trilogy *Drömlandet* (Dreamland, 1909), *Bendel & Co.* (1910), and *Fata Morgana* (1911), which formed the first sequence of realistic autobiographical fictions in Swedish since *The Son of a Servant*. Over the five years their correspondence lasted, Strindberg was to prove a critical but appreciative reader of Berger's work. There are thirteen extant letters from Strindberg to Berger.

24 May 1906

Henning Berger,

Thank you for your friendly letter!

Loneliness has closed about me; I'm writing a Balzacian story for *Idun*,[1] and am oblivious to the world in which I'm living. I've nothing to relate, nothing to philosophize about, since this present mood devours everything.

Yes, our politics has shown us old ones what we already knew: that the world is pretty much itself whatever happens. Just when the Danes finally got a Liberal government and corporal punishment, so we got one too, which muzzled us![2]

I can no longer distinguish left from right; besides, if one turns on one's heel, right is left and vice versa. Or one sails so far to the west that one comes up in the east!

Isidora [*sic*] Duncan left! I didn't see her!

If you read the papers, you know as much as I do. But I know no more about you than what you write; and yet you know people are interested in what you're doing. Your next book will probably be decisive, provided you don't throw yourself into drama, as you may.[3] Swedish Drama has so far been too simple, formless. Your writings have a formal elegance and should prove successful, as long as you don't grow careless when you approach the theatre.

Well, that's it really!

All the best!

Yours,
August Strindberg

548. To HARRIET BOSSE AND ANNE-MARIE STRINDBERG

6 July 1906

My dear Ones,

I hardly had time to say hello to you before you were gone.[1] And then I got pains in my throat and chest, and last night a fever as well, so that the whole day has been as black as pitch. Today is really the first sultry day, and the apartment is unfriendly, gloomy.

What have I done? I usually ask. Don't know! – Should I go away? Where? After all, it's the same everywhere.

I've discovered that I've been making gold for ten years, but thrown it away because it always appeared as black as soot, brown like snuff. But I haven't the energy to kick up a fuss, for no one would believe me. I'm sending you a formula to use after my death.

Form.

Green vitriol
Copper nitrate } Extremely weak solutions.
Silver nitrate

(Heat, preferably with a piece of paper in the bottom of the cooking-utensil)

May be varied *ad infinitum* by one solution and one precipitant.

That is the secret; so one can produce Any metal from each one's Solution and Precipitant.

But Gold is produced by one Copper and one Silver salt, precipitated with Green Vitriol, or with Oxalic Acid, or with Tartaric Acid Ammoniac, or with Stannous Chloride, or with Quicksilver Oxidul Nitrate. Keep this letter, just for fun!

The gilded silver you saw is produced like this: the Silver Leaf is immersed in a weak solution of $Cu\ SO^4+Fe\ SO^4+Na\ SO^2$; and heated. Then coated in Borax and dissolved in water. One can then see a *blue* liquid with an iridescent brown lustre, which is characteristic of a gold solution.

Enjoy yourselves, and think of me!

Your
August Sg

549. To JÖRGEN LANZ-LIEBENFELS

Jörgen Lanz-Liebenfels (1874–1954), Austrian writer and racist, whose theories were to influence Hitler. He and Strindberg can have met while the latter was staying at Klam and Saxen in 1896. Although he sent Strindberg his books and pamphlets as they appeared, the latter did not bother to read them all. Nevertheless, he derived the term '*äffling*', applied in *A Blue Book* to the epigones of Naturalism and Darwin, from Lanz-Liebenfels' notion of 'Der Affenmensch', or Ape Man. This is the only letter of Strindberg's to him that survives.

10 July 1906

Dear Sir,

I have read your book[1] all in one go and – am astonished.

If it isn't the light itself, it is at least a source of light.

I haven't heard such a prophetic voice since *Rembrandt als Erzieher*.[2]

My warmest greetings!

August Strindberg

550. To GRETA STRINDBERG

11 September 1906

Dear Greta,

I have to write this letter, for it is my duty, even if it does no good.

Be careful how you behave, for we do not have the same loose morals here as in Finland. Do not receive men in your room after 9 in the evening, for if you do, you will be given notice to quit your lodgings, and that would be a disgrace.[1]

Do not interfere in other people's lives,[2] for if you do, doors will be closed to you, and you will be absolutely alone, without any respectable company.

Do not go to the café every evening, and do not go out alone at night, for that arouses the attention of the police, and can have incalculable consequences.

Things have already gone so far that only a change in your conduct can save your reputation.

August Strindberg

551. To ADOLF PAUL

40 Karlavägen, Sthlm. 6 January 1907

Adolf Paul,

Will you send me *Teufelskirche*[1] to read, preferably in Swedish. An intimate theatre for *Moderne Kunst* is being set up here,[2] and to judge from the reviews, I think there is something new in your Drama.

If you write anything new, then get in touch, but seek the intimate in form, a restricted subject, treated in depth, few characters, large points of view, free imagination, but based on observation, experience, carefully studied; simple, but not too simple; no great apparatus, no superfluous minor roles, no regular five-acters or 'old machines', no long-drawn-out whole evenings.

Here *Miss Julie* (without an interval) has stood the test of fire and shown itself to be the form demanded by the impatient man of today. Thorough but brief.[3]

Firstly then: *Teufelskirche*!

Yrs,
August Strindberg

552. To EMIL SCHERING

[28 January 1907]

Dear Herr Schering,

But why doesn't Reinhardt want *The Father*, which has never been performed in Berlin (as good as)? Or *Damascus*? Or *The Nightingale*, which is intimate? Or *The Comrades*? Or *The Dream Play*, which is now going to be performed at the Swedish Theatre using Sciopticons for the scenery? Two Sciopticons, bought in Dresden and used at the theatre there.

Or *Easter* (intimate!)? Or???

Yours sincerely,
Aug Sg

When is Vallentin's theatre opening?[1]

553. To EMIL SCHERING

27 March 1907

Dear Herr Schering,

By today's post I am sending you a Second Chamber Play (Opus 3), called *A Spook Sonata*[1] (with the subtitle Kama Loka,[2] though this ought not to be included). It is *schauderhaft*[3] like life, when the scales fall from our eyes and we see *Das Ding an Sich*.[4]

It has form and content: the Wisdom that comes with the years when our knowledge of life has accumulated and we have acquired the ability to comprehend it. That is how 'The World Weaver' weaves men's destinies; secrets like these are to be found in *every* home. People are too proud to admit it; most of them boast about their imaginary happiness, and generally hide their misery. The Colonel plays his auto-comedy to the end; illusion (Maya)[5] has become reality to him – the Mummy wakes up first, but cannot wake others . . . .

I have suffered as though in Kama Loka (Scheol)[6] while writing it, and my hands have bled (literally).

What has saved my soul from darkness during this work is my Religion (= *Anschluss med Jenseits*).[7] The hope of a better life to come, and the firm conviction that we live in a world of folly and delusion (illusion), from which we must struggle to free ourselves.

For me, however, things have grown brighter, and I have written with the feeling that these are my 'Last Sonatas'.

When you've given me your impression of *The Spook Sonata*, I'll send you Opus 1 of The Chamber Plays, an excellent piece for philistines, which can 'go'.[8]

Opus 4 is in progress![9]

N.B. Don't let any Swede get an inkling of the title or content of my Chamber Plays!

Yours very sincerely,
August Strindberg

554. To EMIL SCHERING

1 April 1907

Dear Herr Schering,

It was a great and novel pleasure for me in my Easter suffering to find you so quickly taken by *The Ghost Sonata* (that's what it should be called, both after Beethoven's Ghost Sonata in D minor and his Ghost Trio, not 'Spook' therefore).[1] And you are the first to read it! I hardly knew myself what I had done, but sensed it was something sublime, which made me shudder, the same overwhelming feeling as when one weeps with joy or (like Frederick the Great) witnesses a noble deed in one's old age.

Now, in parenthesis: let me have the manuscripts back when you've finished with them.

The Dream Play opens in a week! If you could get here, it would help you greatly in ascertaining its stage-worthiness.

I have written a Prologue in verse; among the clouds Indra's Daughter talks with her invisible father about going down to see what life is like for mankind. The music for this is from Beethoven's *Pastoral* Symphony, the *Gewitter und Sturm*[2] movement.

Opus IV of the Chamber Plays is in progress: it is more dreadful than the others!

I throw it aside, but it pursues me; and with bleeding hands, I bare my misery, sacrificing myself for my work, burning up consideration, shame, gratitude, every human feeling. I suffer, but regret nothing; I must drink the cup (see *Master Olof*, I:i. Cf. Jeremiah I:i).[3] How cruel life is, more cruel than we!

Yours very sincerely,
August Strindberg

555. To EMIL SCHERING

2 April 1907

Dear Herr Schering,

No, the task was too heavy, and today I burned Opus IV, or 'The Bleeding Hand'.

Now I beg you, read my new dramas only as that; they are mosaic work as usual, from my own and other people's lives, but please don't take them as autobiography or confessions. Whatever doesn't correspond with the facts is poetry, not lies.

It seems to be part of my Karma or Fate that I may not defend myself; in other words, I am condemned in certain important things to suffer innocently (but not in others). And if I try to defend myself, I am punished for what seems like a crime against the law of my Fate (Karma). I am therefore no saint, far from it, but in many ways, people have done me an injustice. However: 'As against God we are always in the wrong'.[1]

The burned Opus IV was a self-defence, that's why it was burned.

It's probable that I am now entering upon something new. I long for the light, have always done so, yet have never found it.

Is it the end that is approaching? I don't know, but that's what it seems like to me. Life is squeezing me out, as it were, or forcing me to leave, and I have long since rested my hopes on 'the other side', with which I am in contact (like Swedenborg).

A feeling has also come over me that I have completed my task, and have no more to say. My whole life often seems to me as if it had been staged for me, so that I might both suffer and portray it. Therefore my actions might, from one point of view, be regarded as immaterial (morally speaking); but that doesn't mean I don't suffer from the dirt I've been dragged through, a suffering which has acted as *conscientia scrupulosa* (pangs of conscience). And the strange thing is that those deeds (?) with which I have reproached myself, have been dependent upon, or necessary for, my development, and have often only arisen as involuntary responses to provocations from without. Thus I have struck back when others have struck me, but it has nevertheless hurt me more to strike than to be struck.

Now we'll see: *Was will jetzt kommen*?[2]

Yours very sincerely,
August Strindberg

556. To BIRGER MÖRNER

In duplo: Raise a stone to Solander on his Cape, 13/23 May this year!

[7 April 1907]

Dear B.M.

In duplo! As well as the picture postcard,[1] I'm sending you this since the former can be defaced by the postmarks! Remembered that there was a Cape Solander near Sydney: Solander was a pupil of Linneaus, and travelled with Cook (not the travel bureau but the round the world sailor of 1770). As the anniversary of Linnaeus' birth is to be celebrated 13/23

May, you can celebrate Solander and find out what's happened to his Cape. (Botany Bay lay between 'Vorgebirgen Banks und Solander' (*Brockhaus Lex.*, 1851). Solander was a somebody, and merits a stone on his Cape.) This is my contribution to Scandinavianism in Sydney. All best wishes!

Yrs, August Strindberg

557. To EMIL SCHERING

[7 April 1907]

Dear Herr Schering,

Forgot to ask you to tell the Doctor[1] that I don't want to write anything in the way of Psychiatry, but that there is a considerable amount on the subject in *Gothic Rooms* and the unpublished Breviary.[2]

Don't you think the following could be inserted into the last scene of *The Ghost Sonata*, or made visible in letters of fire above *Toten-Insel*:[3]

'And God shall wipe away all tears from their eyes; and there shall be no more death, neither sorrow, nor crying, neither shall there be any more pain (*Leiden*): for the former things are passed away.' (*Revelation*, 21, 4.)

My *Dream Play* will be performed this coming week!

N.B. Don't forget the Soya bottle,[4] the colouring, which I've now been suffering for thirty days; eaten coloured water!

Yours very sincerely,
August Strindberg

558. To EMIL SCHERING

17 April 1907

Dear Herr Schering,

It is 8 in the evening (the 17th) and the curtain is now rising on *The Dream Play* while, as usual with premières, I am sitting at home.

The day before yesterday I saw the dress rehearsal – and all my cheerful confidence in my best loved Play, the child of my greatest pain, vanished. I became gloomy, got it into my head that it ought never to be performed – people ought not to be told these things, and they mustn't grumble over their fate. – I have been waiting for some catastrophe to intervene and prevent the performance! But as I said, it is now 8 o'clock!

Furthermore, these insubstantial images cannot be made substantial – or so it seems to me, the author! Perhaps I'm not the right judge!?

Writing *The Roofing Feast* was a great pleasure, and I originally conceived it as a play. The tension rises along with the house, which grows over the crime. The *leitmotiv* is the green eye, revenge which is extinguished by suffering and ends with the flag being hoisted – all this is *Zur Schau,* stage effects – He must not lie in bed, however, but sit on a chair – until the moment he is laid to eternal rest.[1]

But I need the manuscript, so please can you let me have it! Then we'll see!

(The curious thing is, the whole story is from life! for the most part. See my Diary 1896–1907.)

The Green Eye has nothing to do with Adolf P.[2] but my first wife's former husband . . . And when I moved in here[3] in 1901 with my third wife, C.G.W. lived opposite, on Narvavägen, so his window was visible from our Bedroom. Two years ago another house was erected in between, concealing his. Etc!

Who is Antonie Toran in Halensee? She is a Swedenborgian and has written me a couple of letters, quite personal without being offensive.

The Dream Play has unnerved me – 'God is angry with me' – and yet I had the best of intentions, this time! I don't think people like hearing they are unhappy either! Everyone flatters themselves over their relative happiness, which they take to mean that they are 'better' than those who are unhappy.

Now that the monologue is back in fashion and the one in *The Roofing Feast* is specifically motivated by the garrulity brought on by the effect of the morphine, will the drama form a single, giant monologue?? . . . (No?)

But I shall probably have to interweave the destinies of the three characters so that the Nurse and the Doctor have played a greater role in the fate of the dying man.

The episode with his wife and child must either be a Prelude (or be left out); and The Green Eye will then be the first husband.

11 p.m. Telephone call from Bosse and Ranft that *The Dream Play* was a success!

Good Night!
Yours very sincerely,
August Strindberg

559. To EMIL SCHERING

[24 April 1907]

Dear Herr Schering,

As you can see from my Chamber Plays, after having read *Clavigo, Stella,* etc.[1] I have gone back to long speeches and monologues. The French form of dialogue has degenerated into catechistic questioning and precludes profound and exhaustive treatment.

The incomplete (abortive) intentions should be retained, because they give a naturalness to the portrayal of life, since life is full of frustrated plans, passing fancies, projects which serve to fill out a conversation yet still constitute sources of energy. The Bishop's funeral is only part of the scene-setting; it contributes to the atmosphere and perhaps means something, but I no longer remember what; maybe 'an undeserved glory', hinting at the emptiness of all things, and the glorification of emptiness![2]

Yours sincerely,
Aug Sg

560. To AXEL STRINDBERG

25 April 1907

Dear Brother,

With reference to our harp experiment this evening, the following:

The Chopin *Impromptu Fantaisie*, Op. 66, could be transcribed like this: the base remains the same, but the string of pearly notes in the treble is changed into chords, which, especially on page 2, are indescribably beautiful (accompanied by the base).

Now the question is: since arpeggios sound best on the harp and should be in the treble, couldn't one reverse them, and put the present bass into the treble and convert the pearly string of the treble into bass *chords*?

What do you say to that?

That this must be included in *Swanwhite* is for sure![1]

I've also an eye on the Nocturne, Opus 37; the leitmotif, that is! But it's harder to fathom!

Please don't do the instrumentation of the Etude, Opus 25, which I wanted as an overture (for orchestra), but tell me if the bass solo might not suit the oboe. You would no doubt prefer the cello,[2] but it doesn't sing as well as the oboe, which is my favourite. Or the horn, since one appears in the play?[3]

R.S.V.P. when convenient.

Yrs,
August

561. To EMIL SCHERING

26 April 1907

Dear Herr Schering,

You've probably been misled by Hedberg's review, because *The Dream Play* was received splendidly, and is being performed today, for the 10th time, in a benefit performance for Bosse; it will join the repertory, which is why it's coming off on Sunday, when in any case the company is going on tour.[1]

There aren't any good pictures.

I had begun a major Chamber Play with *'Toteninsel'* (Böcklin's) as a setting.[2] The beginning was good (Kama-Loka) but I lost interest, as though I'd lost interest in life, and had a presentiment of the end. For ten years I have been preparing myself for death and have lived, as it were, 'on the other side'.

I am now reading the proofs of *Black Banners*, in which, as you know, I break with the 'Black Ones'. They will no doubt murder me, but I accept that as my calling, and am accustomed to it!

My breviary is still in manuscript and is called 'A Blue Book Dedicated to Those Whom It Concerns'. Will probably be an *Œuvre posthume*.

I am wondering whether to take up my wanderer's staff again and go out into the world of illusion? But I am 60, tired, and hate the dirt of hotels, and dirty habits.

Only one journey tempts me, the last of all, and I want to die in my own country!

However, *The Crown Bride* and *Swanwhite* are now being prepared for the Swedish Theatre this autumn.

Yours sincerely,
August Strindberg

N.B. About the Chamber Plays. One doesn't ask such questions! Discretion – *s'il vous plaît*!

There one lives in a world of Intimations, where people speak in half tones, mutedly, because they are ashamed of being human!

However: cut Marie Antoinette![3]

562. To EMIL SCHERING

6 May 1907

Dear Herr Schering,

Yes, that is the secret of all my novels, stories, and tales, they are plays.

During those long periods when, as you know, the theatre was closed to me, I hit upon the idea of writing my plays in epic form – for future use.

I have told my grown-up children (who write a little) this secret, and encouraged them to turn their stories into plays, like Charlotte Birch-Pfeiffer.[1] But they daren't! – For they believe the old notion that a play must be a conventional 5–acter with set roles and act endings (for applause). Now I believe that with a more modern, informal notion of drama, it might be possible to take the narratives *exactly as they are*! That would be novel! – There would be frequent changes of scene, but that is after all only Shakespeare's *ubiquité*; the author's reflections would become monologues. Or one could also introduce a new character (corresponding to the Greek chorus), who would be – the Prompter, half visible, reading the descriptions (of landscapes, etc.), and narrating or reflecting on events while the scenery was changed (in so far as one need employ any). A permanent arch and the Shakespeare Bühne from Munich[2] would solve everything.

Since it is now a matter of finding a collaborator, I wonder if you wouldn't like to be the dramaturge I am seeking? You know my aims and the way I think, so you wouldn't introduce anything that wasn't in accordance with the author's intentions, would you?

Shall we start with *The Roofing Feast*? And then go on to *The Scapegoat*? *The Roofing Feast* is straightforward: the effect is achieved by the green lamp (the eye) and then the growing house, and the flag pole with the flag. But the man must sit in a chair, not lie in bed, and like the nurse's, the doctor's fate must be interwoven with the dying man's. The nurse could be his Wife in disguise (?), in that way the play would gain suspense. The rider and the women with the dog must be explained, and appear on stage. 'The Green Eye' could always be the Doctor, who the Dying Man fails to recognize.[3] This may resemble the Italian *Commedia*, but does that really matter? Aren't all forms permitted nowadays?

Don't you think that after having been a translator, becoming a dramaturge would be a real vocation? We have a hundred dramas to create!! But I must be there at your side to *plan* them, for that is my forte!

But first: the contemporary subjects, then the historical ones!

Dare I say the word: Come here! – That makes me responsible, but he who dares!???

I understand from your silence that Reinhardt has refused all three Chamber Plays!?[4]

Yours sincerely,
August Strindberg

563. To KARL BÖRJESSON

Karl Börjesson (1877–1941), publisher and bookseller. The firm Björck and Börjesson was founded in 1900 by Albert Björck as an antiquarian bookshop. Börjesson joined him as a partner in 1901 and became its sole owner in 1906, having also started publishing books in 1903. Strindberg's collaboration with Börjesson had its origin in the difficulties he experienced over *Black Banners*. He sent him the novel in January 1907 after two years' vain search for a publisher. All his regular contacts declined the book, rightly fearing the outcry which followed its publication on 29 May 1907. Until 1911 their subsequent relationship was conducted exclusively by post, using a polite form of address. It produced some four hundred and sixty-seven items on Strindberg's side, and even survived a dispute over the advisability of publishing a second edition of *Black Banners*. Börjesson, meanwhile, often supplied Strindberg with books or assisted him financially, while Strindberg gave him several manuscripts cheaply in return. Börjesson brought out *A Blue Book* according to Strindberg's wishes, with each section on a separate, double-columned page with a red margin and red titles, for a modest 5 *kronor*; he also published the *Open Letters to the Intimate Theatre*, three history plays, *The Last Knight, The Regent*, and *The Earl of Bjälbo*, and two works of linguistics, *China and Japan* and *The Origin of the Chinese Language*. But if his intervention in Strindberg's life was certainly opportune, Börjesson's commitment to his writings was clear; in a letter dated 14 May 1908, he wrote: 'Delight and happiness have been my feelings while working on the *Blue Book*. When the manuscript of the *Banners* was in press, I often felt uneasy and afraid, not for me but for my wife and child, for my business, etc. However, I understood so well what this work had cost you, and what it meant for public morality and a new sense of justice. But when I first held your *Blue Book* in my hands . . . I was overwhelmed with happiness at being the one through whom it would be published and read.'

8 May 1907

Herr Börjesson,

Since you represent your firm in its dealings with me, I am sending you, in strict confidence, a new manuscript, 'A Blue Book', which forms a commentary to *Black Banners*. But I do not know where you stand on the highest questions, therefore please do not take it amiss if I turn to Herr Björck[1] as a known Swedenborgian, and ask if he might read the manuscript.

So far as the text is concerned, it covers some of the same ground as *Black Banners*, but otherwise it constitutes my manifesto, whereby I solemnly abjure all fellowship with The Black Banners, for whom I've been made the scapegoat, even though they've always disavowed and denied me, yet stolen my name whenever necessary.

I know the risk, but here I stand! Amen!

However, it ought to appear at the same time as *Black Banners,* or just afterwards; a small, tasteful One-Kronor's Book (like my Tales), in two columns as in the manuscript!

The details later!

Yours sincerely,
August Strindberg

564. To HARRIET BOSSE

12 May 1907

Harriet,

Need I write to you? You know my thoughts and feelings, as I know yours. What you wrote to me, I already knew, and who was tormenting you, though no one had told me. When you suffer I am near you and suffer with you, but when you are happy I cannot always be there, since life then places you among my enemies. I cannot rejoice over an unwarrented success at my expense!

I am now growing accustomed to the great loneliness of this summer, and no longer hope for anything from life, since everything has shown itself to be unstable, transitory, fugitive. Even my child has gone, now that strangers have turned her against me, but it is a mercy not to feel the pain of my loss, and with the severing of every bond, I hasten my release from this prison.

Let me now be dumb! I encounter you best in silence, unembodied as I imagine you, as you appear to me, without a stranger's weft in your fabric . . .

I cannot bear to see your home, because there are strangers there, and yet your home is as perfectly beautiful as if I had myself wished it into being for the two of you, you and the child; I cannot speak to you, for I have nothing to say that can be said, I do not long to see you, for I see you when and as I will.

People and life sought to part us, in one way, but I believe we still meet sometimes, in another place, for we are kin, and can never cease to be so . . .

Your
Nameless One

565. To EMIL SCHERING

16 May 1908

Dear Herr Schering,

I am truly delighted by your choice of Karl Ulfsson, for I love that story, and the little unconscious Queen is my most beautiful and truest portrait of woman in all her naive criminality.[1]

But, do you think it is long enough? Its 31 printed pages need expanding to 100. You must transform all my reflections and summaries into dialogue, and weave the characters together.

Friar Birger and Doctor Laurentius mustn't fade out but recur in the plot, trying to save Karl U., and appear in the final act.

Further: You must abandon all thought of a Chamber Play, and make it 5 Acts. *Ergo* a lively 1st Act, with a street scene; exposition, introduction, prehistory.

You must compose the dialogue in my manner; the long speeches must be cut short by brief replies. However, we mustn't turn it into an old-fashioned 'machine' with a lot of unnecessary minor characters, crowd scenes etc., but achieve a compromise with the concentration of a Chamber Play.

If you can get hold of Birgitta's Revelations in German, there'll be material for the dialogue there.[2]

This is what I've now got in mind: When you've completed your German reworking, I'll have it translated into Swedish. Insert matter where I think it's necessary. And then offer the piece to our new national theatre!

N.B. Be careful not to promote misogyny, and likewise gynolatry! The Queen mustn't throw the blame on the king she's killed (like Nora!), she kills naively because he stood in the way of her love of pleasure.

And you mustn't belittle Birgitta as a woman, but as a *Schafskopf*.[3]

If you wish to consult German sources about Queen Johanna, my story takes place in 1372 when Johanna I was married for the 3rd time to Jakob III of Majorca.

The dramatic aspect of Birgitta's psyche is: She hates Johanna but must avail herself of her protection in order to get to Jerusalem. Her ambition lures her into making ignominious compromises, even with Cardinal Orsini who you must make the villain! Include Birgitta's spiritual struggles here!

The pious Friar Birger ought probably to be presented as a contrast to Karl. And the daughter, Katrina, should be developed and inserted into a scene here and there. N.B. Nothing ridiculous! – Serious!

The first rule of writing is: Don't be impatient! It mustn't go quickly! Four weeks for four acts! Never *invita Minerva*![4] but carefully planned. However, *nulla dies sine linea*,[5] a little every day, otherwise one loses the thread!

And in drama: Keep to the subject! Don't forget the leitmotiv! Weave people's fates together, the warp and the weft! The dialogue full, not too clipped (short); *prepare* the entrances well, round out the exits! Don't disclose all your secrets in the 1st Act. Put some by, dispose of them piecemeal! A scene = an electrical discharge! But charge first, long and well!

Yours sincerely,
August Strindberg

But tell me how you envisage your drama in 100 pages, and don't follow my plan blindly.

In 1372 the Pope was Gregorius XI, the one who returned to Rome from Avignon in 1377 at the entreaty of Katarina *of Sienna*!

Maybe we should introduce Katarina of Sienna? as a rival!

Alfonso,[6] the gallant priest, Birgitta's spiritual lover, mustn't be forgotten! There's a type! But no ridicule! Otherwise we'll have an operetta. Spiritual struggles are not to be smiled at!

566. To EMIL SCHERING

18 May 1907

Dear Herr Schering,

Now I've read it!

1. It can't be called 'Birgitta' because Germany's 20 million Catholics consider her a saint.

2. This is a beginner's way of writing plays, but *it can be improved*!

It's sketchy! too simple, and lacks tension. If there were 20 scenes, they could be that short, but not as it is now! This is how I wrote my first plays at 19!

I've begun by cutting the boat journey, they must remain on land; then it grows dark in the final scene! There mustn't be a time shift at that point!

I can now see 2 ways of utilizing your drama!

Primo: Turn it into *one* act, taking place at Castel Nuovo; but with inserted scenes: between Katarina and her mother; Boccaccio and Katarina (B's last flame!), Alfonso and Karl; Alfonso and Johanna (Birgitta becomes jealous! There's a scene!). No curtain!

Secundo: 4 long, carefully constructed acts.

The main fault is the lack of a build-up! The build-up is achieved by means of minor characters!

You've been in too much of a hurry! Impatience is a writer's mortal sin, the youthful sin to which I and everyone else have yielded!

Further: It is too artless!

Think of the world weaver who weaves people's fates!

Drama is conflict and confrontation! Here there is no confrontation!

Don't lose courage now, for it's through failure that one approaches success.

It's a good sketch! But now *fill it out*! With care!

And don't show it to anyone connected with the theatre!

Now invent the missing scenes! They are self-evident!

At present I go for One Act! everything at Castel Nuovo; but a bench and table in the foreground!

Let them say Naples instead of Rome!

There are presently 42 pages! Make it 75, so it lasts a whole evening!

The exits must be rounded out with more detail; the entrances prepared.

'Mother and Son' is a good title.

Doctor Laurentius must be there at the end, Alfonso and Katarina too!

So, courage! And a fresh start!

Yours sincerely,

August Strindberg

One Act at Castel Nuovo

567. To EMIL SCHERING

10 June 1907

Poor Herr Schering,

So, you too! The greatest of afflictions, which I have wept my way through three times, and which I'm still caught up in![1]

This is surely the stern law of Providence, which has some secret meaning and purposes well.

It is at such moments, when everything comes crashing down, when the emptiness of life reveals itself so clearly, that one gropes one's way over to *Jenseits*, and begins to live on the other shore, where one must go sometime!

Will it console you if I talk about myself? Well, anyway:

Black Banners leaves me standing alone on a rock in the sea, with the starry sky above me and my conscience within.[2] I have no longer any friends, no wife, and my last child has been stolen from me, that too!

I read some years ago in a German magazine that Przybyszewski 'was Strindberg's greatest enemy and best friend'.

So it is with Fru B![3] She hates me, because she feels the bond. She hates Falck's theatre, because she can't be part of it! She hated the *Dream Play*, which once she loved, and even intrigued against its performance, yes, she tried to 'play it away'. When it succeeded, she was furious, and three days later she went to a protest party (Boston) aimed at the *Dream Play*. Tor Hedberg (at 50) had signed the manifesto 'Youth (!) Shall Enjoy Itself!'[4]

She hasn't read my Chamber Plays, which is why I warned you against having anything to do with her, for I thought she would borrow them from you and let the Hedbergs run them down in the press! Therefore, once again! Be on your guard! – That's how she is!

What shall I say to you? Write yourself, write out your pain! You write such masterly letters! and are thus a writer.

Merely seek the form, and take care over the execution! That's the art! The whole art!

Where are you going to live now? if this can be called life? when everything breaks?

I have wept over your fate, and send you a kindly thought in consolation!

Yours sincerely,
August Strindberg

568. To EMIL SCHERING

19 June 1907

Dear Herr Schering,

Reinhardt's acceptance[1] was the first fruit. Let's hope Vallentin is intelligent enough to take *The Ghost Sonata*![2]

I've now completed a fourth Chamber Play; it is *schauderhaft*,[3] but good![4]

Your silence in reply to my warning about Fru B. worries me. I know you've written to each other. I'm now warning Vallentin as well against wasting time in writing to her. For she'll never act in Germany! But she'll use his offer for self-promotion in our papers! has done so already!

Falck has enormous difficulties to contend with in working for me. *Die dummen Schweden*[5] hates everything original, but loves copies, bad copies!

Folly bordering upon insanity, and a wickedness that goes with folly!

It's frightful!

Yours sincerely,
August Strindberg

569. To AUGUST FALCK

August Falck (1882–1938), actor and theatre manager. The son of August Falck, who mounted the Swedish première of *The Father* at the New Theatre in 1888. Falck, or Brother Junior as Strindberg addresses him in this first letter, had studied acting in Stockholm and worked in Helsinki and Gothenburg before forming his own company in 1906. A passionate admirer of Strindberg's work, he followed up a successful tour of *Miss Julie,* including the play's Stockholm première, by forming the Intimate Theatre with the aim of providing it with a permanent stage. Strindberg co-operated actively in the venture, and the collaboration with Falck, who helped him realize his long-standing dream of a theatre devoted to his own plays, was a close if turbulent one, frequently wracked by financial problems. The venture eventually foundered upon Falck's determination to stage other dramatists besides Strindberg, but by then (December 1910), it had made possible a series of premières or major productions of twenty-four of his plays, including *The Pelican, The Ghost Sonata,* and *To Damascus*. In terms of an audience, however, its great successes were *Miss Julie, Swanwhite* and *Easter*. Falck performed in many of the Intimate Theatre's productions, and was a notable Captain in *The Father* and *The Dance of Death,* and Jean in *Miss Julie,* the role for which he is probably best remembered. His book *Fem år med Strindberg* (Five Years with Strindberg, 1935), in which versions of many of the letters he received from Strindberg were first published, remains the main source of information about the Intimate Theatre and, together with the *Open Letters to the Intimate Theatre,* it affords a valuable insight into Strindberg's ideas about the theatre during the period when he was most actively engaged in its production side. Some two hundred and twenty-four letters and notes from Strindberg to Falck have survived.

28 June 1907

Brother Junior,

Do not neglect me! I am a credulous soul filled with the suspicion of a lifetime.

All day I've sat waiting for you to ring, and passed the time in trying to raise some cash for you.

If the authorities refuse you a license, I will come forward and apply for one!

I've so much to tell you about *The Pelican.*

And listen! if the play isn't out for copying, let me borrow it for a day, so I may furnish it with 'atmosphere'!

Yrs,
August Strindberg

570. To EMIL SCHERING

7 July 1907

Dear Herr Schering,

Drop *Black Banners*! We might be prosecuted under Heinze![1]

I shall probably send *The Pelican*, which Falck values most highly and wants to open with! There will be a copy ready in a couple of days!

Now there are so many theatres, why not one for the Beautiful, True and Good? Which calls what's wicked wicked and what's filthy filth.

Yours sincerely,
August Strindberg

571. To EMIL SCHERING

25 August 1907

Dear Herr Schering,

In spring 1893 a Herr Levy (Loewy?) made a bust of me at the Hotel Linden. Do you know where Levy is, and if the bust can be bought in plaster? Falck may want it for the foyer.[1]

Perhaps Schleich, Dehmel, Paul ('*Der Paul weiss Alles*')[2] knows where Levy and his bust are to be found.

Thank you for Hoffmann's ballad, which recalls a certain Swede.[3]

The Crown Bride will be performed here on 10 September at the New Theatre![4]

Falck will open in October with *The Pelican*, which we are calling 'The Sleepwalker' so as not to reveal the theme of motherly love yet. He's been rehearsing for a fortnight already, all four Chamber Plays. Places 'The Sleepwalker'[5] highest!

He is absolutely the man for the undertaking! as Manager, Director, and Actor!

I am more alone than ever since I lost my last child, since I had to break with her mother . . . who also parted me from friends and relatives!

Do you know Lanz-Liebenfels' *Theo-Zoologie* (The Ape Men of Sodom's Religion). A formidable attack upon the New-Heathens![6]

Yrs,
August Strindberg

572. To CARL LARSSON

6 October 1907

Carl Larsson,

It's in your capacity as a farmer that I'm writing to you this time, though to some extent as an Artist too, one who keeps his eyes open.

It's the Corncrake again![1]

This curious creature cannot fly; only (according to no less an authority than Brehm)[2] flap his wings, yet he's supposed to migrate to Egypt all the same, of course. How he crosses the Öresund without using a steamer or the ferry is beyond me, and crossing the Alps is not something he picked up from Hannibal or Napoleon. It seems he wanders to Africa (Brehm)!

But now for something even more extraordinary! The Corncrake isn't to be found in any of the specialist works in which I've investigated the fauna of Egypt. So he can't be there! But where is he then?

What do your rustics think, above all your forester?

A parallel! Our Scanian stork, *Ciconia Alba*, is also supposed to go off to Egypt; but he *doesn't show up there*! On the other hand, every Egyptian village has its stork, which is *a different species*! It remains there all year round! and breeds there!

There is reason to believe that most so-called birds of passage stay put. If, during the winter, one were to examine swallows' nests, the nesting boxes of starlings, hollow trees, roof tiles, hay-ricks, and particularly barn roofs, one might well come across these sleeping 'birds of passage'. After all, millions of bats stay on, mostly hanging up inside hollow trees! Bears sleep without eating for 6 months, and aren't easy to find; why shouldn't birds do so too? I'm not asking you to do anything elaborate now, just to sound out some of your old codgers when you've a moment. It would be a pity to let young lads loose on the sleeping birds, and it's not really lawful to let the rascals go climbing trees!

But it would do no harm if you were to have a look in your own swallows' nests yourself, would it? – Well! Just a thought!

Thanks for your last letter, all hail!

Yrs,
August Strindberg

573. To KARL OTTO BONNIER

21 October 1907

My dear Bonnier,

Since you have acquired my prose works anyway, and particularly the

Biografica, I am now forced to offer you my greatest *œuvre posthume*. My '*Occult Diary*', kept since the Hôtel Orfila in Paris 1896, thus in its 11th year. It comprises 548 octavo pages (274 large folio).

But this is an *affaire de confidence* and *confiance*, with confidence and in confidence. Since it is still in progress and continues to grow, you must have such confidence in me as to allow me to retain the Diary in my care, while a copy is made of the same, this being your property.

As regards publication, well, that will have to be after my death, but all the wonderful things I've experienced are there, intimate things, but with the names often spelt in Greek . . .

It will create problems afterwards . . .

I'm selling it because by 12 tomorrow I have to have 2,000 *kronor* or the bailiffs will be in (not Ranft, however)!

This is thus a request for help rather than business!

If you see any other way out than this, then tell me!

Yrs,
August Strindberg

P.S. You may naturally see the Diary here.

574. To RICHARD BERGH

1 November 1907

Richard Bergh,

I returned the books simply because they haunted me, and were beginning to weigh heavily upon my sense of justice!

I went off into the desert when the last storm was about to break in order to meditate, and to settle some old accounts;[1] I also wanted to break off all contact with my experiences from the last seven years, and the impressions they have left behind; and I found my situation as regards my own circle unclear, at times false; we needed to go our separate ways, and your circles sometimes intersected with mine.

That is more or less the gist of it!

And I'm sure we shall meet again, as before, though not quite as before, even if nearly so, when the time is right, gathered in innocent delight around Beethoven.

I have no pretensions as a prophet or moralist, and am not a 'pietist', though I have written the *Blue Book*.

I feel happy that after ten years of struggle I have attained the childlike clarity of vision with which the highest problems should be viewed, and that I may build upon burned sites . . .

So, until sometime in the future, soon or otherwise!

Yrs,
August Strindberg

575. To AUGUST FALCK

14 November 1907

August Falck,

After this morning's visit I am convinced that with that set and this play[1] our enterprise is doomed! For four months I have been collecting and studying *Art Nouveau* and yet the result was 'The Southside Theatre' 40 years ago!

Time's running out! So have them rub in a little colour and gold! Put the chaise longue to the right of the door; and a large photograph on the wall above the chaise longue, framed by two curtains, as in my drawing-room!

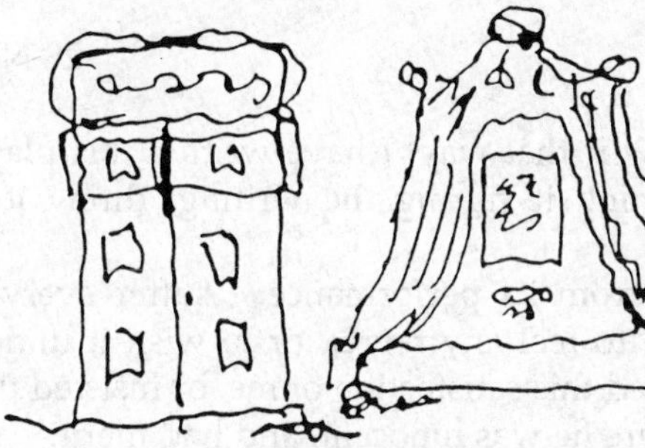

In short: conceal whatever can be concealed! With curtains, *portières*, screens, small tables, palms, flowers in vases, etc.

And another thing: play everything downstage, at the front, otherwise nothing will be visible from the expensive seats! and then there'll be trouble!

It's well-known that a writer cannot bear to see the products of his imagination made real, for they never come up to expectation. That is even more true of a play! I don't think I dare watch you! I might perhaps leave, even if you acted well, and thus dishearten you! Be prepared for that; and try to understand what I mean!

The Burned Site is a more attractive piece with which to open! easier to present, has greater breadth and perspective!

Consider it!

I'm not downhearted, only dubious about the outcome!

Tomorrow is Friday! That's when the inspection is due! Let me know the decision at once![2] And then: permission to perform!

If we had time, we should order a white drawing-room in gold (Gustav III, Haga)[3] right away, but really white, not lampblack! however, we haven't time!

Do what can be done!

Yrs,
August Strindberg

P.S. I'm tired, for I have influenza and a cough, so I'd only disturb your rehearsals!

576. To AXEL STRINDBERG

29 November 1907

Dear Axel,

I'm glad that you saw it that way! I have written this play[1] against my will; I thought of burning it during the writing, threw it aside; but it returned, pursued me!

I have also suffered from its performance, I suffer every evening, but have still not been able to feel any regret, or to wish it undone. It is as if the 'departed'[2] demanded this satisfaction of me, or insisted that I also saw him from that side, where he was innocent, and had merit.

No *harm* can come of it, for it's really a good thing if people who walk in their sleep out on the guttering are awakened.

Nevertheless, it makes me suffer, and the art of hurting others isn't easy.

Yrs,
August

577. To TOR AULIN

Tor Bernhard Wilhelm Aulin (1866–1914), violinist, conductor and composer. He founded the Aulin String Quartet in 1887 and was for many years first violin at the Royal Opera House, where Axel Strindberg was a cellist. He later enjoyed numerous appointments as a conductor. As a composer he is best remembered for the last of his three violin concertos. His friendship with Strindberg, in which he was cast as David to the latter's Saul, was marked by mutual respect and warmth on both sides. Aulin's participation in Strindberg's Beethoven evenings, on one occasion with his quartet, was always well received, and Strindberg often encouraged Aulin, who was diffident about his ability as a composer. Their extant correspondence amounts to some sixty-eight items, thirty-nine of them by Strindberg.

20 January 1908

Tor Aulin,

I am old and tired, and have the right to be so; I spend the day working in order to build and plant on the sites where once I pulled things down.[1] Have therefore to sleep at night, and consequently forego one of life's pleasures: the company of those with whom one enters into harmony and beauty.

That's how it is!

When I first called on you seven years ago, I did so from instinct; you were born with music in your hands and soul. But you retreated, believing you had no calling. Only last spring you drew back. But then fate intervened (perhaps you call it that) and drove us to work together.[2]

I know you have succeeded, I even believe you will have a critical success. And as far as I'm concerned, the reason for this is that you aren't plagued by scholarship (Lindegren),[3] and that you take your art as a game, but a divine game, not as research or mathematics or algebra (the Fugue!).

You have a tonal sense, and your notes possess colour.

Bon! Since you recently suggested a new collaboration (on 'The Journey to Town'),[4] I'm asking: Why not an opera?

But not something Swedish. That would either turn into *The Bewitched*[5] in an endless C major and A minor (and only a small part of an opera is song) or *Waldemar's Treasure*,[6] a combination of Skansen,[7] Wagner and Waldteuffel.[8]

My reponse to your suggestion is: the *Dream Play*! There you have a text which has been tried and tested! But it must be cut as the composer pleases; all the comic moments deleted; the number of characters reduced; and the orchestra restricted to Mozart's instrumentation (your current usage). And brief! A Musical Chamber Play in which all philosophizing is omitted, and only 'the Scenes' remain. Not a sung novel, therefore, as in that French thing at the Swedish Theatre, you remember![9] Dramatic-lyrical music but not theatrical-recitative, discursive.

Simple, but not too simple. Gluck by all means (*Orfeo*), but lined with Beethoven, yet not wholly Beethoven!

Otherwise and 2nd, I have an Old Testament subject, which I have long had it in mind to treat. An idyll like Joseph in Egypt, a Chamber Play, 4–5 characters, but a better text!

Retire again now, but think it over! You will no doubt come round!

Yrs,
Strindberg

578. To NILS ANDERSSON

26 January 1908

Good Nils Andersson,

Those two rooms at the widow's attract me most, if she doesn't hold gatherings that can be heard *verbatim* through the door.[1]

I'll pay more than she wants, and eat once a day, preferably fish, but not gruels: i.e. cabbage, peas, or strong soups. A small *smörgåsbord* with cheese, anchovies, reindeer, fried fish. In the evening a little milk – nothing else. (Coffee in the morning with an egg, of course!)

But I'll never put my foot in Lund! *Ein mal und nicht wieder*![2] I'd get off at the station to the north of Barsebäck, if I came. What's it called?

And then: is it in the town or a fishing village?

Perhaps March then!

In haste. Yours,
August Strindberg

Is there a shop and a tavern? Can one buy meat, goose, poultry?

Thank you for offering me your hospitality! But – you know me! I must live alone – but near company!

579. To TOR AULIN

28 January 1908

Dear Friend,

Yesterday evening I communed with you alone in silence. And among other things I said: The reason why we (Swedes) have no music is undoubtedly this: that we have an Academy and a Lindegren (= antique pedantry). Emil Sjögren,[1] who once possessed a few natural notes and heard songs in the wind, went to Lindegren and was in danger of getting caught up in orthodox cadences, but fled, and sang like a bird in the open air – for a time! I don't know why he went silent, it was probably in his nature that autumn should come early. Since then there's been no one! The good Stenhammar isn't a born composer, *or so I think*; for if he was, his notes would also have reached me, who am so willing to listen; Hallén (sorry about this slip of the pen!)[2] is a bold pot-pourrist; but what then? When an art form has developed over a long period and become complex (Wagner) and turned into a form of higher mathematics, as music has done, there is usually a return to simplicity.

I was in Paris when Gluck's *Orfeo* was performed! Mankind caught its breath! Simple, but not *too* simple, not clumsy, artistic but not artificial.

And then I continued: it has become my *idée fixe* (a call) that you should become a composer. You know the whole literature, as a conductor you have all the instruments in your bones, as well as every tone, rhythm and harmony. The tones (you replied) are there already in the instruments, harmony one learns, but rhythm, that is mine. That little folk song you arranged became yours by virtue of its rhythm! You have an advantage as a composer in not being a pianist, because so many figures from the piano arrangements remain in a pianist's fingers, the conventional forms of harmony and études. You know enough of what has been done in the past to avoid academic jingle-jangle, and must sing for the present, for today. That doesn't mean you need give us the noise of tramcars or the ding-a-ling of a telephone, as Strauss does, for tone painting is imitative art, parody theatre, ventriloquism. And when a 40–strong orchestra with 6 double bases and 6 bassoons is meant to accompany a young girl's voice, then music (opera) is absurd. It's crazy! Seeking new combinations of tones simply to avoid the old ones is affected, not effective! Discords? By all means, but as transitions, contrasting effects, discords yes, but beautiful discords, not ugly ones! not wicked, not foul! – The musical novel is something perverse! Recitative, which can as a last resort be used for supporting roles, cannot become opera; and where the text has any pretension to characterization and psychology, it is best without music. A complex plot isn't singable, and the portrayal of street scenes is best left to painters! . . .

So what is the way? – Well, I have in mind your chamber music as a starting point, an intimate, concentrated form (= Musical Chamber Play) for our tired and impatient contemporaries, whose ears are worn out with the hullabaloo of café orchestras, where the composer can abandon himself to, and become absorbed in, an atmosphere rather than in characterization with leitmotivs, for it is not music's task to portray characters or philosophize about 'issues', to embrace heaven and earth, or to dig up idols, old or new. – – –

And so I took back *The Dream Play*![3] And asked you: What kind of subject attracts you most? – Modern, romantic, classical, biblical, national? At this point I interjected as follows: – Let us be practical! Start from what we have to hand! You have your orchestra, one that isn't so large that it overwhelms a human voice, and a new theatre large enough for the text to be heard.

Right! I have already arranged a composition from my *Fairy Tales*,[4] with the Dormouse (the Composer) as the axis around which it revolves; the Shell Shop is there too, and the Pilot, etc.

Or: 'Saint Gotthard's Tale'.

Or: 'Bluewing seeks the Golden Saxifrage'.[5]

Or: Shall we write a light, Scandinavian 'Midsummer Night's Dream'? I have already mapped it out and offered it to the new Royal Theatre for its première, saw it so clearly last spring . . . but then things grew dark! It is called 'The Dove Spring'! . . .[6]

But light! *Licht*! More *Licht*![7]

It seemed to me yesterday evening that you heard what I said, and went along with me!

But last night I dreamt about you. You didn't agree, and asked: 'What do you want with me? What are you trying to teach me, that I don't already know better myself?'

It seemed to me you were right, and I was reduced to silence, even though I was obeying a call within me!

Then your letter arrived! I thought of what the wise say: that dreams must be fashioned back to front since they can be read in a mirror!

I'm tired after leading a dog's life for 60 years, not of work, which is my rest, but only of company, and especially of those who don't share the same ground as I do; however, I'm always ready for a genial *Zweigespräch*[8] [*sic*] between 7 and 9; if I'm not *very* tired, and the subject touches upon my work, then, as you know, I'm happy to go on sitting at table, only too happy!

Summa Summarum: Reflect and sleep on it! Let us then get together in order to try and do something new! light, beautiful! And liberate music just a little from its old bonds, just a little!

Yours,
August Strindberg

If I can only buy or borrow Lindegren's hymnal, we can discuss it!

580. To KARL OTTO BONNIER

29 January 1908

My dear Bonnier,

When I came to reflect on the sale of my intimate Diary, it felt as if I'd sold my corpse to the dissecting room. Therefore let me do an exchange!

Three suggestions: you credit the sum to my account; or you get all my Poems; or my scientific Collections (= Two cupboards).

What disturbs me most is that the Diary also contains other people's secrets![1]

R.S.V.P.

Yrs,

August Strindberg

581. To AUGUST FALCK

29 January 1908

My dear Falck,

As a result of yesterday morning: you must have an interval in *The Bond*, for you will tire, Fröken Flygare[1] will tire, the audience will tire! But with an interval you and Fr. Fl. can *speak more slowly*, the audience catch what is said better, and the play will profit by it.

If you insist on the principle of One Act (which you ought not to do), then put: '*The Bond*, One Act (with curtain)'.

Also: tell Westergård[2] that he was good, but should be more severe, almost frightening; no smiling, a county sheriff isn't to be trifled with.

And tell all the jurors that there is no humour at the Assizes, where people's fates are decided, it is all terribly serious, which is also clear from the text. Their make-up mustn't evoke the Southside Theatre;[3] they are all 'trustworthy and honourable men'.

If you have an interval, you don't need to tell Fr. Fl. to articulate better, for at present she gets tired, but she won't if she can catch her breath.

And you can speak more slowly too, unforced, because at present it goes too fast. One can't keep up with you and hear what's said.

When you speak to her, your posture (with your arms) should be more relaxed, intimate; one hand in your waistcoat pocket, on your lapel, behind your back; only when you speak to the judge could your arms hang at your sides, signifying respect for authority.

The final scene should be taken *ritardando* – – – a slower tempo with pauses – The last phrase to be said after a pause, with deep feeling, accentuated, almost with emphasis. And both partners should leave the stage inspiring fear (for 'Fate') and arousing sympathy.

The action is so rich, and the plot so artistic, what with the letters, Alexandersson's[4] unexpected testimony, and the Baron's manoeuvre with the child, that the piece can take an interval, indeed it requires one.

I have to say this: you and Fl. almost gabbled at times. The great *legato* was missing! The words were unable to make their effect, couldn't be caught! And you tired! You saw Fl.

Now follow my advice! and it will go well!

Yrs,

August Strindberg

And Alexandersson must arouse sympathy; not a trace of humour; when one's hopes are in ruins, one isn't a humorist.

Tell the whole cast: this is a *tragedy*, even if it is set in the present!

582. To SVEA ÅHMAN

Svea Åhman (1876–1937), actress, engaged at the Intimate Theatre from 1907 to 1908 when she played the Mother in *The Pelican* and the Mummy in *The Ghost Sonata*.

[31 January 1908]

Fröken Svea Åhman,

I praised your 'Mummy' in *The Ghost Sonata*, and do so still.

But I have to tell you that, if you want to save yourself from complete disaster this evening, you must heed the advice I am going to give you here!

It is a comedy,[1] not a farce; a very serious comedy where people hide their tragedies beneath a certain cynicism.

And the young wife is both well-bred and familiar with the way of world. Thus, to arouse the love of a serious man, she must be modest and yet possess a feminine charm. Remember how he (Ljungqvist)[2] portrays her. And use that to make the role plausible! At present one is amazed that this simple coquette of yours has been able to charm him, and the play doesn't make sense.

If you want to save your role and yourself, observe the following:

Move as little as possible on stage, rather sit still;

Don't accompany every word with a facial expression or gesture;

Restrict your voice to one register, and don't run up and down the scale; above all, don't squeak;

Speak more slowly, monotonously like educated people, almost as if you were going over it in your memory, without any nuances –

Be extremely reserved, like a young wife from a good family, who conceals her emotions;

Positively no flirting, for that frightens a man off . . .

The lines themselves say enough, and become cynical if they are accompanied by facial expressions . . .

Don't snap, and don't sneer, that is just repelling . . .

Show in your disposition what attracts him: dignity, a little reserved . . .

You are 'too explicit', as they say, and I asked the Director right at the beginning to remind you and the others of the Royal Theatre's way of playing comedy; converse, don't chat; moderation in gestures and facial expression . . . the greatest moderation!

I really had a reserved character in mind, who only assumes a way of speaking that is foreign to her nature through consorting with artists . . .

What I saw from you today was old and antiquated! And we are here to try and renew things.

These are hard words, but they must be said.

Follow my advice today, and you won't grieve tomorrow, when it will be too late! For otherwise you will be slammed; and people will so easily forget what an excellent actress you were in *The Ghost Sonata*!

Yours sincerely,
August Strindberg

Take your cue from Ljungqvist, and be as reserved as he is. And first and last: Comedy! Not farce!

583. To HELGE WAHLGREN

Helge Wahlgren (1883–1958), actor and theatre director. He made his debut with August Falck in Malmö as Pelleas in *Pelleas et Mélisande*, and followed him to the Intimate Theatre, where he remained until 1910. Between 1926 and 1936 he was head of the Royal Theatre's drama school and subsequently director at the Gothenburg City Theatre. Six letters from Strindberg to Wahlgren survive.

2 February 1908

Dear Sir,

I found nothing to remark on in your Judge in *The Bond*, it was excellent, and you have my thanks and congratulations.

But in *The Ghost Sonata* you did not play my part: the dashing student, the new, sceptical young man, who 'doesn't go on about eternal love'. Therefore I could do nothing to change it. You weren't affected, but something else, which I can't find the words for. But I said to the Director: this has a gravity and a profundity for the future.

That is what you exhibited in *The Bond*, where your performance was perfection![1]

I don't really know what I can teach you. But I urge you next time in *The Ghost Sonata*: speak to the girl, it is with thoughts and words that he enters her soul.

And stress the poisonous effect of the flowers, which drives him mad like his father, and motivates his eruption.

In the final scene try gently to recall her to life, or at least take her hand and see if she is dead!

To go down on your knees before death, not to the Madonna, would make the tableau more beautiful.

Don't take any more lessons. Those who give them are already out-of-date! And your technique is complete.

But when studying your part, look at what the other characters say about you; for unless they are slandering you behind your back (I mean in the play) they give your characterization.

And the next time you get a part, try not to be the same, but look and speak as the role requires.

Create a character, but not a caricature. In so far as one can do, step out of yourself! Fredrikson has never been able to, Lindberg seldom. Therefore they have been forced to choose their roles.[2]

We should also choose for you, so that you find your 'métier', but you mustn't stop growing and always be the same.

Don't regard the stage as a tribune from which to preach, but as a place where you portray people. If you only want to use your role as a mouthpiece, you are taking the writer's part, not the actor's.

Take it seriously, as you do now, but not so terribly seriously!

You have begun well! My thanks! and fare well in future, in freedom and following your own due reflection!

Yours sincerely,
August Strindberg

584. To ANNA FLYGARE

Anna Flygare (1880–1968), actress. After four years as a school teacher and a year with Albert Ranft at his Östermalm Theatre, she was engaged at the Intimate Theatre from 1907 to 1910. She won considerable acclaim for her performance as The Baroness in *The Bond*, and later appeared as Alice in *The Dance of Death*, but her greatest success was as Eleonora in *Easter*: indeed, this was to be the most successful production in the Intimate Theatre's short history. After her marriage to the architect Ernst Stenhammar, her stage appearances became infrequent. Twenty-two letters from Strindberg to her survive.

[3 February 1908]

Fröken Flygare,

In *The Ghost Sonata* I let the director praise you comprehensively.

In *The Bond* as well; but now accept these comments along with my thanks and my congratulations on your success.

The art of the actor today, for today's tired, reserved, but over-intelligent people, is doubtless as follows: the spoken word as the chief thing; but no disturbing emphases, which the public might find offensive, assuming you speak clearly enough for every word to be heard. This can only occur if you keep the phrase together (*legato*), and not *staccato*.

Take it broadly like a singer, enjoy hearing your own voice, and even if you increase the pace, maintain this *legato*.

Then each word doesn't require facial expressions and gestures, for that is old-fashioned.

Economize on your glances; Astri Torsell[1] 'worked with her eyes', and that was why Maeterlinck's wife[2] failed in Berlin (*Die Dame arbeitet mit den Augen*).[3]

You can't be accused of that at the moment, but it may arise if I don't warn you against it now.

Even if the line is vehement, don't sneer, don't bite. Even if the Baroness[4] is angry, she must appear charming in order to motivate the Baron's love for her, and to retain the audience's good will.

Some say that you shouldn't show your profile so frequently, but face the audience; this may or may not be according to the role, but I think that the full face, with the gaze out towards the audience, is more winning, and puts the actress in touch with those for whom she is speaking.

I conclude: *legato*, not *staccato*; economical with gestures and facial expressions; graceful even in what's less beautiful.

And, as I began: thank you and my good wishes.

Yours sincerely,
August Strindberg

585. To IVAR NILSSON

Ivar Nilsson (1877–1929), actor. Played Gustav Vasa in the premières of *The Last Knight* (1909) and *The Regent* (1911), and was highly praised as the Officer in Max Reinhardt's 1921 Stockholm production of *A Dream Play*. Strindberg first wrote to him in 1908 when he was a last-minute replacement for Anders de Wahl as Olof in the production of the verse edition of *Master Olof* which inaugurated the new Royal Theatre. He became an occasional visitor at Strindberg's Beethoven evenings. Thirty-three of Strindberg's letters to Nilsson have survived.

16 February 1908

Herr Nilsson,

Once again: play the role as I have written it, and you will succeed!

He is no elegiac Hamlet, but an 'angry man'. It says so in the text.

'The pale cleric', sharp in logic; thinks a lot, etc.

'To fight with such a man calls for the Devil himself.'

And M.O. says of himself: 'I have lived on a war footing and slept on my sword, and had the strength to defy a world.' Later someone says of him:

'Stood on the battlements and sounded the call.'
'Brazen – very young!
He is as proud as a king.
He is sharp, venomous and sullen.'[1]

Elsewhere, when Brother Lars asks if Olof would be willing to make way for someone stronger, M.O. replies: 'There is no one!'[2] (stronger, that is). A man of iron, then, with an extraordinary self-assurance, who isn't sympathetic and doesn't try to be.

Most actors have made the mistake of playing him with warmth instead of fire, and have insisted on being sympathetic or playing to the public rather than paying heed to the characterization the author has given them, thus depicting him as worn and emotional. This way of interpreting the role subjectively has the drawback of undermining the whole play, because when their rendering of the part doesn't accord with the characterization provided by the other figures, there is of course a discrepancy between the two (sullen, brazen, king, etc.).

His speech is always arrogant, no matter who he is addressing, whether bishop, king or peasant!

M. Olof has been called our Luther, and like the latter, he was a 'bear on every path'; the 'loudest mouth in the Kingdom', etc.

Strong, almost brutal; fire, but no so-called warmth; even at his mother's death, he is hard, but is overwhelmed by sleep and weariness, as he himself says.

If you act the part as it is written and get blamed for it, you have leave to quote me (and the text) as authority, for on this matter, that is without doubt what I am.

I have heard good things of you from yesterday's rehearsal, but have my fears nevertheless!

Remember that you are the driving force of the whole play, keep that in mind, even when you are not on stage! Therefore make sure you can carry them all with you!

The play was written 40 years ago; many have played your role, for the most part like Hamlet, and one of them as a cheap Don Juan! Let us now, in the new White House,[3] see my M. Olof, our Luther, for the first time! If so, it will be an epoch-making achievement!

Yours sincerely,
August Strindberg

Why won't you call on me? At least let me know whether you've received my letters.

586. To AUGUST FALCK

[22 February 1908]

My dear Falck,

One has most to fear from success![1] Therefore consider any obstacles to *Sir B's Wife* and *Christina* carefully! The solution is: The Shakespeare curtain! You can play S B's W retaining the Castle Hall throughout. The curtain with a crucifix painted on it and a prie-dieu will give you the convent. Another curtain the Castle cottage!

Christina can be performed: either with curtains or: the Molière Stage! Think about it, and keep it as an 'escape hatch' in case the authorities descend![2]

I have redesigned *Gustav III* as a Chamber Play, and that can be played on the Molière Stage too. [See Ring's Theatre Book.][3]

Am enclosing it! Just as 'amusing' as *Christina*! A real Box-Office success! People always want to see Gustav III!

Have a look through the roles and distribute them in good time!

Don't paint expensive scenery which may be forbidden!

The R.T.[4] is now the greatest danger, for they are well-in with the Authorities!

Or also ask permission from Olbers![5] It must all be above board!

[no signature]

587. To AUGUST FALCK

28 February 1908

My dear Falck,

The reason I've cut 'Kerstin' and 'Little' is because the role was written for Bosse, whom they fitted. But as the more regal Fru Björling is to play *Christina*, these changes are necessary.

Further: since her speech from the throne in the last act was added later, it is necessary to make adjustments to the role in what has gone before, so that it hangs together.

The dialogue here, with its quite complicated motives, won't bear any scene changes. *Sir Bengt's Wife*, more decorative and simple, demanded something that caught the eye. Everything according to its kind!

However, I have a feeling that you would like to 'do a job' on *Christina*. Don't, for you will destroy its unity and beauty of composition.

Moreover, if you finish at 11 p.m. our friends from the suburbs, whose train goes at 11.30, will stay away, thus wrecking the season!

Give Fru Björling the role in two words: the Amazon who fights for her legitimate freedom, but who is finally conquered in battle when she encounters a love 'stronger than death'. Tott[1] was Christina's only love! The rest was simply mischief and a desire to dominate! At first she merely plays, arousing Tott's love, then it overwhelms her, she falls in love herself, and suffers.

And never forget the Queen for the coquette! The Queen first and last! She sometimes makes herself small when she wants to obtain something, but this is only hypocrisy! 'A Cat'! She must never *be* small.

Remember what I told you about her make-up. Big eyes, unusually big, high eyebrows, like eagle's wings, , a clear brow, strong nose, the corners of her mouth curved; her lower lip thicker, dark hair as in the portrait.

The costume for the final act, Pandora according to taste, but preferably a Greek chiton, hair *à la grec,* dress becoming.

[I'll sacrifice my candelabra, which is Roman, for the moment when she throws away the crown. The throne with gilded feet and my red mohair with gold crowns (royal )].[2]

This morning I saw Karl X on horseback outside the Nord. Museum.[3] He's not someone to be played with even if Christina does allow herself to do so! He was a great drinker, of course, but even if that is instrumental in his proposal, it mustn't be noticeable . . . .

Be careful with the Danes![4] They don't understand Swedish and are hardly well-disposed after Roskilde:[5] also it's by no means certain that you can convey the atmosphere that seems bound to the crypt in Bantorget[6] to Copenhagen! Give it some thought! so you don't catch the tone of Copenhagen's Tivoli, or its Cash Register!

Yrs,
August Strindberg

P.S. De la Gardie[7] is certainly the despised and rejected; but a good fellow, who doesn't take his revenge. But never pathetic, for he has humour, and can smile at himself. Always the Grand Seigneur, the State Councillor! Remember that!

Tott, the infatuated madman, all poetry and madness! beneath which his coarseness nevertheless shines through here and there.

Oxenstierna,[8] the statue, the Great Man, has already undergone his apotheosis, with the Thirty Years' War and the Peace of Westphalia behind him. Authority, Swedish History, a whiff of Gustav Adolf, age and wisdom; majesty!

Karl X![9] Well! 32 but the generalissimo of the Swedish army, Count Palatine, the Crown Prince, victorious on the field of battle, 'a real man' who's not to be played with, although Christina does, but without him becoming more ridiculous than a suitor normally is.

In the final act he's every inch the King! A complete change of character!

When Christina has made her exit in the last act have Oxenstjerna and Karl X shake hands or something, for now a new age is beginning! Try to find an appropriate ending. Both men, who have had their knocks of late, must gather themselves up! Draw a sigh of relief or something! (Feel your way!) Are reconciled! for they weren't friends before! as can be deduced from what O. says in the second act!

The other roles play themselves. However, Holm[10] must be very discreet, no hint of intimacy.

Aug Sg

588. To AUGUST FALCK

[13 March 1908]

Since I've no objections to what you suggest, we'll go on![1]

But, as everything is so uncertain, and also to keep the cast occupied, interested, and in good spirits, couldn't you let them double the roles, though only as a last resort? e.g. Flygare as Christina.

And to resolve the Swanwhite question, tell them that the author wants Geijer[2] and Falkner to compete for the prize = the role. If, however, you've already promised it to Geijer, then ask her if she'd be willing, for *my* sake, to let Falkner alternate with her!

Easter at Easter? With Falkner and Wahlgren?[3] Have they made a start? Do you want music, an organ? Opening on Maunday Thursday?

Don't choose the painful *Father*! Even if it's highly successful, it will only run 3 nights!

The Dance of Death is sounder. And Alexandersson[4] must have her chance. She speaks so well!

But we really ought to give up 'court plays' after the success of *Olof Trätälja*.[5] Why not *Gustav III* or *The Nightingale*? G.III has been ruined by Didring,[6] but can't we rehabilitate him?

When you've finished with my books (Becker's *History of the World* and Hildebrand, *Sv.H.*, 7–13),[7] can you let me have them back.

Christina with drapes is fine, but the small balustrades with the urns create 'period' (Logården), and divert attention from what is otherwise lacking. Make them narrow if necessary, and place them in front of the curtain! I shall miss them if they're not there.

Miss Julie is proscribed in Copenhagen! You know that! Why not something new? – And the Dagmar Theatre has already done *Pariah*![8]

Omit the tailors![9] But aren't you going to have more than *one* backcloth? Otherwise open up the back wall!

You know I always long for depth in the staging! An open window at least, through which one can see a green tree.

In every Dutch tavern scene there is always a small opening in the wall through which one can see the sky and a green branch. It's so pleasant on the eye, and lets out the smoke and fug.

[no signature]

589. To AUGUST FALCK

[13 March 1908]

Advise Fru B.[1] against the costume you refer to! But have a look at the other book (Crane), where there are some genuine Greek costumes for Pandora.[2] Otherwise see the illustration of Greek Vases in your folder.

Don't forget to buy the Easter decorations now, while there still are some, and order some daffodils (yellow).

If you want music (organ) for *Easter*, I'll commission my brother.[3]

It ought to be Maundy Thursday (or Wednesday).[4]

Ask Kjellgren to keep himself slim (thin) for *Easter*, then I'll believe in him! Fröken Falkner ditto.[5]

Fru B. ought really to have a cloak of royal purple with (false) ermine for the speech from the throne in the last act!

Don't make a jest of Karl X! He survives in Djurgården![6]

Shouldn't we put '*Queen Christina*' on the poster?

[no signature]

590. To AUGUST FALCK

28 March 1908

In future! And so as to save me endless confusion on the phone, etc., may I, on receipt of a calling card, have complementary tickets left for me at the box-office? as is usual for an author. I won't abuse this, as you know.

Someone must stand in for me there, who can also report back with their personal impressions!

Nota Bene: a standing set, which affords unity, requires simple furniture: a few essential *matching* pieces, which don't clash! If we go in for elaborate furniture and props again, we'll be back in the old groove of Molander–Michaelson![1] and undo our new fabric!

The Treasury scene was superb – but it would have worked without the shelves! We can regard it as a transitional form! Think over what I said about the unity of costume! And the minor roles!

Distinct: they are so important!

A table and two chairs! The ideal! The biggest scenes in *Christina* were performed with a table and two chairs.

The table gives so much support; and such rich opportunities for beautiful, living gestures; it becomes a hyphen between the two speakers, keeping the dialogue together; separating but joining. It's like the duet in opera!

I now see Ebba Brahe as a silent role, and Ebba Sparre ditto, they ought to have been cut! They don't keep the promise they give in the 1st Act. Cut them! It's also hard on the actors![2]

You understand that I was pleased with yesterday,[3] but to praise is harder. And like you, I am looking for perfection; therefore I pick up on things, even small ones! My praise is of such little use, my approval you can feel in the air, and it gives fresh courage.

I congratulate you (and myself!) on such artists!

A Lord *White-field* is pronounced *Wittfild*, curiously enough! (The man really was called Witt-lock, although he spelt it 'White'.)[4]

[no signature]

591. To AUGUST FALCK

[30 March 1908]

Have someone take a photograph of the *Christina* set, *on its own*, but the third act, that is, with the beautiful table and chairs, and I'll send it to Schering together with a long letter for publication in a Berlin paper. If you can afford it, take all four sets without any actors. But don't forget the plants in the urns!

Make sure I get those of you, Fru B., and Oxenstierna!

You have solved the problem, yet fail! Others will make use of it!

It's appalling! My finest work, technically perfect, the characters realized in detail, the greatest female role in Swedish, the most beautiful of all declarations of love; fine to look at, played as reality itself – and then murdered and plundered by a robber band, for whom [commital to] Rindön and/or Långholmen would be an act of mercy, an unmerited paradise![1]

Take *Christina* with you (if you tour!). Show it! Have a prologue! But take no furniture! You'll always find a table and chairs! Pack some big tablecloths though! to hide their condition!

However: tell your players to use the performances here as dress rehearsals . . . and acquire composure and poise. We shall come again! Everything does!

I heard that de Verdier[2] has been discovered! The lyricist! I'm pleased!

You are certainly too good for Stockholm! Oh Land! Land! You are sinking! – Spend millions on a palace for – who? The least worthy, who has seven theatres and takes no care of any of them![3] It's appalling!

[no signature]

592. To AUGUST FALCK

6 April 1908

P.M. to *Easter*!

Flygare should be *Backfisch*.[1] Her dress short to the ankles, so that her feet are visible; a plait down her back; shiny leather hat  ; fitted cardigan  ; dark hair (not red operetta hair, which is called blond).

Kjellgren[2] the schoolboy: fitted jacket; possibly walking boots  ; collar  ; not like this  as he has at present, and which is *horrible*! A *slight* suggestion of sport! Only slight!

The mother mustn't be morose and pathetic.

The fiancée mustn't hiss and bite!

The Old Man must be good-natured, kind, and only *pretend* to be malevolent! Grunts and growls, but is good!

A big, edifying sorrow, but no lamentations; submission to the hand of Providence (Fate). The girl has discovered her 'fate' and bears it! Sometimes sighs under the burden, but doesn't complain. (She is in 'The Gothic Rooms'.)[3]

When, by using draperies, one has got rid of the whole material side, the piece will appear as if played in the clouds; but it should also be acted in the same way.

Don't encumber the stage with props and furniture! Let the actors get on with it, for only when they hear the dialogue can they get the right tone.

Hire a big organ from that piano firm of yours. Axel can come just the once, his Company has promoted him on condition that he gives up the theatre and music!

Flygare isn't to alter her nose, for it suits her, but best *en face*.

I sent you those things about Christina[4] so you could see the sure basis on which my portrait of her rests. Moreover, in my youth there were popular traditions about Christina, her Hunting Lodge (summer-house, *petite maison* on Stallmästargården, e.g.) and other details, which I can't elaborate on.

Concerning the trial of the Messeniusses,[5] Starbäck says that Christina first pressed for an intensification of the death penalty (torture), but two years later, when she drove past Gallow's Hill at Norrtull (Generalsbacken where as boys we laid our heads on the block!), she said that their judge had deserved their (the Messeniusses') punishment.

Starbäck says with a fair degree of certainty that Pimentelli[6] was her lover. When she lived at Ulriksdal and Uppsala Castle, P. always stayed on the floor below her. And the last night, before P.'s departure, he stayed in the Queen's room until morning!

I think I've handled this filth with decorum! For it is filthy for a woman to go with several at once (like a bitch); but a steady inclination (love) without the bond of marriage, that one respects!

[no signature]

593. To HARRIET BOSSE

[8 April 1908]

When you told me last Saturday that you were engaged,[1] I almost knew it already. But I could not wish you happiness, for since it does not exist, I do not believe in it. I felt no anxiety about the child, for I believe in God.

I would, however, have liked to say goodbye, and – to thank you, in spite of everything, for everything, for those spring months seven years ago when, after 20 years of misery, I was allowed a glimpse of light. But I could not bring myself to write; I sensed things which made me hesitate. Sunday passed, Monday too, in work and calm resignation. You noticed I stopped visiting you exactly a year ago, and you know why.

Then came yesterday, Tuesday! When I went out in the morning I thought it was Sunday. The city looked different, and so did my rooms here. You were dead! And then began the apotheosis of my memories; all day, for twelve hours, I simply lived through these 7 years.

Reproaches, pangs of conscience for everything left undone, every harsh word, all, all, just as after the death of a loved one. The less beautiful things were obliterated, only the beautiful remained. Faced with the fact that all was over, I had a definite impression: Dead! I mourned you as someone dead, and thus could not wish you back, since you no longer existed!

I recalled 'The Easter Girl', *Damascus*, Djurgården with military honours and the King's salute, Rydberg[2] and Drottningholm.

I wept, not this time from the pain of losing you, but from joy at having had these moments from you, with you!

Today is the day of *Swanwhite*! It opens tonight with Sibelius' music.[3]

You gave me that, as I've already written, and though I've sometimes doubted it, I nevertheless believe it! That is how I see you now, Harriet, after your death! although I've always known who you were, your nature, your inclinations! I have explained this in *Christina*! Your *Swanwhite*, which I had from you, and you from me, and which you were never to act.

Today I have had the feeling that . . . You weren't dead![4]

You have my goodwill, and despite everything I am forever your friend, and your child's.

But I am concerned about you; and something is happening here that I don't understand! I have in fact not understood anything of this last business, but I can't write to you, and there's perhaps no need to either!

If only you knew how dangerous it is to get entangled in people's fates, and to play with thunder!

Disentangling oneself is so painful, you remember how long and painful a process it was for us!

You are satisfied as long as you can arouse a man's interest; then you drop him. But there is more to it than just turning on your heel and walking away! . . . Much more!

Just one thing! Let me have Lillan when you marry! Or would you rather I went a long way away?

To pass each other in the streets here would be painful and unclean. And the child ought to be kept out of it!

Shall I go away? I think my influence here is disturbing, and from this apartment invisible wires reach out, carrying inaudible sound waves that nevertheless reach their goal . . .

Our bond is not broken, but it has to be severed . . . for otherwise we shall be defiled . . . You remember our first days, when alien spirits radiating malice disturbed and destroyed us merely by thinking of us!

Tell me what you wish done! but make sure it does not drag us down into the murky depths I dread . . .

A telegram about your *Swanwhite* just arrived! in spite of everything!

Why didn't you want to be the creature I created? I didn't pull you down, like you said! I don't believe it!

One word more, just one! Don't sink, Harriet! For then I'll weep again! over the fact that everything beautiful vanishes! . . .

Your *Swanwhite*, which I had from you, and you from me!

[no signature]

594. To HARRIET BOSSE

9 April 1908

I must finish my letter and tell you plainly, in a few words, what I mean. You know I wanted to be free and to give you back your freedom; and every time you turned your feelings from me to someone else, I was free until you began to think of me again. Then things got confused, and afterwards I reproached myself . . .

So now, when there is no going back, I beg you: do not think of me, neither with good will nor evil; never speak of me, do not mention my name, and if others do so, turn away, or remain silent!

I do not wish to live this double life, ensnared in other people's eroticism . . . I would rather mourn you as dead than remember you as someone else's wife. And you are bringing disharmony into your own life, for it isn't only you and I who 'live on the astral plane'. Lightning can strike backwards or to the side, and one of us can die, perhaps the one you now would miss the most.

You know yourself how often you have been ill and even felt weary of life (suicidal mania); the cause? Why, all those people whose feelings you've aroused have cast the currents you awakened back at you, hence your suffering. That you weren't killed on one occasion (1901) was a miracle, and that I didn't kill myself a still greater one.

I sometimes believe you intended to kill me. Dear child, I wished for nothing better; but what would have been gained? Like other sinners, I would no doubt have been washed clean once dead, my soul would have lived on in those of my works which have the power to survive, my name on the posters in the city would always remind you of me; at least for a while, our child would perhaps torture you by saying my name, though not for very long! So the only person to benefit would be me, who was born with a loathing for life, and who would gladly depart it, though in a decent manner.

I sometimes think it would be better and more fitting if we parted in hate, real hate (loathing); then it would be over. You may say: but we have parted in hate! so many times! – And then we met again!

Why do you, who have suffered so much from your games, and spread so much misery and sorrow, go on playing with love (I know one man who died as a result!)? I once believed you were playing with me too, but it seemed improbable to me that a beautiful young woman would give herself to an old man just to be able to murder him, and hence the difficulty we had in parting from each other seemed to indicate a certain liking.

Now I beg you: Leave me in peace! In my sleep I am as defenceless as everyone else, irresponsible . . . and afterwards I feel ashamed – now I think it a crime!

And note: I wasn't the one who began this, for I didn't understand such things, I was more childlike than you believed, when you initiated me!

[no signature]

595. To HARRIET BOSSE

[10 April 1908]

This morning I have rediscovered our correspondence – which had never really been lost! When I said that, it was a *lapsus linguæ*[1] (without thinking, in anger!) for I *never* lied to you, though I sometimes remained silent, with justification.

When one enters into a new alliance, it is customary to return each other's letters, or to burn them. I have dipped into ours and spent a couple of sublime hours. These letters contain the best of us, our souls in their Sunday best, as life in the flesh so seldom is. They are not artistically composed, but truthful, there is no posing here, nor any illusions – and if illusions are taken to mean something unreal, then this is the very highest reality.

This is how it was, not only how it appeared to be! Ought I to burn this? I am sending you a few of mine to sample. I have some two hundred of yours, all of them beautiful, like mine; not an unseemly word, not an ugly thought! You see, my child, you live in your letters and reveal yourself as 'The Great Woman' I divined you to be; that your everyday person doesn't match up to this is the fault of life, which is so hideous, and affords such foul situations.

You often spoke about your sister D.M.,[2] whose first husband still, in spite of everything, saw in her 'The Great Woman'; I didn't understand this then, but now I wonder if her second husband ever got to see her like that; if he could see her so. And I wonder now if her first husband lives a kind of higher life together with her . . . which would immediately become foul were they to meet and begin speaking. Words on the tongue are so impure that they are unable to express the highest things; what is written on the white paper is more pure! – To burn your letters would be to burn you, and that I cannot do! – Tell me what you want me to do![3]

But forget me! Give me back my freedom, which I need; you will need it, too, in your new union! Do this, or we shall all be unhappy, all of us! and I cannot live in crime and discord, in sin!

When I read the letter to me from the poor photographer, which he ends with a 'blessing', after you had saved him and his family with a single word, I wept for 'the little heart', and felt as if he were a better person than I – and I the worst of all living beings! – But am I? Am I?[4]

[no signature]

596. To HARRIET BOSSE

11 April 1908

Must write another word![1]

When I wrote to Castegren yesterday, I did so with sincere contrition after two days of weeping and reading our letters. But I wasn't certain of my honesty of heart and prayed to God not to let me become a hypocrite, which it is easy to do at such a moment. Then I fell asleep! . . .

This morning I feel like a wretch, indeed almost a hypocrite, although at the time the feelings I expressed in my letter to C-n were genuine. I know that he can die if he is struck by a short circuit in our terrible alternating currents, I know that from experience, and I believe he has seen us in the dark of night. This is woeful! and the most dreadful thing I've ever experienced! It was also the one thing I feared when you got engaged, yes, I feel it every time he[2] caresses you, and then I struggle against suicide.

This is what you have been playing with, Child, in childish folly!

Fortunately, I have never seen him, but yesterday I saw his photograph!

He resembled me; but his self was dead, and he had become an offshoot of my soul, both from acting in my plays and associating with you! He was me – as in my large Ljus photograph[3] – me in youthful guise, which I did not begrudge you for taking in exchange for my old one. But he himself was dead!

What does this mean? Can souls bear offspring? Yes, I've read as much in a profound book.

But why do you have to ignite such deadly fires, dear Child?

One thing I know: I shan't survive your wedding night; not out of envy, but simply from imagining what will happen.

Well, in that case I'll celebrate my blood wedding! God will allow me that after all I've suffered! And I must depart before my self, my immortal soul, is defiled!

It is no good my saying to myself: Why should he touch my woman? – She was not mine in the usual sense, and he had the right, but she was my creation all the same, and there was something of me in her which he now touches . . . it is me he caresses, that is why I must depart!

Why won't you let me go? What do you want with my old body? Take my soul if you wish, but let me go!

This will end badly!

But that you let yourself drift with events! That unlike me, it has never occurred to you to seek the only Anchor which holds!

I've just sent the letter to C-n! But it is no longer pure-hearted as it was yesterday! God preserve us all!

The only solution is for me to go far, far away, and not know when you marry! For if I stay, I cannot remain in touch with you through our child, for Lillan smells of you, and can also talk! In short, I can never see her again!

Don't try to stop me! And don't lead me into sin!

He must accept our writing to each other before the marriage. We must unravel the past and make arrangements for the child! Tell him that, frankly!

Will one of us die as a result of this? I will gladly sacrifice myself! It's the only way. And then no one will be to blame! No one! I absolve you!

He almost died two years ago, you know. Did he perhaps die, but get a new soul from you, whom he had loved ever since you met him in Finland? Has his character changed since his illness? And what brought on his illness? You? Or me? Perhaps!

You, you have been playing with puppets, so . . .

Didn't you notice that many of those who wanted to take you from me came to harm, died, lost wives and children? I had no part in this, hardly dared to wish them harm, for I knew how dangerous it was!

That's why I am afraid of disturbing you, for if I do I shall suffer for it!

Therefore let me go!

You may not have more than one! Two is murder, criminal!

[no signature]

597. To HARRIET BOSSE

11–12 April 1908

After your dear letter today, but only after your confession, I believe I have the right to say this. Our hearts are unreliable, counterfeit, and I am partial in the matter; I cannot trust in any noble motives when wishing to advise you, which is the worst thing one can do when it concerns an engaged couple. (You were also given advice once before, and so was I, but it didn't do any good!)

Well, you know what this man amounts to! You know he's had several women during your relationship, that he deceives you, that he has incorporated you in his harem, you, my Lioness! my Bride!, and thereby drawn us into the atmosphere of other women! And he is to be father to my child, our dear child! He will hold Lillan, caress her with lips that bear the poison of other women!

I haven't mentioned Lillan before, because I didn't dare think of her fate!

He didn't suffer while consoling you, he has lied to you, seduced you, so as to be able to boast of it!

Lillan's father!

What have you been thinking of?

I thought you loved him, and so I bent before the power of almighty love, admired you, who in spite of everything, could love him!

But you named his sickness a good two years ago! And when you didn't recoil at it, I believed your love was infinite! I was almost warmed by it at a distance![1]

But now! Swanwhite, since you don't love him, what are you then?

And were you to have a child? What then?

What have you done, poor Harriet? Dear Heart, what have you done?

There is only One who can help! That is the Almighty and all Powerful God!

Now you are sinking! Harriet!

And our child! Lillan! Linda Gold! Anne-Marie! Oh God in Heaven, help us!

Palm Sunday Morning.

– – – Nothing now remains but to ask you, as I did when I proposed to you: Will you have a little child with me? And in reply you smiled, smiled as Anne-Marie sometimes smiles.

I knew all this last Saturday night of course, but I wasn't conceited enough to believe it.

Will you have a little child by me, Harriet?

[no signature]

598. To HARRIET BOSSE

14 April 1908

What happened yesterday evening between 10.30 and 11.30 I do not know, but *you two* were near to bursting my heart!

Your little heart was beating so hard in *my* breast that I had to lay my hand upon it – and behold, it quietened down and ceased to beat, so that I thought you were dead.

But then, as I lay in the moonlight in the faithful blue bed, that has never thought of any woman but you, you lay on my arm, I could see your little face, feel your breath; and I took your little hand in the dark, kissed it and whispered, as before: Good night, my beloved, beloved wife![1]

Is this what Beethoven meant by *Die ferne Geliebte*?[2] This is the truth, but I was too much of a child to grasp it before you crossed my path. What is this? A higher life on a higher plane, which only we *Götterkinder*[3] can live! And an earthworm is to be introduced, initiated, into it! No, Agnes, Indra's Daughter! No! No profane being! Such a one must remain outside the temple!

At first I shrank back as from a crime! I will not be a hypocrite, I cried to God! And I begged Him to strike me as a sign that He disapproved of me.

But He did not strike me, he let the moon shine into my room, and at midnight He laid my beautiful little wife upon my arm! I may do it! I have permission! – But mark well, only in the soft darkness of the night which renders this mystery innocent!

During the day, by daylight, it is a sin! Then there is a pounding on all the walls!

I think I know that your engagement was stillborn, and is dead! I believe I know why, and also why you took him *par dépit*![4]

I recently saved a burning woman![5] If I've now saved you, I am your good Ariel, your servant for life, unto death, and after!

But what will happen now?

You see, my Child, the purest love was the strongest, and remains so!

[no signature]

599. To HARRIET BOSSE

17 April 1908

Yesterday, Thursday morning, I awoke with the feeling that I was newly married again, and begged of you one word; you know the one I mean, that people wish to say to me, but which I only want to hear from your mouth.

I did you no harm yesterday, neither in word nor thought, not even with looks!

In the evening came your reply!

You sent your child to me wearing the Thrall's[1] bracelet! At that moment the child ceased to be mine! I renounced her, I renounce her! I never want to see her again, to protect her little soul from your evil, you, the most wicked of all created beings!

The Thrall struck you, and now as his woman, you will bear his necklace!

You have now sunk so low that only One, the Almighty, can raise you up out of the abyss.

I didn't weep yesterday, I was turned to stone!

You Black Swanwhite! You took away all my good thoughts with you!

Now take everything with you, everything, the child too! And go!

But then you sought me out at dawn! And found not my better self but my lower one at home! That is what you love, or hate, whatever I'm to call it, but my soul alone can give you joy! And that you'll never possess again![2]

Now the child is his! from this moment on; the Earl's daughter becomes the Thrall's, and her mother likewise!

Oh woe!

And I who believed this time! Who had such beautiful thoughts about you, and took such care of our secret, even though I was proud – such care that I did not even dare mention your name or betray by my expression in the street how happy and restored to favour I felt!

And during these 14 days I have written so beautifully, speaking in my heart to you! If you should ever chance to read a certain 36 pages in that book,[3] you will recognize them, and ask: Where did he get this from?

[no signature]

600. To AUGUST FALCK

[18? April 1908]

That's where the secret lay! It was therefore our undertaking was never blessed: yes, because I let loose old demons, those I was in duty bound to suppress. I was wrong, and other people right, but with reservations. I misjudged them, believing the public wanted the other things! but it now feels as if they were better than I . . . That is a terrible feeling! – Now, I beg you, in future and at once, to delete every insult to religion or what is holy, beginning with *The Father*! I know you're not that way inclined; I don't know either whether Fru Björling has any feeling for what we call religion, but I believe that Flygare has. In any case: let those two, beg those two, to help us delete these things, you know which ones, from the acting and prompt copies of *Easter*, *Miss Julie*, *The Bond* (not so many) and the rest! – It will free me from this sense of being at odds with myself, since I'm responsible there for the preaching of false doctrines, ones that I now preach against! and no longer profess! Only then can I pray for a blessing upon the little temple in Bantorget![1] and then the blessing will be given!

[no signature]

601. To HARRIET BOSSE

[19 April 1908]

After a Good Friday, about which you know, when everything was one huge, sad mockery, evening came . . . Then I grew calmer, and someone whispered in my ear: that inoffensive bracelet was just a worthless plaything of which no one wanted to deprive the child, it was no great treasure.[1]

There I was, humbled, again, yet I could hardly wish the ordeal we had gone through undone, for it was necessary, or at least beneficial.

Was it so?

In any case, I asked your forgiveness 1,000 times! and do so still, even if it was not so but, as I believed, a demon had spoken ill of me!

Of me! who can never be other than faithful to you in my heart, if not always in my words!

My only question, which you have perhaps misunderstood, is this: Are you free?

That is the vital question for me, for I will not live as a criminal! Why don't you answer? I shall of course keep your reply to myself!

Don't let Anne-Marie come here before that question is answered. The little creature talks, and what she says is obscure, sometimes deadly!

Your *Easter* has been performed![2] I have thanked you for it before but do so now, over and over again! The first time you read it, I received your beautiful little soul in my mouth for the first time! And *that*, and only that, is so sweet . . .

Last night you sought me like fire and roses, roses in my mouth!

Every morning at sunrise, I have a desire to give you something! But my hand is so clumsy, my gifts are always such mistakes, causing pain where they only seek to do good . . .

Whisper a wish to me, great or small! Preferably great! I want to sacrifice something, to take something valuable away from myself in order to give you something in return for the joy you give me by loving me! the joy that only a love between souls can give. You see!

But once and for all: Answer! Are you free?

This need have no other consequences than those you desire! Whatever you wish, as you wish!

Lastly, once again! Thank you for your *Easter* and your Easter girl, who was yours! It has given people joy of the right kind! But those ungrateful creatures didn't know that it was you who donated it with your little hand! You, who had suffered for me! And they don't know that she sits in the

Green Room, and that I whisper to her, hold my hand over her, pat her heart, and say: Forgive me!

When you had read your *Easter* for the first time, you came and asked God to bless me!

Now He has heard your prayer!

[no signature]

602. To ANNA FLYGARE

25 April 1908

Dear Fröken Flygare,

Because I had done so in my mind, and often get things muddled, I thought I had already thanked you, but it seems I haven't done so. However, every evening now I feel both your pleasure in having been able to come up into the light, and how you suffer my Eleonora's sufferings, because I wrote this play.

A writer of tragedies often forgets that an actor, evening after evening, goes through hours of agony for him. I only came upon the idea when I saw you being tortured in *The Bond*, and was made aware of my guilt for the first time.

'Poor Eleonora-Flygare!' I say every evening at 8 o'clock, and then play (badly) *Sieben Worte*[1] or 'The Waves of Sound'[2] so as to relieve her suffering!

May a little happiness now come your way!

[no signature]

603. To HARRIET BOSSE

3 May 1908

It is now seven years since we were married! Was this the seven fires; could it be the seven roses are coming with the white dove in the corn? Why do we 'meet' only now? When it is too late?[1]

Why did we part right at the beginning?

I don't know! I was childishly ignorant and loved you so enormously that I couldn't step down and . . . I could only kiss you, as you called it, for to me that alone was beautiful. I understood no better and thought what now exists was brutal. It wasn't selfishness, it was a sense of beauty and want of judgement.

The strange thing is, I still believe I acted correctly!

Faithful and gentle, 'as the wave kisses the shore', I wanted to love you, for love is gentle; and the long, imposing waves of a human embrace told me that the little one, who was waiting to be born, wanted to be cradled in your womb and not harshly shaken from the tree with the fruits of life.

That is surely how it is!

I now have your soul in a little Japanese box on my desk. There lie all your letters, a ring with many smaller rings on it (one is missing); your bridal crown and veil; the gold pen! Let me write something else of beauty with it! Beloved! and two little bags of lavender, keepsakes from Denmark (1901), one red and one green, joined by an indissoluble knot.

The most beautiful letters are from 1904 (at the time of our divorce). I am reading one in which you respond to my application for a divorce with a cry of anguish and defeated love! It reads like a cry of woe to heaven, and makes me roar with pain!

My bride of seven years ago! And now another's! And yet not!

Can you untie this bond? Can you? I can't!

[no signature]

P.S. I 'intend' to write a book on the Art of Acting. Will you therefore let me have the beautiful portraits of yourself from *Johannes*?[2] Right away? Then I'll lend you some beautiful reproductions of modern art, connected with the theatre!

After two weeks of negotiations with Ranft about your *Swanwhite*, he left town yesterday, without giving me an answer. Unless he takes the play, there's nothing we can do.

Would you want me to lose this favourable opportunity and wait for you? You know I'm used to waiting! But you have so many other things, and I have so little! And there's a possibility I may get *Swanwhite* put on at the Royal Theatre. Only a possibility, mind you! Falck will always put it on, Ranft knows that, and with a young child of seventeen,[3] who looks like you and can smile like you, but who is given to melancholy. She is educated, and from a good family. If need be, won't you adopt her as your pupil, your spiritual child, since you don't wish to have an earthly one? In that way you would still be acting, but through her.

I can't understand why you will not let your talent give birth to talent in others, and why you are unwilling to let your strong, exceptional soul have any descendants. After all, anyone can bring ordinary children into the world, but only *Götterkinder*[4] can beget life within a human soul.

I sometimes wonder if small creatures of a spiritual kind will result from our *Übermenschliche Ehe*.[5] Something must surely come of such a union, in which extraordinary spiritual forces meet and merge with each other.

Sometimes I believe that you will have another child by me, though I do not know how. And it will be born in love and become a power on earth, of poor estate but powerful in word and deed. It seems to me that some little soul is waiting to have us as parents, and that I saw her little face one night in the moonlight on a white sheet.

I'm taking this opportunity of telling you, so you won't be frightened if anything should happen. I have read in 'a book' that there is such a thing as phantom pregnancy, with all the symptoms but without the reality! I wonder if we might not expect something in that way. I have also read, but still doubt it, that genuine *conception immaculée*[6] can take place, that is to say telepathically! What should we believe, what would the world say?

But whatever happens, I shall know it through my senses; for I have your bodily soul within me. My body knew when your last period began, and when it ended! I know your every emotion. When you are happy, when someone is tormenting you (then I get a spike in my heart), and when He is angry with me, then there's an explosion in my breast.

[no signature]

604. To AUGUST FALCK

[9 May 1908]

My dear Falck,

I think we've lost our way and failed ourselves and our task, which is to simplify the amount of clutter. By keeping the staging simple, one establishes order on stage, and a little comfort and ease behind the scenes, which the poor actors require. At the moment it's like unloading and loading a boat; disturbing, unsightly, laborious, making it difficult for the artists to create the right illusion and atmosphere, and perhaps forcing them to sometimes lend a hand themselves.

Simplicity provides the solemn calm and silence which alone makes it possible for the artist to hear his role. By keeping the scenery simple, what matters emerges: the character, role, speech, expression, gestures. It is often a waste of effort to reset the stage for a short scene; the spectator doesn't have time to take it all in, for he is fully occupied with listening to and making sense of what is being said!

'In the beginning was the word!' Yes, the spoken word is all! You know the complex artistic interweaving of destinies and wills in *Christina*. But it can be performed anywhere, even in front of a Smyrna rug hung up in a cellar in the provinces,[1]

605. To HARRIET BOSSE

[14 May 1908]

Thrice have I written and burnt these words, from the depths of my heart:

Will you be my lawful wedded wife,
In the eyes of God, the law and the world,
For better and for worse
In faithful love
Now and for evermore?

Must this be burnt too?
Yes? or No?

But you must be free to marry, so that you can receive into your womb a longed-for and a blessed child, in my arms! which have never been opened for another woman but you ever since I saw you, not even in thought!

When you speak or write to me, remember that it is to a man who cannot, dare not utter a word that is not true! Isn't it reassuring to be able to place your trust in a single human being? You must not deceive or play with him! That is sinful![1]

[no signature]

606. To HARRIET BOSSE

[15 May 1908]

To Let!
(immediately.)
40 Karlavägen, 3 (*third*) floor.
Four rooms and kitchen, etc.
The rent need not be paid![1]

607. To AXEL STRINDBERG

[Not sent]

26 May 1908

To My Brother Axel,

It is turning out as I said it would!

I cannot live in sin and crime when every day I condemn sin in *A Blue Book*![1]

I have asked God to free me from this sin, but he doesn't hear me!

I have begged the Lord to take my life, but He has concealed Himself!

Now I believe He is calling me! I shall go myself, to show confidence in Him; and will sacrifice my life, in order to confirm my teachings!

If I go on living, I shall sink, and I do not want to sink! may not!

Thank you for all your help and friendship! You could not love me, because of the difference in our natures, but I did not ask it!

Try to save my poor body from the Dissecting-Room! For the sake of our relatives! That can only be done through intervention in high places (Richard Bergh – Prince Eugen).

Farewell then, Axel! I feel as if I am dying quite free from guilt! But why I can't say! Yes, because I've suffered so immensely. Mostly for my impiety.

August

You are to have my 'Occult Diary' in a red cover in the 3rd drawer of the desk in my study, under the Eagle.[2] It must never be published! It was in pawn to Bonnier, but has now been redeemed![3] The letter is in the Diary.

I have 1,000 *kronor* in the Enskilda Bank at Nybron. About 100 in my wallet.

Lay the crucifix on my breast in the coffin. My brown cape over the coffin.

Place only a black wooden cross on my grave with: *O crux, ave spex unica*! An obscure, simple place! Never a monument![4]

That is what I want!

In the Drawing-Room under Beethoven[5] there is a Japanese box containing all Harriet's *beautiful* letters. Hide them!

I believe I may die without laying hands on my own life! For this sickness, the nature of which escapes me, is stopping my heart!

608. To FANNY FALKNER

Fanny Falkner (1891–1963), painter and actress. The eldest daughter of Meta Falkner, who was shortly to become Strindberg's landlady at 85 Drottninggatan. She studied art in Stockholm and Copenhagen but was drawn into the activities of the Intimate Theatre by Amanda Björling, who also lodged with the Falkners for a time. Her talent as an actress was modest, but as with Bosse, whom she replaced in his affections, Strindberg soon wished to allot her a central role in his life as well as on stage in his plays. Though they were twice engaged, however, marriage was never a serious proposition. Nevertheless, his death affected her deeply. The young man with whom she was then in love committed suicide, and she became seriously ill. She abandoned painting for several years and even though, following a move to Denmark in the 1930s, she enjoyed a small reputation as a miniaturist, the trauma of her time with Strindberg was never resolved. She grew increasingly melancholy and self-absorbed, and died unmarried, leaving a brief account of their relationship in *August Strindberg i Blå tornet* (August Strindberg in the Blue Tower, 1921), which she dictated to Algot Ruhe. Strindberg's surviving correspondence with Fanny amounts to over two hundred items, many of them only brief notes.

30 May 1908

Fröken Falkner,

I will now give you my impressions of your reading today, and what you can learn from it.

It was beautiful, intelligent, and sounded well.

But, you see, it was conversational, fit for a small room; in a larger space, like the theatre, everything must be enlarged in proportion, without the voice needing to be amplified to any great extent.

1. Speak slowly, *legato*, every word in the phrase linked; the punctuation marks must not create a *staccato* effect, one glides over them with a little sound, which I shall teach you.

2. Speak naturally, but don't chatter!

3. Expansive delivery; to start with what people call a little artificial; imagine you are making a speech or preaching, without shouting, however.

4. Begin by speaking grammatically, and get into the habit of talking a little pedantically in everyday life, as if you were reading aloud or giving a lecture. Leave off chattering or gabbling in normal circumstances. In short: don't be slovenly, but speak slowly!

5. Take care over your consonants, particularly the R; the vowels are clearly audible.

6. If you grow accustomed to speaking elegantly in normal circumstances, you won't need to read so much.

7. Speak, accent, phrase like a singer; listen to your own voice and take pleasure in it when it sounds well.

8. Flygare[1] speaks with refinement in normal circumstances, listen to her, imitate her! It should sound a little pretentious, important!

The whole secret of speech is: Slowly, evenly, *legato*.

Beginners chatter rather than speak. They staccato-ize! which is abominable!

Go out and walk in the open air; speak to yourself there, poetry you know by heart; it strengthens the voice.

And then: learn to breath through the nose when you speak, then you'll achieve this expansive delivery.

I have written to Axelsson[2] this evening and am awaiting a reply!

Call on me tomorrow, Sunday, at 1 p.m. so you can hear what he has to say.

I have received a clear summons to make a great actress of you; but you must take the matter seriously and work, for it's no game!

Keep this letter, read it often, and think over my advice.

Yrs,
August Strindberg

X

Letters 609–679 June 1908–April 1912

Shortly after what proved to be the final break with Harriet, Strindberg closed his *Occult Diary* and moved from the apartment they had once shared at 40 Karlavägen to his final residence at 85 Drottninggatan, near the site of the two houses on Norrtullsgatan where he had spent much of his childhood, and where, in 1875, he had first met Siri von Essen. He christened the building, which now houses the Strindberg Museum, Blå tornet (The Blue Tower), hired three small rooms on the fourth floor, and had his meals provided by his landlady, Meta Falkner, who lived on the floor above. Strindberg already knew one of her daughters, Fanny, from the Intimate Theatre where, in spite of August Falck's misgivings, he sought to foster her career as an actress. At Strindberg's insistence she played both Eleonora in *Easter* and the title role in *Swanwhite*, and when the theatre foundered in 1910, following unresolvable differences with Falck over its repertoire, he helped to find her commissions as a portrait painter. He also proposed to her twice, but both engagements were quickly terminated, not least because he was over forty years her senior, and increasingly infirm.

Nevertheless, although he experienced several periods of ill health during the years he spent in Blå tornet, the impression that Strindberg sometimes liked to give of living there as a recluse is largely false. He saw Fanny and her family every day, continued to hold his Beethoven evenings with (among others) Richard Bergh, Tor Aulin, his brother Axel and Carlheim-Gyllensköld, corresponded regularly with Nils Andersson in Skåne, was involved in publishing projects with both Bonniers and Karl Börjesson, and maintained a keen interest in the affairs of the Intimate Theatre. Indeed, for a period, while Falck was fully occupied playing the lead in *The Father*, he took over as director and, in reponse to the practical demands of staging his plays, produced the *Open Letters to the Intimate Theatre* on acting, Shakespeare, and the writing of historical drama. He also wrote his final set of history plays, *The Last Knight*, *The Regent*, and *The Earl of Bjälbo*, a play for children, *Abu Casem's Slippers*, a morality for Christmas, *The Black Glove*, and his dramatic epitaph in verse, *The Great Highway*, besides adding to *A Blue Book* and devoting much time and energy to the studies in linguistics which make up a substantial volume in the collected edition of his works that Karl Otto Bonnier contracted to publish in 1911.

Although his reputation abroad was growing, many of his finest plays remained unperformed in Sweden except by the Intimate Theatre. However, his sixtieth birthday was honoured at several theatres throughout the country and, following a celebration at Folkets Hus, members of the Social Democratic Youth Movement marched in procession to Blå tornet, where they sang the *Internationale* beneath his window. Their homage, in the year of a bitter general strike, anticipated the often savage polemics on political, religious, literary and social topics, now known as the 'Strindberg Feud', upon which he embarked in 1910. His immediate targets were Verner von Heidenstam and the explorer Sven Hedin, who represented an increasingly reactionary establishment, but the real issues raised by the feud were more far-reaching than the personal abuse which often accompanied it, and the affair, which lasted several years, precluded a just estimate of Strindberg in Sweden until long after his death.

The hostility of the Swedish literary and political establishment to the now ailing writer was further exacerbated when, following the award of the Nobel Prize for 1909 to a representative of the literary nineties, Selma Lagerlöf, a working man named Adolf Lundgrehn wrote to *Afton-Tidning* suggesting the launch of a nation-wide appeal for Strindberg, to which ordinary men and women might contribute. The idea was adopted and a subscription started in April 1911, supported by over two hundred signatories and publicised by an exhibition of Strindberg's paintings, manuscripts, letters, portraits and photographs, which was displayed in Stockholm throughout the summer. Many of the contributions to what became known as the Anti-Nobel Prize were small but all the more valuable to Strindberg for that, coming as they did from the underclass with whom he again identified. The money (in all some 50,000 *kronor*) was handed over by Hjalmar Branting in March 1912, following the celebration of his sixty-third birthday by a huge torchlit procession of workers, a banquet in his honour at Berns', and productions of his plays in Sweden, Germany, Finland, Austria and Chicago, where August Lindberg played the title role in *Gustav Vasa*. However, his condition was now critical and he died on 14 May 1912, less than a month after Siri von Essen.

609. To KARL OTTO BONNIER

24 June 1908

My dear Bonnier,

The Italian lady[1] is welcome to translate what she likes, for my Italians abandoned me many years ago.

Thank you for the statement; had it been a little less on the minus side, I would have gone to Switzerland, for I'm certain I have stomach cancer, am in pain for twelve hours out of 24, and gradually ceasing to eat and sleep.

But I would like some company on the journey.

However, perhaps I'll stay here, until I'm hounded out of this cycle, now I've been allowed to build and plant on my burned sites.[2]

Yrs,
August Strindberg

610. To ALF AHLQUIST

Alf Ahlquist (1890–1960), Anne-Marie's cousin, the son of Harriet Bosse's sister, Inez Ahlquist. This is the only letter that Strindberg is known to have addressed to him.

29 June 1908

My good Alf,

Since I can't pay the rent, please let me give these 100 *Kr.* to Mamma Inez as a small expression of my gratitude for the care she is giving, and has given, my beloved child.[1]

I am so ill (stomach cancer – or an ulcer?) that I can't go out, and spend most of the day lying down. Therefore I'm unable to come, and ought not to either. Now Anne-Marie has a new father, I can't maintain our connection, and so get involved in a new relationship, which would tear us both apart. It is better to let sorrow run its course and enter upon a life of purity than to live in muddy waters!

Yrs,
August Sg

611. To TOR AULIN

6 July 1908

Dear Tor Aulin,

The Ghost Sonata was only to show you the form I am seeking for the new music drama; starting from chamber music, condensed, concentrated, with only a few voices.

I began 'St Gotthard',[1] but have been interrupted by my illness, which keeps me to my bed in pain almost the entire day.

But *The Ghost Sonata* has another side! To extract atmosphere (poetry!) out of contemporary, everyday reality without descending to the Orient or Medievalism of the Fairy-Tale play!

Sluggish from strychnine, atropine, bromine, etc., I can say no more today!

Wishing you a good recovery,[2] and that we can meet soon.

Yrs,
August Strindberg

612. To MANDA BJÖRLING

Amanda (Manda) Björling (1876–1960) made her stage debut as Roxane in Rostand's *Cyrano de Bergerac* under Hjalmar Selander's direction in Malmö, but she came to prominence as an actress under August Falck, with whom she appeared in the Stockholm première of *Miss Julie* in 1906. Together with Falck, whom she married in 1909, she appeared in numerous productions at the Intimate Theatre between 1907 and 1911. Her most celebrated Strindberg roles were Queen Christina, Miss Julie, Laura in *The Father*, Tekla in *Creditors*, Alice in *The Dance of Death*, and Henrietta in *Crimes and Crimes*, but she was also known for her performances as Mélisande in Maeterlinck's *Pelléas et Mélisande*, Katherine in *The Taming of the Shrew*, Hermione in *The Winter's Tale*, and the title role in Ibsen's *Hedda Gabler*.

[16 July 1908]

Fru Björling,

Now it only remains for me to thank and congratulate you!

Yesterday morning I finally got to see and hear your great talent! It is of course my fault for not having been able to see you before, but I get so wrought-up and devastated when I am confronted by the ghosts of my imagination alive on stage.

We now have a new Swedish art of acting, which began with Fru Björling and August Falck in *Miss Julie* around Christmas 1906![1]

I shall try not to forget this!

Yours sincerely,
AUGUST STRINDBERG[2]

613. To MANDA BJÖRLING

[16 July 1908]

Dear Fru Björling,

I saw you just now fully live up to your high reputation: I thanked you, gripped by your great, beautiful and truthful acting, and I must once again express my admiration for you. You made it possible for this piece to be seen, and by me as well. And you fooled me into liking the play, which others have fooled me into detesting for 20 years.[1]

But now comes a 'but'! When gesture, posture, facial expression and appearance were all perfect, and the plotting admirable, the diction ought also to be of the highest class. If, today, you spoke as you do in ordinary performances, it seems to me you have been slovenly in your articulation from the beginning. You spoke too rapidly and abruptly, as in comedy – but this is a tragedy! N.B. that! I had difficulty in hearing at times, for it became staccato, or slovenly. You should act up a little, give yourself airs, deliver it like poetry, for there is a concealed rhythm in this prose, where every word counts. Her story to Jean about the family situation was good, with shading and pauses and accompanied by all the right changes of facial expression. But then the tempo increased, and the words got jumbled up.

Listen to your own voice when you speak, and hear how beautiful it sounds when the vowels and consonants are given equal weight.

If you say that things are different during the evening performances, then these comments of mine are redundant, and I beg your pardon; all the same, however, I would be glad if you took my observations as generally applicable, and for all future occasions.

As a tragedienne (that's what you are, and you should never take lightweight roles!), you ought also to cultivate your speech. Full, expansive, rhythmically delivered without becoming declamatory!

I know that this is a stumbling-block for those of us who seek to be natural, and thereby easily become banal.

Simple, yes, but not vulgar: fluent, but not slovenly!

I think it would improve things if you learnt your roles slowly, pedantically. Then one can increase the tempo, and in that way all the words will remain audible.

And follow your part, and keep to your most beautiful register.

These are small things, but important ones; they are the grammar, the rudiments, which can and should be learnt.

What cannot be learnt, you already have, it is yours, that plus an indescribably rich and captivating way of giving expression to every aspect of the role, which is what I admired today, and have also wanted and waited to be able to admire in Christina.

We ought to seek perfection, and that is why I am making these comments. Use them! even if this time they are unwarranted!

A detail! Make your exit in the final scene like a sleepwalker, slowly, with your arms outstretched in front of you, gliding out, as if seeking support from the air in order not to fall over a stone or something; out, irresistibly, towards the last great darkness.[2]

[no signature]

614. To MANDA BJÖRLING

17 July 1908

Dear Fru Björling,

I subtract not a word of my praise for your Miss Julie yesterday; it was truly yours, and more beautiful and human than mine, and it gives me a further, genuine pleasure to be able to repeat my praise today, having reviewed in memory your beautiful portrait of a poor creature, to whom I was perhaps too hard in my own hard days, when everyone's hand was raised against me, and mine against everyone!

But, now comes the 'but', I believe this very dinnertime I have discovered your secret: you do not speak with your larynx, where the tone is formed, but with the lips, tongue, teeth and palate, in short with your mouth.

Now it's accepted that when conversing in a small room, you moderate your voice, that is to say, speak with the mouth. But on stage, even if you are conversing with someone at table, you have always also to speak to the mass of people called the public, which fills the great auditorium.

Remember, therefore, that however intimate the scene behind the curtain, you are nevertheless a 'public speaker' making a speech which must be audible to everyone.

In short, you must speak with the larynx; that's where your notes are, that's where the tone is, for this organ exists for the voice alone, and dwells nearer the breast and heart. The tongue and teeth have other tasks, and only contribute to the shaping of the sound.

Think of your chest tones; and don't lose any of your consonants; they are what gives colour and sonority, and support and sinew to the voice: in the falsetto there is no firmness of register. I don't believe I'm mistaken on this point, and the answer is: Don't be timid or shy on stage, for that extinguishes the voice. Talk big (I mean use the larynx, which contains the vocal cords), but without arrogance; speak to the multitude out there at the same time as you are involved in the scene on stage.

I now have the right to lecture you like this of course, since I have the honour to sign myself

The Director[1]

615. To KARIN ALEXANDERSSON

Karin Alexandersson (1878–1948), actress. A member of the Intimate Theatre from 1908 to 1910. She played Laura in the 1908 production of *The Father* with which it finally established its critical reputation as well as

Kristin in *Miss Julie*, Mme Catherine in *Crimes and Crimes*, and the Mother in *To Damascus*.

30 July 1908

Fröken Alexandersson,

With reference to our most recent conversation about the role of Laura, I only want to make a few general observations.

Analyse your role carefully, but don't pick it to pieces; don't brood upon it, looking for depths where there are none.

What the Captain, her Brother and the Nurse say about her when she is off-stage contributes to her characterization, of course. You ought to know what she was like as a child, as a sister to the Pastor, what she is like as a wife, a mother, a mistress (to the Nurse). Listen to what they say about you from the wings, when you are offstage. They can always be lying, or embroidering, or exaggerating, but that's not what we are to believe is the case here. Her Brother speaks of her morbid stubbornness and craving for power, etc. That is surely the *leitmotiv* which you ought to stress. But we mustn't turn her into a monster, and you haven't. Nevertheless, by illuminating a figure from many sides, it easily becomes shallow, unfocused, insipid. Perhaps a one-sided light is best on stage; the shadows certainly emerge as blacker, and the light brighter, but the figure stands out in relief. I think you showed a little too much human feeling in the role; but I'm not certain about that. And if you've created a vital image of Laura, then keep it, I won't pull it to pieces.

You may well reply that your image wasn't sufficiently 'developed' yet, or that it was 'underexposed' (veiled). Therefore we'll wait until later before commenting. And these must only be regarded as preliminary, general observations.

The role has always been a striking one, and has never failed. It is regarded as easy and transparent because it has perhaps been done too simply. Erik Skram (at the première in Copenhagen in 1889)[1] compared this drama to a duel between a Boa constrictor and a Lion. That is perhaps an exaggeration, for there is really so much that is human in the duellists.

The Director

616. To NILS ANDERSSON

1 August 1908

Nils Andersson,

40 Karlavägen has ceased to exist! A 7 year period has come to an end! 'The Lord gave and the Lord took!'

Now, if you come to Sthlm, I am living as a boarder at 85 Drottninggatan, 4th Floor,[1] where we should feel as comfortable as before, in a threeroomer, with all the necessaries except a cook and kitchen (incl. sponger). Self-serving table,[2] wine from Cederlunds, piano with Beethoven, but everything new!

I've been ill, but am now well again!

The furniture and my library went to the Pawnbrokers! By all means let W.B.[3] know that, if it's suitable!

Where are you?

Yrs,
August Strindberg

Tel: 56.22

617. To RENÉ SCHICKELE

René Schickele (1883–1940), since 1904 the editor of *Neuen Magazins für Literatur* in Berlin.

[Original in German]

2 August 1908

Dear Sir,

The Intimate Theatre is closed and doesn't open until the 15th.

I am only to be met with in my works, not in person.

Yours faithfully,
August Strindberg

618. To NILS ANDERSSON

21 August 1908

My dear Friend,

It wasn't only a matter of money, it was a violent crisis in my life when my last, beloved little child was torn, living, from me and given to – such a stepfather! Life had kept the worst of all until my 60th year. I made myself ill with grieving, and begged God to let me die, but came through!

To do so I wrenched myself free from the past with a mighty tug – the flat was let, the furniture and books had to go, there was nothing for it but the pawnbroker. But, everything worked out to my advantage! Freed from memories and books, my muse broke through! And now I'm living the life that suits me best.

I am just completing the Third Act of a young Gustav Vasa,[1] and freed from everything to do with keeping house, life is pure joy.

Don't mention money, don't even think about it; the past is over and done with! It had to happen, and was my liberation! Congratulate me!

It would be good if W.B.[2] were to repay what he's borrowed, for I'm expecting to have to bury my first wife in Finland![3]

Now believe what I say, and come and enjoy yourself with me in my 'Green Tower'[4] at the top of Drottninggatan. It's visible from the Riksdag building, has a green roof, laurel wreaths and horns of plenty, balconies, a shower room, everything! And I have the urge to write, good food, and Beethoven!

Sometimes a cloud crosses my memory, but I have wept for four months, my tears are beginning to abate, and life turn green again; the past is like a poem, already printed and published, awaiting the new!

Thank you, however, for your friendly letter! And when your evil day comes, think of mine, and remember where I found the wonderful help that enabled me to endure.

It's a wonder I am still alive!

Kindest regards,
August Strindberg

619. To META FALKNER

Meta Falkner (d.1927), the Danish-born wife of an unsuccessful singer and businessman who hired two floors of the newly built house at 85 Drottninggatan with the intention of taking lodgers. Strindberg moved into three rooms on the fourth floor on 11 July 1908, and Meta Falkner, who lived on the floor above, provided all his meals. Strindberg's response to her attentions was expressed mainly through the many notes he sent her, in which his frequent requests and genuine appreciation alternated with lapidary explosions such as 'Are you trying to poison me?', 'Keep your Danish pigswill', or simply: 'Eskimo food'.

[August 1908]

Regulations

1. *If* the hall door is bolted, give two short rings, and it will be opened at once.
2. Do not disturb me with trivial matters, such as letters or parcels that require no answer, nor with magazines, but wait until mealtimes.
3. Do not bring down cleaned glasses, etc. except at mealtimes.
4. Do not admit strangers (workmen) without permission, so that I need not be taken unawares by unknown persons in my rooms.
5. *If* the hall door is bolted, I am not 'angry', I simply do not wish to be disturbed!

Sg

620. To KARL BÖRJESSON

11 November 1908

I've had occasion to thank you for *The Toilers of the Sea*, but why not also publish Victor Hugo's *The Man Who Laughs*? The most sublime and beautiful book ever written! I finished it this morning with a feeling of sorrow and loss! I hadn't read it since 1866! And now realized it was my teacher, my starting point, and my radical-religious programme, the whole long, winding way.

Sg

621. To AUGUST FALCK

17 November 1908

Come by for a while this evening and have a look at the 'Scenery' I've created here at home,[1] in this home which is now my widower's residence, mine! as long as it lasts!

And let me also talk to you about the possibility of the Intimate Theatre doing the Christmas Play[2] I'm going to start writing tomorrow!

Yrs,
Strindberg

622. To KARL BÖRJESSON

[20? November 1908]

Herr Börjesson,

Herewith a letter to read about B.B.[1] from 'Germany's greatest living Lyric Poet', Richard Dehmel.[2] But it's not to be used for Advertising now; though have it copied and translated, so it can be included one day as a literary curiosity.

I don't know what the dream means.

Have you room for a large trunk containing several thousand slips of paper with 25 years of notes for B.B. (was originally called 'The Green Sack', then became *Antibarbarus*, etc., and finally the *Blue Book*)? The trunk has now landed up in the attic, where rats and the damp will wreak havoc on it! But if you can take it for safe-keeping, then don't put it up in an attic or in the cellar! The trunk is fine enough to stand in a room, preferably under a coverlet; or have it made into a 'pouffe' (a settle) to sit on!

Yours ever,
Sg

623. To FANNY FALKNER

29 December 1908

Fröken Fanny Falkner,

When you told me how cold and hungry you were on the last tour (3rd Class), I wanted at least to give you a fur coat for the next one. Since you have acted in my plays, and there was no Christmas box from the Director, this gift seemed to me both suitable and justified.

But since you tell me that your parents consider it improper, I am sending you instead a gratuity of 120 *kronor*, to be used as seems best.

It is possible that my innocent gift was improper.

Therefore, and to avoid anything that might disturb the peace, I must ask you not to visit me alone again in my room.

Our old agreement, with its weekly remuneration, still stands.[1]

If you have anything to ask or say, then do so by open notes.

As before,
Strindberg

624. To ALGOT RUHE

14 January 1909

Algot Ruhe,

Prevent any demonstrations that you get wind of.[1] My incarnations are as numerous as the cast list of a play, and in such disarray that I don't know who people wish to celebrate.

If you're commissioned to do anything by D.N.,[2] then let me have a questionnaire!

Yrs,
Strindberg

625. To SOCIAL-DEMOKRATEN

[23 January 1909]

Social-Demokraten, Stockholm.

My thanks for your greeting, you spokesmen of the common people, among whom, being the Son of a Servant, I shall always count myself.

626. To FREDRIK AND GERDA VULT VON STEIJERN

25 January 1909

Dear Friends,

Distance – and some of the other things that life has to offer – separated us a little; but in memory I am always near you!

Yours ever,
Strindberg

627. To IVAR NILSSON

[27 January 1909]

New signal, secret, because the previous one has been abused by traitors. 2 double! That is, two times 2 quick rings with a pause in between.

628. To ALGOT RUHE

15 February 1909

Algot Ruhe,

When you stage your plays,[1] take all the Facades in one evening (they only require a table and some chairs); but create a frame for them: 1. instead of the proscenium paint a modern house façade cut out in the form of an arch (the stage opening); 2. compose a kind of 'Prologue', a fantastic figure like Asmodeus in *Gil Blas*,[2] who lifts the roofs off the houses and reveals their insides. (Introduces and concludes the play, and perhaps interpolates between the acts. But in costume.) Then you'll have a fine full evening, and an original one.

You've a director in Nycander,[3] for having been an actor is all one needs to understand what goes on behind the scenes.

But you must be the manager! However, hold a read through first, attract some attention! – A little money does no harm!

Yrs,
Sg

629. To KNUT MICHAELSON

Knut Gottlieb Michaelson (1841–1915), businessman, writer, and theatre director. His well-made, artificial comedies and history plays were largely anathema to Strindberg, but in 1907, when the Royal Theatre moved to its present site at Nybroplan, Michaelson was appointed its director, and hence became someone with whom he had to deal. Michaelson established a varied repertoire at the Royal Theatre where his stress on historical accuracy in scenery and costume betrayed the influence of the famous Meiningen Theatre; he also enjoyed considerable popularity among the actors, but was forced to resign in 1910, after a long-running conflict with his board of directors. His initial contact with Strindberg came through their mutual friend Pehr Staaff, but their relationship remained a business one. Twenty-four of Strindberg's letters to him survive, all of them written between 1907 and 1910.

4 March 1909

Herr Director,
Knut Michaelson,

You promised to spare my text, but now I'm told the 4th Act is to be cut.

My composition isn't that slack, that one can remove a whole act!

Sture forgives Trolle three times.[1]

1. He recommends his election. 2. Pays for his pallium! 3. Spares his life. This last is the climax, the high point, when Trolle responds to his noble action by excommunicating him and calling upon Christian.[2]

The cock crows thrice; why should one cut the third instance, which is decisive for Sture's whole understanding of people and life.

History itself gave me the three moments, without my needing to go looking for them. (In Starbäck,[3] Volume II, p.655, it says, after the capture of Stäke:[4] 'The enraged peasantry was ready to cut the traitor in pieces (Trolle) and it was with difficulty that Sir Sten was able to save him.') This find led me to make Sture the central character, since together with Trolle he formed a powerful duo, which gave the play its dynamic.

But the consequences of this cut! The Third Act ends with the taking up of the gauntlet and the promise to meet at Stäke. The audience expects to see Sture perform a manly deed, which doesn't now take place: in other words, it is disappointed, and that always has a depressing effect.

And so the 5th Act! Sture is excommunicated because he laid hands on Stäke; but like this one doesn't know he's ever captured it: in other words, the motivation has disappeared.

The Chancellor, who conveys the excommunication, ought to prove an old acquaintance from Stäke, but now he ends up a dumb extra, for he lacks his short prehistory; and alludes to things unknown. But the 4th Act also ends with Hemming Gadh's[5] return, which is linked to his disappearance in Act I, and Gadh bears with him an important piece of news: that Christian is approaching with a vast army, and that 'Sweden's last battle' is at hand. This is surely important preparation for Act V. (Göran

Siggesson's treachery is also prepared for in Act IV.)

If the 4th Act really had caused problems, we would have played it downstage, using a simple backdrop. So I don't understand the reason and purpose of the cut.

One can take away the first or the last link of a chain without it falling apart, but if one takes the middle, everything gives way!

I read recently in a book on drama about the '4th Act' in a five-act play. The 4th Act has always been considered difficult. It must prepare for the conclusion after the climax of the 3rd Act; but it mustn't dissipate the impression made by the 3rd Act, it must keep what the 3rd Act has promised and contribute something itself to the 5th Act. My 4th Act fulfils these conditions. The gauntlet from the 3rd is taken up; Sture appears as the warrior and a noble victor; Gadh returns, 'the Last Battle is announced'.

How can one cut it then? especially as in doing so one renders the 5th Act incomprehensible by removing its motivation and destroying the context.

Gustav Vasa, who represents the future, also loses an important scene.

The capture of Stäke is also a turning point in Swedish History, for it is the immediate cause of the Stockholm Bloodbath[6] and the war of liberation.

And practically: the public needs to see Sture at least once as the warrior from Dufnäs, so that his nobility doesn't appear the reverse of weakness.

I have spoken up because I don't want to be judged unheard; especially as there are people who, in their ignorance, think I've invented Sture's sparing of Trolle's life!

Yours sincerely,
August Strindberg

630. To META FALKNER

[23? March 1909]

Director Falck has invited himself to dinner today. My first impulse was to say no, after the last dinner, when I was so shamelessly plundered that I considered moving.

I am now asking for an ordinary dinner, as before, but if I see the slightest sign of malice, I shall move, and you know what that means.

Furthermore, please let me have Billström's bill for Herr de Wahl's[1] flowers yesterday.

Sg

So that you don't mistake my kindness for naivety, I shall not pay my board until the legal day, the 10th, if I decide to stay that is, depending on your behaviour.

631. To META FALKNER

12 June 1909

Fru Falkner,

My brother has said yes,[1] and provided you have no objection, the children can leave as soon as his letter arrives.

They will have their own room, a big garden with a greenhouse, a park with a swannery, smithies and hammers, a castle, and lots more to see and enjoy.

Baron de Geer[2] is a youngish, unmarried man and a kindly soul.

My brother is 50, married, with a daughter of 20; he is a good and steady person, who likes children (is a big child himself).

I don't know his wife, but have heard only good of her.

The house has a piano!

If you approve, then let me know.

It's assumed they'll stay until 1 August.

Yours, Strindberg

632. To FANNY FALKNER

[June? 1909]

I am no company for a young girl. Go to the country and find some young people. Go with Dir. F.[1] today. Tell me before you leave and you shall have some money; but if you give away a single penny, I shall regard it as fraud (the right word)!

633. To AUGUST FALCK

26 June 1909

Dear Falck,

If I am to make arrangements for *The Crown Bride* in Mora, I want a guarantee that your Café Diva with her recruiting songs from Fröding[1] won't be involved. Adelswärd disapproved of the latter, and so, still more, did I! Why do you have to drag that old Vampire into my plays? Have you good reason? or is it sheer spite?

If you don't intend to perform *The Crown Bride* this summer, you should tell me; I have others who could do it. To make a promise one doesn't mean to keep, is bad tactics. One loses all credit.

Strindberg

P.S. (to my letter)

I had thought of collecting a company together myself to put on some open-air performances; with *The Secret of the Guild* and *The Crown Bride*.

In order to have something to do, and casting it myself, as I think fit.

Sg

If I don't get a satisfactory reply by return, I shall carry out my plan, and go along myself, too!

634. To TURE RANGSTRÖM

Ture Rangström (1884–1947), Swedish composer, notably of lieder. A passionate admirer of Strindberg, the first of his four symphonies, written in 1914, bears the title 'August Strindberg In Memoriam'. This is the only known letter from Strindberg to Rangström.

27 June 1909

Dear Sir,

We have made a rapid examination of your compositions (an experienced musician[1] and I). There is something bold and novel about them.

But remember one thing: Be on your guard against Norwegian harmonies! All that is their property, and as soon as people hear them, they say: Grieg!

If you want to discover the tones of the Swedish lyre, study the music in my *Crown Bride*.[2] (There is a misprint, a 'b' missing in the first horn call, etc. in some editions.)

N.B. too the violin melody in 'The River God's Song'. There's no Grieg there!

It seems you're also after the Greek Modes. They're only to be found in the short musical addendum to Geijer and Afzelius' *Sw. Folk Songs* (not Höijer and Bergström's)[3], and here and there in Lindegren's Hymnal[4] (not in Haeffner,[5] although it says so).

Who will find the key to the Swedish lyre?

Söderman[6] came close, but got entangled in the Norwegian!

Seek it out! In 'There is a Dove . . . At Midsummer.'????[7]

I am sending your songs to a proper musician.[8] Then you can come and hear the response in person from me.

Yours sincerely,
Strindberg

P.S. To someone recently surprised by Beethoven's 9/8 time in the 30th Piano Sonata, your 8/4 was striking.

635. To RICHARD BERGH

8 July 1909

The Blue Tower is turning green!
What does it mean?[1]

Richard Bergh,

Sympaskómenos,[2] as Kierkegaard called it! I've written 100 pages of a play (verse and prose),[3] but for three months now have considered it worthless, and scrapped it (though without burning it!). Will you give over an evening (with C.G.)[4] to listening to it, and judge? It only takes an hour! Then we can talk about other things, and ask Axel to play some Chopin! Combine this with another errand you have in town, for I don't wish to lure you in from the country!

This morning they began turning on the streetlamps! They will be lit on the 14th (*Quatorze Juillet = Fête nationale de la Bastille*!),[5] and then the first star in the Northern hemisphere (= Capella!) will be visible. With that the worst will be over! (Cf. *Thunder in the Air*, Opus I of the Chamber Plays.)[6]

Yrs,
Strix

A.56.22 is open again, but *pro amicis*[7] only.

636. To FANNY FALKNER

11 July 1909

Fröken Fanny Falkner,

As long as you remain close to your family and discuss everything with them, I cannot speak to you frankly. You must emancipate yourself.

I am glad you didn't come home, where they take away your clothes and money, and beat you.

Try to find some way of getting away from your home without making a complete break.

By all means go and see the Lindbergs,[1] where you can discuss the theatre and keep your interest in it alive, but be careful what you say!

Stay there until things have blown over here at home. Astri[2] is leaving; the reason isn't pleasant but not a secret, since there are *no* secrets.

I have always known what constitutes your life's great pain and sorrow. But you ought to try and find a way out of this, and above all heed this warning. Don't mention this when you ring today as usual, for if you do I shall withdraw, and cease to confide in you.

Your
Sg

637. To KARL BÖRJESSON

11 July 1909

Herr Börjesson,

I am herewith sending you 'the most remarkable book ever written' (as Kipling's young man put it).[1]

I ask nothing for it. But to make its publication possible, we must seek out Esperanto's vast public. They acted my *Miss Julie* last year in Dresden.[2] And we must print it on the cheapest paper with the cheapest type at the cheapest printers.

I *know* how remarkable the book is, but we can't count on the learned Sadducees, who hate the light.

If you daren't take it, I shall try Koppel first;[3] then ruin myself to publish it! For published it must be!

Yours sincerely,
August Strindberg

638. To ANNA FLYGARE

18 July 1909

Fröken Anna Flygare,

Since that's the way things are, we'll drop the idea.[1]

But to wait at my age is imprudent. I've been waiting ten years for *The Dance of Death* to be performed; ten years for *Swanwhite, Gustav Adolf, Gustav III, Damascus II* and *III, Christina,* etc.

I waited 20 (!) years for *Miss Julie, The Father, The Bond*. I waited ten years for *The Crown Bride* to be put on outside Stockholm, my most Swedish play, with its Swedish music.

I may well give it to another company now! since Falck didn't keep his promise![2]

We'll meet again in a fortnight!

What should I say to you about your *role*?[3] Nothing! It plays itself! But for your sake: don't be too unattractive, so that you alienate the audience. Keep the different sides of the role apart, divide it up, so that it becomes a whole gallery of figures (incarnations), which people are in general anyway . . .

So, that was that!

Yours sincerely,
August Strindberg

639. To FANNY FALKNER

[29? August 1909]

Do I really have to write this letter? I learned only a week ago that there was talk of my intention to enter into a new marriage, with a young girl.

I found it so absurd and such a poor invention that I, old and ailing, should seek to bind a young person to my heavy fate, which nature will soon bring to its appointed close. It isn't my fault that your name was involved. When my last child was taken from me, I lost all interest in life, and only sought for someone to help in an unselfish way. That was all!

Do not reply to this, only trust in me as before, and the gossip will die down!

[no signature]

640. To FANNY FALKNER

[August? 1909]

Tired of sitting and growing grey in my tower, I long to see *my* Djurgården again, which I have been unable to do since 10 July last year. But as long as the bridge is guarded from number 57, I cannot bring myself to go there. What I need to know now is: have they parted yet, i.e. is my last, beloved child still in Another Man's hands.[1] You who helped me leave Karlavägen, now help me leave the tower to which you brought me.

Use the telephone if necessary! The ? is: Have they separated? i.e. do they live apart?

Sg

641. To ADOLF STRÖMSTEDT

2 September (the day of Sedan!) 1909

Adolf Strömstedt,

Old Friend from the Inferno years, which have been succeeded by this Purgatory pending The Lost Paradise that is only to be found on the Other Side.

Two wives since we parted[1] – for me involving earthquakes and great conflagrations – which I have, however, made use of for my never finished education, and in my writing.

Your friendly letter and kind words have banished the depression to which your silence reduced me last Spring.

By way of reply, I shall in due course send you 'my last symphony', the Pilgrim Play *The Great Highway* (in verse and prose).

In the meantime, this autumn you can see my most beautiful drama, *The Last Knight* (with Selander in Gbg).[2]

Wishing you all that is good!

Yrs,
Strindberg

642. To KERSTIN STRINDBERG

[Original in German]

85 Drottninggatan, Stockholm.
5 September 1909

My Child,

I have not received a letter from Dornach. And am now so alien to everything that has anything to do with Austria – more than alien. It seems to me like an ancient fairy tale, incredible, and yet once it was true.

Is your rich old ur-grandmother[1] still alive? She was rich, wasn't she? Is Aunt Melanie alive? I know nothing, and am not eager to know anything, since everything has become quite alien to me.

I am sixty years old and live in a boardinghouse . . . But I am a writer, and for me life is simply material for plays, mostly tragedies! – – .

Adieu! And think of me only as a memory!

Your Father[2]

643. To ANNA FLYGARE

8 September 1909

Anna Flygare,

Brilliant, charming, a wholly natural technique . . .

But, a small note of great importance. Retain your beautiful, striking glissando, *but* phrase better (accentuate): speak more clearly, for the auditorium is larger than you think; and yesterday some lines were lost.

De Verdier[1] mustn't manhandle you so that you lose your hat, but keep the hat, for it is becoming and provides a contrast.

– Otherwise nothing, only praise: big A (*Laudatur*). 1st Prize and gold medal.

Yours sincerely,
Sg

644. To ANNA FLYGARE

9 September 1909

Anna Flygare,

Yesterday I could only thank you! Today I can give you my congratulations! And thank you once again! Particularly for the way you ennobled the brutal scenes, and won compassion for Alice as a human being.

You have now come through – though one never arrives, as Gustav Vasa said – just keep yourself there! The path of honour is surrounded with pitfalls!

Your original technique in this role is all your own – but don't develop it *too* far, so that it begins to stand out (= become mannered).

Yours sincerely,
Strindberg

645. To AUGUST FALCK

19 January 1910

Dear Friend,

You must call on me briefly every day now over the next week or so, so that alien, evil influences do not destroy our work!

Yrs,
Sg

646. To WILLIAM MOLARD

William Molard (1862–1937), musician and civil servant in the French Ministry of Agriculture. Molard was born in Norway and had married the Swedish sculptor, Ida Ericson, who was an old friend of Strindberg's companion of the early 1890s, Per Hasselberg. It was through the Molards that Strindberg first met Gauguin, whose atelier was above their residence at 6 rue Vercingetorix. Molard, who took care of Gauguin's affairs when he returned to Tahiti, edited Strindberg's letter on Gauguin's painting for the catalogue of his 1895 exhibition at the Hôtel Drouet. Strindberg was a regular visitor to the Molards between December 1894 and early 1896 (it was there that he celebrated the Christmas described in the first chapter of *Inferno*) and Ida Molard was one of the initiative takers for the collection made on his behalf among the Scandinavian community in Paris, in 1894. Although this act of generosity may have contributed to his break with the Molards, he often looked back with affection to this period of his life. 'I long for Montparnasse, Madame Charlotte, Ida Molard, absinthe, *Merlan frit*, du Blanc, *Le Figaro* and Lilas!,' he wrote to Richard Bergh, in 1904. Only seven letters from Strindberg to Molard have survived.

85 Drottninggatan, 27 January 1910

My Good William Molard,

I doubtless had half a thought of your translating my best play,[1] but while this hardly seems worth the effort involved, it may nevertheless serve as a pretext for keeping in touch. I see neither the possibility of a performance nor its publication in Paris. It has been given here at the Swedish Theatre, without any difficulty, and might well have been put on at a variety theatre in Paris, but didn't reach the right public.

Lugné-Poë has been sitting on a translation for 5 years, and I've a copy here – so that – but it can wait!

The Dance of Death might work at the Odéon, however. It's been translated and is with Philippe Garnier,[2] who'd be the man to play it; I think Loiseau also has a copy. He said it was too 'intense' = profound. But we've[3] performed both parts in one evening, 7.30–10.30, almost 100 times.

Just for fun I'm sending *The Great Highway*, so you can see where I stand now, after the Inferno year 1906, and following . . .

With best wishes to Ida, to the rue Vercingetorix, whither I'm often drawn in memory, and where many fates were decided.

Yours ever,
August Strindberg

647. To VALFRID SPÅNGBERG

Valfrid Spångberg (1871–1946), journalist, editor, and writer. After a period with *Aftonbladet* between 1896 and 1905, Spångberg started the daily *Afton-Tidning* in 1909, where he sought to forge links between radical liberalism and the Social Democrats. Its offices were situated at 83 Drottninggatan, and in 1910 Strindberg, who had earlier declined an invitation from Spångberg to write for him, now urged their collaboration. Spångberg agreed and over the next two years published many of his articles on historical, social and political questions in what became known as the Strindberg Feud. There are forty-seven extant letters and notes from Strindberg to Spångberg.

85 Drottninggatan, 24 April 1910

Herr Editor,

If you would really like to publish this article, let me know on A.199.23.

I write without payment; but request proofs, and beg to be excused negative editorial comment.

Yours sincerely,
A. Strindberg

648. To VALFRID SPÅNGBERG

25 May 1910

Herr Editor,

I would rather a modest place in your columns, as long as the headline is visible.

I am old, have no time to lose, and waiting is hard when I feel I have so much that might clarify my unclear position both in literature and other matters left unsaid.

Yours sincerely,
Sg

649. To KARL BÖRJESSON

21 June 1910

Herr Börjesson,

This is what I would reply to your adversaries, if I were in your place: (in a Circular)[1]

'When Bl.B. was published, I announced on the last page:

"This book is only printed in a limited edition. No new edition will be published."

At the time this was my genuine intention, which the Author bound himself in our contract never to oppose.

After a year had passed and the Swedish bookshops were selling German and Danish editions of Bl.B. quite freely, my good intention was thus rendered null and void.

And when my Auth. realized it was futile to try and keep the book within the circle of the initiated, he asked me to release him from the stipulation in the contract regarding a new edition. I released him from an odious bond, so much more so since I now had reason to consider the stipulation worthless, and inasmuch as my declared intention constituted neither a promise nor my word of honour! Now, finally, having been informed that Bl.B. is to be dramatized and published in Swedish as a play, my original good intention is annulled, through no fault of my own.

In what is now taking place I have, however, no part, and those who believe that they have reason to reproach me for the publication of a new edition may, when they wish to misrepresent my announcement and make of it a promise, like to bear in mind that *I* did not publish it. And hence I regard myself as not a party to the case in which the Auth., as plaintiff, will surely reply with all due force – should that be necessary!

Börjesson'

650. To VALFRID SPÅNGBERG

[Not sent]

[26? June 1910]

Herr Editor,

When I left my lair and sacrificed my peace as a writer, I was following a powerful call; and you could see I was disinterested, since by working for nothing, I ended in poverty.

But what is the point of writing when you cut everything I write?

I'd intended opening a war of liberation against stupidity and snobbery, and timeserving in literature and government . . . but I was interrupted.

If you wish to resume contact, then do so with a diversion – by speaking of something else. Print 'The Signature Stamp' and 'Gustaf Björlin's Saga'.[1]

As long as these articles remain unpublished, I can't produce.

Under no circumstances can I wrangle with madmen; and I refuse to discuss matters with people who are so hide-bound that they are incapable of enlightenment.[2]

651. To ZETH HÖGLUND

Carl Zeth Höglund (1884–1956), politician and journalist. On the left wing of the Social Democrats, Höglund edited the weekly *Stormklockan* between 1908 and 1918. His fierce anti-militarism brought him two prison sentences while in 1917 his radical Marxism led to a split with Branting's more cautious revisionism, and he helped form what became the Swedish Communist Party. A further split brought him back to the Social Democrats in 1926. He wrote a major biography of Branting, whose works he edited, and during the 1930s he also edited *Social-Demokraten*. Although he and Strindberg never met, they were natural allies in many of the issues on which the latter fought the Strindberg Feud.

20 June 1910

Dear Sir,

If you promote atheism, I won't write for your paper!

However, if you want to reprint in their entirety all the articles in *Afton-Tidning* and *Social-Demokraten*, I believe you have the right to do so, since I didn't sell them, but wrote them gratis.

Just one word beforehand!

Watch out for liberal Junkers who make a big noise, who offer universal suffrage with one hand and demand a million for the army with the other, who can't distinguish right from left, ready to defend every injustice, everything foul, everything abnormal; who point left but ultimately align themselves with the right . . .

Yours faithfully,
Strindberg

P.S. I haven't broken my contract with Börjesson!

Don't believe the fables about me in the right-wing press! for now 'it's starting'.

My regards to Fabian Månsson,[1] and thank him for his splendid pamphlet, which I shall quote.

But tell me, who is 'The Lord of Ljusne', who became a Count (Hallwyl?), and what was he called before as a 'common book-keeper'?[2]

652. To AUGUST FALCK

14 September 1910

If I am to continue taking an interest in the Intimate Theatre, its programme must be implemented: i.e. first my unperformed plays! and not an outsider's!

I can't afford to make sacrifices for Maeterlinck, although I admire him!

And my well-wishers and the friends of the theatre are prepared to make new sacrifices – for *my* sake, not that of foreigners or beginners (they have the Royal Theatre!).[1]

A word of advice: beware of Uddgren[2] . . . He's written a play that he wants put on – when he doesn't get permission, he'll destroy the theatre. He's the one who inspired those articles,[3] so as to create a split and, ultimately, to get at the theatre!

Lindholm[4] presents no danger at present, but he can do the moment you perform anyone else but me. He knows the ropes and how to obtain capital; is something of a lickspittle, and has a good nose!

The Intimate Theatre *is* under threat! Repel these attacks by remaining loyal to me – and don't believe I'm done for. For every new enemy, I'll get back two old friends – have done!

I shall probably refuse the Anti-Nobel Prize – and suggest a fund for the Intimate Theatre on the one, simple condition: that they perform me!

Further: Don't always put on the same things!

You've the *Dream Play*, *Damascus* (both with roles for your wife), and also *The Black Glove*, which you insultingly refused!

Strindberg

653. To AUGUST FALCK

20 October 1910

There's nothing to be had here!

Sell up and close; or find a partner, but not Ranft.

My well-wishers lost interest when I did, you know the reasons why.

Don't approach Bonnier or Bergh![1] You'll get nothing!

But when I'm asked for rent, I shall naturally act as the tenant and thus decide the theatre's fate.

Sg

654. To TOR HEDBERG

24 October 1910

Tor Hedberg,

It has taken me three days to consider whether you are right in your criticism of the final act of *The Regent*, namely that it is weak and cumbersome.

I cannot see that's so! – The act resolves all the tragic knots: Gustav has sacrificed his Mother and Sister, Kristina G. her Norrby, Lars Siggeson his brother.[1]

Old Trolle, who arranged the feast in the same setting as Act 1 of

The Knight,[2] is now exiled as Johan Månsson was then. (= Parallelism! Nemesis.) The Innkeeper remains himself whatever happens; the Dalecarlians continue their disputes, which issues in the 1st Act of my *Gustav Vasa*; Herman Israel wants to be paid (*Zahlen*! *Zahlen*!)[3] as usual. But the lighter points?

Rejoicing and bells! The Brännkyrka banner[4] and the bridesmaids' Ballad of St George. Young Sture gets his mother back, Kristina G. her son. Brask is reconciled by the sparing of Munkeboda.

The new age is heralded by the entry of Master Olof, whose arrival is prepared for by his false entrance in a previous scene at the Hanseatic Offices, where the act ends with his being announced (but not seen).

The main knot, Christian the Tyrant, is severed by his dethronement (the letter).

That is surely light, but serious too, for the victor has deep sorrows (his mother and sister).[5]

In short: The last act is rich in motifs but short, as a last act should be, and the continuation (the Reformation = M. Olof) is announced.

Of course I know how I might improve this final act. But Gustav I was no public speaker, and an oratorical ending would be tasteless.

That he became serious after ordeals like his imprisonment in Kalö[6] and his dog's life in Dalarna, is part of his character, and he's no longer young. He has also become king, with all that stormy future (= the Reformation, the conflict with Dacke, the uprising in Dalarna, his children's uneasy fates, the relationship with their Stepmother (Erik XIV)) ahead of him, as the audience knows.

But so as not to expose *The Regent* to the same risks as *The Last Knight*, which was drawn out by over-long scene changes, it ought to be played rapidly, particularly towards the end. In fact the play is short and contains no superfluous scenes. For the underlying idea (the concept) is expressed in the composition: 'repeat again'; 'never arrive'; 'retrace one's steps'. During the long journey, the wanderers remain pretty much the same (cf. the Innkeeper, who has served others, no matter whom, all his life, but never changes).

Hence, the composition isn't just a piece of bravura for the sake of surmounting the problems it presents, but determined by the theme. Therefore I can't alter it without altering the whole conception and aim, which is impossible!

I can say no more!

Yrs,
Strindberg

655. To J. P. A. MUHR

Julius Per Abraham Muhr (1847–?), factory owner and Quaker. Muhr had written to Strindberg after reading an essay in *Afton-Tidning* in which he had maintained the possibility of a link between the tribes of Israel and the Indians of North America. In turn, Muhr wondered whether the Scandinavians might not belong 'to the Lordly tribe of Benjamin'. Of the nine surviving letters from Muhr to Strindberg, two are in English.

18 January 1911

Dear Sir,

Let me first thank you for your interest, and for the valuable information. However, I shall now take this opportunity to ask you something that has long been bothering me:

Nyström's Concordance[1] mentions an Anglo-Israelite school of thought which maintains that the English are one of the ten tribes. That is my view, too; but where can I read about it?

Ghibrith, Ibrith, Ibri = Hebrews; but it also says Iberer = Spaniards, Britons (Britania [*sic*]!) and Brittany.

The English appear to have inherited the covenant, which will be fulfilled in America, where it has been mapped by Zebaoth himself – but only after America has passed through purgatory.

I also believe that 'Dan–ia' is 'Dan'; that the Pelasgians were Pelescheth = פלשת = Philistines, etc., something I am now working on. I have a clue to Sweden, which I shall follow up, but it won't be the tribe of Benjamin. And the cult of Odin didn't come from Israel, but from Phoenicia. Read the hideous account of the temple at Uppsala with Freya-Priapus, obscene dances (Brides of Horga) and human sacrifice. (See my *New Swedish Destinies*, 1st story.)[2]

The Eddas are more recent, and Christianized; that's where the Old Testament borrowings come from.

There's something of mine in this evening's *Afton-Tidning* about 'Israel in Tibet' (today, Wednesday).[3] As someone who knows the Bible in Hebrew, where can I find 'Amene Pada(m) Hem'?[4] Help me to look in the Psalms, Isaiah and Jeremiah. For I am all in,

Yours sincerely,
Strindberg

656. To BIRGER MÖRNER

22 January 1911

Birger Mörner,

I've now read your book! All right! But you must tell about yourself, about the important, remarkable things you have yourself experienced, otherwise it will amount to nothing, or mere bagatelles = the art of writing about nothing (Sw. Ac.). But you don't want to, because cutting open one's belly is painful (= Harakiri) . . . [1]

Tired and ill, am 62 today; regards to F.U.W.[2]

Yrs,
Strindberg

657. To KARL OTTO BONNIER

21 February 1911

My dear Bonnier,

Tomorrow, Wednesday, I shall call on your foreman. Kainz' *Chinese Grammar* is published in Vienna, by Reisser and Werthner (Hartlebens).[1] However, the typeface seems to be lithographed.

Your big proposal worries me.[2] For, like Tolstoy, I have grown afraid of money, and don't think it befits me, now that the end is approaching. And I have no more wishes in that way, neither a country cottage nor the cutter which I never had, and don't want now as a gift.

And those troublesome obligations which come with wealth – the bother of keeping it, the fear of losing it . . .

Then there are the children! And that makes me so uncertain . . . that I don't know what to do.

I daren't let the plays go to the theatre, and cannot either. Nor the translations. Not on account of the money, because there won't be any! This causes me more headaches than poverty – already!

Yrs,
Strindberg

658. To KARL BÖRJESSON

21 April 1911

Herr Börjesson,

Thank you for the Huc, I'd already got it from Klemmings though! Read, however, page 333: 'The Swallows in Winter'.[1]

When M. and H. have had so much from the State for publishing their works,[2] the price of their books ought to be low; but how much do they cost now? H's = 300, M's = 500? Enquire! This is extortion.

The exhibition?[3] My 40 Åtvidaberg boxes full of 30 years of notes for the *Blue Book* ought really to be exhibited, then people could see how I have used my time (*apart from* that spent on literature), be put on show for those who believe that I have spent half my life in the tavern, and for those who called me 'the laziest man ever born'. But certain people are fated not to be able to defend themselves. 'If one tries to defend oneself, they go their way' (*The Great Highway*).[4]

Yours ever,
Strindberg

659. To NILS ANDERSSON

27 April 1911

Dear Nils Andersson,

You have had your Easter too!

I've had four weeks of additional trials – my daughter's life in danger with her first child, which died the day it was born[1] (that's why I didn't receive W.B.);[2] I've also been ill twice myself, persecuted, betrayed, etc. However, I did read the proofs of my Universal Dictionary,[3] which was both a great strain and a pleasure.

But it's as you say: one's soul feels best when 'this foul carcass' is tormented. And even mental suffering contributes to our fructification. In Switzerland they say that walnut trees should be beaten with sticks when the nuts are harvested, beaten so that the leaves and branches are whipped up: 'for then the tree yields more fruit the following year'.

Three years ago I suffered such spiritual anguish that I found life sublime, each and every day, and was so tormented while passing through this hell, that I lived in heaven.

However, old age is here; I have had warnings and premonitions. My 'Last Will' is in the desk drawer; my papers are in order – everything is ready! The Beethoven suppers are a thing of the past. Seldom give dinners; live like a recluse with the daughter I've won back, and my son-in-law (a practising doctor).[4] I want nothing, hope for nothing – on this side.

As for what is to come, I'm not sure: I anticipate a purifying bath like a Russian sauna, but it surely can't resemble this present misery! That would be unreasonable! for here one cannot realize one's good intentions, nor practise the beautiful things in which one believes.

One morning at 8 o'clock, as the bell tolls for matins, my remains will be carried out; no one is to speak at the graveside, not even the priest, and no ritual; that is what my 'Last Will' says.

Just now someone was playing the 'Appassionata' in one of the apartments below – I seldom hear it, for Axel is as tired as I am, Aulin away, my friends absent with their troubles. So one loosens the bonds – so it must be!

But should you come, there is still a bottle of 'supernatural' Sauternes in the cupboard, and then Axel will bring along the Nils Andersson symphony, and we shall have an illusion of something which, although only an imitation, is nevertheless a beautiful one!

Adieu! And my regards to Hans Larsson,

fr. your friend,
Strindberg

660. To NILS ANDERSSON

12 June 1911

Dear Nils Andersson,

In poor health for the past two months; probably an as yet unexplained latent internal complaint, which the doctor (my son-in-law) can't make out. All my entrails in commotion, bursting; no room for them in my skin, although I'm half-starving myself and have given up my evening grog (my usual). It is as though a mad soul inhabited the wrong body – it has always felt that way – that is why wine has always been of help in making my soul feel at home.

With fasting and abstinence comes weakness, even cowardice. Self-examination, a *conscientia scrupulosa*, which reproaches one for everything, even for what one has never done. Also, when my last great interest ended – *The Roots of World Languages* – life went flat. So enormous a task without encouragement is not uplifting. Although I have proved conclusively that e.g. Chinese characters are monograms of Syrian, Hebrew, Arabic and Greek, made up like the Turkish 'Tülüt' (Sülüs),[1] which we see on their tapestries – well, it doesn't help. Then one goes dumb and dries, like an actor who doesn't get his cue.

This unhappy couple H.[2] of whom you speak, ought to read Melsted, whom I discovered through *Milla*, *The Phantom*, and *The Pharisee's Wife*.[3] M. is profound. This 'discord' between married couples is something constant and essential, a vital ingredient. Reversals of current are necessary, otherwise everything comes to a standstill, and goes out. It *has* to be like that, otherwise married life is dead! The intermittent reconciliations compensate for the sufferings one endures, and these sufferings seem *unreal* afterwards. Prescribe those unfortunate people M.'s *Milla* to start with.

And we'll let *Tschandala* remain buried. It is sometimes dangerous to dig up the past and accuse one's self. You could say to H.L.[4] what you can imagine I would feel after – yes, what?

Welcome when you come!

Yrs,
August Strindberg

I can't move from where I am; had thought of hiring a fisherman's cottage, but have abandoned the idea. I am staying here and waiting – for something unknown! Feared, but with a degree of calm.

661. To HENNING BERGER

27 June 1911

Henning Berger,

Old, tired, worn out, I now thank you, belatedly, for your friendly greetings and midsummer wishes, sent to Blå tornet, where I am on the way to the New Churchyard, past the Burned Site, my childhood home.[1]

Have recently been reading your *Dreamland*;[2] and it is doubtless so, that the beautiful dreams come afterwards; those here aren't beautiful.

Yrs,
Strindberg

662. To KARL OTTO BONNIER

28 June 1911

My dear Bonnier,

Your offers appear to be aimed at getting my Collected Works gratis.

When you offered 150 thousand *kronor*, it was really nothing, since this sum could be brought in by performance rights and foreign translations.

Your new offer is a little better, but also fanciful since you include Danish and Norwegian editions, which *You* can sell for a high price, but I can't.

Now make a reasonable offer; these two must be regarded as unreasonable since, according to an expert estimate, my Collected Works are credited at 50 volumes.[1]

Yrs,
Strindberg

663. To TOR BONNIER

Tor Bonnier (1883–1976), Karl Otto Bonnier's son, publisher. His early memories of Strindberg are recorded in *Längesen* (Long Ago, 1972).

11 July 1911

Dear Herr Bonnier,

Forgive me for troubling you with a trifle, but your father has other things to attend to.

In your grandfather's time, around 1865–66 (?), a tree was planted in the courtyard of the Lyceum at 17 Ålandsgatan.[1] What I would like to know is simply whether it is the same tree I saw again the other morning, or if the first one died and was replaced by a new one? *Item*: what kind of tree the first one was? And, in the event of replanting, what kind the second one was.

Herr Banck[2] ought to remember this, if your father has forgotten.

If I get some precise information, I'll let you know the reason for my strange question another time.

Yours sincerely,
August Strindberg

664. To NILS ANDERSSON

[12 July 1911]

Nils Andersson,

If you want to tempt me south, it would have to be a house with a large garden in Lund itself, south facing (the southern Promenade). And if necessary my own, so I can play at creating a botanical garden, and realize all my plans in that line from the 1870s (not 80s!). Not newly planted! Old, gone to seed; but with a greenhouse!

Perhaps one has to make a pilgrimage backwards, become aware of the contrast between past and present, reconcile oneself with the past – but also break camp, withdraw, and go, living, into the grave.

Tegnér called Stockholm 'this Sodom and Abdera'.[1] That's as may be, but I long to get away from here! Not to the country, for I must have people, a Bookshop, and a Vintners!

So: a house in Lund with a large old garden, greenhouse and the sun.

Yrs,
August Strindberg

665. To NILS ANDERSSON

20 July 1911

Nils Andersson,

Some ten days ago I wrote you a letter about a house with a garden in Lund. I believed then that a change of address might revive me; now I no longer believe that, for I have been ill again, and cannot move my limbs, much less move house.

It is no doubt all downhill now; although I brightened up during your last visit, it was, as I predicted, only to collapse again.

It was probably in the foreknowledge of this that I put my worldly affairs in order for the children; this gives me peace, and gave me great joy.

These last three years have told on me; in this 'tower' there was nothing beautiful; in the previous one still something – there was the child, and a couple of Christmas Eves.

So I shall stay where I am, and wait . . . Adieu!

Yrs,
Strindberg

666. To NILS ANDERSSON

[18 September 1911]

Nils Andersson,

The two cases were interesting but gruesome, and have much to teach us. The railway boy seems to be an instance of split personality (*dédoublement de la personnalité*) in which the 'two natures' appear intermittently.[1] If I say I understand him, I don't want it held against me. His momentary insensitivity to other people's sufferings is doubtless confined to his imagination. Do you remember the Mandarin in *Père Goriot* (Balzac), whom no one thought twice about killing at a distance?[2] We often wish our enemy would go to h-ll, or that he might meet with an accident, but if a disaster were to befall him, we would weep and help him.

I understand the boy's aversion to physical work well enough; his intellect was greater than his physique, and claimed him for itself. He was certainly born to something better than minding animals, which I find loathsome, though without feeling contempt for those whose task it is.

His Neronian idea needn't imply *l'homme criminal*, but be an improvisation of his imagination. However, that doesn't resolve the matter, for there is probably more behind it – something inexplicable. When he occasionally smiles at his thoughts, it reminds me of Petőfi,[3] who wanted to fill a volcano with gunpowder and blow the whole lot up. When he confesses everything, he stands above it all, but then his lack of remorse indicates a view of life that stems from a truly frightful childhood.

The other one and the hay stack, I don't understand; but we can know nothing of taciturn natures and their thought processes. One can live together with someone for 50 years without suspecting the chasms in his soul. I think, however, that they both received the correct sentence: not punishment (revenge) but a necessary measure – a kindly attempt at reform!

Nevertheless, one shudders while reading this, and thinks of all the dangerous impulses one has been close to giving way to at certain moments, and which one really has given vent to in one's mind; what one has, through no merit of one's own, only just avoided.

Yrs,
Aug Strindberg

667. To NILS ANDERSSON

19 September 1911

P.S.

Having thought some more about the railway boy, I wonder if he isn't a quite ordinary person, only more honest than other people.

After all, when home and school eradicate all our finer feelings, and bring us up to be Redskins, one finally becomes insensitive.

If a child hurts itself and complains, we make fun of it instead of comforting it. If someone wrongs a child, it isn't allowed to defend itself, which is called 'blaming someone else'. This simply produces villains who suppress all their better feelings. Someone who isn't allowed to feel compassion for his own suffering doesn't give a damn for others later on, but is forced by the social lie to feign sympathy.

The explanation surely lies in the boy's appalling childhood, and not his idiocy. And owing to the fact that the underclass's work is so badly paid, such children are neglected, for want of servants and care; it's all quite simple!

And school, with its systematic training in brutality, only produces savages, who are then educated as bandits in barracks, or as overclass egotists at University. Upper House spongers and highborn ruffians, Academy and Court and Ministerial rabble – that's the state, which even a sane man sometimes wishes to see shut up in a train about to crash!

But one can't say that!

Perhaps the boy with the hayrick was unjustly treated. Perhaps he chased the younger one out of the stable because he was up to no good, something dangerous for which the older one would be punished because 'he hadn't prevented it'. They got him for doing his duty – which was unjust; and he doubtless felt his master's child was 'favoured'. All the underling's hatred then erupted, and found its traditional expression in arson. Perhaps that's what happened??

Sg

668. To BIRGER MÖRNER

3 October 1911

I have now read your book,[1] and with interest, for it is interesting to see someone with innards under their coat. And it has form, too, colour and shading, caught by, and comprehensible to, 'the sound five' (realism!). It is good! Really good!

Yrs,
Strindberg

669. To NILS ANDERSSON

8 November 1911

N.A.

What you say about the relationship which children have with *Jenseits*[1] is probably true. Therefore every child's birth entails something indescribable, and the delight afforded by these little ones is quite unique.

Anrep's *Genealogy*[2] mentions a family tradition (I've forgotten the name, but it's no doubt also in Hofberg's *Sw. Country Districts*)[3] about a little child in the country who vanished in broad daylight, in the presence of its nurse. A search was made by the entire parish: in vain. After 2 (or 1) years, there was the child, on the selfsame spot; but it hadn't grown! Hemberg[4] relates something similar from Lapland.

Prof. Med. Carl Ludwig Schleich (from the Ferkel in Berlin) had a nephew who was friendly with a Daimon. He called this Invisible creature his Air-Robert. He (the boy) often seemed to stand quite still (like Socrates) and consult his Air-Robert. If the boy was asked: 'Do you really intend to do this or that?', he would reply: 'I shall ask Air-Robert first.'

When she was 5, my youngest daughter saw sprites; but she complained that she didn't see them 'properly'. I want to see them '*properly*', she often said.

I am ill! Sometimes go to bed at 7, as I cannot fit into my clothes. It's worst during the day! All right in bed and at night. Best when I have visitors. The doctors don't understand what it is. Almost the same symptoms as in 1896 – (Inferno). Personally I believe it is people's deadly hatred. The presence of visitors seems to divert the currents of hate.

I must have made some great discoveries, which certain people have noticed, but they remain silent – and hate.

Adieu! and welcome when you come!

Yrs,
August Strindberg

670. To BIRGER MÖRNER

7 December 1911

Birger Mörner,

Thank you for your letter! Old, tired, sick; the last three years in Blå tornet have taken their toll. A Swedish Dictionary (A–B) has done its bit.[1]

Your Poems were compared with Snoilsky's in D.N.[2]

I admire Maeterlinck's works, and have written some fine things about them – but one should never meet.[3] One can't talk about what one has written . . . and the rest isn't worth talking about! Can you let him know this – in case he thinks I am expecting a visit from him – without offending him?

Yrs,
Aug Sg

671. To RICHARD BERGH

17 January 1912

Richard Bergh,

Will you tell Branting that if that's how things are I must naturally greet them;[1] and that I will come out on to the balcony; but they are not to stop or make speeches or sing, for in that case I might be obliged to kill myself, out of politeness. I'm actually still ill, even though I fancied I was well. Haven't been out.

So that the procession will recognize my balcony among all the others, I'll set out my most beautiful electric lamp with its red eye facing Tegnérlunden.

If I'm really ill, I'll get someone to telephone Folkets Hus; but illuminate the window as a sign of my appreciation and thanks; perhaps stand in the living-room window.

For fear of overtaxing my strength, I daren't invite anyone to dinner apart from my daughter, son-in-law, and Axel.

Explain all this to Branting!

Yrs,
August Strindberg

672. To HJALMAR BRANTING AND GERHARD MAGNUSSON

23 January 1912

To Branting and Magnusson,[1]
Folkets Hus.

Thank you good friends! Now that I have finally rediscovered my self and my position, which on account of my work as a writer could not be resolute, you know where you have me; and all distrust should now disappear.

Convey my thanks for their fine words on my birthday to the organizations and groups which come under the banner of Folkets Hus, for I haven't the strength myself, tired as I am with the emotions of yesterday.

Yours sincerely,
August Strindberg

673. To ANNE-MARIE STRINDBERG

17 February 1912

Good day little child; dreamt of you last night; it was summer . . .

Father

674. To NATHAN SÖDERBLOM

Nathan Söderblom (1866–1931), Archbishop of Uppsala. In 1895, when Swedish pastor in Paris, he helped organize the collection that enabled Strindberg to receive treatment for his psoriasis at the Hôpital Saint-Louis. Söderblom, who never met Strindberg, held him in great respect, both as a man and a writer. One of the very few of his contemporaries to praise *Black Banners*, he was a member of the committee formed to administer the national collection, and also officiated at Strindberg's funeral.

675. To Charlotte Futterer

18 March 1912

Herr Professor,

I had so much to say to you about a great many things, but sick and old, I must put my house in order and settle my accounts.

— — — — —

About 1892(?) I found myself, through no fault of my own, reduced to poverty in Paris, and by roundabout ways received some 200 francs in assistance from the Swedish Church Relief Fund.[1]

I have tried to console myself with the thought that since then, during these last ten better years, I have given substantial relief to others. But it doesn't help: that must be met with this.

And so, since I don't know its Paris address, I am sending the enclosed 1,000 *kronor* to you, and beg you to please forward it to the Relief Fund for compatriots in need.

As a repayment it can of course in no way be regarded as charity!

One little word is missing from this short letter, that small word which is so hard to say: Thank you! for your help then, and for the trouble you are kindly taking upon yourself now.

Yours sincerely,
August Strindberg

675. To CHARLOTTE FUTTERER

[Original in French]

85 Drottninggatan, Stockholm, 28 March 1912

Chère Madame Charlotte,

Yes, it's true, I am successful; only too late to know it and to be able to enjoy it in the fashion of this world. Old, worn, nearly always ill, I am preparing for my final voyage. Even money has begun to rain down on me, but what good is that to someone who desires nothing: it is all for the poor and for my children.

You mustn't imagine that this brings me – almost indifferent to glory and the rest, who wants nothing – any happiness: the old bitternesses and new sorrows do not cease to obliterate the good fortune of the moment.

That's how life is! You know my endless litanies from the time of the *Crémerie* and of my misery!

Since you, Madame, delight in a tranquil existence, I still wish you some good days, for you and your son.

Your old and obliged guest,
August Strindberg

676. To KARL PETRÉN

Karl Anders Petrén (1868–1927), Professor of Practical Medicine in Lund. One of the Lund radicals and, together with his close friend Bengt Lidforss, a founder of the discussion group, The Young Gaffers. His opinion had now been sought on Strindberg's illness and, in response to the replies he received from Strindberg to a detailed questionnaire, he diagnosed cancer of the stomach.

7 April 1912

Dear Karl Petrén,

With thanks for your friendly communication, I am making haste to reply while I am still alert.

Four years ago there was a periodicity, which is now lacking.

Now the pain is there day and night, irrespective of what I eat; sometimes the pain is dull, sometimes more intense, but I am never free of it. Whether I sit, walk or lie down.

I go to bed to avoid wearing my clothes, but this no longer helps.

If I lie on my face, the pain ceases; on my left side is better than my right, but on my back is worst.

I am losing my appetite; I now have an aversion to all kinds of food; and my distaste for life is becoming more intense. Sleep may come for an hour or two, then the pain wakes me. The twelve hours of night (8–) are endless!

However, we shall now undertake the examinations you have suggested! And now I am going to bed!

Gratefully yrs,
August Strindberg

677. To ANNE-MARIE STRINDBERG

19 April 1912

My dear little daughter,

Thank you for your red flowers! But you mustn't try to see me. There are so many medicine bottles, doctors and things here that it is no fun.

Rejoice in your youth, among the young, and do not grieve for an old man, whose only wish is to depart.

Father

678. To HJALMAR AND ANNA BRANTING

22 April 1912

Hjalmar and Anna Branting,

Thank you for your roses amongst all the iodine and morphine, etc. – – – Her death[1] yesterday awoke memories of 1880, the Crypt, Kymmendö, Ludvig Josephson, Frithiof Kjellberg, Pelle Janzon, Stuxberg, the Alhambra and Svante Hedin, P. and K. S-ff, Erik Thys. and others. Long ago, but just like yesterday!

Yours ever,
AugStr.

679. To THE EDITORIAL STAFF OF *SOCIAL-DEMOKRATEN*

25 April 1912

To the Ed. of *Social-Demokraten.*

Thanks good friends and colleagues for the beautiful flower.

I still had a great deal to say in the paper when my pen fell from my hand – my fountain pen! so forgive the pencil.

Yours sincerely,
August Strindberg

VI

Notes to Letters 285–326

November 1892–11 August 1894

285. To BIRGER MÖRNER

[1] Mörner had met Rod (see Letter 278) in Geneva and tried to interest him in publishing a volume of Strindberg's stories; Strindberg himself pressed for *The People of Hemsö*.

[2] See Letter 283.

[3] Justin Huntley McCarthy (1860–1936), whose essay on Strindberg in the September issue of the *Fortnightly Review* was the first significant response to his work in England. Strindberg's letters to McCarthy have been lost; there are two from McCarthy to Strindberg, both dating from 1892, in the Royal Library, Stockholm.

[4] Mörner had taken the initiative for a kind of *Festschrift* on Strindberg, a venture in which the latter took a lively interest. It eventually appeared as *En bok om Strindberg* (A Book About Strindberg) in 1894, edited by Gustaf Fröding (see headnote to Letter 422), and included a long extract from McCarthy's essay in translation.

[5] Strindberg had broken with the Hanssons shortly after arriving in Berlin. According to one account, he suspected them of intercepting his mail; according to Hansson, 'he came in to us late one evening; he had his guitar with him, and played, danced and sang, all very nice. The next morning he was gone . . . we never saw him go.'

[6] See Letter 282.

286. To STANISLAW PRZYBYSZEWSKI

[1] The tavern owned by Herr Gustav Türke on the corner of Unter den Linden and Neue Wilhelmstrasse, which Strindberg dubbed *'Zum schwarzen Ferkel'*. Officially known as Türke's Weinhandlung und Probierstube. See Letter 372.

[2] Strindberg, who wished to escape from a young Norwegian woman in the pension where he was now staying, went to Weimar, not Prague.

[3] In German.

287. To ADOLF PAUL

[1] Presumably the Castle Park, laid out by Goethe. Strindberg had gone to Weimar at the beginning of the month, but was back in Berlin by the 13th.

[2] Fru Mathilde Prager (1844–1921), Austrian translator. See headnote to Letter 359.

[3] Piersons in Dresden published a translation of *By the Open Sea* by Maria von Borch (1853–95) in 1893.

289. To BIRGER MÖRNER

1 Strictly private.
2 The terrible year '92.
3 *Creditors* with Rosa Bertens as Tekla, Rudolf Rittner as Adolf, and Josef Jarno as Gustav, was a public success at the Residenztheater, in a triple bill with *Facing Death* and *The First Warning*. Bertens (1860–1934) had already appeared in *Miss Julie* at the Freie Bühne and went on to play a series of major Strindberg roles over the next two decades while Jarno (1866–1932) later mounted an important series of Strindberg productions at the Theater in der Josefstadt, Vienna, where he worked from 1899.
4 Gunnar Heiberg (1857–1929), Norwegian dramatist.
5 Edvard Munch (1863–1944), Norwegian painter. See headnote to Letter 373.
6 At a party given by the publisher Felix Lehmann to celebrate the première on 7 January of *Heimat* (Home) by the German dramatist and novelist Hermann Sudermann (1857–1928), Sudermann declared: '*Vom Norden her kommt uns das Licht!*' (The Light has come to us from the North), to which one of the guests replied '*Das Nordlicht!*' (The Northern Lights). In identifying this as a significant moment in literary history, Strindberg anticipates many subsequent literary historians.
7 *Miss Julie* was performed at the Théâtre Libre, on 16 January 1893, in a triple bill with Edmond de Goncourt's *A bas le progrès* (Down with Progress) and *Le Ménage Brésil* by Romain Coolus (1868–1952). According to Antoine, the play was '*une énorme sensation*'; the critical reception, however, was less favourable, though it did bring Strindberg to the attention of the Parisian literary world.
8 Of the French translation of *Miss Julie*.
9 This translation (by Antoine's secretary, Rodolphe Darzens, who also translated *Ghosts*) was not published.
10 Strindberg had been approached by J. T. Grein (1862–1935), the founder of the Independent Theatre in London, with an offer to stage *The Father* 'in private, for I fear the play will never pass the censorship'. This plan, too, came to nothing.
11 Like the others in this catalogue of names, Strindberg saw Rydberg as sick with envy over his success. The character of Lars in Rydberg's novel *Vapensmeden* (1891) is generally acknowledged to derive from Strindberg.
12 *Stockholms Dagblad*'s Paris correspondent, Johan Janzon.

291. To FRIDA UHL

1 Frida had written: 'Regard me as your old and devoted friend, who would so like to help you.'

292. To FRIDA UHL

1 Frida had sent Strindberg an extensive list of questions as to his financial situation and prospects, one in a series of letters in which the two explored the possible basis for marriage.
2 Frida told Strindberg he would always preserve his independence: 'You are free to do as you please. Above all, don't believe you have to remain faithful to me.'
3 The queen of Lydia, in whose service Hercules, dressed as a woman, spun wool and performed other womanly tasks for three years while she assumed his lion skin and club.

[4] The enchantress of Arthurian legend, Merlin's mistress. Part One of *To Damascus*, where this material is reworked, was originally called 'Merlin' or 'Merlin et Viviane'.

293. To BIRGER MÖRNER

[1] After numerous vicissitudes the wedding took place on Heligoland, 2 May 1893, with two local pilots as witnesses. Britain had ceded Heligoland to Germany in 1890 in exchange for Zanzibar, and under the British marriage regulations which still obtained, no banns were required.

[2] Dagny Juel (1867–1901), the erotic and iconographic centre of '*Zum schwarzen Ferkel*', where she was introduced by Edvard Munch (he painted her portrait in 1893, and her image appears in several of his most famous paintings of the 1890s, notably the *Madonnas* of 1894 and 1895 and *Woman in Three Stages*, 1894). Dubbed 'Aspasia' by Strindberg and as such the object of one of his later French vivisections from 1894, 'La Genèse d'une Aspasie', she also stood model for Henriette in *Crimes and Crimes*. A Norwegian doctor's daughter and member of the Christiania *bohême*, she was also a minor poet and dramatist. Before coming to Berlin in 1893 to study music she had met Lidforss in Lund where he had fallen passionately in love with her, although as Strindberg (and others) say, the syphilis from which he eventually died prevented him from pursuing his suit to the end. In a different version, it was not Lidforss to whom Strindberg 'donated' Juel but another member of the circle, Dr Ludwig Schleich (1859–1922), an innovator in the field of local anaesthesia. However, in August 1893 she married Przybyszewski and eventually accompanied him back to Poland. She died in Tiflis at the hands of another of her admirers, Wladyslaw Emeryk, who then shot himself.

[3] The Karlstrasse.

294. To ADOLF PAUL

[1] The Isle of Women, i.e. England, where Strindberg and Frida went mainly in response to J. T. Grein's invitation to discuss the projected production of *The Father*. He had also heard that William Heinemann wanted to publish a translation of *Somnambulist Nights*. Heinemann corresponded briefly with Strindberg but had no such plans.

[2] Original in English.

295. To BIRGER MÖRNER

[1] After ten days at Gravesend, Strindberg and Frida moved into J. T. Grein's flat in Pimlico while Grein, to the detriment of any production of *The Father*, went abroad. Strindberg stayed for nearly three weeks before returning to Germany, Frida somewhat longer.

[2] Following Strindberg's account of their predicament in Letter 293, an expedition was mounted in Lund to bring both Juel and Lidforss back from Berlin. In the confusion and recrimination that followed, Mörner reproached Strindberg for the extravagance of his reporting.

[3] Abominable.

296. To FRIDA UHL

1 After stopping briefly in Hamburg on his way back from England, Strindberg proceeded to the Baltic island of Rügen where Adolf Paul and Karl August Tavastjerna were spending the summer.

2 Black devils.

3 Second spring.

4 The wife of the German actor, Joseph Kainz (1858–1910). Strindberg had hoped to interest her in his plans to open a theatre in Berlin.

297. To FRITZ KJERRMAN

1 *Dagens Nyheter* had announced on 23 June that *Budkaflen* would start publishing *A Madman's Defence* as a *feuilleton* later that week. This was an unauthorized translation of the German edition, which had appeared in May under the title *Die Beichte eines Thoren*. Strindberg received nothing for it except censure.

2 See Letters 197 and 201.

3 Albert Savine (1859–1927), French publisher. Although the novel went to press, Savine did not release it.

4 Carl Gustaf Wrangel.

299. To FRIDA UHL

1 Max Burckhardt (1871–1934), the director of the Burgtheater in Vienna, planned to stage *The Secret of the Guild*. Nothing came of the idea.

2 A restaurant on the Dorothéenstrasse.

3 Since the beginning of August Strindberg had been staying with Frida's family at Mondsee, near Salzburg.

4 On 8 December 1894, when their relationship had disintegrated, Strindberg wrote to her: 'I'll not take revenge. To write a second *Plaidoyer* would be to rewrite the first. And to what end? A vulgar, common type like you doesn't interest me.'

300. To ALBERT BONNIER

1 Strindberg is recalling *Naturens grundämnen* (The Elements of Nature, 1875), which he later maintained had influenced him in his alchemical speculations.

2 See Letter 322.

3 Carl von Bergen (1838–97), whose early radicalism and interest in psychology had given way to spiritism.

4 The portmanteau in which Strindberg preserved his manuscripts and notes during this most itinerant part of his life; even when back in Stockholm, it remained the name by which he referred to his scientific material.

5 Carl Ludwig Schleich and another member of the Ferkel circle, the gynaecologist Max Asch.

6 Robert Koch (1843–1910), German bacteriologist, who discovered the bacillus of tubuculosis (1882) and cholera (1883).

301. To BENGT LIDFORSS

[1] Strindberg had discovered the works of the French naturalist Georges Louis Buffon (1707–88) in the library of Frida Uhl's grandfather at Dornach, where he and Frida were now staying.

302. To CARL LARSSON

[1] Albert Bonnier had quoted from Strindberg's letter of 21 November on *Antibarbarus* in an interview in *Aftonbladet*, 16 December 1893.
[2] In an article entitled 'Narcissistic Literature' in *Ur dagens krönika*, October 1890, Otto Sjögren had compared *By the Open Sea* with *Konstiga kroppar* (Strange Bodies) by Karl Eneroth (pen name 'Chicot' (1843–1907)) to Strindberg's disadvantage.
[3] *Vapensmeden.*
[4] One of Rydberg's major poems, 'Den nya Grottesången' (The New Song of Grotte) portrayed the sufferings and conflicts endemic in nineteenth-century industrial capitalism.
[5] Harald Molander.
[6] Larsson had been commissioned to paint the frescoes in the entrance hall of the National Museum in Stockholm. In reply, he confessed to having become a nationalist and an admirer of Charles XII.

303. To BENGT LIDFORSS

[1] Przybyszewski, now married to Dagny Juel.
[2] 'M. Auguste Strindberg et *La Confession d'un fou*' by Gustave Valbert (pseudonym for Victor Cherbuliez (1829–99), secretary of the Académie Française), 1 November 1893.
[3] Albert Ranft (1858–1938), actor and theatre manager. See headnote to Letter 455.
[4] *En stor man* (A Great Man, 1894) by Anna Wahlenberg (1858–1933), *Nattrocken* (The Dressing Gown, 1894) by Frans Hedberg's son, Tor (1862–1931), *En stormig nyårsnatt* (A Stormy New Year's Eve, 1893) by Staaff and Geijerstam, and Ola Hansson's *Fru Ester Bruce* (1893), in which Strindberg figured as the painter Ödman, a name suggesting fate, desolation and devastation.
[5] Where Ola Hansson lived with Laura Marholm.
[6] Sense of Power.

304. To CARL LARSSON

[1] Larsson wrote that his wife thought Strindberg was being too 'modest' in reproaching a bunch of journeymen for following in his footsteps. According to Larsson, only Viktor Rydberg could compare with him in stature, but Rydberg's achievement belonged to an earlier period.
[2] A large-scale historical novel of ideas from 1859 which depicts the conflict between Christianity and Classical humanism under the Emperor Julian. Its portrait of an age in transition had clear parallels with the mid-century.
[3] Book learning.

4 David Friedrich Strauss (1808–74), German theologian and biographer, and Ernest Renan (1823–92), French Hebrew scholar, philologist, and historian of religion. Both writers had applied the theory of myths to the study of Christianity in *Das Leben Jesu* (The Life of Jesus, 1835) and *La Vie de Jesus* (The Life of Jesus, 1863) respectively. Rydberg's book in fact anticipated Renan's by a year but he remained indebted to him (as he was to Strauss) through the *Études d'histoire religieuse* (Studies in Religious History) of 1857.

5 Frans Hodell (1840–90), journalist, editor and, from 1881, owner of *Söndags-Nisse.*

6 1891.

7 In Scandinavian mythology it was Loki who gave the blind god Höder a shaft of mistletoe with which to shoot the young Balder, who was otherwise immune to harm; however, Strindberg is also recalling one of his most famous early poems, 'Loki's Blasphemies' (1883), where Loki is presented as a Promethean figure in the cause of World Revolution, thus challenging one of Rydberg's most celebrated poems, 'Prometheus and Ahasuerus' (1877).

305. To ADOLF PAUL

1 Otto Julius Bierbaum (1865–1910), German poet, compiler of the volume of German cabaret songs, *Deutsche Chansons* (1900). Przybyszewski reviewed Munch's painting in *Neue deutsche Rundschau* (as the *Freie Bühne* was now called) and edited the first book on his work, in 1894. *Ganz*: Quite.

2 Uteruses.

3 Sun spots.

4 In an essay in *Die Nation*, 20 May 1893.

5 Karl August Tavastjerna's wife, Gabrielle, with whom Strindberg claimed to have had a brief affair in 1892. With his help, she was now engaged at the Residenztheater in Berlin by Siegmund Lautenburg (1851–1918), who had been responsible for the 1893 production of *Creditors* there.

6 Helge Bäckström (1865–1932), Dagny Juel's brother-in-law, part of the expedition mounted from Lund to save her and Lidforss. Bäckström, a mineralogist, also reviewed *Antibarbarus* in *Aftonbladet* as '78 pages full of incomprehension, misrepresentation and hasty conclusions.'

7 Having helped Strindberg translate *Antibarbarus* into German, Lidforss published a review of the book in *Dagens Nyheter* (13 April 1894) called 'Strindberg against Science'. Whereas his letters had frequently shown enthusiasm, and even respect, for some of Strindberg's scientific ideas, the review, about which he gave Strindberg no warning, was critical, almost scornful in tone: 'Strindberg's old opponents will no doubt take this excellent opportunity to make capital out of the work's many eccentricities, while the trained professional will mostly dismiss it with a shrug of the shoulders and a few words about genius and madness . . . *Antibarbarus* proves one important point: Strindberg is neither a reformer nor a philosopher but purely and simply a poet . . . in whom the boundaries between fact, hypothesis and fantasy have been obliterated.'

306. To ADOLF PAUL

1 Asch and Schleich on *Antibarbarus*.

2 Lidforss. See Letter 305, note 7. Poland = Przybyszewski.

3 Where *A Book About Strindberg* had just been published.
4 Where *The First Warning* had failed after only two performances.
5 Maurice Bigeon (1871–94), whose study of Scandinavian literature appeared in 1893.
6 According to *Aftonbladet*, *The Father* had been whistled at the final curtain.
7 *Lucky Peter's Journey* had been a great success there in 1893.
8 Where *The People of Hemsö* and a selection from *Getting Married* had recently been published.
9 Dead man.
10 For the Académie Française. The interview appeared in *L'Éclair* (30 May 1894), not *Le Figaro*.
11 The Bibliographisches Bureau in Berlin, run by Julius Steinschneider. The Bureau published his six one-act plays from 1892, *Antibarbarus*, and the German edition of *A Madman's Defence*, which was banned under the Lex Heinze for immorality after an anonymous denunciation. (Torsten Eklund, who edited these letters in Swedish, suggests the writer may have been Marie David.) No such novel was written though Strindberg wrote a story, 'La Genèse d'un Aspasie', in 1894
12 The Past, i.e. Volume IV of *The Son of a Servant*.

307. To GEORG BRANDES

1 From Ernst Haeckel, to whom Strindberg had sent *Antibarbarus*. Haeckel was cautious but polite: 'I find nothing in your book – in so far as I understand it – that could, in my subjective opinion, be characterized as absolutely absurd or "crazy"'. Though promising to publish the letter in full, Brandes contented himself with quoting from it in a review of *Antibarbarus* in *Politiken*, 24 June.
2 Brilliant.

308. To GEORGES LOISEAU

1 Lugné-Poë had decided to put on *Creditors*, which Loiseau was translating from the German, at the Théâtre de l'Œuvre.
2 A line from the final scene of *Creditors*.
3 Double, counterpart.
4 Herman Bang, now Lugné-Poë's adviser on Scandinavian drama. Strindberg's correspondence with Bang is lost.
5 Bang had declined the part of Adolf, saying that he feared contracting the epilepsy from which the character suffers if he were to assume the role.
6 The Mörner-Fröding *En bok om Strindberg*.
7 Philippe Rameau, who played Gustav. Lugné-Poë himself played Adolf and Lucienne Dorsy, Tekla.

309. To LEOPOLD LITTMANSSON

1 The bust by Ville Vallgren from 1885.
2 A waxwork of Strindberg had been on display in Copenhagen since 1885.
3 Hjalmar Hirsch (1853–97), actor, son of a wealthy Jewish business man, Adolf Hirsch, and member of the Red Room circle. Strindberg's fascination with the

family manifests itself at this time in the essay 'Cristaux de remplacement' (False Crystals), written July-August 1894.

[4] Francisque Sarcey (1827–99), the doyen of nineteenth-century Parisian drama critics. He dismissed *Miss Julie* by this *'génie norvégien'* [*sic*] as incomprehensible, though he was more positive about *Creditors*.

[5] What's New from Stockholm.

[6] The painter Per Ekström (1844–1935), on whom Strindberg based the character of Sellén in *The Red Room*.

310. To ADOLF PAUL

[1] Strindberg had asked Paul if he would translate Parts Two and Three of *Antibarbarus* into German.

[2] Pietro Mascagni (1863–1945), whose *Cavalleria rusticana* (1890) represented a new realism (*Verismo*) in opera.

[3] Play upon Mascagni's inescapable coupling, Ruggiero Leoncavallo (1858–1919), composer of *I Pagliacci* (1892). *'Liljekonvalje'* in Swedish = lily of the valley.

311. To GEORG BRANDES

[1] Edvard Munch.

[2] Schleich.

[3] Strindberg originally mistook the signature to Lidforss' review as 'B.D.', not 'B.L.'.

[4] Perfidious youth.

[5] Mugger.

[6] Writing to Strindberg on 6 February 1894, Lidforss told him he was planning a book on 'Modern Scientists' in which Strindberg would appear alongside Haeckel, Lombroso, and others.

312. To RICHARD BERGH

[1] *The Keys of Heaven*.

[2] Cornelius and Marie Reischl, with whom Strindberg had a dispute over whether or not his newly-born daughter should be baptized a Roman Catholic.

[3] Paul Ollendorff, who published 'Les Relations de la France avec la Suède' and Georges Loiseau's translations of *Creditors*, *The Bond*, and *Playing with Fire*, and Zola's publisher, Georges Charpentier (1846–1905).

[4] François Coppée (1842–1908), French poet and dramatist, at one time engaged at the Institut Rudy where Strindberg lectured in 1885 on 'The Literary Reaction in Sweden'. Coppée, the *'poète des humbles'*, had been elected to the Académie Française in 1884 and ended a committed anti-Dreyfusard. Strindberg's positive attitude to France in his essay disarmed an old hostility.

[5] Allan Österlind (1855–1938), Swedish artist. See headnote to Letter 346.

[6] A district judge and harbour master whom Strindberg met in Gothenburg in 1892. Bergh was staying at Varberg, outside Gothenburg, along with Karl Nordström, and had invited Strindberg to join them there.

[7] Strindberg trained as a telegraphist in 1873. Like several of his other schemes

for making a living, this proposal is not as whimsical as it appears. Generally, Swedish writers had hitherto survived as academics or civil servants, and wrote on the side. Elias Sehlstedt, for example, about whom Strindberg had written his first pieces for *Dagens Nyheter*, had been a customs inspector on Sandhamn.

313. To RICHARD BERGH

[1] Strindberg believed von Steijern and *Dagens Nyheter* were boycotting him because of his antipathy for Geijerstam.

[2] An allusion to the charges against *A Madman's Defence*, pressed in Berlin on 17 July.

[3] Pehr Staaff, Gustaf af Geijerstam.

[4] Albert Ulrik Bååth (1853–1912), scholar and poet. Most of Strindberg's letters to Bååth have been mutilated by their addressee.

[5] Rydberg's translation of Goethe's *Faust* appeared in 1876.

[6] Gustaf Håkon Ljunggren (1823–1905), Professor of Aesthetics, Literature and Art History in Lund; member of the Swedish Academy.

[7] Gunnar Wennerberg (1817–1901), poet, composer, and politician.

314. To LEOPOLD LITTMANSSON

[1] I.e. a follower of Zarathustra.

[2] *Creditors* had opened at the Théâtre de l'Œuvre on 21 June.

[3] *L'Amour brode* (Embroidered Love) by François de Curel (1854–1928).

[4] Forward!

[5] *ta Valget*: make the choice (in Kierkegaardian terms between the aesthetic and ethical standpoints). When writing to Littmansson, Strindberg frequently employs the Kierkegaardian discourse of their youth.

[6] *The Life and Soul of Matter: Studies in Dynamic Chemistry* and *The Metamorphosis of Matter*. Of the two, Jollivet-Castelot (1874–?) came to mean the most for him: 'I've just read your book and am stupefied,' he wrote to him, on 22 July, 'but also comforted to see that I am not alone in this madness that has cost me my family happiness, my reputation, everything!' He contributed frequently to Castelot's journal *L'Hyperchimie*, while the latter discussed his work at length in *L'Hylozoisme, l'alchimie, les chimistes unitaires* (Hylozoism, Alchemy and the Unitarian Chemists, 1896) and *Comment on devient alchimiste* (How One Becomes an Alchemist, 1897). He also published the many letters Strindberg sent him on scientific, alchemical, and occult subjects as *Bréviaire alchimique* (Alchemical Breviary, 1912).

[7] It is a joy to be alive. The German suggests the book he sent Littmansson may have been by Nietzsche, possibly *Beyond Good and Evil*.

315. To LEOPOLD LITTMANSSON

[1] Léon Daudet (1867–1942), French novelist and publicist, son of Alphonse Daudet. He had originally studied medicine and this novel, published in 1892, dealt with the question of heredity.

[2] Life is ours!

317. To LEOPOLD LITTMANSSON

[1] From the term coined by the German chemist and disciple of Mesmer, Karl von Reichenbach (1788–1869), for a hypothetical force formerly thought to be responsible for many natural phenomena, such as magnetism, light and hypnotism. *Le culte du moi*: the cult of the self.

[2] Unconsciously.

[3] 'Moi', one of the French vivisections written during 1894 with Paris in mind but not published until a bilingual edition in 1958.

[4] Ludwig Andreas Feuerbach (1804–72), German materialist philosopher, author of *Das Wesen des Christentums* (The Essence of Christianity, 1841) where he maintains God is merely an outward projection of man's inner self.

[5] David Friedrich Strauss. See Letter 304.

[6] Moses Mendelssohn (1729–86), German Jewish philosopher, best known for *Jerusalem* (1783), in which he defends Judaism and appeals for religious toleration.

[7] Ludwig Büchner (1824–99), German materialist philosopher and physician; author of *Kraft und Stoff* (Force and Matter, 1855), in which he sought to demonstrate the indestructability of matter and force. For Büchner, nature is purely physical, without purpose, will or laws imposed by extraneous authority.

[8] Theodore Parker (1810–60), American Unitarian freethinker whose writings (translated into Swedish in ten volumes, 1866–74) once exerted considerable influence on Strindberg, especially on his early play *The Freethinker* (1869).

[9] Littmansson's mother-in-law.

[10] In both Dostoyevsky's *Crime and Punishment* (1866) and Bulwer Lytton's *Eugene Aram* (1832) the protagonist commits a murder on theoretical grounds.

[11] J. M. Hoene Wronski (1778–1853), Polish mathematician and thinker whom Littmansson admired and Strindberg disparaged. Wronski, who lived the latter part of his life in Paris, was introduced by Balzac into *Le Peau de chagrin* (The Wild Ass's Skin, 1831) and *La Recherche de l'absolu* (The Quest of the Absolute, 1834), and his occult system influenced the ideas of the movement's key figure in France, Eliphas Levi (1810–75), who linked the Parisian occultism of the *fin de siècle* with the mystic-cabbalistic tradition of Böhme, Swedenborg, and Saint-Martin. Against Wronski (and Littmansson's) desire for system, Strindberg argued the modernity of Nietzsche in resisting one. 'I do not believe in zoösperms from the stars,' he observed, 'but admit them provisionally, since they advance disorder' (29 July 1894).

[12] See Letter 272.

[13] Anarchia.

[14] Adolf Hirsch's second son, who worked for his uncle, the music publisher Abraham Hirsch (1815–1900).

318. To TORSTEN HEDLUND

[1] See Letter 272.

[2] Overwrought.

[3] Ch. Théodore Tiffereau (1819–?), chemist and alchemist, author of *L'Or et la transmutation des métaux* (Gold and the Transmutation of Metals, 1889) and *L'Art de faire de l'or* (The Art of Gold Making, 1892).

[4] Sir William Crookes (1832–1919), eminent English chemist and physicist, who became a firm adherent of spiritism.

319. To LEOPOLD LITTMANSSON

[1] Littmansson, himself Jewish, doubtless commented on some remarks of Strindberg's in a letter not translated here, in which he pursued his analysis of the Hirsch family: 'Hjalmar is part negro, you don't know that. But I saw it in Philip's lips, old Adolf's legs and Ivan's hair; even Hjalmar's long-gone hair was nigger, i.e. half-ape.' John Jacobsson (1835–1909), cantor in Stockholm.
[2] Joseph Josephson (1849–1883), member of the Runa society.
[3] I. The world for me!
[4] A word coined by Strindberg in the Littmansson letters for sexual intercourse.

320. To LEOPOLD LITTMANSSON

[1] For his fare to Paris.
[2] Jollivet-Castelot.
[3] Original in English. *Machtgefühl! Alles*!: Feeling of Power! Everything!

321. To LEOPOLD LITTMANSSON

[1] Strindberg is playing with a quotation from Balzac which he had sent Littmansson without comment on a previous postcard (27 July): '*Les femmes sont habituées par je ne sais quelle pente de leur esprit, à ne voir dans un homme de talent que ses défauts, et dans un sot que ses qualités; elles éprouvent de grandes sympathies pour les qualités du sot qui sont une flatterie perpétuelle de leurs propres défauts*' (women are accustomed by I know not what inclination of their spirit to see in a man of talent only his faults and in a fool only his qualities; they experience great sympathy for those qualities in the fool which are a constant flattery of their own qualities).
[2] The quotation, from Goethe's poem 'Rechenschaft', should read: '*Nur die Lumpe sind bescheiden,/ Braue freuen sich der That*' (Only rogues are modest,/Upright men take pleasure in deeds).
[3] Old Sweden.
[4] One of the names of Buddha, whose identity Strindberg here assumes. According to legend, Buddha left his wife and child to become a hermit and live in purity as Strindberg now thought to do. By earth mother he means a wet nurse.
[5] Ludvig Josephson. Cf. the speculations in Letter 319.
[6] Hjalmar Hirsch. See Letter 17.
[7] Otto Samson (1846–1916), director of the Life Insurance Company Nordstjernan, for whom Strindberg worked briefly in 1873 as editor of the *Svensk Försäkringstidning*. The European and Eagle were British Insurance Companies for which Samson was the agent.

322. To LEOPOLD LITTMANSSON

[1] Where the question of money arises, Buddhism ends. A play on the phrase 'Bei Geldfragen hört die Gemütlichkeit auf' (In matters of money, geniality ceases), uttered not by Goethe but by David Hausemann in the first German Parliament of 1847.
[2] Slow goods service.
[3] The Art of Chance.

[4] 'Des arts nouveaux! ou Le hasard dans la production artistique' (The New Arts, or The Role of Chance in Artistic Creation). First published in the *Revue des Revues*, 5 November 1894, this article, with its stress on the role of chance and the unconscious in art, is a key text for understanding Strindberg's later work, and an important early manifesto heralding both literary and artistic modernism. It also helps clarify the attitude he adopts to his everyday experiences during the Inferno crisis.

[5] A copy of a sculpture of his son, Hans, which Strindberg made in 1891 and now considered an example of the automatic art he described in 'Des arts nouveaux'.

[6] 'En Støvring omkring Jorden' (A Ring of Dust Round the Earth), *Politiken*, 23 July 1894. Following a recent theory that zodiacal light was a ring of cosmic matter surrounding the earth, Nordenskiöld had linked this matter with a rain of particles that occurred in Denmark and Southern Sweden in May 1894. Strindberg claimed to have dealt with the subject in the unpublished second part of *Antibarbarus*.

[7] These two motifs are reproduced as colour plates VII and VIII in Torsten Måtte Schmidt, ed., *Strindbergs måleri* (Stockholm, 1972).

[8] The volume of French vivisections.

[9] Here Strindberg includes a sketch of the three crosses.

[10] Know thyself. The inscription on the temple of Apollo at Delphi.

[11] An allusion to *The Keys of Heaven*, Act 1, Scene 4.

[12] At pleasure.

323. To GEORG BRANDES

[1] See Letter 316.

[2] An allusion to Brandes' *Main Currents in 19th Century Literature* (1872–90).

[3] Emil Petersen, who had commented disparagingly on Strindberg's methods in a letter to Brandes on which the latter drew for his review of *Antibarbarus*.

324. To LEOPOLD LITTMANSSON

[1] Seligmann was married to one of Littmansson's sisters.

[2] Fru Svedbom-Limnell (1816–92), noted for her literary salon.

[3] One of the founders of the Swedish branch of the Federation for the Abolition of Prostitution.

[4] God (?) breathed and they are scattered!

[5] C. O. Berg (1839–1903), one of Strindberg's bitterest opponents during his trial in 1884, (not 1889, as Strindberg writes here), had been committed to Långholm prison for financial irregularities.

[6] Let's get down to work.

325. To LEOPOLD LITTMANSSON

[1] An aristocracy of the spirit and not of money.

[2] I.e. Nordstjernan (The North Star).

[3] See headnote to Letter 219.

[4] Always flexible tempo.

[5] Seligmann.

[6] Littmansson originally worked in a bank, then planned to take his university

entrance exam and become a doctor, but soon gave up the idea and went briefly to America. Joseph Seligmann administered his inheritance on the death of his father in 1867. In a previous letter, Strindberg had called Hjalmar Hirsch (here, 'Jallmar') a 'Shaker for want of anything to live on'. The Shakers were an American millenarian sect, founded in 1747 as an offshoot of the Quakers, and given to ecstatic shaking, the advocacy of celibacy, and the common ownership of property.

7 Pacemakers, or avant-garde.

326. To TORSTEN HEDLUND

1 Hedlund's response, outlining the doctrines of theosophy, survives. The letter came to mean a great deal to Strindberg, who wrote of it in *Inferno*: 'at this critical moment in my life I received [a] letter from this unknown man, a letter that struck an elevated, almost prophetic, note. In it he foretold for me a future that would be rich in suffering and in honour. Into the bargain he gave me his motive for renewing our correspondence. This arose from a presentiment that he had that I was at that moment passing through a spiritual crisis and that a word of comfort was perhaps necessary.' *Inferno*, p.167.

2 Hedlund wrote: 'The black French school is regarded by theosophists as an especially dangerous intellectual current for the development of mankind. It probably amounts to nothing more than an unhealthy reaction to an unhealthy materialism.' Like the distinction later in this letter between flying and retaining a feel of the ground, this contrast between black and white often recurs in Strindberg's correspondence with Hedlund.

VII

Notes to Letters 327–394

November 1892–11 August 1894

327. To FRIDA UHL

[1] Albert Langen (1869–1909), German publisher, later renowned for the satirical journal *Simplicissimus*, active 1893–95 in Paris where he interested himself in Scandinavian literature, particularly the work of Knut Hamsun.

[2] Willy Pedersen (alias Grétor, 1868–1923), confidence trickster. Grétor, who dealt in – among other things – art, some of it forged, encouraged Strindberg's painting and lent him a flat in the rue de Ranelagh, Passy, belonging to one of his mistresses, the painter Rosa Pfaeffinger. The German dramatist Frank Wedekind (1864–1918), also a member of the Langen circle, based the protagonist of his play *Der Marquis von Keith* (1901) on Grétor.

[3] Man-servant.

[4] Brandes' three-volume study of Shakespeare appeared in 1895–96. For Cherbuliez, see Letter 303.

[5] Strindberg had been critical of Becque's masterpiece, *Les Corbeaux*, in the essay 'On Modern Drama and Modern Theatre' (1889).

[6] A symbolist journal, which also held literary evenings.

[7] Strindberg never took up Zola's invitation.

328. To FRIDA UHL

[1] Grétor.

329. To FRIDA UHL

[1] *Mein Verhängnis*: my fate.

[2] Strindberg had asked for a folder of notes marked 'France' on 24 August. Frida misread *carnet* for *cahier*.

[3] Littmansson.

330. To FRIDA UHL

[1] Littmansson.

[2] The continuing prosecution of *A Madman's Defence* in Germany.

331. To FRIDA UHL

[1] Dornach.

[2] Any old how; cat and dog existence.
[3] Dear master.
[4] *The Future*, a cultural weekly edited by Maximilian Harden (1861–1927).

332. To FRIDA UHL

[1] Grétor's mistress, Rosa Pfeiffinger.
[2] The kept man.
[3] But you will be installed there in true Parisian style.
[4] The pictures were sent to a lawyer in Gothenburg, Algot Carlander (1847–1910), partly because, as this letter implies, Strindberg was alert to Grétor's criminal traffic in forged paintings.

333. To BIRGER MÖRNER

[1] During an autumn tour of Scandinavia, Lugné-Poë and the Théâtre de l'Œuvre, for whom Bang acted as literary adviser and co-director on Scandinavian material, performed Maeterlinck's *L'Intruse* (The Intruder, 1890) and *Pelléas et Mélisande* (1892). In a lecture in Copenhagen, Bang criticized Naturalism and paid tribute to Maeterlinck as the leader of a new literary movement.
[2] Paul Hervieu (1857–1915), French novelist and dramatist with whom Strindberg was acquainted, and Marcel Prévost (1862–1941), whose psychological novels marked a reaction against Naturalism.
[3] Echo. Strindberg also dismissed Maeterlinck for echoes of style and material in the vivisection 'L'Origine d'un style' (1894).
[4] Pierre Loti, pseudonym of L. M. Julien Viaud (1850–1923), French novelist, known for his sensualism and exoticism.
[5] Over again. Novalis, pseudonym of Friedrich von Hardenberg (1772–1801), and Ludwig Tieck (1773–1853), German romantic poets and novelists (Tieck was also a dramatist) whom Strindberg saw revived in Maeterlinck. He later reversed his opinion of all three.
[6] Arvid August Afzelius (1785–1871), Swedish writer and folklorist. His *Svenska folkets sagohäfder* (Tales of the Swedish People, 1839–70) was one of the sources for Strindberg's later history plays *The Saga of the Folkungs* and *Gustav Vasa* as well as for the Icelandic 'Song of the Sun' introduced at the close of *The Ghost Sonata*.
[7] Erik Wilhelm Dahlgren (1848–1934), librarian and fellow pupil at Klara school. Strindberg had asked Mörner to send Dahlgren some of the Chinese material left in his keeping so that he might respond on Strindberg's behalf to an enquiry he had received concerning early Swedish contacts with the Far East.
[8] *Le Figaro littéraire* for 30 September included Strindberg's article 'Césarine' on Alexandre Dumas' drama *La Femme de Claude* (1873), which had been revived with Sarah Bernhardt at the Comédie Française.
[9] What one has wished for in one's youth.
[10] *Salig Friherrinan* (The Blessed Baroness) in Norway.
[11] 'Strindberg as Painter', an appreciative article by Sven Lange (1868–1930), a Danish playwright and member of the Langen circle, appeared in *Politiken*, 22 October 1894.
[12] The protagonist of Ludvig Holberg's comedy *Jeppe paa Bjerget* (1722) awakens from the drunken stupor into which he retreats from his social and marital commitments on a dunghill, having spent the preceding acts in a dream-like

situation, enjoying the rights of a local aristocrat.

13 Oscar Norén and Alfred Hedenstierna.

14 Simon Broomé, editor of *Skånska Aftonbladet*; Strindberg had asked Mörner to find out if he would publish Part Two of *Antibarbarus*.

334. To FRIDA UHL

1 *Le Jour de tous les morts 1894 et morticules.* A play on the title of Léon Daudet's novel *Les Morticoles* (The Sawbones, 1894). Actually 1 November.

2 Presumably Birger Mörner.

3 The Norwegian painter Johan Frederik (Frits) Thaulow (1849–1906), a good friend of Strindberg's, who spent several days at his home in Dieppe, in October 1894.

4 Max Burckhardt, who broke his promise to stage *The Secret of the Guild.* See Letter 299.

5 Frida had been in Paris from mid-September. On 21 October, when Frida returned to care for their child in Dornach, she and Strindberg parted quite cordially outside the department store Printemps. They never saw each other again.

335. To FRIDA UHL

1 Ladybird.

2 Name of the famous cabaret opened by Rodolphe Salis (1852–97) in Montmartre in 1881. The Chat Noir was renowned for its shadow plays (Théâtre d'Ombres) devised by Henri Rivière (1864–1951), who used zinc silhouettes against a background lit through coloured glass and accompanied by narration, music, and sometimes a backstage chorus.

3 Normally distracted, half-mad, but as used in Parisian *fin-de-siècle* literary circles an accolade, denoting extreme sensitivity and intellectual refinement. Strindberg published an experimental essay, entitled 'Sensations détraquées', in *Le Figaro littéraire*, November 1894–February 1895.

4 A literary cabaret on the Left Bank.

5 'Goatee', i.e. Loiseau.

336. To FRIDA UHL

1 Parenthesis in Swedish.

2 See Letter 327, note 1.

337. To FRIDA UHL

1 Catulle Mendès (1841–1909), French Parnassian poet, novelist, and dramatist, critic of *Le Journal*.

2 The cottage in Dornach where Strindberg and Frida spent perhaps the happiest period of their marriage. *La morticole*: see Letter 334, note 1.

3 Letter 336.

4 That is good.

338. To FRIDA UHL

[1] Strindberg commented on this letter in *Inferno*: 'In an attack of righteous indignation, and overwhelmed by a furious desire to do myself an injury, I committed suicide by despatching an infamous, unpardonable letter, casting off wife and child for ever, and giving her to understand that I was involved in a new love affair. My bullet hit the mark and my wife replied by demanding a divorce' (p.103).

[2] Grétor.

[3] In her memoirs, Frida Uhl reveals that it was Grétor, not Langen, who really attracted her; when he proved unresponsive, she initiated a close friendship with Frank Wedekind to arouse his jealousy. The ruse failed but her affair with Wedekind led in 1897 to the birth of a son.

[4] William Heinemann.

[5] Clotilde's final line in Henry Becque's *La Parisienne*: 'Confidence, that is the only system which is successful with us women!'

339. To RICHARD BERGH

[1] An allusion to his daily absinthe and to a passage in 'Sensations détraquées', in which he claims to have heard the sounds of Paris caught in the auricle formed by the wings of the palace of Versailles. The idea is based upon an ancient account of a system for spying on prisoners installed by Dionysus the Elder in his prison at Syracuse.

[2] Bergh had written to Strindberg on 30 June, inviting him to join him at Varberg on the Swedish west coast.

340. To FRIDA UHL

[1] In the Hôtel des Américains.

[2] Henry Bauër (1851–1915), theatre critic of *L'Echo de Paris*. An admirer of Strindberg's work, he adapted *The Father* for the 1894 production by Lugné-Poë. Strindberg dedicated the French edition of *A Madman's Defence* to him.

[3] Of these translations, only 'The Romantic Organist' appeared, but not until 15 January 1909, and then in the *Revue de Paris*.

[4] An allusion to the quotation from *La Parisienne* in Letter 338.

341. To AURÉLIEN LUGNÉ-POË

[1] Strindberg had stayed away both from the dress rehearsal and the première of *The Father*, which opened on 13 December.

[2] Lugné-Poë had used Loiseau's translation but Strindberg felt the latter sometimes put his own interests before the author's.

342. To AURÉLIEN LUGNÉ-POË

[1] Strindberg had heard that Lugné-Poë intended to use the success of *The Father* to mount a revival of *An Enemy of the People*. In 1895 he produced both *Little Eyolf* and *Brand*.

343. To FRIDA UHL

[1] From 11 to 31 January 1895 Strindberg was a patient of the eminent dermatologist, Professor Henri Hallopeau (1842–1919), at the Hôpital Saint-Louis. He had suffered for many years from psoriasis, now probably exacerbated by the almost daily handling of chemicals. His treatment was assisted by a collection among the Scandinavian community in Paris, administered by the pastor of the Swedish Church there, Nathan Söderblom. (See headnote to Letter 674.)

[2] Frida had repeatedly asked Strindberg to send on the luggage she had left behind.

344. To LEOPOLD LITTMANSSON

[1] This association with leprosy became a motif in the Inferno material, where his affliction is linked to the system of guilt and suffering he explored in his autobiographical fiction: 'Swedenborg explained to me the reason for my stay in the Hôpital Saint-Louis thus: Alchemists are attacked by leprosy, which produces itching scabs like fish-scales – my incurable skin disease in fact' (p.257).

[2] Is it really true that the earth revolves? No!

[3] You see. Refers to Strindberg's long-standing misgivings about the composition of air. Ekazote ≐ Eka-nitrogen.

345. To FRIDA UHL

[1] In *Inferno* Strindberg writes of a nun at the hospital who 'took a special fancy to me, treated me like a baby and called me "my child", while I, like all the others, called her "Mother" ' (p.107).

[2] The warmth of the maternal breast.

348. To PAUL GAUGUIN

[1] Strindberg spent three weeks in Paris in October 1876, travelling there via Norway with the painter Johan Dahlbom (1850–86).

[2] *L'Assommoir* appeared in 1877.

[3] See Letter 59.

[4] During the 1880s, the Durand-Ruel Gallery became the main dealer in Impressionist painting.

[5] 'From Café de l'Ermitage to Marly-le-Roi', which discussed paintings by Sisley and Monet, appeared in *Dagens Nyheter*, 30 November and 9 December 1876.

[6] Julien Bastien-Lepage (1848–1884), an academic painter of realistic subjects from the lives of the common people, popular in the official Salons.

[7] The essays on aesthetics by Taine which Strindberg read during the 1870s eventually appeared as *Philosophie de l'art*, 1882.

[8] The formula 'une œuvre d'art est un coin de la nature vu à travers un tempérament' is one which Zola uses several times: in *Mes haines* (My Hates, 1866), the *Salon de 1866*, and 'Le Naturalisme au théâtre'.

[9] Pierre Puvis de Chavannes (1824–98), decorative painter and muralist whose work was characterized by allegorical or literary subjects, muted colours, and spare, monumental composition. *Le Pauvre pêcheur* (The Poor Fisherman) was first

exhibited at the Salon of 1881.

[10] Georges Leopold Chrétien Cuvier (1769–1832), French naturalist, founder of comparative anatomy.

[11] Aztec war god whose worship entailed human sacrifice.

349. To ANDERS ELIASSON

[1] Strindberg feared a link, often made in the nineteenth century, between psoriasis and syphilis. This was not the case though rumours may have circulated to that effect (the venereal patient in Edvard Munch's lithograph *In the Clinic* (1896), for example, has Strindberg's features).

352. To BIRGER MÖRNER

[1] Strindberg's scientific studies had been treated with respect in the French press; he corresponded with the eminent chemist Marcelin Berthelot (1827–1907), and at the end of April had gained permission to undertake experiments at the Sorbonne. See *Inferno*, p.117.

[2] *Le Figaro*'s science correspondent, Émile Gautier (1853-?), published *La Science Française,* where a discussion of Strindberg's theories appeared on 8 February. Gautier also wrote a respectful article, 'Strindberg chimiste', in *Le Figaro* on 15 February. These articles attracted the interest of an industrial chemist in Rouen, André Dubosc. See headnote to Letter 360.

[3] In chapter four (*Samlade skrifter*, 27, p.199).

[4] 'L'Iode comme un dérivé de houilles' (Iodine as a Derivative of Coal), which appeared in *Le Temps*, 14 May 1895, not *La Science Française.*

[5] Strindberg saw the discovery of Argon in 1894 as confirmation that his long-standing doubts concerning the composition of air were justified.

353. To FRIDA UHL

[1] In Paris and Brussels.

354. To ANDERS ELIASSON

[1] Eliasson had sent Strindberg the fare so that he could visit him in Ystad. He left Paris on 10 June, only to return there on 14 July.

[2] Bengt Lidforss.

355. To TORSTEN HEDLUND

[1] Parisian occult journal, edited by Dr Papus (Gérard Encausse, 1865–1916). The August 1895 issue contained an article by Jollivet-Castelot, 'Les Chimistes unitaires', in which Strindberg was accorded great respect. Strindberg published ten articles on astronomy, photography and related subjects in *L'Initiation* during 1896. Except for one letter, his quite substantial correspondence with Papus, perhaps the leading Parisian occultist of the day, was lost during

the Second World War. However, it may be worth recording the confidence he expressed in Papus when writing to Hedlund on 11 July 1896: 'I have suggested to Papus that I should "kill" myself with Cyanide and he recall me to life following my prescription; but he's reluctant to do so because a medical commission would only say: "All right, but as you see, he wasn't really dead." '

2 Jules Michelet (1798–1874), French historian and writer; his lyrical study *La Mer* appeared in 1861.

357. To TORSTEN HEDLUND

1 The idea originated with Daniel Grant, a well-wisher and businessman who lived in Barcelona. When it failed to materialize, this mysterious gift haunted Strindberg's imagination for weeks.

2 Or Sakyamuni = Buddha. Derived from Sakya, where he was born.

3 Siri von Essen was blond, Frida Uhl dark-haired.

4 The *Moniteur industriel,* which published a positive review of Strindberg's theories about iodine on 8 June 1895.

358. To TORSTEN HEDLUND

1 Hedlund's term for Strindberg in one of his letters.

2 Lit. lost children. Cf. *Sentinelle perdue*: advanced sentry.

3 The Molards. Cf. Strindberg's retrospective account in *Inferno,* p.114.

4 In *'Uber die Weiber'* (On Women) from his *Parerga und Paralipomena* (1851), *Sämtliche Werke,* vol. V, p.679.

5 See Letter 357.

359. To MATHILDE PRAGER

1 *Sylva Sylvarum,* containing four essays later published in Swedish as *Jardin des Plantes,* appeared in French, in January 1896. The title was taken from a posthumous work by Francis Bacon, whose aphoristic mode of presentation Strindberg partly adopted.

2 Reprint and free translation.

3 His *Introduction à une chimie unitaire,* published by *Mercure de France,* 1895.

4 The allusion is to Langen and Grétor. The idea that his experiments might be linked to anarchist actions against the Third Republic was a recurring one, particularly after Caserio's assassination of President Carnot in June 1894. See *Inferno,* p.102. The interviews both appeared on 14 January 1895.

5 See Letter 352.

6 Among Strindberg's unpublished papers is an 'Open Letter to Berthelot on Sulphur'; he published 'L'Affaire soufre' (The Question of Sulphur) in *Le Figaro,* 12 February 1895, and 'L'Avenir du soufre' (The Future of Sulphur) in *La Science Française,* 15 March 1895.

7 Alfred Naquet (1834–1916), chemist and politician. A Boulangist, Naquet was involved in the Panama scandel. See *Inferno,* p.122.

360. To ANDRÉ DUBOSC

[1] See Letter 318.

361. To TORSTEN HEDLUND

[1] Strindberg had sent a copy of *Sylva Sylvarum* to Hedlund, who replied with an English theosophist tract, *Light on the Path*. This drew an abusive response from Strindberg, who accused him of wanting to force him 'to bow the knee to your Gods and Godesses'. The correspondence lapsed for seven weeks.

[2] An allusion to the recent (1895) discovery of x-rays by the German physicist, Wilhelm Röntgen (1845–1923).

[3] The identification with Orpheus, hounded by women, recurs in *Inferno*, pp.242–3.

362. To TORSTEN HEDLUND

[1] Mateo José Bonaventura Orfila (1787–1853), French physician of Spanish parentage, who founded the science of toxicology. Strindberg's discovery of Orfila's *Eléments de chimie, appliquée à la médecine et aux arts* (The Elements of Chemistry, applied to Medicine and the Arts, 1831), and the almost supernatural authority it came to possess for him, is recorded in *Inferno*, p.116. See also Letter 377.

[2] Strindberg had approached Hedlund's cousin, the journalist and politician Henrik Hedlund (1851–1932), about publishing his essay, 'A Memory of the Sorbonne', in *Göteborgs Handels- och Sjöfartstidning*.

[3] Destiny or fate; in Theosophy the doctrine of inevitable consequence; in Buddhism a principle of retributive justice determining a person's state of life.

[4] Albert de Rochas d'Aiglun (1837–1914), French occultist, author of *Les États profonds de l'hypnose* (The Deep States of Hypnosis, 1892) and *L'Extériorisation de la sensibilité* (The Externalization of the Sensibility, 1895). Rochas, a mesmerist, attempted to show experimentally that suggestion and hypnotic phenomena were occasioned by electrical-like currents. Hedlund had himself linked Rochas with Charcot's experiments at the Salpêtrière, and as his essay 'The Irradiation and Extensibility of the Soul' in *L'Initiation* (1896) indicates, Strindberg found what seemed to him a likely explanation for his own experiences in Rochas.

363. To TORSTEN HEDLUND

[1] Hedlund had arranged financial support for Strindberg from a Gothenburg businessman, August Röhss (1836–1904), who donated 1,200 *kronor*, the money being paid in monthly instalments from March to July, sometimes directly to the Hôtel Orfila, where he was now living, and to the *Crémerie* at 13 rue de la Grande Chaumière, where he ate. The surplus carried him through to September.

[2] *Göteborgs Handels- och Sjöfartstidningen*.

364. To TORSTEN HEDLUND

1 Outside Gothenburg.
2 A fact.
3 *Dans l'Inde* (In India), p.184. 'Le Vase de Benares. Le Grand désordre' was the original working title for the material that Strindberg was now gathering, which eventually issued in *Inferno*.
4 The 1895 bust by his friend, Agnes de Frumerie (1869–1937). See Plate 19.

365. To BIRGER MÖRNER

1 Small spills of paper, brownish-yellow at one end, which Strindberg dipped in his experimental solutions and sent out as evidence that he had produced gold.

367. To TORSTEN HEDLUND

1 Here 'critics' but elsewhere in his correspondence with Hedlund, members of a fraternity of occult demons. See Letter 383.
2 The German painter Paul Herrmann (Henri Héran, 1864–1940), one of the pallbearers at Oscar Wilde's funeral in 1900. This episode is recounted in *Inferno* (p.141) where, as in the *Occult Diary*, it unfolds on Good Friday. Strindberg suspected Herrmann, who lived in the United States during the early 1890s, of being the *Doppelgänger* of a notorious American faith-healer, Francis Schlatter.
3 Cf. *Inferno*, p.144, where Strindberg also documents his as yet relatively superficial acquaintance with Emanuel Swedenborg (1688–1772), the Swedish scientist and theologian whose ideas were later to exert a profound influence on him. Chapter Nine of *Inferno* provides a partial account of the role that Swedenborg played in helping Strindberg resolve his spiritual crisis, but his presence is also to be discerned in the structure and imagery of many of his later literary works.
4 Pseudonym for H. L. D. Rivail (1803–69), spiritist and author of *Le Livre des esprits* (The Book of Spirits, 1857), dictated, according to Kardec, by 'esprits supérieurs'.
5 Original in English.
6 See *Inferno*, p.136. Strindberg's sketches of these gnome-like coal figures are reproduced in *Strindbergs måleri*, facing p.144.
7 Actually Theodor Kittelsen (1857–1914), who illustrated Asbjørnsen and Moe's *Norske folkeeventyr* (Norwegian Fairy Tales).

368. To TORSTEN HEDLUND

1 Megalomania.
2 The Molards.

369. To MATHILDE PRAGER

1 Presumably the May number in which Papus wrote: 'Our eminent author, August Strindberg, who combines vast knowledge with his great talents as a writer, has just achieved a synthesis of gold from iron. August Strindberg

has an absolute contempt for riches and has never kept any of his methods secret, consequently he immediately gave us his procedure, which confirms all the assertions of the alchemists.'

[2] Hugo and Anna Philp had recently visited Strindberg in Paris.

[3] François Charles Barlet (pseud. of Alfred Faucheux, 1838–?), minor civil servant and alchemist, later head of the Cabbalistic Order of the Rosy Cross, author of *La Science secrète* (The Secret Science, 1890) and the *Essai de chimie synthétique* (An Essay on Synthetic Chemistry, 1894).

[4] Conceivably Albert-Louis Caillet (1869–1928), who compiled a three-volume *Manuel bibliographique des sciences psychiques et occultes* (Bibliographical Handbook of Psychical and Occult Sciences, Paris, 1912).

[5] Besides Mendès and Darzens (see Letter 278), the poet and novelist Maurice Beaubourg (1866–1943) and the dramatist and novelist Léon Hennique (1851–1935), one of the authors of the *Soirées de Medan* (1880), and a friend of Zola.

[6] Megalomania.

370. To TORSTEN HEDLUND

[1] See Letter 326.

[2] Willy Grétor and his confederates.

[3] A small town, some seventy-five miles north-west of Stockholm.

[4] A mountain range, formerly rich in mineral resources, on the border between Germany and Czechoslovakia.

[5] Erik Werenskiold (1855–1938), Norwegian landscape painter, also illustrated Asbjørnsen and Moe's *Norwegian Fairy Tales*. See Letter 367.

[6] Presumably a reference to the Buddhist concept of *Gomukha*, or life force.

[7] Cf. *Inferno*, p.147.

[8] Albert Stockenström (1867–1954), among Strindberg's closest acquaintances in Paris. See *Inferno*, pp.140, 148.

371. To TORSTEN HEDLUND

[1] Strindberg had been keeping his *Occult Diary*, at first only a collection of undated notes, since 21 February, when he moved into the Hôtel Orfila. It forms a parallel, not always quite consistent record of these months with the Hedlund letters, and he drew on it when composing *Inferno*. He continued to keep the diary until he moved to his final residence at 85 Drottninggatan, in July 1908. The excerpts here enlarge slightly upon the original entries. Jonas Lie's clock also figures in *Inferno*, p.150.

[2] Two sketches showing the cross section of a walnut. See *Strindberg's måleri*, facing p.145.

[3] The inventor Gustav de Laval (1845–1913). Strindberg had sent Mörner a 'Memorandum' on profitable scientific projects (see Letter 370), and speculated on the possibility of a collaboration with de Laval. The 'Memorandum' was to be sent on to Hedlund. When this didn't happen, Strindberg assumed that Mörner and de Laval were trying to cozen him. The following paragraph hints that Mörner was behind Hugo Philp's visit to Paris that summer to determine (or so Strindberg believed) his sanity.

[4] Fate.

372. To ANDERS ELIASSON

[1] Przybyszewski.
[2] *Bierkarte* (from *Briefkarte* = correspondence card).

373. To EDVARD MUNCH

[1] Martha Foerder, with whom Przybyszewski lived before marrying Dagny Juel, had committed suicide, but without in fact harming their children. According to the *Occult Diary*, the information had come in a letter from Eliasson that morning; the entry continues: 'Found an ace of clubs (*joie, argent, bonnes nouvelles*)', i.e. joy, money, good news.
[2] A prison in Berlin.

374. To ANDRÉ DUBOSC

[1] See Letter 362.
[2] Therefore.
[3] Joseph Louis Proust (1754–1826), French chemist who formulated the law of constant proportions. Strindberg encountered Proust's discovery that gold leaf dissolved in hydrochloric acid in Orfila's *Élements de chimie* (see Letters 362 and 377).
[4] It is proved.
[5] I say.
[6] Nothing.
[7] The fact is.

375. To EDVARD MUNCH

[1] M. E. Bäckström (1827–97), the father of Dagny Juel's brother-in-law, Helge Bäckström.
[2] Hoax.

376. To TORSTEN HEDLUND

[1] This is the first in a sequence of seven letters to Hedlund written between 6 and 22 July on manuscript paper rather than Strindberg's customary writing paper. Since they are interspersed with other letters to Hedlund on ordinary writing paper, it seems clear that he regarded them as distinct from the remainder of their correspondence. They are numbered consecutively pp. 1–59 and represent a kind of trial run for what eventually became *Inferno*. (The opening of Letter 377, for example, reads like a draft for the early chapters of his autobiographical fiction.)
[2] Megalomania.
[3] Rehabilitation, whitewash.
[4] A widely used term in French occult circles to describe murderous attempts from afar by adepts in black magic. The most notorious contemporary instance involved the novelist Huysmans, who accused the Rosicrucians of having used

envoûtement to murder his friend, the Abbé Boullan (1824–93). Huysmans' novel *Là-bas* (1891) is based on this episode.

5 A notorious pickpocket, then awaiting trial in Sweden for murder.

6 The painting in question is reproduced in Ingrid Langaard, *Edvard Munch: Modningsår* (Oslo, 1960), p.239, where it is dated 1893–94.

7 Ossian Ekbohrn, on Sandhamn. Strindberg elaborates upon this account in *Inferno* (p.169) and in the second of the vivisections he called 'Nemesis Divina', written in French in 1894.

8 See Letter 371.

9 The reverse of a piece of paper attached to the letter at this point reads: 'Birger Mörner will end up in the dock if he doesn't watch out for his foul proclivities. 6 July 1896.'

377. To TORSTEN HEDLUND

1 Letter two in the Orfila series, paginated 13–20.

2 The chemists Sir Humphry Davy (1778–1829) and Claude Berthollet (1748–1822).

3 André Dubosc.

4 I.e. Good fortune, luck.

5 Strindberg visited Kinnekulle, a mountain near Lake Vänem noted for its occult associations, in October 1890.

6 A page torn from a book. It contains a poem describing the skylark, a short fable entitled 'The Two Sparrows', and an account of the woodpecker and its habits.

7 Accompanying the letter is a coloured print of a Viking ship. The pansies which stand in for the faces of its seven-man crew are expressively human in their markings. Cf. *Inferno*, p.148. For Stockenström, see Letter 370.

8 Rudolf Weyr (1847–1914), married to Frida Uhl's sister, Marie.

9 Megalomania.

10 Cf. *Inferno*, p.164.

11 L. E. Vial, author of *L'Attraction moléculaire*, which he sent Strindberg in 1895.

12 See headnote to Letter 540.

13 Shah Nasreddin (1831–96) had recently been murdered by an anarchist; the Swedish nobleman Oskar von Vegesack (b.1837) died 30 April 1896 while on a visit to Paris with Oscar II.

14 Like the previous two, this paragraph follows closely a series of (differently dated) entries in the *Occult Diary* where he identifies his correspondent as 'the illustrator Westergren' (i.e. Magnus Westergren (1844–?), a member of the Red Room circle who left Sweden in 1886 and eventually moved to America, where he illustrated (among other things) the works of Agassiz). Leif Eriksson (d.1021), the discoverer of Vinland (America).

378. To TORSTEN HEDLUND

1 The fifth letter in the Orfila sequence, paginated 37–46.

2 Cf. *Inferno*, p.136.

3 Bengt Lidforss.

4 See *Strindberg's måleri*, p.146, for the frottage of a crab's shell which accompanied this letter.

[5] See *Strindberg's måleri*, p.151.

[6] Don't let Nemesis hear of it!

[7] In *A Blue Book* (1907), Strindberg recounts a macabre joke of G. E. Klemming's, who arranged for a letter to be posted to a close friend some days after his death. Strindberg was much haunted by Klemming's spirit at this time.

[8] The spectacular fire which destroyed Sweden's first steam-mill took place on 31 October 1878.

[9] Strabo (*c.* 64 B.C.–A.D. 19), stoic and traveller, author of the *Geographica* in seventeen books.

[10] Fr. Svenonius, *Stenriket och jordens byggnad* (1888).

[11] René Just Haüy (1743–1822), author of the *Théorie sur la structure des cristaux* (Theory of the Structure of Crystals, 1793) and a *Traité de cristallographie* (Treatise on Cristallography, 1822).

[12] Piazzi Smyth, *Our Inheritance in the Great Pyramid*, fourth and much enlarged edition, London, 1880. Smyth, the Astronomer-Royal for Scotland, investigated the claim that the Pyramid had been built by Noah and provided a perfect system of weights and measures. When challenged, his conclusion that the Pyramid was a meteorological observatory for the whole world and part of a divine plan vindicating the ways of God to man brought about his resignation from the Royal Society.

379. To TORSTEN HEDLUND

[1] Letter seven in the Orfila sequence, paginated 47–52. Above the date Strindberg has written '(We'll see if this is the last letter)'. At 1.15 the same day he sent Hedlund a telegram in French declaring: 'Accident. Adresse incognito 4 rue de la Clé Paris. Mandats Strindberg' (Accident. Address incognito 4 rue de la Clé Paris. Money Orders Strindberg) The experiences described here are recounted in similar fashion in *Inferno*, p.172.

[2] See Letter 373.

[3] Strindberg did leave Paris for Dieppe to stay with the Norwegian painter Frits Thaulow, but not until 24 July.

[4] Prior to his first visit to Paris, in 1876, Strindberg wrote to the Deputy Editor of *Dagens Nyheter*, Carl Henrik Atterling: 'If . . . I were to shoot myself on Mt Dovre or in a garret in Mont-Martre – say a few kind words in D.N.'

[5] See Letter 371 and *Inferno*, p.163. In the *Occult Diary*, however, the hind (or Frida Uhl) beckons him to 'the southeast (the Danube)'.

380. To EDVARD MUNCH

[1] Max von Pettenkofer (1818–1901), German chemist, one of the founders of scientific hygiene. Among his publications is *Beziehungen der Luft zur Kleidung, Wohnung und Boden* (The Movement of Air through Clothing, Rooms and Floors), 4th edition, 1877.

381. To TORSTEN HEDLUND

[1] *La Lumière d'Egypte. La Science des astres et de l'âme* (The Light of Egypt. The Science of the Stars and of the Soul, 1896).

[2] Strindberg was actually born under Aquarius, though he may (just) have been conceived in Aries (21 March-19 April).

[3] The author of the *Astronomica,* a Latin didactic poem in five books in which he sees design and 'heavenly reason' in the organization of the universe.

[4] Olaus Magnus (1490–1557), historian, churchman and cartographer. In 1523 he went to Rome where, from 1526, he lived in exile, even after being appointed Catholic archbishop of Sweden in 1544.

[5] Megalomania.

[6] See Letter 369.

382. To TORSTEN HEDLUND

[1] Cf. the account in *Inferno,* p.182.

[2] This identification with Jacob, already apparent in *Inferno,* becomes central in a subsequent autobiographical text, *Jacob Wrestles* (1898).

383. To TORSTEN HEDLUND

[1] Two newspaper cuttings, one reporting an earthquake and flood in Japan, the other dealing with a case of split identity from William James' *Principles of Psychology* (1890).

[2] According to both the *Occult Diary* and *Inferno* (p.187), the Jardin des Plantes was devastated by a cyclone on 26 July, the same day that the Swedish engineer and explorer S. A. Andrée (1854–97) was to have embarked on a voyage by balloon to the North Pole with Strindberg's nephew, Nils. See Letter 402.

[3] See Letter 367.

384. To TORSTEN HEDLUND

[1] A letter from Frida Uhl inviting him to Austria. Cf. *Inferno,* p.120: 'For me this was like being recalled to life.' For the significance of 13 August, see Letter 371.

[2] Strindberg left Dieppe on the 28 July and arrived in Ystad by boat and train on the 30th.

[3] 'The Synthesis of Gold', published as a brochure in 1896.

385. To TORSTEN HEDLUND

[1] Hedlund had just attended a conference of theosophists in Dublin where he met a group of Americans calling themselves the 'Crusaders' for the salvation of Europe. He urged Strindberg to devote himself to an undertaking of this kind.

[2] Superman.

[3] August Röhss' 1,200 *kronor* (see Letter 363) were now all but exhausted.

[4] 'The Synthesis of Gold'.

387. To F. U. WRANGEL

[1] Strindberg had taken up an invitation to visit his daughter Kerstin in Austria.

[2] Both these collections are seemingly lost; the Austrian material, however, is now in the Royal Library, Stockholm.

[3] At your discretion.

[4] Heraclitus' '*panta rei*', or state of flux.

[5] The jeweller Jean Jahnsson (1854–1944), who bought a collection of manuscript material from Strindberg through Wrangel, which he donated to the Swedish Society of Authors.

[6] Daniel Fallström (1858–1937), writer and journalist, one of the six-man committee of the Society which handled the affair.

389. To TORSTEN HEDLUND

[1] Strindberg had long been fascinated by certain giant stones near Ystad. He pondered their origin as fossils, prehistoric sculptures, or communications from on high, and wondered (in another letter to Hedlund, 21 September) if they might not substantiate Rydberg's theory in *Undersökningar i germanisk mytologi* (Studies in Germanic Mythology, 1886–89) that 'Southern Sweden was an ancient cultural centre stemming perhaps directly from the original source, India.'

[2] Linnaeus' *Gotland Journey*, 1 July 1741.

390. To TORSTEN HEDLUND

[1] The same sentence appears on page one of the *Occult Diary*, but without the ironic allusion to Madame Blavatsky's *The Secret Doctrine*.

[2] An allusion to Bjørnson's play *Over Ævne* (Beyond Our Power).

[3] See Letter 378.

[4] Bernardin de Saint-Pierre (1737–1814), French naturalist and novelist (*Paul et Virginie*, 1787). A friend and disciple of Rousseau, he was placed in charge of the Jardin des Plantes in 1792. His writings on natural history, *Harmonies de la nature*, are characterized by acute if idiosyncratic powers of observation. They exerted considerable influence on Strindberg's similarly endowed speculations, most evidently in his essay 'The Sunflower' (1896).

[5] His experimental essay in 'rational mysticism', 'The Death's-Head Moth', included in both *Sylva Sylvarum* and *Jardin des Plantes*.

[6] 'Ash and Vine', the first pair of the *Voluspá* in the *Poetic Edda*.

[7] *The Expression of the Emotions in Man and the Animals* (1872).

[8] *Wärend och Wirdarne*, 2 volumes (1863–68), by the Swedish ethnologist Gunnar Olof Hyltén-Cavallius (1818–89), one of only fourteen books which appear in all three of Strindberg's book collections. For the illustrations, see volume I, p.110.

[9] Stuxberg (since 1882 keeper of the zoological collection at Gothenburg Museum) translated *The Great Sea-Serpent. An Historical and Critical Treatise* (Leiden, 1892) by Anthonie Cornelis Oudemans.

[10] See headnote to Letter 422.

391. To TORSTEN HEDLUND

[1] Literally 'Alder King'.

[2] One of Strindberg's boldest speculations in *The Swedish People* was to try and distinguish between the original racial groups in Sweden on the basis of the names

given the ladybird in different parts of the country. While not without error, his findings have been largely confirmed by later scholarship.

[3] This passage (from *L'Événement*, 26 October 1896) is incorporated into the text of *Inferno* (p.242), as is the cyclone which struck the Jardin des Plantes on 26 July. To Strindberg, ever alert against *envoûtement*, such events readily assumed a personal significance as emissions of psychic power.

[4] 'L'Exposition d'Edward Munch', *La Revue Blanche*, 1 June 1896.

[5] Jules Lermina (1839–1915), occultist and editor of the *Revue universelle internationale*. This correspondence has been lost.

[6] Strindberg's landlady in the rue de la Clef. In fact a friend of Hedberg's, Carl Lagerberg (1859–1922), had just arranged for Strindberg's belongings to be sent on to him. According to Lagerberg, Strindberg had accused Mme Kahn of having caused the September cyclone.

[7] Release.

[8] *Dagens Nyheter* reported (26 October) that a photograph of Gustav Adolf's burial vault in Riddarholm Church revealed an apparition of the king. It turned out to be a case of double exposure.

[9] See Letter 376, note 4.

[10] According to the *Occult Diary* (10 July 1897), *To Damascus* was originally called 'Robert le Diable' (and also 'Merlin').

[11] François Ravaillac (1578–1610), Henry IV's assassin.

[12] Besides the Chinese character Strindberg enclosed two illustrations of dragonflies.

[13] Hedlund had sent Madame Blavatsky's book to Strindberg, who replied (26 September) that nothing altered the opinion he had formed in 1884, namely that 'she hasn't had any visions; that she read it up in libraries and used other people's writings, that she is unoriginal.'

392. To F. U. WRANGEL

[1] The essay 'Etudes funèbres', first published in *Revue des Revues*, 15 July 1896; Strindberg now wished to rescind the permission he had given for a Swedish translation in *Vintergatan*, a yearbook published by the Association of Swedish Authors.

[2] A fairy-tale from the Swedish province of Småland, first published in Gunnar Olof Hyltén-Cavallius and George Stephens, *Svenska folk-sagor och äventyr* (Swedish Folk Tales and Adventures, 1844, p.119), which Strindberg frequently quoted, both in his letters and his works.

[3] Poverty comes from the Gods eternal.

[4] Kierkegaard's term 'the Individual'.

393. To TORSTEN HEDLUND

[1] This sentence is not to be found in any of the extant letters to Hedlund.

[2] An association with the name Azarias, assumed by the archangel Raphael when guiding the blind Tobit and his son Tobias in the Book of Tobit: 'I ought to call you Azarias because you lead me like Tobias,' Strindberg had written to Hedlund on 21 June 1896. 'Ariel' in Hebrew signifies 'the Lion of God', though Milton casts him as one of the fallen angels in *Paradise Lost*.

394. To GEORG BRANDES

[1] Brandes described their encounter in a letter to Geijerstam (7 December 1896): 'Strindberg, who was in Copenhagen . . . had left a card asking me to spend the evening with him. I went at once; he was already in bed and had been asleep for a while, but got up and we drank a glass of wine together at a café. He has never looked better: more remarkable, more serious, yet more careworn. He told me at once that his death was imminent, and returned to this again and again. He was suffering from persecution mania and explained to me that an enemy had driven him from France and was now driving him from place to place by magic, by sticking nails in his portrait and thus ruining his night's sleep, giving him raging palpitations of the heart and the like. He talked the whole time of magic. Magic was the latest phenomenon of the age and of the future. It was a natural power akin to those discovered by Charcot. But it was a mystery, terrible, a power from afar . . . Literature . . . no longer exists for him. A great mind broken.'

VIII

Notes to Letters 395–450

December 1896–May 1899

395. To ANDERS ELIASSON

[1] According to Marie Uhl, who wrote to Nilsson from Austria, Strindberg was suffering from persecution mania and believed that she and her sister wished to kill him by black magic. Her letter repeats Strindberg's claim that Nilsson (1855–1933), whom he first met in Skurup in 1891, was the only person in whom he had confidence because of his similar experiences.

[2] Strindberg interpreted the present climate as the fulfilment of a remark attributed to the eminent neurologist Charcot, which he was fond of quoting: '*Avant 50 ans d'ici, disait Charcot peu de temps avant sa mort, les procès de sorcellerie reparaîtront sous un autre nom*' (Before fifty years have passed, said Charcot, shortly before his death, the witch trials will reappear under another name, *Le Gaulois*, 2 July 1896).

[3] The Marquis Stanislas de Guaita (1861–97), founder of the Cabbalistic Order of the Rosy Cross and author of *Essais des sciences maudits*, 3 volumes (Essays on Damned Sciences, 1886–97). It was de Guiata who led the widely reported *envoûtement* of Huysman's friend, the Abbé Boullan, in 1893.

[4] See Letter 376, note 4 and R. Baldick, *J. -K. Huysmans* (Oxford, 1955), p.170.

[5] Sir Kenhelm Digby (1603–65), son of Sir Everard Digby, who was executed for his part in the Gunpowder Plot, and author of *The Nature of Bodies* (1644) and *The Nature of Man's Soul* (1644).

[6] What's to be done?

[7] Torsten Hedlund.

396. To KERSTIN STRINDBERG

[1] Here Strindberg includes a now faded sketch.

[2] The landscape around Klam, and particularly the sunken road or gorge known locally as the *Schluchtweg*, made a deep impression on Strindberg, who linked it with the topography of the hells he had read about in Dante, Viktor Rydberg, and Swedenborg. He introduced it into both *To Damascus* and *Inferno* (see especially pp.212–14). To mark the centenary of Strindberg's birth in 1949, the pass at Klam was renamed the 'Strindberg Weg'.

[3] A six-year-old relation to Kerstin, a dog and a cat respectively.

[4] In Austria it is customary to give children presents on St Nicholas' Day (6 December).

397. To MARIE UHL

[1] Strindberg was now learning to ride a bike and gathering material for 'Scanian

Landscapes', a series of articles he wrote for *Malmö-Tidningen* (The Malmö Paper).

[2] On 14 February, he had written to Austria of his impending departure for Paris, where he intended to remain 'for the rest of my life'.

[3] For chemistry, though the following week he wrote again: 'What would I like most? To spend the spring in Klam with my child, and there, in two months, write my most beautiful book – *Inferno*, so beautifully written that I should win the Nobel Prize for Literature. That is 300,000 francs.'

398. To MARIE UHL

[1] Casting himself as Napoleon, whose second marriage was also to an Austrian, Strindberg elaborated a series of parallels between himself, Frida Uhl's family, and the French Emperor. As Nils Norman has shown ('Strindberg och Napoleon', *Svensk litteraturtidskrift*, 22:4 (1959), 151–70), this half-serious, half-playful exercise in script writing and associational thinking has left traces in several of his works besides the letters.

[2] Having let matters lie during the latter part of 1896, Frida, who without Strindberg's knowledge was pregnant by Frank Wedekind, made a new application for divorce on 5 February 1897.

[3] Strindberg had found yet another correlative for himself in Edward Bulwer-Lytton's novel *Zanoni* (1842), where the magician Zanoni is placed between two women, Viola (for Strindberg, Frida Uhl) and Fillida (Dagny Juel). As in *Inferno*, the protagonist of Lytton's novel must choose between love and wisdom.

399. To VILHELM CARLHEIM-GYLLENSKÖLD

[1] See Letter 381. Between 1894 and 1897, Gyllensköld was an astronomer at the Stockholm Observatory.

[2] This idea is clarified in a letter to Hedlund (31 October 1896): 'The world view that has evolved in me comes closest to that of Pythagoras, which Origen later adopted. We are in hell for sins committed in a previous existence. Therefore pray for nothing save resignation! and expect nothing, absolutely nothing from life. Be happy, if possible, in adversity: for with each misfortune an entry is deleted from your deficit column! Though he did not intend it as such, Swedenborg's description of Inferno is so close to earthly life, so exact, that I am convinced.' Strindberg in fact derives the idea of earth as a penal colony for crimes committed in a previous existence from Schopenhauer's *Parerga und Paralipomena*, II, section 157, which also refers to Pythagoras and Origen.

[3] 'Un regard vers le Ciel', *L'Initiation*, April 1896.

400. To KERSTIN STRINDBERG

[1] In Strindberg's *Inferno*, Kerstin is allotted the role of Beatrice.

[2] Joseph (called Joséphin) Péladan (1859–1918), French writer and occultist, self-styled Magus and Sâr, founder (with Stanislas de Guaita) of the Ordre de la Rose-Croix, whose Grand Master he became in 1890. *Comment on devient mage* (How One Becomes a Magus) appeared in 1892. See Letter 426 and headnote to Letter 526.

[3] Pappa.

401. To GUSTAF AF GEIJERSTAM

[1] *Inferno.* Geijerstam became literary editor at Gernandts in January 1897 and had approached Strindberg on their behalf, the first letter to pass between them since 1892. Over the next few years, he acted virtually as Strindberg's Stockholm agent.

[2] *Inferno* was written in French, and Strindberg equipped the edition which appeared in Paris in 1898 with a Prelude. This comprised the 1876 Postlude to the verse *Master Olof,* which is modelled on a 16th century fragment, *De Creatione Mundi or Mankind's Creation and Fall.* He also inserted three additional chapters (following p.127 in the Penguin text) taken from *Sylva Sylvarum* and including the essays 'The Death's-Head Moth' and 'Etudes funèbres'. These items had already been published elsewhere in Sweden.

[3] Eugène Fahlstedt was again entrusted with translating Strindberg's French into Swedish.

402. To JOHAN OSCAR STRINDBERG

[1] Strindberg last wrote to his cousin in March 1891.

[2] Nils Strindberg (1872–97), a member of the three-man Andrée expedition which attempted to reach the North Pole by balloon. The balloon lifted off from Spitzbergen on 11 July 1897 but came down some sixty-five hours later on pack ice. Travelling with the ice, the three men reached White Island, where they perished. The remains of the expedition, including Andrée's diary, were discovered in 1930.

[3] Strindberg's youthful pseudonym, 'Örnen' (The Eagle), was also the name of Andrée's balloon.

403. To GUSTAF AF GEIJERSTAM

[1] Before the people. Strindberg placed the expression at the head of the French text of *Inferno.*

[2] Strindberg had heard she was translating *Inferno* into German.

[3] 'Vilse i livet' (Lost in Life).

[4] Geijerstam's novel, *Medusas huvud* (The Head of Medusa, 1895).

[5] The sequel to *Inferno.*

404. To GUSTAF AF GEIJERSTAM

[1] See Letter 367.

[2] Paul Herrmann. See Letter 367 and *Inferno,* p.138.

[3] Such, for example, is the one reported in the *Revue spirite* for February 1859, page 41, under the heading: My friend Hermann (!). It concerns a young German, in high society, quiet, kind and of the most honourable character who every evening, at sunset, falls into a state resembling death; during this time his spirit comes to life in the Antipodes, in Australia, in the body of a wicked scoundrel, who ends up being hanged. (Cf. my Herrmann, who slept till 6 p.m. on Good Friday. – Aren't you on the Cross? . . .)

[4] *Kåserier i mystik* (1897).

[5] Preparatory School.

407. To KERSTIN STRINDBERG

[1] The German edition of *Inferno* appeared in November 1897.

408. To GUSTAF AF GEIJERSTAM

[1] Strindberg had written to Geijerstam on 2 November, fearing that *Inferno* might be prosecuted for blasphemy.
[2] Georg Bondi (1865–?). His Skandinavische Bibliotek, edited by Geijerstam, specialized in contemporary works published by Gernandts.
[3] Pilgrimage.
[4] [payable] on sight.
[5] Erik Sjöstedt (pen name Osborne, 1866–1929), *Dagens Nyheter*'s Paris correspondent.
[6] Refers to events surrounding the installation of the astronomer Carl Charlier (1862–1934) as Professor in Lund on 30 September 1897. The conservative majority among the students opposed him for his involvement in the radical Verdandi group in Uppsala, but at a dinner in his honour Bengt Lidforss spoke up on his behalf, and also revealed that as a schoolboy, he had been similarly blind to the virtues of Strindberg's *Getting Married.*
[7] I serve and we serve higher powers.
[8] Bengt Lidforss' sister, who was engaged to Geijerstam's brother, Emanuel (1867–1928). They married in 1899.
[9] Strindberg means Tavastjerna's verse narrative *Laureatus* (1897).
[10] See headnote to Letter 422.
[11] The painter Ernst Josephson's much publicized mental breakdown occurred in 1888, at a time when he and Allan Österlind were occupied with spiritism.
[12] See Letter 404.
[13] A German journal for modern art and literature, founded 1894.
[14] I hate! hate everything and everybody apart from myself . . . No, I love myself . . . because I hate everybody else.
[15] Marcel Réja. See headnote to Letter 410.
[16] The astral plane.

409. To WALDEMAR BÜLOW

[1] My dear Waldemar Bülow.
[2] *Skånska Aftonbladet*, which had accused Strindberg of plagiarizing Huysman's novel *En route* (1895) in *Inferno.*
[3] This tallies with the *Occult Diary* where the entry for 18 September reads: 'Read Huysmans' *En route*, which I didn't know. It's strange how his development runs like mine. From magic and Satanism to Catholicism.'
[4] See Letter 47. Leopold von Sacher Masoch (1836–95), Austrian novelist, author of *Venus in Pelz* (Venus in Furs, 1870).
[5] Strindberg is referring to an account of his youthful Manichean speculations in Volume 3 of *The Son of a Servant* (*Samlade skrifter*, 19, p.81). He made the same claim three years earlier in a letter to Littmansson: 'Do you remember how we anticipated the whole current *fin-de-siècle* movement and even Satanism out there on Kymmendö? Do you remember "Strindberg's Religion" with Satan as the ruler of the world! . . . We were further on then than Huysmans is now!' (17 July 1894).
[6] Strindberg's rebuttal was published in *Folkets Tidning*, 22 November 1897.

410. To MARCEL RÉJA

1 Should read 25 June 1897.
2 See Letter 401, note 2.

411. To AXEL HERRLIN

1 Strindberg, who had been hoping Herrlin would come to Paris, heard he had returned to Germany after visiting Florence with the sculptor Axel Ebbe (1868–1941).

2 Strindberg's interjection. The remarks on Calvin occur in section 798 of the *Vera christiana religio* (True Christian Religion, 1771).

3 The Abbot of the Benedictine Monastery at Solesmes in Belgium had been dismissed for immorality.

4 Clarified in *Legends* as the divinities of religions past and present, who struggle with one another for mastery of the world. Herrlin had ventured the opinion that Zola had a propaedeutic role to play in this on the side of Christ through his intervention in the Dreyfus Affair. Strindberg disagreed.

5 St Louis and Joan of Arc have pity on France.

6 *Jacob Wrestles*.

7 Cf. *Inferno*, p.193.

8 See Letter 422, note 6.

9 On 21 December 1897.

10 Refers to a *cause célèbre* involving accusations of murder and illegitimacy among the Swedish aristocracy.

11 The terms derive from Swedenborg. See *Inferno*, p.257.

412. To GUSTAF AF GEIJERSTAM

1 *To Damascus I*.
2 Viggo Adler, who was translating *Legends* into Danish.

413. To GUSTAF AF GEIJERSTAM

1 *To Damascus I*.

414. To AXEL HERRLIN

1 In a letter now appended to the *Occult Diary*, Herrlin had informed Strindberg that he had obtained proofs of *Legends* only minutes before the book went to press. He requested the omission of certain details, mainly to do with his sexual experiences as depicted by Strindberg. The cuts were made in the Swedish edition, but not in the Norwegian or French. Herrlin then moved on to discuss a number of infernal events in his life which prompted Strindberg's response in the remainder of this letter.

2 The Beyond.

3 Gustaf Brand. See headnote to Letter 429. Strindberg planned a play entitled 'Magnus the Good'. The material was eventually used in *The Saga of the Folkungs*,

but not for another twelve months.

415. To GUSTAF AF GEIJERSTAM

[1] Maredsous, where his friend Gustaf Brand had been converted to Catholicism. The visit took place, but not until the summer. See Letter 427.

[2] Attraction.

[3] The Luxembourg Gardens, which figure prominently in *Jacob Wrestles*.

[4] Emil Hillberg, and Albert Ranft, who had staged *Master Olof* to great acclaim at the Vasa Theatre in 1897.

416. To GUSTAF AF GEIJERSTAM

[1] *To Damascus I*.

[2] In *Gjentagelsen* (Repetition, 1843), which Strindberg first read in 1871.

[3] In *To Damascus I*, the final eight scenes retrace the path taken by the protagonist during the first eight, the journey out and back pivoting upon the episode in the Asylum, which is the only setting not to be duplicated.

[4] Unconscious.

[5] August Lindberg.

[6] Viggo Adler. Nothing came of this idea.

[7] It's theatrical, for the theatre.

[8] In order to conceal his identity, references in *Legends* to Herrlin as 'the young doctor' and 'the young professor' were replaced by 'the young man'. (See Letter 414.)

417. To WALDEMAR BÜLOW

[1] Bülow's housekeeper.

418. To ELISABETH STRINDBERG

[1] Strindberg returned to Lund at the beginning of April, and remained there a further fourteen months.

[2] Elisabeth Strindberg was suffering from deep depression and feelings of persecution. She was admitted to a mental hospital later that year.

419. To ALGOT RUHE

[1] French writer (1865–1901), close friend of Gauguin and of Strindberg.

[2] *Mercure de France*, who published Strindberg's novel in 1898.

[3] *Det yttersta skäret* (1898).

421. To KARIN, GRETA AND HANS STRINDBERG

[1] *To Damascus I*.

422. To GUSTAF FRÖDING

[1] Strindberg, who heard about them second-hand from Bengt Lidforss, had recounted a number of Fröding's recent experiences in *Legends*.

[2] Fröding's latest volume of poems, *Gralstänk*, which had just appeared.

[3] Strindberg means the story 'Nature the Criminal'.

[4] An allusion to the poem 'Esplanadsystemet' (1883), one of the most direct expressions of Strindberg's early radicalism. The Burned Site (*Brända tomten*) became the title of his second Chamber Play, written in 1907.

[5] Louis-Claude de Saint-Martin (1743–1803), French mystic and freemason, greatly influenced by the ideas of Jakob Böhme and also by Swedenborg.

[6] Pseudonym of Alphonse Louis Constant (1810–75), author of a *Histoire de la magie* (History of Magic, 1860) and *La Clé des grandes mystères* (The Key to the Great Mysteries, 1861). Perhaps the central figure in the French occult revival, Levi's teaching owed much to the Cabbala.

[7] Strindberg alludes to the exchanges between Io and Prometheus, lines 756–80, and to Prometheus' next two speeches.

423. To EMIL SCHERING

[1] A letter from the Freie Bühne's lawyer demanding repayment of the money which Strindberg had received from them in 1892. (See Letter 283.)

[2] *Quickborn*. Schering was preparing a special number on Strindberg and Munch, though Strindberg had doubts about the venture, which he communicated to Schering: 'As for Munch, who is my enemy, I am unwilling to be paired with him, particularly as I'm certain he won't miss an opportunity of sticking me with a poisoned knife, especially if he's supposed to be illustrating my pieces' (10 June 1898). Nevertheless, the issue appeared in January 1899 and included ten poems from the 1883 volume, the opening section of *Somnambulist Nights*, *Simoom*, and the stories 'Towards the Sun' and 'The Silver Marsh'.

[3] Richard Dehmel (1863–1920), German lyric poet (*Weib und Welt*, [Woman and World], 1896), a member of the Ferkel circle and good friend of Strindberg's in Berlin.

[4] 'Types and Prototypes', written and published to commemorate the fiftieth anniversary of the Swedish chemist Jöns Jakob Berzelius (1779–1848).

[5] Ermete Zacconi (1867–1948), the outstanding Italian actor of his generation. He performed *The Father* in Venice (1897) and Milan (1898).

[6] Schering's wife, who translated *Simoom* and four of the poems for *Quickborn*.

425. To EMIL KLÉEN

[1] Leonard Wistén (1857–1921), teacher, a mutual friend.

[2] I.e. Marcel Réja and Paul Herrmann (Schlatter).

[3] Kleksography entailed placing a blob of ink in a fold of paper and pressing the two sides together, thus forming a butterfly-like figure which Strindberg hoped would resemble a Death's-Head Moth. See *Kleksographie* (1890), a posthumous work by the German romantic, Justinus Kerner (1786–1862).

[4] *To Damascus II*.

[5] I am sad.

[6] Strindberg was perplexed as to how the corncrake, which according to Pliny

could neither fly nor swim, was able to migrate. See Letter 572.

[7] A tavern in Lund much frequented by Strindberg and his friends.

426. To EMIL KLÉEN

[1] Superman.

[2] Strindberg reproduces this assessment of Péladan almost verbatim in *Gothic Rooms* (1904). The contrast with Zola was a common one. Péladan himself conceived *La Décadence latine*, a sequence of fourteen novels commencing in 1884 with *Le Vice suprême*, as a complement and rejoinder to Zola's *Les Rougon-Macquart* cycle.

[3] Zola's address during the trial which followed his writing *J'accuse*, and from where he escaped to London on 22 July.

427. To KERSTIN STRINDBERG

[1] Heyst-aan-zee, on the Belgian coast.

[2] A renowned Benedictine monastery on the Danube, not far from Klam.

[3] Albert Langen, who Strindberg believed had 'abducted' Frida Uhl. In fact he had married Bjørnson's youngest daughter, Dagny, in 1896. The other allusions remain obscure.

428. To EMIL KLÉEN

[1] On 24 August Nicholas II had invited the other European nations to arms limitation talks, which led to the first Peace Conference at the Hague, in 1899.

[2] Colonel Hubert Henry, the officer in the Statistical (or counter-espionage) Section of the French War Office whose investigations had set the Dreyfus Affair in motion, committed suicide on 1 September after admitting to having forged a document in order to sustain the case against Dreyfus. Strindberg's reactionary stance over Dreyfus was linked to the notions of guilt and suffering that he had evolved during the Inferno crisis. Quite simply, having suffered so much (in a real penal colony), Dreyfus had to be guilty if any sense was to be made of his experience. Were Dreyfus' sufferings without cause, then maybe his own afflictions had no meaning. As he wrote, in the *Occult Diary* (14 April 1899): 'No one suffers innocently, D. must be guilty to suffer so immeasurably.'

[3] I believe it because it's absurd.

[4] Fröding remained in hospital in Uppsala, Georg Brandes had been in Sicily and was bedridden with phlebitis.

429. To GUSTAF BRAND

[1] Kléen was in a sanitorium in Jämtland; Johan Mortensen (1864–1940), who wrote an interesting volume of memoirs, *Strindberg som jag minnes honom* (Strindberg as I Remember Him, 1931), was Professor of Literature in Gothenburg. For Strömstedt, see headnote to Letter 451.

430. To GUSTAF BRAND

1 *Nichts passiert*: Nothing happened.

431. To GUSTAF AF GEIJERSTAM

1 Geijerstam's six-year-old son, Sven, had recently died.

432. To GUSTAF AF GEIJERSTAM

1 Geijerstam's wife, Eugenia.
2 Following his seventieth birthday on 3 March 1898, Ibsen had visited Stockholm, where he was received with great acclaim.
3 In honour of his fiftieth birthday.

433. To GUSTAF AF GEIJERSTAM

1 His children in Finland.
2 *The Cloister*.
3 Here: mental energy, inspiration.
4 Hedberg had reviewed *To Damascus* favourably in *Svenska Dagbladet*.

434. To GUSTAF AF GEIJERSTAM

1 See Letter 432.

435. To EMIL KLÉEN

1 Kléen had now been admitted to hospital in Lund, where he died on 12 December.
2 *Advent*.

436. To ANON

1 Meir Aron Goldschmidt (1819–87), Danish novelist whose autobiography, *Livs-erindringer og Resultater* (Life's Memories and Results, 1877), articulates a belief in retributive justice. Although he refers here to Goldschmidt, whom he was reading at the time, Strindberg had long been familiar with the concept through Linnaeus' posthumously published collection of examples, *Nemesis Divina*.

437. To GUSTAF AF GEIJERSTAM

1 *Advent*.
2 To Stockholm.

439. To KARIN, GRETA AND HANS STRINDBERG

1 Greta had been engaged by the Folkteater in Helsinki from January 1899.
2 *Advent.*
3 *The Saga of the Folkungs.*

440. To GUSTAF AF GEIJERSTAM

1 The original title was 'The Mausoleum' after the resplendent tomb which the wealthy judge and his wife – based on Frida Uhl's grandparents, the Reischls – have erected for themselves at the start of the play.
2 Geijerstam had suggested asking the eminent Swedish composer Wilhelm Stenhammar (1871–1927) to provide a musical score. Nothing came of this idea, but Stenhammar later composed incidental music to both *A Dream Play* and *The Saga of the Folkungs.*

441. To HJALMAR BRANTING

1 In congratulating Strindberg on reaching fifty, Branting had revived the idea of a state pension.
2 Beyond.
3 Distance, background.

442. To CARL LARSSON

1 Strindberg had last written to Larsson in January 1894.
2 On the occasion of Strindberg's fiftieth birthday.
3 Roughly the years that *Master Olof* remained unperformed.

443. To KERSTIN STRINDBERG

1 Original in English.
2 *Crimes and Crimes.*

444. To RICHARD BERGH

1 Presumably the drawings in *Quickborn*. See Letter 423.
2 On 24 February, Strindberg told Geijerstam he 'had read eight volumes of Kipling with increasing admiration.' He listed several of his favourite stories, including 'The Brushwood Boy', 'The Mask of the Beast', 'The Conversion of Aurelian McGoggin', and 'The Finest Story Ever Told', on the cover of the *Occult Diary*.

445. To GRETA STRINDBERG

1 Greta had made her debut as an amateur in a verse drama, *Kan ej* (Can Not),

by Finland's national poet, Johan Ludvig Runeberg (1804–77).

[2] In Berns' restaurant in Stockholm, previously the location of the Red Room.

[3] On 30 May 1896 Strindberg had written to Karin, Greta and Hans from the Hôtel Orfila, reminding them that in the event of his death they had his Collected Works as security. If necessary they were to obtain Count Snoilsky's assistance in their sale. When Siri von Essen sought the latter's help, Snoilsky replied that he could do nothing without Strindberg's written authorization. When, and in what form, this authorization was given is unclear.

[4] In February 1886 Bonnier absolved Strindberg of all his outstanding debts to the firm, amounting to some 8,000 *kronor*.

446. To LEOPOLD LITTMANSSON

[1] A pun on his own initials which can also mean 'swine' in Swedish.

[2] Strindberg had sent Littmansson *Crimes and Crimes* for him to turn into French.

[3] The stage directions for Act II, Scene 1, of *Crimes and Crimes* specify a pianist in an adjoining room practising the finale of Beethoven's Piano Sonata Opus 31, No. 2, generally known as 'The Tempest' but often called 'The Ghost Sonata' by Strindberg (see Letter 554).

[4] Roughly: 'common woman', or 'prostitute', 'strumpet', and 'these women' in Act III, Scene 2, where Henriette is shadowed by two detectives and accused of being a whore, thus implementing a dénouement Strindberg had plotted for Dagny Juel five years earlier (not ten, as he suggests in the next letter) when writing to Bengt Lidforss on 3 January 1894: 'If it concerned me, I'd have the police take her for a whore one dark night when she's out on the prowl.'

447. To GUSTAF AF GEIJERSTAM

[1] An alternative title for *Crimes and Crimes*.

[2] Already.

[3] The triad of Hindu Gods Brahma, Vishnu and Siva, but here a tripartite pun or rhyming witticism such as Strindberg often used to employ, usually in his letters to Littmansson, and generally untranslatable.

[4] Geijerstam's eldest son.

448. To GUSTAF AF GEIJERSTAM

[1] Geijerstam's wife suffered from renal tuberculosis and had tried to commit suicide.

[2] Curious everyday events which Strindberg thought to make the basis of a book on the lines of *Antikrists Mirakler* (Miracles of Antichrist, 1897) by Selma Lagerlöf (1858–1940).

449. To KARL OTTO BONNIER

[1] Bonnier had relinquished the rights on those novels and stories he had published to Gernandts, for a collected edition. This began to appear in October 1899.

[2] Lorentz Henrik Dietrichson (1834–1917), Norwegian writer on art and literature, resident in Sweden 1869–75 as a popular lecturer at the Academy of the Free Arts in Stockholm. In his memoirs, *En norrmans minnen från Sverige* (A Norwegian's Memories of Sweden, 1901–02), Dietrichson tells of how, at the start of Strindberg's career, he 'did him a kindness which he never forgot'.
[3] Bonnier sent Strindberg the required information.

450. To AUGUST LINDBERG

[1] *Gustav Vasa.*

IX

Notes to Letters 451–608
June 1899–May 1908

451. To ADOLF STRÖMSTEDT

1 The Island of the Blessed.
2 *The Saga of the Folkungs*, published autumn 1899 but not staged until 1901.

452. To KERSTIN STRINDBERG

1 Kerstin had been placed in a boarding school in the Austrian village Haag; Strindberg pretended to believe she was in Den Haag for the peace conference.
2 Bertha von Suttner (1843–1914), novelist and founder of the Austrian Pacifist Society. Awarded the Nobel Peace Prize in 1905.
3 Cf. the Rose Room in *Inferno* (p.206) and *To Damascus I*, Scenes 8 and 10.
4 Anna Philp.

454. To NILS ANDERSSON

1 Erik Johan Stagnelius (1793–1823), Swedish Romantic poet who, following a severe personal crisis in 1817, adopted a fervent but heretical form of Christianity derived from Plato, Plotinus, Swedenborg, the Pythagoreans and the Gnostics.
2 Strindberg made sketches for a play on Karl IX but never wrote one.
3 Anders de Wahl (1869–1959), stage and film actor. Engaged by Albert Ranft, he played leading roles in a series of Strindberg productions during the 1890s, including Lucky Peter, Gustav Vasa and Erik XIV. De Wahl was also a friend of Andersson.

455. To ALBERT RANFT

1 The première took place on 17 October with Emil Hillberg in the title role.
2 Now Ranft's literary advisor.
3 *Erik XIV* opened on 30 November, but not with this cast.
4 Julia Håkansson (1853–1940), renowned for her performances in Ibsen.

456. To HARALD MOLANDER

1 Should read Göran Persson, Erik's friend and adviser.
2 Strindberg had played a nobleman in Bjørnson's *Mary Stuart in Scotland* at the Royal Theatre in 1869. According to *The Son of a Servant*, he disliked the play.
3 Andreas Peter Berggreen, *Folkesange og Melodier*, 2nd ed., 11 vols (Copenhagen,

1861–71).
[4] Anders de Wahl, who played Erik.

457. To OSCAR STRINDBERG

[1] Strindberg's brother Olof, master gardener at the Lövsta iron works in North Uppland.

459. To EMIL SCHERING

[1] Presumably written for insertion in a journal in Germany. See Letter 479.

460. To GUSTAF AF GEIJERSTAM

[1] Strindberg visited Geijerstam, whose wife had died after a long illness, on 6 May.

461. To NILS ANDERSSON

[1] Håkon Gillberg (1862–1924), a lawyer. Both the Lawyer in *A Dream Play* and Edvard Libotz in the novella *The Scapegoat* are drawn with Gillberg in mind.

462. To EMIL GRANDINSON

[1] Bjørn Halldén (1862–1935), conductor of the Royal Theatre Orchestra, later a *conférencier* in cabaret.
[2] For the première of *To Damascus* on 19 November 1900, Strindberg specified that the second movement of Beethoven's Piano Sonata Opus 10, No. 3 should be played before the curtain rose.

463. To LEOPOLD LITTMANSSON

[1] Presumably Littmansson's translation of *Crimes and Crimes*.
[2] Loiseau's Paris address; he, Strindberg and Littmansson had come into conflict over translating *By the Open Sea* in 1894.
[3] Nietzsche.
[4] With his new play *Casper's Shrove Tuesday* in mind, Strindberg had asked Littmansson the names of the characters which figured in French Punch and Judy shows.

464. To NILS PERSONNE

[1] *Easter* and *Casper's Shrove Tuesday*.
[2] In *Easter*.
[3] See headnote to Letter 465.

[4] August Palme (1856–1924). He and Harriet Bosse appeared in the Swedish première of *Easter*, which took place at the Royal Theatre, 4 April 1901.

465. To HARRIET BOSSE

[1] Their highly-charged encounter at the dress rehearsal, including a mysterious kiss that Strindberg believed Bosse had given him, is recorded in detail in the *Occult Diary* (see *Inferno*, p.277). The entry also records the first of many erotic dreams in which she featured, both before, during, and after their marriage.

469. To EMIL SCHERING

[1] Part Two of *The Dance of Death* or an extract from it. Part One had been written the previous October.

470. To RICHARD BERGH

[1] *Hinsides* (Beyond, 1900) by the Danish writer Hannah Joël (pseudonym for Helga Johansen, 1852–1912), which depicts a spiritual crisis she had undergone.
[2] Amalie Skram (1847–1905), Danish–Norwegian writer. Her novel *Professor Hieronymus* (1895) depicted neurotic patients in hospital, and followed closely upon her own experience. It deeply impressed Strindberg when he read it in September 1899. (The character of Hieronymus was based on Doctor Knud Pontopiddan at the Roskilde mental hospital outside Copenhagen, whom Strindberg had consulted about his health in 1887, shortly after writing *The Father*.)
[3] *Vie de Saint François d'Assise* (1893) by the French theologian, Paul Sabatier (1858–1928).
[4] The collection of essays *Le Trésor des humbles* (The Treasure of the Humble, 1896), part of which (including 'Le Réveil de l'âme' – The Awakening of the Soul) Strindberg translated as a gift for Harriet Bosse.
[5] It is said that a spiritual epoch is upon us . . . and signs of life that we cannot explain are everywhere, vibrating by the side of the life of every day . . . and on the *sensibility* as well as the *extraordinary presence* of the soul . . . Signs and words no longer count for anything, and in mystic circles it is the mere presence that decides almost all . . . Far above words and acts do they judge their fellows – nay, far above thought – for that which they see, though they understand it not, lies well beyond the domain of thought. *The Treasure of the Humble*, translated by Alfred Sutro, pocket edition (London, 1908), pp.25, 27, 35, 40–41.
[6] Geijerstam.

471. To HARRIET BOSSE

[1] The singer Dagmar Möller (1866–1954) and her husband, the architect Carl Möller (1857–1933). Cf. Möller the Murderer in Strindberg's last play, *The Great Highway*, in which he gives vent to his feeling that the Möllers had come between him and Bosse.
[2] *The Crown Bride*.
[3] Maeterlinck's first play, published in 1889.

472. To RICHARD BERGH

[1] *La Prométhéide, Trilogie d'Eschyle en quatre tableaux* (1895).

[2] Per Hallström (1866–1960), Swedish writer remembered, if at all, for his novels and short stories. Strindberg corresponded briefly with Hallström, and the two met in 1902. However, they were never close and Hallström grew to be critical of Strindberg, both as a man and a writer. Strindberg, he concluded, in a letter to Geijerstam, was not the sort of person one could admit to one's home.

[3] Jules-Amédée Barbey d'Aurevilly (1808–89), French Catholic writer; his collection of short stories *Les Diaboliques* (The She-Devils) appeared in 1874.

475. To HARRIET BOSSE

[1] A play by Péladan.

[2] The bridegroom and the bride of humanity.

[3] Anna Boberg's (1864–1935) libretto for an opera of that name by Wilhelm Stenhammar, first performed in 1898.

476. To HARRIET BOSSE

[1] On 4 March Harriet Bosse confirmed in writing that the Stranger of *To Damascus III* should forget all about the monastery he contemplated entering and remain in the world with the Lady, though her letter betrayed a fear that the latter might not be strong enough to sustain her role (see *Inferno*, p.295). On 5 March the two became engaged.

477. To KERSTIN STRINDBERG

[1] The *Schluchtweg*. See Letter 396.

479. To EMIL SCHERING

[1] In a recent letter (5 March), Strindberg had asked Schering to find out if *A Midsummer Night's Dream* was currently being performed in Germany. With Bosse's success as Puck in mind, he continued: 'If so we could always offer them a guest performance – in Swedish. For after all, what Puck says is unimportant and familiar to the audience – in any case, the Swedish language sounds so mild – but her movements, the wonderful play of her body, that most captivating childlike smile on her little face, with its two rows of milk teeth, the youthful proportions of her slender figure, all this makes it worth seeing, like music for the eye.' Schering responded with the news that Alfred Halm, who had staged *Crimes and Crimes* in Breslau in 1900, now planned a production of *Gustav Adolf*.

[2] The part of the ten-year-old Trumpeter Nils in *Gustav Adolf* has sometimes been played by an actress.

[3] Photographs of Bosse in the role.

[4] During 1901 Schering published three pamphlets containing comments by Strindberg and others on his work.

[5] Alfred Dreyfus (1876–?), who wrote on Strindberg in the *Deutsch-Französische*

Rundschau. It was probably to Dreyfus that Strindberg directed the comment in Letter 459.

480. To HARRIET BOSSE

[1] The leading part in the play of that name which depicts the apotheosis of a pure love and provided Harriet Bosse with, as it were, a role model for their marriage. To Emil Grandinson, he described it as 'a morning gift for my wife' (23 March 1901).

[2] Fredrik Nycander (1867–1944), writer and critic.

[3] Pehr Staaff and Tor Hedberg.

[4] The heroine of *The Crown Bride*, a peasant girl who gives her illegitimate child to the midwife to kill and bury, so that she may appear at her wedding wearing a virgin's crown.

481. To KARIN, GRETA AND HANS STRINDBERG

[1] Both Greta and Karin had written to say that the money he was sending them (700 marks in December, 500 in February, 300 in March) was insufficient.

482. To HARRIET BOSSE

[1] Den Okände, the name of the protagonist in *To Damascus* whose identity Strindberg here conflates with his own.

[2] An allusion to two separate remarks in Scene One of *To Damascus I*.

483. To HARRIET BOSSE

[1] Strindberg's third marriage had begun ominously. Though a honeymoon to Germany and Switzerland was planned, Strindberg surprised Harriet on the morning of their departure by telling her: 'We aren't going, the Powers won't allow it.' Harriet left on her own for Hornbæk in Denmark, where Strindberg joined her at the beginning of July. They proceeded to Berlin but clashed again at the Café Bauer, which Strindberg described as a 'whore's café' ('The things you then imputed to me have so sullied me that the most loving words you could utter would never wash them away or cover them up,' Harriet wrote to him on 27 August). They returned to Stockholm on 7 August; two days later it was confirmed that Harriet was pregnant. On 22 August, while Strindberg was writing *A Dream Play*, Harriet left him a letter saying she had 'gone forever'.

[2] According to the *Occult Diary* (20 August), Harriet informed him that 'the child's name was to be Bosse. Tit for tat!'

[3] Anna Hofman-Uddgren (1868–1947), a well-known variety actress who married Strindberg's friend, the journalist Gustaf Uddgren (1865–1927), and later filmed both *The Father* and *Miss Julie*.

[4] *Easter*.

[5] A bewitching figure in a story by Jonas Lie, who exercises a magnetic power over men. The story had been dramatized in 1897.

[6] Where Harriet's sisters, Inez Ahlquist and Dagmar Möller, had their homes

484. To HARRIET BOSSE

[1] Emanuel Swedenborg's fiancée, who figures in *Charles XII*, the play which Strindberg completed on the eve of Harriet's departure for Denmark. The role was written for her, but her pregnancy prevented her acting it at the première on 13 February 1902.
[2] See Letter 465 and *Inferno*, p.277.
[3] Their bedroom at 40 Karlavägen was decorated in yellow.
[4] The Norwegian-born Axel Hansson (1869–1911), who played opposite Bosse in *Easter*. Strindberg suspected them of having a relationship.
[5] Harriet's sister, Inez Ahlquist (1863–1947).

485. To HARRIET BOSSE

[1] On 27 August Harriet had written to him: 'Remember what I always said: "I'll do anything you like, if only you're kind to me." '
[2] Emil Sjögren (1853–1918), Swedish composer, notably of lieder.
[3] Cf. Letter 292.

486. To ANNE-MARIE STRINDBERG

[1] Harriet Bosse's mother was Danish.
[2] Hornbæk.
[3] Berlin.
[4] Bosse replied the same day: 'My child thanks you for your kind and beautiful message!'

487. To EMIL SCHERING

[1] The cabaret Schall und Rauch (Sound and Smoke), started by Max Reinhardt (1873–1943) in Berlin, in 1901. Two members of Reinhardt's company, Gertrud Eysoldt and Rosa Bertens, performed *The Stronger* there in 1902.

488. To HARRIET BOSSE

[1] Parenthesis inserted at a later date.
[2] See Letter 203, note 1.

489. To HARRIET BOSSE

[1] Informed.
[2] Anders Fryxell (1795–1881), Swedish historian whose *Berättelser ur svenska historien* in 46 vols (Tales from Swedish History, 1823–79), contains a detailed account of Christina's life and reign in volumes 7–11. Bosse replied the same day, saying she had been unable to find a copy at Engström's bookshop in Birger Jarlsgatan.
[3] Claes Theodor Odhner (1836–1904), Swedish historian. Strindberg himself

owned the *Lärobok i fäderneslandets historia* (Textbook in the History of the Fatherland, 1899).

[4] Walter Crane (1845–1915), Pre-Raphaelite painter, designer and illustrator. Strindberg modelled the queen's costume in Act IV on Crane's illustration 'Pandora Desires to Open the Box' in Nathanael Hawthorne's *A Wonder Book for Boys and Girls* (London, 1892).

[5] In *En skugga* (A Shade), which opened at the Swedish Theatre on 24 February 1900, Knut Michaelson had portrayed Christina's later years in exile in Rome.

[6] A play by the Danish writer Henrik Hertz (1797–1870), in which Bosse was appearing at the Royal Theatre that autumn in the role of Iolanthe.

490. To HARRIET BOSSE

[1] Also an actress, Alma (1863–1947) was married to the Norwegian theatre manager, Johan Fahlstrøm (1867–1938).

[2] Strindberg's diary for 23 September records: 'Drove with Harriet to Lidingöbro and had lunch. Most extraordinary day! *C'est la vie*! Complete harmony, everything hopeful! *Christina* finished!'

491. To HARRIET BOSSE

[1] Harriet's name for Strindberg; she disliked August. See Letter 515.

[2] See Letter 489.

[3] A maid.

[4] Harriet returned to Strindberg on 5 October.

492. To CARL LARSSON

[1] The six frescoes which Larsson had painted on the walls of the main staircase in the National Museum in 1896.

[2] Larsson had asked Strindberg to contribute a foreword to an album he published in 1902.

[3] The premières took place on 13 February 1902 and 3 December 1901 respectively.

493. To EMIL SCHERING

[1] Both the historical drama *Engelbrekt* in Sweden and *Easter* on its German première in Frankfurt had failed.

[2] Gertrud Eysoldt (1870–1950) had played Eleonora in Frankfurt and again in Munich.

[3] A dramatic fragment by Schiller, left uncompleted at his death in 1805.

[4] When the Nobel Prize was awarded for the first time in 1901 to the French poet Sully-Prudhomme, forty-two Swedish writers signed a letter of protest and apology to Tolstoy, whom they considered a more appropriate recipient. The conservative *Nya Dagligt Allehanda* and a number of other Swedish papers suggested Strindberg had only signed it out of chagrin at not being awarded the prize himself.

494. To EMIL SCHERING

[1] Bertens had appeared in the première of *Creditors* on 22 January 1893. See Letter 289 for the subsequent festivities.

[2] For her performance as Eleonora in the unsuccessful production of *Easter* in Frankfurt.

[3] The title given to *Crimes and Crimes* in Germany.

495. To TOR HEDBERG

[1] The first collection of stories by Maxim Gorky to appear in Sweden was published in 1901 in a translation by Hedberg's sister, Valborg. Gorky was born Aleksey Mikhaylovich Peshkov in 1868. He was elected an Honorary Academician in 1902, but the election was immediately revoked by the Tsar.

[2] The German encyclopedia *Meyers Konversations-Lexikon*, 21 vols (1897–1901), which Strindberg owned and used assiduously.

[3] The Polish writers Adam Mickiewicz (1798–1855), who wrote *Forefathers' Eve* (1832) and *Pan Tadeusz* (1834), and Henryk Sienkiewicz (1846–1916), the author of *Quo vadis* (1896), who was awarded the Nobel Prize for Literature in 1905.

496. To EMIL SCHERING

[1] A collection of observations on diverse subjects, written in 1770 but published posthumously in 1846. Strindberg, who told Schering on 23 April that he had now completed his Dramatic Works in Swedish, was turning back to science and speculation. He had come across a reference by Goethe to 'my mystical, cabbalistic chemistry' in Book Ten of his autobiography *Aus meinem Leben*, and wished to study his conclusions. The *Ephemerides*, however, which Schering had sent him because he saw it included some extracts from Paracelsus, contained almost nothing on chemistry.

[2] Goethe's play *Götz von Berlichingen* (1771–3).

[3] A historical drama by Gerhart Hauptmann (1862–1946), written in 1896 and revised 1902. Strindberg later clarified what he had in mind in another letter to Schering (31 December 1903): 'Every dramatic subject has its own form, and for historical epics like the life of Luther, it has to be the Shakespeare-Götz form! Hauptmann has ruined *Florian Geijer*, which is an epic drama, with his straightjacket!'

497. To HARRIET BOSSE

[1] When it became clear that Strindberg did not intend to leave Stockholm at all that summer as she had hoped, Harriet Bosse made arrangements for herself and Anne-Marie to go to Räfnäs, near Mariefred on Lake Mälaren. The day before she was due to leave, Strindberg left this letter in her room while she was out.

[2] A reference to the poem *Chrysaëtos* in which Strindberg describes his feelings during their marriage crisis in September 1901. He gave Harriet the poem on 21 June 1902.

498. To HARRIET BOSSE

[1] Where Strindberg lived in 1899–1900 before he set up home with Harriet Bosse at 40 Karlavägen in May 1900.
[2] Such is life; what do you want?
[3] A maid.

499. To EMIL SCHERING

[1] *Crimes and Crimes* which Max Reinhardt was rehearsing at the Kleines Theater in Berlin with Emanuel Reicher as Maurice and Gertrud Eysoldt as Henriette.

500. To LEOPOLD LITTMANSSON

[1] The sonata played in Act IV of *Crimes and Crimes*. See Letter 446.
[2] Ivan Hirsch, who now worked for his cousin Isaac, a builder. See Letters 317 and 319.
[3] The Home of Peace. In his letters to Littmansson during 1894, Strindberg had often dreamt of founding a monastic order for intellectuals (see e.g. Letter 315). Such a monastery features in the novel *Black Banners*, where it is situated on Siklaön, opposite Blockhusudden, on the main fairway into Stockholm, as is the small town of Vaxholm.

501. To LEOPOLD LITTMANSSON

[1] In 1900 Littmansson and his wife had been planning a separation. However, in 1901 she died, leaving him with twin daughters, born 1885.
[2] Buddha.
[3] Cf. Letter 406.

502. To EMIL SCHERING

[1] Strindberg's ideas on staging were influenced at this time by the so-called Shakespeare stage, introduced in Munich by Karl von Perfall, Karl Lautenschläger and Jocza Savits in 1889 (there is an annotated copy of Savits' book *Die Shakespeare-Bühne in München* (1899) in his last library). These ideas were partly implemented in the scenography which he and Emil Grandinson devised for the première of *To Damascus I* in 1900, where the action was not only framed by the proscenium arch but also by a further permanent, curved arch and an upstage row of steps. This created the effect of an inner stage which gave both formal depth and an hallucinatory psychological intensity to the action. It facilitated rapid scene changes, in contrast to the generally ponderous stage architecture of the nineteenth century, and Strindberg often refers to it in his letters.
[2] Otto Devrient (1838–94), actor and dramatist, whose pageant play *Gustav Adolf. Historisches Charakterbild in fünf Aufzügen* (1891) had been widely performed in Germany.

[3] John Hertz (pseudonym for John Emil Jönsson, 1875–1952), writer and journalist. Hertz was privy to Strindberg's ideas on the theatre, and had access through Schering to some of his as yet unpublished material.

503. To EMIL SCHERING

[1] An allusion to Ellen Key's celebrated book *Barnets århundrade* (The Century of the Child, 1900).

[2] The director of the Residenztheater in Berlin; *Creditors* had been performed there in 1893.

[3] Otto Neumann-Hofer (1857–1941), journalist, editor, and director of the Berlin Lessing Theater; close friend of Frida Uhl as well as of Strindberg.

[4] *Erik XIV* was to be performed in Schwerin, *Pariah* in Breslau.

[5] Of *Crimes and Crimes* in Berlin.

[6] The *Norddeutsche Allgemeine Zeitung* had declared *To Damascus* unsuitable for public performance because of its intimate, autobiographical nature. In support of his argument, Strindberg enclosed the relevant passage from Goethe's autobiography ending: '*Alles . . . sind nur Bruchstücke einer grossen Konfession*' (All of it . . . forms only fragments of a great confession).

504. To EMIL SCHERING

[1] *Fairhaven and Foulstrand*, a volume of short stories including a lightly masked adaptation of his most recent autobiographical fiction, *The Cloister*.

[2] Tale.

[3] A mythological hero whose untimely death was celebrated in a dirge, the 'Song of Linus', sung annually from Homeric days at harvest time.

[4] Strindberg tried them all, beginning with the essay 'The Mysticism of World History', first published in *Svenska Dagbladet* in 1903. This was followed by four plays, *Moses, Socrates, Christ* and *The Nightingale of Wittenberg*, all in 1903, and comprising numbers one, two, three and eleven in an incomplete cycle of world historical dramas. Then came two volumes of tales and stories, *Historical Miniatures* (1905) and *Memories of the Chieftains* (1906).

[5] Strindberg is straining the notion of synchronicity somewhat. The *Vasantasena*, or *Little Clay Cart*, a Sanskrit drama in ten acts attributed to King Sudraka, was probably written about 400 A.D., or a little earlier. The play enjoyed a considerable vogue in Western Europe at the close of the nineteenth century; an adaptation, directed by Lugné-Poë, was performed at the Théâtre de l'Œuvre in 1895.

505. To OTTO WEININGER

[1] On 21 July 1903 Strindberg wrote to Schering: 'Dr Otto Weininger of Vienna has sent me *Geschlecht und Charakter*, a formidable book but one which has probably solved the hardest of all problems. He quotes *Creditors*, but ought to know *The Father* and *Miss Julie*. Would you send him them? I spelled it out, but he pieced the words together. *Voilà un homme*!'

506. To LEOPOLD LITTMANSSON

[1] On 21 June Strindberg had written: 'We meet in Beethoven, but not the 9th, joy was never really me, therefore I find the 'Ode to Joy' banal, as Beethoven can become when he tries to be joyous. No, I meet him in the *Appassionata* and the last movement of the *Moonlight*. For me, that's the summit (and I detest Mozart!).'

[2] Jacques Auguste Monnier (1871–?), French writer who translated *The People of Hemsö* with Littmansson. He and Strindberg were trying to extract Littmansson's translation of *Crimes and Crimes* from Antoine.

[3] Axel Strindberg's wife, who had died after a long illness.

507. To HJALMAR SELANDER

[1] See Letter 502. In fact Strindberg and Grandinson had abandoned the notion of using projections on a back cloth when staging *To Damascus I*, but the idea of using a Sciopticon or some kind of Magic Lantern was one which Strindberg had cherished since 1889, when he sought to interest August Lindberg in using a Camera Lucida in a never-written drama on the French Revolution.

[2] Strindberg had written to Branting on 13 June to arrange a visit to the newly built Folkets Hus (People's House), which included a theatre as well as the offices of the socialist newspaper, *Social-Demokraten*, and the Social Democratic Party, of which Branting was leader.

[3] William Engelbrecht had played the role in Gothenburg in 1887 and may well have retained an option on the play; nevertheless, fearing the problems posed by *A Dream Play*, Selander still bought the rights for *Lucky Peter's Journey*.

508. To EMIL SCHERING

[1] R. M. Meyer, *Goethe*, 3 vols (Berlin, 1895).

[2] Cf. Letter 361.

510. To ARTUR GERBER

[1] Paraphrase of an entry in the *Occult Diary* for 6 September 1901. In his letter Gerber told Strindberg that Weininger committed suicide because he felt he neither was, nor could become, a 'good' human being.

[2] *Erdgeist*. Cf. the title of Wedekind's *Der Erdgeist* (1895) and *To Damascus III* (1901): 'In woman I sought an angel who would lend me her wings, and I fell into the arms of the earth spirit who stifled me under bolsters she had filled with her wing feathers – I sought an Ariel and found a Caliban.'

[3] Between 1901 and 1904, Maeterlinck was married to the actress Georgette Leblanc (1867–1941) who appeared, scantily dressed, in his play *Mona Vanna* (1902), on a European tour that came to Stockholm in 1901. Strindberg develops the idea in *A Blue Book*, where it is applied as much to himself as to Maeterlinck.

511. To EMIL SCHERING

[1] Johan Banér (1596–1641), one of Gustav Adolf's ablest commanders.

[2] An allusion to The Linköping Massacre of 1600 when Gustav Adolf's father, Karl IX, had those Swedish Lords who remained loyal to the Polish branch of the Vasas under Sigismund executed. A devout Catholic, Sigismund's claim to the Swedish throne, which he occupied from 1592 to 1599 before being deposed by Karl, was in some respects stronger than Gustav Adolf's.

[3] *The Nightingale of Wittenberg*.

[4] Fritz Henriksson (1872–1941), journalist, G.H.T.'s Berlin correspondent and a friend of Schering. Both felt *The Nightingale of Wittenberg* would shock the Germans in its presentation of Luther.

[5] 'To become German, yes fine, but to Germanize Gustav Adolf, I'd rather not. Rather nothing. My last word! Amen! Here I stand and can do no other.'

512. To ALGOT RUHE

[1] His novel *Den tredje Adam* (The Third Adam, 1903).

513. To ARTUR GERBER

[1] Weininger spent his last night in the house where Beethoven, whom he greatly admired, had died.

514. To HJALMAR BRANTING

[1] Wrongly dated for 1904.

515. To HARRIET BOSSE

[1] A pencilled note on the envelope indicates this letter was never sent. Strindberg and Harriet Bosse had been living apart since August 1903, although they dined together regularly on Sundays and saw each other quite frequently at other times. According to Harriet, this way of life brought an end to their quarrelling, and their meetings were happy and festive. As a diary entry for 2 December suggests, they remained lovers: 'Harriet to dinner. Subsequently in the yellow room! In dread of a child' (*Inferno*, p.331).

[2] See Letter 491.

516. To CARL LARSSON

[1] Henrik Koppel (1871–1934), publisher who planned a cheap edition of *Swedish Destinies and Adventures* and wanted Carl Larsson to do the illustrations. Larsson declined.

517. To HARRIET BOSSE

[1] Though their relationship remained intimate, Harriet had written asking for a divorce.

[2] According to the *Occult Diary* (28 May 1903): 'At 1.30 she woke me up and let fly at me the most appalling scolding because she believed I was having an improper affair with our maid, Ellen. It is simply not true, I swear it! Poor Harriet, who tried to poison me by making me jealous. Now the demon has taken hold of her' (*Inferno*, p.328).

519. To HARRIET BOSSE

[1] A diminutive for Anne-Marie, now two.
[2] The villa in the Archipelago which Strindberg was renting for the summer.
[3] Harriet's sister and her son.

520. To HARRIET BOSSE

[1] The *Occult Diary* for 1 June 1904 records: 'Left for Furusund at 1 o'clock with Lillan. Harriet, who was leaving for Copenhagen that evening to facilitate her divorce, stood on the quay waving to us. I experienced no emotion, merely noted, with complete detachment, that I had had a beautiful young wife and felt grateful for that, and justifiably proud' (*Inferno*, pp.338–9).

521. To HARRIET BOSSE

[1] James Millar (1862–1943), the lawyer who was arranging their divorce. He also assisted Strindberg in his action against Marie David, in 1892.
[2] On Storgatan in Stockholm, where Strindberg was a customer.
[3] A servant.
[4] Cf. Letter 333.
[5] A German theatre journal in which Schering had written an exposition of Strindberg's ideas on staging, based on his comments about the Shakespeare stage in Munich and the production techniques he advocated for *To Damascus*.

522. To HARRIET BOSSE

[1] The glass door in the rue de Fleurus is described in *Inferno* as bearing 'my own initials, A.S., poised on a silvery-white cloud and surmounted by a rainbow. *Omen accipio*. The words of Genesis came into my mind: "I do set my bow in the cloud, and it shall be for a token of a covenant between me and the earth" ' (p.116). The letter contains a sketch of the door.
[2] Olof Teodor (Tore) Svennberg (1858–1941), actor and theatre manager, played Göran Persson in the premières of both *Gustav Vasa* and *Erik XIV*.
[3] Loti had been a naval officer, and derived his pseudonym from a nickname given him by native women in the South Seas.
[4] *Alt-Heidelberg* (1901) by the popular German writer, Wilhelm Meyer-Förster (1862–1934).
[5] Harriet returned from France to rejoin Strindberg at Furusund on 22 June, and they resumed their intimacy: 'Harriet's return from Paris to Furusund is one of my loveliest memories. When she left my bed that night she did not look like herself. Her face was long and oval . . . and sometimes makes me

think she must be a being from a very high sphere, not an ordinary mortal' (*Inferno*, pp.340–41). They spent seven weeks together in apparent harmony until 9 August, when Strindberg noted: 'Left Furusund without saying good-bye to Harriet.'

523. To EMIL SCHERING

[1] Novalis' novel *Heinrich von Ofterdingen*, published posthumously in 1802.

[2] See Letter 521.

[3] Strindberg had previously refused to sign a tribute to Harden (see Letter 331), but now gave way. '*Zukunft* is a parliament, a free Reichstag/Landstag,' he told Schering on 4 July 1904, 'anyone who wants to study the future can do so in *Zukunft*.'

[4] In *Black Banners*, Strindberg refers to both Kepler's *Mysterium cosmographicum* (1596) and Newton's *Observations on the Prophecies of Daniel and the Apocalypse of St John*, published posthumously in 1733.

[5] Jakob Böhme (1575–1624), German mystic.

[6] Certainly.

[7] James John Garth Wilkinson (1812–99), the Swedenborgian friend of Emerson and Dickens who edited and translated numerous volumes of Swedenborg, including the *Oeconomia regni animalis* (The Economy of the Animal Kingdom, 1740–41). *De cultu et amore Dei* (The Worship and Love of God, 1745).

524. To RICHARD BERGH

[1] Elin Svensson (1860–?), who ran a theatre school on Blasieholmen in Stockholm, and knew Bergh well.

[2] Prince Eugen (1865–1947), the youngest son of Oscar II, who was not only a patron of the arts but also a professional painter, primarily of landscapes. He and Strindberg became acquainted in 1908 when the latter sought support for his Intimate Theatre, but the two were never close.

[3] *Balkonen* (1894) by Strindberg's old Berlin acquaintance Gunnar Heiberg depicted the latter's triangular relationship with the painter Christian Krohg (1852–1925) and Krohg's wife, Oda.

[4] In Max Reinhardt's highly successful production with Gertrud Eysoldt and Hans Wassmann.

[5] It makes a difference.

525. To RICHARD BERGH

[1] See Letter 507.

[2] Arthur Sjögren (1874–1951), painter and book designer, who illustrated a number of Strindberg's works in Art Nouveau style, including the autobiographical fiction *Alone*, the volume of poems *Word-Play and Minor Art*, and new editions of *Antibarbarus* and *Swedish Nature*.

[3] Presumably a play upon a slogan of the Social Democrats, who owned Folkets Hus.

[4] See Letter 521.

[5] Strindberg had fallen out with his sister Anna and her husband after *The Dance*

of Death (1900) in which they recognized a version of their marriage (Philp was reputed to have flung the book on the fire in fury and disgust). The phrase 'everything comes back' (*allt går igen*) is a key one in the play, where it evokes one of the central motifs of Strindberg's later work as a whole.

[6] Such is life, eh? . . . What do I know?

527. To NILS ANDERSSON

[1] *L'Initiation.* Its editor, Papus, was a doctor.

[2] Carl du Prel (1839–99), German philosopher and psychologist whose works Strindberg read with admiration. His last book collection contained undated copies of *Der Spiritismus* (Spiritualism) and *Das Rätsel* (The Riddle), but it was du Prel's *Die Philosophie der Mystik* (1885 – entitled 'The Hidden Life of the Soul' in Swedish) that meant most to him, as it did to Freud, who in 1914 added a note to later editions of *The Interpretation of Dreams* acknowledging 'That brilliant mystic du Prel, one of the few authors for whose neglect in early editions of this book I should wish to express my regret' (*Complete Psychological Works*, 24 vols (London, 1953–74), 4, p.63). For du Prel, whose theory of the unconscious and its ability in sleep to condense ideas and characters in dreams clearly prefigures Freud, the dreamer is a dramatist in whose plays an empirical and a transcendental self are in conflict with each other.

[3] For Andersson's musical interests, see headnote to Letter 453.

528. To HARRIET BOSSE

[1] The divorce was made absolute on 27 October. In spite of that, when Harriet returned from Helsinki, where she had been engaged by the Swedish Theatre to play, among other parts, the Lady in *To Damascus I*, their intimacy continued. For Millar, see Letter 521.

529. To HUGO GEBER

[1] *Black Banners*, Strindberg's grim, ruthless, and yet often grotesquely comic settling of accounts with many of his old acquaintances, including Karl Warburg, Ellen Key and Gustaf af Geijerstam. Geber refused the book, which remained unpublished until 1907.

531. To EMIL SCHERING

[1] Raoul Francé (1874–1943), German writer of works in a popular scientific vein, combining speculation with literary reflections on (for example) the love life of plants in *Das Liebesle ben der Pflanzen*.

[2] Scientist.

[3] German poet and writer on science, in the tradition of Gustav Fechner (1801–87), the founder of psychophysics. Pastor's *Lebensgeschichte der Erde* (The Life History of the Earth, 1903) accepts Strindberg's theory that plants draw carbon dioxide from the earth rather than from the air.

532. To HARRIET BOSSE

1 Grieg's Piano Sonata in E minor.

2 Anne-Marie's doll.

3 Henning Berger (1872–1924), Swedish novelist and playwright. See headnote to Letter 547.

4 Strindberg's maidservant and Anne-Marie's nursemaid.

5 A reference to *Memories of the Chieftains*, a volume of short stories drawn from Swedish history, which Strindberg was then writing.

6 The immediate idea of writing monodramas for Harriet Bosse, who according to Strindberg was unhappy with the roles she was currently being offered, may well have been prompted by the recent solo performances of the Danish actress, Charlotte Wiehe (1865–1947), but his old friend August Lindberg had given a series of one-man performances of *The Tempest*, *Faust*, *Peer Gynt* and *Oedipus* between 1900 and 1903, and the genre was implicit in certain trends within the drama and the theatre of the time.

7 The poems *Word-Play and Minor Art*, illustrated by Arthur Sjögren.

8 Betty Nansen (1873–1943), Danish stage and film actress; in fact her autumn season at the Swedish Theatre was a great success.

533. To HARRIET BOSSE

1 Strindberg had given a party for a number of younger Swedish writers: Henning Berger, Bo Bergman (1869–1967), Albert Engström (1869–1940), Gustaf Janson (1866–1913), Henning von Melsted (1875–1953), Algot Ruhe and Hjalmar Söderberg (1869–1941). Of these Berger, Ruhe and Engström, who wrote a volume of memoirs entitled *Strindberg och jag* (Strindberg and I, 1923), were, or became, his friends, while the novelist and playwright Söderberg was incontestably the major writer of the group.

2 Negotiations at Karlstad, overshadowed by mobilization, had led to an agreement on the dissolution of the Union between Norway and Sweden.

534. To HARRIET BOSSE

1 Among Strindberg's papers in the Royal Library there are numerous plans and sketches for a variety of monodramas; the most extensive is an adaptation of Schiller's *Die Jungfrau von Orleans* (The Maid of Orleans, 1801) in which the role of Joan of Arc has been separated from the remainder of the play.

2 See Letter 532.

3 The famous three-act mime play The Infant Prodigy by Michel Carré and André Wurmser, first staged in 1890; it had also been performed as a shadow play at the Chat Noir in 1895 while Strindberg was in Paris and interested in the cabaret.

4 Harriet was appearing in Shakespeare's tragedy at the Grand Theatre in Gothenburg.

535. To HARRIET BOSSE

1 Illusion.

2 The then open view over Ladugårdsgärdet in North-East Stockholm, including

a military barracks and exercise ground. The barracks, with its curious bud-shaped baldachin surmounting a pillared balcony on the top of its dome, was for Strindberg the Growing Castle of *A Dream Play*.

536. To HARRIET BOSSE

[1] Spring 1901, prior to their marriage, when Strindberg wrote *Swanwhite* and Harriet acted in *Easter* at the Royal Theatre. *Easter*, which features both daffodil (or Easter lily) and rod, had just been performed again in Gothenburg, with Harriet as Eleonora.

[2] A well-known restaurant in Djurgården.

537. To HARRIET BOSSE

[1] Harriet returned from Gothenburg on 6 November; Strindberg means he has had no telepathic visitation from her of the type which, according to the *Occult Diary*, he was accustomed to receive, especially at night.

[2] Richard Bergh.

538. To HARRIET BOSSE

[1] Colour plate XI in *Strindbergs måleri*. Three of the other paintings were sold to the banker and art collector Ernest Thiel (1859–1947), and are now on display in the Thielska Gallery in Stockholm. The others he gave away.

[2] On 30 November Strindberg had suggested they take a flat together in Grunewald, outside Berlin, close to the Scherings.

[3] Lies, delusion and illusion.

539. To HARRIET BOSSE

[1] Harriet Bosse had gone to Vienna to audition for the part of Biskra in *Simoom* – a role she played with great success at the Royal Theatre in 1902.

540. To CHARLOTTE FUTTERER

[1] Carl Eldh (1873–1954), who executed four major busts and statues of Strindberg, including the titanic monument, erected some thirty years after the writer's death, in Tegnérlunden. Eldh studied in Paris from 1896 to 1904, and followed Strindberg in patronizing Mme Charlotte's *crémerie* since for much of that time he had an atelier in the same street.

541. To HARRIET BOSSE

[1] Harriet was in Helsinki, then a semi-independent Grand Duchy of Russia, fulfilling an engagement at the Swedish Theatre.

[2] Edward Gordon Craig (1872–1966), English theatre designer, actor and director,

at the time the lover of the American dancer, Isadora Duncan (1878–1927). Craig had designed sets for Ibsen's *The Vikings at Helgeland* and *Rosmersholm* and, according to Albert Engström, had come to Stockholm solely to meet Strindberg. He also contacted Engström about 'the play which Strindberg says he has written without words' (*Strindberg och jag*, p.38), which might, had it existed, have suited his notion of a theatre of *Über-Marionettes*. As so often happened, Strindberg recoiled from direct contact with an eminent visitor; however, he knew Craig's *On the Art of the Theatre*, and the latter's ideas on staging and design doubtless influenced him (the references to screens in Letters 507, 525 and 533 may well have derived, at least in part, from Craig).

3 *Svenska Dagbladet*.

4 He was too handsome (beautiful) for me.

5 A doll given her by Birger Mörner.

6 Architect and master builder, who lived at 99 Regeringsgatan. *Elle dine en ville*: she is dining out.

7 Nothing else!

542. To HARRIET BOSSE

1 Refers again to her telepathic visitations; Harriet was still in Finland.

2 Albert Ranft and Knut Michaelson were both contenders to run the new Royal Theatre on Nybroplan, then under construction. It opened in 1908 with the verse *Master Olof*.

3 Gabriele D'Annunzio (1863–1938), Italian poet, novelist and dramatist. The two novels were *Il piacere* (1889) and *L'innocente* (1891).

543. To HARRIET BOSSE

1 Albert Ranft had offered Bosse a position at the Swedish Theatre in Stockholm; in December 1905 she signed a five year contract with him, giving her an annual salary of 10,000 *kronor*.

2 Greta Strindberg.

3 Olof Rubenson, journalist on the illustrated weekly *Hvar 8 Dag* (Each Week), which had published a picture of Eldh's 1905 bronze bust of Strindberg. Rubenson acquired Strindberg's novella *The Roofing Feast* as a *feuilleton* for 1906.

4 A poem by Jon Ulrik Ekmarck (1794–1830) to the second movement of Beethoven's Seventh Symphony.

5 In her autobiography *My Life* (1928), Duncan writes: 'While I was in Stockholm I sent an invitation to Strindberg, whom I greatly admired, to come and see me dance. He replied that he never went anywhere, that he hated human beings. I offered him a seat on the stage, but even then he did not come' (2nd ed., London, 1966, p.203).

6 Martin Fallas Shaw (1875–1958), composer, pianist and organist; Craig's collaborator on *Dido and Aeneas* in 1900 and *The Masque of Love* later the same year. Shaw also composed music for Craig's production of *The Vikings at Helgeland*.

7 Konni Wetzer (1871–1940), director at the Swedish Theatre in Helsinki.

544. To HARRIET BOSSE

[1] See Letter 490.
[2] See Letter 545.
[3] Tore Svennberg.

545. To HARRIET BOSSE

[1] With Bosse as Eleonora at the Swedish Theatre in Helsinki.
[2] Hilda Borgström (1871–1953), who played the role at the Royal Theatre, had previously played Lisa in *Lucky Peter's Journey* for Harald Molander in 1896.
[3] Vesuvius erupted on 4 April 1906.
[4] The flat which Harriet shared with her sister Inez before her marriage to Strindberg.

546. To HARRIET BOSSE

[1] The première of *The Crown Bride* took place in Helsinki on 24 April with Harriet as Kersti and Gunnar Wingård (1878–1912), whom she later married, as Mats. Though the role was originally written for Greta Strindberg, Bosse would make the part her own; in 1917 she again scored a great success in it at the Lorensberg Theatre in Gothenburg.
[2] Romans 7, 19–24.

547. To HENNING BERGER

[1] *The Scapegoat*.
[2] Karl Staaff's short-lived Liberal government of 1905–6 had introduced a law against anti-military propaganda; one in a succession of Liberal governments in Denmark had introduced corporal punishment for actual bodily harm and certain sexual offences.
[3] Berger was currently writing a play, *Syndafloden* (The Deluge, 1907); Strindberg conjectured that he might be responding to a call from Albert Ranft for writers to turn their novels into plays.

548. To HARRIET BOSSE AND ANNE-MARIE STRINDBERG

[1] Harriet and Anne-Marie had spent a month in Hornbæk; they now travelled via Stockholm to Åre, a mountain resort close to the Swedish border with Norway.

549. To JÖRGEN LANZ-LIEBENFELS

[1] *Theozoologie oder die Kunde von den Sodoms-Äfflingen und dem Götter-Elektron* (Vienna, 1906).
[2] By Julius Langbehn. See Letter 271.

550. To GRETA STRINDBERG

[1] According to Greta's response, she had twice invited her cousin, Henry Philp, to tea. On 21 December the two became engaged.

[2] A reference to Henry's sister, Märta Philp, who married Hugo Fröding on 9 October 1906.

551. To ADOLF PAUL

[1] The Devil's Church, a comedy in three acts, from 1905. Paul now wrote mainly in German; the play was translated into Swedish the following year, but had a large cast and did not meet Strindberg's demands.

[2] The Intimate Theatre, which Strindberg was planning with the young actor-manager August Falck (see headnote to Letter 569), partly stimulated by the example of Max Reinhardt's Kammerspiele, which opened in Berlin in 1906.

[3] *Miss Julie* received its first professional performance in Sweden on 18 December 1906, directed by Falck with August Palme as Jean and Manda Björling as Julie. Later that year Falck took over Palme's role, and the play was at last performed in Stockholm.

552. To EMIL SCHERING

[1] The Hebbel Theater (later the Theater am der Königgrätzerstrasse) opened in autumn 1907 under the direction of Richard Vallentin. In 1906, Vallentin had wanted Harriet Bosse to play Mariamne in Hebbel's *Herodus und Mariamne* (1850).

553. To EMIL SCHERING

[1] See Letter 554 for the definitive title.

[2] Derived from Sanskrit, Kama Loka is the name given by Theosophists to the first stage which the soul enters after death, where it is released from the 'ghosts' of earthly life, the animal desires by which it has been possessed. Strindberg adopts the term from Annie Besant's *Death and After* (1893), although he readily combined the notion with the post-mortem topography of Swedenborg that he had been using since 1896.

[3] Horrible, dreadful.

[4] Immanuel Kant's 'The Thing-in-itself' from *The Critique of Pure Reason* (1781).

[5] The veil of illusion which, according to Schopenhauer, conceals the true nature of reality.

[6] From the Hebrew, used in the Old Testament to denote the kingdom of death where the dead live a shadowy existence in a kind of trance or torpor. Sometimes described as a gated city where silence and oblivion reign.

[7] Contact with the beyond.

[8] *Thunder in the Air*.

[9] Not *The Pelican*, which was published as Opus IV, but a play Strindberg destroyed. See Letter 555.

554. To EMIL SCHERING

[1] I.e. the Piano Sonata Opus 31, No. 2, and the Piano Trio Opus 70, No. 1, traditionally known as the 'Ghost Trio'.

[2] Thunder and storm; the fourth movement.

[3] *Master Olof* opens with the summoning of Olof to his mission in the words of the Lord to Jeremiah.

555. To EMIL SCHERING

[1] The quotation is from Kierkegaard's *Either-Or*, and forms the subject of the concluding reflections of Volume Two.

[2] What will come now?

556. To BIRGER MÖRNER

[1] Strindberg had already sent Mörner a picture postcard of himself earlier that day, likewise asking him to honour the memory of the Swedish scientist Daniel Solander (1733–82), who had accompanied Cook on his voyage of 1768–71 (hence *In Duplo*: in duplicate). Mörner, who had just been appointed the first Swedish consul in Australia, fulfilled the commission: a monument of Swedish granite was raised at Botany Bay in 1914.

557. To EMIL SCHERING

[1] Sigismund Rahmer (1866–1912), a German doctor whose psychological study, *August Strindberg, eine pathologische Studie*, appeared in Munich in 1907.

[2] *A Blue Book*. Strindberg originally conceived its short sections as suitable for daily meditation.

[3] The Island of the Dead. At the close of *The Ghost Sonata* a reproduction of the painting *Toten-Insel* by the Swiss artist Arnold Böcklin (1827–1901) appears in the background. The painting enjoyed a considerable vogue at the end of the century; Strindberg listed it among his favourite works of art, and had a reproduction hung in the auditorium of the Intimate Theatre.

[4] A bottle of colouring carried by the Cook in *The Ghost Sonata*. Used to adulterate food, it is part of the play's complex network of imagery to do with falsification and illusion.

558. To EMIL SCHERING

[1] As he lies dying the protagonist of Strindberg's novella witnesses the building of a house. At the end of the narrative, much of it virtually an inner monologue, the topping out ceremony, with its flags and garlands, coincides with his last moments, but not before the new structure has concealed a green lamp visible in the window of an old adversary – in reality, as the letter indicates, Carl Gustaf Wrangel.

[2] Paul.

[3] 40 Karlavägen.

559. To EMIL SCHERING

[1] Both plays by Goethe.
[2] In the second Chamber Play, *The Burned Site*, there is a passing reference to a Bishop Stecksén, over whose grave a monument is to be raised.

560. To AXEL STRINDBERG

[1] The stage directions for Act II of *Swanwhite* specify harp music.
[2] Axel was a cellist.
[3] In Act III.

561. To EMIL SCHERING

[1] Tor Hedberg's review had been critical of the play and of Harriet Bosse as Indra's Daughter.
[2] A fragment remains which is sometimes used as a framing device for the eventual Opus IV, *The Pelican*, written in May–June 1907.
[3] Strindberg is referring to a passage from *Historical Miniatures* where Marie Antoinette is described as leading a dissolute life at night, and having an 'illicit relationship with her son'. An entry in the *Occult Diary* for 19 May 1907 clarifies this as an allusion to Harriet Bosse.

562. To EMIL SCHERING

[1] Besides *Jane Eyre* (see Letter 18), Charlotte Birch-Pfeiffer dramatized novels by, among others, Victor Hugo, George Sand, and Alexandre Dumas.
[2] See Letter 502.
[3] See Letter 558.
[4] Of the three Chamber Plays which Strindberg had thus far sent Schering (*Thunder in the Air*, *The Burned Site*, and *The Ghost Sonata*), Reinhardt directed the first and the third, though not until 1913 and 1916 respectively.

563. To KARL BÖRJESSON

[1] Albert Björck (1856–1938), Börjesson's erstwhile partner, was a Swedenborgian pastor, and had written a short study of Swedenborg and Strindberg.

565. To EMIL SCHERING

[1] In response to Letter 562, Schering had chosen to dramatize Strindberg's story 'Karl Ulfsson and his Mother' from the collection *Memories of the Chieftains*. An outline by Strindberg for a dramatization of the same story in four acts also survives. The Queen referred to is Johanna I of Naples (1326–82), who was implicated in the murder of her first husband.
[2] St Birgitta (*c.* 1303–73), who believed herself to be God's 'bride and mouthpiece'. Her visions and the messages she received are recorded in over

six hundred *Revelationes* and *Revelationes Extravagantes*, published in both Swedish and Latin.
[3] Muttonhead.
[4] Against the grain.
[5] No day without its line.
[6] The Spanish ex-bishop Alfons of Jaén, who translated many of Birgitta's visions into Latin.

567. To EMIL SCHERING

[1] Schering's American wife had returned to the United States together with their two children.
[2] A version of Immanuel Kant's phrase '*Der bestirnte Himmel über mir und das moralische Gesetz in mir*' from *The Critique of Practical Reason* (1788).
[3] Harriet Bosse.
[4] Precisely to what Strindberg is alluding here is unclear.

568. To EMIL SCHERING

[1] *Thunder in the Air*, which Max Reinhardt put on at his Kammerspielhaus, but not until 1913.
[2] Richard Vallentin, who wanted Harriet Bosse to act in Germany. See Letter 552.
[3] Horrible.
[4] *The Pelican*.
[5] Stupid Sweden.

570. To EMIL SCHERING

[1] The Lex Heinze, introduced in Germany in 1892, derived its name from a pimp and murderer whose trial in 1891 brought to light the 'moral corruption' of the Berlin underworld. Once passed, however, it was employed against 'indecency' in the arts.

571. To EMIL SCHERING

[1] Max Levi (1865–1912). Max Reinhardt had placed Levi's bust in the foyer of the Kammerspielhaus at the Deutsches Theater in Berlin. A copy was made for the Intimate Theatre.
[2] That Paul knows everything.
[3] Probably an allusion to the song sung by Hoffmann in the prologue and epilogue of Offenbach's *Les Contes de Hoffmann* about the dwarf Klein-Zach from E. T. A. Hoffmann's story 'Klein Zaches, gennant Zinnober' (1819). This is the ancestor of Strindberg's 'Little Zachris, called Cinnober' in *Black Banners*, i.e. Gustaf af Geijerstam.
[4] With Harriet Bosse and Gunnar Wingård in the leading roles.
[5] An alternative title for *The Pelican*.
[6] See Letter 549.

572. To CARL LARSSON

1 Strindberg discusses the corncrake in a section of *A Blue Book* entitled 'The Secrets of the Birds: A' (*Samlade skrifter*, 46, p.305). The idea that birds of passage do not migrate is one to which he periodically returns (see e.g. Letter 378). Among his *Nachlass* is an anonymous item, possibly supplied by Waldemar Bülow, depicting several corncrake on the Malmö–Copenhagen ferry.

2 Strindberg's reference is to A. E. Brehm, *Das Leben der Vögel*, 2 vols (The Life of Birds, 1859–61), which he possessed in Swedish translation.

574. To RICHARD BERGH

1 An allusion to *Black Banners*.

575. To AUGUST FALCK

1 *The Pelican*

2 Final permission to use the rebuilt venue at Norra Bantorget as a theatre was granted on 20 November, only six days before the première of *The Pelican*.

3 The pavillion built by Gustav III in Haga Park on the outskirts of Stockholm.

576. To AXEL STRINDBERG

1 *The Pelican*, in which Axel might have recognized their sister, Anna, in the mother who sucks her family dry.

2 Hugo Philp, who had died in January 1906. The family depicted in *The Pelican* has just lost its father, and the daughter's marriage, to a man with whom the mother is conducting an affair, might conceivably be linked with Märta Philp's marriage to Hugo Fröding that same year.

577. To TOR AULIN

1 *Där jag rifvit*, an allusion to the poem 'Esplanadsystemet', one of the clearest expressions of Strindberg's early radicalism.

2 On the verse edition of *Master Olof* for which Aulin composed the incidental music. Strindberg had first invited Aulin to co-operate with him on the music for *The Crown Bride* in 1900, but he did not take up the offer.

3 Johan Lindegren (1842–1908), composer and musicologist, whose standard hymnal was published in 1905.

4 'Stadsresan', a poem in hexameters in the collection *Word-Play and Minor Art*.

5 'Den bergtagna', an opera based upon a well-known folk song of that name by Ivar Hallström (1826–1901).

6 *Valdemarsskatten*, an opera by Johan Andreas Hallén (1846–1925), strongly influenced by Wagner and premièred at the Stockholm Royal Opera in 1899.

7 The national open-air folk museum, founded in 1891 by Artur Hazelius (1833–1901), and situated in Djurgården.

8 Emil Waldteufel (1837–1915), composer of 'The Skaters' Waltz'.

9 Presumably Massenet's *Manon Lescaut*, which is based on Prévost's novel. It

had been premièred at The Swedish Theatre on 18 January 1896.

578. To NILS ANDERSSON

1 Strindberg was considering spending the spring and summer in Skåne, and had asked Nils Andersson to find him somewhere suitable to live.

2 Once and never again.

579. To TOR AULIN

1 Strindberg had recently been trying to interest Sjögren (see Letter 485) in setting the lyrics of *Word-Play and Minor Art* to music.

2 Strindberg had originally written Halldén, i.e. the popular conductor Björn (Nalle) Halldén (see Letter 462), but then altered it to Hallén (see Letter 577).

3 See Letter 577. Aulin had responded positively to Strindberg's suggestion of *A Dream Play* as an opera text.

4 Published 1903. Of the stories he mentions here, Strindberg took the idea of dramatizing 'Saint Gotthard's Tale' most seriously, though he went no further than sketching out a first act.

5 Actually entitled 'Bluewing finds the Golden Saxefrage'.

6 Sketches for a drama in five acts with this title survive; the tale of 'Bluewing' was to have been incorporated in it.

7 Words attributed to Goethe on his deathbed by Eckermann.

8 *Zwiegespräch*: dialogue.

580. To KARL OTTO BONNIER

1 Bonnier chose the first option and credited the Diary against future works, new or reprinted.

581. To AUGUST FALCK

1 See headnote to Letter 584.

2 Axel Westergård, who played the District Officer.

3 Renowned for its lighter repertoire.

4 A farmer in *The Bond*, who is taken to court by a servant for calling her a thief.

582. To SVEA ÅHMAN

1 *Playing with Fire*, which was to have its première at the Intimate Theatre that day, in a double-bill with *The Bond*.

2 Johan Ljungqvist, who played the Friend.

583. To HELGE WAHLGREN

[1] Where Wahlgren played the Judge.
[2] Gustaf Fredrikson and August Lindberg.

584. To ANNA FLYGARE

[1] Astri Torsell (1879–1951), a frequent performer at both The Swedish Theatre, where she played Cecilia in *The Secret of the Guild* in 1906, and The Royal Theatre, where she played Kristina in *Master Olof* in 1908.
[2] The actress Georgette Leblanc. See Letter 510.
[3] The woman works with her eyes.
[4] In *The Bond*.

585. To IVAR NILSSON

[1] The references are to Act I, Scenes 1, 4 and 6 of the verse edition respectively.
[2] Act II, Scene 2.
[3] I.e. the new Royal Theatre.

586. To AUGUST FALCK

[1] The Intimate Theatre's production of *The Bond* had been a success.
[2] According to Falk, the fire regulations only permitted one set on stage at a time, thus rendering quick scene changes impossible.
[3] H. A. Ring, *Teaterns historia* (The History of the Theatre, Stockholm, 1898), from which Strindberg derived a number of ideas for simplifying the staging of his plays. The 'Molière Stage' refers to an illustration in Ring depicting actors on stage at the Hôtel de Bourgogne. The square brackets are Strindberg's.
[4] Royal Theatre.
[5] Levin Olbers, clerk to the Police Authority.

587. To AUGUST FALCK

[1] Claes Tott (1630–74), the Queen's favourite, a great-grandson of Erik XIV.
[2] The square brackets are Strindberg's.
[3] A statue.
[4] Falck was planning to take the Intimate Theatre on tour to Denmark.
[5] By the Peace of Roskilde in 1658 Denmark ceded the provinces of Skåne, Halland, Blekinge and Bohuslän to Sweden.
[6] I.e. the Intimate Theatre, which was located at Norra Bantorget.
[7] Magnus Gabriel de la Gardie (1622–86), Christina's former favourite.
[8] Axel Oxenstierna (1583–1654), the eminent statesman who virtually ruled Sweden during Christina's childhood and youth.
[9] Karl Gustav (1622–60), once Christina's suitor, king of Sweden following her abdication.
[10] Johan Holm (d.1687), became court tailor in 1642 and the Queen's valet shortly afterwards. He was ennobled in 1653.

588. To AUGUST FALCK

[1] Falck had written (12 March): 'Concerning the set for *Christina*: because the stage is so small, it isn't possible to comply with your wishes.' He suggested they make use of the three sets of velvet curtains they already had. Strindberg, who wanted them to adhere to what he called the 'Molière Scene' (see Letter 586), agreed but insisted on retaining two balustrades downstage left and right on which properties could be set to indicate time and place.

[2] Mona Geijer (1887–?). In fact the role of Swanwhite came down to a choice between Fanny Falkner (see headnote to Letter 608) and the more experienced Anna Flygare.

[3] Helge Wahlgren.

[4] See headnote to Letter 615.

[5] A tragedy in five acts by Axel Klinckowström (1867–1936), which had recently won the most prestigious of the national prizes awarded by the Swedish Academy.

[6] A reference to Ernst Didring's play, *Två konungar* (Two Kings), performed at the Swedish Theatre in 1908.

[7] A translation in 6 volumes of K. F. Becker's *Weltgeschichte* (World History) in twelve volumes (Stuttgart, Berlin, Leipzig, 1890) and *Sveriges historia intill tjugonde seklet* (Swedish History Up To The Twentieth Century, 1900–09), edited by Emil Hildebrand.

[8] In spite of Strindberg's misgivings, which date back to the Scandinavian Experimental Theatre, the Intimate Theatre performed both *Miss Julie* and *Pariah* in Copenhagen in March 1908.

[9] Falck wished to omit the opening scene of Act III, set in Holm's tailor's shop, because of the demands it made on staging.

589. To AUGUST FALCK

[1] Manda Björling. See headnote to Letter 612.

[2] On this costume for Christina, see Letter 489.

[3] In the text, Strindberg specifies that each act of *Easter* should be introduced by an extract from Haydn's *Seven Last Words from the Cross.*

[4] The first night of *Easter*.

[5] Alrik Kjellgren (1883–1964) played Benjamin and Anna Flygare Eleonora. However, *Easter* remained in the Intimate Theatre's repertoire until November 1910; by then Fanny Falkner had also played the role of Eleonora.

[6] As a statue.

590. To AUGUST FALCK

[1] Harald Molander and Knut Michaelson.

[2] Ebba Brahe (1596–1674) has four lines in the printed text, Ebba Sparre (1626–62) none.

[3] The première of *Christina* at the Intimate Theatre.

[4] Concerns the pronounciation of 'Whitelock', the emissary sent to Christina by Cromwell to secure an alliance with Sweden. In reality Bulstrode Whitlocke (1605–75).

591. To AUGUST FALCK

[1] The critical response to *Christina* had been almost uniformly hostile. Sven Söderman in *Stockholms Dagblad* wrote: 'Even if one can overlook its misrepresentation of history, the play has no literary weight . . . and we are left with only a vulgar, ignorant and inartistic work by a writer who is both intellectually and morally flawed.' In spite of this, the play was a success, and after sixty-five performances at the Intimate Theatre the production went on tour. Rindön, like Långholmen, a prison.

[2] Anton de Verdier (1878–1954), who played Tott.

[3] Albert Ranft currently controlled seven theatres, and was widely tipped to head the new Royal Theatre.

592. To AUGUST FALCK

[1] A slip of a girl.

[2] Alrik Kjellgren, who played Benjamin.

[3] In Strindberg's novel *Gothic Rooms*, Esther and Max encounter a girl who tells them: 'I suffer for my father's misdeeds; he hasn't the time to serve his sentence, for he has to work for his family.' *Samlade Skrifter*, 40, p.293.

[4] A volume of Georg Starbäck and P.O. Bäckström's *Berättelser ur Svenska Historien* (Tales from Swedish History, 1885–86) and an essay later published in the third supplement to *A Blue Book*. Strindberg had been severely criticized for what were considered the historical inaccuracies in his portrayal of Christina and her reign.

[5] Arnold Johan Messenius (1608–51) and his son, Arnold (1629–51), who were executed for writing a pamphlet attacking, among other things, the Queen's extravagance and misgovernment.

[6] Don Antonio Pimentel de Prado (1604–71), the Spanish Minister in Stockholm 1652–54.

593. To HARRIET BOSSE

[1] To the actor Gunnar Wingård (1878–1912), who had played opposite her as Mats in *The Crown Bride* at the Swedish Theatre in Helsinki, in 1906.

[2] Not Viktor Rydberg but a hotel, then situated in Gustav Adolf's Square. According to the *Occult Diary*, their encounter with the King occurred during a drive in Djurgården on 8 March 1901.

[3] The intention had been for *Swanwhite* to have its première at the Swedish Theatre in Stockholm with Harriet in the title role, but this project was abandoned, and the play was first performed in Helsinki, without her but with the addition of Sibelius' incidental music, which had been composed at Harriet's instigation.

[4] On 7 April Strindberg wrote in the *Occult Diary*: 'She is now as one dead, and *therefore* I only see her as beautiful.' On the 8th, however, he observed: 'Experienced warm contact with H-t the whole day. She sought me.'

595. To HARRIET BOSSE

1 Slip of the tongue.

2 The singer Dagmar Möller. Between 1887 and 1895 she was married to the musician Adolf Teodor Sterky. In 1896 she married the architect Carl Möller.

3 Bosse eventually burned her own letters to Strindberg herself. She also destroyed three of Strindberg's which dealt with Dagmar Möller, Gunnar Wingård and Frida Uhl respectively.

4 A reference to the photographer Herman Anderson (1856–1909), who became something of a 'court-photographer' to Strindberg during the first years of the century. Early on in their aquaintance, Strindberg had helped Anderson financially, apparently at Harriet's request, and Anderson had written to thank him. As well as taking several of the most striking later portraits of Strindberg, he also participated in his photographic and chemical experiments.

596. To HARRIET BOSSE

1 This letter follows up a note to Bosse, also dated 11 April, in which Strindberg asked whether or not he should send a further letter, about *Swanwhite*, to the theatre director Victor Castegren (1861–1941). He also sent her a copy of the letter, in which he suggested Wingård appear with Bosse in 'her' play.

2 Her fiancé, Gunnar Wingård, not Castegren.

3 By Herman Anderson and used as a frontispiece to an edition of *Swedish Destinies and Adventures*, published by Henrik Koppel's firm, Ljus, in 1904.

597. To HARRIET BOSSE

1 According to the *Occult Diary* for 14 April 1908 'This W. resembles me but looks like a dead man; he almost died 18 months ago (of lues), but recovered.'

598. To HARRIET BOSSE

1 On 13 April Strindberg wrote in the *Occult Diary*: 'Continuous contact with H-t all evening. At 10.30 I had such violent palpitations that I had to put my hand on my heart, but when I did so I fancied it was Harriet's heart. It quietened down, then stopped. I thought she was dying, but it started to beat again, only more tranquilly. I slept. At 11.30 the feeling of anxiety returned (I believed this time that he was striking her! She told me in her letter that 'she had fought and been struck'). By 12 o'clock she was lying on my arm, calm, friendly! I was woken three times during the night and received her as my wife.'

2 The Distant Beloved. A reference to Beethoven's song cycle *An die ferne Geliebte*, Opus 98 (1816), which may include an allusion to the Immortal Beloved of one of his most famous letters, a figure he could only love at a remove.

3 Children of the Gods.

4 Out of spite.

5 In the *Occult Diary* (19 March 1908), Strindberg relates how he saw a servant girl rush out into the snow from a house on Karlavägen with her clothes on fire, and how he smothered the flames with his overcoat.

599. To HARRIET BOSSE

[1] I.e. Gunnar Wingård.
[2] According to the *Occult Diary*: 'At 10.30 H-t began to seek me, but irresolutely, and this continued all night until 5 o'clock, when she found me, but without joy. Hatred came between us! There was no soul! And without soul (love), no joy.' *Inferno*, p.385.
[3] Refers to a series of short essays included in the second volume of *A Blue Book*, which Börjesson published in 1908.

600. To AUGUST FALCK

[1] Where the Intimate Theatre was situated.

601. To HARRIET BOSSE

[1] See Letter 599.
[2] At the Intimate Theatre, with Anna Flygare as Eleonora.

602. To ANNA FLYGARE

[1] According to the *Occult Diary*, on 16 April Strindberg 'Played Haydn's *Seven Last Words* while they were performing *Easter* at the Intimate Theatre.'
[2] See Letter 543.

603. To HARRIET BOSSE

[1] Strindberg and Harriet were married on 6 May 1901. The allusions here are to an amulet that Strindberg had been given, and which he passed on to Harriet. The motif is treated in his poem 'Seven Roses and Seven Fires' in *Word-Play and Minor Art*.
[2] Harriet had recently played the part of Salome in Hermann Sudermann's *Johannes* at the Swedish Theatre.
[3] Fanny Falkner. See headnote to Letter 608.
[4] Children of the Gods.
[5] Supernatural marriage.
[6] Immaculate conception.

604. To AUGUST FALCK

[1] The remainder of this letter is lost.

605. To HARRIET BOSSE

[1] On the envelope Strindberg has written: '*A lire Sans peur! (Ohne Vorsicht!)*': To be read Without Fear! (Without Precaution!).

606. To HARRIET BOSSE

[1] That is, Strindberg offers her the appartment beneath his at the same address. The same day Strindberg wrote in the *Occult Diary*: 'Sent H-t another card this morning telling her that the flat under mine is vacant . . . I am calm, have a feeling that my fate has been decided! It would be ideal if she and Lillan lived in the flat below. I think it is going to happen! We shall see!' (*Inferno*, p. 405).

607. To AXEL STRINDBERG

[1] Harriet married Gunnar Wingård on 24 May. However, according to the *Occult Diary* her spirit continued to seek Strindberg out at night 'in eros'. On the 26th he wrote in his diary: 'Harriet persecuted me erotically all morning and finally I was forced to embrace her or burn up (even though she is married to W!) . . . At noon I wrote two farewell letters . . . one to H-t and one to Axel, intending to shoot myself before evening! Drank a lot of wine. Slept saved!'

[2] A stuffed eagle, which accompanied Strindberg throughout his last years.

[3] See Letter 573.

[4] Although a monument (Carl Eldh's statue) was raised to him in Tegnérlunden, Strindberg's wishes regarding the cross and its Latin inscription (Oh Cross, hail you my only hope) were observed.

[5] Both in Karlavägen and at his last residence at 85 Drottninggatan, Strindberg kept a copy of Beethoven's death mask on the wall.

608. To FANNY FALKNER

[1] Anna Flygare.

[2] Konstantin Axelsson (1848–1915), an actor at the Swedish Theatre whom Strindberg thought to engage as Fanny Falkner's tutor. He later joined the Intimate Theatre.

X

Notes to Letters 609–679

June 1908–April 1912

609. To KARL OTTO BONNIER

[1] Giulia Peyretti, who had offered to translate *The Dance of Death* and *Crimes and Crimes*. Nothing came of the plan.

[2] *Mina brända tomter*, another echo of Strindberg's second chamber play, *Brända tomten* (The Burned Site).

610. To ALF AHLQUIST

[1] Anne-Marie.

611. To TOR AULIN

[1] See Letter 579.

[2] In telling Strindberg how 'deeply gripped and shaken' he was by *The Ghost Sonata*, Aulin had mentioned that he was overstrained and suffering from rheumatism.

612. To MANDA BJÖRLING

[1] Strindberg refers to the original Stockholm première of his play, given by Björling and Falck on 13 December 1906. The current production, in which the same artists appeared together with Karin Alexandersson as Kristin, had been in the repertoire of the Intimate Theatre since 2 December 1907.

[2] The name is printed on the visiting card containing the message.

613. To MANDA BJÖRLING

[1] *Miss Julie.* Strindberg had now seen the Intimate Theatre's production of his play at a specially arranged performance in honour of Bernard Shaw, who was visiting Stockholm.

[2] The last paragraph is added in pencil.

614. To MANDA BJÖRLING

[1] For a brief period in the late summer and autumn of 1908 Strindberg took over the task of director at the Intimate Theatre from Falck, who was fully occupied

in rehearsing and performing the title role in *The Father*. Rather than intervene in rehearsals, Strindberg sent his cast numerous notes and letters for, as he concluded a long epistle to Anton de Verdier, who played Doctor Östermarck: 'If you will let your comrades read this, I shan't need to repeat myself. It may contain some observations which could be of use to others! I am no speaker, therefore I write!' (30 July 1908).

615. To KARIN ALEXANDERSSON

1 Skram had reviewed H. R. Hunderup's Copenhagen production, which took place in 1887, not 1889, for *Illustreret Tidende*.

616. To NILS ANDERSSON

1 According to the *Occult Diary*, Strindberg moved to 85 Drottninggatan on 11 July.

2 An allusion to the arrangement Strindberg had come to with Fru Meta Falkner whereby she prepared his meals in her apartment. His own flat had no kitchen.

3 Waldemar Bülow who owed Strindberg 200 *Kr*.

618. To NILS ANDERSSON

1 *The Last Knight*, in which Gustav Vasa is depicted as a young man. According to the *Occult Diary*, it was written 17–27 August.

2 Waldemar Bülow.

3 Although not in good health, Siri's impending death was only a rumour.

4 85 Drottninggatan originally had a high, green-roofed tower in which, once they were redeemed, Strindberg kept his books. Not long after moving in, he began calling the building 'Blå tornet' (The Blue Tower), after a prison of that name in Copenhagen, where several famous Swedes had been incarcerated. The roof of the building was painted its present blue in the 1920s.

621. To AUGUST FALCK

1 Strindberg had just refurbished his rooms, using 2,000 *kronor* he had received from the theatre director Karin Swanström (1873–1942) for his play *Abu Casem's Slippers*.

2 *The Black Glove*.

622. To KARL BÖRJESSON

1 *A Blue Book*.

2 See Letter 423.

623. To FANNY FALKNER

[1] At one time Strindberg paid Fanny, whom he sometimes called his 'secretary', 60 *kronor* a month for the errands she ran for him, more or less daily.

624. To ALGOT RUHE

[1] In connection with his sixtieth birthday. In fact the Young Socialists arranged a celebration in Folkets Hus at which Ruhe was a speaker, and their journal *Stormklockan* brought out a special Strindberg number.

[2] *Dagens Nyheter*.

628. To ALGOT RUHE

[1] A sequence of stories, mainly in dialogue, entitled *Bakom fasaden* (Behind the Façade).

[2] Asmodeus appears in Alain-René Lesage's novel *Le Diable boiteux* (1707), not his *Gil Blas*. The Asmodeus idea recalls a motif in *The Ghost Sonata*, where what lies behind a house façade is also central to the play's action.

[3] The actor and dramatist Fredrik Nycander (1867–1944).

629. To KNUT MICHAELSON

[1] Sten Sture (*c.* 1492–1520), a proponent of Swedish independence from Denmark, and his chief opponent, Archbishop Gustav Trolle (1488–1535) in *The Last Knight*.

[2] Christian II (1481–1559) of Denmark.

[3] G. Starbäck's *Berättelser ur svenska historien* (1885–86), one of Strindberg's principal sources for his historical dramas.

[4] Trolle's fortified castle on Lake Mälaren, north-west of Stockholm.

[5] The patriotic warrior Bishop of Linköping, *c.* 1439–1520.

[6] Following the capture of Stockholm by Christian in 1520, over one hundred leading Swedes were executed, partly at Trolle's instigation and in spite of Christian's assurances of amnesty.

630. To META FALKNER

[1] Anders de Wahl, who had taken over the title role in *The Last Knight* at the Royal Theatre on 22 March.

631. To META FALKNER

[1] Strindberg had arranged for the three youngest Falkner children, Ada, Eva, and Stella, to spend their holidays at Lövsta Bruk, in North Uppland, where his brother Olle was head gardener.

[2] The owner of the iron works at Lövsta.

632. To FANNY FALKNER

[1] August Falck.

633. To AUGUST FALCK

[1] The Intimate Theatre had recently given an open-air performance of *Swanwhite* at Adelsnäs, in Östergötland, as part of a festival arranged by the industrialist and Liberal politician, Baron Theodor Adelswärd (1860–1929). Following the performance, the singer Anna Norrie (1860–1957) had, at Adelswärd's request, sung a number of songs, including several with lyrics by Gustaf Fröding.

634. To TURE RANGSTRÖM

[1] Presumably Axel Strindberg. Rangström had sent Strindberg his *Four Songs*, set to texts from *Word-Play and Minor Art*.
[2] Scene One of *The Crown Bride* is constructed around a song taken from *Svenska vallvisor och hornlåtar* (Swedish Herdsmen's Songs and Horn Melodies, 1846) by Richard Dybeck (1811–77). The melody to 'The River God's Song' in Act I is by Strindberg himself.
[3] *Svenska folkvisor*, the most celebrated collection of Swedish Folk Songs, published in 1814–18 by Erik Gustaf Geijer (1783–1847) and Arvid August Afzelius (1785–1871). Johan Höijer (1815–84) and Strindberg's old teacher, Richard Bergström (1828–93), were responsible for a new, enlarged edition, published in 1880.
[4] See Letter 577.
[5] Johann Christian Friedrich Haeffner (1759–1833), German conductor and composer who, in spite of his poor Swedish, helped Geijer harmonize the melodies of *Swedish Folk Songs*. He also produced a *Swedish Hymnal* (1820).
[6] The composer August Söderman (1832–76).
[7] The reference is to one of Strindberg's own stories in the collection *Fairy Tales* (1903).
[8] Tor Aulin.

635. To RICHARD BERGH

[1] Strindberg sometimes cut out the logo of a grocer's shop on the ground floor of Blå tornet and attached it to his writing paper as a letterhead. It depicted the tower, and was coloured blue and yellow.
[2] Sympathy.
[3] *The Great Highway*.
[4] Carlheim-Gyllensköld.
[5] The fourteenth of July = National Holiday of the Bastille.
[6] A prominent motif in *Thunder in the Air* is the lighting of the street-lamps, heralding autumn and old age, at the close of a torrid late summer's day.
[7] For friends.

636. To FANNY FALKNER

1 August and Augusta Lindberg.
2 The Falkner's maid, who often carried Strindberg's food down to him.

637. To KARL BÖRJESSON

1 *Biblical Proper Names: Linguistic Studies.* The Kipling reference is to 'The Finest Story Ever Told'.
2 At an Esperanto congress. *Miss Julie* and *Pariah* were translated into Esperanto in 1908.
3 The book was eventually taken by Bonniers and published in 1910.

638. To ANNA FLYGARE

1 Flygare had declined Strindberg's invitation to join a company he thought of forming to mount an open-air production of *The Crown Bride* in Dalarna.
2 See Letter 633.
3 As Alice in *The Dance of Death.*

639. To FANNY FALKNER

1 At the time of writing, Strindberg had not yet proposed to Fanny.

640. To FANNY FALKNER

1 Strindberg had heard rumours that Harriet and Gunnar Wingård, who lived at 57 Strandvägen, near Djurgården, were in the process of separating.

641. To ADOLF STRÖMSTEDT

1 Harriet Bosse and Gerda Comstedt, whom Strömstedt married in 1899, in Gothenburg.
2 Hjalmar Selander. The production did not materialize.

642. To KERSTIN STRINDBERG

1 Marie Reischl.
2 This was Strindberg's last letter to Kerstin.

643. To ANNA FLYGARE

1 Anton de Verdier, who played Kurt in the Intimate Theatre's Swedish première of *The Dance of Death,* opposite Flygare as Alice.

646. To WILLIAM MOLARD

[1] *A Dream Play.*
[2] The French actor who played the Captain in Lugné-Poë's production of *The Father* in 1894.
[3] The Intimate Theatre.

649. To KARL BÖRJESSON

[1] Börjesson always opposed Strindberg's wish for a second edition of *Black Banners.* The edition which appeared in 1910 was published by Åhlén & Åkerlund in Gothenburg. Nevertheless Börjesson remained sensitive to criticism, and Strindberg consequently sought to reassure him.

650. To VALFRID SPÅNGBERG

[1] Spångberg remained adamant and the articles (the second of which plays on the title of Selma Lagerlöf's novel *Gösta Berlings saga*) appeared in *Social-Demokraten.*
[2] The letter breaks off here.

651. To ZETH HÖGLUND

[1] Radical Socialist writer and politician (1872–1938).
[2] Refers to an article which Strindberg had read in *Stormklockan.*

652. To AUGUST FALCK

[1] Falck wished to put on Maeterlinck's *L'Intruse.* In spite of Strindberg's admonitions, he staged it on 23 September, thus sealing the fate of the Intimate Theatre which, without Strindberg's support, closed in December.
[2] Gustaf Uddgren.
[3] According to Eklund, Strindberg's own in *Afton-Tidning.*
[4] Uno Lindholm, who had acted with the Intimate Theatre and was now looking to set up his own company.

653. To AUGUST FALCK

[1] On 26 October Strindberg wrote to Richard Bergh: 'If Falck comes begging in my name, treat him as a traitor. Please warn Bonnier and the Prince [Eugen].'

654. To TOR HEDBERG

[1] The characters referred to in this letter are, respectively: Gustav Vasa (*c.* 1494–1560), the Regent and later King of Sweden, Kristina Gyllenstierna (1494–1559), the wife of Sten Sture the Younger (*c.* 1492–1520), the last of the

knights, Sören Norrby (d.1530), a Danish naval hero and Baltic pirate, Lars Siggesson (d.1554), a loyal supporter of Gustav Vasa, Erik Trolle (*c.* 1460–*c.* 1529), a powerful nobleman and ally of Denmark, Johan Månsson (d.1520), whose father had murdered the Engelbrekt about whom Strindberg had written a previous play, Herman Israel, the merchant from Lübeck who is also a central character in *Gustav Vasa*, Bishop Brask (1464–1538), the last Catholic Bishop of Sweden, whose fortress at Munkeboda Gustav Vasa had spared, Olaus Petri (or Master Olof, 1493–1552), Christian II of Denmark (1481–1559), and Nils Dacke, the leader of a yoemen's revolt against Gustav Vasa in 1542–43. The stepmother is Vasa's second wife, Margareta Leijonhuvud (1516–51).

[2] *The Last Knight*. The settings of the two plays repeat each other in reverse order, just as the first eight scenes of *To Damascus I* are retraced in the final eight. Strindberg explains his intention in a note to the text: 'The same settings as in *The Last Knight*, but in reverse order. This contrapuntal form which I have borrowed from music and used in *To Damascus I* has the effect of awakening in the theatergoer memories of the various places in which earlier actions took place, and thereby the drama has the effect of happening much later in life with a great deal behind it; accumulated impressions arise; there are echoes from better times; the hard reality of maturity dominates; the defeated are counted; crushed hopes are recalled; and the drama *The Last Knight* serves as the saga of youth in contrast to the heavy struggle of *The Regent*.' Walter Johnson, *The Last of the Knights, The Regent, Earl Birger of Bjälbo* (Seattle, 1956), p.99.

[3] Payment! Payment!

[4] Scene of a battle in 1518 where the Swedish forces defeated those of Christian II. Gustav Vasa is reputed to have been the Swedish standard-bearer.

[5] Gustav Vasa's mother and sister had died of starvation during their incarceration in the Blue Tower in Denmark.

[6] Kalö castle on Jylland, where Gustav Vasa was imprisoned by Christian II in 1518.

655. To J. P. A. MUHR

[1] E. Nyström, *Biblisk ordbok för hemmet och skolan* (A Biblical Dictionary for the Home and School, 4th edn., Stockholm, 1906).

[2] 'Hildur the Bride of Horga', in which Strindberg depicts the cult of Odin and its blood sacrifices, is actually the second story in *New Swedish Destinies*.

[3] An article entitled 'Tibetankska språket' (The Language of Tibet).

[4] Strindberg is here seeking to link a phrase from the Bible, which in the article he translates as 'Oh you faithful (God), save them!', with a Tibetan prayer, *Om mani padme hum*, meaning 'The Jewel is in the Lotus Blossom'. Muhr responded by listing all the references to 'hem' (Sw. 'home') in Dr James Strong's Concordance, adding (in English): 'This is as near as I can make it.'

656. To BIRGER MÖRNER

[1] Strindberg refers to *Gyllene bin* (Golden Bees), a cycle of poems about Napoleon in which the word 'Harakiri' occurs. 'Sw. Ac.' = The Swedish Academy.

[2] Fredrik Ulrik Wrangel (see headnote to Letter 387).

657. To KARL OTTO BONNIER

[1] C. Kainz, *Praktische Grammatik der chinesischen Sprache für den Selbstunterricht* (Practical Grammar of the Chinese Language for Self-Instruction, Wien, Pest, Leipzig, n.d.). Strindberg had recurring problems in setting the text of his essays in linguistics.

[2] Bonnier had written on 10 February 1911, offering to buy Strindberg's collected works in exchange for an annuity during his lifetime and an outright payment to his heirs after his death.

658. To KARL BÖRJESSON

[1] Klemming's Bookshop, not Gustaf Klemming. *Resa i Kina* (Travels in China, 1864) by the French missionary and explorer Évariste Régis Huc.

[2] The archaeologist Oscar Montelius (1843–1921) and Strindberg's old adversary, the explorer Sven Hedin (1865–1952). According to Börjesson, Hedin had received 75,000 *kronor* for his *Scientific Results of a Journey in Central Asia 1899–1902*, 6 vols with Atlas (Stockholm, 1904–07), the largest sum ever awarded to a Swedish writer for a scientific work.

[3] Börjesson was helping to arrange a Strindberg Exhibition, including paintings, letters, photographs, portraits, and manuscripts, in connection with the nationwide subscription on his behalf. Strindberg thought of adding the contents of his Green Sack, now filed in boxes, to the items on exhibition. The exhibition opened on 11 June.

[4] Paraphrase of a line spoken by The Hunter in the play's final scene: 'They always leave when one seeks to defend oneself,' *Samlade Skrifter*, 51, p.95.

659. To NILS ANDERSSON

[1] Greta Philp gave birth on 29 March 1911; as Strindberg writes, the child died the same day.

[2] Waldemar Bülow.

[3] *The Roots of World Languages*, published by Bonnier in June 1911.

[4] Greta's husband, Dr Henry Philp (1877–1920), who cared for Strindberg during his last years.

660. To NILS ANDERSSON

[1] A style of Arabic script with large letters, also spelt Thülüth (Strindberg omits the 'h's).

[2] Andersson was engaged in helping his close friends, the Hamiltons, who were divorcing.

[3] All novels by Henning von Melsted.

[4] The philosopher Hans Larsson (1862–1944), whom Strindberg had known in Lund. On 10 June, Strindberg had written to Andersson, wondering if it might not be the right moment to rehabilitate his reputation in the Skovlyst affair of 1888. See Letters 207 and 208.

661. To HENNING BERGER

[1] Strindberg means 14 Norrtullsgatan, the family home on three occasions between 1856–69. It provides the setting for the second of his Chamber Plays, *The Burned Site.* The house was demolished in 1904. The route from his final residence at 85 Drottninggatan to the churchyard where he lies buried passes along Norrtullsgatan.

[2] Berger's novel *Drömlandet* (1909).

662. To KARL OTTO BONNIER

[1] Bonnier now raised his initial offer from 150,000 to 200,000 *kronor*, to be paid in four instalments over the next four years. In return he obtained the publication rights in perpetuity to all Strindberg's published works plus *He and She*, but not the performing or foreign rights. When published, the by no means complete edition comprised 55 volumes.

663. To TOR BONNIER

[1] From 1865 Albert Bonnier's office was located at 17 Ålandsgatan (now Mäster Samuelsgatan). The Stockholm Lyceum, where Strindberg once studied, was also situated there in 1865.

[2] Gustaf Banck, for many years chief cashier at Bonniers.

664. To NILS ANDERSSON

[1] A city in Thrace, reputedly built by Hercules to the memory of his beloved Abderus, and renowned for the stupidity of its inhabitants.

666. To NILS ANDERSSON

[1] Andersson had supplied Strindberg with the proceedings of two trials held in Malmö, one for endangering life by placing obstacles across a railway line, the other for arson, which raised questions about the defendants' psychological responsibility for their actions.

[2] A reference to *Le Père Goriot* where Rastignac asks: 'Do you remember the passage where Rousseau asks the reader what he would do if he could make a fortune by killing an old mandarin in China simply by exerting his will, without stirring from Paris?' The attribution to Rousseau is an error; the question was put by Chateaubriand in *Le Génie de Christianisme* (1802).

[3] Sändor Petöfi (1823–49), Hungarian poet and patriot.

668. To BIRGER MÖRNER

[1] *Mot aftonglöden* (Towards the Glow of Evening), the second of two volumes of poetry which Mörner published during 1911. Cf. Letter 656.

669. To NILS ANDERSSON

[1] [The] Beyond.
[2] G. Anrep, *Svenska adelns ättartaflor* (Genealogies of the Swedish Nobility), 4 vols (Stockholm, 1858–64).
[3] H. Hofberg, *Genom Sveriges bygder* (Through the Districts of Sweden, 3rd edn., Stockholm, 1896).
[4] Eugen Hemberg, *På obanade stigar* (On Untrodden Paths, Stockholm, 1896).

670. To BIRGER MÖRNER

[1] A reference to his study *The Origins of Our Mother Tongue* (1911).
[2] See Letter 673.
[3] Maeterlinck had been awarded the Nobel Prize and came to Stockholm to receive it on 10 December 1911. The two writers did not meet.

671. To RICHARD BERGH

[1] To mark his sixty-third birthday, the Social Democrats held a torchlight procession past Blå tornet. Over 15,000 took part, acclaiming 'The People's Strindberg' and 'The Poet King'. Strindberg acknowledged them from his balcony, with Anne-Marie at his side.

672. To HJALMAR BRANTING AND GERHARD MAGNUSSON

[1] Gerhard Magnusson (1872–1940), typographer and *Social-Demokraten*'s editor-in-chief 1910–12.

674. To NATHAN SÖDERBLOM

[1] See Letter 343.

678. To HJALMAR AND ANNA BRANTING

[1] Siri von Essen died in Helsinki on 21 April. According to Karin Smirnoff: 'When Greta told Strindberg . . . that [I] had written of mother's death, he asked to be allowed to hear the letter. Utterly emaciated, with his now sparse, almost white mane of hair damp with the strain of staying upright, he sat in his old brown check dressing-gown and listened. The letter was factual, restrained, almost cold in the dryness of its style, yet he sobbed while it was read, and blew his nose unceasingly. When Greta had finished, he went into the next room and returned wearing an old black dressing-gown and a white necktie, as if in mourning.' According to Axel Strindberg, however, he fell silent for a few minutes; then he remarked: 'She was just as hard, as cold, as unfeeling to the end.'

Sources of Letters: Volume Two

The sources of the letters in this volume of the English edition are as follows (Brev plus roman numeral = the relevant volume of the 16 volumes so far published in the Swedish edition of *August Strindbergs brev*. (Stockholm, 1948–); MSS plus arabic numeral = the relevant issue of the *Meddelanden från Strindbergssällskapet*; KB = manuscript in Kungliga Biblioteket, Stockholm, and SS followed by an arabic numeral = the relevant volume of Strindberg's *Samlade Skrifter*):

285	Brev IX
286	Brev IX
287	Brev IX
288	Brev IX
289	Brev IX
290	Brev IX
291	Brev IX
292	Brev IX
293	Brev IX
294	Brev IX
295	Brev IX
296	Brev IX
297	Brev IX
298	Brev IX
299	Brev IX
300	Brev IX
301	Brev IX
302	Brev IX
303	Brev IX
304	Brev IX
305	Brev X
306	Brev X
307	Brev X
308	Brev X
309	Brev X
310	Brev X
311	Brev X
312	Brev X
313	Brev X
314	Brev X
315	Brev X
316	Brev X
317	Brev X
318	Brev X
319	Brev X
320	Brev X
321	Brev X
322	Brev X
323	Brev X
324	Brev X
325	Brev X
326	Brev X
327	Brev X
328	Brev X
329	Brev X
330	Brev X
331	Brev X
332	Brev X
333	Brev X
334	Brev X
335	Brev X
336	Brev X
337	Brev X
338	Brev X
339	Brev X
340	Brev X
341	Brev X
342	Brev X
343	Brev X
344	Brev X
345	Brev X
346	Brev X
347	Brev X
348	SS 27
349	Brev X
350	Brev X
351	Brev X
352	Brev XI
353	Brev XI
354	Brev XI
355	Brev XI
356	Brev XI
357	Brev XI
358	Brev XI
359	Brev XI
360	Brev XI
361	Brev XI
362	Brev XI
363	Brev XI
364	Brev XI
365	Brev XI

366	Brev XI	410	Brev XII	454	Brev XIII
367	Brev XI	411	Brev XII	455	MSS 61–62
368	Brev XI	412	Brev XII	456	Brev XIV
369	Brev XI	413	Brev XII	457	MSS 61–62
370	Brev XI	414	Brev XII	458	Brev XIV
371	Brev XI	415	Brev XII	459	Brev XIV
372	Brev XI	416	Brev XII	460	Brev XIV
373	Brev XI	417	Brev XII	461	Brev XIV
374	Brev XI	418	Brev XII	462	Brev XIV
375	Brev XI	419	Brev XII	463	Brev XIV
376	Brev XI	420	Brev XII	464	Brev XIV
377	Brev XI	421	Brev XII	465	Brev XIV
378	Brev XI	422	Brev XII	466	Brev XIV
379	Brev XI	423	Brev XII	467	Brev XIV
380	Brev XI	424	Brev XII	468	Brev XIV
381	Brev XI	425	Brev XII	469	Brev XIV
382	Brev XI	426	Brev XII	470	Brev XIV
383	Brev XI	427	Brev XIII	471	Brev XIV
384	Brev XI	428	Brev XIII	472	Brev XIV
385	Brev XI	429	Brev XIII	473	Brev XIV
386	Brev XI	430	Brev XIII	474	Brev XIV
387	Brev XI	431	Brev XIII	475	Brev XIV
388	Brev XI	432	Brev XIII	476	Brev XIV
389	Brev XI	433	Brev XIII	477	Brev XIV
390	Brev XI	434	Brev XIII	478	Brev XIV
391	Brev XI	435	Brev XIII	479	Brev XIV
392	Brev XI	436	Brev XIII	480	Brev XIV
393	Brev XI	437	Brev XIII	481	Brev XIV
394	Brev XI	438	Brev XIII	482	Brev XIV
395	Brev XII	439	Brev XIII	483	Brev XIV
396	Brev XII	440	Brev XIII	484	Brev XIV
397	Brev XII	441	Brev XIII	485	Brev XIV
398	Brev XII	442	Brev XIII	486	Brev XIV
399	Brev XII	443	Brev XIII	487	Brev XIV
400	Brev XII	444	Brev XIII	488	Brev XIV
401	Brev XII	445	Brev XIII	489	Brev XIV
402	Brev XII	446	Brev XIII	490	Brev XIV
403	Brev XII	447	Brev XIII	491	Brev XIV
404	Brev XII	448	Brev XIII	492	Brev XIV
405	Brev XII	449	Brev XIII	493	Brev XIV
406	Brev XII	450	Brev XIII	494	Brev XIV
407	Brev XII	451	Brev XIII	495	Brev XIV
408	Brev XII	452	Brev XIII	496	Brev XIV
409	Brev XII	453	Brev XIII	497	Brev XIV

498	Brev XIV
499	Brev XIV
500	Brev XIV
501	Brev XIV
502	Brev XIV
503	Brev XIV
504	Brev XIV
505	Brev XIV
506	Brev XIV
507	MSS 61–62
508	Brev XIV
509	Brev XIV
510	Brev XIV
511	Brev XIV
512	Brev XIV
513	Brev XIV
514	Brev XIV
515	Brev XIV
516	Brev XIV
517	Brev XV
518	Brev XV
519	Brev XV
520	Brev XV
521	Brev XV
522	Brev XV
523	Brev XV
524	Brev XV
525	Brev XV
526	Brev XV
527	Brev XV
528	Brev XV
529	Brev XV
530	Brev XV
531	Brev XV
532	Brev XV
533	Brev XV
534	Brev XV
535	Brev XV
536	Brev XV
537	Brev XV
538	Brev XV
539	Brev XV
540	Brev XV
541	Brev XV
542	Brev XV
543	Brev XV
544	Brev XV
545	Brev XV
546	Brev XV
547	Brev XV
548	Brev XV
549	Brev XV
550	Brev XV
551	Brev XV
552	Brev XV
553	Brev XV
554	Brev XV
555	Brev XV
556	Brev XV
557	Brev XV
558	Brev XV
559	Brev XV
560	Brev XV
561	Brev XV
562	Brev XVI
563	Brev XVI
564	Brev XVI
565	Brev XVI
566	Brev XVI
567	Brev XVI
568	Brev XVI
569	Brev XVI
570	Brev XVI
571	Brev XVI
572	Brev XVI
573	Brev XVI
574	Brev XVI
575	Brev XVI
576	Brev XVI
577	Brev XVI
578	Brev XVI
579	Brev XVI
580	Brev XVI
581	Brev XVI
582	Brev XVI
583	Brev XVI
584	Brev XVI
585	Brev XVI
586	Brev XVI
587	Brev XVI
588	Brev XVI
589	Brev XVI
590	Brev XVI
591	Brev XVI
592	Brev XVI
593	Brev XVI
595	Brev XVI
595	Brev XVI
596	Brev XVI
597	Brev XVI
598	Brev XVI
599	Brev XVI
600	Brev XVI
601	Brev XVI
602	Brev XVI
603	Brev XVI
604	Brev XVI
605	Brev XVI
606	Brev XVI
607	Brev XVI
608	Brev XVI
609	Brev XVI
610	Brev XVI
611	Brev XVI
612	KB
613	KB
614	KB
615	KB
616	KB
617	KB
618	KB
619	KB
620	KB
621	KB
622	KB
623	KB
624	KB
625	KB
626	KB
627	KB
628	KB
629	KB

630	KB
631	KB
632	KB
633	KB
634	KB
635	KB
636	KB
637	KB
638	KB
639	KB
640	KB
641	KB
642	KB
643	KB
644	KB
645	KB
646	KB
647	KB
648	KB
649	KB
650	KB
651	KB
652	KB
653	KB
654	KB
655	KB
656	KB
657	KB
658	KB
659	KB
660	KB
661	KB
662	KB
663	KB
664	KB
665	KB
666	KB
667	KB
668	KB
669	KB
670	KB
671	KB
672	KB
673	KB
674	KB
675	KB
676	KB
677	KB
678	KB
679	KB

Index

References in bold italics denote letters from Strindberg to the named addressee. The first such entry also denotes a headnote about Strindberg's correspondent. On occasion there may be two letters to a single correspondent on the same page; in that case the italicized entry carries an asterisk. The Swedish letters å and ä are listed under a, and ö under o.